LET'S GO:
Rome

"Its yearly revision by a new crop of Harvard students makes it as valuable as ever." —*The New York Times*

"Value-packed, unbeatable, accurate, and comprehensive." —*The Los Angeles Times*

"A world-wise traveling companion—always ready with friendly advice and helpful hints, all sprinkled with a bit of wit." —*The Philadelphia Inquirer*

"Lighthearted and sophisticated, informative and fun to read. [Let's Go] helps the novice traveler navigate like a knowledgeable old hand." —*Atlanta Journal-Constitution*

"All the essential information you need, from making a phone call to exchanging money to contacting your embassy. [Let's Go] provides maps to help you find your way from every train station to a full range of youth hostels and hotels." —*Minneapolis Star Tribune*

"Unbeatable: good sight-seeing advice; up-to-date-info on restaurants, hotels, and inns; a commitment to money-saving travel; and a wry style that brightens nearly every page." —*The Washington Post*

▪ Let's Go researchers have to make it on their own.

"The writers seem to have experienced every rooster-packed bus and lunar-surfaced mattress about which they write." —*The New York Times*

"Retains the spirit of the student-written publication it is: candid, opinionated, resourceful, amusing info for the traveler of limited means but broad curiosity." —*Mademoiselle*

▪ No other guidebook is as comprehensive.

"Whether you're touring the United States, Europe, Southeast Asia, or Central America, a Let's Go guide will clue you in to the cheapest, yet safe, hotels and hostels, food and transportation. Going beyond the call of duty, the guides reveal a country's latest news, cultural hints, and off-beat information that any tourist is likely to miss." —*Tulsa World*

▪ Let's Go is completely revised each year.

"Up-to-date travel tips for touring four continents on skimpy budgets." —*Time*

"Inimitable.... Let's Go's 24 guides are updated yearly (as opposed to the general guidebook standard of every two to three years), and in a marvelously spunky way." —*The New York Times*

Let's Go Publications

Let's Go: Alaska & The Pacific Northwest
Let's Go: Britain & Ireland
Let's Go: California
Let's Go: Central America
Let's Go: Eastern Europe
Let's Go: Ecuador & The Galápagos Islands
Let's Go: Europe
Let's Go: France
Let's Go: Germany
Let's Go: Greece & Turkey
Let's Go: India & Nepal
Let's Go: Ireland
Let's Go: Israel & Egypt
Let's Go: Italy
Let's Go: London
Let's Go: Mexico
Let's Go: New York City
Let's Go: Paris
Let's Go: Rome
Let's Go: Southeast Asia
Let's Go: Spain & Portugal
Let's Go: Switzerland & Austria
Let's Go: USA
Let's Go: Washington, D.C.

Let's Go **Map Guide:** Boston
Let's Go **Map Guide:** London
Let's Go **Map Guide:** New York City
Let's Go **Map Guide:** Paris
Let's Go **Map Guide:** San Francisco
Let's Go **Map Guide:** Washington, D.C.

LET'S GO

The Budget Guide to
Rome
1997

William G. Ferullo
Editor

St. Martin's Press ✖ New York

HELPING LET'S GO

If you want to share your discoveries, suggestions, or corrections, please drop us a line. We read every piece of correspondence, whether a postcard, a 10-page e-mail, or a coconut. All suggestions are passed along to our researcher-writers. Please note that mail received after May 1997 may be too late for the 1998 book, but will be retained for the following edition. **Address mail to:**

> **Let's Go: Rome**
> **67 Mt. Auburn Street**
> **Cambridge, MA 02138**
> **USA**

Visit Let's Go at **http://www.letsgo.com,** or send e-mail to:

> **Fanmail@letsgo.com**
> **Subject: "Rome"**

In addition to the invaluable travel advice our readers share with us, many are kind enough to offer their services as researchers or editors. Unfortunately, the charter of Let's Go, Inc. enables us to employ only currently enrolled Harvard-Radcliffe students.

Maps by David Lindroth copyright © 1997, 1996, 1995, 1994, 1993, 1992, 1991, 1990, 1989, 1988 by St. Martin's Press, Inc.

Map revisions pp. xii, xiii, 82, 83, 100, 101, 138, 139, 170, 171, 193, 199, 221, 275 by Let's Go, Inc.

Distributed outside the USA and Canada by Macmillan.

ISBN: 0-312-14663-9

First edition
10 9 8 7 6 5 4 3 2 1

Let's Go: Rome is written by Let's Go Publications, 67 Mt. Auburn Street, Cambridge, MA 02138, USA.

Let's Go® and the thumb logo are trademarks of Let's Go, Inc. Printed in the USA on recycled paper with biodegradable soy ink.

About Let's Go

THIRTY-SIX YEARS OF WISDOM

Back in 1960, a few students at Harvard University banded together to produce a 20-page pamphlet offering a collection of tips on budget travel in Europe. This modest, mimeographed packet, offered as an extra to passengers on student charter flights to Europe, met with instant popularity. The following year, students traveling to Europe researched the first, full-fledged edition of *Let's Go: Europe*, a pocket-sized book featuring honest, irreverent writing and a decidedly youthful outlook on the world. Throughout the 60s, our guides reflected the times; the 1969 guide to America led off by inviting travelers to "dig the scene" at San Francisco's Haight-Ashbury. During the 70s and 80s, we gradually added regional guides and expanded coverage into the Middle East and Central America. With the addition of our in-depth city guides, handy map guides, and extensive coverage of Asia, the 90s are also proving to be a time of explosive growth for Let's Go, and there's certainly no end in sight. The first editions of *Let's Go: India & Nepal* and *Let's Go: Ecuador & The Galapagos Islands* hit the shelves this year, and work toward next year's series has already begun.

We've seen a lot in 37 years. *Let's Go: Europe* is now the world's bestselling international guide, translated into seven languages. And our new guides bring Let's Go's total number of titles, with their spirit of adventure and their reputation for honesty, accuracy, and editorial integrity, to 30. But some things never change: our guides are still researched, written, and produced entirely by students who know first-hand how to see the world on the cheap.

HOW WE DO IT

Each guide is completely revised and thoroughly updated every year by a well-traveled set of 200 students. Every winter, we recruit over 120 researchers and 60 editors to write the books anew. After several months of training, Researcher-Writers hit the road for seven weeks of exploration, from Anchorage to Ankara, Estonia to El Salvador, Iceland to Indonesia. Hired for their rare combination of budget travel sense, writing ability, stamina, and courage, these adventurous travelers know that train strikes, stolen luggage, food poisoning, and marriage proposals are all part of a day's work. Back at our offices, editors work from spring to fall, massaging copy written on Himalayan bus rides into witty yet informative prose. A student staff of typesetters, cartographers, publicists, and managers keeps our lively team together. In September, the collected efforts of the summer are delivered to our printer, who turns them into books in record time, so that you have the most up-to-date information available for *your* vacation. And even as you read this, work on next year's editions is well underway.

WHY WE DO IT

At Let's Go, our goal is to give you a great vacation. We don't think of budget travel as the last recourse of the destitute; we believe that it's the only way to travel. Living cheaply and simply brings you closer to the people and places you've been saving up to visit. Our books will ease your anxieties and answer your questions about the basics—so you can get off the beaten track and explore. Once you learn the ropes, we encourage you to put Let's Go away now and then to strike out on your own. As any seasoned traveler will tell you, the best discoveries are often those you make yourself. When you find something worth sharing, drop us a line. We're Let's Go Publications, 67 Mt. Auburn St., Cambridge, MA 02138, USA (e-mail: fanmail@letsgo.com).

HAPPY TRAVELS!

Stuck for cash? Don't panic. With Western Union, money is transferred to you in minutes. It's easy. All you've got to do is ask someone at home to give Western Union a call on US 1 800 3256000. Minutes later you can collect the cash.

WESTERN UNION | MONEY TRANSFER

The fastest way to send money worldwide.

Contents

*E*scape to ancient cities and

 journey to exotic islands with

CNN Travel Guide, a wealth of valuable advice.

Host Valerie Voss will take you

to all of your favorite destinations,

 including those off the beaten path.

Tune - in to your passport to the world.

SATURDAY 12:30 PMET
SUNDAY 4:30 PMET **CNN. TRAVEL GUIDE**

Maps

Color Maps

Acknowledgements

Grazie mille to everyone who has helped me with this guide (and there have been many of you): **Alex S.** and **Emily,** my power-packed researchers, and **Alex T.,** A.K.A. Hawkeye, who not only could spot an italicized period from a mile away, but who also contributed to this book with his mind-boggling command of linguistic rules and interesting minutiae related and unrelated (from Italian cinema to the construction of the perfect mousetrap). All that and familial ties to Verdi ... Thanks to my fellow members of the **Romance Room: Lauren, Tom, Julie, Alexa,** and **Greg,** who provided me with a complete education in the ways of Ben Tucker and the Beatles; **Lisa** and **Amy** who answered my every question about Italy outside of the Eternal City; **Corey,** my *paisàn* from Italian classes and countless other things Italian for the last few years, who was always quick to share both language and cooking tips. Thanks also to **Catherine, Dan O., Michelle** and **SoRelle** for last-minute help, and to proofers **Doug** and **Nina.**

Infinite thanks go to **Pierluigi** and **Fulvia** for everything they've done for us, from finding shelter for Alex and Emily to providing up-to-the-minute information on a city that's anything but static. Thanks also to everyone in the Romance Languages and Literatures departments who has helped me out, especially **Elvira,** who has given me so much good advice over the last four years, including suggesting that I apply for a job at *Let's Go,* and **Marilina,** whose Italian Tables, classes, and general amicability taught me an even greater respect for *l'Italia meridionale.*

Special thanks to **F@mily Fun (Matthew** and **Jeremy)** and to **Ali** for her ebullience and all-around boudjieness. Most of all, thank you to **Mom, Dad, Leah,** and **Ashley,** all of whom I love very much.

-WGF

Editor	William G. Ferullo
Managing Editor	Alexander H. Travelli
Publishing Director	Michelle C. Sullivan
Production Manager	Daniel O. Williams
Associate Production Manager	Michael S. Campbell
Cartography Manager	Amanda K. Bean
Editorial Manager	John R. Brooks
Editorial Manager	Allison Crapo
Financial Manager	Stephen P. Janiak
Personnel Manager	Alexander H. Travelli
Publicity Manager	SoRelle B. Braun
Associate Publicity Manager	David Fagundes
Associate Publicity Manager	Elisabeth Mayer
Assistant Cartographer	Jonathan D. Kibera
Assistant Cartographer	Mark C. Staloff
Office Coordinator	Jennifer L. Schuberth
Director of Advertising and Sales	Amit Tiwari
Senior Sales Executives	Andrew T. Rourke
	Nicholas A. Valtz, Charles E. Varner
General Manager	Richard Olken
Assistant General Manager	Anne E. Chisholm

Researcher-Writers

Alejandro Sepulveda *Rome, Northern Lazio, Colli Albani,*
the Beaches, Tivoli

Alex bounded off to Rome with every intention of returning immediately after his itinerary. Forty-eight pub-hopping days later, he decided that *la dolce vita* couldn't be fully experienced in just a couple of months and chose instead to stay the summer. Alex not only sent back volumes and volumes of excellent copy, but also found time to hang out with twins Mario and Luigi and to become acquainted with a whole slew of new Roman friends and family. Sooner or later, however, he will have to come back to school, where he will continue his studies in linguistics and his quest for mastery of Spanish pronominal clitics.

Emily M. Tucker *Rome, Vatican City, Ostia, Cerveteri, Pontine Islands*

Emily is well on her way to becoming a true *romana da Roma*. Braving a flooded apartment shortly after her arrival in Rome, she managed to install herself once again in her old Trastevere stomping-grounds. Emily's expertise in all things Roman helped her handle the transition from last year's editor to this year's researcher with ease, providing more information on entertainment than the average *Roma C'è*, making crystal-clear every intricacy of the complex world of Roman transportation, and politely (and sometimes not so politely) explaining that she is not *tedesca*. Upon her return, Emily will prepare for her job teaching Latin at the Dana Hall School outside of Boston.

Kathleen Christian *Pompeii, Herculaneum, Paestum*

Kathleen's art-historian's eye was imported from Team Italy in order to help out with these three well-preserved ancient cities.

Salvatore Gogliormella *Orvieto and Tarquinia*

Sal covered Sardinia and Tuscany for the Italy guide and also donated his impeccably printed (think typewriter) notes on Umbria and Etruria to us.

Map of Maps

Villa Borghese

Termini & San Lorenzo

Spanish
Steps

Barberini

Trevi
Fountain

Palazzo del
Quirinale

AZZA
NEZIA

MONTE
PALATINO

NTINO

Appian Way

V. Dalmazia

Viale Regina Margherita

Via Salaria

Via Po

V. Isonzo

Via Nizza

Via Nomentana

Via Piave

Via V. Veneto

Via Boncompagni

V. Ludovisi

Via Sistina

Via del Tritone

Via Barberini

Via Barberini

PIAZZA
DELLA
REPUBBLICA

Via XX Settembre

Biblioteca
Nazionale

SALARIO

Museo
Nazionale
Romano
PIAZZA DEL
CINQUECENTO

Enjoy
Rome

Policlinico
Universita

Viale Regina Elena

Via dell'Universita

Via Castro Pretorio

Via Palestro

Stazione
Termini

Via Nazionale

Via Cavour

Via Panisperna

Via Cavour

Via Giovanni Lanza

Via Marsala

Via Giovanni Giolitti

Via Tiburtina

Via Meridiana

PIAZZA
VITTORIO
EMANUELE

PIAZZA DEL
COLOSSEO

Via Labicana

Colosseum

Parco del
Celio

CELIO

Via di S. Gregorio

Via Claudia

Via di S. Stefano Rotondo

Via dell'Amba Aradam

Via delle Terme

P. DI SAN
GIOVANNI
IN LATERANO

San Giovanni in
Laterano

Viale Manzoni

Via Emanuele Filiberto

V. S. Croce in Gerusalemme

V. Statilia

PIAZZA
DI PTA.
MAGGIORE

Via d. Laterani

Via Gallia

Via Magnagrecia

Via Cervetari

P. DEI RE
DI ROMA

Via Appia
Nuova

Via Etruria

Terme di
Caracalla

Viale Aventino

Via di Porta Latina

Via di Porta Sebastiano

Viale Metronio

Via Satrico

Via Vetulonia

Via Concordia

Via Siria

Guida Baccelli

Viale Giotto

XV

How To Use This Book

Let's Go: Rome begins with a **general introduction** which describes 2750 years of Roman political, historical, and cultural events in about 30 pages. The **Essentials** section will tell you all about what to do before you leave for Rome, how to get there, and how to get around once you are there. The next chapter contains listings of **accommodations** that won't make you feel guilty about spending those extra *lire* on another *gelato*. The **restaurants** section suggests places to enjoy yummy Roman food at a budget price and lists the best places to go for coffee, desserts, and wine. Our **sights** chapter will help you navigate Rome's labyrinth of sight-packed streets and alleys, beginning with the Ancient City and working its way along chronologically through the city, before crossing the Tiber to Trastevere and the **Vatican City**. Then we offer some advice on **entertainment** *alla romana,* including details on nightlife, music, theater, film, shopping, sports, and more. The next section suggests some **daytrips,** from explorations of ancient ruins to a day at the beach, which will help you escape the chaos of Roman life. The appendix includes a climate chart, a glossary of important terms, an explanation of the basics of Italian pronunciation, and a list of helpful words and phrases. Maps have been included throughout the guide to help you find your way to that hip *caffè* or romantic *trattoria*. The Rome overview map is a good place to start, but other, more detailed maps have been included throughout the sights section. Above all, however, remember not to get too tied down to maps or guide books. The number of things to do and see in Rome can seem overwhelming, but wandering around on your own, you may discover a beautiful, little-known church or a specatcular, hidden *gelateria*. *Buon viaggio!*

Rome: A Brief History

TIME LINE

c. 1,000,000-70,000 BC Human settlement in Italy.

c. 2000: Italic tribes settle the peninsula.

c. 1200: Arrival of the belligerent but cultured Etruscans.

c. 800: Greeks settle in southern Italy.

753: Mythical founding of Rome by Romulus and Remus.

616: Forum and Circus Maximus laid out.

509: Romans rebel against Etruscan rule, found republic.

474: Etruscans defeated at Cuma.

378: "Servian Wall" built around the city.

312: Appian Way and Aqua Appia begin.

275: Romans defeat Pyrrhus, last defender of the Greeks, seizing control of the entire peninsula.

264-241: First Punic War against Carthage for control of the Mediterranean.

219: Second Punic War—Hannibal crosses the Alps.

202: Battle of Zama ends Carthage's power.

167: First Roman public library built.

149-46: Third Punic War. Carthage razed.

106: Birth of Cicero.

100: Birth of Julius Caesar.

91-89: Social War—tribes throughout the peninsula fight for extension of Roman citizenship rights.

73: Slave rebellion led by Spartacus, put down by Pompey.

60-50: First Triumvirate rules Rome: Caesar, Pompey, and Crassus.

48: Caesar in Egypt with Cleopatra.

45: Caesar declared *imperator*.

44: Caesar done in by Brutus *et al.* on his way to Senate.

27: Caesar's nephew Octavian founds the Roman Empire, takes the title "Caesar Augustus," and initiates the *Pax Romana* era of peace throughout the empire.

19: Publication of Virgil's *Aeneid*.

4 BC: Birth of Jesus in Bethlehem.

29 AD: Jesus condemned to death.

64: Great fire destroys much of Rome. Nero, a suspect, plays fiddle.

67: Martyrdom of Sts. Peter and Paul.

69-96: The Flavian Emperors.

79: Pompeii and Herculaneum buried by Vesuvius.

80: Completion of Colosseum.

96-192: The Adopted Emperors.

98-117: Emperor Trajan rules the Roman empire at its largest.

117-125: Completion of Pantheon.

193-235: The Severi Emperors.

235-305: The Soldier Emperors.

247: Rome celebrates its 1000th year: empire crumbling; bacchanalia in the streets.

271-276: Emperor Aurelian erects walls around the city.

284: Diocletian divides empire into East and West.

296: Diocletian persecutes Christians.

315: Constantine declares Christianity the official state religion.

326: First Basilica of St. Peter built.

330: Constantine transfers capital of empire to Byzantium, renames city Constantinople .

391: Persecution of non-Christians.

395: End of imperial unity. Western empire in death throes.

410: Rome taken by the Visigoths.

455: Rome sacked by the Vandals.

476: Odoacer, King of the Ostrogoths, crowned king of Italy; deposes last emperor.

498: Rival popes brawl in the streets.

567-751: Lombard Kingdom in Italy.

752: Lombards threaten Rome; Pope Stephen II appeals to Pepin the Short, king of the Franks.

754: Pepin defeats Lombards; founds Papal States.

778: Frankish Charlemagne vanquishes last Lombard king, takes his title.

800: Pope Leo III crowns Charlemagne Holy Roman Emperor.

852: Walls built around the Vatican.

962:	Refounding of the Holy Roman Empire, when Otto I of Saxony is crowned by Pope John XII. Emperor holds power to invest clergy.
1075:	Gregory VII puts his foot down and prohibits lay investiture (king can't appoint bishops). Investiture conflict between church and empire.
1122:	Concordat of Worms settles investiture conflict; the state wins.
1204:	Pope allows sack of Constantinople. Eastern Roman Empire maimed.
1303:	French insult and assault Pope (end of papal supremacy).
1309:	Clement V moves papacy to Avignon, a sort of Rome away from Rome. Beginning of the "Babylonian Captivity."
1378-1417:	Great Schism: two popes, one in Rome and one in Avignon.
1453:	Ottoman Turks overrun Constantinople.
1494:	Charles VIII invades Italy; first decisive use of artillery.
1508:	Michelangelo begins Sistine Chapel ceiling.
1517:	Martin Luther initiates The Protestant Reformation.
1534:	Michelangelo paints the *Last Judgement,* the final stage of his Sistine Chapel project.
1563:	Council of Trent Counter-Reformation.
1600:	Giordano Bruno burned at the stake for heresy.
1626:	Consecration of St. Peter's.
1762:	Completion of Trevi Fountain.
1773:	Expulsion of Jesuits from Rome.
1798:	French kidnap the Pope.
1806:	Holy Roman Empire eliminated by Napoleon
1808:	Napoleon annexes Rome to French empire.
1849-66:	French rule Rome.
1870:	September 20: Italian troops enter Rome.
1870:	October: Rome made capital of recently united Italy.
1922:	October 28-29: Mussolini leads Fascist March on Rome.
1944:	June 4: Allies liberate Rome from Nazis.
1946:	Italian Republic reestablished by national referendum.
1957:	Treaty of Rome establishes the Common Market.
1959:	Fellini's *La Dolce Vita.*
1960:	Rome hosts the Olympic Games.
1962:	Vatican II—they're back.
1965:	Vatican II dissolves.
1978:	Christian Democratic presidential candidate Aldo Moro murdered by Red Brigade.
1981:	Pope John Paul II shot and wounded in St. Peter's Square.
1984:	Marriage and education secularized by new Concordat.
1987	Porn star, La Cicciolina, is elected to Parliament
1991:	50th Italian Government collapses.
1992:	President Scalfaro elected.
1994:	Silvio Berlusconi's right-wing Freedom Alliance gains power.
1995:	Berlusconi forced to resign.

■ Ancient Rome

HISTORY

Roman history traditionally begins with Aeneas, who, driven by fate from his native Troy, came to the shores of Latium and settled in the Tiber valley. After many struggles, the legendary father of the Roman people and his fellow Trojans intermarried peaceably with the locals, eschewing their culture for that of the Italians. The city of Rome itself owes its foundation to Aeneas' descendants, the equally legendary twins, **Romulus and Remus.** The two brothers were abandoned on the banks of the Tiber by their mother, a Vestal Virgin, who had been exposed by her uncle for having broken her vow of chastity. Suckled by a passing she-wolf and raised by a kindly shepherd, the forgotten twins grew up to found Rome in 753 BC. Out of anger, greed, or duty, depending on the version of the legend, Romulus slew Remus and became the first king of the city named after him, Rome. The kingdom flourished under two centuries of Etruscan rule, until the son of the king **Tarquinius Superbus** raped the virtuous Roman matron **Lucretia.** She committed public suicide, and her outraged family led the Roman populace in overthrowing the Tarquins in 510 BC.

Free from foreign domination, the Romans set about establishing a republic, an oligarchy in which land-owning patricians (and, later on, wealthy plebeians) gathered in the Senate to make laws, hear trials, and declare war. A complex system of magistracies and administrative positions, with titles such as praetor, quaestor, aedile, and tribune, oversaw the city's growing infrastructure; under their care Rome blossomed with temples, roads, bridges, and aqueducts. From its power base in the Tiber valley, the city quickly began to expand, conquering its neighbors with unflinching efficiency. They won the voluntary submission of once-independent tribes with shrewd imperialist policies, such as gradual enfranchisement, and they required military service from their youth instead of harsh taxes, allowing the "Roman" republic to spread throughout Italy.

In the two-and-a-half centuries following the expulsion of the Etruscan kings, Latin Rome managed to conquer and absorb the Etruscans to its north, along with the indigenous Latin, Sabine, and Umbrian tribes closer to home. The 3rd-century BC **Samnite Wars** won the city control over the entire southern peninsula, with the exception of the Greek cities. The Greeks invited peerless **King Pyrrhus** of Epirus to defend them; while winning a series of battles against the republic, Pyrrhus invariably failed to press his advantage, assuring his eventual defeat and lending his name to the term "Pyrrhic victor." After losing to Rome at Beneventum in 275 BC, Pyrrhus quit Italy, leaving the rest of the boot open to Roman heels.

After Italy was conquered, the most important battles of the republic were the three **Punic Wars,** waged against Carthage (264-146 BC), in modern-day Tunisia, for control of important Mediterranean trade routes, as well as for territory in Spain and Sicily. During the second of these wars, the Carthaginian general **Hannibal** unexpectedly transported his army—elephants and all—up through Spain and across the Alps. Surprising a series of Roman generals as he swooped down the peninsula, Hannibal made it all the way to the walls of Rome, but failed to breach them. His campaign petered out into a cat-and-mouse game played with the Roman general **Fabius Maximus,** who eluded the overeager Carthiginian for several years until Hannibal's army, starving and exhausted, retreated home. Carthage was decisively defeated at Zama, in Africa, in 202 BC. Pressing the advantage, Cato the Censor (of *Carthago delenda est* fame) egged his fellow Romans on to utterly destroy the powerless Carthage in the Third Punic War of 146 BC, all for political hype. Roman soldiers sowed Carthaginian fields with salt to prevent the city from ever thriving again. It was during the Punic Wars that Rome began to see itself as a pre-eminent world power. Rome would later conquer and subjugate Sardinia, Corsica, Greece, and North Africa, as well as vast areas of Europe, Asia, and the Middle East; their accomplished aim was to consolidate control over Mediterranean trade and shipping, and to supplement their military dominance with economic superiority.

Traditional Roman society had been austere and religious in character. Drowning in riches from its many successful conquests, Rome became a festering swamp of greed and corruption. Yeoman farmers were pushed off their land by avaricious landowners and driven into slavery or starvation. Social upheaval quickly followed; by 131 BC, slave, farmer, and plebeian demands for land redistribution led to popular riots against the corrupt patrician class, culminating in the **Social War** (91-87 BC); tribes throughout the peninsula fought successfully for the extension of Roman citizenship and the many social and economic benefits which accompanied it. **Sulla,** the patrician general who had led Rome's troops during the conflict, then marched his armies into Rome (an unprecedented move), taking control of the city in a bloody military coup: over 1600 nobles and senators were executed without the benefit of a trial.

Sulla's strong-arm tactics set a dangerous precedent for the republic as generals once sworn to the service of the state now amassed large private armies, funded by their own huge fortunes. The century-old conflict between conservative patricians and the more radical, yet similarly unscrupulous, popular party (who advocated expanding Roman citizenship, extending rights to Italians, and limiting the ancient power of the Senate) exploded in a series of blood-lettings during which the Republican government gave way to the machinations of power-hungry warlords. In 73 BC, **Spartacus,** an escaped gladiatorial slave, led a 70,000-man-strong army of slaves and farmers in a two-year rampage down the peninsula. When the dust cleared, **Pompey the Great,** a close associate of Sulla, effectively took control of the city, but soon found himself in conflict with his sometime co-rulers **Julius Caesar** and Crassus. Caesar, the charismatic conqueror of Gaul, finally emerged victorious, but a small senatorial faction, fearful of his growing power, assassinated him on the Ides (15th) of March in 44 BC. Command of the city and its provinces eluded several would-be heirs, including Brutus (of "Et tu, Brute" fame) and Marc Antony, before falling to his grand-nephew and adopted son, Octavian. Under the title of **Augustus,** he consolidated and concentrated power and started assembling an imperial government in 27 BC. His reign (27 BC-14 AD) is generally considered the golden age of Rome, a brilliant flourishing of culture ushering in the 200 years of the **Pax Romana** (Roman peace). Rome gained a virtual monopoly on all Mediterranean trade, while at home the city benefited from a building boom of magnificent new constructions. Poets and authors thrived, transforming the sturdy Latin language into a tool of remarkable complexity and expression.

Within a few years of Augustus' death, however, the power he had amassed began to corrode. The princes of the Julio-Claudian house proved unequal to the task of world government, as their minds, intoxicated by power, slipped into fevers of cruelty, debauchery, and even insanity. Dour **Tiberius** (who could allegedly push his thumb through a man's skull), deranged **Caligula,** drooling **Claudius,** and sadistic **Nero** drained the imperial treasury to support their increasingly decadent lifestyles. While the behavior of many of Octavian's successors pushed the limits of credulity, the Roman war machine remained oblivious. In the first century, what are now Britain, Palestine, Syria, and parts of Germany fell at the hands of well-trained Roman soldiers. When Nero's inanities grew intolerable, the **Flavian** generals from the successful legions staged a coup and took control. The soldier-emperor **Trajan** (98-117 AD) expanded the empire to its greatest size, conquering Dacia (modern Romania) and areas along the Danube River with feats of engineering and tactical brilliance. While conquering Persia, however, Trajan suddenly died. General **Hadrian** seized the moment and the title. As the first **Antonine** emperor, Hadrian (118-138) preferred philosophy to war and concentrated on decorating Rome with his own architectural

---

Nero

Elected emperor at the tender age of 16, this son of Claudius' fourth wife (from a previous marriage) began a sadistic reign of terror, torture, and bad poetry readings. Nero started out rather humanely, guided by his overbearing but well-meaning mother; he was too timid even to sign the standard death warrants. But soon he proved to be one of the most vicious, destructive, and untalented teens in world history. He transmogrified into a megalomaniacal monster, and ordered the cruel murder of his mother, Agrippina, as well as the death of his 19-year-old wife, who was found tied up in cords in a hot bath with all her veins slashed. He even made his best buddy and advisor, the philosopher Seneca, slash his own wrists. Nero was haunted by paranoid visions; he often woke up screaming from nightmares of his dead mother, and he initiated a one-man witch-hunt through his palace, condemning senators, army officers, aristocrats, and various others to be beheaded as traitors. Nero may even have set the famous fire of 64 BC on purpose; he certainly took advantage of its destruction, commandeering acres of burnt-out land in the middle of the city to construct the Domus Aurea, a gargantuan palace which stretched from the Palatine Hill to above the Colosseum. Ultimately, Nero tried the patience and the coffers of his republic too severely, and the Senate sentenced him to death by flogging. Nero, in disguise, rode on horseback to the home of a former servant. He couldn't bring himself to commit suicide, so he had his servant slice his neck with a dagger. He did, however, have enough gall to utter in his last moments, "What an artist dies with me."

designs, including the **Pantheon** and his own colossal mausoleum. The city clung to its status as *caput mundi* (head of the world) until the death of **Marcus Aurelius** in 180 AD. By then, the empire had grown too large to defend. Emperors, required to delegate huge amounts of money and power to their generals in the field, lay vulnerable to military coups, and the tumultuous 3rd century AD saw no fewer than 30 emperors take the throne—only one managed to die of natural causes. Despite occasionally enlightened administrations (of the African Septimius Severus, for example), the brutality and depravity of despots like **Commodus, Caracalla,** and the confused **Elegabalus,** who believed he was the sun, did much to undermine the stability of the empire.

LITERATURE

Roman literature exists in many forms, including plays, historical writings, philosophical treatises, lyric and epic poetry, and satires. **Plautus** (c.220-184 BC) wrote popular farces which entertained the masses much as sitcoms do today. His comedy *Pseudolus* later became the basis for the Broadway musical *A Funny Thing Happened on the Way to the Forum*. The poetry of **Catullus** (84-54 BC), on the other hand, set a high standard for passion, while providing a source of Latin obscenities for future generations of Classics students. **Livy** (c.59 BC-AD17) set down the authorized history of Rome from the city's founding to his own time, while **Julius Caesar** (100-44 BC) gave a first-hand account of the final shredding of the Republic, in his *De Bello Civili;* his *De Bello Gallico* recounts his experiences on the front lines of the Gallic wars. Caesar's close contemporary **Cicero** (106-43 BC), an orator, statesman, and philosopher, penned numerous works noteworthy for their carefully crafted Latin, including the political speech *In Catilinam* ("O tempora, O mores!"), *De Republica* (just one of many philosophical treatises), and several collections of letters to his family and friends.

Augustan Rome, despite a government prone to banishing the impolitic, produced some of the greatest Latin authors of antiquity. **Virgil** (70-19 BC), revered by posterity as the only Roman poet worthy of comparison with Homer, wrote the *Aeneid,* an epic recounting the adventures of the Trojan hero Aeneas in his flight from the ruins of his homeland and his eventual settlement on the Tiber, thus founding the Roman people. **Horace's** (65-8 BC) verse derives more from his personal experiences, which he worked into his prolific *Odes, Epodes, Satires,* and *Epistles.* Both Virgil and Horace also praised the simple life of the country-dweller, in response to the growing squalor and chaos of first-century BC Rome. Self-proclaimed city-lover, **Ovid** (43 BC-AD17), though originally employed by Augustus, was later banished to Romania, apparently because of his involvement in the escapades of Augustus' rebellious and promiscuous daughter and grand-daughter, both named Julia. His poems, among them the *Amores,* the mythological *Metamorphoses* (in which the narrator briefly urges his readers to convert to vegetarianism), and the *Ars Amatoria* (a tongue-in-cheek guide to scamming on the opposite sex), are much more light-hearted than those of his contemporaries and surprisingly in touch with 20th-century Western culture.

From the post-Augustan empire, **Petronius'** (1st century AD) *Satyricon* is a blunt look at the decadence of the age of Nero, while **Suetonius'** (c.AD 69 -c.130) *De Vita Caesarum* was the gossipy version of imperial history. **Tacitus'** (c. AD 56-after 116) *Histories* summarize Roman war, diplomacy, scandal, and rumor in the years after Nero's death. His *Annals* look down from the upright Rome of Trajan's reign onto the scandalous activities of the Julio-Claudian emperors. Finally, **Marcus Aurelius'** (AD 121-180) *Meditations* bring us the musings of a philosopher-king.

ART AND ARCHITECTURE

Some have said that ancient Roman culture was borrowed entirely from the Greeks, and, indeed, the two civilizations share more than a few features in common in terms of religion, literary tradition, art, and architecture. Even before Rome's conquest of Greece in the 2nd century BC, many elements of Greek art and architecture had already found their way into the Roman repertoire, through the Greek-influenced Etruscans. With hundreds of years of Greek art at their disposal, Romans were able to pick and choose from among many different styles. Roman sculpture, however, did not merely reproduce the art of the Greeks. Roman portraiture, for example, was much less idealized than its Greek counterpart; sculptors strove to create an accurate, realistic, and individualized representation of the subject. The events and people that artists chose to depict were also more commonplace and earthy than the lofty sculptures of the Greeks. The collections of the Capitoline and Vatican Museums contain numerous works in this typically Roman style.

Another distinctively Roman art form was household or private art. The interior walls of houses and shops were often extensively painted, usually in the **fresco** style of paint on wet plaster. Sometimes a wall would be painted to look like a beautiful outdoor scene, as in the villa of the Empress Livia at Prima Porta, or *trompe l'oeil* doors or columns would be painted in to make the house look bigger. In other cases, mythological or still-life scenes would be painted on walls or executed in **mosaic,** a popular genre in Roman art from the Hellenistic period onward. A favorite design is the watchdog, sometimes painted on the exterior wall of a house, or else executed in mosaic on the vestibule floor; the *cave canem* ("beware of dog") mosaic at Pompeii is the most famous example.

The Romans' greatest contribution to architecture was the development of the arch. With this simple architectural innovation, the Romans constructed aqueducts, bridges, and triumphal arches. The arch was also incorporated into building types, new and old: the semicircular **theater** (where plays were put on), the oval **amphitheater** (for gladiatorial and military displays, of which the Colosseum (AD 80) in Rome is the most famous example), and the **basilica** (a type of multi-purpose building created in the second century BC). The basilica floor-plan was later used in the design and construction of early Christian churches, and the word *basilica* is still used today to describe the four patriarchal churches in Rome—St. Peter's, Santa Maria Maggiore, San Paolo fuori le Mura, and San Giovanni in Laterano—as well as many other churches throughout the city.

■ The Rise of Christianity and the Fall of Rome

THE AGE OF MARTYRS

Weak leadership and the invasions of Germanic tribes combined to create a state of near-anarchy in the 3rd century AD. **Diocletian** secured control of the fragmented empire in 284 AD, established order, divided the empire into eastern and western halves, and escalated the persecution of Christians. This period became known as "the age of martyrs." The persecution began in 64 when the Emperor Nero, a poetaster and dedicated sadist, needed a patsy for the immense and destructive fire he was widely believed to have started. While Nero made a show of trying Christians in court, the Roman people were diverted and appeased by the entertaining sight of Christians dressed in the hides of animals and torn to shreds by savage canines or set on fire as lamps so law-abiding citizens could do a little reading before bed. The Christians who died came to be known as "martyrs," from the Greek for "witnesses," an apt term for those who experienced first-hand the full extent of Roman cruelty. In spite of this hazardous environment, by the end of Diocletian's violent reign there were approximately 30,000 Christians gathered in Rome.

The fortunes of local Christians took a turn for the better when **Constantine,** Diocletian's successor, saw a huge cross in the wartime sky along with the letters, *"In hoc signo vinces"* (By this sign you shall conquer). Sure enough, victory followed the vision, and Constantine, combining military strategy with spiritual conversion, conquered his co-emperor Maxentius in 312 and declared Christianity the state religion in 315. Constantine hastened the end of Rome's supremacy by moving the capital of the empire east in 330, to the renamed city of Constantinople. As city officials lost touch with their far-off imperial government, Christian bishops began to assume some traditional civic duties, such as caring for the poor and hungry. Meanwhile, huge armies of barbarian mercenaries broke through neglected fortifications along the empire's northern borders and ultimately descended on Rome. In 410, **Alaric,** king of the Visigoths, sacked the city. Sacker-extraordinaire **Attila the Hun** arrived on tour in 452; despite the absence of an opposing army to greet him in Rome, fast-talker Pope Leo I convinced him to pillage elsewhere. The ensuing scramble for power wasn't fully resolved until 476, when **Odoacer,** an Ostrogoth chieftain, deposed **Romulus Augustus,** the last of Rome's western emperors, and was crowned King of Italy. The Christian Byzantines were harder to appease; their brutal sack of Rome during the **Gothic Wars** (535-553) outdid the worst of the barbarians.

LITERATURE

The upheaval and turmoil of the late empire did not exactly foster the growth of literature. During these years, the field was dominated almost entirely by the early Christian writers, among whom **St. Augustine** (354-430) was the most well known, as well as one of the only native Romans. Born of Christian mother and pagan father, St. Augustine credited his own conversion to his mother's prayers and his extensive studies of religion and philosophy. Though quite prolific, he is most famous for his *Confessions*, an autobiographical work in the form of a letter to God.

ART AND ARCHITECTURE

Given the chaos of the 3rd and 4th centuries, emperors' minds tended to focus on making war, not art. Painting of the time consisted mostly of wall **frescoes** done by anonymous artisans. The color, composition, and treatment of subjects in the **Christian catacombs** (see p. 160) recall Roman wall painting, with togate figures representing Christ and the apostles. Mosaics from this period abound in Rome, especially in the early churches, such as Santa Maria Maggiore and Santa Pudenziana (see p. 164). Virtuosi working for wealthy patrons used *tessarae* (tiles) as miniscule as 1/32 of an inch. The taste of Roman emperors, however, tended to run towards the gargantuan. Witness the humongous head of Constantine, located in the Palazzo dei Conservatori on the Capitoline Hill, 6 ft. high and weighing nine tons. The magnitude of the **Arch of Constantine,** a tribute from the Senate in 315 for his victory over Maxentius, compensates for its lack of artistic complexity.

The most significant architectural contributions of the late empire to the city of Rome were the first official buildings of the burgeoning western Church. The first Christian churches in Rome lacked a unique architectural style, and simply took the form of renovated Roman basilicas, rectangular spaces supported by columns. The great hall of Constantine's mother's palace was transformed into a basilica now known as **Santa Croce in Gerusalemme** (see p. 166). Constantine is credited with building the first of many versions of the **Basilica di San Lorenzo fuori le Mura,** a sanctuary for pilgrims visiting the tomb of St. Lawrence. It was during these turbulent centuries that the pagan structures of ancient Rome began to fall into disrepair. The barbarians of the early 5th century can't take all the credit, though—for years before the invasions, native Romans had been dismantling the city's monuments for valuable metals and building materials

■ The Middle Ages

Diocletian's bisection of the empire increased its instability; in every year during the next two centuries, at least one of the two empires was at war. The eastern Roman (Byzantine) emperor **Justinian** brutally conquered much of the western division between 535 and 554 AD and imposed the *corpus juris,* or codified law of the empire, which served as the legal model for European nations for half a millennium. Unfortunately, much of the quarrel between the two divisions of the empire revolved around Rome; the city suffered the consequences of war like never before. By the 6th century, the eternal city, once home to as many as a million people, could support just several thousand. When the Goths slashed the aqueducts in 546 AD, they sealed the city's fate. The hills of Rome, once crowded with houses, baths, and splashing fountains, were deserted as the remaining citizens crowded into the unhealthy neighborhoods along the Tiber banks. It was in these days that some of the most famous neighborhoods of Rome—Trastevere, Campo dei Fiori, and the streets around Piazza Navona—were first heavily settled. In the ramshackle alleyways swarming round the river, starvation and plague ran rampant, relieved only by the periodic invasions of barbarians.

The struggle for Rome required a temporary friendship with the papacy for protection. Since Constantine made Catholicism the official religion, Roman nobility had gradually turned toward the Church as a new means of maintaining their power and status in the increasingly unstable realm of politics. Rome owed its salvation from the turbulence of the Dark Ages in large part to the wealthy popes, who kept up a decent tourist industry attracting cash-laden pilgrims and invoked the wrath of God to intimidate would-be invaders. Pope **Gregory the Great** (reigning from 590-604 AD) devised new, efficient strategies for distributing food and sent the word of God via missionaries all over Europe.

MEDIEVAL CHAOS, PART I

When Rome was faced with the threat of invasion from the German Lombards, Pope Stephen II was forced to ask for help from the Frankish warlord Pepin the Short. Under Pepin's benevolent protection, **Hadrian I** repaired the city's aqueducts and restored its churches. Hadrian's successor Pope Leo III slipped a crown on the unsuspecting head of Pepin's son **Charlemagne** on Christmas Day, 800, declaring him "Emperor of the Romans," a title later known as Holy Roman Emperor.

Peace was short lived. Charlemagne's death in 814 AD set off another 200 years of near-anarchy. In 846, Muslim Saracens rowed up the Tiber and plundered St. Peter's and San Paolo fuori le Mura. With the gradual weakening of Frankish power in Europe, three powers—the Church, Roman nobility, and imperialist forces—engaged in a shockingly bloody and absurd struggle for control over Rome and the papal seat. By far the most ridiculous tale from these years is the posthumous trial of Pope Formosus. Formosus' successor Pope Stephen VI dug up Formosus' corpse, dressed it in ecclesiastical robes, and put it on trial. Not surprisingly, the corpse was convicted on all counts, its three blessing fingers ripped off (just in case) and the body chucked into the Tiber. Stephen was later murdered, the next Pope brutally overthrown, and the Pope after that murdered as well. In the years around the turn of the 9th century, there were eight popes in eight years; nine popes were murdered during the 10th century. It just wasn't a good time to be Pope.

The first major figure to emerge in this two-century game of king-of-the-mountain was **Alberic the Younger** in 932. The son of a powerful aristocratic Roman family, Alberic attempted to wrest control of Rome away from the Church and steer it towards a secular governmental structure or *comune*. (Of course, Alberic had no idea how mammoth this task was: the Vatican wouldn't officially butt out of Rome's political affairs until nearly a millenium later, under the Lateran treaty of 1929.) On his deathbed in 964, however, Alberic appointed his degenerate teenage son **John XII** as Pope, to combine the powers of the Church and Rome's aristocracy once more. (After his father's death, John installed a harem at the Vatican.) Brilliantly indecisive, John crowned the German monarch **Otto I** as Holy Roman Emperor, largely for protection against Berengar, a Northern Italian ruler; panicked by thoughts that he had appealed to the weaker leader, John subsequently asked Berengar for similar protection from Otto. Otto emerged the victor, controller of both the city and the papacy, but the next 100 years of Roman history were dominated by the gruesome tit-for-tat of Romans revolting against imperialist papal appointments and popes imposing imperialist punishments on the rebels. Around the turn of the 11th century, Otto's violent grandson **Otto III** developed a penchant for ripping out the eyes of members of the **Crescenzi** family, the persistent and powerful nobility who would periodically storm the papal fortress, Castel Sant'Angelo.

After the German Emperors had straightened out the church (in their favor), the late 11th-century **Hildebrand,** a crusading monk, won a position as Pope Gregory VII. Hildebrand was so successful at demanding universal church authority that Emperor Henry II, whom he had excommunicated, was forced to beg in the snow for forgiveness. It all turned out to be a trick, however, and the second time the emperor was excommunicated he laid siege to Rome, and Hildebrand's followers jumped ship. In 1084, the Norman conqueror **Robert Guiscard** (who had also fought on behalf of Hildebrand) remembered—a little ahead of schedule—that Rome was due for its tricentennial sacking. Eleven years later, Pope Urban II asked Guiscard's son, Bohemond, and the Frankish nobility to "liberate" the Holy Land, resulting in mass slaughter and religious animosity that continues to this day.

MEDIEVAL CHAOS, PART II

All over Rome you'll see streets, buildings, bridges, and *piazze* named after the city's first families: Orsini, Colonna, Pierleoni, Frangipani, Vitelleschi, Tebaldi, Savelli, Papareschi, Annibaldi. Despite foreign emperors, popes, and anti-popes, ever since the fall of the Empire, these tightly knit clans vied for control of Rome's *rioni* (neighborhoods) and their daily operation. By the mid-12th century, a new class of citizens had coalesced in Rome: large numbers of businessmen, lesser clergy and nobles, and expert craftsmen had prospered but remained disenfranchised from the political system, such as it was. Inspired by the radical preaching of reformist monk **Arnold da Brescia,** in 1143 these Romans rose against their noble superiors, looted their houses, declared Rome a republic, and demanded that the church give up its temporal power. It almost worked, but subsequent popes were able to strike bargains with foreign emperors (mostly German) and reinstate themselves and Rome's families as rulers of the city. Brescia was tortured and hanged, but the church faced more Republican rioting for the next 45 years.

Romans managed to win limited self-determination about the same time that King John was buying time by signing the Magna Carta in England. It wasn't until **Pope Clement III,** a Roman by birth who could claim to have the city's interests at heart, that the rebels and the papacy struck a bargain. The Church's temporal powers were accepted, and members of the Senate swore their loyalty to the Pope and returned seized church property. In exchange, the church agreed to recognize the city of Rome as a *comune,* with its own power to declare war or peace. This agreement paved the way for the unprecedented power of Pope **Innocent III.** Innocent was a skilled mixture of politician and dictator. He can be credited with elevating the Church's power in Europe to its highest level up to that point.

After Innocent's death, the Vatican was again under assault from disgruntled German emperors and the increasingly demanding Senate; in order to break the sway of the city's noble families, strong man Senator **Brancaleone di Andalò** demolished 140 family towers and made an example of two Annibaldis by publicly hanging them. The following pope, French-born **Charles d'Anjou,** heralded a brief period of French dominance in Rome; in the 1260s and 1270s six French-born popes and 21 French or French-allied cardinals (about a third of the cardinals invested in that period) were elected. The Pope who broke the French hold over the Vatican was the much-reviled **Boniface VII,** elected in 1294. After he antagonized nearly every ruler in Europe with a string of excommunications and the demanding papal edict *Unam Sanctam,* the French (aided by the Colonnas, only too happy to help out, since the Church had seized much of their property) assaulted Boniface in his home and accused him of such crimes as sodomy and keeping a demon as a pet. Boniface died of shock, and the **Babylonian Captivity** began six years later; for most of the 14th century, popes would conduct their business from Avignon, France under the thumb of French kings (though rival popes kept cropping up in Rome, making the Church look even more ridiculous).

After hearing the convincing words of St. Catherine of Siena, **Pope Gregory XI** agreed to return the papal seat to Rome and restore the city's greatest source of income, the papal court. This, combined with a hugely successful Jubilee celebration in 1390, positioned Rome to take full advantage of the cultural and intellectual prosperity of the Renaissance.

LITERATURE

During the Middle Ages, the literary language of choice was Latin, in spite of the fact that the Latin of Caesar and Cicero hadn't been spoken by the people since the days of the early Empire. This gap between the written language and the vernacular, or *volgare,* led to a wide-spread rejection of Latin among writers and poets, throughout the Romance-speaking parts of Europe. In Italy, the forerunners in this movement took the form of a triumvirate of Tuscans—Dante, Petrarch, and Boccaccio—who helped to elevate Tuscan to its position as the most prestigious dialect and, ultimately, the standard form of Italian. **Dante Alighieri** (1265-1321), considered as much the father of the modern Italian language as of its literature, was one of the first European poets to eschew Latin. After the death of his young love Beatrice in 1290, Dante began writing his masterpiece, *La Divina Commedia,* partially as a form of personal solace. Dante's allegorical journey through the afterlife is guided by his ancient Roman counterpart, Virgil, author of the great Latin epic poem, the *Aeneid.* Among the *Commedia's* charms are Dante's acid descriptions of Italian cities and their inhabitants. His lines on Rome are particularly haunting and mourn its bloody history. Of Constantine's "gift" (handing Rome over to the papacy) he writes "Ah, Constantine, what evil was spawned not by your conversion but by that gift which the first rich Pope accepted from you." *The Divine Comedy* is believed by many to be the prime expression of the High Medieval world-view.

Although he preferred to write in Latin, **Francesco Petrarca** (1304-1374) was perhaps more influential than Dante in establishing a model for future writers of Tuscan poetry. The language of his *Canzoniere,* his only work in Italian, is careful, consistent, and, above all, not prone to the excesses and fancies so common in his fellow poets' works. The third member of the medieval literary triumvirate, **Giovanni Boccaccio** (1313-1375), was a friend of Pertrach, but owes little to his sonnet-writing pal. The *Decameron,* Boccaccio's collection of 100 stories supposedly told by 10 young Florentines fleeing their plague-ridden city, ranges in tone from suggestive to downright bawdy; in one story, a hard-working gardener has his way with an entire convent. The *Decameron* also includes one of the only contemporary descriptions of the Black Plague and its symptoms.

ART AND ARCHITECTURE

As early as the 6th century, Pope Gregory the Great was calling for art which would edify the illiterate masses, art that would not glorify the individual or the earthly world in which he lived but rather laud the world beyond. The gaze of the Christian art which eventually emerged in the Middle Ages was fixed firmly on heaven. The lack of proportion, the disregard for the body, the monochromatic backgrounds, and the landscapes cluttered with obscure symbols are striking; these paintings are supposed to combine a disregard for this world with the placement of the individual in a larger hierarchy of symbols and belief.

The first important non-Classical style introduced into Italian art was the religious and highly-stylized **Byzantine.** Byzantine art made its first big splash in Rome with the mosaics of **Sant'Agnese fuori le Mura** (638 AD; see p. 197). Byzantine influence made its most profound impact in architecture, however, both by perfecting the blueprint of the Christian basilica and by crowning these churches with domes and vaults. The earliest Italian churches to bear the Byzantine influence are in Ravenna, notably the Church of San Vitale. In Rome, that ultra-serious architecture known as Romanesque rose to an extended prominence. From roughly 500 to 1200 AD churches in the Romanesque style dominated Europe. These churches are unmistakable due to their small, rounded arches resting on massive stone piers, creating a sense of heaviness and power. This heaviness was unavoidable; if large windows were placed in the walls, the weight of the roof would push the walls apart and the church would collapse.

When you spot a Romanesque church, check inside for characteristic art—either distorted, stylized, Byzantine-type artwork or Classical relief sculpture in the stone of the buildings themselves—and note how little light invades the interior. The great Italian Romanesque churches include the Cathedral of Pisa, the Church of San Ambrogio in Milan, the Cathedral of Massa Marittima, and the Church of San Miniato in Florence. Luckily, in Rome the 12th century saw the appearance of the **Cosmati** families who filled these grave monuments (S. Maria in Cosmedin, S. Maria in Trastevere and S. Clemente) with luminous mosaics.

■ The Renaissance and the Baroque

HISTORY

The no-nonsense **Pope Martin V** (a member of the powerful Colonna family) seized power in 1420, marking the beginning of the Renaissance urbanity and absolute papal rule of Rome that lasted until 1870. He wasn't much for art and architecture, but he established a strong administration that made Rome the capital of a Church-controlled Renaissance state. The roads were widened and paved, and buildings in the new style were erected; unfortunately, many ancient structures were demolished to provide building materials for these projects. **Julius II** (in power 1503-13) began an enormous building program, setting out plans for St. Peter's dome and the rest of the city. He hired the architect Bramante, who demolished medieval Rome with such enthusiasm and intent that Raphael nicknamed him *Ruinante*.

When Protestant upstart and Renaissance foe **Martin Luther** returned to Rome in 1510, he was sorely disappointed by the city's aesthetic indulgence and spiritual dissolution. He could barely recognize "the footprints of ancient Rome, as the old buildings were now buried beneath the new, so deep lieth the rubbish." He was enraged at the Church's blatant pursuit of worldly happiness and the utter confidence in salvation. He was revolted by the sight of Raphael's ornate *Stanze* in the Vatican, in which Christian and pagan symbols mingled, in the buff, no less. While the Pope went "triumphing about with fair-decked stallions, the priests gabbled Mass," Luther went about writing the 95 Theses of the **Protestant Reformation**.

After excommunicating that pesky Luther, **Pope Leo X** (in power 1513-1521) asserted his interest in the humanities, drawing up his own plans for a new St. Peter's dome and commissioning artists Michelangelo and Raphael. However, despite these popes' profound patronage of the arts, the political health of Italy only deteriorated. Their blatant disregard for honest politicking and for the well-being of the country undermined Italy's unity and military force. To supplement their pocket money, most of these popes heavily taxed Romans and their country cousins. Previously prosperous Lazio and Umbria soon filed for bankruptcy, and much of the distressed agricultural population just up and left for better regions. The popes also curried favor with assorted foreign nations—whichever suited them best at the time—extracting money from whomever they could. These fragmented alliances left Rome vulnerable to invasion, and soon proved fatal.

The Sack of Rome

Although Rome had been sacked numerous times in the past, on the morning of May 7, 1527 the city faced *the* **Sack of Rome,** an intense eight-day pillage courtesy of German warriors, Spanish marauders, and 15,000 Lutheran mercenaries, after Italy became a bone of contention between France and Spain. The city fell into the hands of the blood thirsty imperialist troops, who stormed through the Borgo, killing everyone and everything in sight and destroying thousands of churches, palaces, and houses. The troops broke down the doors of churches, convents, palaces, monaster-

Disease and Disaster

Along with the humanist ideals of Petrarch, creations of Michelangelo and Raphael, and licentious happenings at *carnevale*, Renaissance Italy encountered a humiliating obstacle to its achievements: namely, **syphilis.** Scientists now believe the disease had existed on the continent for millennia, but Europeans had developed antibodies to combat it. Unfortunately, a second strain of the virus was waiting in the New World, and when Columbus reached America the two strains mingled, creating a malady that would rock both continents. French soldiers contracted the disease from prostitutes in Naples and nicknamed it the "Neapolitan disease;" in turn, the Italians called it *morbo gallico* (disease of the Gauls). In Rome, the disease spread like wildfire, infecting 17 members of the Pope's family and court, including Cesare Borgia, who was treated for it within two months of its first appearance.

To add to the horrors of the city's inundation by venereal disease, the Tiber produced a violent **flood** in 1495, with water gushing into the streets and surging through churches and homes until it was suppressed by the fortified walls of the city's palaces. Many people were drowned, including the prisoners in the fearsome Tor di Nona, which overlooked the (now-called) Ponte Umberto, a stark prison that once held astronomer-*cum*-heretic Giordano Bruno and sculptor-*cum*-jewel-thief Benvenuto Cellini.

The ascetic Florentine Dominican friar **Girolamo Savonarola** soon proclaimed these calamities the wages of sin to be paid by the decadent Church and inaugurated an all-out rampage on the papal and municipal excesses of Rome. He condemned the Church for its whoring and its profligacy. He warned the city of famine, pestilence, and catastrophe if it neglected to clean up its act; he even envisioned a black cross rising from the hills of Rome emblazoned with the words, "The Cross of God's Anger." He later felt the wrath of the city of Florence and met his death at the hands of the executioner.

ies, and studios, hurling their contents into the street. They broke into tombs, including the one holding Pope Julius II, and ripped the jewelry from the corpses. Priceless religious ornaments were used for mockery, and some troops launched a fake papal procession through the streets. Some sporty raiders even took St. Andrew's and St. John's heads to use as kick balls. The invaders tortured men in order to force them to reveal the hiding-places of valuables or made them pay ransom for their lives or the lives of their families. One report relates the horrors of one sect of torturers, who force-fed Roman captives their own roasted testicles. Priests were made to utter blasphemies on pain of death, or to take part in profane travesties. One priest was murdered because he refused to kneel and give the Holy Communion to a donkey. They targeted convents for sexual assault; nuns were auctioned off as whores or used as gambling chips. Women of the Roman aristocracy were also dragged to the desecrated convents. There never was an official body count, and as one Spaniard wrote, "I know nothing wherewith I can compare it, except it be the destruction of Jerusalem. I do not believe that if I had lived for two hundred years, I should see the like again." The Pope managed to escape the sack and died 10 years later of a fever.

By 1600 Rome was again a thriving metropolis facing little political unrest. Having created such havoc earlier in the century, the popes lost much of their political relevance in the play between European powers during the Thirty Years War.

LITERATURE

Fifteenth- and 16th-century Italian authors branched out from the genres of their predecessors. **Leon Battista Alberti** and **Palladio** (Andrea di Pietro) wrote treatises on architecture and art theory; **Baldassare Castiglione's** *The Courtier* instructed the inquiring Renaissance man on deportment, etiquette, and other fine points of behavior; **Vasari** took time off from redecorations of Florence's churches to produce a primer on art history and criticism *(The Lives of the Artists)*. One of the most lasting works of the Renaissance, **Nicolò Macchiavelli's** *Il Principe (The Prince)*, is a sophisticated assessment of what it takes to gain and hold political power. Although Macchiavelli did not make many friends with his candid and brutal suggestions, he is now regarded as the father of modern political theory.

In attempts at living up to the title of "Renaissance men," non-professionals often tried their hands at writing as well. Among Renaissance artists, **Benvenuto Cellini** wrote about the most interesting of all subjects, himself, in *The Autobiography;* **Michelangelo** wrote enough sonnets to fuel a fire, while **Leonardo da Vinci** wrote about anything and everything *(The Notebook)*. The scathing and brilliant **Pietro Aretino** created new possibilities for literature when he began accepting payment from notable targets for *not* writing about them.

ART AND ARCHITECTURE

...if cleanliness is next to godliness, it is a very distant neighbor to chiaroscuro.

—Henry James

The succession of wealthy popes who were eager to leave their mark on the city in the form of new buildings, paintings, and sculpture gave a sagging Rome its most gorgeous makeover since its ancient days of monumental glory. Hailing from Rome's secular noble families, the popes nevertheless bolstered the Church's supremacy and spiritual optimism by commissioning artists to depict conversion scenes and martyrdoms. This age heralded the split between science and faith, and the Church condemned both Galileo and Giordano Bruno for their astronomical assertions that the earth was not the center of the universe. Painters, sculptors, and architects relied heavily on subjective experience, exploiting its emotional and dramatic potential, all while employing the most advanced technical and scientific discoveries the Age of Science had to offer.

The new scientific understandings of anatomy contributed to the discovery of perspective and the perfection of human musculature in two-dimensional representation. The rediscovery of Roman and Greek forms and the new "worldly" concerns of the Church further revitalized the interest in the human form as well as realism. Nudity came back into vogue; both Christian and pagan themes were explored with new interest. Though the rational Age of Enlightenment was right around the corner, it was faith who played muse to the creative brilliance of this period.

Michelangelo

The supreme artist with the supremely tortured soul, **Michelangelo Buonarroti** (1475-1564) grew up among the stone-masons of Tuscany; "With my wet-nurse's milk, I sucked in the hammer and chisels I use for my statues," Michelangelo asserted. After serving as an apprentice to Domenico Ghirlandaio and attending an art academy, he was discovered by Lorenzo the Magnificent, who nurtured the young genius in the palace's court circle of artists and humanists. During this period, Michelangelo honed his knowledge of the human body after he swapped his crucifix for the privilege of dissecting corpses in the Cloisters of San Spirito. At the age of 21 he headed to Rome, already commissioned by the Pope for some minor works, to seek his fortune. His first claim to fame was a marble cupid which imitated the ancients so perfectly that admirers claimed it could be mistaken for an authentic one. He received a flood of commissions; on one of them, he created the profoundly sorrowful and sensuous **Pietà** in St. Peter's, which made him the leading sculptor of marble and quite a celebrity. He returned to Florence for a decade, agonizingly carving his colossal and heroic **David** out of a huge piece of inferior marble; the confidence, pride and perfection of the statue inspired Florence to make it its symbol instead of the *duomo,* and they parked it outside of the town hall. This larger-than-life nude male figure initiated a mad rush of other sculptors, including Benvenuto Cellini, trying to outdo Michelangelo.

In 1502, Pope Julius II sent for Michelangelo, at the time almost thirty and at the height of his career, to return to Rome to build a **tomb** (in San Pietro in Vincoli, see p. 167). The relationship that was to last 10 years between overbearing, irascible, and demanding Julius II and the arrogant, introverted, and temperamental Michelangelo was not a meeting of like minds. Julius first commissioned Michelangelo to construct a colossal tomb, which was left unfinished when Julius got carried away instead with his grandiose plans for St. Peter's.

Infuriated and fed up, Michelangelo fled Rome in 1504. Julius managed to sweet-talk the moody artist into returning to Rome to paint the **Sistine Chapel** ceiling. Michelangelo agreed, and spent the next four years slaving over, or rather under, the problem-ridden project. However, Michelangelo first had to learn how to paint frescoes before he could even begin working. A perfectionist and type-A personality, Michelangelo fired all his assistants for their incompetence and took up even the most menial tasks himself. He threw away the Pope's original pictorial design and got permission to do the whole job himself, a considerable challenge from which he never fully recovered. Michelangelo spent days standing and craning his neck and head up to the ceiling until they were practically dislocated. The chapel was suffocatingly hot in the summer, and freezing in the winter. On a daily basis he had paint and plaster dripping into his face, causing a rash. Julius sometimes climbed up on the scaffolding to prod Michelangelo along.

The ceiling was finished in 1512, four months before Julius's death, and Michelangelo escaped to Florence. Thirty years later, Michelangelo returned to Rome, greeted by the new Pope Paul II, who commissioned the aged Michelangelo to return to the Sistine Chapel for his most important work, *The Last Judgement.* By contrast to the idealized figures, careful details and more optimistic images of the Sistine ceiling, *The Last Judgment* reveals Michelangelo's terrifying vision of the Apocalypse, anticipating the swirling colors, dark, emotional drama, bleak decor, and imperfect figures of the Mannerist period. Michelangelo continued in his architectural designs but never painted again. He died at the age of 89, but before his death he expressed his wish to be buried in Florence. In order to circumvent the Romans, who would certainly want to bury Michelangelo's body in their city, his casket was smuggled to Florence and buried.

Caravaggio

Michelangelo Merisi da Caravaggio (1573-1610) was as "refined" in his life as he was in his art. While his attacks of anxiety drove him to introspection and isolation, Caravaggio violently vented his frustrations on other people. Often drunk, the sight of a uniform made him particularly irascible: 16th-century police reports reveal that Caravaggio stabbed a captain of the papal guards, went to jail for lobbing stones at a policeman, and was picked up after verbally abusing an officer who, understandably, wanted to see his permit for carrying firearms. Born in Caravaggio (near Milan), he moved to Rome when he was around 20. Although he had plenty of work as a painter, he chose to live and work in the seedy Roman underworld of prostitution and gambling. His acquaintances from the underbelly of the city appeared as holy and revered characters in his paintings: a pouty male prostitute posed for *Boy with a Basket of Fruit;* his St. Paul in the *Conversion of St. Paul* is ruggedly blue-collar-esque; St. Paul's horse, usually grandly depicted, could be any bored work horse (see p. 188).

Caravaggio participated in the art world on his own terms. While some patrons were put off by his reputation and those of his models, Caravaggio had a fruitful relationship with the Catholic Church; Church officials recognized the raw, intense spirituality in Caravaggio's work that the Baroque Church wanted (and needed) to illustrate; his figures would "speak to the people," as it were. After stabbing and killing an acquaintance in a dispute over a ball game, Caravaggio fled Rome. He died of a fever while attempting to return to the city to take advantage of a papal pardon.

Bernini and Borromini

The personality differences between effervescent, cavalier boy-genius **Gianlorenzo Bernini** and dark, temperamental **Francesco Castelli Borromini** are abundantly clear in their works. Known as the "greatest European" in his day, the architect, sculptor, painter, and dandy Bernini more than set the standard for the Baroque during his prolific career. Confident in the precocious genius of his son, Bernini's father, a Florentine sculptor, brought his son to Rome to start work; he was immediately signed on for training and didn't stop working until the age of 80. For Bernini, work was pleasure, and by the end of his life, he had served every pope of his time and had shaped the cityscape more than any other artist in history. His swarthy good looks endeared him to countless patrons and fans, and he was given creative control beyond any artist's wildest fantasy. His mastery of marble is unsurpassed, and his expressive sculptures deny the boundaries of clay and flesh.

Along with his charged **St. Teresa in Ecstasy** (in Santa Maria della Vittoria) Bernini's Hellenistic **David** (in the Villa Borghese Museum) stands in great contrast to Michelangelo's classical version of frozen perfection. The sculpture is a study in energy, expressiveness, and concentration whereas Michelangelo's embodies the restraint and coolness of Greek figures. Like Caravaggio, Bernini was eager to dismiss the generic heroic ideal his predecessors (like Michelangelo and Raphael) sought to emulate. Bernini revolutionized sculpture, taking it from an epic to a temporal form, releasing it from its cold, isolated nature to one of dramatic engagement, movement, and imperfect realism.

Although architecture was only a small portion of Bernini's career, he was one of Rome's greatest architects. The oval of the *piazza* of St. Peter's was the culmination of a life's work; he personally supervised the construction of each and every one of the 284 Doric travertine columns. Only Bernini could manage to transform the overwhelming space into an inviting, even emotional square, which would, as he said, "maternally embrace" the crowds in its colonnade. His churches and monuments (including the grand **baldacchino** at St. Peter's and his own favorite, the **Church of Sant'Andrea al Quirinale)** exemplified his high-flown, theatrical, illusory style that came to define the Baroque.

Tortured, acutely cerebral, non-conformist, and Swiss, **Borromini** spent much of his career repudiating the prevailing *zeitgeist* of the Baroque, with its sumptuous illusions and ornate decoration. His surviving architectural designs, fraught with an endless series of changes and minute details, bespeak the sheer agony and intellectual integrity of Borromini's life work. Where Bernini played with illusion and decoration, Borromini sought purity (though in the most complex terms) and used painfully difficult geometry in creating his architectural structures. Borromini once served as a student of Maderno, and was commissioned to design some of the details on Bernini's *baldacchino.* It became increasingly apparent, however, that Bernini's style and Borromini's own were wholly incompatible. He managed to imbue his work with vigor and animation solely by the undulating movement of concave and convex forms and the play of shadow and light, unadorned with Baroque frippery or excessive ornamentation. He staunchly refused to deck his buildings with the windswept statues which Bernini so loved, and insisted that the painfully wrought structures speak for themselves. In works like the **Church of San Carlo alle Quattro Fontane,** in which the façade appears almost stretched out of shape or distended, creating a sense of tensions and counter-pressures and fusing sculpture and architecture, Gothic and Renaissance, like never before, Borromini created an entirely new architectural vocabulary. Eventually the complexity, tension, and pressure of Borromini's work caught up with him; he became obsessed with his calculations and machinations, and withdrew completely from society. Whereas Bernini wallowed in his fame, attending banquets in his honor throughout Europe, Borromini would be comforted only by an old parish priest. Finally, a few days after burning a series of architectural plans, he put a sword through his chest and died.

MUSIC

The Italians are musical tyrants, as anyone who has studied the piano, belonged to a school band, or slaved over a cello can attest. The *piano, crescendo,* and *allegro* are there for a reason: Italians, with help from the French, invented the system for musical notation used today. Guido D'Arezzo came up with *solfege,* the "do, re, mi" syllable system of expressing the musical scale, and a 16th-century Venetian printed the first musical scores with movable type. Cremona offered violins by Stradivarius and Guarneri; the piano (actually the *pianoforte,* which means "soft-loud") is an Italian invention. Even so, for Italians, vocal music has always occupied a position of undisputed prominence. **Palestrina** and his Roman colleagues, worried that the Council of Trent might banish the use of secular tunes in the liturgy in order to ensure clarity of the texts, pre-empted such repression by eschewing Venetian flamboyance in favor of crystalline harmonies. At the same time, **madrigals,** free-flowing secular songs for three to six voices, grew in popularity.

The 16th century brought the greatest musical innovation in Italian history: opera. Born in Florence, nurtured in Venice, and revered in Milan, **opera** is Italy's most cherished art form. Invented by the **Camerata,** an artsy clique of Florentine poets, noblemen, authors, and musicians, opera began as an attempt to recreate the dramas of ancient Greece (which they decided had been sung) by setting their lengthy poems to music. After several years of effort with only dubious success, one member, Jacobo Peri, composed *Dafne* in 1597, the world's first complete opera. (*Dafne* has since been lost—not a great loss, according to contemporary accounts.) A school of operatic composers soon emerged, eager to master the Camerata's new genre of music. As opera spread from Florence to Venice, Milan, and Rome, the styles and forms of the genre also grew more distinct. Much of early opera featured *stile recitativo,* which attempted to recapture the simple, evocative singing and recitation of classical drama. The first successful opera composer, **Monteverdi,** drew freely from history, blithely juxtaposing high drama, concocted love scenes, and lewd humor. Having charmed his patron with *Orfeo,* Monteverdi assured the survival of the genre. Contemporaneous with the birth of opera was the emergence of the **oratorio.** Introduced by the Roman priest **Saint Filippo Neri,** the oratorio set biblical text to dramatic choral and instrumental accompaniment.

Instrumental music began to establish itself as a legitimate genre in 17th-century Rome. During the **Baroque** period, **Corelli** developed the concerto form with its contrasting moods and tempos, adding drama and emotion to technical expertise. **Antonio Vivaldi** wrote over 400 concerti while teaching at a home for orphaned girls in Venice. Under Vivaldi the concerto assumed its present form, in which the virtuoso playing of the soloist is opposed to and accompanied by the concerted strength of the orchestra. His *Four Seasons* is one of the best known Baroque orchestral works.

CARNIVAL

The decadent nature of Renaissance Rome welcomed back the carnival hi-jinks and horrors of ancient times that had been more or less abandoned in the medieval period. Initially, Pope Paul II (1458-64) set up some races in the spirit of good, clean fun. There were races between kids, with a pair of stockings for the winner. There were races between young Christians, between middle-aged men, between senior citizens, and between buffaloes and donkeys. Thus was born the Roman *carnevale.* Pope Paul II later moved to a new palace, the Palazzo San Marco, overlooking the Via Lata, and decreed that the events take place in view of his window. These windows are visible in the facade of the **Palazzo Venezia,** which eventually replaced the Pope's palace. The races, or *corsi,* were then run from the palace to the Arch of Domitian, which is how Via Lata got its present name, Via del Corso.

The Roman Carnival audience delighted in the most cruel and unusual races, with appalling events harkening back to the evil-entertainment days of the Empire. There was a race reserved for hunchbacks and other cripples that prompted taunting and heckling. The Pope's henchmen kidnapped elderly Jews from the Ghetto, stuffed them with Italian pastry and made them run the course; the organizers added horses to goad them on. Those who refused to participate cheerfully were promptly flogged by a man hired just for that purpose, standing by on nearby Via Cavalletto.

With these elaborations of Carnival came some more innocent festivities. Crowds donned elaborate costumes, parading around as nymphs, gods, heroes, and fairies. A tall greased pole was set up in Piazza Navona for teams of men to climb up and test their machismo and strength—a contest still held during the carnival in New York's Little Italy. Streamers, ribbons, and garlands of flowers decorated buildings and benches. At the end of the day, the Pope hosted a lavish banquet for Roman VIPs and allowed the crowds of masqueraders to take doggie bags home. In one burst of drunken enthusiasm, he strewed money from his balcony to the screaming commoners below.

Queen Christina

One of Europe's most intriguing figures during the 17th century was Sweden's Queen Christina. Christina was a Renaissance man: she eschewed the dress of women, was an expert hunter, and could ride a horse like nobody's business; fluent in many languages and exceptionally well-read, she was also a renowned art collector who possessed one of the greatest art collections ever assembled. Unpopular in Sweden for converting to Catholicism and refusing to bear the nation an heir, Christina abdicated and took off to Rome on the advice of two Jesuit priests. There, the city's greatest artists gathered around her: Alessandro Scarlatti oversaw her private orchestra, while Bernini carved sculptures for her and gave her inside information on the art market. The philosopher René Descartes was her private tutor, and he died from a case of pneumonia he caught while teaching her in her drafty, unheated residence. She is buried in St. Peter's; an inscription welcoming her to the city remains on the Porta del Popolo.

■ The 18th and 19th Centuries

IL SETTECENTO ITALIANO

The first three-quarters of the 18th century in Rome were remarkably quiet politically, especially in comparison with the tumult of previous centuries. When the **Treaty of Westphalia** put an end to the **Thirty Years War** in 1648, its terms were less than favorable to papal power, which waned considerably afterwards. A succession of popes were either incompetent or uninterested in international affairs. **Pope Clement XIV,** faced with overwhelming anti-Jesuit sentiment, expelled the Society of Jesuits from Rome in 1773. His successor, **Pius VI,** mishandled conflicts between the Church and the post-revolution French Assembly. Anti-clerical sentiment exploded in Paris: effigies of Pius were set on fire and a severed head landed in the lap of the Papal Nuncio as he was traveling in his coach. In Rome, envoys of the republic replaced portraits of the Pope in the French Academy with portraits of revolutionary heroes and leaders. In 1793, Romans, roused from their usual complacency, attacked a French delegation that arrived on the Corso over-accessorized in tricolor badges. After murdering one of them, the crowd spread through the streets, vandalizing the homes of French sympathizers, setting the French Academy on fire, shouting "Long live the Pope" and "Long live the Catholic religion."

France's commander-in-chief, **Napoleon,** appeared on the scene in 1796 to deal with the problem and to refill French coffers, emptied by the revolution, with the treasures of Europe. Napoleon refused to depose the Pope altogether for certain strategic reasons, but he brought the Church to its knees by extorting millions in tribute and carrying off precious works of art and mountains of jewels. Romans watched 500 wagons leave the city loaded with booty; in fact, some of the most important pieces of Italian and Roman art are now found in Parisian museums. In 1798, Napoleon's successor as commander-in-chief, General Berthier, stormed the Vatican, kidnapping the Pope and establishing yet another **Roman Republic.** When Napoleon's empire began to crumble, however, the papacy returned to temporal power in Rome in 1815.

ROME AS CAPITAL OF THE KINGDOM OF ITALY

Among the members of the victorious, reactionary, monarchistic coalition that extinguished the flame of French liberty was the calcifying Austro-Hungarian Empire of the Habsburgs. Demanding their haunch of Napoleon's carcass, the Austrians annexed northern Italy, including Rome. But having been given a taste of freedom by Bonaparte, the Italians began to hope for their own nation-state. By 1848, the move toward a unified Italy, known as the **Risorgimento,** had erupted in every major city in the country; underground resistance groups like the **Carbonari** and **Young Italy** organized and sabotaged Austrian institutions. Once again the focus of international politics, Rome provoked the wrath of Catholic Europe by finally voting to abolish the papal state and establish in 1849, you guessed it, another **Roman Republic.** Pope Pius IX appealed to the European heads of state with great success; within three months, Rome was once again besieged by the French and another meddling Bonaparte, Napoleon III. The resistance was led by **Carlo Mazzini** and **Giuseppe Garibaldi,** alumni of the Carbonari and Young Italy respectively. Although the former preached with revolutionary fervor, and the latter, with the aid of his scruffy Garibaldians, steadied Rome against a complacent French force, the French triumphed nonetheless and reinstated Pope Pius IX.

Pius IX was interested in the advances which modern science was making into early Christian history (such as the excavations of the Catacombs) and also in modern gadgets. He had his own train; painted white and gold, one car was specially built to house a mobile chapel. His politics, however, remained firmly medieval; this time, the military impetus for a united Italy engulfed Rome rather than emanated from it. Regional Italian rulers united all of the country except for Rome and Venice, then declared Rome the capital and crowned the first Italian king, **Vittorio Emanuele II.** In 1870, when the French declared war on the Prussians, there was no one to stop the Italian forces (led in part by the resurgent Garibaldi) from crashing through the Vatican. There the Pope "imprisoned" himself, refusing to give up his power and urging all Italians to support him; he died a lonely man in 1878. The new government set about erecting public buildings to house its ministries and new apartment buildings to house its gigantic corps of civil servants.

Meanwhile, the influence of the pope was felt again north of the Alps. The **Ultramontanism** movement of the mid- to late-19th century saw North European bishops increasingly seeking Roman guidance which encouraged Pope Leo XIII to decree the doctrine of **Papal Infallibility** in 1870.

LITERATURE

As Italy slid into international inconsequence, literary production floundered. Among the few bright stars of the 18th century was the prolific dramatist **Carlo Goldoni** (1707-1793), who transformed the traditional theater of the *commedia dell'arte* by replacing its stock figures with original, unpredictable characters in such works as *Il Ventaglio.* By the late 19th century, the written language and the spoken language had once again drifted apart, causing another pro-vernacular movement in the literary world. **Alessandro Manzoni** (1785-1873) was instrumental in promoting the use of the "living and true" spoken language in literature, making the written word accessible to the masses as well as the elite. The publication of Manzoni's epic *I promessi sposi (The Betrothed),* not only encouraged the revival of the *volgare,* but also marked the birth of the modern novel in Italy.

Among a welter of great 19th- and 20th-century writers, Rome's unique contribution was the Roman dialect poets. Three of the greatest were **G.G. Belli** (1791-1863), **Trilussa** (1871-1950), and **Cesare Pascarella** (1858-1940). In his fictional history *ABBA ABBA,* Anthony Burgess imagines a conversation in which Belli explains the

The Grand Tour

If you're one of the thousands of backpacking students Eurailing around Europe in the summer, consider yourself in fine historical company: 18th-century Europeans (the English in particular) were the first to discover the absolute necessity of making the **Grand Tour.** Before the transition from school to employment, marriage, or the military, upper-crusty young gentlemen were sent across the English Channel to visit the glamorous capitals of the Continent, traditionally ending in a visit to the holy places of Rome around Easter. Guided by a tutor and one of the many new travel books available, these young whelps were supposed to carefully inspect the monuments of European history and acquire refined continental tastes and manners. In Rome, not just any *cicerone,* or "tour guide," would do, but only the great **Johann Winkelmann,** a German archaeologist who specialized in Roman antiquities.

While gentlemen were acquiring finesse and polish, they were also getting their hands very dirty. The ulterior motive behind the Grand Tour was to give the sons of England and other nations a chance to sow their wild oats, usually in Italy, and to leave them there. Tutors were known as "bear leaders" because of the often animalistic behavior of their charges. Cunning English gentlemen ditched their bear leaders in time to make Carnival in Italy, where social mores were substantially more relaxed than those at home. **Robert Burns** characterized the behavior of 18th-century British tourists in Italy as "whore-hunting among groves of myrtles."

advantages of local dialects over national language: "A language waves a flag and is blown up by politicians. A dialect keeps to things, things, things, street smells and street noises, life." Writing nearly 3000 sonnets, Belli was known for his vulgar caricatures of important Risorgimento figures..

ART AND ARCHITECTURE

In the late 1700s, southern Italy would provide a new direction for world art and the long-awaited reaction to the Baroque. That reaction was **Neoclassicism.** Inspired by the understandable excitement surrounding the excavations in Pompeii, Herculaneum, and Paestum, Neoclassicist artists reasserted the austere values of Greco-Roman art that the Renaissance had also imitated. The greatest artists of this period weren't Roman, but came logically to Rome, the world's unrivaled source of antiquities. Foremost among the Neoclassicists was **Jacques-Louis David** (1748-1825), who studied in Rome at the French Academy. Like his contemporaries, David was interested in the legends of ancient Rome; his archetypal Neoclassicist painting, the *Oath of the Horatii* (1784), depicts the Horatii swearing to defend Rome against Alba, even at the cost of their lives.

An essential stop on the Grand Tour was a visit to the print shop of **Giovanni Battista Piranesi** (1720-1778). Piranesi was the master of etched *vedute,* or views, of Rome. These black-and-white depictions of monuments are sometimes maligned for their likeness to souvenirs, as well as for their sheer numbers. Anything but blandly commercial, however, studies from his four-volume series *Antichità Romane*—such as the moonlight view of the Colosseum—are hauntingly futuristic. This series of etchings of ancient Roman monuments qualified as a scholarly work: for them Piranesi was elected to the London Society of Antiquaries. Alongside Piranesi and Winkelmann, Neoclassicist sculptor **Antonio Canova** (1757-1822) was equally famous for his devotion to antiquity and for his reinterpretation of it. His statue of Pauline Bonaparte in the Villa Borghese exemplifies his cool, intellectual style.

Pope Benedict XIV preferred restoring Rome for tourists to conducting Church business; for the first time, street signs appeared, as well as historical markers. He commissioned paintings for St. Peter's and mosaics for Santa Maria Maggiore, which had been redesigned by prominent architect **Fernando Fuga.** Except for a few buildings (some by Piranesi) the Baroque managed to withstand the tide of Neoclassicism, as **Nicola Salvi's** Trevi Fountain, completed in 1762, testifies. The last palace built by a pope for his family is one of the largest; **Pope Pius VI** constructed the expansive Palazzo Braschi for his nephew. Pius also made a number of enhancements to St. Peter's and the Vatican museums. The tumultuous Risorgimento put a damper on construction in the mid-1800s; once the country was unified, however, large-scale building took place in Rome to accommodate the new government. The previously undeveloped area east, southeast, and northeast of Termini became crowded with apartment buildings. A number of beautiful buildings were lost to this expansion, including Henry James's favorite, the Villa Ludovisi. Among the examples of uninspired public architecture that began to fill Rome is the large but unattractive late 19th-century monument to Italy's first king, **Vittorio Emanuele II.**

MUSIC

Eighteenth-century Italy exported its music; Italian composers coined the established musical jargon, and their virtuosi dazzled audiences throughout Europe. At mid-century, operatic overtures began to be performed separately, resulting in the creation of a new genre of music: the **sinfonia** was modeled after the melody of operatic overtures and simply detached from their setting. Thus began the symphonic art form. At the same time, the composer **Domenico Scarlatti** wrote over 500 sonatas for the harpsichord and **Sammartini's** creative experimentation furthered symphonic development. In opera, Baroque ostentation yielded to classical standards of moderation, simplicity, and elegance. Italian opera stars, on the other hand, had no use for moderation; many a soloist would demand showy, superfluous arias to showcase his or her skill.

To today's opera buffs, Italian opera means Rossini, Bellini, Donizetti, Verdi, and Puccini—all composers of the 19th and early 20th centuries. With plots relying on wild coincidence and music fit for the angels, Italian opera of this era continues to dominate today's stages. **Giuseppe Verdi** had become a national icon by mid-life, so much so that *Viva Verdi* (which may have been an acronym for Vittorio Emanuele Re D'Italia) was a battle cry of the Risorgimento. One popular story says that Verdi, acting as altar boy at the age of seven, became so distracted by the music of the mass that a harried priest kicked him off the altar; when he returned home bleeding and his parents asked him what had happened, he replied only, "Let me learn music." The music which he later wrote includes both the tragic, triumphal *Aïda* and *La Traviata,* whose "foul and hideous horrors" shocked the London *Times.* Be aware as you listen that much of Verdi's work promoted Italian unity; his operas include frequent allusions to political assassinations, exhortations against tyranny, and jibes at French and Austrian monarchs. Another great composer of the era, **Gioacchino Rossini,** boasted that he could produce music faster than copyists could reproduce it, but he proved such an infamous procrastinator that his agents resorted to locking him in a room with a single plate of spaghetti until he completed his compositions. His *Barber of Seville* remains a favorite with modern audiences. Finally, there is **Giacomo Puccini,** composer of *Madama Butterfly,* noted for the beauty of his music and for the strength, assurance, and compassion of his female characters. Relying on devilish pyrotechnical virtuosity and a personal style marked by mystery and incessant rumors, violinist **Nicolò Paganini** brought musical Europe to its knees and filled its ears with, in the words of Brahms, "angelic singing." One of the first musicians to make highly publicized concert tours, Paganini inspired **Franz Lizst** to become a virtuoso pianist; the pair were the 19th-century equivalent of rock stars, complete with groupies.

■ The 20th Century

HISTORY

The *fascisti* of the 1920s, not the first army to invoke the Roman Empire, took their name from the symbol of authority in ancient Rome, the *fasces,* a bundle of sticks tightly wound around an axe-blade. Mussolini had grown so powerful elsewhere in Italy that the 1922 **March on Rome** was just for show, as were the reports that 3000 fascist martyrs had died in the attempt. Rome managed to avoid the new destructive power that was unleashed in World War II; carefully-aimed Allied bombs fell on sparsely populated areas and Hitler declared Rome an "open" city when he withdrew from it. While many Jews had been driven out of the country, a sizeable number survived by being hidden by neighbors in private homes, convents, and monasteries. After the war, many of the Jews who had escaped or fled fascist persecution returned to Italy and continue to live there today.

Benito 'il Duce' Mussolini

One-time schoolteacher, journalist, socialist, and (believe it or not) pacifist, Mussolini was a ruthless and ambitious chameleon, a political maverick, a grandiloquent orator, and a master of manipulation. *Il Duce,* "the Leader," as he made himself known, began his political career with the militant PSI (the *Partito Sinistra Italiano*—the "party of the left"). He went to prison for party-related activities but eventually cut his ties to the party over the issue of World War I (he argued for Italy to enter the Great War). Mussolini traded his *Marxist Reader* for the Nationalist flag and began to attract a following as early as 1918 (he was then only 25 years old), calling for the appointment of a dictator over all of Italy. He described this leader as "a man ruthless and energetic enough to make a clean sweep," hinting three months later that he was the man. His followers were a motley crew of disgruntled anarchists, socialists, and republicans, revolutionaries looking for a cause, conservative monarchists, and agitated soldiers. In 1919, Mussolini assembled army veterans and young men to form paramilitary combat groups (the *fasci di combattimenti*), also known as the **Black-shirts.** These militant right-wing squadrons (*squadristi*) waged a fierce, anti-leftist campaign for power shaped by Mussolini's taste for the theatrical. Shouting patriotic slogans, belting out nationalist ditties, and rather ironically sporting the trademark black shirts of the anarchists, these groups broke labor strikes for industrialists, terrorized Socialists and Communists, raided newspapers sympathetic to Bolshevism, and forcefully established mini-dictatorships in small towns and cities while the police and the army turned a blind eye. To gain widespread support, Mussolini played on the anxieties of the middle class, whose businesses and life-savings were in peril from rising inflation.

Seeking still more popular support, Mussolini formed the parliamentary **National Fascist Party** (*Partito Nazionale Fascista,* or PNF) in 1921, which won 35 seats in the Chamber of Deputies. The party platform was a list of vague concerns for financial stability, international power, and national order. Mussolini felt that the Fascist party represented an attitude and an ill-defined need for action, not a specific ideology. In 1922, Victor Emanuel II commanded Mussolini to form a government and serve as its Prime Minister. Thus Mussolini forged a totalitarian state in Italy, controlling every aspect of Italian life, suppressing opposition parties, regulating the press, and demolishing all labor unions. His few pieces of constructive legislation include his proverbial revamping of the train system to promote efficiency and the **Lateran Pact of 1929,** which regulated relations between the Vatican and Italy. The provisions of the Lateran Pact were later included in the Italian constitution in 1948.

Mussolini was so impressed with German efficiency that he joined forces with Hitler in 1939. Mussolini relied on propaganda rather than strength in fighting WWII, and he ignominiously squandered his army in France, Russia, and Greece, until a coup and the Allied forces deposed *il Duce* in mid-war. The disorganization of the Italian army is humorously portrayed in the 1991 film *Mediterraneo.* Roberto Rossellini's neo-realist film, *Roma, città aperta,* depicts some of the terrible living conditions in Rome under the German seizure of the city right before liberation.

In 1929, Mussolini moved his office to **Palazzo Venezia,** from which he delivered his famous speeches with his trademark style of oratory. He would stand on the balcony, uttering mixed metaphors and clever allusions with the most histrionic seriousness, flapping his arms wildly, and then, from time to time, he would halt for a pregnant pause and a knowing glance at the screaming spectators below. More than anything, Mussolini loved spectacle: he became increasingly restless in meetings, preferring to devote his energies to media junkets—shaking hands with farmers, hosting international delegations, or reviewing troops—all while being photographed. During the later days of his career, he kept candles perpetually lit in his office so that people would think he was working all through the night, earning him the nickname "The Sleepless One."

Part of Mussolini's drive for spectacular success was his revival of imperial images. He fancied himself an emperor in the grandest tradition and was determined to mark Rome as his empire by a series of fortunately unexecuted gargantuan architectural schemes. Under his aegis, the government spent more than 33 billion *lire* on public works, excavations, and rebuilding. He plowed down many important medieval, Renaissance, and Baroque works, as well as over three-quarters of the ruins he claimed to be preserving, to create the wide processional street, **Via dei Fori Imperiali** (see p. 156) to carry him past the great monuments of empire, like the Forum and the Colosseum, and to establish a link between his headquarters at Piazza Venezia and those of the ancient Empire; ironically, the constant coughing of car pollution along this street is now the major cause of the monuments' rapid deterioration. He commissioned numerous archaeological excavations, including the Curia at the Forum and one at Largo Argentina (though it is rumored that he stumbled upon the latter when attempting to raze the area for a new construction and was forced to cancel his plans for destruction). He even refurbished the Ara Pacis and the Mausoleum of Augustus, perhaps for use as his own tomb. Finally, to symbolize the grand achievements of the Fascists, Mussolini envisioned a huge Forum named after himself that would make St. Peter's and the Colosseum look like day-old cabbages. For the centerpiece for his Foro Mussoliano (now the Foro Italico) he commissioned a statue of himself as Hercules, 263 ft. tall, with its right hand raised in the Fascist sign for respect. One hundred tons of metal and part of an enormous foot and head later, the project came to an end. Most of Mussolini's archaeological projects went unfinished, the outrageous sums of money were pocketed by corrupt officials, and most of his more ambitious schemes drifted into oblivion. The dreary **EUR** neighborhood and the flagstones bearing the inscription "DUCE" near the Foro Italico stand as continual reminders of Mussolini's unsettling vision, destructive course, and ultimate failure. Today, his legacy lives on through his granddaughter, **Alessandra Mussolini,** who is trying to revive the Fascist party. She was elected to Parliament a few years ago and ran (unsuccessfully) for mayor of Naples in 1993.

POST-WAR POLITICS

The end of World War II ushered in sweeping changes of the Italian system of government, but no clear leader emerged to marshal the new but battered republic in its turbulent early years. The **Italian Constitution,** adopted in 1948 and still going strong, established a new **Italian Republic** with a president, a bicameral Parliament with a 315-member Senate and a 630-member Chamber of Deputies, and an independent judiciary. The president, elected for a seven-year term by an electoral college, is the head of state and appoints the Prime Minister. Chief executive authority rests with the Prime Minister and his Council of Ministers. Within this framework, the **Christian Democratic Party** (DC), bolstered by enormous sums of American money and military aid (and, as has been recently suggested, Mafia collusion), bested the Socialists and surfaced as the consistent ruling party in the new republic. But domination by a single party did not give the country stability; continual political turmoil has reigned, along with more than 50 different governments since World War II. Until recently, the Italian party system traditionally followed a pattern of "polarized centrism"—a multi-party system with most voters belonging either to the right-leaning Christian Democrats or to one of the left-leaning parties: the **Socialist Unity Party** (PSU, though usually referred to by its old name, the PSI) or the **Democratic Party of the Left** (PDS, a less radical version of the old Communist Party, the PCI). Since no ingle party can claim a majority of the voters, Italian governments are formed with volatile and tenuous party coalitions.

The instability of the postwar era, during which the Italian economy sped through industrialization at an unprecedented rate, gave way to violence in the 1970s. The *autunno caldo* (hot autumn) of 1969, a season of strikes, demonstrations, and riots, came on the heels of the international mayhem of 1968 and foreshadowed the violence of the 70s, to which the Italian government was at a loss to respond. Perhaps most shocking was the 1978 kidnapping and murder of ex-Prime Minister **Aldo Moro,** commemorated by a plaque in the Jewish ghetto of Rome, where his body was dumped by the leftist *Brigate Rosse.*

Divisions in Italy are not just between frightened citizens and organized criminals. Because the nation is still very young, city and regional bonds often prove stronger than nationalist sentiment. The most pronounced split exists between the north's highly industrialized European areas and the south's agrarian Mediterranean territories. Native Italians will often treat foreigners better than their co-nationals from the city of Rome.

Recent Political Developments

The chaos of Italian politics disillusions even its leaders. After three long years, Socialist **Bettino Craxi,** lamenting his inability to work with the Christian Democratic majority, resigned from the prime minister's chair in March 1987. After Craxi's fall, three Christian Democrats took office in quick succession. Then, following a rare period of relative stability, the musical chairs of Italian politics resumed in April 1992, when Prime Minister **Giulio Andreotti** resigned and President **Francesco Cossiga** announced his retirement. On May 27, 1992, after disputes over voting procedures, a fist-fight between the neo-fascists and Christian Democrats, and 10 days and 15 rounds of voting that produced no majority, **Oscar Luigi Scalfaro** was finally elected Italy's new president, pledging his support for significant institutional reform of government, including a streamlining of the cabinet.

Since that time the slow and painful process of reforming electoral laws has resulted in "Tangentopoli" ("Kickback City"), an unprecedented political crisis in which over 2600 politicians have been implicated in corruption scandals. Reaction to the continued uncovering and prosecution of mass corruption has included such acts of violence as the May 1993 bombing of the Uffizi, Florence's premier art museum, and the "suicides" of 10 indicted officials over the past three years, not to mention the unleashing of open Mafia retaliation against judges. Until the winter of 1994, rightwing former Prime Minister **Silvio Berlusconi** (who moonlights as a billionaire publishing tycoon and owner of three national TV channels as well as of the ubiquitous STANDA supermarket chain), presided over a tenuous "Freedom Alliance" of three parties: his conservative Forza Italia (the traditional rally cry for the Italian soccer team), the highly reactionary Northern League (Lega Nord), and the neo-fascist National Alliance. When the Northern League pulled out of the Alliance, Berlusconi lost his Parliamentary majority and was forced to resign. By far the most important recent political event in Italy is the election, in the spring of 1996, of the recently formed leftist coalition, *l'Ulivo* ("the olive tree"), led by the PDS and composed largely of former Communists and Socialists. After this book goes to print, anything may happen.

In spite of the conservative national government, Rome's municipal government is rather progressive. The current mayor, **Francesco Rutelli,** elected in November of 1993, is a member of the liberal Green party. His opponent in the 1993 election was none other than **Gianfranco Fini,** leader of the National Alliance, which went on to win the national elections only a few months later in coalition with Berlusconi.

ITALIAN CINEMA

In the early 20th century, expatriate artists who had once flocked to Rome and fostered the Eternal City's art and culture began taking their inspiration from the City of Light. Nonetheless, the **Galleria d'Arte Moderne** in Rome houses the works of

Porn in Parliament

In 1987, the Radical Party's candidate **Ilona Staller,** commonly known as the ex-porn star "La Cicciolina," was elected to the House of Deputies, the Italian equivalent of the U.S. House of Representatives. The buxom blonde celebrated her win by baring her breasts to the eternally grateful city in a victory parade. In 1991, Staller married American kitsch *artiste* Jeff Koons, whose major works include an enormous sculpture of himself and Ilona as Adam and Eve in the Garden of Eden. She also made an innovative attempt at a peace plan during the Gulf War, offering Saddam Hussein her body if he would agree to pull out (of Kuwait). She has since retired from the House of Deputies and has divorced Koons.

household names from around the world as well as many lesser modern Roman artists. Modern Roman architecture leaves something—well, everything—to be desired. City planners are still dealing with Fascist gaffes such as the **Via dei Fori Imperiali,** which cuts through the ancient Imperial Fora and endangers the Colosseum with the smog of its daily traffic jams. Except for a few blocks of imaginative Art Nouveau apartment buildings around Via Doria, budget-crunched Rome has had to forego the artful innovations that 20th-century architects have had to offer.

For Rome's contributions to the arts in this century, don't go to the museum—go to the movies. Years before Hollywood began producing films, the **Cines** studios thrived in Rome. Constructed in 1905-6, Cines created the so-called Italian "super-spectacle," extravagant, larger-than-life re-creations of momentous historical events. One of these, Enrico Guzzani's incredible *Quo Vadis,* enjoyed international success as the first "blockbuster" hit in film history.

Immediately before World War I, Italy's star system *(divismo)* emerged, and the public appeal and economic success of films became increasingly dependent upon the presence of famous individuals—particularly *dive* ("goddesses") like Lydia Borelli and Francesca Bertini, who epitomized the suffering yet destructive Italian *femme fatale.* With the advent of World War I and the rise of Fascism, government leaders and supporters became more and more visible in the film scene. Recognizing the power of popular cinema, Mussolini created the *Centro Sperimentale della Cinematografia,* a national film school, and the gargantuan **Cinecittà studios.** The famous director and covert Marxist **Luigi Chiarini** attracted many students—including **Roberto Rosselini** and **Michelangelo Antonioni**—who both rose to directorial fame after the war. Mussolini avoided most aesthetic questions of film, but enforced a few "imperial edicts," one of which forbade laughing at the Marx Brothers's *Duck Soup.*

When Fascism fell, a generation of young filmmakers enjoyed freedom from the constraints of the discredited regime. Mussolini's nationalized film industry produced no great films, but sparked the subsequent explosion of **neo-realist cinema** (1943-50). Rejecting sets and professional actors, this new style emphasized location shooting and authentic drama. Low budget productions, partly necessitated by postwar economic circumstances, soon shaped a revolution in film. Neo-realists first gained attention in Italy with **Luchino Visconti's** 1942 *Ossessione,* based on James Cain's pulp-novel *The Postman Always Rings Twice.* **Roberto Rosselini's** widely acclaimed *Roma, città aperta* (Open City), a 1946 movie of a Resistance leader trying to escape the Gestapo, was filmed mostly on the streets of Rome. Because of its neo-realist documentary style and authentic setting, the movie appears to be actual newsreel footage. Perhaps the most famous and commercially successful neo-realist film, **Vittorio de Sica's** *The Bicycle Thief* (1948) is also set in Rome.

When neo-realism turned its wobbly camera from the Resistance to social critique, it lost its popularity and, after 1950, gave way to individual expressions of Italian genius. Post-neo-realist directors **Federico Fellini** and **Michelangelo Antonioni** rejected the mechanics of plots and characters to portray a world of moments and witnesses. In Fellini's autobiographical *Roma,* a gorgeous stand-in for the director encounters an otherwise grotesque cast of characters. *La Dolce Vita* (1960), banned by the Pope but widely regarded as *the* representative Italian film, scrutinizes the stylish Rome of the 1950s. Antonioni's Italian films include *L'Eclisse* (1962), *Deserto Rosso* (1964), and *Blow-Up,* his 1966 English-language hit about mime, murder, and mod London. Antonioni's *L'Avventura,* a story of bored young aristocrats, has been hailed the second-greatest film of all time—maybe the idea was still original back then.

Pier Paolo Pasolini—who spent as much time on trial for his politics as he did making films—was one of the greatest and most controversial Italian directors. Already considered Italy's premier poet when he began directing, Pasolini brought his intense vision to the screen. For Pasolini, Rome was not only a birthplace, but also a major source of inspiration. Politics and religion (particularly Communism and Catholicism) usually take center stage in Pasolini's productions, despite the fact that he was expelled from the Communist party and excommunicated from the Catholic Church. Nevertheless an ardent Marxist, he set his first films in Italian shanty neighborhoods and in the Roman underworld of poverty and prostitution. His masterpiece, *Hawks and Sparrows,* investigates the philosophical and poetic possibilities of film. Pasolini's radical political views, his homosexuality, and his alleged pedophilia may have contributed to his extreme unpopularity among right-wing political groups and, ultimately, his assassination in Ostia in 1975.

Time, aging old-boy directors, and the lack of money for Italian film production led to another era in directing: in 1974, **Lina Wertmuller's** *Swept Away*—the story of a rich Milanese woman stranded on a desert island with a chauvinist provincial sailor—left many feminists fuming. Those familiar with **Bernardo Bertolucci's** *Last Tango in Paris* and *Last Emperor* should see his 1970 *Il Conformista* (The Conformist), about a man hired to assassinate his former teacher. Other major modern Italian films include **Vittorio De Sica's** *Il giardino dei Finzi-Contini* (Garden of the Finzi-Continis) and **Francesco Rosi's** *Cristo si è fermato a Eboli* (Christ Stopped at Eboli). In the 1980s, the **Taviani** brothers catapulted to fame with *Kaos,* a film based on stories by Pirandello, and *La Notte di San Lorenzo* (Night of the Shooting Stars), which depicts an Italian village during the tragic and ludicrous final days of World War II. Neo-realism has recognizably influenced most serious Italian film since the war. Its founder, Cesare Zavattini, declared that "the ideal film would be ninety minutes of the life of a man to whom nothing happens."

Fortunately, Italian film isn't all gloom and doom. The Oscar-winning *Cinema Paradiso,* directed by **Giuseppe Tornatore,** warmed the hearts of Italians and Americans alike, along with **Gabriele Salvatore's** light comedy *Mediterraneo* (also an Oscar winner), which chronicles the experiences of Italian soldiers forgotten on a Greek island during WWII. One of the latest Italian films to be released abroad, *Il Postino,* is a story about the friendship between a semi-literate postman and the renowned Chilean poet Pablo Neruda. **Massimo Troisi**, an Academy Award nominee for Best Actor for his role as the postman, who tragically died only a few hours after the film was completed, was one of Italy's favorite comic actors. Another wildly popular Italian comic is **Roberto Benigni,** who stars in countless Italian films, including the hilarious *Johnny Stecchino,* as well as several films by American director Jim Jarmusch. For a truly Italian take on comedy, see any of the classic films of **Totò,** known for his dignified antics and his clever wordplay. Also worth a trip to the video store are the films of the balding, middle-aged Roman, **Carlo Verdone,** whose characters always manage to have affairs with adolescent girls, and **Nanni Moretti,** whose cynical, left-wing humor and scathing commentaries on the state of Italian middle-class society will bring a smile to anyone's face.

For a more American take on Rome, try **Audrey Hepburn's** first film, the delightful romantic comedy *Roman Holiday* (1953). The Rome she and **Gregory Peck** explore will leave you drooling in anticipation of your own trip. A movie best appreciated on the big screen but available at many video stores is *Belly of An Architect,* directed by British bad-boy Peter Greenaway. Greenaway's painterly eye picks out and presents some of Rome's most glorious scenery in broad tableaux.

20TH-CENTURY LITERATURE

Twentieth-century exposure to communism, socialism, and fascism gave rise to anti-traditional literary achievements among Italian writers. Nobel Prize-winning playwright **Luigi Pirandello** (1867-1936) became the father of modern experimental theater with his exploration of the relativity of truth in works like *Sei personaggi in cerca d'un autore (Six Characters in Search of an Author)*. Another unconventional writer, **Italo Svevo,** has three great works on the bourgeois mind: *Una vita (A Life)*, *La coscienza di Zeno (The Confessions of Zeno)*, and *Senilità (Senility)*.

Italy was a center of Modernist innovation in poetry. The most flamboyant and controversial of Modernism's early poets is **Gabriele d'Annunzio,** whose cavalier heroics and sexual escapades earned him as much fame as his eccentric, over-the-top verse. D'Annunzio was a child of pleasure, or *Il Piacere,* the title of his novel set in Rome. In the mid- and late-20th century, **Salvatore Quasimodo, Eugenio Montale** and **Giuseppe Ungaretti** dominated the scene. Montale and Quasimodo founded the "hermetic movement," but both became more accessible and politically committed after the Second World War, each snagging a Nobel Prize along the way. Ungaretti brought to Italy many of the innovations of the French Symbolists; his collection *L'allegria* set a trend toward increased purity of language and clarity of meaning in poetry. Ungaretti was drawn to Rome to study Keats and Shelley, and during his stay he disseminated his ideas to hundreds of college students.

The 1930s heralded the heyday of a group of young Italian writers who were much influenced by the experimental narratives and themes of social alienation in the works of U.S. writers like Ernest Hemingway, John Dos Passos, and John Steinbeck. This school included **Cesare Pavese, Ignazio Silone, Vasco Pratolini,** and **Elio Vittorini.** One of the most representative works of 1930s Italian literature is Silone's *Pane e Vino* (Bread and Wine), written while the left-wing intellectual and political-activist author was in exile. The most prolific of these writers, **Alberto Moravia,**

The Mafia

The well known **Mafia** are much more of a cultural element of Italian society than their well dressed, gun-toting image implies. In spite of numerous government attempts to curtail organized crime, the loosely affiliated leaders of these nebulous organizations (each one has a different name; only the one in Sicily is called *mafia)* still command great and unseen control over Italy's society, politics, and economy, especially in the South and Sicily. With nearly complete control over the black market, the Mafia has become the pillar, however crooked, of the Italian economy. Some of the *mafiosi's* success stems from the cultural acceptance of their activities (in the good old days, members were regarded not as thugs, but as men of honor and strength). But today's Mafia—with its heightened passion for drug-running and violence—inspires universal fear and resentment among Italians. The Italian parliament passed an unprecedented anti-Mafia law in 1982, followed by the Palermo *maxi processi* (trials), the largest Mafia trials in history. In 1993, numerous high-ranking bosses were arrested. At the same time, however, terrorist bombings heavily damaged major Italian monuments, including the Uffizi Museum in Florence and the Churches of San Giorgio in Velabro and San Giovanni in Laterano, in Rome. Although no group has claimed responsibility for these attacks, they are widely believed to have been the work of the Mafia.

---

wrote the ground-breaking *Gli Indifferenti* ("The Time of Indifference") which launched an attack on the Fascist regime and was promptly censored. To evade the stiff government censors, Moravia employed experimental, surreal forms in his subsequent works. His later works, up to the 1970s, use sex to symbolize the violence and spiritual impotence of modern Italy.

One of the Italian authors most widely translated into English is **Italo Calvino.** His writing—full of intellectual play and magical realism—is exemplified in, among other wrote the ground-breaking *Gli Indifferenti* ("The Time of Indifference") which launched an attack on the Fascist regime and was promptly censored. To evade the stiff government censors, Moravia employed experimental, surreal forms in his subsequent works. His later works, up to the 1970s, use sex to symbolize the violence and spiritual impotence of modern Italy.

One of the Italian authors most widely translated into English is **Italo Calvino.** His writing—full of intellectual play and magical realism—is exemplified in, among other works, *Invisible Cities,* a collection of cities described by Marco Polo to Kubla Kahn. The more traditional narrative *If on a winter's night a traveler...* is a boisterous romp about authors, readers, and the insatiable urge to read, but perhaps most enjoyable for the traveler is *Italian Folktales,* Calvino's collection of traditional regional fairy tales.

Umberto Eco's wildly popular *The Name of the Rose,* a richly-textured mystery set in a 14th-century monastery, somehow manages to keep readers on edge while making the history of the revolutionary crisis in medieval Catholicism vaguely intelligible. Eco's latest novel, *L'isola del Giorno Prima (The Island of the Day Before)*, supposedly uses only those Italian words in existence during the 17th century and includes a 70-page manual on the terminology of boats.

TELEVISION

A few hours in front of the boob tube in Rome may prove harmful to your otherwise glorious impression of the Eternal City. Italian television comes in two varieties—the three vaguely educational, state-owned **RAI** channels and the often shamelessly insipid networks owned by the former Prime Minister, Silvio Berlusconi. Italia Uno, Rete 4, and Canale 5 transmit all your favorite American trash, including "Beverly Hills 90210" and "Saved by the Bell" (called "Bayside School"), as well as a few indigenous crimes against human intelligence.

Eight-year-old girls and adolescent boys rush home every day at two o'clock to watch **"Non E' La RAI,"** a variety show featuring scantily clad high-school age girls dancing and lip-synching to all your favorite tunes. You can even catch a glimpse of Ambra, the hostess, outside the studios near S. Giovanni in Laterano. Though waning in popularity since its original host, Fiorello, moved on to bigger and better things, **"Karaoke"** is almost as bad. The name says it all—every day is a new contest to see who can karaoke the best to the latest hits and old favorites. Though almost intolerable, Karaoke can be educational; the words to the songs appear at the bottom of the screen so that you can sing along and learn Italian at the same time.

People who have studied Italian should also try to watch the news on the RAI stations, the National Geographic specials, and the movies that are shown almost every night. Soccer and basketball are often on the tube on weekends, but beware Sunday programming. Many stations have variety show marathons, with washed-up movie and TV personalities and busty, blonde bimbos singing, dancing, acting out skits, and participating in and officiating game show-type contests. One last word of warning about *la tivvù*: if your name is Brooke, Carolyn, Ridge, or Thorn, don't be too flattered if Italians exclaim "beautiful" when they meet you—it's more likely the name of their favorite soap opera character; the U.S. soap opera, (the Bold and the) **Beautiful,** hit Italy five years ago with full force, and seemingly every Italian—housewives, students, and businessmen alike—now spends a portion of his/her afternoon break following the vicissitudes of big-haired blondes and hunky heartthrobs dressed in Gitanos. *O tempora, O mores!*

MUSIC, POPULAR AND OTHERWISE

Italian classical **music** continues to grow in the 20th century. **Ottorino Respighi,** composer of the popular *Pines of Rome* and *Fountains of Rome,* experimented with shimmering, rapidly shifting orchestral textures. **Giancarlo Menotti,** now a U.S. resident, has written short, opera-like works such as *Amahl and the Night Visitors,* but is probably best known as the creator of the Two Worlds Art Festival in Spoleto.

Popular music in Italy, though, has seen better days. Once upon a time, Italian pop had its own unique and indigenous character that blended Italian folk songs and Mediterranean rhythms with pop beats. **Pino Daniele, Vasco Rossi, Lucio Battisti,** and others used to perform their folk-inspired ballads for captive audiences of university students. In recent years, however, these Italianate Billy Joels, James Taylors, and Stings, though still popular and revered, can't compete with the mass-produced British and American dance music that pollutes the airwaves and the discotheques. The Swedish uber-stars, **Ace of Base,** are even more popular in Italy than they are in the States, so don't be surprised if someone asks for a translation of "All that she wants is another baby."

Equally inescapable in Italy are the native talents, **Eros Ramazzotti, Laura Pausini,** and **883** *(Otto otto tre)*. Pausini's "Non C'è" and "La Solitudine" express the angst felt by all 15-year-olds, while 883's ballad "Come Mai" was suggested by some as the new Italian national anthem. Believe it or not, Italian rap exists and it's not that bad. **99 Posse**'s reggae and rap hybrid music was featured in the controversial film *Sud,* while rapper **Jovanotti** has risen from TV-variety-show pop star to semi-alternative singer-songwriter.

Eighties music buffs won't miss home at all, since Laura Brannigan's "Gloria" is actually a cover of an (overplayed) Italian song of the same title. The legacy of Old Blue Eyes lives on in his mother country with "My Way." If you learn one Italian song in Italy, make it **"Volare."** This song has been covered by nearly every artist in the country, as well as countless Italian-lovers in the U.S. and Latin America.

Popular music in Italy, however, is not all frivolous. In fact, Italian popular music, much more so than American music, often has a political agenda. **Lucio Dalla** was one of the first musicians to use pop music as a vehicle for political protest. Today, many socially conscious bands from southern Italy promote improving relations between the industrial North and the impoverished South, while others address issues such as corruption in the government and the Mafia.

NEWSPAPERS AND MAGAZINES

Panorama and *L'Espresso* are the *Time* and *Newsweek* of Italy, but with more photos of naked or near-naked women. *Il Messaggero* and *La Repubblica* are Rome's newspapers. Every Thursday, *La Repubblica* publishes *Trovaroma,* a guide to culture and entertainment in Rome.

Essentials

PLANNING YOUR TRIP

■ When To Go

Swarms of tourists converge on Rome in July and August, which means that if you choose to join them, you'll be scaling the walls of booked hotel rooms and sharing your first experience of the Sistine Chapel with 4000 other tourists. Hotels legally charge more in the high season, and their rooms are populated by lemming-like tour groups. While the tourist industry opens in the summer, Romans abandon ship for their own vacations, particularly around August 15, the mass exodus/holiday known as *Ferragosto*. By mid-August, you'll be lucky to find a Roman, let alone an open restaurant. Easter seems to be the hot time for a pilgrimage to the Vatican; the festivities of Holy Week include several processions featuring the Pope and extended hours at the Vatican Museums. The best time to see Rome is in the mid-spring or fall; the weather is temperate, there are fewer tourists, hotel prices go down, and you can attend the autumnal olive and wine harvests in Lazio or the springtime flower shows in the city. Though winter in Rome is rather mild, *caffè*, restaurants, and the general population move indoors (see Climate, p. 282).

■ Useful Information

TOURIST OFFICES

Italian Government Tourist Board (ENIT), 630 Fifth Ave., #1565, **New York, NY** 10111 (tel. (212) 245-4822; fax 586-9249). Write for their guide *Italia: General Information for Travelers to Italy* (containing train and ferry schedules), and for regional information as available. Branch offices: 12400 Wilshire Blvd., #550, **Los Angeles,** CA 90025 (tel. (310) 820-0098; fax 820-6357); 1 Pl. Ville Marie, #1914, **Montréal,** Qué. H3B 3M9 (tel. (514) 866-7667; fax 392-1429); 1 Princes St., **London,** England WIR 8AY (tel. (0171) 408 12 54; fax 493 66 95).

Italian Cultural Institute, 686 Park Ave., New York, NY 10021 (tel. (212) 879-4242), is often more prompt and helpful than ENIT. Request the booklet entitled "Mia Italia," which is full of maps and suggestions for less touristed sites.

TRAVEL ORGANIZATIONS

Council on International Educational Exchange (Council), 205 East 42nd St., New York, NY 10017-5706 (tel. (888) COUNCIL (268-6245); fax (212) 822-2699; e-mail info@ciee.org; http://www.ciee.org). A private, nonprofit organization, Council administers work, volunteer, and academic programs around the world. They also offer identity cards (including the ISIC and the GO25) and a range of publications (see Useful Publications, below). Call or write for more information.

Federation of International Youth Travel Organizations (FIYTO), Bredgade 25H, DK-1260 Copenhagen K, Denmark (tel. (33) 33 96 00; fax 93 96 76; e-mail mailbox@fiyto.org), is an international organization promoting educational, cultural, and social travel for young people. Member organizations include language schools, educational travel companies, national tourist boards, accommodation centers, and other suppliers of travel services to youth and students. FIYTO also sponsors the GO25 Card (see p. 37).

International Student Travel Confederation, Herengracht 479, 1017 BS Amsterdam, The Netherlands (tel. (31) 204 212 800; fax 204 212 810; e-mail istcinfo@istc.org; http://www.istc.org). A non-profit confederation of student travel organizations, including International Student Rail Association (ISRA), Student Air Travel Association (SATA), ISIS Travel Insurance, and the International Association for Educational and Work Exchange Programs (IAEWEP).

USEFUL PUBLICATIONS

Adventurous Traveler Bookstore, P.O. Box 1468, Williston, VT 05495 (tel. (801) 860-6776; fax 860-6607; both at (800) 282-3963; e-mail books@atbook.com; http://www.gorp.com/atbook.htm). Free 40-page catalogue upon request. Specializes in outdoor adventure travel books and maps for the U.S. and abroad. Their web site offers extensive browsing opportunities.

Bon Voyage!, 2069 W. Bullard Ave., Fresno, CA 93711-1200 (tel. (800) 995-9716, from abroad (209) 447-8441; e-mail 70754.3511@compuserve.com). Annual mail-order catalog offers a range of products for everyone from the luxury traveler to the die-hard trekker. Books, travel accessories, luggage, electrical converters, maps, videos, and more. All merchandise may be returned for exchange or refund within 30 days of purchase, and prices are guaranteed. (Lower advertised prices from their competitors will be matched and merchandise is shipped free.)

The College Connection, Inc., 1295 Prospect St., Suite A, La Jolla, CA 92037 (tel. (619) 551-9770; fax 551-9987; e-mail eurailnow@aol.com; http://www.eurail-pass.com). Publishes *The Passport,* a booklet listing hints about every aspect of traveling and studying abroad. This booklet is free to *Let's Go* readers; send your request by e-mail or fax only. The College Rail Connection, a division of the College Connection, sells railpasses and flights with student discounts.

Council (see Travel Organizations, above) has a number of useful publications, among them the magazine *Student Travels* (free), *The High School Student's Guide to Study, Travel and Adventure Abroad* (US$14, postage US$1.50), *Work, Study, Travel Abroad: The Whole World Handbook,* and *Volunteer! The Comprehensive Guide to Voluntary Service in the U.S. and Abroad.* They are available at Council Travel offices (see Budget Travel Organizations, below), campus study abroad offices, or by mail. Write to Council, Marketing Services Dept., 205 E. 42nd St., New York, NY 10017-5706.

The European Festivals Association, 120B, rue de Lausanne, 1202 Geneva, Switzerland (tel. (22) 732 28 03; fax 738 40 12). Publishes the free booklet *Festivals,* which lists dates and programs of many major European festivals, including music, ballet, and theater events.

Forsyth Travel Library, P.O. Box 480800, Kansas City, MO 64148 (tel. (800) 367-7984; fax (816) 942-6969; http://www.forsyth.com). A mail-order service that stocks a wide range of city, area, and country maps, as well as guides for rail and ferry travel in Europe, including the *Thomas Cook European Timetable* for trains. Also sells rail tickets and passes, and offers reservation services. Call or write for a free catalogue, or visit their web site.

Hippocrene Books, Inc., 171 Madison Ave., New York, NY 10016 (tel. (212) 685-4371; orders (718) 454-2366; fax 454-1391). Free catalog. Publishes travel reference books, travel guides, foreign language dictionaries, and language-learning guides which cover over 100 languages.

Hunter Publishing, 300 Raritan Center Parkway, Edison, NJ 08818 (tel. (908) 225-1900; fax 417-0482). Has an extensive catalog of travel books, guides, language. learning tapes, and quality maps. Ask about the *Charming Small Hotel Guide*s to Italy, as well as other European countries (each US$13).

John Muir Publications, P.O. Box 613, Sante Fe, NM 87504 (tel. (800) 888-7504; fax (505) 988-1680). In addition to many travel guides, John Muir publishes an excellent series of books by veteran traveler Rick Steves. *Europe though the Back Door* offers great advice on the dos and don'ts of budget travel (US$19), and *Mona Winks: Self-Guided Tours of Europe's Top Museums* (US$18) will allow you to bypass a tour guide. Also available in bookstores.

Michelin Travel Publications, Michelin Tire Corporation, P.O. Box 19001, Greenville, SC 29602-9001 (tel. (800) 423-0485; fax (803) 458-5665). Publishes travel-related material, including the *Green Guides,* for sight-seeing info, maps, and driving itineraries. Also offers detailed, reliable road maps and atlases, available at bookstores and distributors throughout the world.

Specialty Travel Index, 305 San Anselmo Avenue, #313, San Anselmo, CA 94960 (tel. (415) 459-4900; fax 459-4974; email spectrav@ix.netcom.com; http://www.spectrav.com). Published twice yearly, this index is an extensive listing of off-the-beaten track and specialty travel opportunities. One copy US$6, one-year subscription (2 copies) US$10.

Superintendent of Documents, U.S. Government Printing Office, P.O. Box 371954, Pittsburgh, PA 15250-7954 (tel. (202) 512-1800; fax 512-2250). Publishes *Your Trip Abroad* (US$1.25), *Health Information for International Travel* (US$14), and "Background Notes" on all countries (US $1 each). Postage is included in the prices.

Transitions Abroad, 18 Hulst Rd., P.O. Box 1300, Amherst, MA 01004-1300 (tel. (413) 256-3414; fax 256-0375; e-mail trabroad@aol.com). This invaluable magazine lists publications and resources for overseas study, work, and volunteering. Also publishes *The Alternative Travel Directory*, a comprehensive guide to living, learning, and working overseas (US$20; postage US$4).

Travel Books & Language Center, Inc., 4931 Cordell Ave., Bethesda, MD 20814 (tel. (800) 220-2665; fax (301) 951-8546; e-mail travelbks@aol.com). Sells over 75,000 items, including books, cassettes, atlases, dictionaries, and a wide range of specialty travel maps. Free comprehensive catalogue upon request.

Ten Speed Press, P.O. Box 7123, Berkeley, CA 94707 (tel. (800) 841-2665, order dept. (510) 559-1629). *The Packing Book* (US$8) provides various checklists and suggested wardrobes, addresses safety concerns, and imparts packing techniques.

U.S. Customs Service, P.O. Box 7407, Washington, D.C., 20044 (tel. (202) 927-5580). Publishes 35 books, booklets, leaflets, and flyers on various aspects of customs. *Know Before You Go* tells almost everything the international traveler needs to know about customs requirements; *Pocket Hints* is a condensed version.

Wide World Books and Maps, 1911 N. 45th St., Seattle, WA 98103 (tel. (206) 634-3453; fax 634-0558; e-mail travelbk@mail.nwlink.com; http://nwlink.com/travelbk). A good selection of travel guides, accessories, and hard-to-find maps.

INTERNET RESOURCES

Along with everything else in the '90s, budget travel is moving rapidly into the Information Age. With the growing user-friendliness of personal computers and Internet technology, much of this information can be yours with the click of a mouse.

There are a number of ways to access the Internet. The most popular are the commercial Internet providers, such as America On-Line (tel. (800) 827-6394) and Compuserve (tel. (800) 433-0389), both of which charge a user fee. However, many employers and schools also offer gateways to the Internet, often at no cost. Learning how to navigate through cyberspace is not extraordinarily difficult, but it is somewhat beyond the scope of this book. For more information, contact one of the commercial servers, ask a computer-using friend, or check out one of the many comprehensive guides to the Internet now available in most bookstores.

Increasingly the Internet forum of choice, the **World Wide Web** features a variety of "sites" which may interest the budget traveler. The use of search engines (services that look for web pages under specific subjects) can facilitate the search process. Lycos (http://a2z.lycos.com) and Infoseek (http://guide.infoseek.com) are two of the most popular. Yahoo! is a slightly more organized search engine; check out its travel links at http://www.yahoo.com/Recreation/Travel. However, it is often better to know a good site, and start "surfing" from there, through links from one web page to another.

Dr. Memory's Favorite Travel Pages (http://www.access.digex.net/~drmemory/cyber_travel.html) is a great place to start surfing. Dr. Memory has links to hundreds of different web pages of interest to travelers of all kinds.

Big World Magazine (http://boss.cpcnet.com/personal/bigworld/bigworld.htm) specializes in budget travel, and its web site provides great links to travel pages.

The Student and Budget Travel Guide (http://asa.ugl.lib.umich.edu/chdocs/travel/travel-guide.html) is just what it sounds like.

The World At a Discount

Save 20% to 50% on Airfare (major carriers)

Save 10% to 50% on Museums & Theaters

Save 10% on AT&T Calls to the U.S.

International Student Identity Card
Carte Internationale d'étudiant/Carnet Internacional de estudiante

ISIC
1997
Valid Sep. 96–31 Dec. 97

Family name/Nom de famille/Apellido
YOUNG
First names/Prénoms/Nombres
CHRISTOPHER
Born/Né le/Nacido
5/3/77
Nationality/Nationalité/Nacionalidad
USA
Studies at/Établ. d'Enseignement/Estab. de Enseñanza
BROWN UNIVERSITY
STUDENT

Save up to 40% on Train Passes

Save 15% on Greyhound Travel

Save 10% to 30% on Accommodations

Worldwide Discounts in more than 90 countries

The International Student Identity Card
Your Passport to Discounts & Benefits

With the ISIC, you'll receive discounts on airfare, hotels, transportation, computer services, foreign currency exchange, phone calls, major attractions, and more. You'll also receive basic accident and sickness insurance coverage when traveling outside the U.S. and access to a 24-hour, toll-free Help Line. Call now to locate the issuing office nearest you (over 555 across the U.S.) at:

Free 40-page handbook with each card!

1-888-COUNCIL (toll-free)

For an application and complete discount list, you can also visit us at **http://www.ciee.org/**

CIEE: Council on International Educational Exchange

Another popular source of information is a **newsgroup,** which is a forum for discussion of a specific topic. There are thousands of different newsgroups, which means that there is information available on almost any topic you can imagine. Since most newsgroups are unmoderated and unsupervised, however, the reliability of information posted within them is not always certain. Nonetheless, there are still a number of useful newsgroups for travelers.

Usenet, a family of newsgroups, can be accessed easily from most Internet gateways. In UNIX systems, a good newsreader is "tin" (just type "tin" at the prompt). There are several hierarchies of newsgroups. The "soc" groups deal primarily with issues related to society and culture; of interest to travelers to Italy are **soc.culture.italian** and **soc.culture.europe.** The "alt" (alternative) groups form a less organized hierarchy and include **alt.politics.italy** and **alt.currentevents.italy.** "Rec" groups, such as **rec.travel.air** and **rec.travel.europe,** are oriented toward recreational activities which may interest travelers. Finally, **Clari-net** posts Associated Press news wires for many different topics; travelers to Italy should take a look at **clari.world.europe.italy** and **clari.news.europe.**

■ Documents and Formalities

It is strongly recommended that you file applications for all necessary documents well in advance of your planned departure date. Once you have acquired the documents, it is a good idea to photocopy them all (as well as credit cards); leave a copy at home with someone you can easily contact, and carry another one with you.

When you travel, *always carry on your person two or more forms of identification, including at least one photo ID.* Never carry all identification, traveler's checks, and credit cards together. If you plan an extended stay, you might want to register your passport with the nearest embassy or consulate. Consulates also recommend that you carry an expired passport or official copy of your birth certificate in a separate part of your baggage, as well as an extra passport photo or two; these measures will facilitate replacement of a lost passport. If you do find that your passport has been lost or stolen, contact the local police and your embassy or consulate immediately.

ITALIAN EMBASSIES AND CONSULATES

U.S.: Embassy of Italy, 1601 Fuller St. NW, **Washington, D.C.** 20009 (tel. (202) 328-5500; fax 462-3605) and Italian Consulate, 12400 Wilshire Blvd., #300, **Los Angeles,** CA 90025 (tel. (310) 820-0622). Other consulates of Italy at 2590 Webster St., **San Francisco,** CA 94115 (tel. (415) 931-4924); 500 N. Michigan Ave., #1850, **Chicago,** IL 60611 (tel. (312) 467-1550); 630 Camp St., **New Orleans,** LA 70130 (tel. (504) 524-2271); 100 Boylston St., #900, **Boston,** MA 02116 (tel. (617) 542-0483); 535 Griswold, **Detroit,** MI 48226 (tel. (313) 963-8560); 690 Park Ave., **New York,** NY 10021 (tel. (212) 737-9100); Public Ledger Building, 100 S. Sixth St., #1026, **Philadelphia,** PA 19106 (tel. (215) 592-7329); 1300 Post Oak Blvd., #660, **Houston,** TX 77056 (tel. (713) 850-7520).

Canada: Embassy of Italy, 275 Slater St., 21st Floor, **Ottawa,** Ont. K1P 5H9 (tel. (613) 232-2401); Consulate of Italy, 3489 Drummond St., **Montréal,** Qué. H3G 1X6 (tel. (514) 849-7113).

U.K.: Embassy of Italy, 14 Three Kings Yard, **London,** W1Y 2EH (tel. (0171) 312 22 00; fax 312 22 30); Consulate General of Italy, 38 Eaton Place, London, SW1 8AN (tel. (0171) 235 9371); Italian Consulate in Manchester, 111 Piccadilly, **Manchester,** M1 2HY (tel. (0161) 236 90 24); Consulate General of Italy in Scotland and Northern Ireland, 32 Melville St., **Edinburgh,** EH3 7HA (tel. (0131) 220 36 95).

Australia: Embassy of Italy, 12 Grey St., Deakin, Canberra City A.C.T. 2600 (tel. +61 (06) 273 3333; fax 273 4223).

New Zealand: Embassy of Italy, P.O. Box 463, 36 Grant Rd., Wellington (tel. (644) 473 53 39 or 472 93 02; fax 472 72 55).

South Africa: Embassy of Italy, 796 George Ave., Arcadia, Pretoria (tel. (12) 43 55 41/2/3/4; fax 43 55 47).

ESSENTIALS

PASSPORTS

Citizens of the U.S., Canada, the U.K., Ireland, Australia, New Zealand, and South Africa all need valid passports to enter Italy and to re-enter their own countries. Some countries will not allow entrance if the holder's passport will expire in less than six months, and returning to the U.S. with an expired passport may result in a fine. Some countries require travelers under 16 to have passports.

Your passport is a public document that belongs to your government and may not be withheld without your consent. You may be asked to surrender it to an Italian government official; if you don't get it back in a reasonable amount of time, you should inform the nearest embassy or consulate of your country. In Italy, hotel proprietors are apt to ask you to leave your passport with them overnight as collateral. Even though this is an accepted custom, you are not *required* to leave it for any longer than it takes to write the number down.

United States Citizens may apply for a passport, valid for 10 years (five years if under 18) at any authorized federal or state courthouse or post office, or at a U.S. Passport Agency, located in Boston, Chicago, Honolulu, Houston, Los Angeles, Miami, New Orleans, New York, Philadelphia, San Francisco, Seattle, Stamford, CT, or Washington, D.C . Parents must apply in person for children under age 13. You must apply in person if this is your first passport, if you're under age 18, or if your current passport is more than 12 years old or was issued before your 18th birthday. You must submit proof of U.S. citizenship (a certified birth certificate, certification of naturalization or of citizenship, or a previous passport), identification bearing your signature and either your photograph or physical description, and two identical, passport-size photographs. It will cost US$65 (under 18 US$40). You can renew your passport by mail or in person for US$55. Processing takes two to four weeks. Passport agencies offer rush service for a surcharge of US$30 if you have proof that you're departing within ten working days (e.g., an airplane ticket or itinerary). Abroad, a U.S. embassy or consulate can usually issue a new passport, given proof of citizenship. If your passport is lost or stolen in the U.S., report it in writing to Passport Services, U.S. Department of State, 111 19th St. NW, Washington DC, 20522-1705 or to the nearest passport agency. For more info, contact the U.S. Passport Information's 24-hour recorded message (tel. (202) 647-0518).

Canada Application forms in English and French are available at all passport offices, post offices, and most travel agencies. Citizens may apply in person at any one of 28 regional passport offices across Canada. Along with the application form, a citizen must provide citizenship documentation and a CDN$60 fee. The application must also be signed by an eligible guarantor. Processing takes approximately five business days for in-person applications and three weeks for mailed ones. A passport is valid for five years and is not renewable. If a passport is lost abroad, Canadians must be able to prove citizenship with another document. For additional info, call (800) 567-6868 (24hr.; from Canada only). Regional offices are located in Metro Toronto (tel. (416) 973-3251), Montréal (tel. (514) 283-2152), and Quebec (tel. (819) 994-3500). Refer to the booklet *Bon Voyage, But...* for further information and a list of Canadian embassies and consulates abroad. It is available free of charge from any passport office.

United Kingdom British citizens, British Dependent Territories citizens, British Nationals (overseas), and British Overseas citizens may apply for a **full passport.** Residents of the U.K., the Channel Islands, and the Isle of Man also have the option of applying for a more restricted **British Visitor's Passport.** For a full passport, valid for 10 years (5 years if under 16), apply in person or by mail to a passport office, located in London, Liverpool, Newport, Peterborough, Glasgow, or Belfast (UK£18). Processing by mail takes four to six weeks. The London office offers same-day, walk-in rush service, but you must arrive early in the morning.

Ireland Citizens can apply for a passport by mail to either the Department of Foreign Affairs, Passport Office, Setanta Centre, Molesworth St., Dublin 2 (tel. (01) 671 16 33), or the Passport Office, 1A South Mall, Cork (tel. (021) 627 25 25). Obtain an application at a local Garda station or request one from a passport office. The new Passport Express Service offers a two-week turn-around and is available through post offices for an extra IR£3. Passports cost IR£45 and are valid for 10 years. Citizens under 18 or over 65 can request a three-year passport that costs IR£10.

Australia Citizens must apply for a passport in person at a post office, a passport office, or an Australian diplomatic mission overseas. An appointment may be necessary. Passport offices are located in Adelaide, Brisbane, Canberra City, Darwin, Hobart, Melbourne, Newcastle, Perth, and Sydney. A parent may file an application for a child who is under 18 and unmarried. Application fees are adjusted frequently. For more info, call toll-free (in Australia) 13 12 32.

New Zealand Application forms for passports are available in New Zealand from travel agents and Department of Internal Affairs Link Centres. Completed applications may be lodged at Link Centres and at overseas posts, or forwarded to the Passport Office, P.O. Box 10-526, Wellington, New Zealand. Processing time is 10 working days from receipt of a correctly completed application. An urgent passport service is also available. The application fee is NZ$80 in New Zealand, and NZ$130 for applications submitted from overseas under the standard service.

South Africa Citizens can apply for a passport at any Home Affairs Office. Two photos, either a birth certificate or an identity book, and a SAR12 fee must accompany a completed application. South African passports are valid for 10 years. For more information, contact the nearest Department of Home Affairs Office.

VISAS

A **visa** is a stamp that permits you to visit another country; it is placed on your passport by a foreign government. Tourists from the U.S., Canada, United Kingdom, Australia, New Zealand, and South Africa do not need a visa to visit Italy for three months or less. If you intend to travel for more than three months, consider obtaining a long-term visa before departure. You may do so either by applying directly to the nearest Italian consulate or through the **Center for International Business and Travel (CIBT),** 25 West 43rd St., #1420, New York, NY 10036 (tel. (800) 925-2428 or (212) 575-2811 from NYC). The CIBT secures visas for travel to and from all countries for various fees. Travelers from countries other than those listed above should be sure to check with the Italian Government Travel Office or an Italian embassy or consulate; Italy may require visas from citizens of your country.

Entrance to Italy as a tourist does not include permission to study or work there. There are special requirements for **student and work visas,** which can be obtained from the nearest Italian consulate.

CUSTOMS: ENTERING

Make a list of any valuables you are bringing with you from home and register it with customs as you depart in order to avoid import duty charges upon your return. Do not attempt to carry firearms, explosives, ammunition, fireworks, controlled drugs, most plants and animals, or pornographic materials into Italy. To avoid problems when you transport prescription drugs, ensure that the bottles are clearly marked, and carry a copy of the prescription.

CUSTOMS: GOING HOME

Unless you plan to import a BMW or a barnyard beast, you will probably pass right over the customs barrier and into the arms of relieved relations with minimal ado. Upon returning home, you must declare all articles you acquired abroad and must pay a duty on the value of those articles that exceed the allowance established by your country's customs service. Goods and gifts purchased at duty-free shops abroad are not exempt from duty or sales tax at your point of return; "duty-free" merely means that you need not pay a tax in the country of purchase.

United States Citizens returning home may bring US$400 worth of accompanying goods duty-free and must pay a 10% tax on the next US$1000. You must declare all purchases, so have sales slips ready. Goods are considered duty-free if they are for personal or household use (this includes gifts) and cannot include more than 100 cigars, 200 cigarettes (1 carton), and 1L of wine or liquor. You must be over 21 to bring liquor into the U.S. If you mail home personal goods of U.S. origin, you can avoid duty charges by marking the package "American goods returned." For more information, consult the brochure *Know Before You Go,* available from the U.S. Customs Service, Box 7407, Washington, D.C. 20044 (tel. (202) 927-6724).

Canada Citizens who remain abroad for at least one week may return with up to CDN$500 worth of goods duty-free once per calendar year. Canadian citizens or residents who travel for a period between 48 hours and six days can bring back up to CDN$200, with the exception of tobacco and alcohol. You are permitted to ship goods except tobacco and alcohol home under this exemption as long as you declare them when you arrive. Citizens of legal age (which varies by province) may import on their person up to 200 cigarettes, 50 cigars, 400g loose tobacco, 400 tobacco sticks, 1.14L wine or alcohol, and 24 355ml cans/bottles of beer; the value of these products is included in the CDN$500. For more information, write to Canadian Customs, 2265 St. Laurent Blvd., Ottawa, Ontario K1G 4K3 (tel. (613) 993-0534).

United Kingdom Citizens or visitors arriving in the U.K. from outside the EU must declare any goods in excess of the following allowances: 200 cigarettes, 100 cigarillos, 50 cigars, or 250g loose tobacco; 2L table wine, 1L strong liqueurs of over 22% alcohol content, or 2L sparkling wine and other liqueurs; 60cc/ml perfume, 250cc/ml toilet water; and UK£145 worth of all other goods including gifts and souvenirs. You must be over 17 to import liquor or tobacco. These allowances also apply to duty-free purchases within the EU, with the exception of gifts and souvenirs, which has an allowance of UK£75. Goods obtained duty- and tax-paid for personal use (regulated according to set guide levels) within the EU do not require any further customs duty. For more info about U.K. customs, contact Her Majesty's Customs and Excise, Custom House, Nettleton Road, Heathrow Airport, Hounslow, Middlesex TW6 2LA (tel. (0181) 910 37 44; fax 910 37 65).

Ireland Citizens must declare everything in excess of IR£34 (IR£17 per traveler under 15 years of age) obtained outside the EU or duty- and tax-free in the EU above the following allowances: 200 cigarettes, 100 cigarillos, 50 cigars, or 250g loose tobacco; 1L liquor, 2L wine, or 2L still wine; 50g perfume or 250ml toilet water. Goods obtained duty and tax paid in another EU country up to a value of IR£460 (IR£115 per traveler under 15) will not be subject to additional customs duties. You must be over 17 to import liquor or tobacco. For more information, contact The Revenue Commissioners, Dublin Castle (tel. (01) 679 27 77; fax 671 20 21; e-mail taxes@ior.ie; http:\\www.revenue.ie) or The Collector of Customs and Excise, The Custom House, Dublin 1.

Australia Citizens may import AUS$400 (under 18 AUS$200) of goods duty-free, in addition to the allowance of 1.125L alcohol and 250 cigarettes or 250g tobacco. You must be over 18 to import either of these substances. There is no limit to the amount of Australian and/or foreign cash that may be brought into or taken out of the country. However, amounts of AUS$5000 or more, or the equivalent in foreign currency, must be reported. All foodstuffs and animal products must be declared on arrival. For information, contact the Regional Director, Australian Customs Service, GPO Box 8, Sydney NSW 2001(tel. (02) 213 20 00; fax 213 40 00).

New Zealand Citizens may bring home up to NZ$700 worth of goods duty-free if they are intended for personal use or are unsolicited gifts. The concession is 200 cigarettes (1 carton), 250g tobacco, 50 cigars or a combination of all three not to exceed 250g. You may also bring in 4.5L of beer or wine and 1.125L of liquor. Only travelers over 17 may bring tobacco or alcoholic beverages into the country. For more information, consult the *New Zealand Customs Guide for Travelers,* available from customs offices, or contact New Zealand Customs, 50 Anzac Ave., Box 29, Auckland (tel. (09) 377 35 20; fax 309 29 78).

South Africa Citizens may import duty-free up to 400 cigarettes, 50 cigars, 250g tobacco, 2L wine, 1L of spirits, 50mL perfume, 250ml toilet water, and other items up to a value of SAR500. Amounts exceeding this limit but not up to SAR10,000 are taxable at 20%. For more specific information contact the Commissioner for Customs and Excise, Private Bag X47, Pretoria 0001. This agency distributes the pamphlet *South African Customs Information* for visitors and residents who travel abroad. South Africans residing in the U.S. should contact the Embassy of South Africa, 3051 Massachusetts Ave. NW, Washington D.C. 20008 (tel. (202) 232-4400; fax 244-9417) or the South African Home Annex, 3201 New Mexico Ave. NW, #380, Washington, D.C. 20016 (tel. (202) 966-1650).

YOUTH, STUDENT, & TEACHER IDENTIFICATION

The **International Student Identity Card (ISIC)** is the most widely accepted form of student identification. Flashing this card may procure you discounts for sights, theaters, museums, accommodations, train, ferry, and airplane travel, and other services throughout Europe. Make a habit of presenting it and asking about student discounts wherever you go *(c'è uno sconto studentesco?).* Don't be too surprised, though, if it is not honored—student discounts are sometimes exclusively for Italian or EU students. ISIC also provides accident insurance of up to US$3000 with no daily limit. In addition, cardholders have access to a toll-free traveler's assistance hotline whose multilingual staff can provide help in medical, legal, and financial emergencies overseas.

ISICs are issued by many travel offices, including Council Travel, Let's Go Travel, and STA Travel in the U.S.; Travel CUTS in Canada; and any of the organizations under the auspices of the International Student Travel Confederation (ISTC) around the world (see Budget Travel Services, p. 62). When you apply for the card, request a copy of the International Student Identity Card Handbook, which lists some of the available discounts by country. The card is valid until fall semester of the following year. The fee is US$18. Applicants must be at least 12 years old and degree-seeking students of a secondary or post-secondary school. Because of the proliferation of phony ISICs, many airlines and some other services now require another proof of student identity, either your school ID card or a signed and stamped letter from your school's registrar attesting to your student status. The US$19 **International Teacher Identity Card (ITIC)** offers similar but limited discounts, as well as medical insurance coverage. For more info on these handy cards consult the organization's web site (http://www.istc.org).

Federation of International Youth Travel Organisations (FIYTO) issues a discount card to travelers who are not students but are under 26. Known as the **GO25 Card,** this one-year card offers many of the same benefits as the ISIC, and most organizations that sell the ISIC also sell the GO25 Card. A brochure that lists discounts is free when you purchase the card. To apply, bring proof of birthdate (a copy of your birth certificate, a passport, or a valid driver's license) and a passport-sized photo. The fee is US$16, CDN$15, or UK£5. GO25 cards *(carta giovane)* and ISIC are also available in Rome at the CTS office on Via Genova (tel. 467 91; see Budget Travel Services in Rome, p. 73.).

HOSTEL MEMBERSHIPS

A one-year **Hostelling International (HI)** membership permits you to stay at youth hostels in Italy at unbeatable prices (usually US$5-20). You can save yourself potential trouble by procuring a membership card, available at most budget travel organizations (like Council Travel and STA) before you leave home, since not all hostels sell them on the spot. For details on the Italian hostel network, contact the HI affiliate in Rome, the **Associazione Italiana Alberghi per la Gioventù (AIG)**, Via Cavour, 44, 00184 Roma (tel. 487 11 52; fax 488 04 92). For a listing of Rome's youth hostel, see p. 111.

The Internet Guide to Hostelling (http://www.hostels.com) can provide additional information on these accommodations, and the HI International Booking Network (IBN) allows you to make confirmed reservations at over 300 hostels worldwide for a nominal fee. Note that not all the Italian hostels take reservations, however.

The following are national HI affiliates in English-speaking countries. In many cases, **membership must be acquired through the HI affiliate in one's own country,** not abroad. Check with your local organization before you go.

American Youth Hostels (HI-AYH), 733 15th St. NW, Suite 840, Washington, D.C. 20005 (tel. (202) 783-6161; fax 783-6171; http://www.taponline.com/tap/travel/hostels/pages/hosthp.html). HI-AYH maintains 34 local offices, but most budget travel organizations sell memberships as well. Membership cards, which are valid for twelve months from the date of issue, cost US$25, under 18 US$10, over 54 US$15, family card US$35.

Hostelling International-Canada (HI-C), 400-205 Catherine Street, Ottawa, Ontario, K2P 1C3 (tel. (613) 237-7884; fax 237-7868). The Canada-wide membership and customer service line is (800) 663-5777. One-year membership fee CDN$25, under 18 CDN$12; 2-year (over 18) CDN$35; lifetime CDN$175.

Youth Hostels Association of England and Wales (YHA), Trevelyan House, 8 St. Stephen's Hill, St. Albans, Hertfordshire AL1 2DY (tel. (01727) 855 215; fax 844 126). Enrollment fees are UK£9.30 for adults, under 18 UK£3.20, lifetime membership UK£125. Various family memberships are also available.

An Óige (Irish Youth Hostel Association), 61 Mountjoy St., Dublin 7 (tel. (01) 830 45 55; fax 830 58 08; http://www.touchtel.ie). One-year membership is IR£7.50, under 18 IR£4, family IR£7.50 per adult with children under 16 free.

Youth Hostels Association of Northern Ireland (YHANI), 22 Donegall Rd., Belfast BT12 5JN, (tel. (01232) 31 54 35; fax 43 96 99).

Scottish Youth Hostels Association (SYHA), 7 Glebe Crescent, Stirling FK8 2JA (tel. (01786) 45 11 81; fax 45 01 98). Membership UK£6, under 18 UK£2.50.

Australian Youth Hostels Association (AYHA), Level 3, 10 Mallett St., Camperdown NSW, 2050 (tel. (02) 565 16 99; fax 565 13 25; e-mail YHA@zeta.org.au). Cards cost adults AUS$42, under 18 AUS$12, renewal AUS$26.

Youth Hostels Association of New Zealand (YHANZ), P.O. Box 436, 173 Gloucester St., Christchurch 1 (tel. (643) 379 99 70; fax 365 44 76; e-mail hostel.operations@yha.org.nz; http://yha.org.nz/yha). Annual memberships NZ$24.

Hostel Association of South Africa, P.O. Box 4402, Cape Town 8000 (tel. (21) 419 18 53; fax 21 69 37. Adult membership SAR45, students SAR30, group SAR120, family SAR90, lifetime SAR225.

INTERNATIONAL DRIVER'S PERMIT

Italy honors the IDP, although it is not required for car rental in most places. It is probably a good idea to get one anyway, just in case you're in a small town where the police do not read or speak English. The IDP must be issued in your own country before you depart and must be accompanied by your regular driver's license. In Italy you may also need a "green card," or International Insurance Certificate, which can be obtained through the car rental agency.

American Automobile Association (AAA), 1000 AAA Drive (mail stop 28), Heathrow, FL 32746-5080 (tel. (407) 444-4245; fax 444-4247). The IDP is available from any AAA branch in the U.S. or by mail from the address above. The permit is valid for 1 year and costs US$10.

Canadian Automobile Association, CAA Central Ontario, 60 Commerce Valley Dr. E, Thornhill, Ontario L3T 7P9 (tel. (416) 221-4300). The IDP is available from any CAA branch in Canada or by mail from the address above (CDN$10).

Money Matters

This book's prices and exchange rates were compiled in the summer of 1996. Since rates fluctuate considerably, be sure to confirm them before you go. **Prices may have changed as well, so do not demand that businesses honor the ones listed. Your trip will probably be easier if you are financially flexible.**

Generally speaking, you can assume that 10,000 lire equals about six bucks (at the current exchange rate, it's actually worth a little more). When estimating your budget, remember that you will probably need to keep handy a larger amount than usual. Don't sacrifice your health or safety for a cheaper tab.

CURRENCY AND EXCHANGE

US$1 = 1515 lire (L)	L1000 = US$0.66
CDN$1 = L1103	L1000 = CDN$0.91
UK£1 = L2347	L1000 = UK£0.43
IR£1 = L2445	L1000 = IR£0.41
AUS$1 = L1172	L1000 = AUS$0.85
NZ$1 = L1035	L1000 = NZ$0.97
SAR1 = L337	L1000 = SAR2.97

The Italian currency unit is the *lira* (plural: *lire*). Coins are minted in L50, L100, L200 and L500, and the most common bills are L1000, L2000, L5000, L10,000, L50,000, and L100,000. We recommend that, before you leave home, you buy enough *lire* to last for the first 24-72 hours of your trip, in order to avoid a frenzied exchange (at terrible rates) at the airport when you arrive. Otherwise, it is cheaper to buy *lire* in Italy than at home. When exchanging money in Rome, look for *"cambio"* signs, and shop around. Exchange bureaus *(cambi)* very often offer better rates and lower commission than Roman banks. Changing currency at a bank is best done in the morning; banking hours are usually Monday through Friday 8:30am-1:30pm, with an extra hour in the afternoon (often 3-4pm). It also helps to plan ahead: you don't want to get caught without *lire* at night or on a Sunday.

TRAVELER'S CHECKS

Traveler's checks are the safest way to carry large sums of money. Several agencies and many banks sell them, usually for face value plus a 1% commission. Buy them in your home currency (none of the major companies listed below sell checks in *lire*). They are refundable if lost or stolen, and many issuing agencies offer additional services to travelers. Be sure to bring your passport with you when you plan to use traveler's checks; some places won't accept them otherwise. Buying checks in U.S. dollars or British pounds may also facilitate the exchange process.

Refunds on lost or stolen checks can be time-consuming. To accelerate the process and avoid red tape, *keep check receipts and records in a separate place from the checks themselves.* Leave a photocopy of check serial numbers with someone at home as back up in case you lose your copy. Never countersign checks until you're prepared to cash them. Keep careful track of your usage; record the number of each check as you cash it.

American Express (tel. (800) 221-7282 in the U.S. and Canada; (0800) 52 13 13 in the U.K.; (008) 25 19 02 in Australia; (0800) 44 10 68 in New Zealand). Elsewhere, call U.S. collect at (801) 964-6665. **In Italy, call (1678) 720 00.** AmEx traveler's checks are the most widely recognized worldwide and easiest to replace if lost or stolen—just call the information number or the AmEx Travel Office nearest you. AmEx offices cash their own checks commission-free (except where prohibited by law) and sell checks that can be signed by either of 2 people traveling together ("Cheque for Two"). Checks are available in 11 currencies and can be purchased at American Express Travel Service offices, banks, and American Automobile Association offices (AAA members can buy them commission-free). Cardmembers can also purchase checks at American Express Dispensers in Travel Service Offices of airports, or by ordering them by phone (tel. (800) ORDER-TC (673-3782)). Traveler's checks are also available over America On-Line. Request AmEx's *Traveler's Companion,* which gives office addresses and stolen check hotlines for each European country.

Citicorp sells both Citicorp and **Citicorp Visa** traveler's checks in 7 currencies (tel. (800) 645-6556 in the U.S. and Canada, (1812) 97 47 81 in the UK; from elsewhere call the U.S. collect at (813) 623-1709). Commission is 1-2% on check purchases. Checkholders are automatically enrolled for 45 days in the Travel Assist Program (hotline (800) 250-4377, or collect (202) 296-8728), which provides access to English-speaking doctors and lawyers. Citicorp's World Courier Service guarantees hand-delivery of traveler's checks anywhere in the world.

Thomas Cook MasterCard (tel. (800) 223-9920 in the U.S. and Canada; elsewhere call the U.S. collect (609) 987-7300; in the U.K. call (0800) 62 21 01 toll-free, (1733) 50 29 95 or 31 89 50 collect). Checks available in 12 currencies. Commission ranges from 1-2% for purchases. Try buying (and cashing) the checks at a Thomas Cook office for potentially lower commissions.

Visa (tel. (800) 227-6811 in the U.S.; (0800) 89 54 92 in the U.K.; from elsewhere call the U.K. at (1733) 31 89 49, a toll call for which the charges can be reversed) provides info on where you can buy their checks locally. Any kind of Visa traveler's checks (Barclay's or Citicorp) can be reported lost at the Visa number.

CREDIT CARDS

Credit cards for the budget traveler can be a blessing or a curse. On the dark side, many smaller establishments will not accept them, while enticing, pricier, big-city establishments accept them all too willingly. Relying extensively on credit cards while abroad could be a big mistake, especially if doing so leads you to spend more than you would otherwise. However, used sparingly, credit cards can be a great boon to careful spenders and an invaluable resource in case of emergency. Perhaps the most important benefit is that holders of most major credit cards can now get **cash advances** around the clock from associated banks and automatic teller machines (ATMs) throughout Europe, including cities in Italy. Because you make your withdrawal in foreign currency, you benefit from a wholesale exchange rate. This service requires you to have a PIN number, available from your issuing bank (check with them about charges, interest rates, and ATM locations as well). Pay your bill quickly to avoid ruinous interest rates for such advances; only withdraw what you can pay back immediately (or have someone at home take care of it while you're away). You can also reduce conversion fees by charging purchases instead of changing traveler's checks. Remember that MasterCard and Visa have different names in Europe ("Euro-Card" and "Carte Bleue", respectively). Thomas Cook (Piazza Barberini, 21) has a MasterCard service desk, and BankAmericard (Largo del Tritone, 161) has a Visa service desk.

Lost or stolen cards should be reported *immediately,* or you may be held responsible for forged charges; toll-free numbers (within Italy) exist for these cases (AmEx 167 86 40 46; MC 167 87 72 32; Visa 167 87 42 99). Write down the card-cancellation telephone numbers and keep them in a safe place separate from your cards. Always be sure that the carbon receipt has been torn into pieces, and watch as your card is being imprinted; an imprint onto a blank slip can be used later to charge merchandise in your name.

CASH CARDS AND ATMS

There are several types of **ATMs (automatic teller machines)** streets of Rome. One type accepts actual bank notes (US$5, 10, 20, 50, 100; UK£5, 10, 20, 50) in exchange for *lira*, at horrible rat machines have instructions in Italian, English, German, and French. Demachines except in case of emergency, since they seem to exist solely ists. Thankfully, Rome now has ATMs which will give you a **cash advance** **card** and even the familiar ones we know and love that will accept **cash ca** American banks. These ATMs are generally on the street, rather than in the bank itself, and are often indicated by the *Bancomat* (A brand name which has become the generic word for ATM) sign. If you plan to use a credit card to withdraw money from an ATM, check before you leave to make sure you have a large available credit line and a PIN code (see Credit Cards, p. 40.). If you plan to use your American ATM card, memorize your PIN in Numbers rather than letters since ATM keypads in Italy do not always have letters. In general, if you plan to use a cash machine, prepare yourself for immense frustrations. ATMs are few and far between, and the ones you find will often be broken or will mysteriously refuse to process your transaction. Your card may be eaten or demagnetized, so be sure to bring an emergency supply of traveler's checks. The banks with the most reliable ATMs accepting Visa and Mastercard are Banca Nazionale del Lavoro and Banca di Roma. Credit card ATMs also abound on Via Arenula, Via and Largo del Trirone, Via del Corso, and near the Pantheon and Termini. Cirrus claims not to have any ATMs in Rome, but Banca Nazionale del Lavoro, with locations at Via della Rossetta (at the Pantheon) and on the corner of Via Marsala and Via Solferino (near Termini) usually accept Cirrus and PLUS cards.

MONEY FROM HOME

Sending money overseas is a complicated, expensive, and often extremely frustrating adventure. Do your best to avoid it by carrying a credit card or a separate stash of emergency traveler's checks.

The easiest way to get money from home is to bring an **American Express Card.** AmEx allows green card holders to draw cash from their checking accounts at any of its major offices and many of its representatives' offices (up to US$1000 every 21 days, no service charge, no interest). AmEx also offers Express Cash, which allows green-card holders to withdraw up to US$1000 in a seven-day period. There is a 2% transaction fee for each cash withdrawal (US$2.50 minimum). To enroll in Express Cash, cardmembers may call 1-800-CASH NOW/227-4669 (outside the U.S., call collect (904) 565-7875). Another approach is to wire money through the **international money transfer services** operated by **Western Union** (tel. in the U.S. (800) 325-0000 or (800) CALL-CASH/225-5227).

Finally, if you are an American in a life-or-death situation, you can have money sent to you via the **Overseas Citizens Service, American Citizens Services,** Consular Affairs, Public Affairs Staff, Room 4831, U.S. Dept. of State, Washington, D.C. 20520 (tel. (202) 647-5225, after hours and on holidays, 647-4000; fax 647-3000; http://travel.state.gov). For a fee of US$15, the State Department will forward money to the nearest consular office within hours, which will then pass it on according to instructions. In a dire emergency, cable the State Department through Western Union.

VALUE-ADDED TAX

The **Value-Added Tax** (**VAT,** in Italian, *imposto sul valore aggiunta,* or **IVA**) is a form of sales tax levied in the European Union. VAT is generally part of the price paid on goods and services. Tourists who do not reside in an EU country have a legal right to a refund of the VAT, but only for major purchases. The receipt, purchases, and purchaser's passport must be presented to and stamped by the Customs Office as you leave the EU, and the invoice must be returned to the store. Some of the more

...ores offer "Tax-Free Shopping for Tourists," which enables you to get your
...efund in cash when leaving from the airport or crossing borders.

BARGAINING

Bargaining is common in Italy, but use discretion. It is appropriate at outdoor markets, with street vendors, and over unmetered taxi fares (always settle your price *before* getting into the cab). Haggling over prices is out of place almost everywhere else, however, especially in large stores. Hotel haggling is more successful in uncrowded, smaller *pensioni* (*Let's Go* mentions when such activity is common). If you don't speak Italian, at least memorize the numbers. Let the merchant make the first offer and counter with one-half to two-thirds of his or her bid. The merchant will probably act extremely offended by your offer, even if the context warrants bargaining, but stand firm. Never offer anything you are unwilling to pay—you are expected to buy if the merchant accepts your price.

■ Safety

> If you are ever in a potentially dangerous situation in Italy, call the **EMERGENCY ASSISTANCE NUMBER**—113 or 112. 113 is the Public Emergency Assistance number for the State Police and usually has an English interpreter on hand; 112 is the Immediate Action Service of the *carabinieri;* 115 is the nationwide telephone number for the fire department; 116 will bring the *Soccorso Stradali* or ACI (Italian Automobile Club) if you need assistance on the road. Dial 118 for *Pronto Soccorso,* or First Aid.

When exploring a new city, extra vigilance may be wise, but no city should force you to turn precautions into panic. When you get to a place where you'll be spending some time, find out about unsafe areas from tourist information, from the manager of your hotel or hostel, or from a local whom you trust. Especially if you are traveling alone, be sure that someone at home knows your itinerary. Never say that you're traveling alone. Both men and women may want to carry a small **whistle** to scare off attackers or attract attention, and it's not a bad idea to jot down the number of the police. When walking at night, you should turn day-time precautions into mandates. In particular, stay near crowded and well-lit areas and do not attempt to cross through parks, parking lots or any other large, deserted areas. Whenever possible, *Let's Go* warns of unsafe neighborhoods, but only your eyes can tell you for sure if you've wandered into one; buildings in disrepair, vacant lots, and general desertedness are all bad signs. Pay attention to the neighborhood that surrounds you. A district can change character drastically in the course of a single block. Simply being aware of the flow of people can tell you a great deal about the relative safety of the area. Many notoriously dangerous districts have safe sections; look for children playing, women walking in the open, and other signs of an active community.

Tourists are particularly vulnerable to crime for two reasons: they carry large amounts of cash and they are not as savvy as locals. To avoid such unwanted attention, try to blend in as much as possible. If you feel nervous, confused, or lost, walk purposefully into a shop or *caffè*-bar to check your map, rather than checking it on the street. Thefts are often more impromptu than planned; walking with nervous over-the-shoulder glances can be a tip that you have something valuable to protect. Even when unsure, act as though you know exactly where you're going. An obviously bewildered body-builder is more likely to be harassed than a stern and confident 98-pound weakling.

Petty thievery is more common in Rome than in cities of similar size in the U.S., so you should take extra precautions with your valuables. Before you go, **photocopy all important documents** to facilitate their replacement in case of theft or loss. Buy small key or combination locks to lock the zippers on your purse, backpack, and luggage. When in Rome, even though the Romans seem to do it, **it's not a good idea to**

keep your wallet in your back pocket. The crowded streets, markets, buses, and subways make picking back pockets extremely easy for even the most inexperienced thieves. Front pockets, which you can see and keep your hand in, are infinitely better, though still not particularly secure. If you must carry a purse, buy a sturdy one with a strong clasp and wear it across your front, with the clasp facing you, though even these precautions may not suffice, since purse-snatchers, often on mopeds, use knives to cut the straps. The best way to avoid being robbed is to keep your money and documents in a **money belt,** which must be worn inside your clothes to be effective, or a neck pouch. Fanny-packs, even when worn in the front, are among the easiest targets for thieves; they can be unzipped or even slit with a knife, especially on public transportation. Backpacks should also be guarded carefully on buses and the subway; slip a small lock through the zippers, and keep your camera and sunglasses (both popular items for thieves) in the least accessible compartments.

Trains are also notoriously easy spots for thieving. Professionals wait for tourists to fall asleep and then carry off everything they can. When traveling in pairs, sleep in alternating shifts; when alone, use good judgement in selecting a train compartment: never stay in an empty one. Keep important documents and valuables on your person, and try to sleep on top bunks with your luggage stored above you, if not in bed with you. To thwart the evil doings of those thieves that are said to gas train compartments and strip their unconscious occupants of all their belongings, you may also want to leave the train window slightly open.

Among the more colorful aspects of large cities are **con artists.** Con artists and hustlers often work in groups, and children, unfortunately, are often the best at the game. Be aware of certain classics: sob stories that require money, rolls of bills "found" on the street, mustard smudged or saliva spit on your shoulder, distracting you for enough time to steal your bag. Although con artists and thieves come in all shapes and sizes, Rome is especially notorious for (a few of) its **gypsies.** Most of these so-called gypsies are honest refugees from Eastern Europe, but the few criminals among them have given them all a bad name. Common practice among gypsy con artists and their children is to shove a newspaper or piece of cardboard directly under your face or at your waist so you can't see while they clean you out in seconds. Some have had a gypsy mother literally throw her baby (or what looked liked a baby) at them and were pickpocketed while trying to catch the child in the air. Be especially alert in these situations; if approached by gypsies, do not respond or make eye contact, walk quickly away, brandish your umbrella menacingly, and keep a solid grip on your belongings. If gypsy children actually begin to touch you or your belongings, shouting (anything, even in English), making large, threatening gestures are very effective in scaring them away. Contact the police if a hustler or gypsy is particularly insistent or aggressive.

In general, theft is more common in the high season (summer, especially), in touristed neighborhoods (Via dei Fori Imperiali, the Colosseum, etc.), and on public transportation (like the notorious #64 bus), but unfortunately, it is impossible to predict exactly where or when these crimes will occur. Romans are usually embarrassed by their city's reputation as a hotbed of petty crime and they will be helpful, sometimes even warning tourists on public transportation that suspicious-looking characters have boarded the bus. Your best bet is to be cautious, but not hysterical; don't let your fears of being pickpocketed ruin your visit to Rome.

There is no sure-fire set of precautions that will protect you from all of the situations you might encounter when you travel. A good self-defense course will give you more concrete strategies for countering different types of aggression, but it might cost you more money than your trip. **Model Mugging,** a national organization with offices in several major cities, teaches a very effective, comprehensive course on self-defense. Contact Lynn S. Auerbach on the East Coast ((617) 232-7900), Alice Tibits in the Midwest ((612) 645-6189), and Cori Couture on the West Coast ((415) 592-7300). Course prices vary from $400-500 and are offered for both women and men. Community colleges frequently offer self-defense courses at more affordable prices.

For official **United States Department of State** travel advisories, including information on crime and security, call their 24-hour hotline at (202) 647-5225. To order publications, including a pamphlet entitled *A Safe Trip Abroad*, write to the Superintendent of Documents, U.S. Government Printing Office, Washington, D.C. 20402, or call (202) 783-3238.

DRUGS

Travelers should avoid drugs altogether. All foreigners in Italy are subject to Italian law, where drugs (including marijuana) are illegal. Your home country is essentially powerless to interfere in a foreign court. Even if you don't use drugs, beware of the person who asks you to carry a package or drive a car across the border. If you carry prescription drugs, it is vital to carry a copy of the prescription among your important documents. Avoid public drunkenness; it is dangerous and rude, and it may attract police attention.

▓ Health

BEFORE YOU GO

Though no amount of planning can guarantee an accident-free trip, preparation can help minimize the likelihood of contracting a disease and maximize the chances of receiving effective health care in the case of an emergency.

For minor health problems on the road, a compact **first-aid kit** should suffice. You can buy a ready-made kit, but it's just as easy to assemble your own. Items you might want to include are bandages, aspirin or another pain killer, antiseptic soap or antibiotic cream, a thermometer in a sturdy case, a Swiss Army knife with tweezers, a decongestant, a motion sickness remedy, medicine for diarrhea and stomach problems, sunscreen, burn ointment, and an elastic bandage.

People with asthma or allergies should be aware that larger Italian cities often have high levels of air pollution, particularly during the summer, and that, as elsewhere in Europe, "non-smoking" areas are almost nonexistent. Take an **antihistamine, decongestant, inhaler,** etc. (be it prescription or over-the-counter), since there may not be an Italian equivalent with the correct dosage.

Travelers with chronic medical conditions should consult their physicians before leaving the country. Always go prepared with any **medication** you may need while away, as well as a copy of the prescription and/or a statement from your doctor, especially if you will be bringing insulin, syringes, or any narcotics into Italy (some drugs legal at home may not be legal there). Be sure to keep all medication with you in your carry-on luggage. If you wear **glasses** or **contacts,** take a copy of your prescription or bring an extra pair of glasses with you from home. Consider bringing saline solution, enzyme tablets, and appropriate lens cleaners with you, since these products are often more difficult to find and considerably more expensive in Italy.

In your passport, write the names of people you wish to be contacted in case of a medical emergency, and also list any allergies or medical conditions of which you would want doctors to be aware. Take a look at your immunization records before you go. Although Europe is fairly safe, it won't hurt to make sure your vaccinations are up to date. Any traveler with an important medical condition that cannot be easily recognized may want to obtain a **Medic Alert Identification Tag,** which indicates the nature of the bearer's problem, as well as the number of a 24-hour collect-call information number (US$35 the first year, US$15 annually thereafter). Contact Medic Alert Foundation, 2323 Colorado Ave., Turlock, CA 95382 (tel. (800) 825-3785). The **American Diabetes Association,** 1660 Duke St., Alexandria, VA 22314 (tel. (800) 232-3472) provides copies of an article entitled "Travel and Diabetes" and 18-language ID cards explaining the bearer's condition.

Let's Go should not be your only information source on common health problems for tourists in Italy. For general health information, send for the **American Red Cross'**

First-Aid and Safety Handbook (US$15); contact the ARC at 285 Columbus Ave., Boston, MA 02116-5114 (tel. (800) 564-1234), or look for the manual in your local bookstore. In the U.S., the ARC also offers many first-aid and CPR courses, which are well-taught and relatively inexpensive. The **United States Center for Disease Control** (based in Atlanta, Georgia) is an excellent source of general info on health for travelers around the world, and maintains an international traveler's hotline (tel. (404) 332-4559; fax 332-4565; http://www.cdc.gov). You can also write directly to the Centers for Disease Control and Prevention, Traveler's Health, 1600 Clifton Rd. NE, Atlanta, GA 30333. The CDC publishes the booklet *"Health Information for International Travelers"* (US$14), an annual global rundown of disease, immunization, and general health advice, including risks in particular countries.

If you are concerned about being able to access medical support while traveling, contact one of these two services: **Global Emergency Medical Services (GEMS)** provides 24-hour international medical assistance, coordinated through registered nurses. The staff has on-line access to your medical information, your primary physician, and a worldwide network of screened, credentialed English-speaking doctors and hospitals. Subscribers also receive a pocket-sized personal medical record that contains vital information in case of emergencies. For more information call (800) 860-1111, fax (770) 475-0058, or write to 2001 Westside Dr., #120, Alpharetta, GA 30201. The **International Association for Medical Assistance to Travelers (IAMAT)** offers a membership ID card, a directory of English-speaking doctors around the world who treat members for a set fee schedule, and detailed charts on immunization requirements and sanitation. Membership is free, though donations are appreciated and used for further research. Contact chapters in the **U.S.,** 417 Center St., Lewiston, NY 14092 (tel. (716) 754-4883; fax (519) 836-3412; e-mail iamat@sentex.net; http://www.sentex.net/iamat; **Canada,** 40 Regal Rd., Guelph, Ontario, N1K 1B5 (tel. (519) 836-0102) or 1287 St. Clair Ave. W, Toronto, M6E 1B8 (tel. (416) 652-0137; fax (519) 836-3412); or **New Zealand,** P.O. Box 5049, Christchurch 5.

The **United States State Department** compiles Consular Information Sheets on health, entry requirements, and other issues for all countries of the world. Call the Overseas Citizens' Services (tel. (202) 647-5225). If you have access to a fax, you can request these sheets by dialing 647-3000 directly from the fax machine and then following the recorded instructions. You can also obtain copies of the information from the State Department's regional passport agencies in the U.S., from the field offices of the U.S. Chamber of Commerce, and from U.S. embassies and consulates abroad. If you prefer, you can even send a self-addressed, stamped envelope to the Overseas Citizens' Services, Bureau of Consular Affairs, Room 4811, U.S. Department of State, Washington, D.C. 20520. If you are HIV-positive, call (202) 647-1488 for country-specific entry requirements or write to the Bureau of Consular Affairs, CA/P/PA, Department of State, Washington, D.C. 20520.

ON THE ROAD

Common sense is the simplest prescription for good health while you travel: eat well, drink plenty of liquids, get enough sleep, and don't overexert yourself. While traveling, pay attention to signals of pain and discomfort that your body may send you. Because of travel exhaustion and possible exposure to unusual foreign organisms (microbes, that is), you are more susceptible to illness while you are on the road. Some of the milder symptoms that you may safely ignore at home may be signs of more serious problems overseas.

Rome scorches in the summer. Avoid **heat exhaustion:** relax in hot weather, drink lots of non-alcoholic, non-caffeinated fluids, and lie down inside if you are getting too hot. Continuous heat stress can eventually lead to **heatstroke,** characterized by rising body temperature, severe headache, and cessation of sweating. Wear a hat, sunglasses, and a lightweight longsleeve shirt or pants (if you can stand it) to avoid heatstroke. Take advantage of Rome's natural air-conditioning in one of the ubiquitous stone and marble churches. Heatstroke victims should be cooled off with wet towels and taken to a doctor as soon as possible. These conditions are potentially fatal!

Always drink enough liquids to keep your urine clear. Alcoholic beverages are dehydrating, as are coffee, strong tea, and caffeinated sodas. If you'll be sweating a lot, be sure to eat enough salty food to prevent electrolyte depletion, characterized by severe headaches. Less debilitating, but still dangerous, is **sunburn.** If you're prone to sunburn, bring sunscreen with you (it's often more expensive and hard to find when traveling). Apply it liberally and often to avoid burns and the risk of skin cancer. If you get sunburned, drink more fluids than usual.

If you're going to be doing a lot of walking, remember to treat your most valuable resource well: Lavish your **feet** with attention. Wear good walking shoes, change your socks often, apply talcum powder to keep your feet dry, and use moleskin to pad hotspots before they become excruciating blisters. Also, take along some quick-energy foods. You will need to drink plenty of fluids (to prevent dehydration and constipation). Carry a water bottle, and drink from it even when you don't feel thirsty. Roman water is generally safe to drink unless marked *"non potabile,"* or unless it is running water on public transportation (ferries, trains, etc.). Relying on bottled mineral water for a while at the start of your trip minimizes chances of a bad reaction to the few unfamiliar microbes in Italian water.

Food poisoning can spoil any trip. Be cautious with street vendors and perishable food carried for hours in a hot backpack. One of the most common symptoms associated with eating and drinking in another country is **diarrhea.** Many people carry over-the-counter remedies (such as Imodium AD or Pepto-Bismol), but such remedies can complicate serious infections; don't use them if you suspect you have been exposed to contaminated food or water, since you are therefore at risk for cholera, typhoid fever, and other diseases. Dehydration is the most common side effect of diarrhea, and the best remedy is a teaspoon of sugar or honey and a pinch of salt in eight ounces of clean water. Rest, and let the dastardly disease run its course.

AIDS, HIV, AND STDS

On or off the road, you should be concerned about **Acquired Immune Deficiency Syndrome (AIDS),** transmitted through the exchange of body fluids with an infected individual (HIV-positive). The World Health Organization estimates that there are around 13 million people infected with the HIV virus. Over 90% of adults newly infected acquired HIV through heterosexual sex; women now represent 50% of all new diagnoses. Italy has one of the highest HIV rates in Europe.

The easiest mode of HIV transmission is through direct blood-to-blood contact with an HIV+ person; *never* share intravenous drug, tattooing, or other needles. The most common mode of transmission is sexual intercourse. Remember that *it is impossible to tell who may be infected* without a blood test. Health professionals recommend the use of latex condoms; follow the instructions on the packet. Casual contact (including drinking from the same glass or using the same eating utensils as an infected person) is not believed to pose a risk.

For more information on AIDS, call the **U.S. Center for Disease Control's** 24-hour Hotline at (800) 342-2437 (Spanish (800) 344-7332, daily 8am-2am). Council's brochure, *Travel Safe: AIDS and International Travel,* is available at all Council Travel offices see Travel Organizations, p. 29. In Europe, write to the **World Health Organization,** Attn: Global Program on AIDS, 20 Avenue Appia, 1211 Geneva 27, Switzerland (tel. (22) 791 21 11), for international statistics on AIDS. You can also write to the **Bureau of Consular Affairs,** CA/P/PA, Department of State, Washington, D.C. 20520.

Sexually transmitted diseases (STDs) such as gonorrhea, chlamydia, genital warts, syphilis, and herpes are a lot easier to catch than HIV. It's a wise idea to actually *look* at your partner's genitals before you have sex. If anything looks amiss, that should be a warning signal. When having sex, condoms may protect you from certain STDs, but oral or even tactile contact can lead to transmission.

There are no restrictions on travelers with HIV or AIDS entering Italy, nor is there any obligation to report an infection on arrival in the country or if you find you have it once there. Italians are generally very sensible about medical treatment, and the medical professionals will not pry if you get tested; still, it's not a bad idea to double-check that your test is confidential, or even done anonymously if need be. AIDS education is becoming more prevalent throughout the country, and you will not have any problems finding condoms *(preservativi)* at any pharmacy. The **toll-free AIDS number** for Italy is 167 86 10 61 (call Mon.-Fri. 1-6pm).

AIDS tests, as well as tests for STDs, can be performed at any **Analisi Cliniche** (a private lab that handles all sorts of tests, from allergies to pregnancy). Simply ask for the "AIDS test" or "HIV test"—there isn't an Italian word. (AIDS is pronounced AH-eeds in Italian; HIV is AH-ka-ee-voo.) Tests can be expensive (up to L150,000). Look in the Yellow Pages under *Analisi* for private labs or see Clinics, p. 77, for a list of clinics in Rome.

BIRTH CONTROL AND ABORTIONS

If you are straight and sexually active, you will need to consider contraception. Reliable devices may be difficult to come by while traveling; bring enough to allow for possible loss or extended stays. Women on the Pill should bring a prescription, since it comes in many forms. **Condoms** (profilattici, or in common parlance, preservativi) can be bought over the counter at pharmacies and in some supermarkets. A packet of six costs around L15,000.

Analisi Cliniche will perform tests for venereal disease *(malattia venerea)* as well as pregnancy tests, or you can buy home tests over the counter at pharmacies throughout the city. These labs also do pap smears and cryotherapy.

Abortion is legal in Italy, although not as a means of birth control. Local health units called *consultori* advise women on rights and procedures. Contact a hospital or clinic in Italy for more information.

■ Insurance

Beware of buying unnecessary travel coverage: your current policies may well extend to many travel-related accidents. **Medical insurance** (especially university policies) often covers costs incurred abroad, although **Medicare's** coverage is usually only valid for travel in Mexico and Canada. Canadians are protected by their home province's health insurance plan up to 90 days after leaving the country; check with the provincial Ministry of Health or Health Plan Headquarters for details. Australia has a Reciprocal Health Care Agreement (RCHA) with Italy, providing tourists with basic hospital and medical coverage in case of acute illness or accident. Contact the Commonwealth Department of Human Services and Health for more complete information. Your **homeowners' insurance** (or your family's coverage) often covers theft during travel. Homeowners are generally covered against loss of travel documents (passport, plane ticket, railpass, etc.) up to US$500.

ISIC and **ITIC** provide US$3000 worth of accident and illness insurance and US$100 per day up to 60 days of hospitalization. They also offer up to US$1000 for accidental death or dismemberment and up to US$25,000 if injured due to an airline's negligence or for emergency evacuation due to illness. The cards also give access to a toll-free Traveler's Assistance hotline (in the US and Canada (800) 626-2427; elsewhere call collect to the US (713) 267-2525). The multilingual staff can provide help in emergencies overseas. **Council** (see Travel Organizations, p. 29) offers the inexpensive Trip-Safe plan with options covering medical treatment and hospitalization, accidents, baggage loss, and even charter flights missed due to illness; **STA** offers a more expensive, more comprehensive plan. **American Express** cardholders receive automatic car-rental and flight insurance on purchases made with the card (tel. (800) 528-4800 for customer service).

Insurance companies usually require a copy of the police report for thefts, or evidence of having paid medical expenses (doctor's statements, receipts) before they will honor a claim. There may also be time limits on filing for reimbursement. Always carry policy numbers and proof of insurance, and try to have documents written in English. Check with the insurance carriers listed below for specific info.

Access America, 6600 West Broad St., P.O. Box 11188, Richmond, VA 23230 (tel. (800) 284-8300; fax (804) 673-1491). Covers trip cancellation/interruption, on-the-spot hospital admittance costs, emergency medical evacuation, sickness, and baggage loss. 24-hr. hotline.

The Berkley Group/Carefree Travel Insurance, 100 Garden City Plaza, P.O. Box 9366, Garden City, NY 11530-9366 (tel. (800) 323-3149 or (516) 294-0220; fax (516) 294-1096). Offers two comprehensive packages including coverage for trip cancellation/interruption/delay, accident and sickness, medical, baggage loss, bag delay, accidental death and dismemberment, and travel supplier insolvency. Trip cancellation/interruption may be purchased separately at a rate of US$5.50 per US$100 of coverage. 24-hr. worldwide emergency assistance hotline.

Globalcare Travel Insurance, 220 Broadway Lynnfield, MA 01940 (tel. (800) 821-2488; fax (617) 592-7720); e-mail global@nebc.mv.com). Complete medical, legal, emergency, and travel-related services. On-the-spot payments and special student programs, including benefits for trip cancellation and interruption GTI waives pre-exisitng medical conditions with their Globalcare Economy Plan for cruise and travel, and provides coverage for the bankruptcy or default of cruiselines, airlines, or tour operators.

Travel Assistance International, by Worldwide Assistance Services, Inc., 1133 15th St. NW, Suite 400, Washington, D.C. 20005-2710 (tel. (800) 821-2828 or (202) 828-5894; fax (202) 828-5896; e-mail wassist@aol.com). TAI provides its members with a 24-hr. free hotline for travel emergencies and referrals. Their Per-Trip (starting at US$52) and Frequent Traveler (starting at US$226) plans include medical, travel, and financial insurance, translation, and lost document/item assistance.

Travel Guard International, 1145 Clark St., Stevens Point, WI 54481 (tel. (800) 826-1300 or (715) 345-0505; fax (715) 345-0525). Comprehensive insurance programs starting at US$44. Programs cover trip cancellation and interruption, bankruptcy and financial default, lost luggage, medical coverage abroad, emergency assistance, accidental death. 24-hr. hotline.

Travel Insured International, Inc., 52-S Oakland Ave., P.O. Box 280568, East Hartford, CT 06128-0568 (tel. (800) 243-3174; fax (203) 528-8005). Insurance against accident, baggage loss, sickness, trip cancellation and interruption, travel delay, and default. Covers emergency medical evacuation and automatic flight insurance.

Wallach and Company, Inc., 107 West Federal St., P.O. Box 480, Middleburg, VA 20118-0480 (tel. (800) 237-6615, fax (540) 687–3172) or e-mail wallach.r@media-soft.net). Comprehensive medical insurance including evacuation and repatriation of remains and direct payment of claims to providers of services. Other optional coverages available. 24-hr. toll-free international hotline.

■ Alternatives to Tourism

STUDY

Foreign study may be an alluring possibility, but keep in mind that programs vary tremendously in expense, academic quality, living conditions, and exposure to local students and culture. Most American undergraduates enroll in programs sponsored by domestic universities, and many colleges' advising offices provide information on study abroad. Take advantage of these resources and put in some time in their libraries. Ask for the names of recent participants, and talk to them.

Publications

Council (see Travel Organizations, p. 29) sponsors over 40 study abroad programs throughout the world, and publishes *The High School Student's Guide to Study, Travel and Adventure Abroad* and *Work, Study, Travel Abroad: The Whole World Handbook* (see Useful Publications, p. 30).

Peterson's Guides, P. O. Box 2123, Princeton, NJ 08543-2123 (tel. (800) 338-3282; fax (609) 243-9150; http://www.petersons.com). Their comprehensive *Study Abroad* annual guide lists programs in countries all over the world and provides essential information on the study abroad experience in general. Purchase a copy at your local bookstore (US$27) or call their toll-free number.

Institute of International Education (IIE), 809 United Nations Plaza, New York, NY 10017-3580 (tel. (212) 984-5413 for recorded info; fax 984-5358). Non-profit international and cultural exchange agency. Their library of study abroad resources is open to the public Tues.-Thurs. 11am-3:45pm. Publishes *Academic Year Abroad* (US$43 with US$4 shipping and handling) detailing semester and year-long programs worldwide and *Vacation Study Abroad* ($37 with $4 shipping and handling) which lists over 1600 short-term, summer, and language school programs. Write for a publications list.

Organizations

Centro Turistico Studentesco e Giovanile (CTS) provides information on study in Italy. For contact info, see below, p. 62.

Youth For Understanding (YFU) International Exchange, 3501 Newark St. NW, Washington, D.C. 20016 (tel. (800) TEENAGE or (202) 966-6800; fax 895-1104; http://www.yfu.org). One of the oldest and largest exchange programs, YFU places U.S. high school students with families worldwide for year, semester, and summer homestays.

American Field Service (AFS), 220 E. 42nd St., 3rd floor, New York, NY 10017 (tel. (800) AFS-INFO or 876-2376; fax (212) 949-9379; http://www.afs.org/usa). AFS offers summer, semester, and year-long homestay exchange programs for high school students (including graduating high school seniors) and short-term service projects for adults in Italy and other countries. Financial aid available.

Finally, be aware that study in Italy for longer than three months requires a **student visa**. For info on how to get one, see Visas, p. 35.

Italian Universities

If your Italian is fluent, consider enrolling directly in an Italian university. Universities are overcrowded, but you will probably have a blast and develop a real feel for the culture. For an application, write to the nearest Italian consulate. In Rome, contact the **Segretaria Stranieri,** Città Universitaria, Piazzale delle Scienze, 2 (tel. 499 91; open Mon., Wed., Fri. 8:30am-1pm). For more advice, contact **Ufficio Centrale Studenti Esteri in Italia (UCSEI),** Via Lungotevere dei Vallati, 14, 00186 Roma (tel. 880 40 62; fax 880 40 63), a national organization for foreign students who have already started their course of study in Italy.

Language Schools

If you are planning to be in Rome for two weeks or more, a course at one of the several language schools in the city would improve your Italian immensely as well as facilitate your communication skills for a better trip. These institutions offer courses for students of all ages, interests, and levels of Italian.

Italiaidea, Piazza della Cancelleria, 85, 00186 Rome (tel. 68 30 76 20; fax 689 29 97). Organizes Italian language, arts, and culture courses throughout the year, including vacation courses (specifically for the students) at the seaside or in the mountains during summer months. 1-month intensive language course (meeting 3hrs./day) is L600,000; there's a L30,000 registration fee, and a deposit of L120,000 is required on the first day of class, but the cost of supplies is included. Located in the historic center of Rome. Open Mon.-Fri. 9am-6:30pm.

Istituto Italiano, Via Merulana 139, 00185 Roma (tel. 70 45 21 38; fax 70 08 51 22, e-mail: istital@uni.net), near the San Giovanni Metro stop on Linea A. Courses offered for students who want a slower pace or for those who seek an intensive setting and rapid progress. Seven different language levels accommodate the students according to their needs. A 4-wk. intensive course (22½hrs. per week) is

L960,000. The less intensive 4-wk. program is L700,000. Programs available for any number of weeks (2wks. minimum). Office open Mon.-Fri. 8:30am-7pm.

DILIT, Via Marghera 22, 00185 Roma (tel. 446 26 12; fax 444 08 88), near Termini Station. A school which emphasizes dialogue among students and with the teacher. Resources include a language lab, video and listening center, a computer, and reading room. Intensive courses of 3, 4, or 6 hrs. per day for any number of weeks (2wks. minimum). A 6hrs. per day, 2-wk. program will cost L750,000. Students of all levels of Italian are accommodated according to a placement exam. Also, the school can accommodate students in private quarters or with host families. Office open summer daily 8:30am-8pm.

Torre di Babele, Via Bixio 74, 00185 Roma (tel. 700 84 34; fax 70 49 71 50; e-mail: babele@flashnet.it; http://www.nube.com/babele). Small groups of students (a maximum of 12) enjoy personal attention from the instructor in non-intensive or intensive courses for an even number of weeks (2wks. minimum). The no-nonsense language student may be interested in the 4-wk. super-intensive course (6hrs. every weekday, 2 of which are one-on-one with the instructor) for L2,700,000. The less aggressive student can opt for a 2-wk. intensive program (4hrs. per day) for L470,000. Students can find lodging through the school upon request, for somewhat steep fees.

Academies and Cultural Institutions

Another option is studying at an institute designed for foreigners but run by an Italian university. The following schools and organizations offer a variety of classes in Italian language, art, and culture; contact them directly for more information.

John Cabot University, Via della Lungara 233, Rome 00165 (tel. 687 88 81; fax 638 20 88; e-mail rspitzmi@nexus.it). Located in Trastevere, this American international university offers undergraduate degrees in Art History, Business Administration, English Literature, and International Affairs. Foreign students can enroll for summer-, quarter-, and year-long sessions. Qualifying students can obtain academic internships in business and international organizations in Rome. Apply directly to the Admissions Office.

American Academy in Rome, Via Angelo Masina, 5 (tel. 584 61). Library open to students with a letter of introduction from an American professor responsible for their work. Occasional exhibits open to the public.

British School at Rome, Via Antonio Gramsci, 61 (tel. 321 34 54). Library open to British students with a letter, or occasionally on application in person. Exhibits open to the public.

WORK

The employment situation in Rome is grim for natives and even worse for foreigners. Openings are coveted by herds of would-be expatriates, so competition is fierce. Foreigners are most successful at securing harvest, restaurant, bar, and domestic work, or jobs in the tourism industry, where English-speakers are needed.

Officially, you can hold a job in European countries only with a **work permit,** applied for by your prospective employer (or by you, with supporting papers from your employer). An employer must demonstrate that a potential employee has skills that locals lack. You will also need a **working visa,** obtainable from your local consulate (for requirements, see the section on visas, p. 35). On the other hand, there is the cash-based, untaxable **underground economy**—*economia sommersa* or *economia nera*—which makes up as much as one-third of Italy's economy. Many permitless agricultural workers go untroubled by local authorities, who recognize the need for seasonal labor. **European Union** citizens can work in any other EU country without working papers, and if your parents or grandparents were born in an EU country, you may be able to claim dual citizenship or at least the right to a work permit. Students can check with their university's foreign language departments, which may have official or unofficial access to job openings abroad.

Teaching English, one of the few long-term job possibilities, can be particularly lucrative. No more than minimal Italian is necessary to teach conversation, though many language institutes require a college degree and/or some sort of TEFL or RSA certificate or completion of a shorter TEFL training course. There are numerous English-language institutes in Rome that offer jobs through ads in *Wanted in Rome* (L1500; available in English bookstores) and in Rome's daily newspaper *Il Messagero*. Some schools simply post signs in stores, hair salons, or *caffè*. The language schools are listed under *Scuole di Lingua* in the Italian yellow pages and are also listed in the English yellow pages. **International House,** Viale Manzoni, 22 (tel. 70 47 68 94; open Mon.-Fri. 9am-1pm and 3-7:30pm), near Piazza Barberini, which offers TEFL courses, has a good bulletin board and advertises teaching jobs throughout Italy. Many people poster their services around the university and on the community bulletin boards. A common method is to set up a small class of four-six students for which the going rate, depending on the size of the class, is about L15,000-35,000 per hour. There are numerous "How to Teach English" handbooks at the English bookstores in Rome, but consider buying one before you go. Another short-term option, albeit horrifying, is to be a substitute teacher at one of the American or British schools; generally, you need a college degree, nerves of steel, and a *Codice Fiscale* (tax code).

Publications and Organizations

Remember that many of the organizations listed in books may have very few jobs available and usually have very specific requirements.

Vacation Work Publications, 9 Park End St., Oxford OX1 1HJ (tel. (01865) 24 19 78; fax 79 08 85). Publishes a wide variety of guides and directories with job listings and information for the working traveler. Opportunities for summer or full-time employment in countries all over the world. Write for a catalog of their publications, including those which deal specifically with Italy. Many of their books are also available in bookstores.

Addison-Wesley, Jacob Way, Reading, MA 01867 (tel. (800) 822-6339). Published *International Jobs: Where They Are, How to Get Them* in 1994 (US$16).

InterExchange Program, 161 Sixth Ave., New York, NY 10013 (tel. (212) 924-0446; fax 924-0575). Offers pamphlets on work programs and *au pair* positions.

Childcare International, Ltd., Trafalgar House, Grenville Place, London NW7 3SA (tel. +44 (01819) 59 36 11 or 06 31 16; fax 06 34 61; e-mail office@child-int.demon.co.uk; http://www.ipi.co.uk/childint), offers *au pair* positions in Italy and many other European countries. UK£60 application fee. The organization prefers a long placement but does arrange summer work.

Once in Rome, check out community bulletin boards, as well as the help-wanted columns in the English-language papers *Daily American* and the *International Daily News. Wanted in Rome* (L1500) is available at newsstands, from their office at Via dei Delfini, 17, 00186 Roma (tel. (06) 679 01 90; fax 678 37 98; e-mail 101360.2472@compuserve.com), or in English-language bookstores (see Bookstores, p. 78). *Metropolitan,* an English-language bi-monthly magazine, has a helpful classified ads section and is available at the Economy Bookstore and Video Center (see p. 79).

VOLUNTEERING

Volunteering is a good way to immerse yourself in a foreign culture. *Volunteer! The Comprehensive Guide to Voluntary Service in the U.S. and Abroad,* (US$13, postage US$1.50) offering advice and listings, is available from **Council Travel** offices, or by writing to Council's Voluntary Services Dept., 205 E. 42nd St., New York, NY 10017 (tel. (888) COUNCIL; fax (212) 822-2699; http://www.ciee.org).

Volunteers for Peace, 43 Tiffany Rd., Belmont, VT 05730 (tel. (802) 259-2759; fax 259-2922; e-mail vfp@vermontel.com; http://www.vermontel.com/~vfp/home.htm). A non-profit organization that arranges for speedy placement in one of 800 workcamps, many of which are in Europe. The majority of camps last for 2-3 weeks and are comprised of 10-15 people. The most complete and up-to-date listings can be found in the annual *International Workcamp Directory* (US$12). Registration fee US$175. Some workcamps are open to 16- and 17-year-olds for US$200. Free newsletter.

Council (see Travel Organizations, p. 29) offers 2- to 4-week environmental or community service projects in over 30 countries around the globe through its Voluntary Services Department (US$195 placement fee). Participants must be at least 18 years old. Council also publishes *Volunteer! The Comprehensive Guide to Volunteer Services in the U.S. and Abroad* (see Useful Publications, p. 30).

Service Civil International Voluntary Service (SCI-VS), 5474 Walnut Level Road, Crozet, VA 22932 (tel. (804) 823-1826; fax 823-5027; e-mail sciiv-susa@apc.org). Arranges placement in workcamps in Europe (ages 18 and over), programs in which local organizations sponsor groups for physical or social work. Registration fees for the placement service range from US$50-250.

ARCHAEOLOGICAL DIGS

The **Archaeological Institute of America,** 656 Beacon St., Boston, MA 02215-2010 (tel. (617) 353-9361; fax 353-6550) puts out the *Archaeological Fieldwork Opportunities Bulletin.* This guide lists over 250 field sites throughout the world, costs US$11 for non-members, and is available from Kendall/Hunt Publishing, 4050 Westmark Drive, Dubuque, IA 52002 (tel. (800) 228-0810). For other questions, contact the AIA directly at the first address. For information on anthropology, archaeological digs, and art history in Italy, write to the **Centro Comune di Studi Preistorici,** 25044 Capo di Ponte, Valcmonica (Brescia) (tel. (0364) 420 91; fax 425 72). This research center is involved with the management of cultural property and the organization of congresses, research projects, exhibitions, parks, and museums. They offer volunteer work, grants, tutoring, research assistant positions, and training and apprenticeship in prehistoric and primitive art, research methods, and editing (they publish *BCSP,* the world journal of prehistoric and tribal art).

Local colleges and universities in your home country are another excellent source of information on archaeological digs in Italy and elsewhere. Check with the Departments of Classics, Archaeology, Anthropology, Fine Arts, and/or other relevant area studies; many excavations send information and applications directly to individual professors or departments rather than to the general public.

■ Specific Concerns

WOMEN TRAVELERS

Often spotted on neon Vespas, sporting mirrored Ray-bans, and "working" quite a bit of hair gel, local Roman men show a remarkable interest in your birthplace, your destination, and your desire for, well, them. Italian males consider flirtation both an art form and a game; most comments should not be taken seriously. Women, whether alone or in groups, can avoid most harassment by adopting the attitude of Roman women: walk like you know where you are going; avoid eye contact—sunglasses are indispensable; meet all advances with cold silence and if still troubled, walk or stand near older women, nuns, or couples until you feel safe. A walkman with headphones clearly signals that you are not listening (but be careful—purse-snatchers and pick-pockets will take note of your obliviousness; you need not have the music on). Wearing attire that is perfectly modest but obviously American (college t-shirts, sneakers, shorts, Tevas, and Birkenstocks) can attract unwanted attention. If you are physically harassed on the bus or in some other crowded space, don't talk to the person directly. A well-aimed knee, elbow, or foot may do the job. Most Italians are embarrassed by the treatment that foreign women receive in Italy and will be supportive and helpful if they see that you are being bothered. With luck, you may get the satisfaction of seeing your tormentor get an indignant, rapid-fire Italian tongue-lashing.

When choosing a train compartment, look for other women, couples, or, better yet, nuns. **Never sit in an empty train compartment.** Be especially careful on overnight trains; some men may think that because you are sleeping next to them, you want to sleep with them. A simple *non mi toccare* ("don't touch me") will alert the other riders that you're being bothered and may humiliate your harasser enough to make him leave. Many experienced travelers also recommend wearing a fake (or real, if you've got one) wedding or engagement ring; in a Catholic country like Italy, this token does carry some weight, even with would-be harassers. Blondes and redheads may be harassed more than others with calls of "*Pssssst, biondina*" and German phrases, but even brunettes and native Romans have to deal with harassment, all too frequently.

In Rome, as in any major city, women, especially when alone, should stay in well-lit places and avoid dark alleys. Self-defense courses suggest carrying a whistle or an airhorn on your keychain. Memorize the local emergency numbers and always carry extra money for a phone call or cab ride. In general, trust your instincts; if you feel unsafe, go somewhere else.

When choosing accommodations, avoid small dives in Testaccio and south of Termini in favor of inexpensive *pensioni* in the historic center. Centrally located accommodations are usually safest and easiest to return to after dark. Some religious organizations offer rooms for women. For a list of these institutions, contact the city's archdiocese, write to the tourist office, or contact the **Associazione Cattolica Internazionale al Servizio della Giovane,** Via Urbana, 158, 00184 Roma (tel. 488 14 89) (hostels run by nuns for women ages 18-25; 10pm curfew; L24,000-30,000 per person in doubles or triples). There are a number of women's organizations in Rome which are listed in *Agendonna* (L10,000), a book of addresses of feminist and lesbian groups in Italy, available at the only **women's bookstore** in Rome, **Al Tempo Ritrovato,** Piazza Farnese, 103 (tel. 68 80 37 49), off Campo dei Fiori. There is a small section of English books about Italian and European feminism and politics, as well as American women's writing and lesbian literature. The bookstore is open Mon.-Sat. 10am-1pm and 4-8pm; Oct.-May 10 am-8pm. The **main feminist center** in Rome is the **Virginia Woolf Center** at Via Lungara, 1a (tel. 686 42 01), off Via San Francesco di Sales in Trastevere (the façade of the building is under construction, so the entrance is semi-hidden). It's a pleasantly disorganized center for women which provides resources as well as a hang-out in a beautiful courtyard. Call or stop by in order to find out about seminars, cultural events, gatherings (no men allowed), spontaneous dance nights, and access to their lesbian archives. The women welcome all female visitors and are sure to have the most up-to-date information for women in Rome. The center also runs academic courses in women's studies. The other branch of the Virginia Woolf Center, where the library is located, is at Via dell'Orso, 36. The **anti-violence hotline** *(Telefona Rosa assistenza contro la violenza)* in Rome is 683 26 90 or 683 28 20; Italian-speaking volunteers answer calls (Mon.-Fri. 10am-1pm and 4-7pm).

For more information, consult the following **publications:** *A Journey of One's Own* by Thalia Zepatos (Eighth Mountain Press, US$17) is the latest book on the market and is full of good advice. It also features a specific and manageable bibliography of books and resources. *Women Going Places* is a women's travel and resource guide emphasizing women-owned enterprises. It's geared toward lesbians, but offers advice appropriate for all women. It costs US$14 from Inland Book Company, 1436 W. Randolph St. Chicago, IL 60607 (tel. (800) 243-0138; or you can order it form a local bookstore). *Women Travel: Adventures, Advice & Experience* by Miranda Davies and Natania Jansz (Penguin, US$13) offers info on specific foreign countries plus a decent resource index. The sequel *More Women Travel* costs $15. For more information for women of color, see Minority Travelers, p. 55.

OLDER TRAVELERS

Senior travelers are often entitled to travel-related discounts. Always ask about them, and be prepared to show proof of age (you probably look younger than you are). The following organizations and publications provide information on discounts, tours, and health and travel tips.

AARP (American Association of Retired Persons), 601 E St. NW, Washington, D.C. 20049 (tel. (202) 434-2277). U.S. residents over 50 receive discounts on lodging, car rental, and sight-seeing. US$8 per couple per year; US$75 lifetime.

Elderhostel, 75 Federal St., 3rd Fl., Boston, MA 02110-1941 (tel. (617) 426-7788; fax 426-8351; http://www.elderhostel.org). Those 55 and over are eligible (and may bring a spouse of any age). Programs at colleges, universities, and learning centers in over 50 countries focus on varied subjects and last one to four weeks.

Pilot Books, 103 Cooper St., Babylon, NY 11702 (tel. (516) 422-2225). Publishes *The International Health Guide for Senior Citizens* (US$5, postage US$2) and *The Senior Citizens' Guide to Budget Travel in Europe* (US$6, postage US$2).

Gateway Books, 2023 Clemens Rd., Oakland, CA 94602 (tel. (510) 530-0299; fax 530-0497; donmerwin@aol.com; http://www.hway.com/gateway/). Publishes *Europe the European Way: A Traveler's Guide to Living Affordably in the World's Great Cities* (US$14), and *Adventures Abroad* (US$13), offering general hints for the budget-conscious senior considering a long stay or even retiring abroad. Call (800) 669-0773 for credit card orders.

BISEXUAL, GAY, AND LESBIAN TRAVELERS

Rome is not the site of a particularly "out" gay and lesbian community. A few Italian cities (Bologna, Milan, Turin), however, are gradually outgrowing the prevailing cultural silence surrounding homosexuality, and Rome is beginning to find its own voice with a burgeoning activist community. Roman men and women are open in showing affection for members of the same sex; holding hands or walking arm-in-arm with someone of the same-sex, especially for women, is common. According to a law passed in 1898, sexual acts between members of the same sex are legal for those above the age of consent (16).

You may be astonished by how openly affectionate Roman men are with one another, especially compared to their high-fiving, shoulder-punching American counterparts; remember, however, that this homosocial ease hasn't translated into tolerance for men or women who want to express a *different* kind of affection for one another. The visual clues gay men use elsewhere are often used by all Roman men, straight and gay. There are only a handful of openly gay bars and, as with the rest of Roman nightlife, gay nightlife happens outside (see Gay and Lesbian Entertainment, p. 232, for more information).

The national gay organization is affiliated with the recreational branch of the Communist party, ARCI, which organizes social events, movies, and sports. Write to **ARCI-gay,** P. di Porta Saragozza, 2, PO Box 691, 40123 Bologna (tel. (051) 644 70 54; fax 644 67 22; e-mail arcigl@iperbole.bologna.it) for more information on gay and lesbian life in Italy. The Roman branch of **ARCI-gay** (tel. 41 73 07 52), is located at Via Primo Acciaresi, 7 (off of Via Tiburtina; open Mon.-Fri. 3-7pm, Sat. 4:30-7:30pm). They publish the monthly newsletter *Pegaso.*

In Rome, the **Circolo di Cultura Omosessuale Mario Mieli,** Via Ostiense, 202 and Via Cortino, 5 (tel. 541 39 85; fax 561 39 71), provides loads of information about gay life in Rome. Take the Metro Linea B to Piramide or San Paolo. The eager staff offers group discussions, social events, and information sessions on topics such as gay health concerns.

Unfortunately, there isn't much organized lesbian activity for the traveler in Rome. The best source of info is the **Coordinamento Lesbico Italiano,** a lesbian organization and a branch of the **feminist center** (see p. 53), located at Via S. Francesco di Sales, 1A (tel. 686 42 01), off Via della Lungara in Trastevere. The women there are probably the best source for current resources for women in Rome. Rome's one and only gay bookstore, **Libreria Babele,** Via Paola, 44 (tel. 687 66 28; open Mon.-Sat. 9:30am-7:30pm), across the bridge from Castel Sant'Angelo, hosts a variety of gay literature, films, erotic material, and general information about gay life in Rome. It is also one of the only places which sells the *Gay and Lesbian Map of Rome* (published annually, L12,000). This map offers a guide to all of the bars, baths, beaches, discos, nd restaurants in the Rome area which cater to gay interests. As you might expect, most of the places cater to men, but are friendly to women. The most well known ational gay magazines are *Babilonia* (L8000) and *Adam* (L10,000) published monthly nd available at most newsstands (there is a page or two specifically directed towards women tucked inside). Also check out *Guida Gay,* published by *Babilonia* and avail-ble at newsstands.

The following sources should prove helpful in planning your trip; before ordering ny publications, try the gay and lesbian sections of your local bookstores.

Are You Two...Together? A Gay and Lesbian Travel Guide to Europe. A travel guide with anecdotes and tips for gays and lesbians traveling in Europe. Includes overviews of regional laws relating to gays and lesbians, lists of gay/lesbian organizations, and establishments catering to, friendly to, or indifferent to gays and lesbians. Available in bookstores. Random House, US$18.

Ferrari Guides, PO Box 37887, Phoenix, AZ 85069 (tel. (602) 863-2408; fax 439-3952; e-mail ferrari@q-net.com). Gay and lesbian travel guides: *Ferrari Guides' Gay Travel A to Z* (US$16), *Ferrari Guides' Men's Travel in Your Pocket* (US$14), *Ferrari Guides' Women's Travel in Your Pocket* (US $14), *Ferrari Guides' Inn Places* (US$16), *Ferrari Guides' Paris for Gays & Lesbians* (Fall 1996). Available in bookstores or by mail order (postage/handling US$4.50 for the first item, US$1 for each additional item mailed within the US. Overseas, call or write for shipping cost.)

Gay Europe (Perigee Books, US$14). A gay guide providing a quick look at gay life in countries throughout Europe, including restaurants, clubs, and beaches. Intros to each country cover laws and gay-friendliness. Available in bookstores.

Gay's the Word, 66 Marchmont St., London WC1N 1AB (tel. (0171) 278 7654). The largest gay and lesbian bookshop in the U.K. Mail-order service available. No catalog of listings, but they will provide a list of titles on a given subject. Open Mon.-Sat. 10am-6pm, Thurs. 10am-7pm, Sun. 2-6pm.

Giovanni's Room, 345 S. 12th St., Philadelphia, PA 19107 (tel. (215) 923-2960; fax 923-0813; e-mail gilphilp@netaxs.com). An international feminist, lesbian, and gay bookstore with mail-order service which carries many of the publications listed here.

International Gay Travel Association, Box 4974, Key West, FL 33041 (tel. (800) 448-8550; fax (305) 296-6633; e-mail IGTA@aol.com; http://www.rainbow-mall.com/igta. An organization of over 1100 companies serving gay and lesbian travelers worldwide. Call for lists of travel agents, accommodations, and events.

International Lesbian and Gay Association (ILGA), 81 rue Marché-au-Charbon, B-1000 Bruxelles, Belgium (tel./fax 32-2-502-24 71; e-mail ilga@ilga.org). Not a travel service. Provides political information, such as homosexuality laws of individual countries.

Spartacus International Gay Guides (US$32.95), published by Bruno Gmunder, Postfach 110729, D-10837 Berlin, Germany (tel. (30) 615 00 30; fax 615-9134). Lists bars, restaurants, hotels, and bookstores around the world catering to gays. Also lists hotlines for gays in various countries and homosexuality laws for each country. Available in bookstores and in the U.S. by mail from Giovanni's Room (listed above).

Women Going Places (Inland Book Company, US$14). An international women's travel and resource guide emphasizing women-owned enterprises, geared toward lesbians. Available in bookstores.

MINORITY TRAVELERS

We have been hard-pressed to find any resources that advise members of visibly different ethnicities about specific travel concerns; if you have knowledge of any such institution, please write to us and let us know. At *Let's Go* we ask our researchers not to include establishments known to be discriminatory in their reviews. If, in your travels, you encounter discriminatory treatment, please let us know so that we can, if appropriate, warn other travelers away.

Until recently, the Roman population was relatively homogeneous. Immigration in the latter half of the 20th century from Eastern Europe, North Africa, the Philippines, and former Italian colonies like Somalia and Ethiopia has changed the make-up of the city. Since finding work as a non-EU citizen is next to impossible, these immigrants have resorted to selling sunglasses, flowers, and lighters on the streets, in subway stations, and in bars and restaurants. Many Romans have not quite gotten used to these newcomers and blame them for, among other things, the rise in crime and social unrest. Although immigrants of color do experience discrimination, tourists of color from the West, who are easily distinguishable by western clothes and language, are not the usual targets of racism. In Rome, women of color, such as Asians, Indians, or African-Americans, may find themselves being referred to as *giapponese* (a reference to a woman of any Asian heritage), *indiana*, or merely *bellissima*. Women of color may be seen as exotic, but not unwelcome. Traveling in groups or taking a taxi whenever you are uncomfortable are always good ideas. Your own ethnicity will not necessarily be problematic; you may very well find your visit to Rome trouble-free and your hosts open-minded.

TRAVELERS WITH DISABILITIES

Italians are making an increased effort to meet the needs of people with disabilities. The **Italian Government Travel Office (ENIT)** will let you know whether a certain hotel or other building is handicapped-accessible. When making arrangements with airlines or hotels, specify exactly what you need and allow time for preparation and confirmation of arrangements. Many **train stations** have "Reception Centers" for disabled travelers in the info office, the ticket office, or the stationmaster's office, where they offer a number of services and types of assistance. Look for the awkwardly titled pamphlet *Servicing for Disabled People*, available in most train stations. Major train stations will provide aid as long as you make reservations by telephone 24 hours in advance. You can generally find a *portiere* to assist you for L500 to L1000 per bag. Italy's rail system is modernized, so most trains are wheelchair-accessible. For more info, call the **Italian State Railway Representative** in New York (tel. (212) 697-1482) or **Rail Europe** in the U.S. (tel. (800) 438-7245).

If you plan to bring a seeing-eye dog to Italy, contact your veterinarian and the nearest Italian consulate. You will need an import license, a current certificate of your dog's innoculations, and a letter from your veterinarian certifying your dog's health.

American Foundation for the Blind, 11 Penn Plaza, New York, NY 10011 (tel. (212) 502-7600). Open Mon.-Fri. 8:30am-4:30pm. Provides info and services for the visually impaired. For a catalog of products, contact **Lighthouse** at (800) 829-0500.

Graphic Language Press, P.O. Box 270, Cardiff by the Sea, CA 92007 (tel. (619) 944-9594). Publishes *Wheelchair Through Europe*. Comprehensive advice for the wheelchair-using traveler, including specifics on wheelchair-related resources and accessible sites in various cities throughout Europe.

The Guided Tour Inc., Elkins Park House, Suite 114B, 7900 Old York Road, Elkins Park, PA 19027-2339 (tel. (800) 783-5841 or (215) 782-1370; fax 635-2637). Organizes travel programs for people with developmental and physical challenges as well as for persons requiring renal dialysis. Call or write for a free brochure.

Mobility International, USA (MIUSA), P.O. Box 10767, Eugene, OR 97440 (tel. (514) 343-1284 voice and TDD; fax 343-6812). International headquarters in Brussels, rue de Manchester 25, Brussels, Belgium, B-1070 (tel. (322) 410 62 97; fax 410 68 74). Info on travel programs, international workcamps, accommodations, access guides, and organized tours in 30 countries. Membership US$25 per year, newsletter US$15. Sells the periodically updated and expanded *A World of Options: A Guide to International Educational Exchange, Community Service, and Travel for Persons with Disabilities* (US$14, US$16 for nonmembers). MIUSA also teaches a series of courses on travel strategies for disabled tourists.

Moss Rehab Hospital Travel Information Service, (tel. (215) 456-9600, TDD (215) 456-9602). A telephone information resource center on international travel accessibility and other travel-related concerns for those with disabilities.

Society for the Advancement of Travel for the Handicapped (SATH), 347 Fifth Ave., #610, New York, NY 10016 (tel. (212) 447-7284; fax 725-8253). Publishes quarterly travel newsletter *SATH News* and information booklets (free for members, US$13 each for nonmembers) with advice on trip planning for people with diabilities. Annual membership US$45, students and seniors US$25.

Twin Peaks Press, P.O. Box 129, Vancouver, WA 98666-0129 (tel. (360) 694-2462, orders with MC and Visa (800) 637-2256; fax (360) 696-3210). Publishers of *Travel for the Disabled,* which provides travel tips, lists of accessible tourist attractions, and advice on other resources for disabled travelers (US$20). Also publishes *Directory for Travel Agencies of the Disabled* (US$20), *Wheelchair Vagabond* (US$15), and *Directory of Accessible Van Rentals* (US$10). Postage US$3 for first book, US$1.50 for each additional book.

TRAVELING WITH CHILDREN

Italians are well-known for their love of children, and you will probably encounter more cooing than complications. Most hotels will put a cot in your room for a percentage price increase, and even picky children tend to enjoy the simplest (and cheapest) of Italian foods: pizza, spaghetti, and *gelato*. In addition, train systems in Italy sometimes offer discounts for groups or families. There are **discount Eurailpasses** for groups and children (those under 25 get a flat discount, those under 12 travel at half-price, and those under 4 travel free), and an Italian kilometric ticket can be used by up to five at once. Still, planning ahead and drawing up a detailed itinerary are especially useful for those traveling with small children. Remember that you may have to slow your pace considerably, and that all the new sights and experiences are especially exhausting for kids—you may want to leave room for a mid-afternoon nap for everyone (remember: most businesses and tourist attractions in Italy are closed from around noon to 3pm anyway). For some families, it may be more convenient to travel by rental car, but train travel will often be cheaper, reduce the fidgets, and provide a novel, absorbing experience for children. Finally, make sure that your children have some sort of ID on their person in case they get lost or are faced with an emergency.

Caffè della Palma (near the Pantheon) and Jolly Pop **candy stores** (in Piazza Navona and in the entrance of Termini Station) are always good for a rest stop or a bribe. The **zoo** at Villa Borghese is a cool respite from ancient monuments and churches, and you can rent bicycles or a rowboat to paddle in the small lake. There are **boat rides** down the Tiber and **horse-drawn carriage rides** around the city, originating from Piazza di Spagna. The Sunday **flea market** at Porta Portese is great fun for kids with a penchant for junk. Kids also love the **caricatures** and portraits done in Piazza Navona. There are puppet shows in English on Saturday and Sunday at **Teatro dei Satiri,** Via di Grotta Pinta, 19 (tel. 68 80 62 44), off Campo dei Fiori. Check out the genuine Sicilian puppet shows at the **Teatro Crisogono,** Via S. Gallicano, 8, off Viale di Trastevere. **LunEUR** park (in EUR; see p. 200) is an old-fashioned amusement park, with a hokey wax museum, a roller coaster, sugary snacks, and carnival attractions. There are **playgrounds** at Villa Ada, Villa Celimontana, and the Euro-sculpture park by Porta Ardeatina.

Apart from the obvious, manufactured fun, most kids enjoy the **Colosseum,** the **Trevi Fountain, St. Peter's dome,** the **Villa d'Este** at Tivoli, the **Monster Park** at Bomarzo (outside Rome; see p. 260), and the models exhibit at the **Museum of Roman Civilization** in EUR. For those tykes with a taste for the macabre, check out Castel Sant'Angelo with its **dungeons,** the spooky **catacombs,** and the **Capucin Crypt** off Piazza Barberini, which is decorated with skeletons. Daytrips to nearby lakes and beaches like Lake Bracciano are also a good breather from the city. Then there's the **Baby Park.** It's plain and simple: your kids won't even know they're away from home unless they can read the communist graffiti nearby. They can enjoy their own culture with a jungle gym, merry-go-round, and a playground. It's on Via Tiburtina across from #46 (Pizzeria L'Economica). Take bus #492 and get off at Tiburtina. Turn right.

For more information, order books from the following publishers. **Wilderness Press,** 2440 Bancroft Way, Berkeley, CA 94704 (tel. (800) 443-7227 or (510) 843-8080; fax 548-1355), distributes *Backpacking with Babies and Small Children* (US$10). **Lonely Planet Publications,** Embarcadero West, 155 Filbert St., Suite 251, Oakland, CA 94607 (tel. (800) 275-8555 or (510) 893-8555; fax (510) 893-8563; e-mail info@lonelyplanet.com; http://www.lonelyplanet.com), or P.O. Box 617, Hawthorn, Victoria 3122, Australia, publishes *Travel With Children* (US$12 plus US$1.50). **Mason-Grant Publications,** P.O. Box 6547, Portsmouth, NH 03802 (tel. (603) 436-1608; fax 427-0015; e-mail charriman@masongrant.com) publishes *Take Your Kids to Europe* by Cynthia W. Harriman (US$14), which is geared towards family travel.

KOSHER AND VEGETARIAN CONCERNS

Jewish travelers keeping kosher should consult local tourist boards for a list of kosher restaurants. Sepher-Hermon Press, 1265 46th St., Brooklyn, NY 11219 (tel. (718) 972-9010), publishes *The Jewish Travel Guide,* which lists synagogues, kosher restaurants, and Jewish institutions in over 80 countries. The Jewish quarter in Rome is located by the Piazza Cenci, off Via Arenula. Semi-kosher restaurants and kosher foodstores, wine shops, and bakeries are listed under Food and Wine, p. 114. Check with the synagogue of Rome in the Jewish Ghetto (tel. 687 50 51; see p. 185 for more information). One small but well-supplied kosher grocery and wine shop in Rome is **Billo** (tel. 687 79 66), Via S. Ambrogio, 7, in the Jewish Ghetto. The store also posts meeting times and places for daily minyans of Ashkenazi Jews.

A vegetarian should have no problems in Italian restaurants, since the majority of first courses (*primi,* the pasta course) are meatless, and most restaurants will also supply you a mixed plate of their vegetable side dishes upon request—ask for *verdure miste* (mixed vegetables). *Let's Go* includes some vegetarian restaurants and you can always ask for a dish *senza carne* (without meat). If you aren't sure of the contents of a particular dish, ask *c'è carne?* For more information, consult the *European Vegetarian Guide to Hotels and Restaurants,* which covers most of Western Europe. It is available from the Vegetarian Times Bookshelf (tel. (800) 435-9610, orders only).

TRAVELING WITH PETS

If you are bringing your cat or dog into Italy, you must have a veterinarian's certificate containing the breed, age, sex, and color of the pet, the owner's name and address, and a statement that the beast is in good health and has been vaccinated against rabies between 20 days and 11 months before entry into Italy. Both the Italian Government Travel Office and your local Italian Embassy have these forms, which are valid for 30 days. Parrots, parakeets, rabbits, and hares also need these certificates, and Customs will examine them upon entry into Italy (some cats and dogs may be examined too). A leash or muzzle is required in public.

■ Packing

If you want to get away from it all, don't take it all with you. Plan your packing according to your type of travel and the average temperatures of the region. Set out everything you think you'll need, then pack half the clothes and twice the money. Once you're on the road you'll be thankful; remember, everything you take you have to carry. If you find yourself packing "just in case," remember that almost all supplies are readily available in Italy. (For tips on medical and hygienic supplies you should bring from home, see Health, p. 44.)

LUGGAGE

Backpacks: If you intend to do a lot of hiking, you should have a **frame backpack.** Get one with an internal frame if you'll be hiking on difficult trails that require a lot of bending and maneuvering—internal-frame packs mold better to your back, keep a lower center of gravity, and can flex adequately to follow you through a variety of movements. In addition, internal frame packs are more manageable on crowded planes, trains, and automobiles, and are less likely to be mangled by rough handling. External-frame packs, however, are more comfortable for long hikes over even terrain since they keep the weight higher and distribute it more evenly. These don't travel as well, so be sure to tie down loose straps when dealing with baggage handlers. Make sure your pack has a strong, padded hip belt, which transfers much of the weight from delicate shoulders to sturdier legs. Any serious backpacking requires a pack with at least 4000 cubic inches, while longer trips require around 5000. Tack on an additional 500 cubic inches for internal-frame packs, since you'll have to pack your sleeping bag inside, rather than strap it on the outside as you do with an external-frame pack. Sturdy backpacks cost anywhere from US$125-400. This is one area where it doesn't pay to economize—cheaper packs may be less comfortable, and the straps are more likely to fray or rip quickly. Test-drive a backpack for comfort before you buy it.

Suitcase/trunk/other large or heavy luggage: Fine if you plan to live in one city and explore from there, but a bad idea if you're going to be moving around a lot. Useful features: wheels on suitcases for maneuverability, PVC frame on soft luggage, lightest possible weight, and strong linings to resist bad weather.

Daypack, rucksack, or courier bag: Bringing a smaller bag in addition to your pack or suitcase allows you to leave your big bag in the hotel while you go sightseeing. It should have secure closures for security. Use it also as an airplane carry-on; keep the absolute essentials with you to avoid the lost-luggage blues.

Moneybelt or neck pouch: Guard your money, passport, railpass, and other important articles in one of these, and keep it with you *at all times*. Moneybelts should rest *inside* the waistline of your pants or skirt, and neck pouches should be worn under at least one layer of your clothing. Avoid the ubiquitous "fanny pack," which is an invitation to thieves, even when worn in front.

CLOTHING AND FOOTWEAR

No nation outdresses Italy, so plan to admire rather than compete. Most importantly, be sure to bring clothes appropriate for visits to cathedrals and churches, since shorts, skirts above the knees, and sleeveless or cut-off shirts are usually forbidden there. In general, bring few but comfortable clothes, and keep accessories to a minimum. Climate and convenience should determine your wardrobe. Dark colors will not show the dirt they're bound to accumulate, but light colors will be cooler in hot weather. In addition, solid colors are usually easiest to mix and match. Natural fibers are also good choices since synthetics trap heat. Laundry facilities are expensive in Italy: bring non-wrinkling, quick-drying clothes that you can wash in a sink. Above all, shorts, university t-shirts, and running shoes brand you as a tourist and may be the cause of increased attention in Italy.

Women: During the summer, light cotton pants are the most appropriate travelwear and are a good option for getting by cathedral dress codes. You might also wear a long dress with a lightweight drape or shawl to cover your shoulders for church visits. Jeans may cause you problems on the road—they're hot, and hard to dry after a downpour. Shorts will definitely make you stand out and garner unwanted attention from men. Surprisingly enough, you might be just as comfortable and attract fewer stares in a knee-length skirt. Really.

Men: Again, cotton pants will be more comfortable than jeans. Shorts are more acceptable on men than on women and provide a break from the heat, but remember that they will not pass in cathedrals.

Walking shoes: Not a place to cut corners. For **city** walking, lace-up leather shoes with firm grips provide better support and are more socially acceptable than athletic shoes. If you plan to travel in the **rainy** fall or spring, you can waterproof them. For alpine forays, a good pair of **hiking boots** with adequate ankle support is essential. Wearing a double pair of socks (light silky ones underneath tough wool ones) can help prevent blisters. Teva **sandals** are excellent for airing out your feet after a long day or for braving the fungus in hostel showers. You could also buy a pair of Italian leather sandals once you get there. Don't forget to *break in your shoes before you leave.*

Weather protection: Raingear is absolutely essential. **Gore-Tex** fabric, which is both waterproof and breathable, is a good choice. Pack a light sweater or jacket, even in summer. **Silk bomber jackets** are warm, light, and compact. Gloves and thermal underwear are also useful for northern winters.

CAMPING

The most important things to remember when camping are: stay warm, stay dry, stay hydrated. Always be sure to pay attention to weather forecasts. Purchase the following **equipment** items before you leave. For **backpacks,** see Luggage, p. 59.

Sleeping bag: Choose either down (compact, lightweight, and warm, but useless when wet) or synthetic (cheaper, heavier, more durable, and warmer when wet). Bags are rated according to the lowest outdoor temperature at which they will still keep you warm. A 3-season or 20°F bag (US$135-200 for synthetic, US$150-225 for down) should usually be sufficient in Italy, except in the winter.

Pads: A cushion between your soft body and the hard ground. Closed-cell foam pads start at $13; open-cell foam pads start at $25; an air mattress cushions your back and neck for $25-50. Another good alternative is a **Therm-A-Rest**, a combined foam pad and air-mattress which inflates to full padding when unrolled.

Tents: The ideal models are free-standing, with their own frames and suspension systems. Low-profile dome tents tend to be the best all-around, entailing very little unnecessary bulk. Hikers should carry a small tent weighing less than 3.5lbs. Be sure your tent has a rain fly and that you have a **tarpaulin** or **plastic groundcloth** to put underneath it. Last year's models are often drastically reduced.

Camp stoves: Don't rely on campfire cooking; some regions restrict fires. Simple Coleman stoves start at $30. Or try a GAZ-powered model, which burns propane and is common in Europe. Bring a **mess kit** and a **battery-operated lantern**.

Other: Waterproof matches, calamine lotion, and water-purification pills.

The following **organizations** provide advice and/or supplies:

Family Campers and RVers (NCHA), 4804 Transit Rd., Bldg. 2, Depew, NY 14043 (tel./fax (716) 668-6242). Sells the International Camping Carnet, required at some European campgrounds (US$30 includes membership in the National Campers and Hikers Association, Inc., and a subscription to *Camping Today*).

Recreational Equipment, Inc. (REI), P.O. Box 1700, Sumner, WA 98352-0001 (tel. (800) 426-4840; http://www.rei.com). Publishes *Europa Camping and Caravanning* (US$20), an annually updated catalog of European campsites. REI also sells a wide range of the latest in camping gear and holds great seasonal sales. Huge selection, and many items are guaranteed for life. Merchandise available from 1700 45th St. E, Sumner, WA 98390.

Shop around locally before turning to mail-order firms; this allows you to get an idea of what the different items actually look like (and weigh), so that if you decide later to order by mail you'll have a more exact idea of what you are getting. The mail-order firms listed below offer lower prices that those you're likely to find in stores, and they can also help you determine which item you need.

Campmor, P.O. Box 700, Saddle River, NJ 07458-0700 (tel. (800) 526-4784; http://www.campmor.com). Has a wide selection of name-brand equipment at low prices. One-year guarantee for unused or defective merchandise.

Eastern Mountain Sports (EMS), One Vose Farm Rd., Peterborough, NH 03458 (tel. (603) 924-7231). Call to find the store nearest you. Though slightly higher-priced, they provide excellent service and guaranteed customer satisfaction.

L.L. Bean, Inc., Attn: Product Info, Freeport, ME 04033 (ordering: U.S. and Canada (800) 221-4221, International (207) 865-3111; customer service: U.S. and Canada (800) 341-4341, International (207) 865-3161; fax U.S. (207) 552-3080, Canada and International (207)552-4080; TTY and TDD at (800) 545-0090). Equipment and preppy outdoor clothing. Open 24hrs. per day, 7 days per week, 52 weeks per year.

MISCELLANEOUS

The following is not an exhaustive list. For a **first-aid kit** see Health, p. 44.

Washing clothes: Laundry facilities in Italy are expensive and inconvenient. Washing clothes in your hotel sink is often a better option. Bring a small bar or bottle of detergent soap, a rubber squash ball to stop up the sink, and a travel clothes line (available at camping stores) for drying.

Film: Available but expensive in Italy, as it is all over Europe. Bring lots of film with you and, if you will be seriously upset if the pictures are ruined, develop it at home, too. If you're not a serious photographer, consider bringing a **disposable camera** or two rather than an expensive permanent one. They generally cost US$10-15 (not including developing). Whatever kind of camera you use, be aware that, despite disclaimers, airport security X-rays *can* fog film. To protect it, you can either buy a lead-lined pouch from a camera store or ask the security personnel to hand inspect your film. In any case, be sure to pack it in your carry-on luggage, since higher-intensity X-rays are used on checked bags.

Contact lenses: Travelers who heat-disinfect their lenses should either buy a small converter for their machine (US$20) or take chemicals to use in Italy. Note that chemicals are not safe for all lenses and are rare and expensive overseas.

Also valuable: insect repellent, travel alarm clock, plastic bags that seal shut (for damp clothes, soap, food), sun hat, sunscreen, sewing kit, clothespins, sleepsack (required in many hostels; you can make one by folding a full-size sheet in half the long way and sewing up the sides), sunglasses, walkman, pocketknife, tweezers, plastic water bottle, small flashlight, padlock, towel, and moleskin (for blisters).

■ Electricity and Time

ELECTRIC CURRENT

Your favorite electrical appliances may require an **electrical converter** (which changes the voltage). Voltage is either 125 or 220v AC throughout Italy, although hotels often offer 110v. Check before plugging in or you could zap your appliance into oblivion. Since Italy's prongs are not flat but round (2 prongs), U.S., Canadian, and Australian gadgets need an **adapter** (unless appliance instructions explicitly state otherwise, as with some portable computers), available in Italy or from most travel or hardware stores. The **Franzus Company,** Murtha Industrial Park, PO Box 142, Railroad Ave., Beacon Falls, CT 06403 (tel. (203) 723-6664; fax 723-6666) publishes the free and illuminating pamphlet *Foreign Electricity Is No Deep Dark Secret* (which contains, among other things, a voltage list for countries other than Italy) and sells a variety of adaptors and converters.

TIME ZONES

Italy is in the Western Europe time zone, making it six hours ahead of the East Coast of North America, one hour ahead of Great Britain and Ireland, one hour behind South Africa, nine hours behind Australia, and a whopping eleven hours behind New Zealand. Italy does participate in Daylight Savings, but they will not necessarily change the same weekend as your home country does.

GETTING THERE

The first challenge to the budget traveler is getting there. Students and people under age 26 ("youth") qualify for reduced airfares, which are most readily available from student travel agencies. **TravelHUB** (http://www.travelhub.com) will help you search for travel services on the web.

■ Budget Travel Services

Campus Travel, 52 Grosvenor Gardens, London SW1W 0AG (http://www.campus-travel.co.uk.) 41 branches in the U.K. Student and youth fares on plane, train, boat, and bus travel, including flexible airline tickets. Discount and ID cards for youths and travel insurance for students and those under 35. Provides travel suggestion booklets, maps, and guides. Telephone booking service: in Europe call (0171) 730 3402; in North America call (0171) 730 2101; worldwide call (0171) 730 8111; in Manchester call (0161) 273 1721; in Scotland (0131) 668 3303.

Centro Turistico Studentesco e Giovanile (CTS), Via Genova, 16, 00184 **Roma** (tel. (06) 467 91; fax 467 92 07; e-mail: ctsinfo@mbox.vol.it). With 98 offices throughout Italy, CTS provides travel, accommodation, and sight-seeing discounts, as well as currency exchange and information for students and young people. Sells the *Carta Verde* for discounts on train fares, the International Student Identity Card (ISIC), the International Youth Cards (FIYTO card), and the Euro Youth Card. Branch offices also in **London** and **Paris.** Rome office open Mon.-Fri. 9am-1pm and 3:30-7pm, Sat. 9am-1pm.

CIT Tours, 342 Madison Ave., #207, **New York,** NY 10173 (tel. (212) 697-2100; fax 697-1394; e-mail alr5@ix.netcom.com); 6033 West Century Blvd., #980, **Los Angeles,** CA 90045 (tel. (310) 338-8616); 1450 City Councillors St., #1450, **Montréal,** Qué. H3A 2E6 (tel./fax (800) 361-7799 or (514) 845-9137); **Toronto,** Ont. (tel. (416) 415-1060). Over 100 offices worldwide, with most in Italy. The official representative of the Italian state railways in the US; also sells Eurail passes.

Council Travel (http://www.ciee.org/cts/ctshome.htm), the travel division of Council, is a full-service travel agency specializing in youth and budget travel. They offer discount airfares on scheduled airlines, railpasses, hosteling cards, low-cost accommodations, guidebooks, budget tours, travel gear, and international student (ISIC), youth (GO25), and teacher (ITIC) identity cards. U.S. offices include: Emory Village, 1561 N. Decatur Rd., **Atlanta,** GA 30307 (tel. (404) 377-9997); 2000 Guadalupe, **Austin,** TX 78705 (tel. (512) 472-4931); 273 Newbury St., **Boston,** MA 02116 (tel. (617) 266-1926); 1138 13th St., **Boulder,** CO 80302 (tel. (303) 447-8101); 1153 N. Dearborn, **Chicago,** IL 60610 (tel. (312) 951-0585); 10904 Lindbrook Dr., **Los Angeles,** CA 90024 (tel. (310) 208-3551); 1501 University Ave. SE, **Minneapolis,** MN 55414 (tel. (612) 379-2323); 205 E. 42nd St., **New York,** NY 10017 (tel. (212) 822-2700); 953 Garnet Ave., **San Diego,** CA 92109 (tel. (619) 270-6401); 530 Bush St., **San Francisco,** CA 94108 (tel. (415) 421-3473); 4311½ University Way, **Seattle,** WA 98105 (tel. (206) 632-2448); 3300 M St. NW, **Washington, D.C.** 20007 (tel. (202) 337-6464). **For U.S. cities not listed,** call 800-2-COUNCIL (226-8624). Also 28A Poland St. (Oxford Circus), **London,** W1V 3DB (tel. (0171) 437 7767).

Educational Travel Centre (ETC), 438 North Frances St., Madison, WI 53703 (tel. (800) 747-5551; fax (608) 256-2042; e-mail edtrav@execpc.com). Flights, HI cards, Eurail and regional railpasses. Write for their free pamphlet *Taking Off.*

Let's Go Travel, Harvard Student Agencies, 67 Mt. Auburn St., Cambridge, MA 02138 (tel. (800) 5-LETS GO (553-8746), or (617) 495-9649). Offers railpasses, HI-AYH memberships, ISICs, International Teacher ID cards, FIYTO cards, guidebooks, maps, bargain flights, and a complete line of budget travel gear. All items available by mail; call or write for a catalog.

Rail Europe Inc., 226 Westchester Ave., White Plains, NY 10604 (tel. (800) 438-7245; fax 432-1329; http://www.raileurope.com). Sells all Eurail products and passes, national railpasses, and direct tickets. Up-to-date info on rail travel.

STA Travel, 6560 N. Scottsdale Rd. #F100, Scottsdale, AZ 85253 (tel. (800) 777-0112; fax (602) 922-0793). A student and youth travel organization with over 100 offices worldwide offering discount airfares for young travelers, railpasses, accommodations, tours, insurance, and ISICs. 16 offices in the U.S. including: 297 Newbury Street, **Boston,** MA 02115 (tel. (617) 266-6014); 429 S. Dearborn St., **Chicago,** IL 60605 (tel. (312) 786-9050; 7202 Melrose Ave., **Los Angeles,** CA 90046 (tel. (213) 934-8722); 10 Downing St., Ste. G, **New York,** NY 10003 (tel. (212) 627-3111); 4341 University Way NE, **Seattle,** WA 98105 (tel. (206) 633-5000); 2401 Pennsylvania Ave., **Washington, D.C.** 20037 (tel. (202) 887-0912); 51 Grant Ave., **San Francisco,** CA 94108 (tel. (415) 391-8407), Miami, FL 33133 (tel. (305) 461-3444). In the U.K., 6 Wrights Ln., **London** W8 6TA (tel. (0171) 938 47 11 for North American travel). In New Zealand, 10 High St., **Auckland** (tel. (09) 309 97 23). In Australia, 222 Faraday St., **Melbourne** VIC 3050 (tel. (03) 349 69 11).

Travel CUTS (Canadian University Travel Services, Ltd.), 187 College St., Toronto, Ont. M5T 1P7 (tel. (416) 979-2406; fax 979-8167). Canada's national student travel bureau, with 40 offices across Canada. Also, in the **U.K.,** 295-A Regent St., London W1R 7YA (tel. (0171) 637 31 61). Discounted domestic and international flights. Issues ISIC, FIYTO, GO25, and HI cards, as well as railpasses. Offers free *Student Traveller* magazine, and info on Student Work Abroad Program (SWAP).

Travel Management International (TMI), 3617 Dupont Avenue South, Minneapolis, MN 55409 (tel. (617) 661-8187 or (800) 245-3672). Diligent, prompt, and very helpful travel service offering student fares and discounts.

Unitravel, 117 North Warson Rd., St. Louis, MO 63132 (tel. (800) 325-2222; fax (314) 569-2503). Offers discounted airfares on major scheduled airlines from the U.S. to Europe, Africa, and Asia.

Wasteels, 7041 Grand National Drive #207, Orlando, FL 32819 (tel. (407) 351-2537; in U.K. (0171) 834 70 66). A huge chain in Europe, with 200 locations. For information in English, contact the London office. Sells the Wasteels BIJ tickets, which are discounted (30-45% off regular fare) 2nd-class international point-to-point train tickets with stopovers for those under 26; sold only in Europe.

■ By Plane

Constantly fluctuating prices make estimating airfares impossible, but a few general rules do apply. Most airlines maintain a fare structure that peaks between mid-June and early September. Midweek (Mon.-Thurs. morning) roundtrip flights run about US$40-50 cheaper than those on weekends. If you plan on traveling elsewhere in Europe, consider beginning your trip outside Italy. A flight through Brussels (on **Sabena**) or Amsterdam (on **KLM**) could cost considerably less than one to Milan or Rome. Round-trip tickets from New York or Boston to major cities such as Florence or Rome could cost anywhere from US$400 to $800. Because inexpensive flights from Canada can cost substantially more than the lowest fares from the U.S., Canadians may want to consider leaving from the States. Also check with Travel CUTS for information on special charters (see above).

Have a knowledgable budget travel agent (or better yet, several) guide you through the options. Travel sections in Sunday newspapers often list bargain fares from the local airport. You might also be able to outfox airline reps with the *Official Airline Guide,* available at large libraries. This monthly guide lists nearly every scheduled flight in the world (including prices), along with toll-free phone numbers for all the airlines which will allow you to call in reservations directly. On the web, try the **Air Traveler's Handbook** (http://www.cis.ohio-state.edu/hypertext/faq/usenet/travel/air/handbook/top.html) for very complete information on air travel.

COMMERCIAL AIRLINES

The commercial airlines' lowest regular offer is the **APEX (Advance Purchase Excursion Fare).** Specials advertised in newspapers may be cheaper, but have more restrictions and fewer available seats. APEX fares provide you with confirmed reserva-

tions and allow "open-jaw" tickets (landing in and returning from different cities). Reservations must usually be made seven to 21 days in advance. There are also minimum and maximum stay limitations with hefty cancellation and change fees. For summer travel, book early. **Alitalia,** Italy's national airline, is commonly used by business travelers, but may offer off-season youth fares as well. Its main address in the U.S. is 666 Fifth Avenue, New York, NY 10103 (tel. (800) 223-5730). Look into flights to less popular destinations or on smaller carriers for lower prices. You can call **Icelandair** (tel. (800) 223-5500) for info on last-minute offers.

TICKET CONSOLIDATORS

Ticket consolidators sell unsold tickets on commercial and charter airlines at unpublished fares. The consolidator market is by and large international. Consolidator flights are the best deals if you are traveling on short notice, to an offbeat destination, or in the peak season, when published fares are jacked way up. There is rarely a maximum age or stay limit, but unlike tickets bought through an airline, you won't be able to use your tickets on another flight if you miss yours. You will also have to go back to the consolidator to get a refund, rather than the airline. Keep in mind that these tickets are often for coach seats on connecting (non-direct) flights on foreign airlines, and that frequent-flier miles may not be credited. Decide what you can and can't live with(out) before going with a consolidator.

Consolidators come in three varieties: wholesale only, who sell only to travel agencies; specialty agencies (both wholesale and retail); and **"bucket shops"** or discount retail agencies. You, as a private consumer, can deal directly only with the latter. You have access to a larger market if you use a travel agent, who can also get tickets from wholesale consolidators. Look for bucket shops' tiny ads in weekend papers (in the U.S., the Sunday *New York Times* is best). In London, the real bucket shop center, the Air Travel Advisory Bureau (tel. (0171) 636 50 00) provides a list of consolidators.

Be a smart and careful shopper. Among the many reputable and trustworthy companies are, unfortunately, some shady wheeler-dealers. Contact the local Better Business Bureau to find out how long the company has been in business and its track record. Although not necessary, it is preferable to deal with consolidators close to home so you can visit in person, if necessary. Ask to receive your tickets as quickly as possible so you have time to fix any problems. Insist on a written **receipt** that gives full details about the tickets, refunds, and restrictions, and record who you talked to and when. It may be worth paying with a credit card (despite the 2-5% fee) so you can stop payment if you never receive your tickets. Beware the "bait and switch" gag, in which shady firms will advertise a super-low fare and then tell a caller that it has been sold. Although this is a viable excuse, if they can't offer you a price near the advertised fare on *any* date, it is a scam to lure in customers—report them to the Better Business Bureau. Ask also about accommodations and car rental discounts; some consolidators have access to several different types of resources.

For destinations worldwide, try **Airfare Busters,** offices in Washington, DC (tel. (800) 776-0481), Boca Raton, FL (tel. (800) 881-3273), and Houston, TX (tel. (232-8783) or **Cheap Tickets**, offices in Los Angeles, CA, San Francisco, CA, Honolulu, HI, Overland Park, KS, and New York, NY, (tel. (800) 377-1000). For a processing fee, depending on the number of travelers and the itinerary, **Travel Avenue,** Chicago, IL (tel. (800) 333-3335) will search for the lowest international airfare available and even give you a rebate on fares over US\$300. To Europe, try **Rebel,** Valencia, CA (tel. (800) 227-3235) or Orlando, FL (tel. (800) 732-3588); or **Discount Travel International,** New York, NY (tel. (212) 362-3636; fax 362-3236). To Italy, check with **New Frontiers** in New York, NY (tel. (800) 366-6387) and **Pino Welcome Travel,** New York, NY (tel. (800) 247-6578).

Kelly Monaghan's *Consolidators: Air Travel's Bargain Basement* (US\$7 plus US\$2 shipping) from the Intrepid Traveler, P.O. Box 438, New York, NY 10034 (e-mail intreptrav@aol.com), is an valuable source for more information and lists of consolidators by location and destination. Cyber-resources include **World Wide** (http://www.tmn.com/wwwanderer/WWWa) and Edward Hasbrouck's incredibly informative **Airline Ticket Consolidators and Bucket Shops** (http://www.gnn.com/gnn/wic/wics/trav.97.html).

STAND-BY FLIGHTS

Airhitch, 2641 Broadway, Third Floor, New York, NY 10025 (tel. (800) 326-2009 or (212) 864-2000) and Los Angeles, CA (tel. (310) 726-5000), will add a certain thrill to your itinerary, since you will be unable to control exactly when you leave and where you end up. Complete flexibility on both sides of the Atlantic is necessary. Flights cost US$169 each way when departing from the Northeast, US$269 from the West Coast or Northwest, and US$229 from the Southeast and Midwest. The snag is that instead of buying a ticket, you purchase only a promise that you will get to a destination near where you're intending to go within a window of time (usually 5 days) from a location in a region you've specified. You call in before your date-range to hear all of your flight options for the next seven days and your probability of boarding. You then decide which flights you want to try to make and present a voucher at the airport which grants you the right to board a flight on a space-available basis. This procedure must be followed again for the return trip. Be aware that you may only receive a refund if *all* available flights which departed within your date and destination-range were full. There are several offices in Europe, so you can wait to register for your return. The main one is in Paris (tel. (1) 47 00 16 30).

Air-Tech, Ltd., 584 Broadway, #1007, New York, NY 10012 (tel. (212) 219-7000, fax 219-0066) offers a very similar service. Their travel window is one to four days; rates to and from Europe are generally the following: Northeast US$169; West Coast US$249; Midwest/Southeast US$199. Upon registration and payment, Air-Tech sends you a FlightPass with a contact date when you are to call them for flight instructions. Note that the service is one-way—you must go through the same procedure to return—and that *no refunds* are granted unless the company fails to get you a seat before your travel window expires. Be advised that clients' vouchers will not be honored if an airline fails to receive payment in time.

Contact the Better Business Bureau before contracting with either company.

CHARTER FLIGHTS

The theory behind a charter is that a tour operator contracts with an airline (usually one specializing in charters) to fly extra loads of passengers to peak-season destinations. Charter flights fly less frequently than major airlines and have more restrictions, particularly on refunds. They are also almost always fully booked, and schedules and itineraries may change or be cancelled as late as 48 hours before the trip, and without a full refund. You'll be much better off purchasing a charter ticket on a regularly scheduled airline. As always, pay with a credit card if you can, and consider traveler's insurance against trip interruption. Try **Interworld** (tel. (305) 443-4929) or **Travac** (tel. (800) 872-8800). Don't be afraid to call many numbers and hunt for the best deal.

Eleventh-hour **discount clubs** and **fare brokers** offer savings on European travel, including charter flights and tour packages. Research your options carefully. **Last Minute Travel Club,** 1249 Boylston St., Boston, MA 02215 (tel. (800) 527-8646 or (617) 267-9800), and **Discount Travel International,** New York, NY (tel. (212) 362-3636; fax 362-3236) are among the few travel clubs that don't charge a membership fee. Others (which charge US$25-50 membership fees) include **Moment's Notice,** New York, NY (tel. (718) 234-6295; fax 234-6450) and **Travelers Advantage,** Stanford, CT, (tel. (800) 835-8747). Study these organizations' contracts closely; you don't want to end up with an unwanted overnight layover.

COURIER COMPANIES AND FREIGHTERS

Those who travel light should consider flying to Europe as a **courier.** The company hiring you will use your checked luggage space for freight; you're only allowed to bring carry-ons. You are responsible for the safe delivery of the baggage claim slips (given to you by a courier company representative) to the representative waiting for you when you arrive—don't screw up or you will be blacklisted as a courier. You will probably never see the cargo you are transporting—the company handles it all—and airport officials know that couriers are not responsible for the baggage checked for them. Restrictions to watch for: you must be over 18, have a valid passport, and procure your own visa (if necessary); most flights are round-trip only with short fixed-length stays (usually one week); only single tickets are issued (but a companion may be able to get a next-day flight); and most flights are from New York. Round-trip fares to Western Europe from the U.S. range from US$250-400 (during the off-season) to US$400-550 (during the summer). **NOW Voyager,** 74 Varick St. #307, New York, NY 10013 (tel. (212) 431-1616), acts as an agent for many courier flights worldwide, primarily from New York. They offer special last-minute deals to such cities as London, Paris, Rome, and Frankfurt for as little as US$200 round-trip plus a US$50 registration fee. Other agents to try are **Halbart Express,** 147-05 176th St., Jamaica, NY 11434 (tel. (718) 656-5000), **Courier Travel Service,** 530 Central Avenue, Cedarhurst, NY 11516 (tel. (516) 763-6898), and **Discount Travel International** (tel. (212) 362-3636).

You can also go directly through courier companies in New York, or check your bookstore or library for handbooks such as *Air Courier Bargains* (US$15 plus US$3.50 shipping from the Intrepid Traveler, P.O. Box 438, New York, NY 10034). *The Courier Air Travel Handbook* (US$10 plus US$3.50 shipping) explains how to travel as an air courier and contains names, phone numbers, and contact points of courier companies. It can be ordered directly from Bookmasters, Inc., P.O. Box 2039, Mansfield, OH 44905 (tel. (800) 507-2665). **Travel Unlimited,** P.O. Box 1058, Allston, MA 02134-1058, publishes a comprehensive, monthly newsletter detailing all possible options for courier travel (often 50% off discount commercial fares). A one-year subscription is US$25 (outside of the U.S. US$35).

A final caveat for the budget conscious: don't get so caught up in the seemingly great deals. Always read the fine print; check for restrictions and hidden fees. There are amazingly cheap fares waiting to be unearthed, but you can't get something for nothing. If you really have travel time to spare, **Ford's Travel Guides,** 19448 Londelius St., Northridge, CA 91324 (tel. (818) 701-7414, fax 701-7415) lists **freighter companies** that will take passengers worldwide. Ask for their *Freighter Travel Guide and Waterways of the World* (US$16, plus US$2.50 postage if mailed outside the U.S.).

■ Getting to and from the Airports

FIUMICINO (LEONARDO DA VINCI INTERNATIONAL)

Most international, domestic, and non-charter flights touch down at **Leonardo da Vinci International Airport** (switchboard tel. 659 51), referred to as **Fiumicino** for the coastal village in which it is located. Two train lines connect Fiumicino with the center of Rome: the **Termini line** and the **Tiburtina/Orte/Farasabina line.** For transfers to domestic flights from the international terminal, follow the signs for "Voli Nazionali/Domestic Flights." It's quite a walk, though almost all by escalators or people-movers. You may want to take the shuttle *(navetta)* to the domestic terminal.

Services in Fiumicino (International Terminal)

EPT (Rome Tourist Authority) (tel. 65 95 44 71). Hotel reservations and brochures. English spoken. Open 8:15am-7pm.

Banca di Roma, Open Mon.-Fri. 8:25am-1:35pm and 3:10-4pm, Sat. 8:25-11:55am. Decent exchange rates. **ATM** on the right as you exit customs (lower floor) accepts Cirrus, MC, and Visa cards. Other ATMs in the domestic terminal.

Post Office, Open Mon.-Fri. 8am-12:50pm and 1:50-6:50pm., Sat. 8am-12:50pm. Also on the right as you exit customs (lower floor).

Public Toilets, on right as you exit customs. Also on upper floor (departures) by service windows at check-in counters A.

Luggage Storage, (lower floor-arrivals). On the right as you exit customs. Open 24hr. L1400 per bag per day ending at midnight.

From Fiumicino to Rome

When leaving customs, follow the signs to your left for **Stazione FS/Railway Station**. You can either take the escalator down to the underground pedestrian walkway and a series of escalators and people-movers up to the station, or take the elevator up two floors to the pedestrian bridge to the airport train station. From here you can take one of the two trains to the center of Rome. The **Termini** line goes directly to Rome's main train station and transportation hub, Termini Station. As of 1996, trains leave Fiumicino for Termini every hour at eight minutes past the hour from 8:08am to 10:08pm. Additional trains leave at 7:38am, 4:38pm, 6:38pm, and 8:38pm. The ride costs L13,000 and takes approximately 30 minutes. Buy a ticket *"Per termini"* at the FS ticket counter, the *tabacchi* on the right, or from one of the machines in the station.

The **Tiburtina/Orte/Fara Sabina** train stops at many of the minor train stations (but NOT Termini) on the outskirts of the city center, all of which are, in turn, connected to the city center by bus or metro. The most convenient way to reach the city center when using this line is to get off at the Tiburtina station which is connected to the Metro Linea B Stop, Tiburtina. When you get off the train (track #1) go down the stairs, following the signs for the *Metropolitana*. Buy a ticket (L1500), validate it, and take Metro Linea B in the direction of Laurentina. Get off at Termini, Rome's main transportation hub and train station. As of 1996, trains leave Fiumicino for Tiburtina every 20-30 minutes from 6:28am to shortly after midnight. Note however that the schedule of trains is erratic on Sundays and in August, and that late trains may arrive at Tiburtina after the metro stops running. The ride costs L7000 and takes approximately 40 minutes. Buy tickets *"Per Tiburtina"* on the right, or from the machines in the station. Note that the final destination of this train may be indicated on the signs by "Orte," "Fara Sabina," "Tiburtina," or "Monte Rotondo." In order to pass through the high-tech turnstiles you must validate a ticket. Keep the ticket with you for the entire train ride; it will be punched by the conductor.

From Rome to Fiumicino

As of 1996, a train leaves **Termini** for Fiumicino every hour at 22 minutes past the hour from 7:22am to 9:22pm, with additional trains at 6:52am, 3:52pm, 5:52pm and 7:52pm. It takes approximately 30 minutes and costs L13,000. Buy tickets at the Alitalia office at track #22 at the window marked "Biglietti Per Fiumicino" or from other designated areas and machines in the station. The train normally leaves from **track #22,** though it occasionally departs from track #23 which is located at the very end of the #22 platform. Validate (and retain) your ticket before boarding.

If you are desperate, you can also reach Fiumicino from **Tiburtina Station,** located at the Tiburtina stop on Metro Linea B. As of 1996, a train leaves Tiburtina for Fiumicino every 20-30 minutes from 5:06am to 11:05pm. Note that the schedule of trains is erratic on Sundays and in August. The ride is approximately 40 minutes and costs L7000. Buy tickets at the ticket booths. The train leaves from track #3. Validate tickets before boarding and retain them.

Early and Late Flights at Fiumicino

If your flight arrives at Fiumicino after 10pm or leaves Fiumicino before 8am, you may have some transportation difficulties. Avoid flying into or out of Rome during these hours. If you must, however, the most reliable, albeit expensive, option is to take a cab, which should cost between L65,000 and 85,000. (Request one at the kiosk in the airport or call 35 70, 49 94, or 66 45.) Otherwise, you must take the **COTRAL bus.**

To get to Rome from Fiumicino in the wee hours, take the blue COTRAL bus to Tiburtina. COTRAL buses in 1996 leave Fiumicino at 1:15am, 2:15am, 3:30am and 5am. Tickets cost L7000; buy them on the bus. Before 1:15am you may be able to take a train to Tiburtina (see From Fiumicino to Rome, above). From Tiburtina, take bus 42N to Termini Station (near which we hope you have reserved a room).

To get to Fiumicino from Rome in the wee hours, take the 42N bus from Termini to Tiburtina (leaves every 20-30min.) and catch the blue COTRAL bus to Fiumicino (L7000). As of 1996, COTRAL buses leave at 12:30am, 1:15am, 2:30am, and 3:45am. Buy tickets on the bus. The first train from Tiburtina to Fiumicino leaves at 5:06am (see From Rome to Fiumicino, p. 68).

CIAMPINO

Most charter and a few domestic flights arrive at **Ciampino** airport (tel. 79 49 41). From here take the blue COTRAL bus to the Anagnina stop on Metro Linea A (L1500; departures every hr. from 6am-11pm.). Linea A takes you to Termini, the Spanish Steps, or the Vatican. Reverse these directions to get to Ciampino from the center of Rome. At night (after 11pm or so), you may have to take a cab to and from Ciampino. Although Ciampino is inside the Rome city limits, there is still a supplement charge of L10,000.

■ By Train

IN EUROPE

The great majority of budget travelers in Europe use the economical and efficient train system. In theory, purchasing a railpass allows you to change your travel plans at will, jumping on any train to any destination at any time. Keep in mind, though, that reservations and additional fees are required for some trains, you must still stand in line for initial validation, and, most importantly, it may not save you money. Ask your travel agent for the Eurail tariff manual, then add up the second-class fares for your planned routes and deduct 5% (listed prices automatically include commission) to see if the purchase will pay off.

Eurailpasses may be used to get to Italy from a number of European countries. They are also valid, though not as economical, for travel within Italy. They are intended for non-Europeans and should be bought before arrival in Europe. All travel agents offer the same prices, which are at set by the EU. There are several varieties (including group passes); investigate the Eurail Youthpass if you are under 26 (US$418 for 15 days, US$598 for one month, US$798 for two months). Eurail passes are not refundable once validated unless you have purchased insurance on it through the Pass Protection Plan (US$10). Contact **Rail Europe, Inc.,** 226-230 Westchester Ave., White Plains, NY 10604 (tel. (800) 438-7245, fax (800) 432-1329 in the U.S.; tel. (800) 361-7245, fax (905) 602-4198 in Canada; http://www.raileurope.com) for the free *Europe on Track* guide to pass options and rail travel.

For travelers under 26, **BIJ tickets** *(Billets Internationals de Jeunesse),* sold under the names **Wasteels, Eurotrain,** and **Route 26,** are a good alternative to railpasses. Available for international trips within Europe and some ferry routes, they knock 25-40% off regular second-class fares. Tickets are good for 60 days after purchase and allow a number of stopovers along the normal direct route of the train journey. Issued for a specific international route between two points, they must be used in the direction and order of the designated route without side- or back-tracking. You must buy BIJ tickets in Europe, at either Wasteels or Eurotrain offices (usually in or near train stations), or try directly at the ticket counter.

The ultimate reference for planning rail trips is the *Thomas Cook European Timetable* (US$28; US$39 includes a map of Europe highlighting all train and ferry routes; add US$4.50 for postage). In the U.S., order it from **Forsyth Travel Library** (see p. 30). The annual *Eurail Guide to Train Travel in the New Europe* (US$15) is available in most bookstores, or by writing to the Houghton Mifflin Co., 222 Berkeley St., Boston, MA 02116 (tel. (617) 351-5974; fax 351-1113).

ESSENTIALS

WITHIN ITALY

If you're traveling to Rome from elsewhere in Italy, you'll probably want to use the economical and efficient nationalized train system, the Ferrovie dello Stato (FS). Most major Italian cities either lie on a direct line from Rome or can be reached with a single change.

Train fares are determined by the number of kilometers between the departure city and the destination. In order to ride on the faster trains, however, you must pay a **supplement** (*il supplemento*). The classes of trains requiring a supplement are: the *IC* (an "InterCity" train running non-stop between major cities), the *EC* (*Eurocity* like the IC but going to a European city outside Italy), the EN (a nocturnal EC train with sleeping cars only), and the *Pendolino* (this costs significantly more).

Tickets can be bought and **reservations** made in Termini Station (or any train station) and at many travel agencies (see Tourist Offices, p. 29). The Ferrovie dello Stato recently began to accept AmEx; beyond that, however, the only foreign-issued card they will take is Diner's Club. Reservations are mandatory for all *pendolino* trains and for some IC and EC/EN trains, and usually cost under L10,000. Reservations are free for other trains and can be made up to three hours in advance. The bold and impatient should try to use the self-service machines opposite the main ticket counter which sell national train tickets with directions in English, Spanish, French, Dutch, Portuguese, and Italian. These machines accept L1000, L5000, L10,000, and L50,000 bills, and Diners Club International.

Students and youths qualify for numerous discounts on the Italian Rail System. Ask a travel agent about the *Carta Verde,* which gives youths under 26 a 20% discount on train fares. If you plan to take several short trips or are traveling with a few people, you may want to buy a kilometric ticket or an Italian State Rail Pass. Check with a travel agent or the ticket booths at Termini for more information. The following prices are for second-class seats, one-way:

Florence: 2-3hrs.;L24,400 (sup. L11,800). **Venice:** 5hrs.;L44,100 (sup. L17,600). **Naples:** 2-2½ hrs.;L17,200 (sup. L9700). **Milan:**. 5-6 hrs.; L47,700 (sup. L18,500). **Bologna:** 3¼-4hrs.;L33,400 (sup. L14,500). **Brindisi:** 6-8hrs.;L47,700 (sup. L18,500). **Palermo:** 11-12hrs.;L68,900 (sup. L23,700).

If you don't feel like waiting in line to obtain information about train times and schedules, never fear. In every train station in Italy, yellow and white charts labeled **Partenze** or **Arrivi** (departures or arrivals) are posted near the tracks and ticket booths, listing the destination and origin, arrival and departure time and intermediary stops of every train entering the station. Comprehensive train schedules covering all of Italy are available at newsstands for about L10,000. Look at the map in the front of the booklet and find the line number that connects the cities between which you wish to travel. Flip to the listing of that number and read the schedule from top to bottom. To determine the price of a particular item, look at the column on the far right labelled "K" for "Kilometer." A chart at the front of the booklet tells you how much it costs to travel per kilometer. Ask a local if you have questions.

TERMINI (AND OTHER TRAIN STATIONS)

Termini, the transportation hub of Rome, is the focal point of most train lines and both subway lines. The various stations on the fringe of town (**Tiburtina, Trastevere, Ostiense, San Lorenzo, Roma Nord, Prenestina**) are connected by bus and/or subway to Termini. Trains that arrive in Rome after midnight and before 5am or so usually arrive at Stazione Tiburtina or Stazione Ostiense, which are connected to Termini during these hours by the 42N and 20N-21N respectively. Be particularly wary of pickpockets in and around the stations. For more tips on how to avoid theft, see Safety, p. 42.

Practical Information

Railway Info, right at the front entrance, facing P. dei Cinquecento where all the buses are. Home to Eurail Office (windows #9 and #10). Open 7am-11pm.

EPT tourist office (tel. 48 89 92 55) between tracks #2 and #3. Makes hotel reservations and has brochures. Open 8:15am-7:15pm daily.

Luggage Storage, at tracks #1 and #22. L5000 per bag per 12hrs. Pay in advance and DON'T LOSE THE RECEIPT. Open daily 6am-10pm.

Train Police (Polizia Ferroviaria) (tel. 481 95 61), on track #1 and between tracks #4 and #5. Report theft in station or on train here. Open 24 hours.

Lost Property: Oggetti Rinvenuti, on track #1. Open daily 7am-11pm.

Police: Carabinieri, on track #1 and between tracks #2 and #3. Same function as Train Police.

Waiting Room (Sala di Attesa) along track #1.

ATMs, San Paolo di Torino, at track #22 and between tracks #11 and #12. Banca di Roma, in the main gallery. (Cirrus, MC, and Visa accepted at both.) BNL, outside the station on corner of Via Marsala and Solferino.

To freshen up between journeys, go downstairs to the **Albergo Diurno** (tel. 48 21 880), where you can find showers (L10,000), baths (L12,000), and a barber, manicurist, and pedicurist (L8000-L25,000). Sheets, towels, and soap are available for modest fees. Or check out the misnamed **Drug Store Termini,** which, as of 1996, provides just about every service imaginable (CONAD supermarket, bakery, bar, candy store, optical store, key repair, shoe repair) except a drugstore; it is downstairs in Termini, accessible by the Metro entrance (open 24hr.).

▓ By Bus

Few people think of buses when planning travel within Europe, but they are available and cheap. Bus travel in Europe is significantly more comfortable than in North America, though you can never have a true non-smoking section, and some companies force you to watch bleary videos or listen to the radio; a walkman will probably come in handy here. Amsterdam, Athens, Istanbul, London, Munich, and Oslo are centers for private lines that offer long-distance rides across Europe and, from time to time, all the way to India. Passes for travel between major European cities are available from **Eurobus,** 355 Palermo Ave., Coral Gables, FL 33134 (tel. (800) 517-7778 or (800) 727-2437 for students). The U.K. address is P.O. Box 5220, London W51GQ (tel. (0181) 991 55 91; fax 991 14 42). **Eurolines,** 4 Cardiff Rd., Luton LU1 1PP (tel. (01582) 40 45 11 or (0171) 730 82 35 in London), is Europe's largest operator of coach services, offering unlimited 30- or 60-day travel between 18 major cities.

ONCE THERE

▓ Embassies and Consulates

Embassies in Rome have a tendency to close on holidays even the Romans don't know about. Call in advance to make sure your embassy is actually open before you wander over. All embassies answer the phone around the clock in case of emergencies and have lists of English-speaking doctors and lawyers. Often, the embassy and consulate for a country are at different addresses and yet in the same building.

United States, Via Veneto, 121 (tel. 467 41; fax 46 74 22 17). Passport and consular services open Mon.-Fri. 8:30-noon and 1:30-3:30pm. Report stolen passports here; new passports can be issued the same day for a US$65 fee (US$40 for minors). Notorials (Tues. and Thurs. 8:30am-noon); visas (8:30-10:30am); immigration and naturalization (8:30am-12:30pm); IRS (9am-noon and 2-4pm); social security

Auberge Internationale des Jeunes

Open 24 hours
Rooms from
2 to 6 beds
Breakfast included
Free showers
New building

Credit cards accepted
(Visa, Mastercard,
American Express)
Traveller's cheques
Change of foreign
currencies

Hostel in the city centre of Paris

81 FRF
from November to February

91 FRF
from March to October

An ideal location for young people, a lively area with many
CAFES, PUBS, RESTAURANTS, DISCOS.
INTERNATIONAL ATMOSPHERE

Other Hostels might be less comfortable, and more expensive...!!

10, rue Trousseau - 75011 PARIS - FRANCE
Tél. : 01 47 00 62 00 - Fax : 01 47 00 33 16

Métro : LEDRU ROLLIN - Line 8 (Next to Bastille)

(8:30am-noon and 2:15-4:30pm by appointment only). Closed on U.S. and Italian holidays.

Canada, Consulate, Via Zara, 30 (tel. 44 59 84 21; fax 44 59 89 12). Near the intersection with Via Nomentana, on the 5th floor. Consular and passport services here open Mon.-Fri. 10am-noon and 2-4pm. A passport issued here costs CDN$60; if you call in the morning, a new passport can be issued by the afternoon. English and French spoken. Embassy, Via G.B. De Rossi, 27 (tel. 44 59 81).

Britain, Via XX Settembre 80/A (tel. 482 54 41; fax 48 90 30 73), near the Porta Pia and the corner with Via Palestro. Consular and passport services open Mon.-Fri. 9:15am-1:30pm and 2-4pm; mid-July-Aug. open Mon.-Fri. 8am-1pm.

Australia, Via Alessandria, 215 (tel. 85 27 21; fax 85 27 23 00). The office has lots of useful information for Australians (or any English-speakers) staying in Rome. Consular and passport services around the corner at Corso Trieste 25, open Mon.-Thurs. 9am-noon and 1:30-5pm, Fri. 9am-noon. Passport costs AUS$106. Australians in Italy are required to obtain a permit of stay from the police within 8 days of arrival and are not allowed to work there.

New Zealand, Via Zara, 28 (tel. 440 29 28/29/30; fax 440 29 84). Consular and passport services Mon.-Fri. 9am-noon. Regular embassy services available Mon.-Fri. 8:30am-12:45pm and 1:45-5pm. Passport L137,000. If you need the passport after hours or during the weekend, a large surcharge is added.

Often, there are restrictions on travel from other countries, so it is a good idea to contact your embassy before leaving to find out what these are. Some other embassies in Rome are: **Austria,** Via Pergolesi, 3 (tel. 855 82 41; fax 854 32 86; e-mail austrianembassyrome@rmnet.it); **Belgium,** Via Monti Parioli, 49 (tel. 360 95 11); **Czech Republic,** Via dei Gracchi, 322 (tel. 32 444 59; fax 32 444 66); **Egypt,** Via Salaria, 265 (tel. 855 53 61); **France,** Piazza Farnese, 67 (tel. 68 60 11); **India,** Via XX Settembre, 5 (tel. 48 84 642; fax 48 19 539); **Ireland,** Piazza Campitelli, 3 (tel. 69 79 121); **Israel,** Via M. Mercati, 12 (tel. 36 19 81); **Mexico,** Via Spallanzani, 16 (tel. 440 44 00); **Spain,**

(*Embassy*) Largo Fontanella Borghese, 19 (tel. 68 78 172), (*Consulate*) Via Campo Marzio, 34 (tel. 686 43 92).

▒ Tourist Offices

In addition to the tourist offices listed below, you may also take advantage of the **Info-Tourism Boxes,** kiosks in the historic center conveniently set up in trailers. They are open Tues.-Sat. 10am-6pm and Sun. 10am-1pm. Locations include those at Largo Carlo Goldoni (tel. 68 75 027), off Via del Corso, across from Via dei Condotti; Largo Corrado Ricci (tel. 67 80 992) near the Colosseum; and on Via Nazionale (tel. 47 45 929), near the Palazzo delle Esposizioni.

Enjoy Rome, Via Varese, 39, 00185 Roma (tel. 445 18 43; fax 445 07 34; http://dbweb.agora.stm.it/markets/magenta39/enjoy.htm). From Termini station, cross Via Marsala (adjacent to the station as you exit the train terminal's main gallery to the right), and head 3 blocks up to Via Varese. Its hip and friendly English-speaking owners, Fulvia and Pierluigi, will handle your questions and concerns with kindness and care, and will provide you with a copy of their very useful guide to the city (also called *Enjoy Rome*), all **free of charge.** They'll help you out with hotel accommodations, short-term apartment rentals, and will help organize 3-hour walking tours (L30,000, under 26 or over 65 years old L25,000), cycling tours (call for prices), and bus tours (L46,000) throughout the city. Very warm and solicitous, they'll even book you a cab back to the airport. Open Mon.-Fri. 8:30am-1:30pm and 3:30-6:30pm, Sat. 8:30am-1:30pm, but hours tend to be extended during the summer. Emergency calls taken Mon.-Sat. until 10pm.

Tourist Office EPT, in the Termini Station (tel. 482 40 70), in front of track #2. Lines can be horrendous. **Central Office,** Via Parigi, 5 (tel. 48 89 92 55 or 48 89 92 53; fax 58 82 50). Walk from the station diagonally to the left across P. Cinquecento (filled with buses) and go straight across P. della Repubblica. Via Parigi starts on the other side of the church, at the Grand Hotel. English spoken. Offices open Mon.-Sat. 8:15am-7pm. At any office, pick up a map and copies of *Romamor.* If you will be traveling in the region around Rome, also ask for *Alberghi di Roma e Provincia,* which lists all hotels and *pensioni* registered with the EPT. Both of these offices will help you find a room; they advise arriving in Rome early in the morning before hotels book up for the night.

ENIT, Via Marghera, 3 (tel. 49 71 282); as you exit the tracks at Termini, head to your right and cross Via Marsala to Via Marghera; it's 2 blocks down on the left. Some information on Rome, but mostly brochures and hotel listings for the rest of Lazio, Italy's provinces, and its major cities. Open Mon.-Fri. 9am-5:30pm.

Centro Turistico Studentesco Giovanile (CTS), Via Genova, 16, 00184 Roma (tel. 467 91; fax 467 92 05). With 90 offices throughout Italy, CTS provides travel, accommodation, and sight-seeing discounts. Sells the *Carta Verde* for discount train fares, the International Student Identity Card (ISIC), the International Youth Card (IYC card), and the Euro Youth Card. Branch offices in London and Paris. Open Mon.-Fri. 9am-1pm and 3-7pm, Sat. 9am-1pm.

▒ Budget Travel Services in Rome

Compagnia Italiana di Turismo (CIT), P. della Repubblica, 64 (tel. 47 46 555; fax 48 18 277). A national travel agency that books discount train tickets and tours. Open Mon.-Fri. 9am-1pm and 2-5:30pm.

Italian Youth Hostels Association (Associazione Italiana Alberghi per la Gioventù), HI-IYHF, Via Cavour, 44 (tel. 487 11 52; fax 488 04 92). Plenty of advice and a list of hostels throughout Italy. IYHA cards L30,000. Open Mon.-Thurs. 7:30am-5pm, Fri. 7:30am-3pm, Sat. 8am-12:30pm.

Transalpino, P. dell'Esquilino, 10Z (tel. 487 08 70; fax 488 30 94). Sells the *Carta Verde* (L40,000) and BIGE tickets (20-30% youth discounts on international train tickets). Ferry information as well. Open Mon.-Fri. 9am-7pm, Sat. 9am-1pm. Also a booth in Termini, at track #22 (tel. 488 05 36), open Mon.-Sat. 8am-8:30pm; summer also Sun. 8:30am-5:30pm.

Wasteels, Via Milazzo, 8/C (tel. 445 66 79 or 482 55 37) (it hits Termini perpendicularly 100 yards to the right of the entrance on Via Marsala). You can get the same prices here on national and international train and plane tickets as you can elsewhere, but there are no big crowds. Sells BIGE and other specialized passes. Open Mon.-Fri. 9am-1pm and 2-5:30pm, Sat. 9am-12:30pm.

Centro Turistico Studentesco (CTS), Via Genova, 16 (tel. 467 91), off Via Nazionale, about halfway between P. della Repubblica and P. Venezia. Open Mon.-Fri. 9am-1pm and 3-7pm, Sat. 9am-1pm. Another office at Via degli Ausoni, 5 (tel. 445 01 41) open Mon.-Fri. 9:30am-1pm and 2:30-6:30pm, Sat. 10am-1pm. Branch offices at Termini at track #22 (tel. 467 92 54; open 8:30am-8:30pm); at Via Appia Nuova, 434 (tel. 780 84 49; open Mon.-Fri. 9:30am-1pm and 3:30-7pm, Sat. 9:30am-1pm); at Corso Vittorio Emanuele II, 297 (tel. 687 26 72; open Mon.-Fri. 9:30am-1:30pm and 2:30-6pm, Sat. 9:30am-noon); and at Terminal Ostiense (tel. 467 92 57; open Mon.-Fri. 9:30am-1:30pm and 2:30-6pm, Sat. 9:30am-noon). ISIC and *Carta Giovane* cards L15,000 each; bring ID photo and proof of student status. Discount plane, train, boat and bus reservations and tickets, plus a free map, and currency exchange. Accommodations service, including out-of-town reservations (done for free). Bulletin boards with notices for rides, companionship, special services, etc. Lines can be aggravatingly slow; if information is all you need, it's better to phone (information tel. 467 91). Excellent English spoken at all locations.

■ Useful Publications

BROCHURES AND PAMPHLETS

The tourist offices Enjoy Rome (Via Varese, 39) and EPT (Via Parigi, 5) have free maps and brochures on Rome and its environs. Enjoy Rome's aptly-titled booklet, *Enjoy Rome,* is packed with vital information about food, sights, embassies, hospitals, etc., geared towards the young, English-speaking budget traveler. The **Tourist's Yellow Pages** references useful services; you can page through a copy at the tourist office. **Un Ospite a Roma (A Guest in Rome)** is a free pamphlet updated weekly, listing events, exhibits, and concerts, as well as vital phone numbers for museums, galleries, and emergency services. It's unavailable at EPT or Enjoy Rome, but you can ask for it at "finer" hotels.

MAGS AND NEWSLETTERS

Metropolitan is an English-language magazine containing all kinds of articles, reviews, helpful advice, entertainment listings, and a classified ads section. The magazine is available at the various English-language bookstores and the newsstand at 11 Largo Torre Argentina, among others (L1500). **Roma C'è** is probably the most useful manual to everything from restaurants to church services to discos. It is written in Italian, but there is a substantial English language section at the end. It comes out every Thursday and is available at most newsstands (L1500). *Trovaroma,* the Thursday publication of *La Reppublica,* lists events and recreational possibilities for the week. **Wanted in Rome,** a highly informative English-language newsletter (published every 2 weeks Sept.-July), contains job and housing classifieds, a calendar of cultural events, and short articles on topics of interest to English speakers (available at newsstands, English-language bookstores and English-speaking institutions for L1500). The Economy Book and Video Center, Via Torino, 136 (tel. 474 68 77), publishes the monthly pamphlet *Happenings* which lists cultural events and discussions affiliated with the bookstore. An erratically published English newspaper called *Nerone* is available at EPT and has interesting articles and lists of upcoming events.

MAPS

Rome's circuitous streets make **maps** indispensable for the traveler. The **EPT Tourist Office** at Via Parigi, 5; **American Express** at Piazza di Spagna; **Enjoy Rome** at Via Varese, 39; and **McDonald's** at Piazza di Spagna, 46/47, offer good maps at no charge. **Editrice Lozzi** publishes a decent but cumbersome transportation map of the city called *Roma Metro-Bus;* it is available at most newsstands and bookstores (L9000). Those who know the general layout of the city and would like a detailed, compact map should check out the weirdly-designed but superb map from **Falk,** also available at newsstands. For a thoroughly indexed street atlas, try *Rome A to Z* (sold with *Lazio A to Z*) which includes a pocket guide of 20 bike itineraries around Rome. A similar street atlas, **StradaRoma,** is available for L12,000, also at newsstands. **Tuttocittà,** distributed to Romans with their phone books each year, has an equally exact atlas. Ask Roman friends or a store owner if you can take a peek.

■ Money

Dealing with the Italian banking system is always an adventure, with broken machines, uncooperative tellers, and usurious exchange rates around every corner. Explore your financial options before you go, and you'll save time, money, and your sanity. For more advice and information, see Money Matters, p. 39.

CHANGING MONEY

When exchanging money in Rome, look for *cambio* signs and shop around. Avoid exchanging at luxury hotels, train stations, and airports. *Cambio* booths often offer the best deal around, but the rates and fees vary greatly. Changing currency is best done in the morning; banking hours are usually Monday-Friday approximately 8:30am-1:30pm with an extra hour in the afternoon. Expect long lines, pushy customers, and cranky tellers who may let natives go in front of you and may close the window just as it is your turn. Decent deals are usually found at banks such as the **Banca di Roma** or the **Banca Nazionale del Lavoro.** Count your money inside the bank or *cambio,* never out on the street, and make sure you are not followed after changing money. Beware of street money-changers, who may give you counterfeit money. If you arrive too late in the day to change money, there are machines scattered throughout the city that change foreign bank notes for lire, but at horrendous exchange rates. Avoid problems by buying some *lire* in your home country before you leave. To change money, head to a bank or any of the institutions below:

American Express, P. di Spagna, 38, Roma 00187 (tel. 67 641; lost or stolen cards and/or checks issued in the U.S. toll-free 24hrs. 167 87 43 33; others call 72 281). Chaotic at times, but fairly efficient, and perfect English spoken. Mail (but not FedEx items) held for free for 30 days if you carry American Express traveler's checks or the card. Mail can be forwarded to another address by surface mail for a L10,000 fee on arrival, or by airmail with prepaid postage. Messages can be left in the office in a stamped envelope for L3000. There's no need to change checks here, as you will find the same rates and shorter lines at any of the small *cambi* all over the city. Excellent maps of Rome are free for the asking. The ATM outside accepts AmEx cards. Open Mon.-Fri. 9am-5:30pm, Sat. 9am-3pm.

Numismatica Internazionale, Piazza d. Cinquecento, 57/58 (tel. 488 50 05), in the arcade on the left side of the Piazza as you face away from the station. Open Mon.-Sat. 8am-7pm.

ACITOUR, Via Marsala, 14A (tel. 446 99 20), inside the Galleria Caracciolo shopping arcade (L1000 flat traveler's check fee; no commission). Open Mon.-Fri. 9am-1pm and 2-6pm.

Thomas Cook, Piazza Barberini, 21A (tel. 482 80 82). No charge for Thomas Cook traveler's checks, 3% commission on all others; open Mon.-Sat. 8:30am-5:30pm, Sun. 9am-1:30pm. Also at Via della Conciliazione, 23/25 (tel. 68 30 04 35), in front of San Pietro; open Mon.-Sat. 8:30am-6pm, Sun. 9am-5pm. Via del Corso, 23 (tel.

323 00 67); open Mon.-Sat. 9am-8pm, Sun. 9am-1:30pm; and Piazza della Repubblica, 65 (tel. 48 64 95), inside CIT; open Mon.-Fri. 9am-6pm with 1-hr. lunch break, Sat. 9am-1pm.

ATMS

Before you decide to depend on ATMs for your money supply, please read the section on Cash Cards and ATMS, p. 41. ATMs, called *Bancomat* or *sportelli automatici* in Italian, are all around the city, but only some of them accept American credit cards and cash cards. The banks with the most reliable ATMs accepting Visa and Mastercard are Banca Nazionale del Lavoro and Banca di Roma. **Credit card ATMs** also abound on Via Arenula, Via and Largo del Tritone, Via del Corso, and near the Pantheon and Termini. The ATM at the American Express office at the Spanish Steps accepts **American Express** cards, as does the Banca Popolare di Milano, with locations in Piazzale Flamina and on Via Veneto. ATMs that accept American **cash cards** are becoming more and more common in Rome. Though **Cirrus** claims not to have any ATMs in Rome, Cirrus cards are accepted quite often at Banca Nazionale del Lavoro, and sometimes at Banca di Roma. **PLUS** cards are also accepted regularly at these banks' ATMs. Below is a list of tried and true locations:

Banca Nazionale del Lavoro, Via Marsala, 6 (near Termini), Via della Rosetta, 1 (at the Pantheon), Piazza Venezia, 6. Takes Cirrus and PLUS.
Banca di Roma, Via Cavour, Via del Corso, Corso Vittorio Emanuele II. Takes PLUS.
Istituto Bancario San Paolo di Torino, in Termini Station at track #22 and track #12. Takes Cirrus only.

OPENING A BANK ACCOUNT

Anyone who's ever tried merely to change a few *lire* will attest to the horrors of the Italian banking administration; employees are snippy, computers crash at the drop of a hat, and the amount of paperwork required is enough to give any Greenpeace member a coronary. Opening a bank account is no exception. In order to open a bank account in Italy you must present a *certificato di residenza* (which you receive from your local *commune* when you register as a resident) or your *permesso di soggiorno,* a passport or photo ID, and a *codice fiscale,* the equivalent to an American Social Security number which you also get from the *commune.* Sound simple? Think again. Getting a *codice fiscale,* like all bureaucratic transactions in Italy, is next to impossible. Check with the institution with which you hope to do business or the international desk of your local bank for requirements and other information.

■ Emergencies, Health, and Help

EMERGENCY NUMBERS

Police: State Police (English interpreter) 113; *Carabinieri* 112
First Aid (Pronto Soccorso): 118
Fire: 115
Roadside Assistance: 116
Ambulance (Red Cross): 5510

MEDICAL HELP

Late-night Pharmacies:
All pharmacies post the names, addresses, and hours of neighboring pharmacies and all-night pharmacies. *La Repubblica* and *Il Messaggero* newspapers publish a list of pharmacies open in August, and the closed pharmacies usually post a list. You can usually get foreign prescriptions at a pharmacy (so you don't have to go to an Italian doctor's office). The following are your best bet, especially in August:

Farmacia Grieco, Piazza della Repubblica, 67 (tel. 488 04 10 or 48 38 61). Steps from Termini. Open 24hr.

Farmacia Piram, Via Nazionale, 228 (tel. 488 07 54). Open 24hr.

Cristo dei Ferroviari, near track #14 in Termini (tel. 488 07 76). Open till 10pm.

Medical Assistance:

International Medical Center, Via Amendola, 7 (tel. 488 23 71; nights and Sundays 488 40 51), 1 block from Termini, on the 2nd floor. On call 24hr. and very helpful. Call them first in case of medical problems. Will refer you to an English-speaking doctor, make an appointment, or send one to your hotel. Each visit L100,000-L170,000. Will provide prescriptions. Mobile paramedic crew on call. Open Mon.-Sat. 8:30am-8pm. Phone lines open 24hr.

Hospitals:

Rome-American Hospital, Via E. Longoni, 69 (tel. 225 33 33, 225 52 90 or 22 551). Private emergency and laboratory services. English information and English-speaking doctor on call 24hr.

Policlinico Umberto I, Viale di Policlinico, 155 (tel. 49 97 09 00 or 499 71), near Termini. Take Metro Linea B to the Policlinico stop. Free first aid (*pronto soccorso*). Open 24hr.

Nuovo Regina Margherita, Via Emilio Morosini, 30 (tel. 58 44), 1 block off Viale Trastevere. Walk-in first aid. Open 24hr.

Dental Hospital:

George Eastman, Viale Regina Elena, 287/B (tel. 49 00 42), take Metro B to Policlinico. On call 24hr. every day. Unless it's an emergency, though, call in the morning for an appointment in the afternoon. Check in *Wanted in Rome* or *Metropolitan* for English-speaking dentists in private practices.

Clinics:

These facilities provide diagnostic testing and some treatment for a variety of ailments, injuries, and illnesses. Call ahead to see if they have the services you need.

Unione Sanitaria Internazionale, Via V. Orsini, 18 (tel. 321 50 53), north of the Vatican, off Piazza della Libertà; or Via Machiavelli, 22 (tel. 70 45 35 44), Metro Linea A, Vittorio Emanuele stop. English spoken. Open for info. 7am-7pm. Open for tests 7am-11am.

Analisi Cliniche Luisa, Via Padova, 96A (tel. 44 29 14 06), take Metro Linea B to Piazza Bologna; it is just south of Viale delle Province. Pregnancy tests, STD and HIV tests (L110,000). Open Mon.-Fri. 7:30am-6pm, Sat. 8am-2pm.

Laboratorio Analisi Cliniche e Specialistiche "Cavour," Via Cavour, 238 (tel. and fax 474 39 48), at the Metro Linea B Cavour stop. Open Mon.-Fri. 7:30-11am and 4-6pm, Sat. 7:30-11am.

Studio Polispecialistico Nomentano, Via Nomentana, 550/552 (tel. 86 89 56 11). Does it all, including AIDS tests. Open 7am-12:30pm and 3-6:30pm.

Gynecology, STDs, and Abortion:

Analisi Cliniche will perform tests for venereal disease (*malattia venerea*) as well as pregnancy tests (see Clinics, p. 77), or you can buy home tests over the counter at pharmacies throughout the city. These labs also do pap smears and cryotherapy. See Medical Vocabulary, p. 288, for medical words and phrases.

Ospedale San Camillo in Monteverde, Circonvallazione Gianicolense, 87 in Gianicolo (tel. 587 01). Abortion on demand is not available; women must have a gynecological exam, discussion with a doctor, and possibly counseling. Open Mon.-Sat. 8-11am.

AIDS Concerns:

Tests can be performed at any **Analisi Cliniche** (a private lab which handles all sorts of tests, from allergies to pregnancy; see Clinics, p. 77). Simply ask for the "AIDS test" or "HIV test" (AIDS is pronounced "AH-eeds" in Italy; HIV is pronounced "A-kah-EE-VOO"). Look in the Yellow Pages under *Analisi* for the private labs or refer to one of the following. Go in the morning for a *prelievo* (withdrawal) and pick up the results (or call) in the afternoon.

> **Mario Miele,** Via Ostiense 202 (tel. 54 13 985; fax 54 13 971), near the Basilica di S. Paolo fuori le Mura, is a gay health service providing counseling and anonymous HIV and STD testing.

HELP LINES

> **Crisis Line: Samaritans,** Via San Giovanni in Laterano, 250 (tel. 70 45 44 44). Native English speakers. A great resource for anyone feeling down, in need of someone to talk to, or in a crisis situation. Anonymous or face-to-face counseling available. Open for calls and visits daily 1-10pm. Call ahead before visiting.
> **Alcoholics Anonymous** (tel.678 03 20). Meetings at various English-language churches around Rome.

POLICE

> **Police: Ufficio Stranieri (Foreigner's Office),** Via San Vitale, 15 (tel. 46 86 27 11). English spoken. Report thefts here in person. Open 24hr.
> **Police Headquarters (Questura),** Via San Vitale, 15 (tel. 468 61). Report thefts in person here.
> **Railway Police,** on track #1 and facing track #2 in Termini.

LOST PROPERTY

If you are robbed, always file a report *(fare una denuncia)* with the police—you'll need it for insurance and it's helpful in case anything is turned in, which may actually happen. Also check at your **embassy,** since wallets and passports are sometimes returned there.

> **Oggetti Rinvenuti,** Via Nicolo Bettoni, 1 (tel. 581 60 40), at the Trastevere train station. Open Mon. and Fri. 8:30am-1pm, Tues.-Wed. 8:30am-1pm and 2:30-6pm, Thurs. 8:30am-6pm, Sat. 8:30am-noon. **Ufficio Stranieri (Foreigner's Office),** Via San Vitale, 15 (tel. 46 86 27 11). English spoken. Report thefts here. Open 24 hrs. **Termini,** at track #1. Open 7am-11pm. **ATAC,** Via Volturno, 65 (tel. 469 51). Open Mon.-Fri. 9am-noon and 2-5pm.

■ Helpful Services

WASHING CLOTHES

OndaBlu, Via Principe Amedeo, 70b (tel. 474 46 647; open daily 8am-10pm), off Via Cavour 2 blocks south of Termini; also Via Milazzo, 8, off of Via Marsala. Rome's first self-serve laundromat; it opened in 1993. A newspaper review inside calls it "almost a nightclub." Pass time while waiting for your laundry by watching Videomusic (Italian for MTV), or better yet, the lively clientele around you. Wash L6,000 per 6.5kg load (40min.). Dry L6000 per load (20min.). Special L10,000 for 16kg. **American Laundry,** Via d'Azeglio, 3-E (tel. 48 20 003), about 50m from Termini as you exit the station on the left (south-west). Coin-operated Maytag machines. Wash 7kg, L7000; dry 7kg L7000. Open Mon.-Fri. 8am-8pm, Sat. mornings only. **Lavaservice,** Via Montebello, 44 (tel. 474 31 52). Northeast of Termini. They'll do your laundry for you for L4000 per kg. Open Mon.-Fri. 7am-6pm.

BOOKSTORES

Viale di Termini, connecting Termini with P. della Repubblica, is lined with booksellers who often sell dirt-cheap used English paperbacks. **Via di Conciliazione,** the broad avenue leading to St. Peter's, has several bookstores selling English-language histories and guidebooks, as well as devotional materials. **Feltrinelli,** an Italian bookstore chain, sells some English-language books, including our favorites, the *Let's Go* series. Try the branch in Largo Argentina at the corner of Corso Vittorio Emanuele and Via di Torre Argentina. **Rare books and prints** are sold in the outdoor market at Piazza Borghese, off Via di Ripetta (open daily).

Economy Book and Video Center, Via Torino, 136 (tel. 474 68 77), off Via Nazionale. Italy's largest selection of English language books, as well as books on tape and greeting cards. Also buys books, gives free maps, and rents videos (L10,000 per night, with L150,000 deposit or credit card). Open Mon.-Fri. 9am-8pm, Sat. 9am-2pm.

The Lion Bookshop, Via del Babuino, 181 (tel. 322 58 37), between Spanish Steps and P. di Popolo. For the literature lover and Anglophile in you. A very well-stocked bookstore with contemporary releases on hand. Poetry, philosophy, history, fiction, and children's books. Community bulletin board here as well (with apartment listings, etc.). Greeting cards and video rental. Closed in Aug. Open Mon. 3:30-7:30pm, Tues.-Fri. 9:30am-1:30pm and 3:30-7:30pm, Sat. 9:30am-1pm.

Anglo-American Bookshop, Via della Vite, 102 (tel. 679 52 52). Steps from P. di Spagna. An astonishing array of titles, including academic works, books on the history and art of Italy, guidebooks to Rome and Italy, and paperback fiction. Open Mon.-Fri. 9am-1pm and 4-8pm, Sat. 9am-1pm.

Open Door Bookshop, Via della Lungaretta, 25 (tel. 589 64 78), off Viale Trastevere. Paperbacks of all languages and a fax machine (L4000 first page, L2000 per additional page, plus phone charges). Also rents videos (L8000 per day with L50,000 deposit). Open Mon. 4-8pm, Tues.-Sat. 10am-1pm and 4-8pm.

Corner Bookshop, Via del Moro, 48, Trastevere (tel. 583 69 42). The usual native Anglophone writers and an impressive assemblage of Italian and international authors in translation. Bulletin board displays ads for rooms, cooking classes, aerobics, etc. Open summer Mon.-Sat. 9:30am-1:30pm and 3:30-8pm, Sun. 11am-1:30pm and 4-8pm. In winter, closed Mon. morning.

Bibli, Via dei Fienaroli, 28 (tel./fax 588 40 97; e-mail info@bibli.it), in Trastevere. Turn right on Viale delle Fratte di Trastevere and right again onto Via dei Fienaroli. This cutting-edge bookstore's most useful feature is its Internet access. Establishing an account here allows you to e-mail friends in far-away places and to telnet to your account at home (10hrs., L50,000, valid 3 months; 25hrs., L100,000, valid 6 months). The comfy computer room is complemented by a *sala da tè* and a growing selection of books in English. Open Sept.-July Mon. 5pm-midnight, Tues.-Sun. 11am-midnight; Aug. daily 5pm-midnight.

ENGLISH LIBRARIES

British Council Library, Via delle Quattro Fontane, 20 (tel. 482 66 41 or 47 81 41), between P. Barberini and Via Nazionale. A font of fiction. Films and lectures in winter. Borrowing privileges with membership. Hours fluctuate. Closed Aug. Call ahead.

Centro Studi Americani, Via Michelangelo Caetani, 32 (tel. 68 80 16 13, ask for the library; fax 68 30 72 56), off P. Mattei in a large *palazzo* on the 2nd floor. Borrowing allowed with deposit. One year membership L30,000-70,000. One-time only borrowing L10,000. Open Mon.-Thurs. 10am-6pm, Fri. 10am-2pm.

ENGLISH-LANGUAGE CHURCHES AND CONFESSIONALS

St. Paul's Church (Episcopalian), Via Napoli, 58 (tel. 488 33 39), at Via Nazionale. A Roman exterior done up in stripes of brick. Sunday Eucharist 8:30am; sung Eucharist 10:30am.

All Saints Anglican, Via del Babuino, 153 (tel. 36 00 18 81 or 36 00 21 71). Victorian outside and in. Sat. Holy Communion 6:30pm; Sun. Communion 8:30am; sung Eucharist 10:30am; First Sun. of the month, sung Matins 10:30am; Eucharist 11:30am.

Rome Baptist Church, Piazza di S. Lorenzo in Lucrina, 35 (tel. 687 66 52), off Via del Corso. Sunday service 10am; Bible study 11am.

San Silvestro (Catholic), P. San Silvestro (tel. 679 77 75). Masses in English.

Ponte Sant'Angelo Methodist Church, Piazza Ponte Sant'Angelo (tel. 686 83 14). Sunday service 10:30am; Communion 1st Sunday of the month.

St. Andrew's Church (Presbyterian), Via XX Settembre, 7 (tel. 482 76 27). Sunday service at 11am.

English Language Confessionals: In St. Peter's, Sta. Maria Maggiore, S. Giovanni in Laterano, S. Paolo fuori le Mura, the Gesù, Sta. Maria sopra Minerva, Sant'Anselmo, Sant'Ignazio, and Santa Sabina.

■ Getting Around

BY SUBWAY

The two lines of the subway **(Metropolitana)** intersect at Termini and can be reached by the stairway inside the station, as well as numerous entrances around the station. Entrances to all stations are marked on the street by a white "M" on a red square. **Linea A** runs from Ottaviano, near the Vatican, through P. di Spagna, P. Barberini, P. della Repubblica, and Termini, before heading to Anagnina and intervening stops in the southeastern suburbs of the city. **Linea B** runs from Rebibbia in the northeastern suburbs, through the university area around P. Bologna, to Termini, then on to the Colosseum, Piramide, and Magliana (change here for trains to Ostia and the beach) before terminating at Laurentina in EUR. The subway is fairly safe, but guard your valuables. Many of Rome's sights are a trek from the nearest subway stop, but for covering large distances fast, the subway beats the bus, especially during the day, during protests, and during rush hour. Remember that the subway runs daily only from 5:30am-11:30pm.

Tickets are L1500 and can be bought in newsstands, *tabacchi,* at coin-operated machines, and machines that accept bills in and near the stations. Most stations do not have ticket booths, but most have ticket machines that accept L1000 and L10,000 bills. It is basically impossible to board the subway without a ticket. Trains to Ostia and the Lido beach, as well as many of the outlying suburbs not on the A and B lines, are not part of the subway and may require a separate ticket.

Bus and Subway Passes and Tickets

Bus and subway tickets are one and the same and can be bought at *tabacchi*, newsstands, some bars, and machines located in stations and at major bus stops. Each ticket is valid for either ONE ride on the Metro or for unlimited bus travel for 75 minutes after the first validation. Once you have stamped a ticket for bus travel, you may not use it on the metro. There is a L50,000-100,000 fine for riding without a validated ticket. If you will be in Rome for more than a few weeks, consider purchasing the *abbonamento mensile,* which allows one month (beginning the first of that month) of unlimited transport on the buses and subways for L50,000. Ask for the pass anywhere bus and subway tickets are sold. Student bus passes are cheaper, but are only for Italian students or foreign students at an Italian university who hold a special document from ATAC stating their financial need for such a pass. Non-Italian students can buy the pass and may get by the bus ticket patrol with the student pass, but if the officials are in a bad mood, those carrying the student pass without the proper documentation will have to pay a hefty fine. Weekly bus/metro passes are also available at the *tabacchi* in Termini, as well as select others for L24,000. The BIG daily bus/subway ticket, also on sale at this booth, costs L6000.

BY BUS

> **Note: Rome is currently revamping its transportation system. Some buses listed may no longer exist, while others may simply be on hiatus and new buses may suddenly appear.**

Rome's extensive bus system is a surprisingly efficient means of getting through the city. Though the network of routes may seem daunting at first, the **ATAC** *(Aziende Tramvie Autobus Communali)* intra-city bus company (tel. 469 51) has myriad booths and a friendly staff who can help you find your way. The more independent may want to buy the in-depth Roma Metro-Bus map, published by Lozzi and available at almost all newsstands for L9000. Each bus stop *(fermata)* is marked by yellow signs listing all routes that stop there, key streets/stops on those routes, and routes with nighttime service *(servizio notturno)*. Regular service route numbers are marked by red shields. Some buses run only on weekdays *(feriali)* or weekends *(festivi)*, while others may have different routes, depending on the day of the week. The hours of service vary from route to route, but most begin around 5 or 6am and stop around midnight.

Night routes *(notturno)* are indicated by black shields on the newer signs or by the letter N following the number, or both. The abbreviation *Pass.* on the signs lists the times the bus will pass that stop during the night. You should signal a night bus to stop by standing right under its sign and motioning with your arm. They run infrequently and you may have to transfer several times to get where you want to go. Don't depend too heavily on *notturno* buses, since they are often unreliable.

Tickets for the bus cost L1500. **Board from the back door (not from the middle or front) then immediately stamp the ticket in the orange machine at the back;** the ticket is then good for any number of transfers over the next 75 minutes. If you exceed 75 minutes during your last ride, stamp the other end of the ticket. Tickets are available at newsstands, *tabacchi,* and kiosks throughout the city. Many people take advantage of ATAC's honor system and ride the bus without a validated ticket or bus pass. This is against the law and is inadvisable, since Italian transportation officials board buses at random and check to see that all passengers have a validated ticket or bus pass. If you're found without a ticket, or if your ticket hasn't been validated, you're in trouble. **There is a strictly enforced L50,000-100,000 fine for not carrying a validated ticket or bus pass.** If you don't have the cash on you, the inspectors will take you to a police station until you can arrange to pay. Playing dumb tourist will make things worse. Buy a number of tickets during the day, since they are difficult to come by at night and on weekends. After midnight, ticket salesmen ride the buses and will sell you a ticket on board. The following is a list of useful **bus routes:**

13 (Tram) S. Giovanni in Laterano, Colosseo, Porta S. Paolo, Viale di Trastevere.

19 (Tram) S. Lorenzo area, Villa Borghese, Via Ottaviano and P. Risorgimento (Vatican Museums).

23 S. Paolo Basilica, Porta S. Paolo, Lungotevere to Vatican. Goes down the other side of the river on the way back from the Vatican.

27 Stazione Trastevere, Testaccio, Colosseo, Via Cavour, Termini (note: does not go to Piazza Sonnino in Trastevere)

30/ (Tram) Porta S. Paolo, Colosseo, S. Giovanni, S. Lorenzo, Villa Borghese.

46 near the Vatican, Corso Vittorio Emanuele II, Largo Argentina, Piazza Venezia.

56 Trastevere, Largo Argentina, Piazza Venezia, Via del Corso San Silvestro, P. Barberini, Via Veneto, Villa Ada.

57 Piazzale Ostiense, Via Nazionale, Termini, Villa Ada (service stops at 10pm).

60 Via Nomentana, Via XX Settembre, Piazza Barberini, San Silvestro, Via del Corso, Piazza Venezia, Largo Argentina, Trastevere.

62 Via XX Settembre, Via del Tritone, San Silvestro, Piazza Venezia, Corso Vittorio Emanuele II, Vatican.

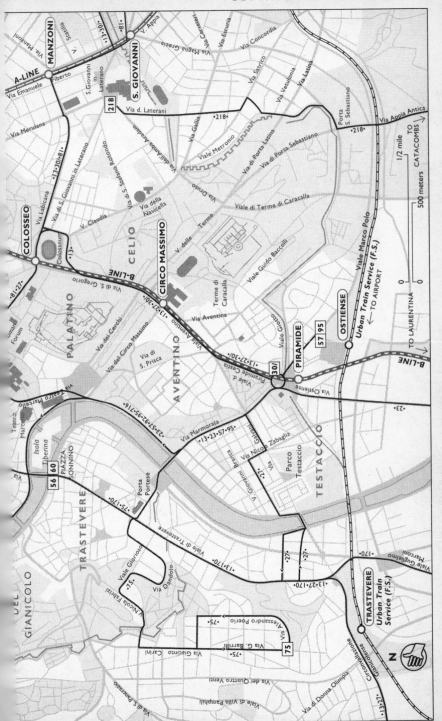

64 Termini, Via Nazionale, Piazza Venezia, Largo Argentina, Corso Vittorio Emanuele II, Vatican (the "wallet-eater"—watch out for pickpockets).

75 Trastevere, Largo Argentina, Piazza Venezia, Via Nazionale, Termini, Piazza Indipendenza.

81 Piazza Malatesta, S. Giovanni, Colosseo, Via Cavour, Via Nazionale, Piazza Venezia, Vatican.

95 Piazzale dei Partigiani, Ostiense, Piazza Venezia, Via del Tritone, Via Veneto.

110 *Giro Turistico* (tour bus; leaves from Termini; L15,000).

119 Mausoleum of Augustus, Pantheon, Piazza di Spagna, Piazza del Popolo, Mausoleum of Augustus.

170 Termini, Via Nazionale, Piazza Venezia, Largo Argentina, Trastevere, S. Paolo Basilica (service ends at 10pm).

492 Tiburtina, Termini, Piazza Barberini, Piazza Venezia, Vatican.

Night *(Notturno)* buses: Be careful at night; bus numbers and routes change, and you must signal a night bus to stop for you. Buses are supposed to come at 30-60 minute intervals but are extremely unreliable. Women waiting at bus stops often endure relentless ride offers and heckling; you may want to take a cab.

20N/21N Piazzale Flaminio, Piazza Cavour (near Vatican), Porta S. Paolo, Colosseo, S. Maria Maggiore, Termini, Piazza Indipendenza, Piazzale Flaminio.

29N/30N Viale Belle Arti, Piazza del Risorgimento, Lungotevere, Porta S. Paolo, Colosseo, San Giovanni, Villa Borghese, Viale Belle Arti.

42N Tiburtina, Termini.

45N Piazza della Rovere (Vatican), Largo Argentina, Piazza Venezia, Piazza San Silvestro.

60N Via Nomentana, Via Veneto, Piazza Venezia, Largo Argentina, Piazza Sonnino (Trastevere).

78N Vatican, Via Flaminia, Piazza Cavour, Corso Rinascimento, Piazza Venezia, Termini.

ATAC also offers a no-frills, three-hour circuit of the city, leaving from P. del Cinquecento (Bus #110, daily at 3:30pm, winter and holidays at 2:30pm; L15,000). They provide a map and some explanation in Italian and quasi-English, whirling you around the city for a comprehensive peek. Otherwise, take plain ol' bus #119 for an orienting glance at some of the city's more visible monuments.

COTRAL bus service between Rome and the province of **Lazio** (tel. 591 55 51) has moved its departure points outside of the city proper to facilitate traffic; you need to take the subway to an outlying area and catch the bus from there. Head to **Anagnina** (last stop on Metro Linea A) for Frascati and the Colli Albani; **Rebibbia** (last stop on Metro Linea B) for Tivoli and Subiaco; **Lepanto** (last stop on Metro Linea A before Ottaviano) for Cerveteri, Tarquinia, Bracciano, Lago Vico, and Civitavecchia. *Let's Go* lists specific transportation information in the Daytrips section. For information, call CTS (tel. 467 91) or any travel agency where English is spoken.

BY TAXI

Taxis are a viable but expensive option. On call 24 hours, they can be flagged down in the streets, but are more easily found at taxi stands. Taxi stands are in Piazza Sonnino on Viale Trastevere (right near the Ponte Garibaldi and next-door to McDonald's), at Piazza Venezia, Piazza della Repubblica, Via Nazionale, Piazza Risorgimento, and at Piazza del Popolo, as well as numerous other places throughout the city. Ride only in yellow or white taxis, and make sure your taxi has a meter; then at least you'll know that you're being robbed legally. Official rates are L4500 for the first 153.8m or 20.6 seconds, then L200 for each successive 153.8m/20.6 seconds. Night surcharge L5000; Sunday surcharge L2000; each suitcase L2000; Fiumicino airport surcharge L11,500-14,000; Ciampino airport surcharge L10,000. Radio taxis (tel. 35 70 or 66 45 or 49 94 or 881 77). Taxis between the city center and the airport cost around L70,000.

BY CAR

To drive in Rome (or in Italy), Americans need to get an International Driver's Permit before leaving the U.S., or an American driver's license that has been officially translated. Those entering Rome by car approach the city center by way of the **Grande Raccordo Anulare (GRA),** the beltway that encircles Rome. You can take any of several exits into the city. If you are coming from the north, enter on **Via Flaminia, Via Salaria,** or **Via Nomentana.** Avoid **Via Cassia** at all costs; the ancient two-chariot lanes can't cope with modern-day traffic. **Via Tiburtina,** to the east, is even worse. Follow the Grande Raccordo around to **Via del Mare** to the south, which connects Rome with **Lido di Ostia.** When leaving the city, don't try to follow the green **Autostrada per Firenze** signs; get on the Grande Raccordo instead and follow it around; it's longer but faster. From the south, **Via del Mare** and **Via Pontina** are the most direct connections from the coastal road from Naples. From the Adriatic coast, take **Via Appia Nuova** or **Via Tuscolana** off the southeastern quadrant of the Raccordo.

We hesitate to comment on the sanity of any traveler wishing to get around Rome by car. But if the aggression of other drivers, the weaving antics of moped maniacs, and the suicide squads of pedestrians don't totally unnerve you, keeping a car in the city does guarantee a high-adrenaline trip. It also assures a high-cost one. Parking is expensive and difficult to find, and if you don't keep your eyes peeled for the little signs, you may drive into a car-free zone and incur a fine. Gas *(benzina)* costs four times as much in Italy as in the U.S. (approximately L1800-1900 per liter). **FINA** gas stations will often accept Visa cards as payment; Exxon, Shell, Mobil, and API will take AmEx. Rental charges are another expense: around L500,000 per week for an economy car with unlimited mileage. Non-residents of Italy are eligible for discounts of up to 60%, usually only by reserving from home. Insurance is required, thereby augmenting the rates by as much as L100,000 a week. Moreover, all agencies require either a credit card or a minimum deposit of L300,000 in cash, and some take only credit cards. You must be over 21 and have a valid International Driver's Permit to rent. An added financial hazard awaits outside the city; if you plan to drive cross-country on major *autostrade,* make sure to budget for extremely expensive tolls. (For instance, Rome-Florence would cost over L20,000.) While cruising the *autostrade,* try to buy gas off the highway in smaller towns, although be aware that smaller stations may not take credit cards. **TCI (Touring Club Italiano),** Via Marsala, 14 (tel. 491 17 41), inside the shopping arcade, sells maps, guides, and books (Italian) for every region of Italy (open Mon.-Fri. 9am-1pm and 4-7pm). There's a branch office at Via Ovidio, 7/A (tel. 687 44 32; open 9am-1pm and 2:30-5:30pm).

If you're still game to rent, Hertz, Maggiore, and Europcar all operate booths on the east side of Termini. You can make arrangements at these booths or at each firm's headquarters in the city, in phone or in person. All firms will let you drop your rental car off in any other Italian city where they have an office (with an additional charge of about L50,000 north of Rome and a monumental L300,000 to the south). English is spoken at all locations.

Maggiore, Main office (tel. 229 15 30), information only; Termini (tel. 488 00 49), open Mon.-Fri. 7am-8pm, Sat. 8am-6pm, Sun. 8:30am-12:30pm; Fiumicino (tel. 65 01 06 78), open Mon.-Sat. 8am-11pm; toll-free national number (167) 86 70 67, open Mon.-Fri. 8:30am-6:30pm, Sat. 9am-1pm.

Hertz, Termini (tel. 47 40 389; fax 47 46 705), open Mon.-Fri. 7am-7pm, Sat. 7am-5pm; Fiumicino (tel. 650 114 48 or 650 115 53), open Mon.-Fri. 7am-midnight, Sat. 7am-11pm.

Europcar, Termini (tel. 488 28 54), open Mon.-Fri. 7am-8pm, Sat. 8am-6pm; Fiumicino (tel. 650 109 77 and 650 010 879), open daily 7am-11pm.

BICYCLES AND MOPEDS

Rome's many hills, cobblestone streets, dense traffic, and lunatic drivers make the city less than ideal for bikes and mopeds. In some areas, however, bikes can be a perfect way to explore the city; bike rides around Rome's parks are a welcome relief from a city of stone. Bicycling down the Appian Way, though quite dangerous, may be the best way to see the many monuments, as well as the long stretches of countryside between them. Bikes generally cost around L5000 per hour or about L15,000 per day, but the length of that "day" varies according to the shop's closing time. In summer, try the unmarked stands at P. di San Lorenzo at Via del Corso or Via di Pontifici at Via del Corso. Both are located near P. di Spagna (open from 10am-1am). Also look for *"noleggio bicicletta"* signs around the city, at P. di Spagna Metro stop, at P. Sidney Sonnino off Viale Trastevere, and in Villa Borghese. While Rome is definitely not the place to take your first moped or scooter ride, moped aficionados can rent mopeds and scooters for between L50,000 and L85,000 a day. You need to be at least 16 years old, but you don't need a driver's license. Take your pick of these zanily titled establishments. **Practice safe cycling and always wear a helmet.**

Rent-a-Scooter, Via F. Turati, 50 (tel. 446 92 92), steps from Termini. "Best prices in Rome:" scooters from L29,000 per day. Also offers scooter tours with native Roman guides. 24-hr. roadside assistance. Open Sun.-Fri. 9am-7pm.

I Bike Rome, Via Veneto, 156 (tel. 322 52 40), which rents from the Villa Borghese's underground parking garage. The subterranean entrance is near the intersection of Via di S. Paolo del Brasile and Via della Magnolie. Bikes L5000 per hour, L13,000 per day, or L38,000 per week. Tandems, too. Mopeds L30,000 per 4hr., and L45,000 all day. Open daily 9am-8pm.

St. Peter Moto, Via di Porto Castello, 43 (tel. 687 49 09), steps east of Castel Sant'Angelo. Mopeds only, L50,000 per day. Open daily 9am-7pm.

Scoot-a-long, Via Cavour, 302-4 (tel. 678 02 06). Motor scooters and Vespas L50,000-80,000 per day. Open daily 9am-8pm.

Scooters for Rent, Via della Purificazione, 84 (tel. 488 54 85), off P. Barberini. Bicycles L15,000 per day, L80,000 per week. Mopeds L50,000 per day. Vespas L60,000 per day. Gas will cost ya. Open Mon.-Sat. 9am-7pm, Sun. 9am-6pm. AmEx, MC, Visa.

BY THUMB

We strongly urge you to consider the risks inherent in hitchhiking. **Let's Go does not recommend hitchhiking as a means of travel, and the information presented below is not intended to do so.**

Many more people hitchhike in Europe than in the U.S., but stop and give it some thought before you decide to do it. Not everyone can fly an airplane, but any bozo can drive a car; hitching means entrusting your life to a random person who decides to stop their car near you on the highway. Don't get in the back of a two-door car, and never let go of your backpack. Don't put anything in the trunk. When you get into a car, make sure you can get out again in a hurry. Couples may avoid hassles with male drivers if the woman sits in the back or next to the door. If you ever feel threatened, experienced hitchers recommend that you insist on being let out immediately, regardless of where you are. If the driver refuses to stop, many people act as though they're going to open the door or vomit on the upholstery.

Those choosing to hitchhike north toward Florence usually take bus #319 to P. Vescovio and #135 onto Via Salaria. They get off at the entrance to the *autostrada;* it's illegal to hitchhike on the highway itself. Those hitching south toward Naples, a dubious proposition in terms of safety and a downright reckless one for women, generally take Metro Linea A to Anagnina (last stop) on Via Tuscolana right at the entrance to the *autostrada*. Hitchers usually check for rideshare offers on bulletin boards at English-language institutes and universities or in publications.

▌Orientation

*The best way to inspect the streets of Rome, if you wish to study as well as
see them, is to break your pocket-compass and burn your maps and
guidebooks ... take Chance for a mentor and lose yourself.*
—George Sala, 1866.

▌AYOUT OF ROME

his *Early History of Rome,* Livy concluded that "the layout of Rome is more like a
quatter's settlement than a properly planned city." Two thousand years of city-plan-
ng later, Rome is still a splendid, unnavigable sea of one-way streets, dead-ends,
andestine *piazze,* incongruous monuments, and incurable traffic. Getting lost is
evitable, but it is also the best way to get to know the city.

No longer defined by the Seven Hills, modern Rome sprawls over a large area
etween the hills of the **Castelli Romani** and the beach at **Ostia.** The major sights,
owever, lie within a much smaller compass. Rome was, until recently, a city built to
e covered on foot. From Termini, the arrival point for most visitors to Rome, the
ittà Universitaria and the student area of **San Lorenzo** are to the east and north-
ast, while to the south are S. Giovanni and the historic Esquiline hill, home to some
f the oldest, biggest, and most beautiful churches in the city. Many of the major tour-
t sights slope down between the hills to the west and southwest toward the Tiber.
ia Nazionale is the central artery connecting Termini with the city center. At one
nd is Piazza della Repubblica; the other end of Via Nazionale is joined by Via IV
ovembre and Via C. Battisti to the immense **Piazza Venezia,** crowned by the con-
picuous white marble pile of the **Vittorio Emanuele II Monument.** From Piazza
enezia, Via dei Fori Imperiale leads southeast to the **Forum** and **Colosseum,** south
f which are the ruins of the **Circus Maximus, the Baths of Caracalla,** and the
ppian Way. Via del Corso** stretches north from Piazza Venezia to **Piazza del
opolo** and the neighboring **Pincio.** East of the Corso, fashionable streets border the
iazza di Spagna** and, beyond that, the lush **Villa Borghese.** South and east are the
revi Fountain, Piazza Barberini,** and the churches of the Quirinal hill. From Piazza
enezia to the west, **Largo Argentina** marks the start of the Corso Vittorio Emanuele,
/hich leads into the *centro storico,* the medieval and Renaissance tangle of alleys,
owers, churches, and fountains around the **Pantheon, Piazza Navona, Campo de'
iori,** and **Piazza Farnese,** before crossing the Tiber to gargantuan **Castel
ant'Angelo** and the **Vatican City.** Also across the Tiber from the *centro storico* is
ne **Trastevere** quarter, home to countless *trattorie* and the best streets for wander-
ng. Back across the Tiber from Trastevere, via the Tiber Island, is the old **Jewish
Ghetto.** To the south of the Ghetto and the Ancient City are the peaceful **Aventine
Hill,** crowned with rose gardens and churches, and the earthy, working-class **Testac-
io** district.

▌OURS

ome's greatest treasures often lie hidden in the perplexingly tangled web of streets:
he Pantheon emerges quite suddenly as you weave your way through narrow, cob-
le-stoned streets and Bramante's Tempietto sits in the small courtyard of a lonely
hurch. On your first morning in Rome, consider hopping on bus #110, *Giro Turis-
ico,* which leaves from Termini, for a whirlwind peek and an orientation tour of the
istorical center (L15,000). If you're staying in Rome for an extended period of time,
reate your own tour on foot. Though it might be more fun to figure out Rome for
ourself, older travelers or those on a very tight schedule may opt for a guided tour
n an air-conditioned bus for the easiest and most convenient way to visit the city's
rincipal sights.

Carrani Tours, Via V.E. Orlando, 95 (tel. 474 25 01). Eleven different bus tours of
Rome and environs (some including meals, admission to sights, or even audience

with or blessing by the Pope) range from L43,000 for a simple 3-hr. tour to L95,000 for a nighttime tour complete with strolling musicians.

Walk Thru the Centuries, Via Silla, 10 (tel. 323 17 33), near the Ottaviano stop on Metro Linea A. Offers two tours: the first covers the essentials of the Historic Center (the Colosseum, Campidoglio, Trevi Fountain, Pantheon, Piazza Navona, and more); the second visits the Vatican Museums (3-hr. tours given daily, often twice daily in summer, L25,000, plus L10,000 for admission on the Vatican tour). Tour can be booked at the office or at Pensione Sandy, Pensione Ottaviano, Pensione Fawlty Towers, or the Enjoy Rome tourist office. Open Mon.-Fri. 9am-1:30pm and 2:30-5:30pm, Sat. 8:30am-1:30pm.

Appian Line, P. dell'Esquilino, 6/7 (tel. 488 41 51). Offers 13 different tours of the city (also including meals, admission to sights, or Papal encounters) from L30,000 for a simple tour to L85,000 for the strolling accordions.

American Express, P. di Spagna, 38 (tel. 676 41), offers a series of bus and walking tours daily (except Sundays and holidays in winter), at 9:30am and 2:30pm (L53,000-63,000 including various admission fees to museums and sights). Open Mon.-Fri. 9am-5:30pm, Sat. 9am-12:30pm.

Enjoy Rome, Via Varese, 39 (tel. 445 18 43), now offers daily walking tours, led by an American archaeologist living in Rome. The tours last 3 hours and cost L23,000. Make reservations for the tours at Enjoy Rome or at Pensione Fawlty Towers, Pensione Ottaviano, or Hotel Sandy.

ATAC offers a no-frills quickie tour (see p. 84).

Secret Walks in Rome (tel. 39 72 87 28) is a new tour company that organizes 1½ hr. strolls through the oft-overlooked alleys of the city. English-speaking guides (better known as "storytellers"), many of them English and American expatriates, give tours such as *The Talking Statues of Rome, The Poets of Trastevere, Domes and Other Hidden Treasures,* and *The Devil and the Holy Water.* They also offer Sunday bike and moped tours of the city and moped tours of its outskirts. Call in advance for the upcoming week's schedule and the appointed meeting places.

■ Keeping in Touch

MAIL

Although the postal system in Italy has justly drawn snickers from the rest of Western Europe, things may be changing. New EU standards may have whipped the *posta* into shape, at least temporarily. Aerograms and airmail letters from Italy take anywhere from one to three weeks to arrive in the U.S., while surface mail—much less expensive—takes a month or longer. Letters and small parcels rarely get lost if sent *raccomandata* (registered), *espresso* (express), or *via aerea* (air mail); they won't necessarily get there any faster, though. Stamps *(francobolli)* are available at face value in *tabacchi* (tobacco shops), but you might want to mail your letters from a post office to be sure they are stamped correctly, since tobacco shop owners may not give you the proper stamp amounts. Overseas letters and postcards are L1250. Letters and postcards within the EU are L750; outside of the EU (but not overseas), L850. Keep in mind that postcards, even with air mail postage affixed, may be sent by boat; don't send important messages by postcard.

Make sure anyone sending you mail in Rome from North America plans on its taking at least two weeks to reach you. Mail from home can be sent to a hotel where you have reservations, but let the proprietor know that you will be expecting mail. The **American Express** office will hold mail up to 30 days for American Express card or traveler's check holders. Have the sender write "client mail" on the envelope with the office's complete address, and with the last name spelled in capital letters and underlined, for example, Leo <u>PIANTES</u>; American Express; Piazza di Spagna, 38; 00187 Roma. Letters addressed to the post office with your name and the phrase **Fermo Posta** (General Delivery) will be held at the post office of any city or town for pick-up. Letters to Rome should look like this: Ali <u>ORDOÑEZ</u>; Fermo Posta; P. San Silvestro, 19; 00187 Roma. You must claim your mail in person with your passport as identification. You may have to pay L300 per piece of mail. In major cities like Rome, the post office handling *Fermo Posta* is usually efficient and open long hours, though they close at noon on Saturday, all day Sunday, and the last day of every month.

Rome's **main post office** is located at the P. San Silvestro, 19, 00187 Roma, south of Piazza di Spagna and accessible by the #56, 60, 71, and 492 buses (open Mon.-Fri. 9am-6pm, Sat. 9am-2pm). Stamps are at booths #23-25, *Fermo Posta* at booth #72. Currency exchange (no checks) is at booths #25-28. Other post offices are scattered throughout the city; some have hours similar to the San Silvestro office, but many are open only in morning. Like all Italian bureaucratic institutions, almost all post offices have ridiculously long lines and a generally chaotic atmosphere.

If you need to get something to or from Italy with celerity, **DHL** operates in Italy, as do several Italian competitors. DHL shipments from North America to anywhere in Italy are guaranteed to arrive within 48 hours; shipments (up to 500g) from Italy are guaranteed anywhere in the world within two days. The cost from the U.S. to Italy for under 220g of documents is about US$30; shipping anything but documents usually involves filling out a commercial invoice. Contact DHL for more information:

DHL in Rome is located at Via Carlo Botta, 41 (tel. 79 08 21), southwest of Termini, between Piazza Vittorio Emanuele II and the Parco Oppio (Parco Traiano). (Open Mon.-Fri. 9am-6:30pm.) In the U.S. and Canada, tel. (800) 225-5345; regional offices in London, tel. (181) 890 93 93; Sydney, tel. (2) 317 83 00; Dublin, tel. (353) 1 844 41 11; Johannesburg, tel. (11) 921 3600.

The post office at S. Silvestro also offers **CAI Post,** a service similar to Federal Express except that it's owned by the public post system. Prices are expensive (about US$30 for parcels up to 500g sent to the U.S.), but they also guarantee two-to-four day service and mail packages up to 20kg. It is located at booth #10 to the right after you enter.

Parcels, unsealed packages under 1kg (500g for Australia), may be mailed from San Silvestro (see CAI Post, above); otherwise they must be mailed from **P. de Caprettari, 69,** near the Pantheon (tel. 68 80 59 01; open Mon.-Fri. 9am-6pm, Sat. 9am-2pm). Packages must be under 20kg and 200cm (length, width, and height), and should wrapped in brown paper, tied with a single string, and the string should be held together by a tiny little weight at the end of it. Postal workers will put these weights on for you if you don't know how, but you'll have to pay for them. There are also boxes for sale in a variety of sizes that they'll help you package correctly. Another parcel office is at **Via Terme di Diocleziano** (entrance on Via Viminale near P. della Repubblica; open Mon.-Fri. 9am-6pm, Sat. 9am-2pm).

The **Vatican** runs its own postal system which some say is more efficient and reliable, with the same prices. You must use Vatican postage. See p. 216 for more details. The generic **postal code** for Rome is 00100; specific codes are elaborations on the 00101, 00102 theme. For *Fermo Posta* at S. Silvestro Post Office and at American Express, the code is 00187.

TELEPHONES

Telephone codes:
Rome's city code: (06) within Italy; (6) from elsewhere
Italy's country code: (39)

Directory Assistance:
for Italy: 12 (*servizio dodici;* free)
for Europe and the Mediterranean: 176 (L1200)
Intercontinental: 17 90 (L1200)

Italian phone numbers range from two to eight digits in length. *Let's Go* makes every effort to get up-to-date and correct numbers, but even the Pope is at the mercy of the

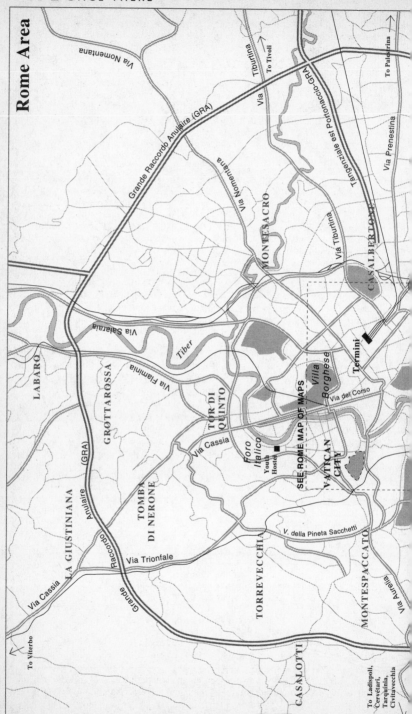

Rome Area

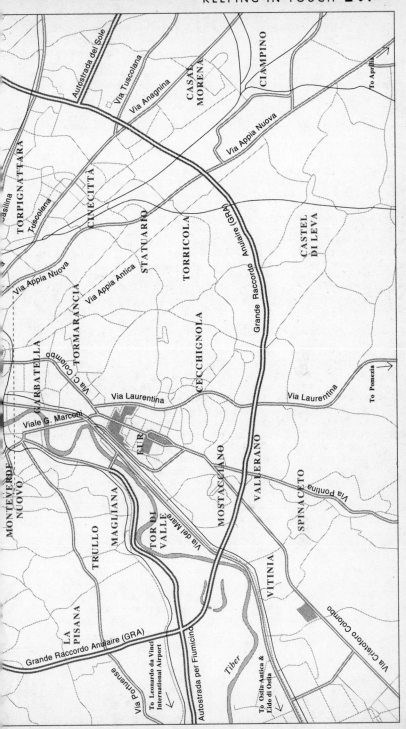

Italian phone system. Rome is in the process of unifying all phone numbers to seven or eight digits, so numbers are changing more frequently than usual. If you call an old number, you may hear a recording of the new number in Italian, possibly followed by an English recap or a message telling you the number is *"inesistente"* (non-existant). Phone books often list two numbers: the first is the number at the time of printing; the second (marked by the word *prenderà*) is what the number will be at some future, unspecified time. For **directory assistance** (in Italian, of course), dial 12. Insert L200 if you are calling from a pay phone, which will be returned when you complete your call. A number beginning with 167 is *numero verde*, or **toll-free.**

Types of Phones

There are several types of **telephones** in Italy: coin phones, card phones, and metered phones *(telefoni a scatti).* There are also combination coin-and-card phones, which, of course, accept both coins and cards. **Coin phones** accept L50, L100, L200, and L500 coins. Local calls in Rome cost L200, allowing you to talk for varying amounts of time depending on the time of day. You will not be warned that your time is running out, although you may hear a beep or a click right before you are cut off. You can make long-distance calls with coins, but be forewarned that it will take a lot of coins. Once upon a time in Italy there were phones that took only *gettoni,* tokens that are the same shape and color as L200 coins. You will probably not find a *gettoni*-only phone in Rome, but you may encounter *gettoni,* which are no longer accepted as currency.

For all kinds of calls, including long-distance and overseas calls, we suggest using a **phone card.** Phone cards are available in denominations of L5000, L10,000, and L15,000 and are sold at *tabacchi,* newsstands, bars, and post offices. You can also buy them from the occasional machine (usually in train stations and Metro stations) and from the TELECOM office. L15,000 cards are often available at post offices. Ask for *"una scheda* (or *una carta) telefonica da x lire."* You must first break off the perforated right corner of the card and then insert that end into the phone. The amount of money on the card will appear on the display. As you talk, you can watch the numbers get smaller and smaller. If you run out in the middle of a call, you can usually feed another card into the phone. Partially used cards may be removed and used again. Telephone cards can be used to call anywhere, even internationally, though a L10,000 card will only give you about three minutes with your parents or significant other in the States. Recently, Ameretel cards of L20,000-40,000 were made available for especially long calls. Buy them at the *tabacchi* in Termini that advertise them.

Scatti (metered) calls are made from a phone run by an operator, who may simply be the proprietor in a bar. According to TELECOM, there are only two in the city of Rome, both at the TELECOM office (see Phone Offices, p. 93). Small towns usually have at least one bar with a *telefono a scatti,* which can be used for international calls. A meter, called a *contascatti,* records the cost of your call, and you pay when you finish. Check with the operator before you lift the receiver, and remember that he or she may tack on a substantial service fee.

Dialing Instructions and Rates

From Italy

International calls from Italy can be made easily from phone card pay phones. In Rome, you should never have to speak to an Italian operator or go to the telephone office. However, if you plan on having a long conversation, don't have a calling card, or simply don't want to feed card after card into the phone, you can also make international calls from Telecom (see Phone Offices, p. 93).

To dial direct internationally, dial **two zeros** and then the **country code** (U.S. and Canada 1, United Kingdom 44, Ireland 353, Australia 61, New Zealand 64, South Africa 27), followed by the area/city code and number. If you normally dial a zero before a long-distance call within your own country, do not do so when calling to your home country from Italy. For example, to call the Italian Embassy in New York from Rome dial (00)-(1)-(212)-737-9100. To call the Italian Embassy in London from Rome dial (00)-(44)-(171)-312 22 00 (no zero before the city code!).

Miraculously enough, rates have actually dropped lately for international calls from Italy. At their most expensive, rates to the U.S. are L2127 for the first minute and L1675 for each minute thereafter. To Australia, New Zealand, and South Africa they're higher and to the UK and Ireland a bit lower. Rates are highest on weekdays 8am-7pm, decrease after 7pm on weekdays and Saturdays from 1 to 10pm. They're at their lowest 11pm-8am, on holidays, and between 2:30pm on Saturday and 8am on Monday.

By far the simplest way to call home to the U.S. is to use the **AT&T Direct** or **MCI World Phone;** dialing a single number will connect you to an overseas, English-speaking operator who will then put through your collect call or calling card call for you. In Italy, you must deposit L200 or insert a phone card when calling the American operator from a pay phone. The money or card will be returned to you when you hang up. Many hotels have managed to block access to the AT&T and MCI numbers, in spite of the fact that it is illegal to do so, so a pay phone is often your best bet. Rome does not yet have touch-tone service compatible with that of the U.S., so don't try to punch in the number you're calling or your card number—you'll have to speak to the helpful operators. When calling the U.S. from Italy, you should be able to reach an **AT&T** operator by dialing **172-1011** or an **MCI** operator with **172-1022.** The **Sprint Express Direct Service** number is **172-1877; Australiadirect** is **172-1061,** and **British Telecom's** direct number is **172-0044.** To reach Canada easily, call **Canada Direct** at **172-1001.** Consider getting a calling card if you plan to make a lot of international calls; although the initial hook-up charge is steep, the cost overall is significantly lower.

There are several ways to make a **collect call.** You can speak to the **Italian operator;** the word for collect call is *contassa a carico del destinatario* or *chiamata collect.* The **English-speaking operator in Italy** can put through collect calls and can be reached by dialing 170. The most reliable and simplest way to call collect to the U.S., however, is with the **AT&T USA Direct** operator. Dial the access number above and ask to make a collect call.

To Italy

Calls to Italy from other countries must be preceded by the international code which enables you to dial out of the country **(011 in the U.S.),** Italy's country code **(39)** and then the city code **(6 for Rome).** When direct-dialing, the zero should be dropped from the beginning of each city code, so, for instance, a call to Rome from the U.S. should begin: 011-39-6 and end with the actual phone number of the establishment.

Within Italy

All long distance calls **within Italy** are preceded by a (0), then the city code. The city code for Rome is (6). To call Rome from elsewhere in Italy, dial (06) then the number as listed in the book. To call Rome while in Rome, do not dial (0) or the city code (6). Dial only the number as listed.

Phone Offices

IRETEL, SIP, and all the other phone companies have been absorbed by the predictably-named übercompany, TELECOM, though traces of SIP still linger throughout the city. Avoid dealing with the Italian telephone bureaucracy by getting a calling card before you leave home or by using magnetic phone cards.

TELECOM, in the main gallery of Termini (this office formerly IRETEL), has two metered phones, apparently the only two in the city. Tell the manager you want to call, dial direct, and pay in full afterwards. The office is open 8am-9:45pm.

TELEGRAMS

The surest way to get an important message across the ocean is by wire service. **Telegrams** are sent from the post office and cost L1000 per word, including the address. They ask for the telephone number of the addressee. In Rome, telegrams can be sent from the post office at P. San Silvestro, at booths #73-76. At night, use the Telegraph Office (P. San Silvestro, 18, next door to the post office) for sending telegrams (open whenever the post office is closed).

FAX

Fax service is more and more common in Rome, at *tabacchi* and photocopy/lamination shops. Also try **Mailboxes, Etc.,** Via dei Mille, 36/38/40 (tel. 446 13 38).

E-MAIL

Access to the Internet is not as difficult to find as one might expect from a city where answering machines are still only slowly beginning to catch on. A few cyber-cafés have begun sprung up around the city, providing those planning an extended visit to the city with an economical (and oh-so- hip) option for keeping in touch with friends and family at home. For a listing of one such café, see Bibli, p. 79.

■ When in Rome ...

No book could possibly list all of the cultural differences that are peculiar to Italy and Rome. We hope, however, that the following tips can save the serious tourist from confusion, frustration, and embarrassment.

Hours

Although the locals seem to approve of them, Roman **business hours,** or lack thereof, can cause problems for tourists. Schedules and timetables are unreliable. Though shop owners usually set their own hours, most **shops** are open in the morning from 8 or 9am to 1pm and again in the afternoon from 4-8pm or so (3:30-7:30pm in the winter). A few stores stay open during the lunch break, *all'americana*. Most shops, businesses, and some *caffè* shut down on Sundays and Monday morning, though restaurants, tourist organizations, some department stores, supermarkets, and nearly everything on Via del Corso remain open for business. In the summer, some shops may also close on Saturday afternoon. Don't forget that **food shops** (*alimentari*) are usually closed on Thursday afternoons. **Churches and museums** keep similar hours though schedules vary from place to place. The seven major basilicas (S. Pietro, S. Maria Maggiore, S. Giovanni in Laterano, S. Paolo fuori le Mura, S. Croce in Gerusalemme, S. Lorenzo fuori le Mura, S. Agnese fuori le Mura) are open all day, though, usually 7am-7pm. Also open all day are some of the ancient monuments, including the Forum and the Colosseum. **Banks** are the worst of all, open in the morning from about 8:45am-1:45pm and then again for an hour in the afternoon. Local post offices keep similar hours, though the main post offices at Piazza San Silvestro and on Via Marmorata stay open all day.

Floors

Europeans count **floors** differently than Americans. What an American would call the first floor (the one on street level) is called in Italian *piano terra,* and usually abbreviated with a "T" on an elevator. The first floor, *primo piano,* is one flight up, what an American would call the second floor. When you take an elevator from your *pensione* and you want to go outside, press T, not 1.

Bus Etiquette

Unless you are a pass holder, you have to get on the bus through the rear door. The middle doors are for getting off only. If you are a young person, you are obliged to give your seat to elderly people and middle-aged women who don't look particularly elderly. People on the bus like to prepare for their descent several stops in advance and if you are standing near the central doors, you will be asked repeatedly *"Scende (la prossima)?"* which means "Are you getting off at the next stop?" Answer appropriately.

Cashiers at the STANDA

You may notice that Italians never seem to have change; even at the STANDA, the cashiers will often ask you if you have coins to cover the hundreds of lire of your total (*Ce l'hai due cento?*), claiming that they have no coins themselves.

Ferragosto

Rome shuts down at the beginning of August, and by *Ferragosto* (Aug. 15), the big Italian summer holiday, you'll be hard-pressed to find a single Roman in the city. Though museums and sights remain open, most offices and restaurants close down completely. You won't starve during this period; a humanitarian law bars bread shops from closing down for more than one day at a time. *La Repubblica* and *Il Messaggero* newspapers each publish daily lists of open pharmacies, *alimentari,* and other essential services. Closed pharmacies usually display a list of open ones.

Church Etiquette

It's not nice to walk into a church in the middle of mass unless you intend to participate. Refrain from speaking loudly, walking directly in front of the altar, and taking flash photographs. While some churches strictly adhere to established dress codes (no shorts, short skirts, bare midriffs, or tank tops), others may not be so adamant. Even in the latter case, however, the usual grubby, cut-off gear sported by tourists will probably attract many disapproving stares from church-going Italians.

Let's Go Picks

Even though Rome is jam-packed with amazing things to see, eat, and drink, we've managed to compile a shortened list of some of our favorite places to visit. Naturally, this list is purely subjective, and we would love to hear about some of your faves for next year's list. Send us a postcard and fill us in.

Best Accomodations: Pensione Papa Germano, Mama, Papa, and the *bambini's* cheerful *pensione* not far from the station. **Pensione Fawlty Towers,** a hip backpacker's paradise with all the fixings. **Hotel Kennedy,** a funky place with more perks than seem imaginable. **Pensione Sandy,** hostel-style beds and prices without the institutional feel. **Hotel San Paolo,** a bright, happy *pensione* decorated with huge puzzles. **Youth Hostel Roma Inn Keiko,** a cozy new hostel-style accommodation with rock-bottom prices. **Hotel Mimosa,** a homey, family-run place decorated with puppy wall-calendars. **Pensione Ottaviano,** another great hostel-style accomodation, this time in the otherwise pricey neighborhood near the Vatican.

Best Restaurants: Pizzeria Baffetto, Pizzeria al Leoncino, and **l'Archetto,** *pizzeria* fare to make your mouth water in anticipation. **Palladini,** lunch-time sandwich place where you choose the fillings. **Margarita,** hidden little lunch-joint with a hand-written menu that changes daily. **Hostaria Grappolo d'Oro, Al Piccolo Arancio,** and **Taverna dei Quaranta,** some of the best of traditional and typically Roman cuisine. **L'Insalata Ricca** and **Il Pulcino Ballerino,** Italian food with a twist; many unexpected concoctions.

Researchers' Favorites: Church of Santa Cecilia and **Church of San Nicola in Carcere,** two churches whose foundations were laid over underground ruins; the ruins have now been excavated and can be visited. **Porta Portese,** an immense flea-market where you can find anything from coffee-makers to clothes. **Gianicolo,** a park near the Vatican with one of the city's greatest views. **Capuchin Crypt,** four chapels decorated with the bones of 4000 Capuchin Friars. **Onda Blu,** a laundromat and so much more; a more active nightlife than many Roman discos.

Accommodations

In July and August, Rome swells with tourists. A great number of rooms meet the high demand for lodging, but quality varies significantly, and hotel prices in Rome are quite often astronomical. Although reservations help, they do not always guarantee that a room awaits you for the full length of your intended stay, or at the decided price, since large groups frequently take precedence over a reserved double in some proprietors' minds. Prices vary substantially with the time of year, and a proprietor's willingness to bargain increases in proportion to the length of your stay, the number of vacancies, and the size of your group. Settle the price before you commit. Knowing a few key words in Italian can greatly ease communication gaps and make your stay more pleasant (see Phrases, p. 284).

A provincial board inspects, classifies, and registers all hotels on a five-star system. An official rate card is then put on the inside of the door of each room. No hotel can legally charge more than the maximum permitted by the inspector, but some proprietors double their prices at the sound of a foreign voice. Under this system, it is not likely that you will really get ripped off by checking into the first place you find, nor will you find an unusual bargain by shopping around for hours. Differences between hotels of the same class are largely a matter of location and character, rather than price or facilities. In general, the more charming places are near the historic center, while cheaper, less attractive joints lie near Termini.

Rates tend to be lower per person in a shared room, and so it may be less expensive for you to share a triple with two friends than to get a single on your own. A single is a *camera singola;* a double with separate beds is called a *camera doppia* and a double with one big bed is *matrimoniale.* Rooms in most economical accommodations do not have private baths, showers, or other bathroom equipment; in order to have these amenities in your room, you must often pay as much as L20,000 extra. Sometimes, even when there are communal facilities, you will have to pay for a shower. Many rooms, however, have sinks and bidets—good for chilling wine, washing clothes, and soaking tired feet. Beware of other hidden costs. A breakfast of dry bread and cold coffee can hike up the price of a room L10,000 or more. Some places offer only full pension *(pensione completa),* which includes room and board (3 meals per day), or half-pension *(mezza pensione),* which includes room, breakfast, and one other meal. This is rare in Rome, but more common in summertime resorts and countryside getaways.

Italian law establishes high and low seasons for areas popular with tourists. Rome's low-season runs October through April, though special occasions like Easter send prices rising. Those without reservations should start looking for a room in the morning or call a day in advance during high season. **Always insist on seeing a room first,** though some proprietors will not be amenable. Check the mattresses, the bathroom, and the water pressure. It is crucial to check the security; test the locks (make sure your room key doesn't open any other rooms). Ask about the curfew or when the front door locks, check how accessible room-keys are to other guests and passers-by, and find out whether someone guards the front desk at all times. Inquire about additional costs. Keep in mind that heating is a relatively new convenience in some parts of Italy, and even if an establishment does have heating, it will probably take advantage of this good fortune only sparingly. Bring warm clothes, if only for sleeping, and ask for extra blankets at the desk.

Many hotels accept phone reservations several days or weeks in advance. English may not be spoken at some smaller places, but this shouldn't dissuade a non-Italian-speaker from calling. Most *pensione* proprietors are used to receiving calls from non-Italian-speakers; phrases helpful for making a room reservation in Italian are included in the appendix (see page 284). If the hotel or *pensione* where you wish to reserve a room asks for a deposit, it is best to send a bank draft. If you do make reservations, though, you probably won't be able to get your deposit back if you have to cancel. It is poor traveling etiquette to fail to cancel a reservation if you change your plans; the hotel proprietor will be turning away other wearied souls who are willing to pay for a spot you're not intending to use. If you plan to arrive late, call and ask a hotel to hold a room for you.

When you check into a hotel or *pensione*, the proprietor will ask for your passport so that you can be registered with the police, as required by Italian law. They should only need it for a few hours—don't forget to retrieve it. According to Italian law, you are not allowed to have unregistered visitors in your room, so don't be surprised or upset if the proprietor won't let you invite your new Italian friend in for a nightcap. Though the law is rarely enforced, it is also illegal to hang laundry out the window or on a balcony.

The **tourist offices** in Rome will scrounge (sometimes reluctantly, in peak season) to find you a room. They offer a list of hotels and their prices and they quote rates over the phone. They can also provide a booklet of the current official prices for all of the hotels and *pensioni* in Rome. The **Enjoy Rome** agency (p. 73) will be both helpful and informative all the time; the **Centro Turistico Studentesco e Giovanile (CTS)** will also be of some help. **Associazione Cattolica Internazionale al Servizio della Giovane** (p. 53) assists women 25 years old or younger in finding convent accommodations and moderately priced rooms during brief visits to Rome.

Termini is full of officials swarming around to find you a place. Many of them are the real thing and have photo IDs issued by the tourist office. Some sneaky imposters, however, issue themselves fake badges and cards and they will likely direct you to a rundown location charging significantly more than the going rate. Ask the officials for maps and directions, but exercise caution.

If the line at the tourist office extends to infinity, check your bags at the station and investigate nearby *pensioni*. It's usually not hard to find a place; several establishments often operate in a single building. There are over 300 *pensioni* in Rome with prices comparable to those listed here. During peak season, some hotels will try to charge more than the official prices and will automatically tell the tourist office they are full. For help, you may do better going to Enjoy Rome, one of the most useful tourist offices around, or consider calling and bargaining on your own.

It is illegal and ill-advised to "camp out" in the public places of Rome. Though violent crime is infrequent, dozing tourists invite trouble. If you must, sleep in groups with designated sentry watches in Termini. Check your bags at the station's luggage storage room or risk serious material loss; Rome's best pickpockets hang out at Termini, waiting to prey on tired tourists. Women, whether alone or in a group, should never sleep outdoors. It is also a good idea to be careful even at designated campgrounds.

HOTELS AND PENSIONI (BY LOCATION)

Most of the following listings do **not** accept credit cards, unless explicitly stated. Expect **price increases** of around 10% for the summer of 1997. When **calling Italy** remember that Italy's country code is (39) and Rome's city code is (6). Please refer to Dialing Instructions and Rates, page 92, for more information.

■ Near Termini Station

NORTH OF TERMINI

There are clusters of clean, reasonably priced *pensioni* and hotels awaiting the weary traveler within five to 15 minutes of Termini. Although once somewhat run-down, this area has recently experienced a renaissance of sorts, making it a trendy haven for budget travelers, cheaper than the historic center to the west and safer than the sometimes seedy Esquiline area south of Termini. All that remains of what used to be

a red-light district are the struggling porn theaters in P. della Repubblica and the occasional, unobtrusive prostitute by the Diocletian baths. There are lots of travelers looking for budget accommodations in summer, so it pays to book a room at least a few
days in advance. The area is reasonably easy to navigate, with a more grid-like organization than you'll find in the older parts of the city. Keep in mind, however, that
street names here change at many major intersections, and even at some minor intersections.

Inside the station, with the trains behind you, exit the station to the right, near
Track 1. You will now be on Via Marsala. If you're already outside the station, look for
the big blue BNL (Banco Nazionale del Lavoro) sign atop a large building. Use this
building to find north/northeast and Via Marsala. Piazza dell'Indipendenza is another
important landmark; from the intersection of Via Marsala and Via Solferino, follow Via
Solferino northeast for one block to arrive at P. dell'Indipendenza. Continue in this
direction through the *piazza* and you'll soon come to Via Palestro, home to many a
pensione. There are plenty of small **Alimentari** along Via Marghera and Via Marsala
(also see Markets, p. 134). A convenient laundromat, **Ondablu** (open daily 8am-
10pm), at Via Milazzo, 8, equipped with English instructions, will enable you to have
6kg of your smelly apparel washed and dried for L12,000.

Pensione Papa Germano, Via Calatafimi, 14A (tel. 48 69 19). With the trains
behind you, exit the station to your right and turn left on Via Marsala, which
shortly becomes Via Volturno; Via Calatafimi will be on your right. Though their
last name might indicate otherwise, Papà Gino and Mamma Pina run this place
with pure Italian charm. Deservedly popular with backpackers and students. Reservations are encouraged during summer. Gino speaks English and will help you find
a place if he's booked. He may also helpfully try to match lone travelers with others
to fill a room. Cheerful flowered walls and bedspreads. No curfew. Check-out
11am. Singles L35,000. Doubles L60,000, with bath L80,000. Triples L75,000, with
bath L90,000. Quads L25,000 per person. 10% reduction Nov.-March. MC, Visa,
AmEx, Eurocard.

Pensione Fawlty Towers (formerly Il Nido), Via Magenta, 39 (tel. 445 03 74). Exit
Termini to the right and cross Via Marsala to Via Marghera. Head up Via Marghera
and turn right on Via Magenta. Look for the yellow sign. Despite the images the
name might conjure up for those who don't catch the reference (to a British sit-
com), there is nothing amiss about this meticulously maintained dormitory-style
pensione. The owners and staff are all English-speakers and are eager to befriend
guests. They will provide all sorts of valuable tourist information so that you may
Enjoy Rome. The communal veranda and terrace are so peacefully detached from
the chaos of Roman life that you might forget you're only a block away from Termini. A comfortable common room equipped with satellite TV, communal fridge,
and travel guides is conducive to meeting other travelers. No curfew; night keys
available. Singles L45,000, with shower L65,000. Doubles L70,000, with shower
L85,000, with full bath L95,000. Triples with shower L90,000, with full bath
L105,000. Co-ed dormitory-style quads L25,000 per person.

Hotel Virginia, Via Montebello, 94 (tel. 488 17 86). Exit Termini to the east (right)
onto Via Marsala, turn left and follow the street until it turns into Via Volturno. Via
Montebello will be on your right. The rooms have a unique and varying decor,
ranging from pink satiny sheets and lacy white curtains to a large portrait of Christ
painted onto the wall above the bed. The fourth floor houses only new, spacious
rooms. Singles L35,000, with shower L40,000. Doubles with shower L50,000-
65,000, with full bath L60,000-80,000. Triples L60,000, with shower L60,000-
75,000. Quads L20,000 per person. Prices vary depending on the season. Breakfast
L1400.

Pensione Tizi, Via Collina, 48 (tel. 48 20 128; fax 47 43 266). A 15-min. walk from
the station. Take Via Goito from P. dell'Indipendenza, cross via XX Settembre onto
Via Piave, then take the first left onto Via Flavia, which leads to Via Collina. In a
safer location than many other accommodations around Termini, this family pensione has welcomed students for years. The rooms are new with marble floors and
rosy wallpaper with pinks and grays. Pristine conditions. Check-out 11am. Singles

ACCOMMODATIONS

Termini & San Lorenzo

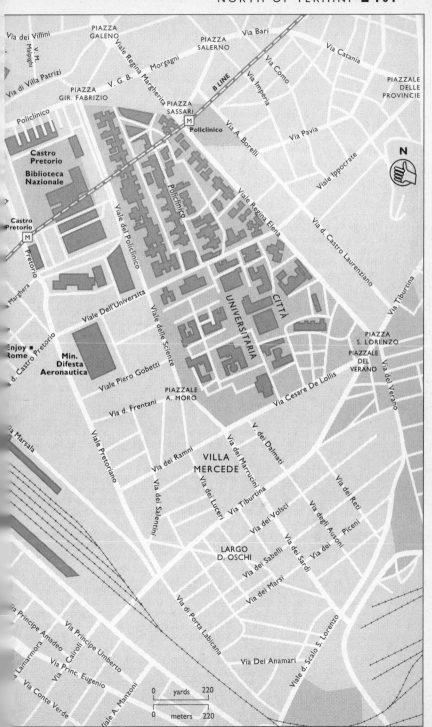

L45,000. Doubles L65,000, with bath L80,000. Triples and quads L30,000 per person, with bath L35,000 per person. Breakfast L7000.

Hotel Matilde, Via Villafranca, 20 (tel. 445 43 65; fax 446 23 68; e-mail hmatilde@mbox.vol.it), off Via S. Martino della Battaglia (what Via Solferino becomes when it crosses P. Indipendenza). Opened by the Riccioni brothers of Hotel Jonella, this establishment is decorated with frescoes and has a safe in every one of its spotless rooms. The decor has seen its day, but the red carpet and the roomy quarters make up for it. They'll help find restaurants, nightlife, and even discounts for parking. Reception open until midnight. Check-out 10am. No curfew. Singles L60,000. Doubles L90,000. Triples L120,000. Quads L140,000. One large room even has space for five. AmEx, Visa, MC.

Pensione Piave, Via Piave, 14 (tel. 474 34 47; fax 487 33 60). Off Via XX Settembre. A step up from the garden variety budget accommodation, and worth the extra *lire.* All rooms have private bath, telephone, and carpeted floors. The singles have double beds and one room even has a little fireplace. English spoken. Check-in at noon. Check-out at 10:30am, but luggage can be left all day. No curfew. Singles L45,000. Doubles with bath L80,000. Triples with bath L95,000. Quads (upon request) with bath L125,000. Washer and dryer available for an extra L15,000-20,000. Personal checks accepted.

Pensione Alessandro, Via Vicenza, 42 (tel. 446 19 58). Across the street from a *pizzeria rustica,* near the corner with Via Palestro. There are 85 beds in all, mostly in the form of bunks, 2, 3, and 4 to a large room. A full-size picture of the Pink Panther greets you as you enter, while other paintings of subjects ranging from cacti to nude women adorn the white walls. The owner, Alessandro, will provide tourist and nightlife information and a nice chat (in English). The low prices make this *pensione* a backpacker's mecca. Coffee and biscuits provided all day. Kitchen with microwave available. No curfew. Reception open 6:30am-11pm. Check-out by 9am. Lock-out noon-3pm. May 1-Sep.31 L25,000 per person. Oct.1-Apr.31 L20,000 per person.

M&J Place, Via Solferino, 9 (tel. 44 62 802). A prime location just off of Via Marsala, north of Termini. The young, English-speaking staff will provide comfortable accommodations and ideas for evening fun. Bunk beds in large dorm-style rooms cater to economically-minded backpackers. Mario can take you out for a night at the pub. Common TV, radio, and fridge. L20,000 per person.

Hotel Home Michele, Via Palestro, 35 (tel. 444 12 04). Cosmic forces have come together to assemble this *pensione's* eclectic atmosphere. Michele, the cat, hangs from pink felt attached to the doors of the five rooms. Oriental furniture mixes with 70s decor. The owner is sweet and carefree. Check-out 10am. Singles L40,000. Doubles L55,000. Triples L25,000 per person. Will accommodate quads. Rates are lower in winter.

Pensione Monaco, Via Flavia, 84 (tel. 474 43 35 or 481 56 49). Around the corner from Tizi and Ercoli. Low lighting, but bathrooms and beds are sparkling clean. A large lounge is available for eating or chatting. Curfew midnight. One shower per day included, L2500 per extra one. Singles L45,000. Doubles L75,000. Triples L30,000 per person. Quads L29,000 per person. Prices lower in the winter.

Pensione Lachea, Via San Martino della Battaglia, 11 (tel. 495 72 56), off P. dell'Indipendenza. *Let's Go's* biggest fan, the warm-hearted owner will ensure every comfort. Small but honest *pensione* with high ceilings and colorful Roman scenes painted right onto the sparkling white walls. Three rooms have balconies. Check-out 11am. Singles L45,000. Doubles L60,000, with bath, L80,000. Triples L80,000, with bath, L110,000. Bargaining is possible if the place isn't full.

Hotel Galli, Via Milazzo, 20 (tel. 445 68 59; fax 446 85 01), off Via Marsala. Clean and close to Termini. Pictures of Rome adorn the halls. The floors and bathrooms gleam, while the comfortable kitchen invites guests to enjoy breakfast for an extra L10,000. Many of the rooms were recently renovated, with brand new bathrooms. Singles L50,000, with bath L75,000. Doubles L75,000, with bath L90,000-120,000. Triples and quads L27,000 per person. MC, Visa, Eurocard.

Hotel Pensione Catherine, Via Volturno, 27 (tel. 48 36 34). A hop, skip, and a leapfrog from Termini. Two uncommonly clean common bathrooms serve spacious singles and doubles. Curfew midnight-1am. *Let's Go* readers are offered a discount if they flash a current edition of the guide. Singles L45,000. Doubles L65,000, with bath L85,000. Triples L38,000 per person.

Hotel Castelfidardo and **Hotel Lazzari,** Via Castelfidardo, 31 (tel. 446 46 38; fax 494 13 78). Both run by the same family. Completely new rooms, clean showers, and helpful management. Renovated rooms painted peach and grey. Four floors of modern, shiny comfort and bodacious bathroom space. Singles L50,000, with bath L70,000. Doubles L65,000, with bath L80,000. Triples L85,000, with bath L110,000. Quads with bath L130,000. AmEx, MC, Visa.

Sant'Andrea, Via XX Settembre, 89 (tel. 48 14 775; fax 48 55 09). Near the British Embassy and the intersection with Via Palestro. If you brush the long, striped curtains aside, there's a view of Michelangelo's nearby Porta Pia. Flowers and incense add a pleasant smell to the impressive view, especially if you ignore the '70s carpet. Bar, TV room, beautiful marble foyer. Twenty-four rooms with bath, TV, and telephone. Check-out 11am. Singles with bath L60,000. Doubles with shower L70,000, with full bath, L90,000. Triples with bath L120,000. Quads with bath L150,000. Travelers checks accepted. AmEx, MC, Visa.

Hotel Rubino and **Hotel Alvisini,** Via Milazzo, 3 (tel./fax 445 23 23). Sister establishments run by two brothers who speak some English. Immaculate hallways with blue walls and plain but pleasant rooms. Same prices for both places. Discount for *Let's Go* users; just show a current edition of the guide. Singles L65,000, with bath L80,000. Doubles L90,000, with shower L100,000, with full bath L110,000. Am Ex, MC, Visa.

Hotel Milazzo, Via Milazzo, 3 (tel. 445 22 83). The decor is plain and the atmosphere staid, and the reduced price for guests staying for 3 or more days should please most. All rooms have showers; baths cost more. Singles L40,000, with bath L60,000. Doubles with full bath L100,000. Triples and quads upon request.

Pensione Ercoli, Via Collina, 48 (tel. 474 54 54; fax 487 33 60). Above the Pensione Tizi on the third floor. The young, English-speaking, Sardinian management is eager to house students and families. Friendly dorm atmosphere. Rooms, lounge, and large common bathrooms are in perfect order. Check-out 10:30am. Rooms scheduled to be renovated in Nov. 96. Singles L50,000. Doubles L65,000, with bath L80,000. Triples L90,000, with bath L100,000. Quads available; 35% increase in price for each bed after three.

Pensione Ester, Viale Castro Pretorio, 25 (tel. 495 71 23), off Via Marsala. Go through the archway to the courtyard and enter the door on the right marked "C." The courtyard downstairs is much cheerier than the dark lobby. Five old-fashioned, spacious rooms with tile floors in a beautiful, tranquil building with a cheery courtyard. Check-out 9am. Curfew midnight. Doubles L70,000, triples L94,500, and quads can be formed from one of the other rooms.

Hotel Bolognese, Via Palestro, 15 (tel./fax 49 00 45). In a land of run-of-the-mill *pensioni*, this place is spruced up by extra amenities which pop up here and there; some bedrooms have attached sitting rooms, some feature bathtubs, and still others feature terraces. There are two tidy bathrooms per floor and an espresso machine for all. Check-in after 11am. Check-out 11am. Curfew 2am. Singles L45,000, with bath L55,000. Doubles L75,000, with bath L80,000. Triples L100,000, with bath L120,000. Quads with bath L150,000.

Hotel Positano, Via Palestro, 49 (tel. 49 03 06; fax 446 91 01). Comfy, family-style place, on the fifth floor. Clean floors, firm beds, breakfast bar, and outdoor patio. All rooms have telephone and television. English spoken. Check-out 10:30am. Singles L50,000, with bath L80,000. Doubles L70,000, with bath L100,000-L150,000. Triples L90,000. Triples and quads with shower L30,000 per person. AmEx, DC, MC, Visa, AmEx.

Hotel Cervia, Via Palestro, 55 (tel. 49 10 56; fax 49 10 57). 21 rooms and 41 beds. A bit dark, but the helpful management speaks English. Common television and lounge with bar. Reception open 5:30am-1am. Check-out noon. Curfew 2am. Singles L40,000, with bath L60,000. Doubles L60,000, with bath L80,000. Triples and quads L25,000 per person, with bath L30,000 per person. MC, Visa.

Pensione Albergo Mari, Via Palestro, 55 (tel. 446 21 37) and **Pensione Albergo Mari 2,** Via Calatafimi, 38 (tel. 474 03 71; fax 482 83 13). Sister establishments. Clean rooms with moderate prices, though the singles are a bit small. Some employees speak a little English. Lounge with bar. Check-out noon. Curfew 1am. Singles L50,000. Doubles L80,000. Triples and quads L30,000 per person. Mari 2 has rooms without baths for these same prices, but also has some rooms with baths. Singles with bath L60,000. Doubles with bath L100,000. Triples and quads with bath L35,000 per person. Breakfast L8000. AmEx, MC, Visa (5% more with credit card).

Hotel Adventure, Hotel Ventura, and **Hotel Philia,** Via Palestro, 88 (tel. 445 19 51). First-floor location is convenient, but noisy at night. All three hotels are owned by the same family. Adventure is a more upscale, three-star hotel, while Ventura's rooms are smaller but newly renovated with television and telephone. Hotel Philia is the most economical, as the rooms attest. **Adventure:** Doubles with bath L140,000-240,000. Triples with bath L180,000-L270,000. **Ventura:** Doubles with bath L80,000. Triples with bath L105,000. Quads L35,000 per person. **Philia:** L30,000 per person.

Hotel Roxena, Via Marghera, 13 (tel 445 68 23; fax 445 26 29). Plain is the operative word here, but the 11 rooms are spacious and clean, with happy light wood furniture. Curfew midnight. Doubles L65,000-75,000, with full bath L85,000-120,000. Triples L90,000, with full bath L120,000. Quads L120,000, with full bath L150,000-160,000. Continental breakfast L10,000. MC, Visa.

Locanda Marini, Via Palestro, 35 (tel. 444 00 58). Across the hall from and in cahoots with Pensione Katty. The interior is warmed by the sprightly proprietress. Extremely clean with high ceilings. Fifth floor rooms are newly renovated. Singles L25,000. Doubles L60,000. Triples L75,000.

Pensione Katty, Via Palestro, 35 (tel. 444 12 16). No-frills place at a no-frills price; the scrupulously clean may be unnerved by the condition of the showers and the ultra-low lighting. Lounge and espresso machine available. Check-out 11am. L2000 key deposit. Singles L35,000-60,000. Doubles L40,000-75,000, with bath L60,000-95,000. Triples L20,000-L30,000 per person, with bath L22,000-38,000.

Hotel Continentale, Via Palestro, 49 (tel. 445 03 82; fax 445 26 29). Exit the station to the right and head up Via Marghera until it hits Via Palestro. Recently renovated rooms in tasteful navy blue. Rooms have telephones and televisions, and some have balconies. Some English spoken. Singles with shower L75,000. Doubles with bath L130,000. Triples with bath L160,000. Quads with bath L200,000. Breakfast included. MC, Visa.

Hotel Pensione Stella, Via Castelfidardo, 51 (tel. 444 10 78). A smiling woman with an ever-ready mop keeps the place clean. The easy-going proprietor will bend over backwards to keep you happy. The whole place is scheduled for renovation in late '96 and should prove to be crispy new with telephones and televisions in all rooms. Singles with bath L70,000-80,000. Doubles with bath L120,000. Triples L150,000. Quads with bath L180,000. AmEx, MC, Visa.

Hotel Fenicia, Via Milazzo, 20 (tel./fax 49 03 42). Friendly, English-speaking management. Rooms are small but clean, and there are well-kept common bathrooms for rooms without private shower and/or toilet. A large sitting room with TV is open to guests. Singles with shower L70,000, with full bath L80,000. Doubles with shower L100,000, with full bath L120,000. Will accommodate parties of 3 or 4 for about L50,000 per person.

Hotel Bruna, Via Marghera, 13 (tel. 495 93 70 or 495 73 96), upstairs from Roxena. All of these flowery rooms have TVs, telephones, and safes. A glass porch fervid with plant life is the scene for breakfast (it's included) and conversation with the spirited family. Doubles L120,000. AmEx, Visa.

SOUTH OF TERMINI

The area south of Termini is often portrayed as busier, noisier, and seedier than other parts of central Rome, and it may still be home to more than its share of pickpockets and tourist traps. Lately, however, the neighborhood has started to clean up its act, with savvy locals and business-minded immigrants catering to the budget traveler and university students who frequent the two nearby dining halls. With good judgement and perseverance, you may find great places and excellent bargains. You *will* see a prostitute here or there, but you'll also be steps away from hip pubs, gorgeous medieval churches, and Termini, Rome's major transportation hub.

Prices tend to be very flexible in this area; they depend on the season, length of stay, how many people are in your group, and how busy the establishment is. As a result, a double which may cost L80,000 in August could drop to L40,000 a few weeks later. Don't be afraid to haggle, but do realize that you will not find too much room to bargain during the peak season, particularly if you're looking for a single or double for just a few nights. Many of the prices listed below are in the form of ranges; expect to pay near or above the maximum during the peak season and closer to the minimum during the off-season.

Via Principe Amedeo runs parallel to the southwest side of the station, two blocks down. It can be reached by taking any of the side streets that intersect with Via Giolitti outside the south-west exit of the station. The closer you get to P. Vittorio Emanuele, which lies to the south-east of the station, the more unsafe and disreputable the area becomes. Via Giolitti, Via Filippo Turati, and Via Principe Amedeo may also seem intimidating at night, so use appropriate caution and watch your pockets.

Pensione Sandy, Via Cavour, 136 (tel. 488 45 85), near Santa Maria Maggiore. No sign; look for the Hotel Valle next door. Buzz to be let in. Run by peppy Americans and a native Roman, Slim, who is proud to say he learned his English from "Beavis and Butthead." At prices like this, even some older folks are willing to make the 4-flight trek to the top. Plain, comfortable, dormitory-like, hostel-style rooms, usually for 3-5 people, in great central location. L25,000 per person during the summer, L20,000 per person in winter (no heat, but lots of blankets). Showers included. They'll lock up small valuables for you, including passports and traveler's checks.

Pensione di Rienzo, Via Principe Amedeo, 79A (tel. 446 71 31 and 446 69 80). A tranquil family-run retreat with spacious, newly-renovated rooms overlooking a peaceful courtyard. Many rooms have balconies and baths, and hall baths are usually shared by only 2-3 people. Warm, friendly, English-speaking staff. No curfew; they give you the keys. Singles L45,000-50,000, with bath up to L80,000. Doubles L60,000-75,000, with bath L80,000-90,000. Triples L100,000-120,000. MC, Visa.

Hotel Kennedy, Via Filippo Turati, 64 (tel. 446 53 73; fax 446 54 17). Trendy rooms with the works. Private bath, color TV with satellite (MTV, CNN, you name it), phone, and even A/C. Hearty all-you-can-eat breakfast includes cornflakes, croissant, and endless varieties of jams, cheese, and tea. Free juice and coffee all day long. They'll organize trips and tell you about all the cultural events going on in the city. Everyone speaks some form of English. The hip, helpful manager stresses the youth and vitality of the staff and offers a 10% discount to *Let's Go* travelers "under 29, like us." Singles L60,000-99,000. Doubles L80,000-155,000. Triples L110,000-180,000. AmEx, MC, Visa.

Pensione Cortorillo, Via Principe Amedeo, 79A (tel. 446 69 34), at Via Gioberti. On the 5th floor (the 6th for Americans). Simple, family-run establishment. Charming rooms with wooden beds. Continental breakfast included. The proprietress will cook dinner for L10,000. Singles with bath L30,000-50,000. Doubles L50,000-70,000. Triples L75,000-90,000. Try bargaining.

Hotel Orlanda, Via Principe Amedeo, 76 (tel. 488 06 37; fax 488 01 83), at Via Gioberti. Take the stairs on the right in the vestibule; on the 3rd floor. Spic-'n'-span, pleasant rooms, all with TV and phone. Guests can leave valuables in the hotel's safes and use their handy guides and maps to plan a tour. English spoken. Singles with bath L70,000-90,000. Doubles L80,000-140,000. AmEx, DC, MC, Visa.

Hotel Sweet Home, Via Principe Amedeo, 47 (tel. 488 09 54; fax 481 76 13), downstairs from the Hotel California. Quiet, stripey, green, clean, and kept by a nice, outgoing family. There is a family room with a double bed, a twin bed, and a crib. Singles L60,000-70,000. Doubles L80,000-100,000, with bath L100,000-150,000. Triples L50,000-70,000 per person. Many discounts offered and lots of room to bargain. MC, Visa.

Hotel Scott House and **Hotel Eliana,** Via Gioberti, 30 (tel. 446 53 92 or 446 53 79; fax 446 49 86). Tidy, clean, pleasant, two stars. The newly renovated rooms all have televisions and bathrooms. English spoken. Curfew 1am, but negotiable.

ACCOMMODATIONS

Prices with *Let's Go* discount: Singles L60,000-80,000. Doubles L80-000-110,000. Credit cards accepted.

Hotel Serena and **Pensione delle Rose,** Via Principe Amedeo, 62 (tel. 481 82 14 or 481 93 39; fax 474 47 07). Breezy, new, tasteful, and antiseptic. Don't bump your head on the ubiquitous crucifixes. There's a common space with a TV and coffee machine. May be further renovated this winter, so don't be surprised by a price hike. **Serena** is slightly more upscale—TVs and bathrooms in most rooms. Singles up to L80,000, with bath L90,000-110,000. Doubles L80,000-110,000, with bath L110,000-150,000. **Delle Rose** singles L60,000-70,000. Doubles L80,000-100,000, with bath L90,000-120,000. MC, Visa. Try bargaining.

Albergo Teti, Via Principe Amedeo, 76 (tel./fax 48 90 40 88); take the stairs at the end of the courtyard. Exceedingly comfortable, and tastefully decorated, though a bit pricey for the neighborhood. The singles and doubles with bathrooms also have TVs. Good English spoken. Singles up to L100,000. Doubles up to L150,000. Breakfast L8000. AmEx, MC, Visa.

Pensione Pezzotti, Hotel Contilia, and **Hotel Tony,** Via Principe Amedeo, 79D (tel. 446 69 42 or 446 68 75; fax 446 69 04). Three *pensioni* with one charming and talkative (in English) management. Go to the Contilia desk on the first floor to check in. New, clean, and pastel, with TV and telephone in every room. A/C costs extra, but breakfast is included. Singles L60,000, with bath L80,000-100,000. Doubles L80,000, with bath L100,000-150,000. Triples and quads L150,000-200,000. Prices drop drastically in the off-season. AmEx, MC, Visa.

Hotel Pelliccioni, Via Cavour, 47 (tel./fax 48 44 27), at Via Farini. That 1970s furniture you sold at a garage sale last year ended up here. Done up in mauve and gray, but clean. Most rooms are heated, have A/C, and contain refrigerators and televisions. Singles and doubles with bath L25,000-80,000 per person depending on room and time of year. Show *Let's Go* for a possible discount. Room for negotiation. AmEx, MC, Visa.

WEST OF TERMINI

The area west and south-west of Termini, though steps away from all the hustle and bustle, has managed to preserve a more authentically Roman atmosphere than any other area near the station. You'll find winding, cobblestone alleyways with family-run businesses and traditional *trattorie*, as well as hip wine shops and trendy Irish pubs. This neighborhood is also home to the city's two women-only establishments.

Youth Hostel Roma Inn Keiko, Via Urbana, 96 (tel. 474 38 45). Ring buzzer at bottom marked "Roma Inn" on 1st (2nd) floor. What you get when you mix a frat house with home sweet home. Recently renovated red-walled rooms for 1-5 people. Enjoy the communal fridge, use your hot plate in the food room, wash your clothes in the sink and hang them on the clothesline. The youthful proprietor organizes late-night excursions. Native English spoken. L30,000 per night in dorm-style rooms. L35,000 in singles and doubles. Reservations possible.

Hotel San Paolo, Via Panisperna, 95 (tel. 474 52 13; fax 474 52 18), follow Via S. Maria Maggiore, just off Via Cavour to your right after S. Maria Maggiore. Far-removed from the hubbub and riff-raff of Termini, in the heart of the older Rioni Monti quarter. Recently renovated, sparkling with white wall tiles and colorful art, San Paolo's modestly-sized rooms provide ample opportunity for relaxation. Some rooms have terraces and most are decorated with enormous puzzles assembled by the proprietor. Hall baths are clean and private. No commission for use of telephone. Free luggage storage after check-out. English spoken. Singles up to L50,000; two bed doubles up to L85,000, *matrimoniale* with bath up to L100,000; triple L115,000. Breakfast L8000. AmEx, MC, Visa. Reservations accepted.

Hotel Giugiu, Via del Viminale, 8 (tel./fax 482 77 34). Steps away from Termini. A warm, friendly family loves hosting young (and not so young) English-speaking travelers year-round. Recently expanded with a breakfast area and 18 large, quiet rooms with high ceilings. Excellent espresso. Show 'em your *Let's Go* for great prices: Singles L45,000-60,000. Doubles L65,000-75,000, with bath L75,000-85,000. Breakfast L8000.

YWCA, Via Cesare Balbo, 4 (tel. 48 80 460 or 48 83 917; fax 48 71 028), off Via Torino, south of Termini. The YWCA (pronounced EEV-kah) is a fantastic place for women travelers who enjoy safety in numbers. It lacks the traditional authenticity of the family-run *pensione,* but has an exceedingly pleasant, cheerful atmosphere with a garden terrace and large TV room. Services include fax and photocopying. Curfew midnight. No men allowed, except those accompanied by their wives. Singles L45,000. Doubles L35,000 per person. Triples and quads L30,000 per person. Showers and breakfast (7:30-8:15am) included. Tell reception by 10am the same day if you want lunch (1-2:15pm, L20,000).

Associazione Cattolica Internationale al Servizio della Giovane, Via Urbana, 158 (tel. 48 80 056). Can make arrangements for women 25 years old or younger who are in Rome for a brief stay. See Religious and Rural Housing, page 112.

■ San Lorenzo

A 10-min. walk from Termini (or a 5-min. bus ride on #492), San Lorenzo is one of the quieter, less touristy sections of Rome. Before WWII, San Lorenzo was occupied by factory workers known for their leftist politics. Towards the end of the war, the Allies bombed San Lorenzo at the behest of the Vatican, to suppress an alleged Communist uprising. Today, remnants of war-torn buildings remain, their walls spray painted with graffiti proclamations like "Guevara still lives." In the 1970s, radical university students were recruited by the Red Brigades *(Brigade Rosse),* the terrorist group blamed for assassinating Prime Minister Aldo Moro in 1978. Artists have been flocking to the area since the 60s and have created a stylish underground community within the "working-class-turned-studio" apartment buildings. In the middle of the summer, the University of Rome often opens up 300 rooms in the **Casa dello Studente** (at Via Cesare Lollis, 20) to foreign students. To find out about possible openings contact the Youth Hostel of Rome, **Foro Italico** (tel. 32 36 267).

Albergo Felice, Via Tiburtina, 30 (tel. 445 33 47), at the corner of Via dei Falisci, across from the baby park. The location of the hotel will make you feel *felice* indeed if you can get one of the 18 rooms. Very clean, with an air-conditioned lobby and noise-proof shutters in the rooms to keep out the already minimal street noise. Singles with showers L75,000. Doubles with sink and bidet L95,000, with shower L125,000. Make reservations a few days before. AmEx, MC, Visa.

Hotel Laurentia, Largo degli Osci, 63 (tel. 445 02 18; fax 445 38 21). From Via Tiburtina, turn left on Via degli Umbri, then right at Largo degli Oschi. For those looking for a bit of luxury, this hotel promises A/C, telephone, color TV, and mini-bar in each room. Overlooking the marketplace of Largo degli Osci, this is a quiet but scenic place to rest those weary bones. Singles with bath L145,000. Doubles with bath L180,000. AmEx, DC, MC, Visa.

■ Centro Storico: Near Piazza Navona and Campo dei Fiori

Il Centro Storico (the Historic Center) is the ideal, if increasingly expensive, base for living as the Romans do. By day, its winding cobblestone streets, hidden *piazze* and numerous *caffè* enchant and mesmerize; by night, the area swarms with boisterous Romans and tourists alike. Most major sights are within walking distance and the day market at nearby Campo dei Fiori yields bounties of cheap fruit, vegetables, and, of course, flowers. Unfortunately, hotel proprietors (mostly English-speaking) successfully exploit this desirable location; you can expect to pay about 10-15% more to finance the charm and the deeper sense of Roman history absent from Termini accommodations. Reservations may be the only way to get a bed, especially in the summer. Most *pensioni*, unless otherwise indicated, do *not* accept credit cards.

Piazza Navona lies to the north of Corso Vittorio Emanuele II, the avenue that cuts through the historic center; Campo dei Fiori is to the south. From Stazione Termini, take bus #64. Also originating near Termini, #75 and #170 stop in Largo Argentina the transportation hub of the historic center. Buses #62 and #60 travel along Via XX Settembre and Via del Tritone and stop at Largo Argentina.

Hotel Mimosa, Via Santa Chiara, 61 (tel. 68 80 17 53; fax 68 33 557), off P. di Minerva behind the Pantheon. Haphazard decoration in spacious rooms in a fantastic location. A matronly woman and her kindly husband preside over this kitschy abode, with puppy wall-calendars and red-checkered tablecloths in the breakfast room. English spoken. Drunkenness not tolerated. Singles L65,000. Doubles L95,000, with bath L120,000. Triples L135,000. Quads L180,000. Prices 10% lower during winter season. Breakfast L5000.

Albergo della Lunetta, P. del Paradiso, 68 (tel. 686 10 80 or 687 76 30; fax 689 20 28), near the Church of Sant'Andrea della Valle. Take Via Chiavari off Corso Vittorio Emanuele II, then the first right off Via Chiavari. An economical Eden in the heart of Old Rome, this is the best value in the Campo dei Fiori area. Tidy rooms with armoires, desks, and phones. Muse in the central garden or the TV lounge, but definitely not in the somewhat cramped common baths. Enjoy the view from two lofty, new terraces. Singles L55,000, with bath L80,000. Doubles L100,000, with bath L180,000. Triples L130,000, with bath L180,000. Quads L160,000, with bath L210,000. Reservations accepted with a credit card. MC, Visa.

Albergo Pomezia, Via dei Chiavari, 12 (tel./fax 686 13 71). The recently renovated section on the 1st floor is far nicer than the old one; all of the re-done rooms have baths. Telephones, matching furniture, heat in the winter, and stylish bathrooms (on the 2nd and 3rd floors). Don't let the hall mirrors fool you—the two managers really are twins. Bar on the first floor (*caffè*, L1300). Breakfast lounge open 8-11am. Singles L77,000, with bath L110,000. Doubles L110,000, with bath L165,000. Triples L132,000, with bath L198,000. Prices drop Nov.-Feb., except at Christmas. Breakfast included. AmEx, DC, MC, Visa.

Pensione Navona, Via dei Sediari, 8 (tel. 686 42 03; fax 68 80 38 02; call before faxing). Take Via dei Canestrari off of the southern end of P. Navona, cross over Corso del Rinascimento, and continue straight. A very helpful Italo-Australian family runs a tight ship in this 16th-century Borromini building, which has served as a *pensione* for over 150 years. During World War II, Jews hid in the extensive network of tunnels leading to the Teatro di Marcello. The entrance is supposedly what remains of the ruins of the ancient Baths of Agrippa. The renovated section puts the older section to shame, but all of the rooms are quiet and clean and most have bathrooms; ask for a room facing the courtyard. Cheery breakfast room. They tend to fill up with larger groups, so call several weeks in advance and send a US$100 deposit to secure a room. If full, they can refer you to other hotels in the area. Checkout 11am. They also organize bus tours to Tivoli (L60,000) and Pompeii (L140,000). Singles L75,000, with bath L85,000. Doubles L120,000, with bath L135,000. Triples L170,000, with bath L180,000. Breakfast included.

Albergo Abruzzi, P. della Rotonda, 69 (tel. 679 20 21). Here the humble can contemplate the great; this *albergo* is located smack dab in front of the Pantheon with a gorgeous view of its façade and its noisy admirers. While cleaner than the Pantheon, it could use some of the Pantheon's overhead lighting. But it's roomy, so don't be gloomy. English spoken. Ask for a room facing the Pantheon, but be prepared to spend L18,000 more than the following prices (for rooms facing the inner courtyards). Singles L65,000. Doubles L92,000. Triples (facing Pantheon only) L148,500. Reservations recommended in summer.

Hotel Piccolo, Via dei Chiavari, 32 (tel. 689 23 30 or 68 80 25 60), off Corso Vittorio Emanuele II, behind Sant'Andrea della Valle. Next to a bustling grocery but off the beaten path. Clean, quiet, and comfortable, with pleasant wood trim in the bathrooms. Spacious singles in a mellow atmosphere. All rooms have telephones. No elevator. Curfew 1:30am. Breakfast L7000. English spoken. Singles L80,000, with bath L100,000. Doubles L100,000, with bath L130,000. Triples with shower L120,000, with bath L140,000. Quads with bath L160,000. Reservations recommended in summer. AmEx, MC, Visa.

Pensione Campo Marzio, Piazza Campo Marzio, 7 (tel. 68 80 14 86). Take Corso del Rinascimento, turn right on Via del Salvatore and then left on Via della Dogana

Vecchia which eventually turns into Via della Scrofa. The hotel is off Via della Stelletta near the government buildings. Stay here for the location, not the faux brick wallpaper. The rooms are big and have heavy wood armoires. Proprietor has young sidekick who speaks some English. Singles L60,000, doubles L90,000, triples L120,000.

Albergo del Sole, Via del Biscione, 76 (tel. 68 80 68 73 or 68 79 446; fax 68 93 787). Off P. Campo dei Fiori. Rooms have top-notch furniture, plush lounging chairs, and matching headboards and dark wood armoires. Telephones, too. A peaceful rooftop terrace is decorated with flowers from the nearby *campo*. Although many of the singles look like those near Termini, the *pensione* is supposedly the oldest in Rome. English (as well as French and German) spoken. Singles L82,500, with shower L93,500, with bath L110,000-120,000. Doubles L110,000-125,000, with bath L155,000-175,000. Add 35% for each additional bed. Parking available, L30,000-40,000.

■ Near the Spanish Steps

Marxist purists, budget travelers, and quiet Amish types be warned: this area of Rome will not be sympathetic to your lifestyle. In this neighborhood, where designer silk suits, leather loafers, mini-skirts, and face-lifts abound, inexpensive accommodations are scarce. However, it may be worthwhile to spend a few extra bucks to sleep in the hippest part of town. For fashion victims who find themselves lingering in front of Fendi after the buses stop running, the following havens are worth a try:

Pensione Parlamento, Via delle Convertite, 5 (tel./fax 67 92 082, for reservations 69 94 16 97). Off Via del Corso, 1 block before the post-office, on the street leading up to P. San Silvestro. 23 rooms. Plant-crowded landing, glamorous roof-top terrace with flowers; safes, hairdryers, telephones, and TVs in every room. High ceilings, balconies and plush-velvet chair seating area with magazines galore. Living room with color TV and bar. Giorgio, the owner, speaks English, as well as French, Spanish, and German. Singles L80,000, with bath L112,000. Doubles L110,000, with bath L140,000. Each additional person L35,000. Reservations recommended. Breakfast included. AmEx, MC, Visa.

Pensione Panda, Via della Croce, 35 (tel. 678 01 79; fax 69 94 21 51), between P. di Spagna and Via del Corso. Repainted every year to keep up a fresh Tom Sawyer decor, this light, airy place may be just the refuge you need from the fashionable chaos below. Big single beds. No curfew, but you'll have to carry the key with you. Singles L60,000, with bath L80,000. Doubles L95,000, with bath L130,000. Triples L120,000, with bath L160,000. Each additional bed L25,000. Reservations recommended. Discount for *Let's Go* readers. AmEx, MC, Visa.

Hotel Marcus, Via del Clementino, 94 (tel. 68 30 03 20; fax 68 30 03 12). Off Via di Ripetta, Via Clementino is an extension of Via deiCondotti and Via della Fontanella di Borghese. Situated on the second floor, this homey hotel is filled with elegant tile-work, a chandelier, and matching wood furniture. All rooms have telephones, TV, heaters in the winter, secure double doors, small baths, and lots of mirrors. Singles L110,000. Doubles L150,000. Triples L180,000. Quads L195,000.

Pensione Fiorella, Via del Babuino, 196 (tel. 361 05 97), just off P. del Popolo. The charming management asks only that you respect the 1am curfew. Airy, comfortable breakfast room. Happening location may lead to motorcycle wake-up calls. Singles L60,000. Doubles L95,000. Breakfast included. No reservations, so arrive early in the morning.

Pensione Jonella, Via delle Croce, 41 (tel. 679 79 66), between P. di Spagna and Via del Corso. A marble stairway becomes continually steeper and narrower on the ascent to effervescent rooms with high ceilings. Luckily, prices aren't as steep. Owned by friendly Carlo and his brothers, who also run Hotel Matilde. Singles L60,000. Doubles L85,000.

Hotel Boccaccio, Via del Boccaccio, 25 (tel. 488 59 62). Off Via del Tritone down from P. Barberini. Patrizia runs this peaceful little establishment with her very own sense of familial comfort. Paisley comforters blend with old wooden heirlooms passed down from Grandma. Singles L60,000. Doubles L85,000, with bath L110,000. Triples L114,000, with bath L150,000.

Hotel Pensione Suisse S.A.S., Via Gregoriana, 54 (tel. 678 36 49; fax 678 12 58). Off P. di Trinità dei Monti; turn right at the top of the Spanish Steps. In the Swiss tradition of pricey perfection and neutral yet endearing location. TV lounge, phone in every room, tidy bathrooms, some with tubs. Cold drinks and soda, as well as fans (on request) for the sweaty summers. Singles L95,000, with bath L110,000. Doubles L125,000, with bath L160,000. Triples L165,000, with bath L210,000. Quads with bath L260,000. Half the bill may be paid by credit card. Breakfast included. MC, Visa.

■ Prati (Near the Vatican)

The *pensioni* on the other side of the Tiber aren't the cheapest in Rome, but they tend to be comfortable, clean, and friendly. Those in **Prati,** near the Vatican, are attractive for their proximity to popular sights and a safer residential area. Bus #64 from Termini ends right near St. Peter's and Metro Linea A runs to Ottaviano, the metro stop in the area.

Pensione Ottaviano, Via Ottaviano, 6 (tel. 39 73 72 53 or 39 73 81 38), off P. del Risorgimento north of P. San Pietro. Steps away from Metro Linea A and minutes from St. Peter's, this is the only hostel-style *pensione* in the area—3 to 6 beds per room. Two doubles also available for L70,000 in summer and L45,000 in winter. English-speaking backpackers' haven, including satellite TV, individual lockers, and fridges. Phantasmagoric wall murals abound. No curfew. The energetic staff speaks English. L20,000-25,000 per person (depending on the time of year) for a bed in a shared room.

Residence Giuggioli, Via Germanico, 198 (tel. 32 42 113). At Via Paolo Emilia, 1st floor. 5 of the best rooms in Rome. Beautiful antiques adorn pristine rooms and the common bath is gleaming and newly renovated. Room #6 is huge and furnished with antiques. The wonderful proprietress will chat with you in Italian. Doubles L100,000; matrimonial suite with private bath L120,000.

Pensione Lady, same building as the Guiggioli, 4th floor (tel. 324 21 12). A loving couple has been running this clean, peaceful *pensione* for 30 years. Recently renovated and restored to its original charm. Check out the wooden ceiling. Spankin' new bathrooms. The rooms that face away from the street are soothingly quiet. The couple takes a few weeks off each year, so call ahead. Singles L85,000; doubles L100,000, with bath L130,000.

Pensione Nautilus, Via Germanico, 198 (tel. 324 21 18), same building as the Guiggioli with reception on the 2nd floor. Not quite as charming as Guiggioli but very spacious with clean bathrooms. Fluent English spoken. Curfew is officially 12:30am, but they occasionally give out keys. Doubles L100,000, with bath L120,000. Triples L130,000, with bath L150,000.

Hotel Florida, Via Cola di Rienzo, 243 (tel. 324 18 72; fax 324 16 08). On the 2nd and 3rd floor, below Hotel Joli. Charming, modern rooms that flaunt their recent renovation, including new wallpaper, floral carpeting, and ceiling fans. Bathrooms are delightfully clean. Telephones and hairdryers in each room. Friendly management. Singles L65,000, with bath L90,000. Doubles L120,000, with bath L135,000. Prices may fluctuate; possible discount in low season. AmEx, MC, Visa.

Hotel Pensione Joli, Via Cola di Rienzo, 243, 6th floor (tel. 324 18 54 or 324 18 93; fax 324 18 93). At Via Tibullo, Scala A. Parquet floors. Comfortable with polished upholstered chairs. A few views of Roman rooftops and St. Peter's cupola. Breakfast included. Singles L65,000, with bath L80,000. Doubles with bath L120,000. Triples with bath L160,000. MC, Visa.

Pensione Ida, Via Germanico, 198 (tel. 324 21 64), on the 1st floor next to Guiggioli. Curfew midnight. Variably sized, slightly mismatched doubles for L80,000.

■ Trastevere

Hedonists and bohemians flock to **Trastevere,** scene of much night-time revelry and home to many young expatriates. Bus #75 from P. Indipendenza and #170 from P. dei Cinquecento run from near Termini to Trastevere. Bus #56 and #60 to Trastevere leave from Via Claudio at Piazza San Silvestro, south of the Spanish Steps.

Pensione Manara, Via Luciano Manara, 25 (tel. 581 47 13). Take a right off Viale di Trastevere onto Via delle Fratte di Trastevere to Via Luciano Manara. Friendly management runs this homey establishment overlooking colorful P. San Cosimato in the heart of Trastevere. Undergoing reconstruction in summer 1996 to brighten up the somber interior. English spoken. Doubles L75,000. Amex, MC, Visa.

Pensione Esty, Viale Trastevere, 108 (tel. 588 12 01), about 1km down Viale di Trastevere from the Ponte Garibaldi. You're almost there when you pass the towering stone municipal building on your right. It's easy to miss; make sure you ring the buzzer on the right, labeled *"pensione."* This clean, quiet *pensione* sits somewhat removed from the rowdy heart of Trastevere. Some rooms have balconies overlooking busy Viale di Trastevere. Singles L50,000, doubles L70,000.

ALTERNATIVE ACCOMMODATIONS

■ Institutional Accommodations

If you are looking for a raucous time in Rome, institutions are not the place to go. Though they provide affordable accommodations, most of them are inconveniently located and difficult to arrange, while curfews at the HI hostel and various religious organizations keep you locked away from *la dolce vita.* Consider other comparably priced accommodations that do not depend so heavily on public transportation.

Ostello del Foro Italico (HI), Viale delle Olimpiadi, 61, 00194 Roma (tel. 323 62 67; fax 324 26 13). Take Metro Linea A to Ottaviano (last stop) and then exit onto Via Barletta and take bus #32 (in the middle of the street) to Cadorna. It's the bus's 5th stop; get off when you see the pink Foro Italico buildings. The entrance is in the back, across the street. Inconvenient location but they have a bus and metro ticket-vending machine. Three hundred and fifty beds. Huge red lockers big enough for 2 packs, but you supply the lock. Bring earplugs. 3-day max. stay when full. Reception open noon-11pm. Lockout 9am-2pm. Sizeable but not superlative lunch or dinner. Bar downstairs open 7am-10:30pm. Curfew midnight. L23,000 with HI card (buy one at the desk for L30,000). Breakfast and curtain-less showers included. Wheelchair accessible.

■ Student Housing

Student residences throughout Italy are inexpensive and theoretically open to foreign students whenever there is room. Unfortunately, these accommodations are often nearly impossible to arrange. Contact **Enjoy Rome,** an agency with a plethora of helpful services, Via Varese, 39 (tel. 445 18 43; fax 445 07 34). They can sometimes arrange short-term accommodations for tourists in rooms rented out by Italian students or families. The **Centro Turistico Studentesco e Giovanile (CTS)** is the Italian student and youth travel organization, which helps people find rooms in *pensioni* or dormitories. The London, Paris, and Athens offices can reserve a room for you in Italy for the first few nights. The central office is at Via Genova, 16, Roma (tel. 467 91) though information should first be sought at the **Ostello del Foro Italico** (tel. 323 62 67).

■ Religious and Rural Housing

Convents, monasteries, and religious houses offer shelter, but unless you have a personal reason for seeking such accommodations, it is inadvisable, as prices often exceed L30,000 per night and strict curfews incarcerate you at 11pm. Guests need not attend services but are expected to make their own beds and, often, to clean up after meals. Generally found in rural settings, monasteries tend to be peaceful. Staying in one can be an enriching option for those who seek a quiet, contemplative experience and a first-hand taste of Italian history. **Associazione Cattolica Internazionale al Servizio della Giovane** at Via Urbana, 158 (tel. 48 80 056), near Termini, can make arrangements for women 25 years old or younger who are in Rome for a brief stay. Carrying an introduction on letterhead from your own local religious leader may facilitate matters, but note that many monasteries will accept only Catholic guests. For more information about specific regions and a list of religious institutions offering accommodations, write to the tourist board in Rome or to the regional office of the area in which you'd like to stay.

   Country Living: For a quiet, non-religious atmosphere, stay in a rural cottage or farmhouse. Usually, you will be given a small room and asked to clean up after yourself, but you will have freedom to come and go as you please. For more information, write to the office of **Agriturist,** Corso V. Emanuele II, 101, 00186 Roma (tel. 685 23 42), or contact any of their offices in the region that you will be visiting. They offer a publication called *Guida dell'ospitalità rurale* which lists various options for rural housing. Write for a copy.

■ Camping

You probably won't catch the malaria that killed Daisy Miller, but there are still plenty of mosquitoes menacing tourists in campgrounds near the city. Though there's often little space between sites, peaceful seclusion is usually steps away. In August, arrive early, well before 11am, to secure yourself a spot. Rates average L9000 per person and another L5000 per car. Many of the campgrounds are downright luxurious, with everything from swimming pools to campground bars, while others may be more primitive. The **Touring Club Italiano,** Corso Italia, 10, 20122 Milano, publishes an annual directory of all camping sites in Italy, *Campeggi in Italia,* available in bookstores throughout Italy. A free map and list of sites is available from the **Italian Government Travel Office** or directly from **Federcampeggio,** Via V. Emanuele, 11, Casella Postale 23, 50041 Calenzano (Firenze).

   Camping on beaches, roads, or any flat, inconspicuous plot is not uncommon, but it is illegal. Respect for property rights is extremely important—always ask permission before bedding down. Campers who don't make fires or litter will lessen their chances of being booted.

   Seven Hills, Via Cassia, 1216 (tel. 30 36 27 51 or 303 31 08 26; fax 303 31 00 39), 8km north of Rome. Take bus #907 from P. Risorgimento to Via Cassia, or the #201 from Flaminio. Ask where to get off—it's a few km past the GRA. From here, follow the country road about 1km until you see the sign. Lots-o-peacocks, goats, deer, and bunnies. Young international campers play volleyball on the manicured grounds. Laze by the poolside and dance the night away in the **disco** (10pm-1am). Completely self-sufficient, it houses a bar, market, BBQ, restaurant, convenience store, and pizzeria. You can't use money, though; you buy a Seven Hills card which you can use all over the campground. The money you don't use is refunded when you leave. If you aren't too embarrassed, they will wash your clothes for you for L15,000. Doctor on hand during the day. Daily Vatican shuttle leaves at 9:30am, returning at 1:30 and 5:30pm (L6000 round-trip). Check-in open 7am-11pm. L11,000 per person, L8000 per tent. Caravan L10,000. Camper L14,000. Bungalow L70,000-110,000. L6000 per car. Open late May-late Oct.
   Flaminio, Via Flaminia Nuova, 821 (tel. 333 14 31), about 7km outside of Rome. Take bus #910 from Termini to Piazza Mancini, then transfer to #200. Get off on

Via Flaminia Nuova when you see the "Philips" or EUCLID building (open 9am-5pm; there are several stops on Via Flaminia Nuova, so keep your eyes peeled) on your right. Shady grass strewn with closely knit enclaves of tents, campers, and bungalows. The landscaping is a bit rough around the edges, but they're outfitted with a pool, market, restaurant, bar, and a disco that rages long into the night. Coin-operated washing machines L500. L10,000 per person, L5700 per tent. Bungalows L33,000; singles and doubles L56,000, triples L89,000, quads L120,000. Open March-Oct.

Capitol Campground, Via di Castel Fusano, 195 (tel. 565 73 44), in Ostia Antica, is 3km from the beach and the ruins and has a swimming pool, tennis courts, markets and bar. From Magliana or Metro line B, take the Ostia Lido-Centro bus to its Capollinea. Then take #05 bus to Casal Palocco. L13,000 per person, L10,000 per tent, L6000 per car. Hot-water showers L1000.

■ Finding an Apartment

Finding an apartment in Rome is downright painful. About 20 years ago, the municipal government passed all kinds of legislation to protect tenants from being evicted. Today, many landlords are reluctant to rent out their apartments for fear of squatters and thus may leave their apartments empty. As a result, the real estate market is extremely tight, especially in the historic center; many families have lived in their houses for generations. The prices have also skyrocketed; expect to pay no less than L1,000,000 for a month in a one-bedroom in the city center. Cheaper areas include the Nomentana neighborhood, and the area around Piazza Bologna and the university. Utilities are inordinately expensive in Rome; they can augment your rent by up to 25%. As a foreigner you may also be required to pay special taxes or fees. Check English **classified ads** in *Wanted in Rome, Metropolitan,* and Italian ads in *Porta Portese.* The community and university **bulletin boards** carry advertisements for roommates. **Real estate agencies** can help, but they can charge hefty fees (from one month's rent on up, though more than one month's rent is suspicious). Avoid working with agencies that charge a non-refundable fee. Prowl around a particular neighborhood you'd like to live in and check for "for rent" *(affitasi)* signs, or ask people in the neighborhood if they know of any apartments. Check with **foreign university programs** as well; they often rent out apartments for their students for the school year, but leave them empty come summertime. Ultimately, the best way to find an apartment is through connections—network, network, network. If you know someone who heard of someone who had a hairdresser who lived in Rome—get that person's phone number. Be sure to check out apartments recommended by strangers.

The following real estate agents specialize in finding apartments for foreigners. Most of their clients are businesses, so they may be out of your price range, but they're often willing to give advice:

Edwards Real Estate Agency, Via Lanciani, 1 (tel. 861 08 71; fax 861 12 62). English, French, and Spanish spoken. Deals with apartments and villas, furnished and unfurnished.

Welcome Home Relocation Services, Via Barbarano Romano, 15 (tel. 303 669 36; fax 30 36 17 06). All kinds of housing plus assistance in documentation and orientation.

Property Network, Viale Angelico, 62 (tel./fax 372 98 95). If they can't help you themselves, they will refer you to other agencies and individuals specializing in lower-budget rentals.

Food and Wine

In ancient Rome, citizens ate only two meals a day: the *prandium* (a light midday meal) and *cena,* the dinner. Dinners were often lavish, festive affairs lasting as long as ten hours, with entertainment, music, and hanky-panky considered as vital as food. Roman writers such as Petronius and Juvenal reported the erotica, exotica, and excess of the Imperial dinner table: peacocks, flamingos, and herons were served with their full plumage meticulously replaced after cooking. Acrobats and fire-eaters distracted the guests between the courses of doormice and camels' feet. Food orgies went on *ad nauseam,* literally, for after gorging themselves, the guests would retreat to a special room called the *vomitorium,* throw it all up, and return to the party. More decorous families forwent the vomit-inducing gluttony, but even the stuffiest of Romans ate without cutlery, lying down, spitting on the floor, and belching their compliments to the chef.

Today, meals in Rome are still lengthy, though more refined, affairs, continuing for hours on end as each course is savored with deliberation. Breakfast, the one exception, is usually just a few sweet biscuits or a *cornetto,* downed with a glass of *caffè latte.* Lunch is traditionally the day's main meal, though some Romans now eat lunch on the go during the week, *all'americana.* Fortunately for the budget traveler, restaurants in Rome cater to most reasonable eating schedules; plop yourself down whenever you feel peckish and you're sure to be satisfied.

When you sit down at that charming *trattoria,* snack on the freshly baked bread, rolls, or breadsticks in the basket on your table as you peruse the menu. First come the **antipasti,** including *carciofi alla giudia* (or *alla romana;* fried artichokes), *fiori di zucca* (zucchini blossoms filled with cheese and fried), and *bruschetta al pomodoro* (thick pieces of bread, toasted and topped with olive oil, basil, and tomatoes). Meat-eaters will love *prosciutto e melone* (thinly-sliced cured ham with melon) or *bresaola e rughetta* (cured beef with arugula). If you're really hungry ask for the *antipasto misto,* usually a variety of peppers, olives, vegetables, cheese, and meats. On Fridays, try the *baccalà,* fried cod.

Next, the **primo piatto** (first course) arrives, usually *risotto* (rice), soup, or pasta. Try *spaghetti alla carbonara* (with bacon and egg) or *penne all'arrabbiata* (a spicy red sauce). On Thursdays, many restaurants serve up homemade *gnocchi,* a dense dumpling of potato or semolina, often in a gorgonzola sauce. Pasta prepared *all'amatriciana* is in a sauce of bacon, white wine, tomato, and pepper, while *spaghetti alle vongole* is served with clams. *Ravioli* filled with spinach and ricotta or porcini mushrooms also frequently appear on Roman menus.

The second course, or **secondo piatto,** usually consists of meat or fish. Common main courses include *saltimbocca* (slices of ham and veal cooked together, literally "jump in the mouth"), *abbacchio alla scottaditto* (tender grilled lamb at the "burnt finger"), *involtini al sugo* (rolled veal cutlets filled with ham, celery, and cheese, smothered in tomato sauce), and *coda alla vaccinara* (stewed oxtail with vegetables). Write home about *trippa* (chopped, sauteed cow intestines) or the rare treat, *pajata* (veal intestine with its mother's milk clotted inside, seasoned with garlic, chili peppers, tomatoes, and white wine). Seafood can be expensive, like the *anguilette in umido* (stewed baby eels from Lake Bracciano). San Giovanni's festival features *lumache* (snails). Vegetarians should try *scamorza alla griglia* (a slab of tasty cheese, grilled).

There are numerous vegetable specialties, **contorni,** served on the side or, more commonly, after the main course. Even the most carnivorous gourmets will enjoy *contorni* like *fagiolini* (early-picked, tender string beans), *zucchini* (tastier than the American or English variety), *melanzana* (eggplant prepared in a variety of ways), *bieta* (swiss chard), *broccoletti* (broccoli greens), and *cicoria* (chicory). Salads are usually eaten after the main course; however they have not experienced the immense degree of popularity, enormity, and variety that they have in the States.

Insalata verde is a green salad; ask for a sprinkling of *rughetta* (arugula to Americans, rocket to the Brits) or *radicchio* to add a tasty bitter touch. *Insalata mista* is a mixed salad (note that tomatoes in Italy are often partially green). *Insalata caprese* has tomatoes, fresh mozzarella, and basil. Fresh fennel, *finnochio*, is often served in raw chunks with a salted olive oil dip as a digestive.

After hours of rumination, and long after those with non-Italian appetites are full, dessert, fruit, cheese, and *espresso* are served. Imported from Venice, homemade *tiramisù* (ladyfingers soaked in espresso, layered with sweet mascarpone cheese, a dash of brandy, and dusted with chocolate) is an out-of-body experience. *Zuppa Inglese* (English soup), despite its name, is actually a trifle-like cake layered with custard and soaked in rum. For the less daring, *macedonia* is a mixed fruit cup.

For your *digestivo*, try *sambuca con le mosche* (anise liquor "with flies"), flaming with coffee beans floating on top. *Grappa,* a potent, doubly distilled clear liqueur made from old grape pressings, is another post-prandial option. A fitting cap to any meal is a leisurely stroll with that amazing and world-famous Italian ice cream, *gelato.* Another tasty summertime treat is the refreshing *grattachecca,* a heaping pile of shaved ice topped with gooey syrups in flavors like mint, cranberry, and coconut.

Emulating the Roman smorgasbord every night will cost you an arm and a leg and a month's membership at the gym. Pasta is generally the cheapest and most satisfying choice on the menu and comes with plenty of sauce to dip your bread in, though ordering only a *primo* will not endear you to the waitstaff. Huge plate-size pizzas satisfy the biggest appetites and the tightest budgets. Multi-course, fixed-price menus, often including wine, are becoming more and more common and are often less expensive than ordering a full feast à la carte. House wine is often as cheap as a bottle of sparkling water. If you want water from the tap, ask for *acqua dal rubinetto.* There's also *acqua minerale,* which comes carbonated *(frizzante, gassata,* or *con gas)* or non-carbonated *(naturale).*

The billing at Roman restaurants can be a bit confusing. Most restaurants will add a charge for **pane** (literally for bread, but actually a crafty way of working in a cover, which Roman restaurants are no longer allowed to charge) of about L1500 per person to the price of your meal, as well as tacking on a service charge **(servizio)** of 10%-15%. Do not be surprised to see your L8000 bowl of pasta inflated to L11,000 after *pane* and *servizio*; keep an eye out for additional charges before you order. Restaurants and stores are also required to give you a **ricevuta fiscale** (receipt) for tax purposes. You are required by law to carry it with you until you are sixty meters away from the restaurant. There is a fine for both the restaurant and the patron if you fail to do so. Such arrests are infrequent, but don't be surprised if your waiter comes chasing you down the street with your receipt if you forget to take it.

CATEGORIES OF RESTAURANTS

Ristorante is generally the most elegant sort, with dolled-up waiters, linen tablecloths, and expensive (though not necessarily better) dishes. A **trattoria** has a more casual atmosphere and lower prices. Occasionally there are no menus, and they just bring you what they are making. In some establishments, you can order a smaller portion of pasta, which gets you a plate two-thirds full for two-thirds the price. If you find an original **osteria** (or **hostaria**), you'll see old locals sitting around a table, chewing the fat, playing cards, downing bottles of wine or beer. However, these casual spots are rare and many so-called *osterie* are overpriced *ristoranti* in disguise. Similarly, *trattorie* can range tremendously in price. Many of the smaller, more authentic lunch spots, called **enoteche**, sometimes sporting the sign **vino e cucina** (wine and cooking), cater to a regular crew of workers and are the last relics of the *osteria* lifestyle. An *enoteca* is actually a wine store (not a bar), and some have added card tables with paper tablecloths to the back room and serve simple fare in a no-nonsense way. We list some of these establishments in a separate section below (see Enoteche (Wine Shops), p. 132).

In Italy there are two kinds of **pizzerias;** at a *pizzeria forno a legno,* you sit down to your own plate-size pizza. A well-prepared pizza is light and crispy and blackened

FOOD & WINE

Eat Your Heart Out, Chef Boyardee

We all know the greatest challenge facing any traveler in Rome. It's not figuring out the bus system, finding a bargain hotel, or climbing the stairs to the top of St. Peter's cupola—it's deciding which pasta to eat. Lucky for you, Marco Polo's souvenir has fathered generations of pasta derivatives designed to meet every picky mamma's needs. Don't even think of belittling the dazzling array of doughy delights; selecting the correct pasta for the dish and cooking it right (*al dente*—literally "to the teeth" and slightly chewy) is as close to Italian hearts as the Madonna herself. *Lasagne* come in at least two forms: flat or *ricce* (one edge crimped). The familiar *spaghetti* has larger, hollow cousins, such as *bucatini* and *maccheroni* (not the Yankee Doodle kind), as well as smaller, more delicate relatives like *capellini*. Flat pastas include the familiar *linguine* and *fettuccine*, with *taglierini* and *tagliatelle* filling in the size gaps. Short, roughly two-inch pasta tubes include *ziti, penne* (cut diagonally and occasionally *rigate*, or ribbed), *sedani* (curved), *rigatoni* (bigger), and *canneloni* (biggest and usually stuffed). Funny-shaped and good for entertaining the stimulation-deprived include *fusilli* (corkscrews), *farfalle* (butterflies or bow-ties), and *ruote* (wheels). Don't be alarmed if you see pastry displays with the label *pasta;* the Italian word refers to anything made of dough and vaguely edible. What we call "pasta" is actually *pasta asciutta* or "dry" pasta.

---

a little around the edges. There are innumerable pizza toppings and combinations, so order exactly what you want. The most common pizzas are the *margherita* (mozzarella and tomato sauce; ask for *basilico:* basil), *napolitana* (*margherita* with anchovies), *capricciosa* (a bit of everything: olives, ham, hard-boiled egg, tomato, cheese), and *funghi* (with mushrooms). Don't neglect the yummy appetizers, like *baccalà* and *bruschetta.* Be warned that asking for "pepperoni" will get you red peppers, not salami. In a *pizzeria rustica* or *a taglio,* you order a slice or a particular weight of any of the pizzas already prepared and displayed at the counter. *Pizza rustica* is thick and square, and often topped with interesting tidbits. Try pizza with *gamberi* (shrimp), potatoes, or even with the chocolate-hazelnut confection, *nutella.* At either pizzeria, be sure to sample *supplì,* rice balls with tomato sauce and mozzarella, battered, and deep-fried.

FOOD ON THE GO

Alimentari are your best bet for standard groceries, stocking dairy, dry goods, and deli items. For specialty cheeses, fresh bread, and meats, head to a **panificio** or a **salumeria.** These shops can fix you a sandwich or simply sell you the ingredients; an **etto** (100g) of anything is usually enough for a sandwich. For produce, seek out the small **frutta e verdure** shops and stands. Food stores are open roughly Mon.-Wed. and Fri. 8am-1pm and 4-8pm, Thurs. and Sat. 8am-1pm. Get a taste of local produce and local haggling techniques at Rome's many outdoor **markets.** The largest markets are at P. Campo de' Fiori, P. Vittorio Emanuele II, and in Piazza San Cosimato in Trastevere. Smaller markets can be found on Via Montebello and Piazza della Pace off Piazza Navona. Markets generally operate Mon.-Sat. 6am-2pm, and sell a large variety of goods, from food and housewares to clothing and antiques—good to remember if you're planning an extended stay and need kitchen supplies. Supermarket **STANDA** offers a huge selection of foodstuffs, produce, toiletries, kitchen supplies, cheap clothing, and anything else you can think of. There is one located on Viale Trastevere, a few blocks down from Piazza Sidney Sonnino, and one on Via Cola di Rienzo, several blocks down from the Ottaviano Metro stop.

A **bar** is an excellent place to have a quick and inexpensive bite, though take care to avoid bars on major tourist thoroughfares, where prices go through the roof. Despite their name, Italian bars are more like what an American would call a "café" (or in this case *caffè*) selling café drinks, pastries, non-alcoholic and alcoholic beverages, as well as hot and cold sandwiches and salads. **Tramezzini** come with an assortment of fillings, often smothered in mayo and surrounded by soft, de-crusted white bread, just like Mom used to make. Try the rolls and *pizza bianca* (what Romans call *focaccia*) stuffed with *prosciutto* (ham), cheese, or even omelettes. You can have any sandwich **scaldato** (heated) in the waffle-iron-like sandwich pressing machine. A **tavola calda** or a **rosticceria** may be cheaper than a sit-down meal, but quality varies. Most offer a broad range of hot and cold dishes, from roast chickens, fried *calamari* (squid), and eggplant parmesan to rice salad and sandwiches.

A few words of advice: when looking for a restaurant, stay away from the area near the train station—most ostensible "bargain" restaurants (offering dirt-cheap, fixed-price menus) are actually second-rate tourist snares which serve nothing resembling Italian cuisine. Instead, hop on a bus to reach the nearby university district of **San Lorenzo** or the working-class neighborhood, **Testaccio.** These are the last truly untouristed neighborhoods in Rome. The areas around **Piazza Navona** and **Campo dei Fiori** harbor some romantic *trattorie,* and **Trastevere** boasts the liveliest pizzerias. Romans generally eat late—around 8 or 9pm; set out early to avoid the rush. Most restaurants close for at least two weeks in August. One final tip; some say the mark of a good restaurant is the presence of voracious *carabinieri* (police), who take their food seriously, so keep an eye out for the blue uniforms.

In order to enhance your Roman culinary experience, we've divided this chapter into five sections: Restaurants (by location), Desserts, Caffè, Wine, and Markets. You choose the category and we provide our suggestions, recommendations, and advice. All neighborhoods are also listed alphabetically in the index as subheadings of the larger restaurant category. *Buon appetito!*

RESTAURANTS (BY LOCATION)

▨ Centro Storico

■ Piazza Navona

Authentic, inexpensive *trattorie* are easy to find in the Piazza Navona area, but steer clear of the main *piazza,* where the restaurants entice witless tourists with English menus and then overcharge them shamelessly. Some of the best restaurants in the city hide along Via Governo Vecchio and the alleys emerging from it; head here for authentic Italian restaurants that cater to real-live Italians. Often, lunch-time favorites are unmarked; look for doorways with bead curtains or follow an Italian worker to a favorite lunch spot. There is no shortage of *alimentari* (grocery stores), *tavole calde* (self-service restaurants that serve hot dishes), and *pizzerie rustiche* lining Via di Ripetta and around the Pantheon. The best ice cream places surround the Pantheon and the main piazza.

★ **Palladini,** Via del Governo Vecchio, 29 (tel. 68 61 237). Really a *salumeria* (deli) rather than a bona fide restaurant. No sign or place to sit, but bustling with a Roman lunch crowd eating seconds-old *panini.* Point to the fillings of your choice and eat outside. Favorites include *prosciutto e fiche* (ham and figs) or *bresaola e rughetta* (cured beef with arugula) sprinkled with parmesan cheese and lemon juice. A plethora of vegetable options—artichoke, peppers, mushrooms, tomatoes, and more—make anything possible. Hearty sandwich L2500-5000. Open summer Mon.-Fri. 8am-2pm and 5-8pm, Sat. 8am-2pm. In winter, closed Thurs. afternoons.

★ **Pizzeria Baffetto,** Via del Governo Vecchio, 114 (tel. 686 16 17), on the corner of Via Sora. Once a meeting place for '60s radicals, Baffetto now overflows with Romans of all political persuasions. The *pizza gigante* could almost feed the entire Forza Italia party, Berlusconi included. Outdoor seating. Harried service. Pizzas L5000-9000. *Vino* L6000. Cover L1000. Open Mon.-Sat. 7:30pm-1am.

Trattoria Gino e Pietro, Via del Governo Vecchio, 106 (tel. 686 15 76), at Vicolo Savelli. Keep your eyes peeled for the reddish wood sign that marks the location of this establishment teetering on the line between *trattoria* and *osteria*. The main menu is always in an exciting state of flux. Delve into the back room for a huge array of homemade *antipasti vegetali* (L7500). *Secondi* L8500-15,000. *Pane* L1000. Open Fri.-Wed. noon-3pm and 6:30-11pm. Closed mid-July to mid-August. Reservations accepted.

L'Insalata Ricca 2, P. Pasquino, 72, right off of the southwest corner of P. Navona. Who ever said sequels disappoint? This spin-off of the original (see p. 118) is just as good. Omelettes cooked to order (L6000). The *gnocchi verdi alla gorgonzola* L9000 are outstanding. *Secondi* L8000-13,000. *Pane* L2000. Open daily noon-3pm and 7-11:30pm. Reservations recommended for Sat.

Il Giardinetto, Via del Governo Vecchio, 125 (tel. 686 86 93), Escape the hard, dusty cobblestones of the area, and dine beneath the leaf-lined ceiling of this Tunisian-run oasis. Edith Piaf's *La Vie en Rose* and soothing Barry Manilow lilt through this pastel heaven. Take your time over the well-seasoned pastas—try the *gnocchetti* (L9000) or the *pennette alla gorgonzola* (L9000) and house wine (L8000 per liter). Portions generous enough to skip the *secondi* (L13,000-15,000). Open Tues.-Sun. 10:30am-3pm and 6pm-midnight. AmEx, DC, MC, Visa.

Pizzeria Corallo, Via del Corallo 10/11 (tel. 68 30 77 03), off Via del Governo Vecchio. Unusual pizzas in a laid-back setting of green arches, crayon graffiti, and a metal palm tree. The waiters are as zesty as the fare. Enjoy wild creations like the *focaccia scamorza fiori di zucca e alici*, a pizza with scamorza cheese topped with zucchini flowers and anchovies (L12,000). Pizzas L7000-13,000. The homemade desserts are sublime (*tiramisù* L5000, *panna cotta* L5000). Outdoor seating. Open Tues.-Sun. 7pm-1am.

La Pentola, Via Metastasio, 21 (tel. 68 80 26 07), off Piazza Firenze. One of the waiters claims to speak 9 languages (11 dialects), but English is definitely one of them. Excellent service and food that might have you moaning aloud (no joke). *Bruschetta* L3000 is a must. Their *pizza caprese* L10,000 defies paltry adjectival expression. Outdoor dining. Open Tues.-Sun. noon-3:30pm and 7pm-12:30am.

■ Ethnic foods

Piedra del Sol, Vicolo Rosini, 6 (tel. 68 73 651), off of Via di Campo Marzio across from Piazza del Parlamente. Countless Aztec calendars, painted Mayan figures, and pictures of Emiliano Zapata adorn the stuccoed walls of this little establishment. If you're craving creamy *enchiladas suizas* with chicken (L17,000) and nachos as an appetizer (L9000), you won't be disappointed. Happy hour upstairs from midnight to 1am. Margarita L10,000. Obligatory chips and salsa L3000 per person. Open Sept.-July daily 7:30pm-12:30am. Closed Sun. in July. AmEx, Visa.

Giardino del Melograno, Vicolo dei Chiodarole, 16/18 (tel. 68 80 34 23), off of Via dei Chiavari near Campo dei Fiori. The most renowned Chinese restaurant in Rome, a vast menu offers an antipasti delight of various kinds of ravioli (L4500). The tourist menu offers a full lunch for L11,000. Shrimp, chicken, and mixed vegetables make up the delectable *pentola cinese* (L10,000). No cover, service, or bread charge. Open Sun.-Tues. and Thurs.-Sat. noon-3pm and 7-11:30pm. Reservations accepted. AmEx, MC, Visa.

■ Campo dei Fiori

For many Romans, this neighborhood is the authentic, pre-commercial Rome of years gone by. Its cobblestone streets, miniature *piazze*, and broad avenues are just as enticing to the uninitiated who are seeking spirited meals and romantic wine bars. There are innumerable restaurants hidden in these streets; try Via Monserrato to the south and west of the *piazza*. *Caffè*, bars, pastry shops, and *alimentari* tempt and tantalize along Via dei Giubbonari.

★**L'Insalata Ricca,** Largo di Chiavari, 85 (tel. 68 80 36 56), off Corso Vittorio Emanuele near P. Sant'Andrea della Valle. Funky modern art, innovative dishes, and an off-beat ambience are successfully combined here with neighborly service and savory, traditional *trattoria* food. New, expanded seating downstairs and outside accommodates the devoted masses. Try the *gnocchetti sardi* (L8500) or request their title dish *insalata ricca,* a robust salad with everything on it (L9000). Whole wheat pasta *integrale* L9000. *Pane* L1500. Open daily 12:30-3:15pm and 6:45-11:15pm. Closed Wednesday in winter.

Hostaria Grappolo d'Oro, Piazza della Cancelleria, 80-81 (tel. 686 41 18), on Via Cancelleria off Corso Vittorio Emanuele II. The owner concentrates on turning his neighborhood *trattoria* into a stellar (but still inexpensive) gastronomic ecstasy. Words are too cheap for his *antipasti* (L10,000) and *penne all'arrabbiata* (L10,000). House white wine L9000. *Pane* L2000. Open Mon.-Sat. noon-3pm and 7-11pm. AmEx, DC, MC, Visa.

Arnaldo ai Satiri, Via di Grotta Pinta, 8 (tel. 686 19 15), take Largo dei Chiavari off of Corso Vittorio Emanuele to Piazza dei Satiri and turn right. Unusual dishes include spicy *fusilli con melanzane* (pasta with eggplant, L10,000), fresh *gazpacho* (L10,000), and the speciality of the house, pasta with cabbage cream sauce (L10,000). Alight with red lightbulbs and candles, the interior looks like a cross between a bordello and a darkroom. Outdoor dining in summer. Open Wed.-Mon. 12:30-3pm and 7:30pm-1am. AmEx, DC, MC, Visa.

Filetti di Baccalà, Largo dei Librari, 88 (tel. 686 40 18). Take Via dei Giubbonari off P. Campo dei Fiori; Largo dei Librari will be on your left. Be sure not to miss this busy, unpretentious little establishment located in a tiny *piazza* beneath a small church. The ideal spot for informal *antipasti* and wine, this self-service favorite makes an unforgettable *filetto di baccalà* (deep-fried cod filet, L5000). Wine L7000 per liter. *Pane* L1500. Open Sept.-July. Mon.-Sat. 5:30-10:40pm, winter open 5-10:40pm.

L'Oasi della Pizza, Via della Corda, 5 (tel. 687 28 76). Off the southern side of Campo dei Fiori. The brick oven in the center of the room is not a mirage. Quiet, simple, yummy. Pizzas L8000-16,000. *Pane* L2000. Open Thurs.-Tues. noon-3pm and 7-11:30pm.

Da Sergio, Vicolo delle Grotte, 27 (tel. 654 66 69). Exit Campo dei Fiori from the southeast corner on Via dei Giubbonari and take your first right. Da Sergio is legendary for its pasta plates, so much so that they occasionally run out. Fortunately, their pizzas are excellent too (L7000-15,000). On summer nights, Romans throng the tables in the cobbled alley outside. Service ranges from Parisian to personal, depending on how often you eat here. *Servizio* L2000. Open Mon.-Sat. 12:30-3pm and 7pm-12:30am.

Pizzeria Vergilio, Campo dei Fiori, 10/A (tel. 68 80 27 46). One of the least expensive spots in a row of bustling *caffè* and *trattorie.* During the day you can watch the market from the shade of an umbrella, while the view of the *piazza* at dusk is unforgettable. Delicious pizzas (L8000-12,000) and rich pasta dishes (the *fettuccine al salmone* is excellent, L12,000). *Pane* L1000. Open Thurs.-Tues. noon-3pm and 7-11pm. MC, Visa.

Om Shanti, Campo dei Fiori, 53-54 (tel. 687 55 30). Portions here at the eastern end of the *piazza* are big (L7000-14,000 for pizza, L7000-12,000 for pasta). It's a cheerful, informal place, with umbrella tables spilling out into the morning market. 15% service charge. Open Tues.-Sun. 11:30am-midnight. AmEX, DC, MC, Visa.

Ristorante la Pollarola, Piazza della Pollarola, 24-25 (tel. 68 80 16 54), take L. Chiavari two blocks south of C. Vittorio Emanuele II. A typical Roman *trattoria* with good eats, charming location, and tolerable prices. Outside dining in the summer. *Spaghetti alla carbonara* L9000. *Fettuccine ai funghi porcini* (fettuccini with porcini mushrooms) L10,000. House wine L8000 per liter. *Pane* L2000. Open Sept.-July Mon.-Sat. 12:30-3:30pm and 7:30-11:30pm. Reservations accepted. Diner's, MC, Visa.

■ The Jewish Ghetto

To the west of the roaring Via Arenula, the former Jewish Ghetto has endured centuries of modernization, anti-Semitism, and tourism to remain a proud community, and to become, these days, an extremely chic locale, with all kinds of Romans trekking

FOOD & WINE

here to sample the home cooking. Many traditional Roman dishes actually originated in this neighborhood, like *carciofi alla giudia* (fried artichokes, also known as *carciofi alla romana*) and *fiori di zucca* (zucchini blossoms filled with cheese, battered, and lightly fried). Keep an eye out for kosher groceries and bakeries.

★ **Margarita,** Via di S. Maria de' Calderari, 30, right next to the big green door to the S. Maria del Pianto church, off of P. delle Cinque Scole. Behind the green rope door (don't look for a sign), locals and RISD European Honors Program students fight over politics in a basement filled with the smoke of frying fish. The place is tiny and almost always packed with customers awaiting delicious homemade treats. The daily specials are scrawled on the single paper menu—on Thursday, you might be able to experience homemade *gnocchi* for L10,000. *Fettuccine* L10,000. *Baccalà* (fried salt cod) L11,000. *Pane* L2000. Open Mon.-Fri. noon-3pm.

Ristorante Il Portico, Via del Portico d'Ottavio, 1E (tel. 68 30 79 37), around the corner from the Teatro di Marcello. Wonderful fresh anchovies with green beans, delicious and unusual kosher pastries in a comfortable outdoor setting. Kosher meat, wine, and marinated vegetables served from the same menu as non-kosher food. *Zuppa di ceci* (chickpeas) L10,000. *Spaghetti cacio e pepe* (grated cheese and pepper) L12,000. *Pane* L2000. Open Wed.-Mon. 12:30-3pm and 7-11:30pm.

Ristorante da Giggetto, Via del Portico Ottavio, 21-22 (tel. 686 11 05). Swallow a lot of the *carciofi alla giudia* (fried artichoke, L8000 each) as you sit at arm's length from the ancient ruins of the Portico d'Ottavio. *Supplì* (a rice ball with mozzarella, tomato sauce, and meat, deep fried) L2000. *Buccatini all'amatriciana* L12,000. *Pane* L3000. Open Tues.-Sun. 12:30pm-3pm and 7:30-11pm.

Ristorante Piperno, Via Monte de' Cenci, 9 (tel. 68 80 66 29), on your right as you walk towards the Tiber from P. delle Cinque Scole. Founded in 1856, this air-conditioned, classy, and pricey locale boasts of having introduced the fried artichoke to the masses (2 for L20,000). They also have *pasta e ceci con taglioni* (with chickpeas, L20,000) and *fritto misto* (L30,000). Pastas L20,000. *Coperto* L6000. Open Tues.-Sat. 12:15-3pm and 8pm-midnight, Sun. 12:15-3pm. Closed in Aug. AmEx, DC, MC, Visa.

■ Near the Spanish Steps

Caveat edax (let the diner beware): the high prices in this flashy district are no guarantee of quality. Although looking for inexpensive meals around Piazza di Spagna is like looking for a bargain at Armani, there are a few places that don't check for gold cards at the door. Skip McDonald's, even if they do have beautiful desserts and *really* nice bathrooms, and opt for a hot *panino* with mozzarella and prosciutto, a salad, or a piece of *pizza rustica* at one of the many bars in this area. There are *alimentari* at Via Laurina, 36 and Via di Ripetta, 233. Produce markets are on Via del Lavatore, near the Trevi Fountain, and halfway down Via Tomacelli between the fountain and Via dell'Arancio. Both are open approximately 8am-1pm.

★ **La Capricciosa,** Largo dei Lombardi, 8 (tel. 687 86 36 or 687 86 36). Right off Via del Corso and across from the intersection of Via del Corso and Via della Croce. This is the home of the famous *capricciosa* pizza, divided into four sections of ham, egg, artichoke, and so on (L9000). The venerable waiters are attentive, serving up perfect pizzas on the outdoor terrace. *Primi* (L8000-11,000), including *ravioli di ricotta e spinaci.* Desserts (L6000). *Pane* L2000. Open Wed.-Mon. 12:30-3pm and 6:30pm-12:30am. Reservations necessary for large groups. AmEx, MC, Visa.

★ **Trattoria da Settimio all'Arancio,** Via dell'Arancio, 50 (tel. 687 61 19). Take Via dei Condotti from P. di Spagna, cross Via del Corso, continue on Via della Fontanella Borghese, take your first right then your first left. A favorite among savvy Romans. Run by the same family that runs Al Piccolo Arancio. Excellent 3-course meals L27,000-45,000. Try the *ossobuco* (braised veal shank in sauce, L15,000) or the *ravioli all'arancia* (with orange), L10,000. Huge portions of fresh vegetables (L4000-8000) and delicious *antipasti.* *Pane* L2000. Fresh fish Tues. and Fri. Open

Mon.-Sat. 12:30-3:30pm and 7:15pm-midnight. Reservations accepted. AmEx, DC, MC, Visa.

Al Piccolo Arancio, Vicolo Scanderberg, 112 (tel. 678 61 39). Near the Trevi Fountain in a little alley off of Via del Lavatore, which is on the right as you face the fountain. The sign says "Hostaria." Delicious pastas and appetizers. Try the *fiori di zucca* (fried zucchini flowers stuffed with mozzarella, L7000) or the *carciofi alla giudia* (a whole fried artichoke, L5000). If you're lucky enough to hit this place on the same day as the fish merchants (Tues. and Fri.), order the homemade *gnocchi al salmone* (L9000) or the *linguine all'aragosta* (lobster linguini;L9000). *Pane* L2000. Arrive early. Open Tues.-Sun. noon-3pm and 7-11:30pm. Closed in Aug. AmEx, DC, MC, Visa.

Pizzeria al Leoncino, Via del Leoncino, 28 (tel. 68 76 306). Take Via Condotti from P. di Spagna, cross Via del Corso, continue on Via della Fontana Borghese, then take your first right onto Via del Leoncino. Fast, inexpensive, and informal. Traditional, hand-prepared pizzas (L8000-12,000) baked in front of you and the hordes of Romans who love the place. Wine L5000 per liter. Open Mon., Tues., Thurs., and Fri. 1-3pm and 7pm-midnight, Sat.-Sun. 7pm-midnight.

Ristorante e Pizzeria Er Buco, Via del Lavatore, 91 (tel. 678 11 54), steps from P. di Trevi. Possibly the oldest pizza oven in the city. It's tiny, so get there early and avoid the crowds. Taste the perfection which is their pizza *"Er Buco"* (tomatoes, cheese, *parmigiano,* and basil) L9000. *Bruschetta alla crema di carciofi* (toast with artichoke paste) L4000. Salmon calzone L10,000. Open Mon.-Sat. noon-3pm and 6:30-11:30pm.

Ristorante Vegetariano Margutta, Via Margutta 119 (tel. 36 00 18 05), off Via del Babuino, a block before Piazza del Popolo. The place to be if you're a rich vegetarian. Unclassifiable music plays in the background and well-dressed waitresses rush by as you drift into oil paint oblivion while your lettuce is prepared. Greek or arugula and parmesan salad (L12,000), *radicchio* and *provola risotto* (L12,000). Bottle of slightly alcoholic apple cider L12,000. Lunch package for L20,000 to L23,000 with wine. Open Sept.-July Mon.-Sat. 1-3:30pm and 7:40-11:40pm. AmEx, MC, Visa.

Centro Macrobiotico Italiano-Naturalist Club, Via della Vite, 14 (tel. 679 25 09), on the third floor, just off Via del Corso. A different batch of wholesome food is made each day, explaining the absence of a lunch menu. Lunch foods and sweets are usually eaten up by 3pm, but the tea room remains open, serving cakes and, well, tea. Dinner features naturist cooking with vegetarian delights and plates with fresh fish as an alternative. They also sell New Age books and natural cosmetics. Membership costs L30,000 per year (which reduces as the year progresses; in the summer months, membership is only about L13,000). Tourists are allowed one meal with a L2000 surcharge and a passport or other foreign ID. A full meal comes to about L15,000. *Cous-cous vegetale* L7200. Open Mon.-Fri. 10am-6:30pm and 7:30pm-midnight.

Trattoria la Buca di Ripetta, Via di Ripetta, 36 (tel. 321 93 91), 2 blocks from P. del Popolo. An air-conditioned sanctuary adorned with wine bottles and copper pots. Baked *lasagne* L9500. *Tortellini in brodo* L9000. Tongue (only in winter) L13,000. Wine L10,000 per liter. *Pane* L2000. One of the few places open for lunch on Sunday. Open Tues.-Sat. 12:15-3pm and 7:30-11pm, Sun. 12:30-3pm. Closed in Aug. Reservations recommended. AmEx, DC, Visa.

Trattoria e Pizzeria del Pollarolo, Via Ripetta 4-5 (tel. 361 02 76). Ten yards from the Piazza del Popolo presides the Pizzeria del Pollarolo. Simple eats, small, and friendly. *Pizza capricciosa* L14,000, other pizzas L10,000-14,000. *Gnocchi* L10,000. *Zuppa di verdure* L8000. Non-alcoholic beer L4000. *Insalata* L5000-6000. *Pane* L2000. Open Sept.-July Fri.-Wed. 12:30pm-3pm and 7-11pm. AmEx, Diner's Club, MC, Visa, all of them.

Ristorante da Ugo al Gran Sasso, Via di Ripetta, 32 (tel. 321 48 83). A lively, bustling place with a grand menu in Italian and English. *Spaghetti alle vongole* (with clam sauce) L10,000. Other pastas L7000-10,000. Tomatoes stuffed with rice L5000. Fish on Fridays. Liter of house wine L7000. *Pane* L1000. Open Sun.-Fri. noon-4pm and 7-11pm. AmEx, DC, Visa.

Hostaria al Vantaggio, Via del Vantaggio, 34 (tel. 323 68 48), off Via del Corso, a few blocks south of Piazza del Popolo. Lovely outdoor dining in summer. Don't confuse the peach tablecloths and massive canvas umbrellas with those of its over-priced neighbors. Filling, elegant meals. Tourist menu (which includes a first and second plate, vegetable dish, and fruit) L24,000. *Pizza gorgonzola* L11,000. Roast chicken L10,000. *Saltimbocca alla romana* (L16,000). *Pane* L1500. Open Mon.-Sat. noon-3pm and 7-11pm. Closed 2 weeks in July. AmEx, DC, MC, Visa.

■ Ethnic foods

Hamasei, Via della Mercede, 35-36 (tel. 67 92 134 or 67 92 413), just off Piazza San Silvestro. Modernistic pine interior with gentle mood lighting is a placid relief from the boisterous neighborhood *trattorie*. Though the complete meal deals are a bit pricey (L40,000), the à la carte dishes, like the yummy *yumen* (hot broth with noodles), or the sumptuous *sashimi* (both L15,000), are delectable and filling, especially if you top it off with a side order of rice (L3500). Lunch special L18,000. Take-out available. Service charge 15%. Open Tues.-Sun. noon-2:30pm and 7-10:30pm.

McDonald's, Piazza di Spagna, 46-47 (tel. 69 92 24 00). See p. 128 for details.

■ Ancient City

Despite its past glory, this area has yet to discover the noble concept of "the affordable restaurant." Flanked on all sides by wide, traffic-ridden streets, you may want to head straight out to the many bars and *tavole calde* on Via Cavour. If you need immediate relief, head to one of the following locales.

★ **Taverna dei Quaranta,** Via Claudia, 24 (tel. 700 05 50). This is the best food you can afford in the shade of the mighty amphitheater. Its cool, tree-shaded outdoor dining provides the ultimate respite from baking in the sun. The ever-changing menu features an outstanding *bruschetta al pomodoro* (toasted bread topped with chopped tomatoes, olive oil, and basil, L3500) and such creations as *linguine alla crema di zucchini* (L9000). Beer from the tap L5000. Open daily noon-3pm and 8pm-midnight. AmEx, MC, Visa.

★ **Hostaria da Nerone,** Via delle Terme di Tito, 96 (tel. 474 52 07). Just steps north of the Colosseum. Perhaps Rome's only openly gay restaurant. With the Colosseum on one side and the ruins of the Baths of Titus on the other, you can feast on *fettucine alla Nerone* (with salami, ham, beans, and mushrooms; L8000), or the more daring *fritto di cervello con zucchine o carciofi* (fried brain with zucchini or artichoke, L14,000). Wash it down with a ¼-liter of red or white wine (L2000). Outdoor dining. *Pane* L2500. 10% service charge added. Open Mon.-Sat. noon-3pm and 7:30-11pm.

Trattoria di Priscilla, Via Appia Antica, 68 (tel. 513 63 79), across from the Domine Quo Vadis, it can be reached from the parking lot of the S. Callisto catacombs. Its sign says simply "Trattoria," so look for the street number. A cozy, family-run establishment hidden in an area where overpriced, tourist-oriented restaurants abound. Takes its name from an upper-class contemporary of Nero, whose tomb is visible in an exposed segment of the back wall. Pasta dishes L8500. *Pollo alla romana* L13,500. Open daily noon-3pm and 8-11pm. AmEx, DC.

Pizzeria Imperiale, Largo C. Ricci, 37 (tel. 678 68 71), at the start of Via Cavour opposite the Roman Forum entrance gate. Recover from ruins under one of the dozens of shady umbrellas. Good pizzas; try the *peccato del frate* (red peppers, zucchini, spicy sausage, olives, and artichokes) for L12,000. Check out the *calzone gigante*. Pasta L9000-13,000. Wine L10,000 per liter. Open daily noon-4pm and 5pm-midnight. MC, Visa.

Bar Martini, Piazza del Colosseo, 3a & 3b (tel. 700 44 31), on the side of the Colosseum opposite the Colosseum entrance. Find relief here in more ways than one. This friendly outdoor *bar/trattoria* sports not only a wide variety of food (pasta L10,000-13,000, sandwiches L4000-7000) but a great big public bathroom for those feeling a little pent up after a day of wandering through insufficiently equipped ancient spaces. A towering Colosseum view. Open July-Aug. daily 9am-2am, Sept.-June Thurs.-Tues. 8am-1am. AmEx, DC, MC, Visa.

Ristoro della Salute, Piazza del Colosseo, 2a (tel. 700 44 56), next door to Bar Martini. Cold tasty things everywhere. Mix your *frulatti* (fruit shakes) with all the fruits you can imagine, L5000. If you're planning to hang out at the forum, try their *frulatti energetico e vitaminico* with granola, L5500. Frappes L3000 and up. *Gelati* and *dolci* L2000-5000. Open daily 8am-2am; Sept.-May Wed.-Mon. 8am-midnight.

■ Trastevere

You can't say you've been to Rome without having savored a pizza and swilled some house wine in one of the rowdy outdoor pizzerias in Trastevere. Just across the river from the historic center and down the river from the Vatican, Trastevere is the site of the city's most raucous beer parlors, hopping pizza joints, and loud bohemian population. By day, these laundry-filled streets rumble only with the sounds of children and the occasional Vespa, but by the time night rolls around, the Piazza di Santa Maria di Trastevere is packed with expatriate hippies and their dogs, howling along with the out-of-tune folk guitars, while the monied diners from the more costly restaurants stroll by.

★ **Taverna della Scala,** P. della Scala, 19 (tel 581 41 00). A *trattoria* with quiet outdoor dining featuring an enormous selection of pizzas and pastas. Start off with a *bruschetta al pomodoro, con melanzane* (eggplant), or *al pâté d'olive* (L2000-4000). Pastas L7000-10,000, pizzas L5000-10,000. Check out the *piatti del giorno* on the board outside, offering specials like *gnocchi con crema di carciofi* (potato dumplings in an artichoke cream sauce). *Pane* L2000. Open Wed.-Mon. 12:30-3pm and 7pm-midnight.

★ **Pizzeria Ivo,** Via di San Francesca a Ripa, 158 (tel. 581 70 82). Take a right on Via delle Fratte di Trastevere off Viale Trastevere and another right on Via J. Francesco a Ripa. Alas, the tourists have finally discovered this Trastevere legend, but the mouth-watering pizza's still well worth the long wait and chaotic atmosphere. Pizza L8000-16,000. Open Sept.-July Wed.-Mon. 5pm-2am.

★ **Hostaria da Augusto,** P. de' Renzi, 15 (580 37 98). Take Via Fonte Olio to the right as you face the church in P.S. Maria in Trastevere, to Vicolo del Piede which leads to P. de' Renzi. Neighborhood crowds spill from this no-frills restaurant into its tiny *piazza.* Daily pasta specials including *gnocchi* on Thursday and *pasta e ceci* on Friday, L6000-7000. Cheap satisfying *secondi* L9000-12,000. No cover. Open Mon.-Sat. noon-3pm, Mon.-Fri. 8-11pm. Closed in Aug.

Pizzeria Sonnino, Viale di Trastevere, 23, 2 doors down from the big movie theater. A hectic, popular *pizza a taglio* joint. Potato with rosemary and *margherita* slices cost L1500 per *etto,* and their *supplì* (vegetarian) and *crochette* are out of this world (L1000 each). Roast half-chicken L6000. *Tavola calda* pasta dishes L6000-8000. Open 8am-midnight. Occasionally closed Mon.

Il Tulipano Nero, Via Roma Libera, 15 (tel. 581 83 09), in P. San Cosimato. A friendly, rowdy pizzeria—dine outdoors in the summer. Iron palates can attempt the *pennette all'elettroshock* (very hot indeed, L10,000), or try the innovative pizza combos. *Pizza tonno, mais, e rughetta* (with tuna, corn, and arugula, L10,000) tastes far better than it sounds. All plates served in small or gigantic *(gigante)* portions. Open daily 6pm-2am.

Hostaria da Corrado, Via della Pelliccia, 39. Arrive early to sample the consistently delectable Roman fare at this charmingly typical *osteria.* Super spicy *penne all'arrabbiata* L7000. Ravioli filled with mushrooms or spinach and ricotta L7000. Traditional Roman *secondi: involtine* (veal rolled around vegetables; L8000), *scamorza* (slab of grilled cheese; L7500). *Pane* L1000. Open daily 12:30-3pm and 7:30-11pm.

Hostaria er Belli, Piazza Sant'Apollonia, 11 (tel. 580 37 82). Off Via della Lungaretta right before P. Santa Maria in Trastevere. A friendly *trattoria* specializing in Sardinian cooking. *Ravioli sardi* (in tomato cream sauce, L11,000); meat tortellini in cream sauce with mushrooms L11,000. *Pane* L2000. Open Tues.-Sun. 12:30-2:30pm and 7:30-11:30pm.

Sala da Te Trastè (tel. 589 44 30), Via della Lungaretta, 76. More of a place to nosh than dine. Crêpes, desserts, salads (L7000-10,000). Tea out the wazoo L5000, herbal and otherwise. Sit at the groovy low couches and tables. Open Tues.-Sun. 5pm-midnight.

■ Ethnic Foods

India House, Via di Santa Cecilia, 8 (tel. 581 85 05). Turn left (east) off Viale Trastevere at McDonald's, continue down Via dei Genovesi, and turn right at its end. On the left, a few meters up the street. Perfumes of a curry sort waft through the stillness of this perfectly beautiful, quiet, and authentically Italian section of Trastevere. No ordering à la carte–the fixed-price menu includes meat, rice, potatoes, vegetables, bread, and dessert for L22,000. Open Tues.-Sun. 7-11pm. Call ahead to find out what the day's menu is.

Ocak Başi, Via del Moro, 24. A Turkish restaurant brimming with the smells and sounds of Istanbul. Good choices include fried eggplant with yogurt (L8000), kebabs with vegetables (L8000), and baklava (L8000). *Pane* L1000. Open Tues.-Sun. 7:30-11:30pm. AmEx, MC, Visa.

McDonald's, Piazza Sonnino, 39-40 (tel. 588 71 27). See p. 128 for details. Open 10:30am-12:30am.

Stardust, Vicolo de' Renzi, 4 (tel. 58 32 08 75). Take a right off Via dell Lungaretta onto Via del Moro right before P.S. Maria in Trastevere. Vicolo de' Renzi is the second street on the left. American food on an American timetable. More than just brunch all day long, Stardust's cuisine is a *menage à trois* of Italian desserts, American breakfast, and Middle-Eastern treats. Bagels with cream cheese (L6000), crêpes with banana and Nutella© (L5000), baba ghanoush (L3000). Beer L4000-6000, mixed dinners L6000-12,000. Live jazz every night. Open Mon.-Fri. 1:30pm-3am, Sat.-Sun. 11:30am-2am.

■ The Borgo and Prati (near the Vatican)

During the day, the streets of the Prati and Borgo fill with foreigners overwhelmed and exhausted by sightseeing in Vatican City. The character of the area changes at night, as the locals head to neighborhood *trattore* and *pizzerie* for classic Roman fare. The residential district around Via Cola di Rienzo hides some great bargains, as well as an immense indoor food market. Take Metro Linea A to Ottaviano.

★ **Hostaria dei Bastioni,** Via Leone IV, 29 (tel. 39 72 30 34), off P. del Risorgimento near the Vatican Museums. A miraculous subterranean restaurant which rightly boasts its seafood specialties. Vegetarians need not be deterred; one of the house specialties is *fettuccine alla bastione,* smothered in a creamy tomato and orange sauce. *Risotto al pescatore* L10,000. Fresh fish dishes L13,000-18,000. Wine L7000 per liter. The buzz of traffic makes for a noisy outdoor lunch. *Pane* L2000. Service 10%. Open Mon.-Sat. noon-3pm and 7pm-1:30am.

★ **L'Archetto,** Via Germanico, 105 (tel. 323 11 63). The kind staff serves up Roman pizzeria grub on this quiet residential street. Pizzas (L6500-12,000), *filetti di baccalà* (fried fish, L3000), *fiori di zucca* (fried zucchini flowers, L2000), salmon bruschetta L4000. Open Tues.-Sun. 7pm-midnight. Closed for part of August.

★ **Pizzeria Il Bersagliere,** Via Candia, 22A/24 (tel. 39 74 22 53), off Via Leone near Via Tolemaide. A squadron of pastel tablecloths draw the weary traveler's eye to mouth-watering pizzas (L8500-10,500); try the *fiori di zucca* pizza (L10,500). The *bruschetta al pomodoro* (L2500) tingles the tongue. *Pane* L2000. Open Tues.-Sun. 7pm-midnight.

Armando, Via Plauto, 38-39 (tel. 68 30 70 62), off Borgo Angelico. Snazzy yet traditional. Delicious *lasagne* is the house specialty at L9000. *Saltimbocca alla Romana* L13,000. *Pane* L2500. Open Thurs.-Tues. 12:30-3pm and 7-11pm.

Non Solo Pizza, Via degli Scipioni, 95 (tel. 372 58 20). Simple decor, but there are plenty of bargain-hunting Italians bumping elbows with you. Pizza comes in every variety and is charged by weight. Round pizzas available to take away. Roast

TESTACCIO ■ 125

chicken L11,000. *Tavola calda* pasta (3 choices per day) L7000; *secondi* L7500. Open Tues.-Sun. 8:30am-9:30pm.

Trattoria La Caravella, Via degli Scipioni, 32 (tel. 39 72 61 61). Near entrance to Vatican Museums. Pasta dishes L6000-12,000. *Menu turistico* L15,000 (soup or spaghetti, *secondo*, fries, salad, and dessert). Pizza too. Open Fri.-Wed. noon-4pm and 7-11pm. AmEx, DC, MC, Visa.

Hostaria l'Etrusco da Vincenzo, Via dei Gracchi, 12-14 (tel. 39 73 31 65). A simple wooden room located compellingly near the Vatican for museum dwellers. Teeny, so no groups, please. Unbelievable pastas, L8000. Open Thurs.-Tues. noon-3pm and 6:30pm-midnight.

Taverna-Ristorante Tre Pupazzi, Borgo Pio, 184 (tel. 68 68 371), at Vicolo del Campanile. Pizzas L8000-11,000, pasta L7000-10,000. Try the homemade *agnolotti* (meat-filled ravioli, L9000) and the delicious *antipasto misto* (L8000). *Menu turistico* L20,000. Open Mon.-Sat. noon-3pm and 7pm-midnight.

■ Testaccio

One of the oldest areas of Rome, yet still unassailed by tourism, Testaccio remains a stronghold of Roman tradition. Food for people who want to get a true taste of Rome, or at least a taste of local animal parts. In the Mattatoio neighborhood around the old slaughterhouses, you can dare to eat as the Romans do at restaurants that serve authentic local delicacies, such as *animelle alla griglia* (grilled sweetbreads) and *fegato* (liver). The hippest **nightclubs** are located here as well (see Discos and Dancing, p. 232), particularly around Monte Testaccio, so you can boogie your oxtail-intake away. Take Metro Linea B to Piramide, bus #27 from Termini or bus #95 from P. Venezia to reach this area south of the historic center.

★ **Pizzeria Ficini,** Via Luca della Robbia, 23 (tel. 57 43 017). Take Via Vanvitelli off Via Marmorata, then take your first left. For those who've lost their carnivorous nerve, a friendly, no-nonsense pizzeria. Pizzas L6000-8000, calzone L8000, wine L6000 per liter. Don't miss the *bruschetta con fagioli* (L2500). Open Sept.-July Tues.-Sun. 6-11:30pm.

Trattoria da Bucantino, Via Luca della Robbia, 84/86 (tel. 574 68 86). Take Via Vanvitelli off Via Marmorata, then take the first left. A Testaccio tavern with fabulous *antipasti*. Indigenous pasta delights like *bucatini all'amatriciana* (L11,000) and *coda alla vaccinara* (stewed oxtail, L12,000). Wine L6000 per liter. *Pane* L2000. Open Tues.-Sun. 12:30-3:30pm and 7-11pm. Closed in Aug.

Il Caffè del Seme e la Foglia, Via Galvani, 18 (tel. 574 30 08), on the corner of Via Nicola Zabaglia. A friendly bar/sandwich-type place that specializes in all possible permutations of salad, while a mostly local clientele crowds around its tables. Salads L8000, creative sandwiches (try the *Indiano* with turkey and curry) L4000 and up. Open daily 7:30am-midnight; lunch served 1-3:30pm, dinner served 8pm-midnight.

Trattoria Turiddo, Via Galvani, 64 (tel. 575 04 47), in the Mattatoio district of Testaccio (take bus #27 from Termini or the Colosseum). Locals come here for food they grew up on, like *rigatoni con pagliata* (with tomato and lamb intestine, L10,000), *coda alla vaccinara* (stewed oxtail, L15,000), and *animelle alla griglia* (grilled sweetbreads, L13,000). Standard Roman specialties available for the weak of stomach. Vegetarians may want to flee in terror. Open Mon.-Tues. and Thurs.-Sat. 12:30-2:20pm and 7:30-10:20pm, Sun. 1-2:30pm; closed Sept.

Trattoria al Vecchio Mattatoio, P. Giustiniani, 2 (tel. 574 13 82). A gutsy Roman eatery that shares an outdoor seating corner with Turrido (see above). Their *tonarelli sugo coda* (thick spaghetti with tangy tomato oxtail sauce, L9000) seconded by *arrosto misto di frattaglie* (a mixed grill of liver, intestines, and sweetbreads, L13,000), washed down with some extra-strong wine (L6000 per liter), will put hair on anyone's back. *Penne all'arrabbiata* (L8000) for less hairy types. Service 12%. Open Mon. 10am-3pm, Wed.-Sun. 10am-midnight; closed second half of August.

▓ San Lorenzo

A five-minute bus ride east of Termini on bus #71 or 492 (get off when the bus turns onto Via Tiburtina by the old city walls), San Lorenzo sits at the edge of the Città Universitaria. This trendy, tourist-free zone is home to Marxist students and cutting-edge artists. Many unpretentious *trattorie* and pizzerias offer grand cuisine for the university students and the traveler who dares to leave the historic center.

★ **Il Pulcino Ballerino,** Via degli Equi, 66/68 (tel. 494 12 55), off Via Tiburtina. An artsy atmosphere with cuisine to match. The cook stirs up an ever-changing menu of unusual dishes like *tagliolini del pulcino* (pasta in a lemon cream sauce, L9000) or *risotto Mirò* (with arugula, radicchio, and *parmigiano*, L10,000). The vegetable *contorni* are to die for—try the spinach with gorgonzola and walnuts (L8000). *Pane* L1000. Open Mon.-Sat. 12:30-2:30pm and 8pm-midnight. Closed first two weeks of August. AmEx.

Pizzeria la Pappardella, Via degli Equi, 56 (tel. 446 93 49), off Via Tiburtina at the Largo dei Falisci. Exquisitely inexpensive, offering a variety of authentic Roman cuisine in a relatively tourist-free atmosphere. Try their *pappardelle* (pasta with sausage, peas, and cream sauce, L6000) or the *canneloni di carne* (L7000). Cheap pizzas, too. Open daily noon-3pm, 6pm-midnight.

Il Capellaio Matto, Via dei Marsi, 25 (tel. 49 08 41). From Via Tiburtina take Via degli Equi and take the 4th right onto Via dei Marsi. Vegetarians rejoice! Numerous pasta and rice dishes for L7000-11,000. Sorceress's salad, with potato, shrimp, chicken, corn, carrot, and egg, L9000. Crêpe dishes around L6500. Spinach and ricotta ravioli L8,000. Menu available in English. *Pane* L2000. Open Wed.-Mon. 8pm-midnight.

La Tana Sarda, Via Tiburtina, 116 (tel. 49 35 50). Personable Sardinians rush from table to table, piling plates with delicacies. Romans rave about the *gnocchetti sardi* (L8000) and the *penne alla gorgonzola* (L8000). For dessert, try the *dolcetti sardi* for L5000. Pizza L8000-10,000. *Pane* L2000. Open Mon.-Sat. noon-2:30pm, 5-11pm. Closed mid-Aug. through mid-Sept.

Super Pizza Rustica a Taglio, Largo degli Oschi, 67, off Via degli Umbri. Wonderful pizza by the slice at non-tourist prices. Pizza with peppers (L1500 per *etto*) and potato with rosemary (L2000 per *etto*). Try the *fiori di zucca* (L1600 per *etto*). Open Mon.-Sat. 8am-9pm.

Armando, Piazzale Tiburtino, 5 (tel. 495 92 70). On the other side of Porta di San Lorenzo at the beginning of Via Tiburtina. Take bus #492 to Tiburtina or a ten-minute walk from Termini along Via Marsala through Porta di San Lorenzo. Lots of people, noise, and outdoor dining. A great place to go with picky eaters since the menu contains everything from meat and fish to vegetable and pasta dishes. A one-trip-only buffet of cold *antipasti* and desserts, L12,000 per plate. Roasted peppers in oil, L5000. Pizza L7000-15,000. Menus in English. Open Sun.-Tues. and Thurs.-Sat. 12:30-3pm, 7:30pm-1am. Reservations accepted.

La Pantera Rosa, Piazzale del Verano, 84/85 (tel. 445 63 91), along Via Tiburtina before Piazza San Lorenzo. Apparently, the Pink Panther likes pizza with salmon and red caviar, since that's the house specialty (L11,000). *Spaghetti alle vongole* (clam sauce) is a favorite among the staff, L12,000. *Penne all'arrabbiata* (short pasta in a spicy red pepper sauce) L7,500. Huge pizzas. Open Sun.-Tues., Thurs.-Sat. noon-3pm, 6:30pm-12:30am. MC, Visa.

Pizzeria l'Economica, Via Tiburtina, 46, after Largo dei Falisci. The mobs of locals and tourists don't bother the family that owns this cheap eatery; they just serve delicious pizza. *Antipasto misto* L6000. *Pizza con funghi* L6500. *Bruschetta* L2000. Go early or late to avoid waiting. Open Sept.-July Mon.-Sat. 6:30-11pm.

Pizzeria il Maratoneta, Via dei Sardi, 20 (tel. 49 00 27), off Via Tiburtina. Four young marathoners bake pizza on the run (L6000-10,000). Tomatoes and marinated seafood cover half of their gorgeous *pizza mare e monte* (sea and mountain pizza), while tomatoes, mozzarella, mushrooms, eggplant, onion, zucchini, and peppers bury the other half. Crowded. Pizza to take out, too. Open Mon.-Sat. 5:30pm-12:30am.

Pizzeria Formula I, Via degli Equi, 13 (tel. 445 38 66) in San Lorenzo, off Via Tiburtina. Romans know their pizza, so when it's as good and cheap as this, expect to wait. Pizza of all varieties L6000-9000; *alla melanzana* L8000. The owner recommends *filetti di baccalà* (fried fish fillet) L2500. Really crowded. Open Mon.-Sat. 6:30pm-12:30am.

Trattoria Colli Emiliani, Via Tiburtina, 104, at the corner of Via degli Umbri. Charming, with homestyle cooking at tables with checkered tablecloths. The grilled *scamorza* (L7000) and *penne all'arrabbiata* (L7500) are especially good. Open Mon.-Sat. noon-3pm and 7:30-11pm.

■ Near Termini Station

There is no reason to subject yourself to the gastronomic nightmare of the tourist-trapping restaurants that flank Termini; a 20-minute stroll from the station can take you to virtually any historic district this side of the Tiber—with quieter streets, tastier viands, and a more relaxing atmosphere. Still, when you've got corns on your feet and hunger pangs in your belly, the following establishments provide excellent service for a largely local clientele.

■ South of Termini

Though stellar restaurants are sparsely distributed throughout this area, there are many tasty treats to be found at the various bars and *pizzerie rustiche* scattered around the neighborhood. These establishments often provide high-quality sandwiches and pizza by the slice at rock-bottom prices. Still, there are a few restaurants that will offer a full meal without the special, inflated tourist price.

★ **Da Silvio, Osteria della "Suburra,"** Via Urbana 67/69 (tel. 48 65 31), off Via Cavour and down the stairs on the right at the Cavour metro stop. One of the few authentic places in the area. A huge variety of traditional Roman fare at low prices. Homemade *fettucine* in a variety of styles (L8000-10,000). *Penne all'arrabbiata* L6000. Excellent *antipasto rustico* L8000. *Pane* L2000. Open Tues.-Sun. 1-3pm and 7-10:30pm.

★ **Osteria da Luciano,** Via Giovanni Amendola, 73/75 (tel. 488 16 40). Head south on Via Cavour from Termini and turn left after one block onto Via G. Amendola. A green bead curtain screens the entrance to this haven for the cheap and hungry. International crowd does not make this place any less Italian. Hearty, generous pasta dishes L3900-5000. Huge marinated half-chicken L7000. Tourist menu a great deal at L15,000. Wine L4500 per liter. *Pane* L1000. Service 10%. Open Mon.-Fri. 11:30am-9pm, Sat. 11:30am-5pm.

Ristorante Due Colonne, Via dei Serpenti, 91 (tel. 48 80 852), on the left, down from P. della Repubblica on Via Nazionale, after the Palazzo delle Esposizioni. By day, Romans on lunch break fill the tables. By night, American tourists struggle with reading the menu. Cheap, excellent pizzas L7000-13,000. *Pasta e fagioli* L6500. Open Mon-Sat. noon-3:30pm and 7pm-midnight. AmEx, MC, Visa.

Trattoria Fulvimari, Via Principe Amedeo, 7 (tel. 474 06 26). As rustic as the area gets. Expansive wall murals show off the famous sights. Pasta dishes L6000-9000. Omelettes L8000. *Bistecca* L13,000. Cover L1500. Open noon-3pm and 6-11pm.

■ North of Termini

La Cantinola da Livio, Via Calabria, 26 (tel. 482 05 19 or 474 39 62). Take Via Piave off Via XX Settembre, then take the 4th left onto Via Calabria. This cozy, lively establishment specializes in *frutti di mare;* live lobsters wait nervously in tanks by the door. Stellar cuisine and impeccable service. Seafood fresh from Sardinia daily. *Spaghetti alla Cantinola* L10,500. *Scampi* L19,000. *Antipasto di mare* L12,000. *Pane* L1500. Open Mon.-Sat. 12:30-3pm and 7:20-11:20pm. AmEx, DC, MC, Visa.

Da Giggetto, Via Alessandria, 43 (tel. 854 34 90), near the Porta Pia. This place claims to be "the king of pizza"—you'll have a festive and satisfying meal deciding if it's true. The savory *bruschetta* with tomatoes and mozzarella (L4000) is just a prelude to the pizza (L7200-13,000). Open Mon.-Sat. 7pm-1am. Closed in August.

Ristorante la Capitale, Via Goito, 50 (tel. 494 13 91), off Piazza Indipendenza. Perfect for those times when your *lire* just can't stretch any further. Tasty and friendly. Pastas and rice dishes L7000-L8000; pizzas L6000-L7000. Discounts for large groups. Open Mon.-Sat. 9am-4pm and 6pm-midnight. AmEx, MC, Visa.

Restaurant Monte Arci, Via Castelfidardo, 33 (tel. 494 13 47). Take Via Solferino past P. dell'Indipendenza and then take the first left past the piazza. Boisterous waiters serve delectable *paglia e fieno al Monte Arci* (a pasta and spinach dish, L12,000) and *gnocchetti* (L8000). Wood-oven pizzas in the evening. *Pane* L2500. Open Mon.-Fri. 12:30-2:30pm and 7-11:30pm, Sat. 7-11:30pm. AmEx, Visa.

■ Ethnic foods

McDonald's, Piazza della Repubblica, 40 (tel. 481 55 10). There's no need to feel guilty for craving the artificial, happy-meal appeal of McDonald's while in Rome. The fare is as good as you're used to at home, and the restaurants are clean, predictable, and blissfully air-conditioned. But the truth is, the two uniquely Roman features of these McDonald's are the most compelling reasons to make the golden-arched pilgrimage: 1. L6900 gets you an *Insalata Deluxe,* a combination of three typically Italian salads from a huge selection. It's one of the tastiest, most affordable vegetarian deals around. 2. McWash: the automatic hand washing/drying unit (it spits out soap, water, and then hot air) that raises hand-washing to a giddier level. In fact, the bathrooms are some of the tidiest in the city and worthy of tourists' attention. The combo meals (i.e. Big Mac, large fries, and a large Coke©) still reign supreme here, all for about L10,000. McD's offers free maps of the city which are good for basic orientation but not detailed enough for in-depth exploration. Seven locations around town: Piazza di Spagna, 46-47 (tel. 69 92 24 00); in EUR, Piazza Don Luigi Sturzo, 21 (tel. 591 66 83); in Trastevere, Piazza Sonnino, 39-40 (tel. 588 71 27); Corso Vittorio Emanuele II, 139, near Campo dei Fiori; on Via G. Giolitti on the southwest side as you exit Termini Station; and Via Nazionale, 58 (tel. 444 16 72).

DESSERTS

Forgive me Father, for I have thinned. It has been three meals since my last confection.

—L.G. Redattore

If you have a sweet tooth, the road from Rome will lead straight to the dentist. Gooey, creamy, and flaky pastries taunt passers-by from every bakery window, while the spectrum of the *gelato* rainbow rivals even the palette from Michelangelo's Sistine ceiling. Fortunately, you can get more than one flavor at a time. Traditional vanilla or chocolate are available, but don't miss out on exotica like *tiramisù, riso,* and kiwi. Usually you can also get a free dollop of whipped cream (*panna*).

★ **Grattachecca da Bruno,** right at the Ottaviano Metro stop on Viale Giulio Cesare, near the corner of Via Vespasiano. Watch Bruno go to work with a hand-made ice shaver as he serves up the yummiest Italian ice you'll ever have. Pick from a variety of fresh fruit. Perfect for after a trip to the museums. Grattaceccha for L3000. Open all day till the wee hours.

★ **Palazzo del Freddo Giovanni Fassi,** Via Principe Eugenio, 65/67 (tel. 446 47 40), off P. Vittorio Emanuele, southeast of Termini. This century-old *gelato* factory is a confectionery altar duly worshiped by many. Try *riso* (rice), try *coco* (coconut), try them all. Some argue that the *gelato* here beats Giolitti's hands down, and we agree. Try both and argue your calories away. Cones L2000-3000. Open Tues.-Sun. noon-midnight. Open Mondays only in the summer, 6pm-midnight.

★ **Giolitti,** Via degli Uffici del Vicario, 40 (tel. 699 12 43). From the Pantheon, follow Via del Pantheon (at the northern end of the piazza) to its end and then take Via della Maddelena (in front of you) to its end; Via degli Uffici del Viccario is on the right. A Roman institution as venerable as the Vatican, Giolitti is revered by many as the home of Rome's greatest *gelato*. Indulge yourself with their gargantuan 10-scoop "Olympico" sundae for L11,000, and don't forget the homemade *panna*. It's futile to make flavor suggestions; you'll just have to try them all yourself. Small cone L2500, medium L3000, large L4000. Open 7am-2am. Nov.-April closed Mon.

★ **Jolly Pop (formerly Sweet Sweet Way),** Via del Corso, 70 (tel. 36 00 18 88), near intersection with Via Vittoria. A bright, colorful candy smorgasbord and perfect remedy for a sudden drop in blood-sugar, perhaps induced by the prices of the clothing in the swanky boutiques near the Spanish Steps. Gargantuan assortment of chewy, sugary morsels for L2000-3500 per 100g, chocolate morsels L4500 per 100g. Open daily, 10am-8pm. AmEx, MC, Visa.

Tre Scalini, Piazza Navona, 30 (tel. 68 80 19 96). This classy, old-fashioned spot is famous for its perfect *tartufo,* a menacing hunk of chocolate ice cream rolled in chocolate shavings, but fame has brought tourists and with them, high prices. Get your *tartufo* at the bar for L5000; still a splurge, but *so* worth it. Bar open Thurs.-Tues. 8am-1am; restaurant open Thurs.-Tues. 12:30-3:30pm and 7:30-9pm.

Gelateria Trevi di A. Cercere, Via del Lavatore, 84/85 (tel. 679 20 60), near the Trevi Fountain. A small *gelateria* of yesteryear whose famous *zabaglione* (L3000) puts the glitzy *gelaterie* down the street to shame. Open daily 10am-2am.

Pascucci, Via Torre Argentina, 20 (tel. 68 64 816), off Corso Emanuele, east of P. Navona. The 6 throttling blenders on the bar have earned this place a reputation throughout the republic; they grind fresh fruit into colorful, frothy *frulatti* frappes (L3300-4500). Open Mon.-Sat. 6:30am-midnight.

Yogufruit, P. G. Tavani Arquati, 118 (tel. 58 79 72), off Via della Lungaretta near Piazza S. Sonnino. No ancient tradition here. Instead, it's filled with the young and the fruitful. Tart frozen yogurt blended with just about anything: fruit, M&Ms, even Cornflakes. Cups or cones L3000-4000. Open Mon.-Sat. noon-2am.

Bar San Giacomo, Via Antonio Canova, 13-15, off Via del Corso. Snow-cones will never be the same after you try the splendid *cremati* (Italian ices) at S. Giacomo. Lemon, melon, and blueberry are among the best in town (L2000-3000).

Il Fornaio, Via dei Baullari, 5-7 (tel. 68 80 39 47), across from P. San Pantaleo, south of Piazza Navona. The smell of baking goodies makes it impossible to walk on by. Every cookie possibility imaginable (*biscotti*, L1800-2600 per *etto*); desserts (*mele in gabbia* L1300 per *etto*). Open daily 7:30am-8:30pm.

Grattachecca (di Ponte Cestio), at the end of the Trastevere side. Rightfully the most popular booth in town. Watch a butterfly tattoo come to life, as the bulging bicep of the man shaving the ice pumps life into your fruit-flavored slushy. Ask for a few syrups on your ice pile—*amarena* (sour cherry) and *mirtillo* (blueberry) are great choices. Regular L3500. The house specialty is lemon and coconut, L3500. Open daily in summer, 11am until around 2am.

Gelateria della Palma, Via della Maddalena, 20 (tel. 68 80 67 52), off P. della Rotonda. So many flavors and fruit toppings, so short a lifetime. A glamorous candy selection to turn Willy Wonka green with envy. Medium cone L2500. Sex horoscope machine L500. Open daily 8am-2:30am.

Selarum, Via dei Fienaroli, 12 (tel. 581 91 30), off Via d. Fratte di Trastevere. A lusciously leafy garden terrace where heftily priced gourmet desserts are served to the lilting tones of live jazz. Dessert wines L8000-13,000. Try one of the specialties like the *mandorlita* (chocolate, amaretto, and whipped cream, L15,000). Open May-Oct. daily 9pm-1:30am (music usually starts around 10:30pm).

Da Quinto, Via di Tor Millina, 15 (tel. 686 56 57) off Piazza Navona. Talk about refreshing. Every combination of ice, milk, fruit, cream, and ice cream imaginable. Possibilities endless. Prices range from L2500-10,000. Open daily noon-2am. Closed Wed. in winter. Hours may vary.

FOOD & WINE

The Scoop on *Gelato*

It may be translated as "ice cream," but *gelato* is in a league of its own. Some tips to guide you through your quest for frozen, flavored perfection:

Look for stores that carry *gelato artigianale* or *propria produzione*—it means they make it themselves.

Singola (single) and *doppia* (double) portions are the most common. Some locales serve *gelato* in a *brioche* (sweet pastry bun), a special treat. Saying *"con panna"* will add a mound of fresh whipped cream to your serving. Some *gelaterie* require you to pay before you eat, so head first for the *cassa* (cashier) and then present your receipt to the scooper when you order.

Some flavorful vocabulary: *mela* (**apple**), *ananas* (**pineapple**), *mirtillo* (**blueberry**), *stracciatella* (**chocolate chip**), *cannella* (**cinnamon**), *noce/cocco* (**coconut**), *nocciola* (**hazelnut**), *miele* (**honey**), *latte/panna* (**milk/cream**), *liquirizia* (**black licorice**), *frutti di bosco* (**forest fruits,** like blackberries), *arancia* (**orange**), *pesca* (PES-kah, **peach**—DON'T say *pesce* (PESH-ay; it means "fish"), *lampone* (**raspberry**), and *fragola* (**strawberry**). There are also some flavors that don't exist in America, like *baci* (chocolate and hazelnut, like the candy), *cassata* (fruity ice cream with nuts and candied fruits), *riso* (**rice**), and *tiramisù* (espresso, sweet cheese, and chocolate—like the dessert).

If you can't find the fresh kind, try the prepackaged *gelati.* Another option is a slushy flavored ice treat called *granita.* Two common flavors are *limone* (**lemon**) and *menta* (**mint,** vaguely reminiscent of mouthwash), but many *gelaterie* also feature *granita di caffè* (slushy frozen espresso), a real treat when topped with *panna.*

Do not pig out. Let's Go does not recommend eating too much *gelato* (unless you really can't help it).

CAFFÈ

In most *caffè* and *bar,* you pay one price to stand and drink at the bar, and a higher price (as much as double) if you sit down at a table. There should be a menu on the wall of the bar listing the prices *al bar* (standing up) and *a tavola* (at a table). Check the prices before you get comfy in your seat: around the historic center and the major piazzas, the price of a *cappuccino* can jump from L1500 to L5000 when your tush hits the chair.

Usually you pay the cashier first and present the receipt with your request to the *barrista.* Don't forget to drop a L200 tip in the dish on the bar. Along with your breakfast cup, you can get a sugar lift from a *cornetto,* a souped-up Italian version of the croissant, served plain or filled with cream *(crema)*, marmalade *(marmalata)*, or chocolate. At lunch you can grab a sandwich *(panino;* see p. 116).

The number of ways you can get your caffeine fix is remarkable. A *caffè* or *espresso,* a large thimbleful of very strong coffee, is the starting point. A **cappuccino** is *espresso* with foamy, steamed milk; ask for a sprinkle of *cacao* (cocoa powder) on top. Generally, Romans only drink it for breakfast, though you can get it (probably accompanied by a disapproving glance) after dinner or any other time. A **caffè latte** adds an entire glass of hot milk to the thimble of espresso. A **latte macchiato** is hot milk with espresso, which can also be had cold; kids love it. **Caffè macchiato** is *espresso* with a spot of milk added, served hot or cold *(caldo* or *freddo)*. **Caffè ristretto** (or **alto**) has less water than usual. A **caffè lungo** has more water than normal, for non-Italian nervous systems. **Caffè corretto** a black espresso "corrected" with a spot of liqueur. **Caffè americano** is just like your favorite greasy spoon used to serve. **Granita di caffè con panna** is coffee poured over shaved ice, topped with whipped cream; look for it at upscale gelato outlets, not the local bar.

If all the caffeine has you running up St. Peter's dome in three minutes flat, it's time to switch beverages. Decaffeinated **(decaffeinato)** coffee is sometimes available, though the leading decaf brand in Italy is actually German. Fresh-squeezed juice, **spremuta,** is available in three different flavors: orange *(arancia)*, lemon *(limone),* and grapefruit *(pompelmo)*. If you want lemonade, ask for *spremuta di limone*, not *limonata*, which will get you lemon soda. Ask for a spritz of *acqua gassata* for a little fizz, and don't forget the sugar. You can also get chamomile tea *(camomilla)* in any bar, with a little honey *(miele)*.

There is no shortage of *caffè* and *bar* in Rome. We point out some of the most notable, though they are sometimes more crowded and pricier than average. The streets around Campo dei Fiori and Trastevere hide some of the best places. The bars lining the streets (Via Condotti, Via Frattina, etc.) that lead to the Spanish Steps cater to monied tourists and are often packed and over priced. Take the few extra steps over towards the river, around Via della Scrofa, or head across the bridge to the neighborhood around Piazza Cavour. Here, there are many *caffè, bar, alimentari,* and *tavole calde*. Avoid the numerous establishments right near the Vatican; the prices are some of the highest in Rome, the quality is poor, and the clientele is not of the budget variety; wander a few blocks over to Via Cola di Rienzo and environs to find a more authentic and reasonable *caffè*.

★ **Caffè Sant'Eustachio,** P. Sant'Eustachio, 82 (tel. 686 13 09), in the *piazza* southwest of the Pantheon. Take Via Monterone off Corso Vittorio Emanuele II. Rome's "coffee empire." Once a favorite haunt of Stendhal and other literary expatriates, now bursting with Romans. Thankfully, neither the recipe nor the decor has changed since it first opened. Sit in the piazza and nurse a steaming cappuccino (L4000, L2000 at the bar). *Granita di caffè* with all the works (L8000, L6000 at the bar), or try their very own *gran caffè speciale* (L5000, L3000 at the bar) for a sweet, frothy, and powerful zap of climactic delight. Buy some beans to take home (.5kg L17,500). Open Tues.-Fri. and Sun. 8:30am-1am, Sat. 8:30am-1:30am.

Bar S. Calisto, P. S. Calisto, 4, in Trastevere (tel. 583 58 69). *Il preferito* across the river, where Trasteverean youth, expatriates, and Roman elders socialize over truly incredible yet inexpensive cappuccino (L1200 sitting or standing) and *granita di limone* (L2000). Open Mon.-Sat. 6am-1:30am, Sun. 4pm-1:30am; winter closed Sun. Crowded.

Caffè della Pace, Via della Pace, 3/7 (tel. 686 12 16), off P. Navona. Not just a L4000 cup of cappuccino, but an entire lifestyle. Come prepared with newspapers, books, letters to write, and clever conversations to start up; get the most out of the *al tavolo* price hike at the dark wood tables. Chic and expensive, beneath vines and church façades. Cappuccino: daytime L3000 at bar, L5000 at table; nighttime L4000 at bar, L8000 at table. Red wine L7000 at bar, L10,000 at table. Open daily 10am-2am.

Tazza d'Oro, Via degli Orfani, 84/86 (tel. 679 27 68), off the northeast corner of P. della Rotonda. The sign reads *"El major del mundo,"* and that may not be far from true. No place to sit down, but a great brew at fantastic prices (*caffè* L1100). Extensive tea, coffee, and coffee bean selection. Superlative *granita di caffè* (L1500) after a hot day of sight-seeing. Extensive coffee bean selection at L32,000-34,000 per kg. Chamomile tea L2000. Open Mon.-Sat. 7am-8:20pm.

L'Antico Caffè Greco, Via Condotti, 86 (tel. 679 17 00), off Piazza di Spagna. One of the oldest *caffè* in the world, this posh house has entertained the likes of European kings, movie stars, and John F. Kennedy since 1760. Happily, this swank establishment has not gentrified its price list, as long as you stand at the bar. Cappuccino L2000. Pot of tea L2400. Hot chocolate with cream L4100. Open Mon.-Sat. 8am-9pm.

WINE

Italy's rocky soil, temperate climate, and hilly landscape have been celebrated as ideal for growing grapes since the days of the Empire. Today, Italy produces more wine than any other country, and it is even served to children. Unfortunately, many wines have remained confined to the neighborhood of their vineyard. Unlike the popularized *Asti Spumante* and *Chianti* from the North or *Marsala* from Sicily, Lazio's harvest never travels far from the wine-maker's own dinner table. While the majority of oenophiles and exporters have long neglected or even snubbed Italian, and especially Latian, wines, you can discover incomparable wine territory at humble vineyards all through the countryside. The major wine-producing region around Rome is to the south and is known as the Castelli Romani for the summer villas built there by bacchanalian patricians. Mostly fruity white wines are produced in this region. *Frascati* is perhaps the most well-known, inspiring Roman dialect poet Trilussa to exclaim of this wine, "in a mouthful, there's such good humor that sings hymns and decks your heart with banners."

The god Bacchus was credited with having first brought "the vine" to the Aegean from India. The beverage caught on, and Italians became supreme wine-makers and consumers. In the highly efficient Roman Republic, wine was so widely produced that vineyards were occasionally demolished in order to check the problem of overproduction. Nowadays, wines from throughout Italy are available in most wine shops and restaurants. While those on a tight budget may not get to taste the legend of Rome, there are numerous, inexpensive, local wines (often named for their towns) that are worth tippling.

Frascati, the most famous local white wine, is fruity, dry, and clear. **Est! Est!! Est!!!** is the famous white wine of Montefiascone (see below). Wine from the **Colli Albani** is pale gold, fruity, and delicate. **Colli Lanuvini** and **Velletri** are, respectively, a dry white and a dry red. Both are good for fish, but the latter is also good for meats and robust pasta. **Cerveteri** wines offer a full-bodied red wine and a slightly bitter, aromatic white. **Zagarola** is a soft white wine, all the rage in the Renaissance. **Monte Compatri Colonna** is yet another local white that goes well with light pasta.

You can usually order by the glass, carafe, or half-carafe, although bars may not serve wine by the glass. *Vecchio* means "old," and *stravecchio* means "very old." *Secco* means "dry" and *abboccato* or *dolce* means "sweet." When in doubt, request the local wine—it will be cheaper and best suited to the Roman or Latian cuisine. Many of the more inexpensive *trattorie* don't have a wine list; instead, they just yank down one of the bottles lining the rafters. Most of the wines from the Roman countryside are served young and are on the sweet side.

Est! Est!! Rest (in Peace)!!!

One of the finest golden wines of the region, grown on the slopes of Montefiascone, owes its name, *Est! Est!! Est!!!,* to a German Cardinal who was traveling through the district. He sent his valet ahead of him to sample the local wines and chalk "Est" on the doors of inns with satisfactory offerings, and "Est Est"if it was particularly good. When the valet reached Montefiascone, he was so enraptured with the harvest that he wrote "Est Est Est," a great piece of publicity for the wine which has since assumed this name. The Cardinal himself unintentionally spent the last, very happy days of his life in Montefascione. He stayed at the inn for several days and drank such vast quantities of the wine that he died a sudden, if not quite giddy death.

■ Enoteche (Wine Shops)

Enoteche (or *bottiglierie*), traditional wine and olive oil shops, have become an economical and more authentic lunchtime alternative to pricey *trattorie*. Originally these shops did not serve the tasty fare for which they are know today. This tradition began in the days when shop proprietors whipped up bowls of pasta to share with the men who delivered barrels of the local harvest. The workers lingered over the long marble counters and slurped up whatever had been prepared by the mother of the house. Eventually, the proprietors extended their modest cooking to the customers, and word got out; laborers and others soon began flocking to these wine shops for a cheap and filling afternoon meal and a game of cards. The wine shops installed card tables, put up signs *"vino e cucina,"* and turned family members into waiters. In the 1960s and 1970s, students, hippies, and political activists gathered here to talk Marx and Marcuse. Today, anyone looking for substantial, inexpensive food in an informal, personable setting will enjoy the cuisine and company in these neighborhood establishments. Most are open only on weekdays during lunchtime (approximately noon-3pm). Arrive early since these places tend to fill up around 12:30pm with workers in no hurry to leave; you may be hard-pressed to find a seat even if you wait. Unfortunately, the prices have risen since days of yore, and a full meal can cost upwards of L20,000, though you generally get a lot for your money. Feel the place out; some of the smaller places expect you to order at least a *primo* and a *secondo* if you're taking the place of a 300-pound construction worker with an appetite to match. Tell them how much you want, and they'll charge you accordingly. You'll have to look carefully to find these places, since most are not marked by more than a small sign or the wandering smell of garlic; explore the areas around Via del Governo Vecchio and in the winding streets behind Via Tomacelli (on the way to Piazza Navona from Via del Corso and the Mausoleum of Augustus) to find more of these modest establishments.

★ **Bar Da Benito,** Via dei Falegnami, 14, in the former Jewish Ghetto, off of Piazza Mattei. You can't get more authentic than this: a tiny 1-room shop lined with wine bottles and hordes of hungry workmen. The daily menu is posted on the door, usually offering some sort of hearty dish of pasta, including the Roman Thursday special, *gnocchi.* A full meal will run you about L16,000. Open Mon.-Sat. 7:20am-8pm, for lunch noon-3pm.

★ **Armando,** Via Plauto, 38-39 (tel. 68 30 70 62), near the Vatican, off Borgo Angelico. A typical *bottiglieria* with enough outstanding *contorni* like swiss chard and *cicoria* to burst any meat-eater's bubble. Lasagna is the house specialty. Pastas L6000-10,000. House wine L7000. The prices are cheaper for lunch. *Pane* L2500. Open Thurs.-Tues. 12:30-3pm and 7-11pm.

Al Parlamento, Via dei Prefetti, 15 (tel. 687 34 46), take Via di Campo Marzio from Via del Corso. Have your morning glass of *chianti* here; they open bright and early. Small selection of dishes but lots of wine and champagne. They also stock cognac dating back to 1830. Open Mon.-Fri. 9am-1:30pm and 4:30-8:15pm, Sat. 9am-1:30pm.

Trimani Wine Bar, Via Cernaia, 37b (tel. 446 96 30). Quiet, classy, and near Termini station, perpendicular to Via Volturno which becomes Via Marsala. It's not the cheapest place around, but if you're willing to splurge for a little fine dining, get their full *menù* (soup, meat, dessert, wine, and coffee) for L24,000, starting at 1pm. Glass of wine or beer L3500. There's also the real wine shop just around the corner at Via Goito, 20, where they stock one of the largest selections of alcohol in the city. Open Mon.-Sat. noon-3pm and 6pm-12:30am.

Antica Enoteca, Via della Croce, 76b (tel. 679 08 96), off Piazza di Spagna, on the corner of Via Bocca di Leone. Soothe your nerves at the elegant semi-circular bar after a long day's visit to Cartier and the Spanish Steps. Plenty of other tourists are here sipping wine (L4000-8000 per glass), but the atmosphere is relaxing, and the menu is enticing. *Melanzane alla parmigiana* (eggplant parmesan) L12,000 and a great variety of salads (L8000-12,000). *Bruschetta* with arugula and tomatoes (L3000). Open Mon.-Sat. 9am-2am. AmEx, MC, Visa.

Billo, Via S. Ambrogio, 7 (tel. 687 79 66), off Via Portico, in the Jewish Ghetto. A small but well-equipped grocery and wine store. Some kosher meats and wines. Meeting times and places for daily minyans of Ashkenazi Jews posted here. Open Mon.-Thurs. 9am-1:30pm and 4-7:30pm, Fri. 2:30-7:15pm.

■ Wine Bars

Many of the best wine bars in Rome are located in clandestine *piazze* or on acutely romantic cobblestone streets. You can nurse a glass of *chianti* for several hours and partake of mellow conversation; don't expect to get roaring drunk, dance on the tables, or play Spin the Bottle with the wait-staff. Many of these establishments serve food, ranging from small plates of cheese to four-course meals.

FOOD & WINE

★ **Vineria,** Campo dei Fiori, 15 (tel. 68 80 32 68). A chic spot for young Romans to sip wine and beer, exchange meaningful glances, and swap phone numbers. Packed and cheap. On summer nights the crowd spills outdoors into the piazza. Chardonnay L2000; Vodka alla frutta L5000. *Tartine* (baguette with cheese, ham and egg, shrimp, etc., L2000) make a tasty complement to the wine. Open Mon.-Sat. 10am-2pm and 6pm-2am.

Cul de Sac, Piazza Pasquino, 73 (tel. 68 80 10 94), off Piazza Navona. A quiet little wine bar that also serves homemade paté and other noshes. Better suited to a languorous outdoor conversation than to a face-stuffing extravaganza. Attracts oenophiles of all ages. Open Tues.-Sun. 12:30-3pm and 6:30pm-12:30am, Mon. 6:30pm-12:30am.

Il Piccolo, Via del Governo Vecchio, 75 (tel. 68 80 17 46), off the southwest corner of P. Navona. *Molto chic* wine bar for Beautiful People. By day, nibble on salad (L5000) or pasta (L6000-8000) while, of course, washing it down with the house wine (L2000). After 6pm, snacks and sweets abound to complement wines from all over Italy. Try the *fragolino* (a sweet, sparkling wine; L6000). L4000 and up for a glass. Open Tues.-Fri. noon-3pm and 5pm-2am, Sat.-Sun. 5:30pm-2am.

Arc-en-Ciel, Via Banco di Santo Spirito, 45, off Corso V. Emanuele II leading to the Ponte Sant'Angelo. They serve up crêpes with a variety of coffees and wines. The tiny place is dark and intimate, but that's just so French. Open 7pm-2am.

MARKETS

■ Outdoor Markets

Going to an outdoor market in Italy is always an adventure; you'll be sure to find the best produce, but you may also be asked to eat live crustaceans. Generally, markets are open Monday-Saturday from 7am-2pm, but hours are never set in stone—markets begin when everyone gets there and end when they get hungry for lunch.

Mercato di Campo dei Fiori. Flowers, fruits, cheese, fish. Weekdays only.

Mercato di Piazza Navona, in Via della Pace (off Governo Vecchio via Via Parione). A fruit market.

Mercato della Piazza del Quirinale, Via Lavatore, in front of Palazzo del Quirinale. It's a fruit and veggie market.

Mercato di Piazza San Cosimato, in Trastevere. A fruit and produce market rages here. Take the #170 bus from Termini to Viale di Trastevere or bus #56 or #60 from P. S. Silvestro, just south of P. di Spagna. Get on at the stop on Via Claudio and get off at the last stop, P. Sonnino. Walk up Viale di Trastevere, turn right on Via Fratte di Trastevere, and turn left on Via S. Cosimato.

Mercato di Piazza Vittorio Emanuele II, near Termini. The usual mayhem, this time with fruits, vegetables, and lots of clothes.

Mercato Trionfale, Via delle Milizie. A short walk from the Vatican museum entrance, up Via Tunisi to its intersection with Via Andrea Doria brings you to an open air market with cheap produce, cheese, bread, and other picnic fixings.

Mercato di Via del Lavatore, near the Spanish Steps, off the piazza in front of the Trevi Fountain. A large market that sells fresh food.

Mercato di Via Milazzo, Via Milazzo, between Via Varese and Via Palestro.

Mercato di Via Montebello, Via Montebello, near Termini.

Mercato di Via Tomacelli, near the Spanish Steps, halfway down Via Tomacelli between the Trevi fountain and Via dell'Arancio.

Produce Market, Piazza Testaccio, on Via Luca della Robbia. Come here for fat-free fodder. Take bus #27 from Termini or bus #92 from P. Venezia to reach this area south of the historic center.

■ Indoor Markets

Mercato di Via Cola Rienzo, Via Cola di Rienzo, 52-54, at Via Porpezio. An immense indoor food market bulges in Ottaviano near the Borgo. Open 7am-2pm.

Alimentari Coreani (Korean Grocery Store), Via Cavour 84 near Piazza di Santa Maria Maggiore. You won't find any spaghetti here; Ramen, soups, frozen foods, and some Korean drugstore products line the shelves of this quiet little surprise. Open Mon.-Sat. 9am-1pm, 4-8pm.

Sidis Supermarket, at Via Luca della Robbia, 49, Testaccio. A grand specimen for the food shopper. Take bus #27 from Termini or bus #92 from P. Venezia to reach this area south of the historic center.

Standa, several locations including Via Cola di Rienzo, 173 (near the Vatican) and Viale di Trastevere, 62. Supermarket with all you could desire, even 90210 party decorations.

Sights

Rome wasn't built in a day, and it's not likely that you'll see any substantial portion of it in 24 hours either. The city practically implodes with monuments—ancient temples, medieval fortresses, Baroque confections of marble and rushing water—crowding next to and even on top of each other on every interwoven street. No other city in the world can lay claim to so many masterpieces of architecture from so many different eras of history, not to mention the treasures of painting and sculpture found inside each of them. Accept the fact that it's impossible to see everything the city has to offer. It is a hot and dusty place in summer (a crowded and chaotic one year-round) and is likely to sap the energy of even the most hardened sightseer. Though you'll probably end up covering the city neighborhood by neighborhood, the following chronological catalogue may help show how the monuments fit together within the context of Roman history.

The **ancient city** of Rome centered on the **Capitoline** and **Palatine Hills** in the southern part of the modern city. These two riverside mounds remain the most famous of Rome's seven hills; the lesser known five include the Quirinal, west of Termini and home to the residence of the President of the Republic; the Viminal, the next rise to the south; the Esquiline, where Sta. Maria Maggiore now presides; the Caelian, rising south of the Colosseum; and the Aventine, overlooking the Tiber, just south of the Circus Maximus. On the low ground between the Capitol and Palatine, the ancients built the magnificent **Forum Romanum,** the city's political and economic center. Close by are the **Colosseum,** the **Imperial Fora** and **Palaces,** and the riverside temples of the **Forum Boarium.**

Elsewhere in the city, the majestic **Pantheon, Hadrian's mausoleum** under Castle Sant'Angelo, and the **Mausoleum of Augustus** bear testament to the architectural ingenuity of the city's ancient inhabitants. Long removed from their original niches, **ancient statues** still evoke the glories of the classical ideal. The best collections are found in the **Musei Capitolini** and the **Museo Pio-Clementino** (inside the Vatican Museums). Outside the city, pagan tombs still line the ancient **Appian Way,** while the forbidding brick ramparts of the third-century **Aurelian Walls** can be seen at many points along the ancient city's perimeter.

When the Goths sacked Rome in 410 AD, they destroyed much of the city's pagan splendor and ushered in the **middle ages.** But when they cut the city's **aqueducts,** they did its monuments an inadvertent favor. Thirsty survivors of the sacks came down off the city's hills and settled anew by the banks of the Tiber, in the elbow-shaped bend to the northeast of the ancient center. Though ancient monuments were relentlessly pillaged for their marble and bronze, those far from the river at least avoided being swallowed entirely by medieval construction. The new riverside neighborhoods bristled with fortified houses and towers, the tangible result of the paranoia gripping the sack-prone city. The densest concentrations of medieval houses make up the picturesque quarters of **Trastevere, Campo dei Fiori,** the **Jewish Ghetto,** and the area around **Piazza Navona.** Here you'll find a labyrinth of cobblestone alleys and crumbling balconied houses (some of them built from pagan marbles) alongside fountains and churches.

Christianity offered a ray of hope to citizens huddling in squalor along the malarial Tiber, and the middle ages saw a boom of church building. **Constantine,** emperor from 306 to 337 AD, legalized the upstart Eastern sect and laid the foundations for the city's first great basilicas: the churches of **Santa Maria Maggiore, San Lorenzo fuori le Mura,** and **Sant'Agnese fuori le Mura.** The basilical form, borrowed from pagan administrative architecture, is marked by a long central nave divided by columns, polychrome marble pavements, and gilded mosaics in the apse over the altar. Other mosaic-studded medieval churches in the city include **Santa Maria in Cosmedin** near the Aventine, **Santa Sabina** on the Aventine, **Santa Maria in Trastevere** across the river, and **Santa Prassede** on the Esquiline Hill.

Rome set about launching its **Renaissance** with particularly self-conscious activity. Medieval squabbling between rival cardinals and their families had led to the **Great Schism,** and during the subsequent "Babylonian Captivity" the city suffered untold neglect. Martin V and his successors, returning to the throne of Peter, set about cleaning up and clearing out the dilapidated city with one goal in mind: the glorification of the papacy's power. The **Vatican Palace** was renovated, a gargantuan project that

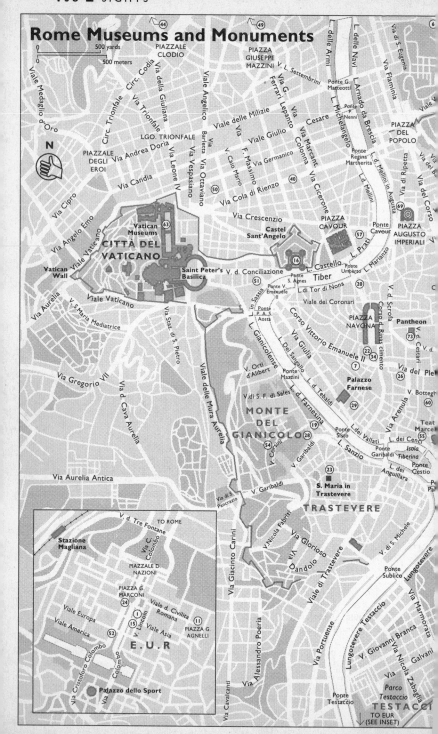

Rome Museums and Monuments

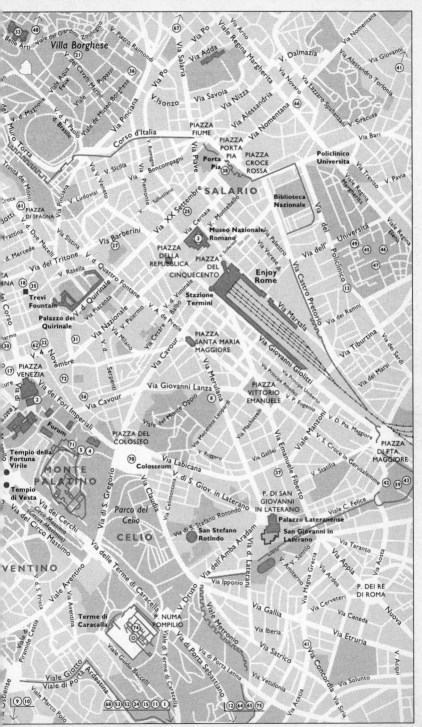

included the construction and decoration of the **Sistine Chapel,** the exquisitely frescoed **Borgia Apartments,** and the **Raphael Rooms.** Construction began on a new **Basilica of St. Peter,** and several new, straight streets were carved out of the welter of medieval alleyways that snaked through the city, among them the **Via Giulia** and the **Via Papalis** (modern Corso Vittorio Emanuele II). Other marks of papal attention in the city include the sublime **Cancelleria** and its neighboring **Palazzo Farnese,** the papal apartments atop **Castel Sant'Angelo,** the exquisitely decorated **Villa Farnesina,** and Bramante's tiny **Tempietto.** More Renaissance treasures hide within many of Rome's churches—**Santa Maria del Popolo** houses masterpieces to cover the growing costs by **Raphael, Caravaggio,** and **Pinturicchio; Sant'Agostino** and **San Luigi dei Francesi** boast more Caravaggios; **Santa Maria sopra Minerva** proudly displays two statues by Michelangelo, while **San Pietro in Vincoli** across town shelters the Florentine master's world-famous **Moses.**

The Renaissance building boom left the popes in command of a richly decorated new city, but some European Catholics weren't too impressed. The crisis of the **Reformation,** incited in part by the church's sale of indulgences to cover the growing construction costs of the new St. Peter's, led Pope Paul III to call the famous **Council of Trent.** The Council's first objective was to reform the church's priestly and monastic orders, but the members also devised new standards for the design of churches. Renaissance interest in classical architecture had inspired a host of circular and Greek-cross churches in which, the Council said, the priest and his altar had been subordinated from their rightful place at the head of the congregation. The new plans, first executed in della Porta's famous **il Gesù,** called for a long central nave, with side chapels replacing the traditional basilical aisles, so that every person could have a view of the altar, whose importance was highlighted by a soaring dome and elaborate altar canopy. This model became the pattern for most of the **Counter-Reformation** and **Baroque** churches in the city.

The 17th-century successors to the Renaissance popes took the Council of Trent's recommendations to heart, but even the "reformed" churches they built were extravagantly constructed, incorporating Counter-Reformation imagery in monuments of Baroque extravagance. A succession of pontiffs employed the rival talents of **Bernini** and **Borromini** to produce artistic and architectural works that would not only glorify the Catholic church but also outshine those of their predecessors. Bernini's works in the city include the ingenious, oval-shaped **Piazza San Pietro,** the elaborate **Fountain of the Four Rivers** in P. Navona, the **Fontana del Tritone** in P. Barberini, and the sublime **Sant'Andrea al Quirinale** on the Quirinal Hill. Bernini's greatest talent lay in sculpture; not even Michelangelo could capture the fleeting expressions of joy, pain, agony, and ecstasy in the way this Baroque genius could. His greatest works include the erotic *St. Theresa in Ecstasy* in Santa Maria della Vittoria, the *Blessed Ludovica Albertoni* in San Francesco a Ripa, and a host of dramatic monoliths housed in the **Galleria Villa Borghese,** including his *David* and *The Rape of Persephone.* In the shadow of such a prolific talent, the cerebral Borromini couldn't help but feel bitter. His lesser-known but equally inspired creations include **Sant'Agnese in Agone** in P. Navona, the celestial **Sant'Ivo** nearby, **San Carlo alle Quattro Fontane** on the Quirinal Hill, the sumptuous interior of **San Giovanni in Laterano,** and the ingenious *trompe l'oeil* perspective at the **Palazzo Spada.** Other lights of the Baroque include **Carlo Maderno,** responsible for the façade of St. Peter's, and **Domenico Fontana,** architect of many of Rome's most beautiful fountains. The churches of **Sant'Andrea della Valle, Sant'Ignazio,** the **Chiesa Nuova,** and **Trinità dei Monti** round out the city's roster of Baroque architectural wonders.

The 17th century was also the age of collecting, and many of Rome's **patrician galleries** house collections from the 16th and 17th centuries. Among them, the **Galleria Doria Pamphili, Galleria Spada,** and **Galleria Colonna** merit a visit for their collections of such Baroque masters as **Guido Reni, Guercino, Domenichino,** and others. The Capitoline and Vatican **Pinacotecas** also house 17th-century paintings.

With the 18th century, the political fortunes of the papacy began to wane, as did the city's centuries-old building boom. Noble Roman families continued to build and rebuild their palaces—as the **Rococo** confections of the **Palazzo Doria Pamphili** and **Palazzo Colonna** attest. The Rococo style (generally translated as "Baroque-gone-berserk") also graces the frothy interiors of the churches of **Santi Apostoli** and **Santi Giovanni e Paolo.** Some of the city's last great projects of urban planning date from the 18th century, including the **Spanish Steps** and the **Trevi Fountain.**

The 19th century counts demolition and overdevelopment among its dubious accomplishments. The now-unified government erected large-scale **public buildings** to house the Italian bureaucracy. The ostentatious, incongruous **Vittorio Emanuele II Monument,** also called "the typewriter" or "the wedding cake," stands as blaring testimony to the garish vision of this era.

In the 20th century, Mussolini combined his pomposity and Fascist Nationalism with a misguided reverence for grandiose Imperial monuments to create the horrific **municipal buildings,** the dreary neighborhood of **EUR,** and most significantly, the **Via dei Fori Imperiali,** where cars spew corrosive pollution on the city's ancient monuments as they roll past.

THE ANCIENT CITY

> Turn all the pages of history, but Fortune never produced a greater
> example of her own fickleness than the city of Rome, once the most
> beautiful and magnificent of all that ever were or will be … not a city in
> truth, but a certain part of heaven.
>
> —Poggio Bracciolini

▓ The Velabrum

The **Velabrum** lies to the south of the old Jewish Ghetto (see Piazza Mattei and the Jewish Ghetto, p. 183) in the shadow of the Capitoline and Palatine Hills. This flat flood-plain of the Tiber was a sacred area for the ancient Romans; it was believed that Hercules kept his cattle here. This is also where Aeneas probably first set foot on what was to become Rome, and where Romulus and Remus were rescued by the she-wolf. During the Republic, the area's proximity to a port on the Tiber made it an ideal spot for the city's cattle and vegetable markets. Civic-minded merchants forested the riverbanks with monuments dedicated to their gods of trade and commerce. Even after the empire fell, the area remained a populous and busy market center, where medieval Romans continued the tradition of sacred building. To get to this area, take any bus to Piazza Venezia and head down Via del Teatro di Marcello, to the right of the Vittorio Emanuele II monument as you face it. Walk past and around the Theaer of Marcellus; Via del Portico d'Ottavia and the Jewish Ghetto are right behind it.

■ Portico d'Ottavia

At the bend of Via del Portico d'Ottavia in the Ghetto (see Piazza Mattei and the Jewish Ghetto, p. 183), a shattered pediment and a few disembodied ivy-covered columns in the shadow of the **Theater of Marcellus** are all that remain of the once magnificent **Portico d'Ottavia,** one of Augustus's grandest contributions to the architecture of the ancient city. The pediment crowned the side entrance to a long, rectangular enclosure whose 300 columns formed a sacred precinct around two important temples to Jupiter and Juno. Augustus planned this whole area as a monument to his own family, dedicating the portico to his sister Octavia and the Teatro di Marcello to his nephew and chosen successor, Marcellus. Medieval Romans, in typical haphazard style, built around, inside, and on top of the marble portico, then filled the remaining open space with a fish market, the Foro Piscario, which functioned until this century.

A quick walk beginning at the arch directly to the left of the portico and continuing around its right, down Via di S. Angelo in Pescheria, brings you to the gleaming white columns of the **Temple of Apollo Sosianus.** In 34 BC, Gaius Sosius rebuilt the temple, dating from 433 BC, thus winning the right to attach his own name to it. The three Corinthian columns support a well-preserved frieze of bulls' skulls and floral garlands. Consider viewing the ruins from Via del Teatro di Marcello on the other side.

■ Theater of Marcellus

The stocky, grey **Theater of Marcellus** *(Teatro di Marcello)* next door bears the name of Augustus' unfortunate nephew, whose early and sudden death remains a bit of a mystery. Augustus was particularly fond of the young Marcellus and was preparing him to be imperial successor. This plan, however, did not appeal to Augustus' wife Livia, who hoped Tiberius, her son from a previous marriage, would be the heir. Whether Marcellus was poisoned by his aunt or simply died of food poisoning (salmonella was not an uncommon cause of death at that time) is still subject to debate.

As for the theater itself, if it strikes you as a Colosseum wanna-be, think again. The pattern of arches and pilasters on the theater's exterior, completed in 11 BC, actually served as a model for the great amphitheater across town. You can still make out the classic arrangement of architectural orders, which grows, in accordance with ancient principles, more complex from the ground up. Plain Doric pilasters support the bottom story, curved Ionic capitals decorate the middle, and, though they're now long gone, elaborate Corinthian columns once crowned the top tier. Vitruvius and other ancient architects called this arrangement the most perfect possible for exterior decoration, inspiring Alberti, Bramante, Michelangelo, and countless other Renaissance architects to copy the pattern. Sadly, the perfect exterior is all that remains of the theater, as a succession of medieval families used its seats and stage as the foundation for their fortified castles. The Pierleoni first set up shop in the 11th century, using the theater's imposing height to control access to the Tiber and its bridges. The money they made from exacting tolls helped vault the family to social and political power, culminating in the election of Anacletus I as the notorious "Jewish Pope." The Savelli family, the theater's next occupants, commissioned Baldassare Peruzzi to design the Renaissance castle that crowns the structure's height. The Orsini, the last family to occupy the building, converted it in this century to an apartment complex, making the ancient monument one of the city's most prestigious addresses. Normally closed to the public, the park around the theater hosts classical concerts on summer nights (tel. 481 48 00 or 67 10 38 19 for more information; open July-Sept. 3-9pm).

Further down Via di Teatro di Marcello towards the Tiber, the remains of the three more Roman temples provide the foundation for the 12th-century **Church of San Nicola in Carcere** (tel. 686 99 72; open Sept.-July daily roughly 7am-noon and 4-7pm; daily mass at 7am, Sunday mass at noon). The three ancient buildings incorporated into the architecture of the church were originally dedicated to the gods Juno, Janus, and Hope. On the right side of the church lies the most complete temple, its Ionic columns scattered on the grass and embedded in the church's wall. The left wall preserves the Doric columns of another temple. The third temple lies buried beneath the sober little church. The deserted interior boasts well-labeled paintings and restored engravings, including part of the church's original dedication from May 12, 1128. The façade was added by Giacomo della Porta in 1599. Call ahead for a brief tour of the excavations below, where, avoiding exposed, seemingly bottomless pits, you can see the remains not only of the three temples, but also of the ancient streets and market which connected them.

■ Foro Boario and the Bocca della Verità

One block further south along Via Luigi Petroselli lies the **Piazza della Bocca della Verità,** the site of the ancient **Forum Boarium** *(foro boario* in Italian), or cattle market. The two ancient **temples** in the Forum Boarium are among the best-preserved in Rome. The rectangular **Temple of Portunus,** once known as the Temple of Fortuna Virilis, shows both Greek and native Etruscan influence in its design. The present construction dates from the late second century BC, though there had probably been

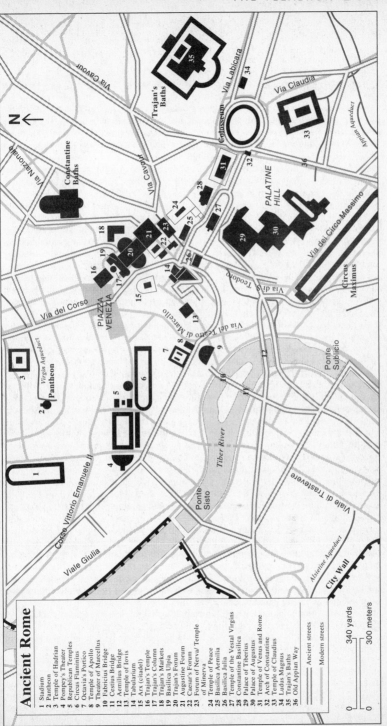

Ancient Rome

1 Stadium
2 Pantheon
3 Temple of Hadrian
4 Pompey's Theater
5 Republican Temples
6 Circus Flaminius
7 Octavia's Portico
8 Temple of Apollo
9 Theater of Marcellus
10 Fabricius Bridge
11 Cestius Bridge
12 Aemilius Bridge
13 Temple of Iovis
14 Tabularium
15 Arx (citadel)
16 Trajan's Temple
17 Trajan's Column
18 Trajan's Markets
19 Basilica Ulpia
20 Trajan's Forum
21 Augustine Forum
22 Caesar's Forum
23 Forum of Nerva/ Temple of Minerva
24 Temple of Peace
25 Basilica Aemilia
26 Basilica Julia
27 Temple of the Vestal Virgins
28 Constantine Basilica
29 Palace of Tiberius
30 Palace of Augustus
31 Temple of Venus and Rome
32 Arch of Constantine
33 Temple of Claudius
34 Ludus Magnus
35 Trajan's Baths
36 Old Appian Way

Ancient streets
Modern streets

0   340 yards
0   300 meters

a temple on the site for some years before. The **circular temple** next door, presently cloaked in scaffolding for restoration, was also built in the late second century BC, making it one of the oldest marble structures in Rome. Once thought to be dedicated to Vesta because of its similarity to the Temple of Vesta in the Forum, it now seems more probable that it was intended to be a temple to Hercules Victor.

Just across the street from the temples, the **Church of Santa Maria in Cosmedin** (also called Church of S. Maria de Scuola Greca) harbors some of Rome's most beautiful medieval decoration. The front porch and bell tower, dating from the 12th century, welcome busloads of tourists every day, all on their way to see the famous **Bocca della Verità** in the portico (portico open 9am-5pm; church open 9am-noon and 3-5pm; Byzantine mass Sun. 10:30am). Originally a drain cover carved as a river god's face, the circular relief was credited with supernatural powers in the Middle Ages. It's said the hoary face will close shut on the hand of a liar, severing his fingers. To keep the superstition alive, the caretaker-priest used to stick a scorpion in the back of the mouth to bite the fingers of suspected fibbers. The *bocca* made a cameo appearance in the movie *Roman Holiday*. During the filming, Gregory Peck put his hand in the mouth and, when he yanked it out, jokingly hid his hand in his sleeve, causing Audrey Hepburn to scream in shock; the scene wasn't scripted, but it worked so well that they kept it in the movie. The dusky interior of the church brims with intricate stonework, from the exquisite choir enclosure and pulpits to the geometric, marble-inlaid floor. Although many of the 11th-century frescoes have peeled away, little mosaic tiles still glitter across the interior. Test the perfidy of your friends at home with clay replicas of the *Bocca* that sell for L3000-70,000 in the shop of the church interior. You'll be lured into the shop by craftily-placed signs guiding you to the gleaming 8th-century mosaic of the epiphany on display inside.

Across the *piazza* to your right as you exit the portico, Via del Velabro climbs a short way toward the Capitoline Hill. Behind the hulking **Arch of Janus,** built in the fourth century as a covered market for cattle traders, the little **Church of San Giorgio in Velabro** was a marvelous medieval edifice, with a ninth century porch and pillars, a simple basilican interior, and a *campanile* (bell tower) built of brick and stone arches. A terrorist car-bombing on July 27, 1993 reduced the church's famed portico to a single arch and part of a stone beam. Both the church and the arch are presently being restored. To the left of the church, the eroded **Arch of the Argentarii** was erected by the money changers *(argentarii)* and cattle merchants who used the *piazza* as a market in the third century AD, in honor of Emperor Septimius Severus and his family. Caracalla, Severus's son and successor, had his brother Geta's name and image erased from the arch (as well as from the arch of Septimius Severus in the Roman Forum) after he had the boy himself rubbed out.

From Via del Velabro, a quick backtrack up Via del Teatro di Marcello offers an excellent view of the ruins of the theater and its surrounding temples, as the road winds up to the **Vittorio Emanuele II Monument** and the steps up to the **Piazza di Campidoglio.** For a less direct but perhaps more aesthetically pleasing path to the Campidoglio, take a short jaunt up Via Giovanni Decollato, on your left as you face the arch of Janus. The street ends at Piazza della Consolazione, originally intended as a final place of consolation for prisoners condemned to execution on the Capitoline Hill. The church is usually closed to the public.

Across the *piazza,* Via del Monte Caprino begins its ascent up the Capitoline, leading to Via Caffarelli. Follow this street to a staircase which, after a moderately tiring climb, leads to a small park at Piazza Caffarelli. Make your way past the benches of affectionate young Italian couples taking advantage of the park's romantic setting for a view of the Theater of Marcellus to your left and Piazza Venezia to your right. At the far end of the park, the curving Via delle tre Pile descends directly into the Piazza di Campidoglio.

Someone back home *really* misses you.
Please call.

With **AT&T Direct**™ Service it's easy to call back to the States from virtually anywhere your travels take you. Just dial the **AT&T Direct** Access Number for the country *you are in* from the chart below. You'll have English-language voice prompts or an AT&T Operator to guide your call. And our clearest,* fastest connections** will help you reach whoever it is that misses you most back home.

AUSTRIA●◇ 022-903-011	GREECE● 00-800-1311	NETHERLANDS●...06-022-9111
BELGIUM● 0-800-100-10	INDIA✖.........................000-117	RUSSIA●▲♪ (Moscow).755-5042
CZECH REP▲ 00-42-000-101	IRELAND............1-800-550-000	SPAIN◇.................900-99-00-11
DENMARK.................8001-0010	ISRAEL.................177-100-2727	SWEDEN................020-795-611
FRANCE...............0 800 99 0011	ITALY● 172-1011	SWITZERLAND●..0-800-550011
GERMANY.................0130-0010	MEXICO▽........95-800-462-4240	U.K.▲ 0800-89-0011

*Non-operator assisted calls to the U.S. only. **Based on customer preference testing. ●Public phones require coin or card deposit. ◇Public phones require local coin payment through call duration. ◇From this country, AT&T Direct calls terminate to designated countries only. ▲May not be available from every phone/pay phone. ✖Not available from public phones. ▽When calling from public phones, use phones marked "Ladatel." ♪Additional charges apply when calling outside of Moscow.

Can't find the Access Number for the country you're calling from? Just ask any operator for AT&T Direct Service.

Greetings from LET'S GO

With pen and notebook in hand, a change of clothes in our backpack, and the tightest of budgets, we've spent our summer roaming the globe in search of travel bargains.

We've put the best of our research into the book that you're now holding. Our intrepid researcher-writers went on the road for months of exploration, from Anchorage to Angkor, Estonia to Ecuador, Iceland to India. Editors worked from spring to fall, massaging copy into witty and informative prose. A brand-new edition of each guide hits the shelves every fall, just months after it is researched, so you know you're getting the most reliable, up-to-date, and comprehensive information available.

We try to make this book an indispensable companion, but sometimes the best discoveries are the ones you make on your own. If you've got something to share, please drop us a line. We're Let's Go Publications, 67 Mount Auburn Street, Cambridge, MA 02138 USA (e-mail: fanmail@letsgo.com). Good luck and happy travels!

■ The Capitoline Hill (Campidoglio)

The original capitol and one of the most sacred parts of the ancient city, the **Capitoline Hill** still serves as the seat of the city's government, perched on high in a spectacular *piazza* of Michelangelo's design. Here you'll also find a rambling complex of museums and unforgettable views of the Forum and Palatine. In ancient times, the hill was dominated by a gilded temple to Jupiter, chief god of the Roman pantheon, along with the state mint and the senatorial archives. The northern peak of the hill once held Juno's sacred flock of geese, which saved the city from ambush by the Gauls, in 390 BC, by honking so loudly that they woke the populace. With such an illustrious past, it's not surprising that successive generations of Romans have exploited the site for its aura of Republican virtues. The original form of the Capitol is now almost entirely obscured by monuments of medieval, Renaissance, and modern civic construction, all trying to capitalize on the memory of the hill's ancient glories. The Campidoglio can be reached by heading down Via dei Fori Imperiali from the Colosseo Metro stop and walking around the Vittorio Emanuele II monument. You can also take any of the myriad buses that stop at Piazza Venezia.

To the right and left of Michelangelo's spacious **Piazza di Campidoglio** stand the twin **Palazzo dei Conservatori** and **Palazzo Nuovo,** while at the far end, opposite the stairs, is the turreted **Palazzo dei Senatori.** Paul III commissioned Michelangelo to remodel the top of the hill for Charles V's visit and had the famous equestrian **statue of Marcus Aurelius** brought here from the Lateran Palace to serve as the focal point. The gilded bronze, which graced the center of the space until recently, was one of a handful of ancient bronzes to escape medieval melt-down, because it was thought to be a portrait of Constantine, the first Christian Emperor. Unfortunately, both man and steed proved too delicate to combat the assault of modern pollution and were removed for restoration in 1981, leaving behind only the pedestal on which they once stood. The emperor now resides in climate-controlled comfort in the courtyard of the Palazzo dei Conservatori. The long-awaited weather-proof copy is scheduled once again to crown the pedestal at the center of the *piazza* in April of 1997. Until then, you can view the construction of the copy in the courtyard of the Palazzo Nuovo. Michelangelo also set up the imposing statues of the twin warriors Castor and Pollux that flank his magnificent staircase, La Cordonata, as well as the two reclining river gods and the statue of the goddess Roma.

■ Capitoline Museums

Housed in the twin *palazzi* on either side of the *piazza* are the **Musei Capitolini** (tel. 67 10 20 71; open Tues.-Sat. 9am-5pm, Sun. 9am-1:30pm; L10,000, L5000 with student ID, under 18 and over 60 free, free-for-all on last Sun. of each month; one ticket covers entrance to both buildings). The museums' collection of ancient sculpture is among the largest in the world, but you may find the *pinacoteca*'s lackluster assortment of 16th-century Italian painting a bit disappointing.

Start at the ticket booth in the **Palazzo Nuovo** (on the left as you enter the *piazza*). In the courtyard, the enigmatic *Marforio*, a colossal river god, reclines beside his splashing fountain. On the right, the original Marcus Aurelius rides his stirrup-less horse behind glass, extending his hand in the gesture of imperial clemency. Though he wears civilian dress, the statue was apparently part of a monument to one of the emperor's overseas victories. In the left end stands an enormous battle-ready Minerva, perhaps warning visitors away from the rest of the ground floor rooms, containing sarcophagi and inscriptions, which are usually closed. A bulky statue of Mars at the right of the entrance glowers toward the staircase and marks the start of the sculpture galleries. Though the Romans owed much of their artistic culture to the Greeks, their taste in sculpture often departed quite radically from the classical Greek tradition. Rather than celebrating ideal concepts of form and beauty, Roman sculpture tried to entertain, to amuse, even to horrify. Ugly or charming, grotesque or endearing, Roman marbles were carved to provoke a reaction. The same is true for portraiture—the crusty personalities of the Roman aristocracy liked accurate portraits of themselves, warts and all. Dismiss your expectations of classical perfection and look instead for a truthful (and not always flattering) picture of ancient Roman taste.

The rooms on the first floor are laid out more like a jumbled curio cabinet than a modern museum. Few works are labeled, and everywhere random heads and limbs have been patched onto bodies, whole sculptures have been placed on alien plinths, and priceless collections of inscriptions and reliefs have been plastered into the walls as decoration. In the first room at the top of the stairs, the morbid *Dying Gaul* heaves through the last moments of life, his chest pierced with wounds and his arm giving way to the heated swoon of death. It's unclear whether the statue portrays a Gaul dying in a Roman arena or in the field of battle, but the work is testament to the Romans' capacity to view suffering as art, and even as entertainment. Note his intricately carved *torque* (necklace), exquisitely polished physique, and Magnum P.I. mustache (c. 1985). *Satyr Rising* is the "Marble Faun" that inspired Hawthorne's book of the same title.

Next door, a porphyry *Laughing Centaur* cavorts with an awful, Oompaloompahesque basalt *Infant Hercules.* Don't miss the monolithic *Boy with Goose* and *Child with Mask.* Beyond lie two rooms crammed with labeled busts, a collection which reads like a roll-call of Roman and Greek notables. Greek philosophers and writers throng the first room (among them Homer, Demosthenes, Pythagoras, and Epicurus), though they've deigned to admit one Roman to their company—the orator and statesman, Marcus Tullius Cicero, who hides in the corner. Next door more Romans, including the emperor Augustus (by the window), an intricately coiffured Flavian woman, a polychrome bust of Emperor Caracalla, a portrait of Lyndon Johnson as the emperor Vespasian, several bearded soldier-emperors from the third century AD, and finally, an iconic head of Constantine. His mother, St. Helena, reclines coyly in the center. The long corridor outside contains more dusty fragments, funerary urns, and inscriptions. Look for the prudish *Venus Pudens* in her skylit nook, a weird *Winged Psyche,* a *Drunken Old Woman* so far gone she's squatting on the ground, and a cabinet with exquisite mosaics of masks and doves from Hadrian's Villa.

The sculpture collections continue across the *piazza* in the **Palazzo dei Conservatori,** admission to which is included in the ticket for the Palazzo Nuovo. The Sale dei Conservatori and the Museo del Palazzo dei Conservatori are on the first floor, while the **Pinacoteca** (p. 147) is on the second. The courtyard houses sundry limbs long separated from their one-time possessor, a colossus of Constantine; this is your chance to get a picture of yourself cradled in the emperor's muscular forearm. On a landing before the first floor, four reliefs from a monument to Marcus Aurelius show scenes of the emperor sacrificing, driving a triumphal chariot, bestowing clemency on captives, with the same gesture as in his equestrian statue, and receiving the mysterious "orb of power."

At the second landing, a door straight ahead leads to the **Sale dei Conservatori.** The Cavaliere d'Arpino frescoed the giant main room with episodes from the reigns of the early kings, telling the typical Italian stories of love, carnage, and religion. Statues of Popes Urban VIII and Innocent X wave at each other across the room. An intricately carved wooden door ushers you into a room filled with more frescoes. The corner salon houses a stark bronze head of Marcus Brutus along with the *Spinario,* a sculpture of a young lad extracting a thorn from his foot. In the next room prowls the famous *Capitoline Wolf,* an Etruscan statue which has symbolized the city of Rome since antiquity. Antonio Pollaiuolo added the cherubic figures of Romulus and Remus in 1509. On the walls are the *Fasti,* the archival records of the ancient Pontifex Maximus, excavated from the Regia in the Forum. Bernini's serpentine *Head of Medusa* highlights the next room, along with a rare ancient greyhound. Tapestries hang in the next room; one of them depicts the birth of the indomitable twins Romulus and Remus. The salons continuing left around the courtyard hold even more frescoes.

The **Museo del Palazzo dei Conservatori** opens up to the left from the landing. The first three rooms have walls covered with lists of the principal officers of Rome since 1640. The long gallery ahead is a showcase of disembodied limbs and limbless torsos. Don't miss the colossal foot and the two pudgy armless boys. To the right at the end of the gallery, a series of rooms leads back to the entrance. Among its attractions are a fifth-century chariot-mounting, more colossal heads, hands, and feet, scattered sarcophagi, an impressive collection of Etruscan red-figure vases, and an understandably perturbed child holding the long since chipped-away remains of what is identified as his dog. At the original landing once again, stairs lead up to the vestibule of the Pinacoteca, with two vibrant polychrome *opus sectile* panels of tigers from the third century AD and an acerbic relief of the *Apotheosis of Sabina*.

At the top of the stairs, the **Pinacoteca** houses a mostly forgettable assortment of 16th- and 17th-century Italian paintings. Much of the collection was pilfered by the Vatican Galleries, leaving an awkward array of poorly-hung canvases. The paintings are carefully labeled in English, however, and the rooms are numbered and unfold ahead of you. Among the masterpieces not purloined by the popes are (in the second room) Bellini's *Portrait of a Young Man*, Titian's *Baptism of Christ*, and a selection of religious scenes by Domenico Tintoretto, son of the more famous Jacopo Tintoretto. In the third room, van Dyck's portrait of the engravers Pieter de Jode, father and son, stands out, while an anonymous portrait of the aged Michelangelo stares gloomily back. Across the room, a young man gently cradles a melon at the dinner table. Note Guido Reni's self-portrait and Rubens' *Romulus and Remus Fed by the Wolf*, which was the model for the similar tapestry in the Sale dei Conservatori. Room 4 is the center of the museum, holding a collection of second-rate 14th- and 15th-century unknown masters. The aesthetically adventurous can continue forward to encounter a horribly ugly bronze statue of Hercules, but less foolhardy souls will branch off right to a gallery full of bronzes and porcelains. If you missed the original of Caravaggio's *St. John the Baptist* in the Galleria Doria, a copy hangs here. Better still is the recently restored *Gypsy Fortune-Teller* by the same artist, in the room across central Room 4. Here also hangs a collection of overindulgent 17th-century Baroque painting. Gasp at the awfulness of Guido Reni's *Lucretia*, *St. Sebastian*, *Beata Anima*, and *Penitent Magdalen*, but hold your breath for the monstrosity of Guercino's vast *St. Petronilla*. Guercino finishes off this angst-filled spectacle with *Antony and Cleopatra*, *St. Matthew and the Angel*, and the *Persian Sybil*.

To the right and left of the Palazzo dei Senatori, paths lead downward to a promontory with a panoramic view of the Forum and the Colosseum; consider returning at night, when the ruins take on a romantic gleam. Stairs also lead up from the right of the Palazzo Nuovo as you face it to the rear entrance of the **Church of Santa Maria in Aracoeli,** a seventh-century church now filled with a jumble of monuments from every century since. Cross the pavement, studded with worn medieval tombs, to the stunning **Bufalini Chapel** (open 7am-noon and 4-7pm; *in restauro* in 1996), home to the *Santo Bambino* (see below), and generally considered among the finest works of Pinturicchio. The master's lively frescoes of the life and death of St. Bernardino of

SIGHTS

The Case of the Burgled Bambino

In a small chapel behind the Bufalini's patchwork medieval-Baroque altar complex, the *Santo Bambino*—a relic supposedly carved from an olive tree in the Garden of Gethsemane—reposes in swaddled majesty and bears suspicious resemblance to a Cabbage Patch Kid. Around the Bambino's cradle lie stacks of letters sent from around the world, often addressed simply to "Bambino. Roma." The Bambino (no relation to the home-run-hitting NY Yankee) used to be carried to the houses of sick children. In recent years, these trips have become less frequent and are usually made by taxi. One legend says that a Roman woman who stole the Bambino promptly fell gravely ill; returning the relic, on the advice of her confessor, she was miraculously healed. Unfortunately, a contemporary thief, perhaps lacking such sound advice, absconded with the Bambino on February 1, 1994 and has not returned. For now, a Holy Copy takes the Holy Baby's place among the piles of mail.

Siena and of St. Francis receiving the stigmata, with four sibyls in the vault, are masterpieces of early Renaissance Roman painting.

Down the hill from the back stairs of the Aracoeli squats the gloomy **Mamertine Prison,** later consecrated as the **Church of Saint Pietro in Carcere** (open daily 9am-noon and 2:30-6pm; admission free but donation requested). In Roman times the dank lower chamber was used as a dungeon for prisoners and captives awaiting execution (though some were simply left to die without ceremony). Among the more unfortunate inmates were Jugurtha, King of Numidia; Vercingetorix, chieftain of the Gauls; the accomplices of the would-be dictator Catiline; and, according to Christian tradition, Saints Peter and Paul, to whom the upper church is now dedicated.

On the open side of the *piazza,* opposite the Palazzo dei Senatori, Michelangelo's magnificent staircase, **La Cordonata,** leads down to Piazza Venezia. Michelangelo built this stepped ramp in 1536 so that Emperor Charles V, apparently penitent over his sack of the city a decade before, could ride his horse right up the hill to meet Pope Paul III during a triumphal visit. On your way down La Cordonata, pause to note on your right a statue of Cola di Rienzo, leader of a popular revolt in 1347 which attempted to reestablish a Roman Republic. The statue marks the spot where the disgruntled populace tore the demagogue limb from limb, where only a short time before they had elected him first consul. At the bottom of La Cordonata, the 124 steep medieval steps to your right climb back up to the unadorned facade of the seventh-century Church of Santa Maria in Aracoeli (p. 147).

A bit further around the bend, you'll come face to face with the **Vittorio Emanuele II Monument,** a colossal confection of gleaming white marble started in 1885 to commemorate the short-lived House of Savoy, whose kings briefly ruled the newly unified Italy. Often dubbed "the wedding cake" or "Mussolini's typewriter," this hideous monstrosity swallows up the north face of the Capitoline hill. Whether it's the blessed air-conditioning or an insatiable curiosity about what's inside the monument that attracts you, make your way around its left side (as you face the steps) and into the tiny **Sacrario delle Bandiere** (open Tues.-Sun. 9am-1pm), a curious military flag museum and the only part of the big white wonder that is open to the public. The museum is essentially a salute to 20th-century Italian war efforts in the form of colorful battle-weary flags in intricate, solemn wood cases. While these deserve a look, the real attraction is the hulking World War I submarine that dominates the two-room museum. In front of the monument begins the Via dei Fori Imperiali, a broad road leading to the Colosseum, which cuts through the imperial fora and past the entrance to the Forum Romanum (on the right about halfway to the Colosseum).

▓ The Roman Forum and the Palatine Hill

The **Forum** and the **Palatine** are open Monday through Saturday 9am to 7pm and Sunday 9am to 2pm in the summer. In the winter the complex generally closes one hour before sunset and may close as early as 3pm on weekdays and 1pm on Sundays and holidays. Admission is L12,000 and last admittance is one hour before closing. The Forum is accessible from the Colosseo Metro stop or any bus that stops in Piazza Venezia (#56, 60, 64, 75, 170, and others).

In the midst of the countless, scattered stones of the Roman Forum there is a small, truncated column that lies almost forgotten at the foot of the Capitoline Hill. This was the **Umbilicus Urbis,** the "navel of the city," set up to mark the geographical center of the ancient *urbs.* More than any other monument in this field of broken treasures it represents what the Roman Forum used to be—not just the physical center of ancient Rome, but also the seat from which the Empire was ruled and to which every Roman citizen from England to Persia looked for government. For a thousand years, these few acres of dusty, low-lying valley were the grandest and most beautiful in existence, the pattern for the ideal European city, and the unquestioned center of the Western world. Today, the vicissitudes of time and neglect have sadly stripped the Forum of its monumental masses, but even the few eroded remains provide daunting testimony to the unparalleled splendor Rome once enjoyed. Though it can be a hot and confusing place on a summer day, when *il Foro* may begin to feel more like *il Forno* ("the oven"), there is still no other place like it on Earth.

The Forum was originally a marshy valley prone to flooding from the Tiber. Rome's earliest Iron Age inhabitants (1000-900 BC) eschewed its low, unhealthy swampiness in favor of the Palatine Hill, descending only to bury their dead. In the seventh and eighth centuries BC, Etruscans and Greeks, using the Tiber Island as a crossing point for their trade and the forum as a weekly market, brought prosperity to the area. The early Romans came down from the Palatine, paved the area, drained it with a covered sewer (the **Cloaca Maxima**), and built their first religious shrines to the vital natural forces of fire and water. By the sixth century BC (the traditionally observed date being 510 BC), the Romans had kicked out their Etruscan overlords and established a republic. The **Curia,** the meeting place of the Senate, the **Comitium Well,** or assembly place, and the **Rostra,** the speaker's platform, were built to serve the infant democracy, along with the earliest **temples** (to Saturn and to Castor and Pollux), dedicated in thanks for the civic revolution.

The conquest of Greece in the second century BC brought new architectural forms to the city, including the lofty basilica, which was first used as a center for business and judicial activities; the wealthiest Roman families, including Julius Caesar's, lined the town square in front of the Curia with basilicas. The Forum was never reserved for any single activity, and it was during these centuries that it was at its busiest, as senators debated the fates of far-flung nations over the din of haggling traders. The Vestal Virgins built their house over a street full of prostitutes, priests sacrificed in the temples, victorious generals led triumphal processions up to the Capitoline, and pickpockets cased the tourists (as they are occasionally wont to do even today).

The Forum witnessed the death throes of the Republic in the tumultuous first century BC. Cicero's orations against the antics of corrupt young aristocrats echoed off the temple walls and Julius Caesar's murdered corpse was cremated amid rioting crowds in the small temple in the Forum that bears his name. Augustus, Caesar's great-nephew, adopted son, and the first emperor, exploited the Forum to support his new government, closing off the old town square with a temple to the newly deified Caesar and a triumphal arch honoring himself. His successors clotted the old markets with successively grander tokens of their own majesty—the marble temples and arches which still stand are mostly remnants of these later autocrats and their insatiable need to glorify themselves. The Forum still resonated with the ideals of republican liberty, however, and increasingly despotic emperors found it convenient to divert the flow of public life away from its archaic precincts. The construction of the imperial palace on the Palatine Hill and of new fora on higher ground to the north cleared out the old neighborhoods that had surrounded the square, and by the second century AD, the Forum, though packed with gleaming white monuments, had become a cold, cavernous, and nearly deserted ceremonial space. Eventually, the imperial court was removed entirely to Ravenna.

Barbarian invaders of the fifth century burned and stripped much of the Forum even before the Christian government of the city ordered the pagan temples closed (see The Rise of Christianity and the Fall of Rome, p. 6). In the Middle Ages, many buildings were converted to churches and alms-houses; what marble remained disappeared into the smoldering lime-kilns of farmers eager for cheap fertilizer. The land itself was slowly taken over by an orchard which crept over the monuments. The Forum, its pavements grown over with weeds and its monuments half-sunk in the ground, became known as the *Campo Vaccino*, a cow-pasture with only the tips of the tallest columns breaking through the tall grass. The last bits of its marble were quarried by Renaissance popes looking to revive Roman glories in their own monumental constructions. Excavations, begun in 1803, have uncovered a vast array of remnants great and trivial, but have also rendered the site extremely confusing—the ruins of structures built over and on top of each other for more than a thousand years are now exposed to a single view.

The best way to see the Forum is to start early in the day, take it slow, and be prepared to be exhausted. It's a big, complicated place and it gets hot and dusty in the

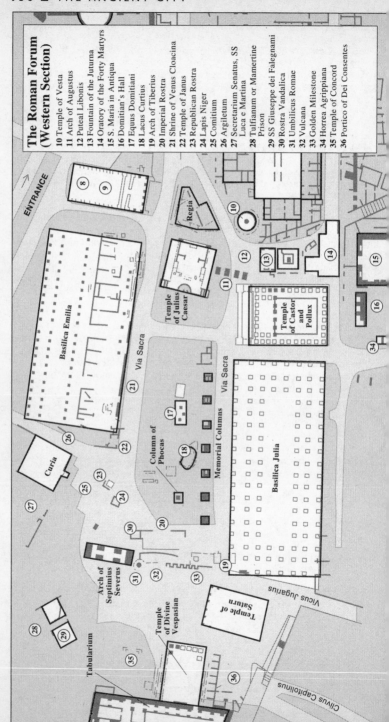

The Roman Forum (Western Section)

10 Temple of Vesta
11 Arch of Augustus
12 Puteal Libonis
13 Fountain of the Juturna
14 Oratory of the Forty Martyrs
15 S. Maria in Antiqua
16 Domitian's Hall
17 Equus Domitiani
18 Lacus Curtius
19 Arch of Tiberius
20 Imperial Rostra
21 Shrine of Venus Cloacina
22 Temple of Janus
23 Republican Rostra
24 Lapis Niger
25 Comitium
26 Argiletum
27 Secretarium Senatus, SS Luca e Martina
28 Tulfianum or Mamertine Prison
29 SS Giuseppe dei Falegnami
30 Rostra Vandalica
31 Umbilicus Romae
32 Vulcana
33 Golden Milestone
34 Horrea Agrippiana
35 Temple of Concord
36 Portico of Dei Consentes

ENTRANCE

Basilica Emilia

Regia

Via Sacra

Temple of Julius Caesar

Temple of Castor and Pollux

Via Sacra

Column of Phocas

Memorial Columns

Basilica Julia

Curia

Arch of Septimius Severus

Temple of Divine Vespasian

Temple of Saturn

Tabularium

Vicus Jugarius

Clivus Capitolinus

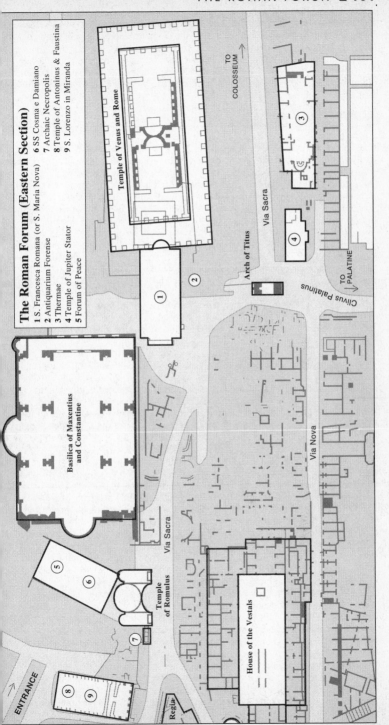

The Roman Forum (Eastern Section)

1 S. Francesca Romana (or S. Maria Nova)
2 Antiquarium Forense
3 Thermae
4 Temple of Jupiter Stator
5 Forum of Peace
6 SS Cosma e Damiano
7 Archaic Necropolis
8 Temple of Antoninus & Faustina
9 S. Lorenzo in Miranda

Temple of Venus and Rome

TO COLOSSEUM

Via Sacra

Arch of Titus

Clivus Palatinus

TO PALATINE

Via Nova

Basilica of Maxentius and Constantine

Via Sacra

Temple of Romulus

House of the Vestals

Regia

ENTRANCE

middle of the day, so take a bottle of water. From the entrance gate on Via dei For Imperiali (across from the end of Via Cavour), a ramp descends, past the Temple o Antoninus and Faustina on the left and the remains of the Basilica Aemilia on the right, to the basalt stones of the **Via Sacra,** the main thoroughfare of the Forum and the oldest street in Rome. The Via Sacra leads right to the slopes of the Capitoline Hill and was once the route of generals trumpeting their military victories while the unfortunate prisoners followed behind.

LOWER FORUM

Turn right at the end of the entrance ramp; you will be on the Via Sacra facing the Capitoline Hill and the Arch of Septimius Severus. The Via Sacra cuts through the old market square and civic center of Republican Rome, bordered by the **Basilica Aemilia** (to your immediate right) and the intact brick **Curia** building (to your right as you walk down to the arch). The Basilica, built in 179 BC, housed the guild of the *argentarii,* or money-changers, who operated the first *cambi* in the city, providing Roman *denarii* for traders and tourists. The basilica was rebuilt several times after fires; in the pavement you can see melted bronze coins which the *argentarii* lost in these blazes. Up the steps of the basilica, the broken bases of columns are all that remains of the great aisled interior, while the row of *tabernae* (shops) that once faced the forum is just visible along the path. In the back right corner of the basilica are casts of the decorative frieze, with reliefs of the *Rape of the Sabine Women* and the *Death of Tarpeia.* After Romulus founded his Palatine city, his pioneer Romans needed brides, and so invited their neighbors, the Sabines, to games and a feast When the Sabines were drunk enough, Romulus gave the signal and his men hauled the Sabine women back up the Palatine. Later, the Roman girl Tarpeia offered to get the women back for the Sabines, but that chivalrous tribe killed her instead for her people's treachery.

The broad space in front of the basilica is the **Forum** itself. The Curia, or Senate House, to the right of the Basilica Aemilia as you exit, was one of the oldest buildings in the Forum, although the present structure dates from the time of Diocletian (303 AD). It was converted to a church in 630 AD and only restored in this century. When the interior is open, you can see an intricate and well-preserved inlaid marble pavement and the steps where the Senators brought their own portable chairs to their meetings. The Curia houses the **Plutei of Trajan,** two sculptured parapets, originally found near the Rostra, which depict the burning of the tax registers (on the left) and the distribution of food to poor children (on the right).

The broad space in front of the Curia was the **Comitium,** or assembly place, where male citizens came to vote and representatives of the people gathered for public discussion. This was also home to the famed Twelve Tables, bronze tablets upon which were inscribed the first codified laws of the Republic. The brick platform to the left of the Curia as you face the arch was the **Rostra,** or speaker's platform, erected by Caesar in 44 BC, just before his death. Senators and consuls orated to the Roman plebs from here, and any citizen could mount to voice his opinion. After his assassination, Cicero's head and hands were put on display here. Augustus' rebellious daughter Julia is said to have voiced her dissenting opinion by engaging in amorous activities with some of her father's greatest enemies here on the very spot where Augustus had proclaimed his new legislation promoting family values.

The hefty **Arch of Septimius Severus** at the end of Via Sacra is an anomaly in this Republican square; dedicated in 203 AD to celebrate that emperor's victories in the Middle East, the arch reliefs depict the imperial family. Though much of the relief has worn away, the small group of men in traditional garb on the column's base is impressive. Severus' son and successor, Caracalla, grabbed the throne by knocking off his brother Geta and then scraped his portrait off the arch. Halfway up the Capitoline Hill, the grey tufa walls of the **Tabularium,** once the repository of Senate archives, now serve as the basement to the Renaissance **Palazzo dei Senatori.**

This part of the Forum, the original market square, was graced by a number of shrines and sacred precincts. Before they built a single marble temple, the Romans revered the forces of nature with quiet, Italic superstition. Between the Curia and the Rostrum, a flat grey stone—the **Lapis Niger** (the black stone)—marks the supposed burial place of Romulus, the legendary founder of the city. The shrine was considered ancient even during the Republic, when its statuary and honorific column were covered by the forbidding grey pavement. Below, one of the oldest Latin inscriptions around, dating from the sixth century BC, warns against dumping garbage on the shrine. Closer to the Basilica Julia, the **Three Sacred Trees** of Rome—olive, fig, and grapevine—have been replanted. On the other side, right across from the Basilica Julia, a circular tufa basin commemorates the **Lacus Curtius,** an ancient spring where, legend says, a gaping chasm opened in 362 BC, into which the Roman patrician Marcus Curtius threw himself in order to save the city. A relief records his sacrifice.

The three great temples of the lower Forum (to Saturn, to the emperor Vespasian, and to Concord) have been closed off during excavations and restoration, although the eight columns of the **Temple of Saturn** have at last shed their cloak of scaffolding. This was the site of the public treasury and an underground stash of sacred treasures. As you round the corner to your left, you'll come to the Basilica Julia.

Rows of deserted column bases are all that remain of the **Basilica Julia.** It was built on the site of an earlier basilica by Julius Caesar in 54 BC, and followed the same plan as the Basilica Aemilia but was far more extensive. The Basilica was used by tribunals of judges for administering justice. Look for inscribed grids and circles in the steps where anxious Romans, waiting their turn to go before the judge, played an ancient version of tic-tac-toe.

At the far end of the Basilica Julia, three white marble columns and a shred of architrave mark the massive podium of the **Temple of Castor and Pollux** (under restoration), dedicated in 484 BC in celebration of the Roman rebellion against their Etruscan king, Tarquinius Superbus, in 510 BC. Tarquin, who had brutally raped the Roman matron Lucretia, was ejected from Rome by her outraged family. He returned with an Etruscan army and would have defeated the Romans at the Battle of Lake Regillus in 496 BC, had the twin gods Castor and Pollux not miraculously routed the enemy.

Legend says that immediately after the battle the twins appeared in the Forum to water their horses at the adjacent **Basin of Juturna** (*Lacus Juturnae*), now marked by a reconstructed marble aedicule to the left of the gods' own temple. The Basin was the site of the ancient city's water administration, and invalids tried to convalesce in the rooms surrounding the spot. Across the way from the Temple of Castor and Pollux is the rectangular base of the **Temple of the Deified Julius** (under restoration), which Augustus built in 29 BC to honor his murdered adoptive father, and to proclaim himself the son of a god. The circular pile of rocks inside probably marks the spot where Caesar's body was cremated in 44 BC (he was assassinated near Largo Argentina); pious Romans still leave flowers here on the Ides of March. In his own glory, Augustus built the **Arch of Augustus,** which framed the Via Sacra and commemorated his triumphs.

The circular building behind the Temple of the Deified Julius is the restored **Temple of Vesta,** on a foundation dating back to the time of the Etruscans. Built in imitation of an archaic round Latin hut, this is where the Vestal Virgins tended the sacred fire of the city (associated with the sanctity of the home), keeping it continuously lit for more than a thousand years. Behind the temple, between the House of Vestal Virgins and the Temple of Antoninus and Faustina, lays the triangular **Regia,** office of the Pontifex Maximus, Rome's high priest and titular ancestor of the Vatican's own pope. The Regia is surrounded by a web of public houses from the same period.

THE UPPER FORUM

The **House of the Vestal Virgins** occupied the sprawling complex of rooms and courtyards behind the temple of Vesta, in the shade of the Palatine Hill. The six virgins who officiated over Vesta's rites, each ordained at the age of seven, lived in spacious seclusion here for thirty years above the din of the Forum. As long as they kept their vows of chastity, the Vestal Virgins were among the most respected people in Ancient Rome, even possessing the power to pardon prisoners condemned to death. Fine living had its price; if a virgin strayed from her celibacy she was buried alive. After her 30 years of service, however, a virgin was free to go and even to marry. In the central, pond-filled courtyard of the Vestals' house are statues of the priestesses, including one whose name was scraped away perhaps after she turned Christian (eighth on the left as you enter the courtyard). A tour through the storerooms and lower rooms of the house brings you back to the Via Sacra and the **Temple of Antoninus and Faustina** (to the immediate right as you face the entrance ramp), whose lofty columns and frieze were incorporated into the **Church of San Lorenzo in Miranda** before the 12th century (its façade dates to the Baroque era). Antoninus, one of the "good emperors" of the second century AD, had the temple built in honor of his wife Faustina, who died in 141; the Roman people returned the favor after his own death, and the temple now stands to commemorate both of them. In the shadow of the temple (to the right as you face it), the archaic **Necropolis**, with Iron Age graves from the 8th century BC, was excavated earlier in this century, lending credence to the Romans' own legendary foundation date of 753 BC. The bodies were found in hollowed-out tree trunks. Here the Via Sacra runs over the **Cloaca Maxima,** the ancient sewer that still drains water from the otherwise marshy valley. The street then passes what is called the **Temple of Romulus** (the round building peeking out from scaffolding), that still retains its ancient bronze doors from the 4th century AD. Not a temple at all, it probably served as the office of the urban praetor during the Empire (no admittance).

THE VELIA

The street now leads out of the Forum proper to the gargantuan **Basilica of Maxentius** (also known as the Basilica of Constantine). The three gaping arches are only the side chapels of an enormous central hall whose coffered ceiling covered the entire gravel court, as well as another three chapels on the other side. The emperor Maxentius began construction of the basilica in 306 AD, but was deposed by Emperor Constantine at the Battle of the Milvian Bridge in 312. Constantine converted to Christianity during the battle, and though he oversaw completion of the basilica, some pagan reverence for the Forum kept him from ever dedicating it as a church. He built the basilica of S. Giovanni in Laterano instead, on much the same plan. Later, Michelangelo studied the architecture of the Basilica, including its powerful domes, before constructing St. Peter's Cathedral.

The Baroque façade of the **Church of S. Francesca Romana** (built over Hadrian's Temple to Venus and Rome) hides the entrance to the **Forum Antiquarium** (open daily, mornings only). Most of the rooms have been closed for years, but a few on the ground floor display funerary urns and skeletons from the necropolis. On the summit of the Velia, the shoulder running down from the Palatine, is the **Arch of Titus,** built by the otherwise ungenerous Emperor Domitian to celebrate his brother Titus's destruction of Jerusalem in 70 AD. The reliefs inside the arch depict the Roman sack of the great Jewish temple, including the pillage of a giant menorah. The Via Sacra leads to an exit on the other side of the hill, an easy way to get to the Colosseum. The path that crosses in front of the arch climbs up to the Palatine Hill.

THE PALATINE HILL

The flowering sculptured gardens and broad grassy expanses of the **Palatine Hill** make for a refreshing change from the dusty Forum—an ideal place to picnic after a morning in the ruins. Though there are lots of remnants of Ancient Rome to see here too, the cool breezes and sweeping views of Rome are reason enough to make the steep climb from below. The best way to begin is from the stairs (to the right after the street turns at the Arch of Titus) which ascend to the **Farnese Gardens.**

The hill, actually a square plateau rising between the Tiber and the Forum, contains some of the oldest and "newest" Roman ruins. The first and final chapters of the ancient Empire unfolded atop its heights. The she-wolf that suckled Romulus and Remus had her den here, and it was here that Romulus built the first walls and houses of the city, a legend supported by the discovery of ninth-century BC huts on the southeastern side of the hill. During the Republic, the Palatine was the city's most fashionable residential quarter, where aristocrats and statesmen, including Cicero, built their homes. Augustus, who was born there, lived in a surprisingly modest house, but later emperors capitalized on the hill's prestige by building progressively more gargantuan quarters for themselves and their courts. By the end of the first century AD, the imperial residence had swallowed up the entire hill, whose Latin name, *Palatium,* became synonymous with the palace that dominated it. After the fall of Rome, the hill suffered the same fate as the Forum, though Byzantine ambassadors and even popes sometimes set up house in the crumbling palace. Various medieval families built fortresses and towers out of the ruins; the Farnese family's gardens still remain partially intact on the side overlooking the Forum.

The staircase, to the right of the path from the Arch of Titus, ascends past the Villa Farnese through the Farnese Gardens, past a *nymphaeum,* or fountain room, to a series of terraces with all-encompassing views of the forum and the city. From the top, take a right through avenues of roses and orange trees until you reach another terrace with a breathtaking view of the Forum, the Imperial Fora, and the Quirinal Hill. The gardens continue along the western side of the hill, where an octagonal box-hedge maze in the center follows the layout of a real maze excavated from the Palace of Tiberius underneath; the maze was excavated early in this century, but the practical Romans decided the gardens had been nicer, and filled the dig back in. At the southwest corner (at the extreme top right of the gardens), another terrace (blocked off for restoration in 1996) looks out over the Capitoline Hill, the Republican temples of the Forum Boarium, and, across the river, the roofs of Trastevere and the ridge of the Gianicolo. Steps lead down to covered excavations of the ninth-century BC village, wishfully labeled the **Casa di Romulo.** The Iron Age inhabitants (who might indeed have included that legendary twin) built their oval huts out of wood, so all that remains are the holes they sunk into the tufa bedrock for their roof-posts. The overgrown lump to the right is the podium of the **Temple of Cybele,** whose cult statue now sits in an arch in the foundation of Tiberius' palace on the left as you ascend the stairs. Further along, to the left of the Temple of Cybele as you make your way from the steps is the **House of Livia.** Livia (Augustus' wife, the first Roman Empress, and according to Robert Graves's *I, Claudius,* an "abominable grandmother") had the house, with its vestibule, courtyard, and three vaulted living rooms, connected to the **House of Augustus** next door (now closed). Take the stairs in the far left corner of the excavation to three rooms decorated with rare Roman wall paintings.

Around the corner, the long, spooky **Cryptoporticus** (really a tunnel which is also reachable by stairs descending from the middle of the Farnese Gardens) connected Tiberius' palace with the later buildings on this side of the hill (closed for renovation in 1996). Used by slaves and imperial couriers, it may have been built by Nero in one of his more paranoid moments as a secret passage. It's easy to imagine the whispers of assassins and informants echoing along its gloomy, stuccoed vaults. The short end of the tunnel, or the path around the House of Augustus, brings you up to the vast ruins of the solemn **Domus Augustana,** the imperial palace built by Domitian (81-96 AD). This was used by most of the subsequent emperors as the headquarters of the empire. To the left, three brick rooms (currently fenced off) served as a basilica, throne room, and shrine to the imperial cult. The exterior walls, even in their ruined state, are so high that archaeologists are still unsure how they were roofed over. The broad square to the right was a huge, open-air colonnaded courtyard, graced by an octagonal fishpond in the center. To the south of the court (moving toward the cliff of the hill), a sunken **Triclinium,** or dining room, hosted imperial banquets between a set of twin oval fishponds (decorated with niches for statuary). On the other side of the Triclinium, a walkway offers a sweeping view of the grassy **Circus Maximus** and, further off to the left, the **Baths of Caracalla.** The ground gives way at the end of the terrace, and the multi-layered labyrinth of the central palace gapes below. Arranged around a central court with yet another fishpond, the private rooms of the Emperor and his household burrow far into the hill. You can't descend into the court, but a few brick rooms are still intact on the surface level. The square holes in the brick-work show where polished marble slabs once lined the palace walls. The **Palatine Antiquarium** remains closed for restoration though its anterior houses public bath-rooms that are open. The easternmost wing of the palace contains the curious **Stadium,** a sunken oval space once surrounded by a colonnade, but now surrounded by fragments of porticoes, statues and fountains. Once thought to have been a private racetrack, it seems now that it was used as a garden. From the palace, a road leads straight down the hill from the throne room, or you can take a path down from the Stadium to an exit on Via di San Gregorio, 100 meters away from the Colosseum.

■ Fori Imperiali

The **Fori Imperiali** sprawl across the street from the old Forum Romanum, a vast con-glomeration of temples, basilicas, and public squares constructed by the emperors of the first and second centuries AD, partly in response to increasing congestion in the old forum. Julius Caesar was the first to expand the city center in this direction, though he was motivated as much by political reasons as by civic spirit. The forum and temple he built in honor of Venus, his legendary ancestress, seriously undercut the prestige of the Senate and its older precinct around the Curia. Augustus, Vespa-sian, Nerva, and Trajan all followed suit, filling the flat space between the Forum and the Quirinal Hill with capacious monuments to their own greater glory. In the 1930s, Mussolini, with imperial aspirations of his own, cleared the area of medieval con-structions and built the Via dei Fori Imperiali to pass through (and over) the newly excavated remains. The fora were only partially excavated, and the broad, barren thoroughfare cuts across the old foundations at an awkward angle (see Ruining the Ruins, p. 156). Although the area immediately around the ruins is not open to the public (with the exception of the Forum of Trajan), the fora can be viewed from above on the Via dei Fori Imperiali.

The **Forum of Trajan,** the largest and most impressive of the lot, spreads across Via dei Fori Imperiali below two Baroque churches at the eastern end of Piazza Venezia.

Ruining the Ruins

When Mussolini created wide, paved roads to circle around the city's ancient monuments in an effort to emphasize their greatness, he also paved the way for their destruction. Today, the Colosseum is facing serious damage and deteriora-tion due to the constant rush of traffic and pollution it creates. Hundreds of thou-sands of cars, scooters, and buses race past the great symbol of Rome each day; the ground beneath it shakes when the subway rumbles by. Homeless people and pickpockets camp under its arches, and young people climb over its iron gates for midnight rendezvous. In 1992, the superintendent of city monuments made an urgent plea to the government to provide funding for its restoration, asking for at least US$43 million (ten times more than the minimal maintenance budget, which just manages to pay for the clean-up of tourists' litter). The Banca di Roma recently pledged US$35 million for rescue work, though that is just a start. For the past quarter-century, the government has been considering mark-ing off the entire area, from Piazza Venezia to beyond the Colosseum, as an "archaeological park" closed to traffic. These restrictions would seriously aggra-vate the already horrible traffic conditions that plague the city, but the park's advocates insist that this is the only way to preserve the ancient monuments from complete collapse. So far, the government has made some minimal efforts to cut down on traffic. Environmentalist Mayor Rutelli's plan to shut the road to all motorized vehicles but city buses, however, was never implemented, although on occasional summer weekends the road is open only to pedestrians.

The complex was built between 107 and 113 AD to celebrate the emperor's victorious Dacian campaign (fought in modern Romania), and included a colossal equestrian statue of Trajan plus a triumphal arch boasting the successful outcome. Today you can see the two neat rows of truncated columns of his enormous **Basilica Ulpia** (the ancient Hall of Justice) and the nearly perfectly preserved spiral of his famous **Trajan's Column**, the greatest specimen of Roman relief-sculpture ever carved. The 200-meter-long continuous frieze wraps around the column like a ribbon and narrates the Emperor's victorious campaigns against the Dacians. From the bottom you can survey Roman legionaries preparing supplies, building a stockaded camp, and loading boats to cross the Danube. Twenty-five hundred figures have been making their way up the column since 113 AD, but they may be somewhat disappointed when they finally reach the top; the statue of their emperor, which crowned the structure in ancient days, was destroyed in the Middle Ages and, in 1588, was replaced by the figure of St. Peter. Stretched out, the spiral frieze would be 656 feet long, one of the most dense and ambitious artistic endeavors of the ancient world. The sculptor faced several problems in creating this narrative. He had to let the pictures speak for themselves (there were no inscriptions) and flow clearly from scene to scene. The pictures also had to be more shallow than normal friezes, because more deeply sculpted figures would produce shadows on the lower scenes. Unfortunately, this shallow carving now makes the friezes especially susceptible to obliteration by air pollution. In the base of the column is a door that leads to the tomb of Trajan and his wife.

Down the street (but with an entrance on Via IV Novembre, 94, up the steps in Via Magnanapoli, to the right of the two Baroque churches behind Trajan's column) are the brick **Markets of Trajan** (tel. 67 90 048; open Tues.-Sat. 9am-6:30pm, Sun. 9am-1:30pm; winter hours vary depending on when the sun sets, and closing may be as early as 1pm; L3750, L2500 with student ID, EU citizens under 18 and over 60 free). The three-floored semicircular complex, which provides a glimpse of daily life in the ancient city (second century AD), is built into the Quirinal Hill and probably sheltered several levels of cavernous *tabernae,* or single-room stores, along cobblestoned streets. Some believe that the structure may have served as public administration offices rather than as a market. Be sure to examine the detailed descriptions of the fora and the scale models of the buildings and temples that once stood as symbols of imperial power. The ground floor and first floor rooms of the markets are now home to an impressive high-tech display of sculpture and statuary found in the imperial fora, including two colossal torsos of Nerva and Agrippa. Stroll along the basalt paving stones and climb to a spectacular view of Trajan's Forum and the Capitoline Hill. The stairs at the end of the entrance hall descend, after a series of maze-like tunnels, stairs, and porticoes, into the forum itself, where you can wander among the crumbling remains of this once thriving commercial center.

Across the Via dei Fori Imperiali, in the shade of the Vittorio Emanuele II Monument, lie the paltry remains of the **Forum of Caesar** (the first of the Imperial fora, undergoing restoration in 1996). A few reconstructed columns are all that remain of Caesar's famous **Temple to Venus Genetrix** (Mother Venus, from whom he claimed descent), but an elaborate cornice lying haphazardly near the columns suggest its past grandeur. The stone façades of the arcades he built into house shops are in better repair.

Adjacent to the Markets of Trajan across Via dei Fori Imperiali, the great grey tufa wall of the **Forum of Augustus** backs up against the side of the Quirinal Hill. Dedicated by the Emperor in 2 BC in honor of Mars Ultor (Mars the Avenger), the huge complex commemorated Augustus' vengeful victory over Julius Caesar's murderers at the Battle of Philippi and the founding of his new imperial dynasty. A few of the partially reconstructed columns from the porch of the central temple, the roof-lines carved into the back wall, and scattered marble floor fragments remain intact. The wall, built to protect the precious new monument from the seamy Suburra slums that once spread up the hill behind it, doesn't run exactly straight. Legend says that when the land was being prepared for construction, even Augustus couldn't convince one stubborn homeowner to give up his domicile, so the great wall was built at an angle around it.

The aptly named **Forum Transitorium** (also called the **Forum of Nerva**) was a narrow, rectangular space connecting Augustus' forum with the old Roman Forum and with the Forum of Vespasian near present-day Via Cavour. Most of it now lies under the street, although new excavations have begun. The emperor Nerva built the forum in 97 AD and wittily gave it a temple to "Minerva," a pun on his own name. All that remains to view is a colossal doorway that once led into **Vespasian's Forum;** between two gorgeous Corinthian columns is a relief of Minerva, the Roman Athena, and a decorative frieze. The only remnant of Vespasian's Forum, which is mostly under the Via Cavour, is the **Church of Santi Cosma e Damiano** (open daily 9am-1pm and 3-7pm) across the street by the Roman forum entrance, built in 527 AD out of a library in Vespasian's complex. The interior is brightened by a rare set of sixth-century mosaics.

Further up Via dei Fori Imperiali, stairs over the Colosseo Metro station lead up to an ill-kept park where the remains of Nero's **Domus Aurea** are secreted inside the Oppian Hill (the site itself is completely closed). The "Golden House" once spread over most of the hill, a labyrinthine collection of domed and vaulted passages, each lined with a precious mosaic or fresco. The decorations of the palace are rightly famous; the *Laocoön* in the Vatican apparently decorated the fun-loving emperor's dining room, while the wall-paintings, discovered in the Renaissance when the subterranean rooms were thought to be grottoes, inspired the *grotteschi* motifs that are a hallmark of Renaissance decorative art. The few ruins you can see today were only part of the emperor's larger complex—having declared himself a living god, Nero took this whole part of Rome as his private quarters, building a palace on the Palatine to match the Domus Aurea here, with a lake in the valley in between (on the present-day site of the Colosseum) and the Caelian Hill as a private garden. He converted the Forum into a vestibule to the palace and crowned it with a colossal statue of himself as the sun—the largest bronze statue ever made (for which the Colosseum is named). The party didn't last long, however. Nero was assassinated only five years after building his gargantuan pleasure garden, and the more civic-minded Flavian emperors replaced all traces of it with monuments built for the public good. These included the Flavian Baths, built on top of the Domus Aurea, and the Colosseum, built over Nero's lake. Hadrian covered the Domus Aurea in 135 with his Temple of Venus and Rome, which in turn was covered by the Church of S. Francesca Romana, accessible from the Roman Forum.

■ Colosseum

> *As long the Colosseum stands, Rome shall stand. When the Colosseum falls, Rome shall fall. When Rome falls, the world shall end.*
> —The Venerable Bede (c. 673-735)

The ground level of the Colosseum is open in summer Monday through Tuesday and Thursday through Saturday 9am to 7pm, Wednesday 9am to 2pm and Sunday 9am to 1pm; in winter, the Colosseum closes one hour before sunset (as early as 3pm); admission is free. The **Upper decks** close one hour earlier than the ground level. Admission to the upper decks is L8000, but EU citizens under 18 and over 60 get in free.

The **Colosseum,** accessible from the Metro stop Colosseo (Metro Linea B—head for the plastic statue vendors across the street), stands as the enduring symbol of the Eternal City—a hollowed-out ghost of somber travertine marble that dwarfs every other ruin in the city. At its inauguration in 80 AD it could hold as many as 50,000 spectators; the first 100 days of operation saw some 5000 wild beasts perish in the bloody arena (from the Latin word for sand, *harena,* which was put on the floor to absorb blood), and the slaughter didn't stop for three centuries. Gladiators fought each other here, and it is sometimes said that the elliptical interior could be flooded for mock sea battles, though archaeologists and native Romans insist that it wouldn't have been possible. The outside of the arena, still well-preserved around three quarters of its circumference, provided the inspiration for countless Renaissance and Baroque architectural confections, with the triple stories of Doric, Ionic, and Corinthian columns considered the ideal orchestration of the classical orders. The raw interior might come as a bit of a disappointment; almost all the marble stands and seats were quarried by Renaissance popes for use in their own grandiose constructions, including St. Peter's Basilica and the Palazzo Barberini. The floor (now gone) lay over a labyrinth of brick cells, corridors, ramps, and elevators used for transporting wild animals from their cages up to the level of the arena. Note the large wooden cross directly across from the side entrance; legend has it that the Colosseum was saved from total destruction at the hand of pillagers when the Pope, in order to commemorate the martyrdom of the thousands of Christians supposedly killed in the stadium, declared the monument a sacred shrine and forbade any further demolition. Later, so the story goes, it was discovered that Christians had not, in fact, participated in the bloody gladiatorial games, and thus, the Colosseum was saved by a very fortunate mistake. The Colosseum continues to play an important role in the celebration of Holy Week.

Between the Colosseum and the Palatine Hill lies the **Arch of Constantine,** one of the latest imperial monuments to grace this area and certainly one of the most intact. Though it has straddled the tail end of the Forum's Via Sacra since its dedication in 315 AD, recent excavations of an earlier garden park have obstructed most access to it (it is now surrounded by an ugly fence). Constantine, after his conversion to Christianity by a vision of a flaming cross, built the arch to commemorate his victory over his rival Maxentius at the Battle of the Milvian Bridge in 312. The triple arch, though well-proportioned, is constructed almost entirely from sculptural fragments pillaged from older Roman monuments. The circular medallions were originally part of a monument to Hadrian and include depictions of his lover Antinous; the rectangular reliefs (restored in 1989) were taken down from Trajan's Forum and show incongruous scenes of that emperor's defeat of the Dacians.

▓ Circus Maximus, Baths of Caracalla, and the Appian Way

Cradled in the valley between the Palatine and Aventine Hills, just a short walk down the shaded Via di S. Gregorio, beginning at the Arch of Constantine in the Piazza del Colosseo, the **Circus Maximus** today offers only a grassy shadow of its former glories. After its construction in about 600 BC, more than 300,000 Romans gathered here to watch the riotous, break-neck careening of chariots round the quarter-mile track. The turning points of the track, now marked by a raised hump, were perilously sharp by design to ensure enough thrills and spills to keep the crowds happy. The best seats in the house were actually the Palatine palaces themselves, where the emperors built special terraces for viewing the carnage. The Circus may have also been the sight of the mythical sea battles that others have attributed to the Colosseum. Nowadays, though, the great athletic feats are performed by dogs and toddlers chasing soccer balls down the grassy banks of the stadium.

From the Piazza di Porta Capena, at the eastern end of the circus, Via delle Terme di Caracalla passes the hulking remains of the **Baths of Caracalla** (open in summer Tues.-Sat. 9am-7pm, Sun. 9am-1pm, Mon. 9am-2pm; in winter, closes 1 hr. before sunset; last entrance 1 hr. before closing; L8000, discount for EU citizens under 18 or over 60), the largest and best-preserved of their kind in the city. Though the ruthless Caracalla wasn't known for his kindly nature, his construction of this monumental complex did do the city some good—some 1600 heat-soaked Romans could sponge themselves off here at the same time. While the occasional mosaic floor is beautiful, particularly in the **Apodyteria** (dressing rooms), it's the sheer magnitude of this proto-health club that boggles the sun-baked mind. These ruins were once the center of the complex: a huge central hall opening onto a cold-water swimming pool on one side and a round warm-water pool on the other. Outside the main complex, remains of a rectangular brick wall mark the outer boundary of the ancient gym; here Romans played sports, sipped juices in snack bars, and exercised their minds in an expansive library. Rome's opera company used to stage Verdi's *Aïda* here each summer, complete with horses and elephants. When it was discovered a few years ago that the performances were causing extensive structural damage to the complex, the company moved to their present location in the Piazza di Siena in the Villa Borghese.

Bad news for pickpockets and fans of early Christian iconography: service has been temporarily suspended for the #118 bus, which used to go from the Colosseum past the Baths of Caracalla and down Via Appia Antica. This leaves two options for those wishing to cap off a morning of sight-seeing at the ruins with an afternoon of the macabre at the tombs along Via Appia and the catacombs. The more cautious should take bus #90b or #714 from the baths (and on the same side of the street as the baths) to Piazza di S. Giovanni in Laterano, where the *capolinea* for bus #218 is located. The #218 bus heads to the Porta San Sebastiano before turning down Via Appia Antica towards the catacombs. For a more adventurous and more aesthetically appealing route, walk down the Via delle Terme di Caracalla until it reaches a fork at Piazzale Numa Pompilio. Directly across the *piazza,* Via di Porta S. Sebastiano heads out past the **Tomb of the Scipios** (closed to the public), one of Rome's most famous families, and the neighboring airy hills of the Parco degli Scipioni, towards the city walls.

The **Porta San Sebastiano** is a fine example of one of the Romans' more ingenious defensive practices: the killing gate. The outside gate was left deceptively weak, but when invaders stormed through they found themselves trapped in the inner court, where archers picked them off like fish in a barrel. The gate houses a **Museum of Walls,** Via di Porta S. Sebastiano, 18 at the end of the road on the right (open Tues., Thurs., and Sat. 9am-1:30pm and 4-7pm; Wed. and Fri 9am-1:30pm; Sun. 9am-1pm; closed Mon.; admission L3750, L2500 with student ID, under 18 and over 60 free). One of the least crowded museums you're likely to come across in Rome, the Museo delle Mura not only houses models and reconstructions of the various walls of the city and restored pieces of the original fortifications, but it also allows visitors to clamber down a long stretch of the third-century Aurelian walls and climb up onto the towers. These towers provide a bird's-eye view of both the Appian Way and the **Arch of Drusus,** which was once part of the aqueduct that supplied the water for the Baths of Caracalla.

Piazza di Porta S. Sebastiano marks the beginning of the **Via Appia Antica,** built in 312 BC and rightly called the queen of roads ever since. The Appian Way once traversed the whole peninsula, providing a straight and narrow path for legions heading to Brindisi and conquests in the East. It also witnessed the grisly crucifixion of Spartacus' rebellious slave army in 71 BC—their bodies are said to have lined the road from Rome all the way to Capua. Mere decades later, Saint Peter took the Appian Way when he first came to Rome with his disciples in 42 AD. Since burial and the erection of funerary monuments inside the city walls were forbidden during ancient times, fashionable Romans made their final resting place along the Via Appia, while early Christians secretly dug the maze-like catacombs right under the ashes of their persecutors. Some of Italy's modern *autostrade* still follow the ancient path, but a sizeable portion leading out of the city remains in its antique state, with basalt paving stones, avenues of cypress trees, views of the Roman countryside, and crumbling necropolis, both pagan and Christian. The narrow, cobblestoned, car-clogged Via Appia Antica can be difficult and dangerous to navigate. Exercise caution when walking on the practically non-existent shoulder, especially when getting on and off the bus.

■ The Catacombs

Outside the city proper lie the **catacombs,** multi-story condos for the dead, stretching tunnel after tunnel for up to 25km on as many as five levels. Of the 60 around Rome, five are open to the public; the most notable are those of **San Sebastiano, San**

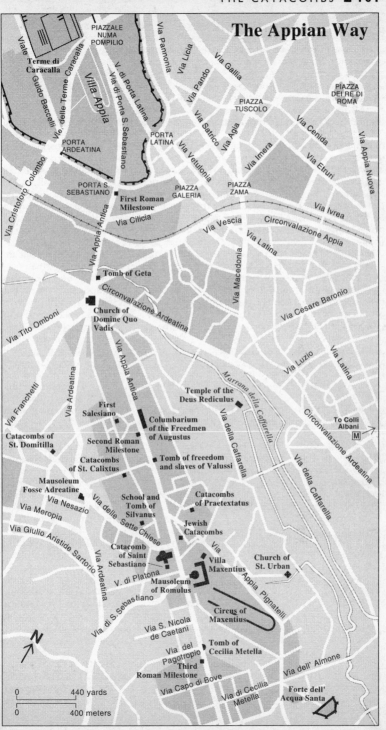

The Appian Way

Callisto, and **Santa Domitilla,** next door to one another in parks on Via Appia Antica south of the city. The best days to visit the catacombs are Friday through Monday, when the standard three are open. To get to the catacombs, take bus #218 from its capolinea at Piazza di S. Giovanni in Laterano (a short walk from the Metro Linea A stop, S. Giovanni) or as it joins Via Appia Antica, just outside the Porta di S. Sebastiano. If you're coming from near the train station, it may be easier to take Metro Linea A in the direction of Anagnina to Colli Albani, where you can switch to bus #660. The #218 proceeds down Via Appia Antica, until the church of Santa Maria in Palmis, also known as **Domine Quo Vadis,** where a fleeing St. Peter had a vision of Christ. Upon being asked "Domine Quo Vadis?" ("Lord, whither goest thou?"), Christ replied that he was going to Rome to be crucified again because of St. Peter's abandoning him. Peter instead returned to Rome and suffered his own martyrdom. Two stops later, the #218 bus, branching off to the right at Domine Quo Vadis, arrives at the gates of the San Callisto catacombs and near the gates of Santa Domitilla. The #660 stops at the gates of San Sebastiano and the far south entrance to San Callisto. Get off when you see the Ristorante Archeologico. You can also walk down the tree-lined path that begins across the street from Domine Quo Vadis, in between the Via Appia Antica and Via Ardeatina, and leads to the entrance to the S. Callisto catacombs.

For the first 200 years of Christianity in Rome, there were no established burial places, since the pagan Romans preferred cremation. From the second to the fifth century, the Christians took their burial business outside the city walls. Little by little, more underground tombs were carved into the volcanic rock (called "tufa") beneath the property of wealthy Romans. As the number of martyrs increased with the persecution of the Christians, the catacombs evolved from burial grounds of relatives to pilgrimage sites. At the height of the Christian persecution, some of the catacombs were officially closed down, but at no time were they used as a refuge or as housing, as some believe. By the fifth century, Christianity was in full swing, and the people's attention shifted from merely expanding the catacombs to creating a city of Christian monuments and churches; all catacombs were abandoned with the exception of St. Sebastian's, which remained a pilgrimage site. Over time, the martyrs' remains were moved into churches in the city, and the tombs were looted for valuables by Rome's various invaders, including the Goths and the Lombards. The long-lost death mazes were rediscovered in the 16th century by Antonio Bosio, but serious excavation didn't begin until the 19th century under Giovanni Battista de Rossi.

All of the catacombs are open six days per week, 8:30am-noon and 2:30-5:30pm (5pm in winter); the closing days are staggered so that at least two catacombs are open at any given time (see below for details). Admission is L8000.

San Callisto, Via Appia Antica, 110 (tel. 513 67 25 or 513 67 27; closed Wed.) can be reached by exiting the #218 bus at Domine Quo Vadis and walking up the tree-lined path between Via Appia Antica and Via Ardeatina. San Callisto is the largest catacomb in Rome, comprising almost 22km of subterranean paths. Its four serpentine levels once held 16 popes (in what now goes by the name of "The Crypt of the Popes" or the more jolly "Little Vatican"), seven bishops, Santa Cecilia (patron saint of music—her remains are now in the Church of Santa Cecilia in Trastevere), and some 500,000 other early Christians interred in the first public Christian cemetery. Look for vertical fish rebuses on the walls. The acronym of the Greek for "Jesus Christ, Son of God, Savior" spells out the Greek word for "fish," and this schematic drawing of a fish became a symbol for his name. Less appealing are the charred remains of babies who fell in vats of boiling oil.

Santa Domitilla, Via delle Sette Chiese, 282 (tel. 511 03 42; closed Tues.) can be reached by exiting S. Callisto at the far gates, where the #218 bus stops, crossing Via Ardeatina, and taking a right on Via delle Sette Chiese. The catacombs are on the left, less than five minutes down this road. Santa Domitilla enjoys acclaim for its paintings—a third-century portrait of Christ and the Apostles is still intact—and for its collection of inscriptions from tombstones and sarcophagi. The tour here is the shortest of all the catacombs.

Perhaps the most impressive is **San Sebastiano,** Via Appia Antica, 136 (tel. 788 70 35; fax 784 37 45; closed Thurs.), whose claim to fame is being the temporary home for the bodies of Peter and Paul (or so ancient graffiti on its walls suggests). San Sebastiano is most easily reached by taking the #660 bus from Colli Albani and exiting at the San Sebastiano stop, just after the Ristorante Archeologico. The entrance will be to your left. This is the only catacomb that was never abandoned. Running for seven miles among three levels and accommodating 174,000, the tunnels here are eerily decorated with animal mosaics, disintegrating skulls, and fantastic symbols of early Christian iconography, still clearly discernible. In the chapel on the first level is Bernini's bust of St. Peter.

In all three catacombs, visitors follow a guided tour in the language of their choice; non-English tours are significantly less crowded (every 20min., free with admission). Santa Domitilla receives very few visitors, so you're almost assured of a personalized tour. Because the catacombs have winding, uneven paths and the tours are conducted briskly (especially in the summer), they are not recommended for people who are claustrophobic or have difficulty walking, nor are they recommended for people who have an irrational fear of death. The **Jewish catacombs,** at Via Appia Antica, 119A, are at a fork in the road between Callisto and Sebastian but are not open to the public.

Down the road from the catacombs, the **Villa of Maxentius** lies half-buried in cricket-filled greenery. The Emperor built the villa in the first decade of the fourth century AD but never got to enjoy it, having been summarily ejected by the newly Christian Constantine at the Battle of the Milvian Bridge in 312. His sprawling circus retains its seats and spina. The **Tomb of Romulus** (tel. 780 13 24; open summer Tues.-Sat. 9am-7pm, Sun. 9am-1pm; winter Tues.-Sat. 9am-5pm, Sun. 9am-1pm; L3750, students L2500), inside a giant brick portico, housed the remains of the emperor's son, who was named for the city's legendary founder.

At the top of the hill, the proud **Mausoleum of Cecilia Metella** (tel. 780 24 65; open Tues.-Sat. 9am-sunset, Sun.-Mon. 9am-1pm; admission free) towers over the road. Built in the 30s BC for the patrician Cecilia, the tomb was preserved by its conversion into a fortress in the Middle Ages when its famous crenulations were added. The rest of the medieval complex, including a ruined gothic church, straddles both sides of the road. Beyond Cecilia's tomb, the Appian Way continues about 7km through progressively more deserted countryside. Here, the denuded remains of circular and turreted tombs, commemorative reliefs and steles, line the road between the country villas of Rome's glitterati. If you're walking, keep in mind that the bus stops its service shortly after the catacombs.

THE ESQUILINE, THE CAELIAN, AND SAN GIOVANNI

The Esquiline and the Caelian, the two most extensive original hills of Rome, are home to some of the most chaotic and seedy parts of the city center, as well as to some of the most spiritual, serene, and aesthetically breathtaking. Between and around the hills, the urban grid of broad avenues and cobblestoned alleyways conceals a surprising collection of ancient basilicas, overgrown parks, and narrow stone stairways. Though made up of several distinct neighborhoods, the region as a whole is filled with relics and monuments of the Christian church in its infant centuries, from the countless mosaics to the Esquiline basilicas to the rustic cloister gardens of the Caelian churches.

■ The Esquiline Hill

The **Basilica of Santa Maria Maggiore,** four blocks down Via Cavour from Termini (open daily 7am-7pm; dress code enforced), occupies the summit of the Esquiline Hill. It is one of the seven major basilicas traditionally visited on the pilgrimage to Rome, as well as one of the five churches in Rome granted extraterritoriality, making it officially part of Vatican City. Both its front and rear façades are Rococo works, but its interior, built in 352 AD, is the best-preserved example of a paleo-Christian basilica in the city.

According to legend, the Virgin Mary appeared before Pope Liberius in August of that year and requested that he build a church in her honor on the spot on the hill that would be covered in snow the next morning. On the morrow, the Pope discovered that snow had indeed fallen in the middle of August on the crest of the Esquiline hill, and promptly set out to design and build the church. Hence, the church's earliest name was Santa Maria della Neve (St. Mary of the Snow). The story is told in a series of 14th-century mosaics on the church's *loggia* (open daily 9:30am-5:40pm; tickets available at the souvenir stand just before you enter the church, L5000). A visit to the *loggia* also grants access to the one-time private chambers of Pope Paul V and a stunning, steep, spiral staircase designed by Bernini.

The church has a long, rectangular plan, divided by ancient columns into a central nave and two side aisles surmounted by clerestory windows, a flat ceiling, and a semi-circular apse behind the altar lined with gleaming mosaics. The coffered ceiling is believed to have been gilded with the first gold sent back from America by Columbus. The mosaics on the upper walls of the nave and on the triumphal arch before the altar date from the fifth century. The apse mosaic, from the 13th century, glitters with a magnificent scene of the *Coronation of the Virgin*.

Descend into the subterranean *confessio* before the altar, where a solemn marble Pope Pius IX kneels in front of a relic of the baby Jesus' crib. Though now sheathed in globs of silver, the crib is revealed each Christmas morning. A dazzling *baldacchino* (canopy) looms over the altar. To the right of the altar, a simple marble slab marks the **tomb of Gianlorenzo Bernini.** In contrast to the medieval simplicity of the central church, the Borghese and Sistine chapels on either side of the nave are monuments to the High Renaissance; vibrant frescoes adorn one chapel dome, while the other chapel is lined with extravagant slabs of colored marble pillaged from nearby Roman ruins. Outside in the Piazza di Santa Maria Maggiore, pigeons flock around a statue of the Virgin perched atop a 15-meter column left over from Constantine's third-century basilica.

Nearby lie two churches named for saints that never were. Saints Prassede and Pudenziana were once believed to have been sisters who witnessed the slaughter of 23 Christians, cleaned up the blood with a sponge, and were later converted to Christianity by St. Peter. Despite hundreds of years of saintly stature, doubts about the origins of this legend led the Church, in 1969, to declare the sisters non-existent and to remove them from the register of saints. Walk around to the back of Santa Maria Maggiore, head down Via A. Depretis one block, and turn left on Via Urbana. Shortly on your right appears the **Church of Santa Pudenziana** (open 8am-noon and 3-6pm; Sun. 9am-noon and 3-6pm) contains the oldest Christian mosaics in Rome, from 390 AD, depicting Christ and the apostles against a backdrop of ancient Roman buildings. From the front of Santa Maria Maggiore, Via Santa Prassede leads from Piazza Santa Maria Maggiore to the **Church of Santa Prassede** (open daily 7am-noon and 4-6:30pm), built in 822 and home to an extraordinary set of ninth-century mosaics. In the apse is the *New Jerusalem,* a triumphal lamb, and a host of celebratory apostles and elders. The tiny, glittering **chapel of Saint Zeno** (lit by a coin-operated machine outside the door, L600), in the right aisle, is lined almost entirely in mosaic. The walls are populated by various saints while in the vault four angels hold up a Byzantine Christ floating in a sea of gold. The chapel also holds part of a black and white column retrieved from Jerusalem in 1228 during the sixth Crusade. Possibly a site of historical scourgings, this is reputedly the column on which Christ was strapped and flagellated.

Down Via Carlo Alberto, which begins directly across from the front steps of S. Maria Maggiore, lurks the shabby **Piazza Vittorio Emanuele II,** home to one of Rome's biggest outdoor markets, which vends fresh fish and fruits, and non-edibles like clothes, shoes, and luggage. The small park also houses the curious remains of a fourth-century fountain, while the **Porta Magica,** a few steps away, reveals an alchemist's ancient instructions for turning lead into gold.

Via Conte Verde, at the eastern end of the *piazza,* turns into Via di Santa Croce in Gerusalemme on its way to the Piazza di Santa Croce in Gerusalemme. Here the Rococo façade (presently *in restauro*) of the **Church of Santa Croce in Gerusalemme** (open daily 8:30-noon and 3:30-6:30pm), welcomes the scores of pilgrims who come to catch a glimpse of the relics housed here. The church is believed to have been built around 326 to house a relic of the "true cross" on which Christ is said to have been crucified, brought from Jerusalem to Rome by St. Helena, mother of the Emperor Constantine. The church was rebuilt in 1144, most notably with the addition of the *campanile,* before the modernization of the facade in 1744.

At the end of the right aisle in the church's interior, the Chapel of St. Helena contains 15th-century mosaics depicting Christ, St. Peter, St. Paul, and St. Helena. The fascist-era Chapel of the Relics houses not only the small piece of the true cross which lends the church its name, but also a healthier chunk of the cross of the Good Thief. Perhaps the eeriest of the chapel's relics is the uncertain, now dismembered, finger used by a dubious St. Thomas to probe Christ's wounds.

Just to the right as you exit the church is the National **Museum of Musical Instruments** (tel. 701 47 96; open Tues. and Thurs. 9am-7pm, Wed. and Fri.-Sat. 9am-2pm, Sun. 9am-1pm; L4000). The museum displays instruments of almost every era, from classical times to the 19th century. Many of the instruments came from the collection of tenor Evangelista Gorga (1865-1957), whose career in the opera ended up taking a back seat to his obsessive collecting. This particular trove, bought by the state when Gorga declared bankruptcy, represents only one of his approximately 30 collections. During the summer, the museum hosts an outdoor festival of dance and music. See *Roma C'è* or call 474 23 19 or 474 22 86 (Mon.-Fri. 10am-1pm and 2:30-6pm) for more information.

■ San Giovanni

On the upper left side of Piazza S. Croce in Gerusalemme, as you look out from the church steps, Viale Carlo Felice leads to the Piazza di Porta San Giovanni and the grandiose **Church of San Giovanni in Laterano** (open daily 7am-6:45pm; winter 7am-6pm; dress code enforced; also accessible from Metro A stop San Giovanni), the cathedral of the diocese of Rome. The church and adjoining Lateran Palace, accorded since 1929 the same rights of extraterritoriality as the Vatican City, were the chief residence and church used by the popes until their flight to Avignon in the 14th century. The church itself is actually the oldest Christian basilica in the city, founded by Constantine in 314 AD. The traditional pilgrimage route from St. Peter's ends here, and the Pope still celebrates festival masses on occasion. On Corpus Christi, the ninth Sunday after Easter, a triumphal procession including the College of Cardinals, the Swiss Guard, and hundreds of Italian girl scouts, leads the pontiff back to the Vatican after the mass. The doors of the main entrance, facing the Porta San Giovanni, were pillaged from the Curia, the Roman Senate House in the Forum. Inside, the old basilical plan, notable for its four aisles, has been obscured by the 17th-century remodeling by Borromini, who encased the antique columns in enormous piers to make niches for statues of the apostles.

The giant Gothic *baldacchino* over the altar houses two golden reliquaries with the heads of Saints Peter and Paul inside. A door to the left of the altar leads to the 13th-century **cloister** (open daily 9am-6pm; winter 9am-5pm; L4000), a modest and peaceful space, and home to the church's collection of sacred relics and regalia (not to mention the bathrooms). The twisted double columns are typical of the work of the Cosmati family, who designed them and many other stone projects, including the pavements of inlaid red and green marble that color many churches in the city. Gold accents gleam from the frescoes and columns that plaster the church. Unfortunately, a terrorist bomb heavily damaged the basilica in 1993, when a simultaneous blast devastated the Church of San Giorgio in Velabro (see p. 185). Most of the damage was done to the façade, especially a part designed by Domenico Fontana in 1586, and some frescoes were left in danger of collapsing. Since San Giovanni is an extraterritorial property of the Vatican, the Vatican state, not the Italian government, must foot the repair bill.

Outside the church and across the street to its left as you exit the church, the sanctuary of the **Scala Santa** (open daily 6:15am-12:15pm and 3:30-7pm, winter 6:15am-12:15pm and 3-6:30pm) houses what are believed to be the marble steps used by Jesus outside Pontius Pilate's house in Jerusalem. Pilgrims earn an indulgence for ascending the covered steps on their knees; if you prefer to walk up to the Sancta Sanctorum, the chapel at the top, use the secular stairs on either side. Across the busy Piazza di S. Giovanni and to the left as you leave the Scala Santa building (on the other side of an egyptian obelisk—the oldest in the city, from the fifth century BC) the **Baptistery of Saint John** (open only for masses and baptisms, almost all day Sunday) was also built by Constantine in the fourth century and was where every Christian was baptized during that era. The octagonal building was probably the model for its more famous cousin baptistery in Florence. The baptistry is part of the original **Lateran Palace,** which is now closed to the public.

■ Caelian Hill

From the northwestern corner of Piazza di San Giovanni in Laterano (in the upper left corner as you walk out of the baptistry of St. John), Via di S. Giovanni in Laterano soon leads to a fork in the road. Walk down the shady, tree-lined Via di S. Stefano Rotondo, taking the left-most road at this fork and the next fork. Just after the immense S. Giovanni hospital, #7 marks the entrance to the **Church of S. Stefano Rotondo** (tel. 481 93 33; open Mon. 3:30-6pm, Tues.-Sat. 9am-1pm and 3:30-5pm; from July 1 to Sept. 3 open Tues.-Sat. morning hours only), one of the oldest and largest circular churches in existence, built in the late fifth century. The original church included three concentric rings, but centuries of decay and remodeling reduced the church to its inner two rings by 1450. In fact, the most recent renovations, finished in 1990, gave the church a hard-wood floor. Considering that much of the church remains inaccessible while restoration continues, it takes some imagination to picture what the original church must have looked like. Nonetheless, the recent renovations have made accessible not only the impressive round structure of the church itself, but also the seventh-century mosaics housed in the first chapel on the left.

Continue down Via di S. Stefano Rotondo and double back to the right down Via Celimontana. Towards the end, Via dei SS. Quattro Coronati climbs steeply to the right to the solemn **Church of Santi Quattro Coronati**. The church itself is remarkable more for its strange shape and overly wide apse than for any decoration, but the little **chapel of San Silvestro** off the entrance courtyard (to the right, after the courtyards, but before the church entrance) contains an extraordinary fresco cycle of the life of Emperor Constantine painted in 1248 (ring the bell of the convent; the cloistered nuns will send you a key on a lazy susan; L1000). Take a break from your climb to the church to sit on the benches that line the cold walls of the chapel and view a series of frescoes from the life of Sylvester, including Constantine presenting him with the papal crown. The medieval, delicate arches of the cloister (ring from inside the church and a sister will let you in) hide one of the prettiest, quietest garden spots in the city.

As you head back down Via SS. Quattro Coronati, take a right on Via dei Quercetti to arrive at the **Churches of San Clemente** (open Mon.-Sat. 9am-12:30pm and 3:30-6:30pm, Sun. and holidays 10am-12:30pm and 3:30-6:30pm). True to Roman architectural traditions, the complex incorporates centuries of handiwork into three-piece layers. The upper church, dating from the 12th century, is built over a fourth-century basilica which in turn rests on the ruins of a first-century Roman house and the second-century **Mithraeum,** all of which cover a still-operative system of Republican drains and sewers, some 30m below the current street level. The stratum of Roman houses is believed to have burned while Nero played his fiddle in 64 AD. The 12th-century courtyard to the upper church is the only medieval atrium extant in Rome. In the upper church are breath-taking 12th-century mosaics of the Crucifixion, saints, and apostles, and, in the **chapel of Santa Caterina,** a fresco cycle by Masolino (possibly executed with help from his pupil Masaccio). Dating from the 1420s, they include scenes of the Annunciation and the Crucifixion. On the left wall that supports the arch of the chapel, there is a fresco of St. Christopher upon which 15th-century pilgrims have scrawled their names. The marble choir enclosure, with its pulpits and Romanesque Paschal candlestick, sits in the center of everything and was originally part of the lower church. It dates from the sixth century. In the sprawling lower church (admission L3000), the original plan is obscured by newer piers and walls built to support the upper church. With a little imagination, you can trace the lines of the original nave, aisles and apse, all of which retain traces of rare 11th-century frescoes. A second stair leads further underground to the dank imperial ruins and Mithraeum (behind iron bars). According to myth, the Persian god Mithras created the world by slaughtering an enormous bull, out of whose slit throat the universe came pouring. Devotees of Mithras's cult always met in these cold, darkened rooms to recreate the slaughter in a festive (and sanguine) banquet. Beyond the creepy Mithraeum, a warren of brick and stone rooms lies over a rushing Republican sewer.

▓ Oppian Hill

Across Via Labicana from the church, Via Tomaso Grossi leads up a staircase at the top of which lies the somewhat unkempt **Parco Traiano**. Also called the Parco Oppio, this patch of lawns and lofty pine trees stretches out in disrepair, as the remnants of the giant brick vaults from the Baths of Trajan and the Flavian Baths crumble in unmown grass. Although at night the young bicycle-riding, balloon-toting Romans give way to older scooter-riding, needle-toting Romans, people still enjoy pleasant strolls past the remains of Nero's Domus Aurea (closed to the public; see p. 158).

Off to the right, between the Parco Traiano and the Piazza Vittorio Emanuele II, hovers the hulking, grey **Palazzo Brancaccio,** at Via Merulana, 19C. It's home to the **Museo Nazionale d'Arte Orientale** (tel. 487 44 15; open Mon., Wed., and Fri. 9am-2pm, Tues. and Thurs. 9am-7pm, Sun. 9am-1pm; admission L8000, under 18 and over 60 free), on the second floor. The museum is a trove of Asian ceramics, weaponry, paintings, and sculpture from the 14th century BC to the 15th century AD.

A few blocks to the west, Via Giovanni Lanza intersects Via Cavour. Head straight down Via Cavour, away from the station, and you'll soon find steps on the left which lead up and under the narrow archway of Via San Francesco di Paola to the *piazza* and **Church of San Pietro in Vincoli** (open 7am-12:30pm and 3:30-7pm). In the right aisle of the church, an unfinished fragment of Michelangelo's *Tomb of Julius II* is testament to the monumental frustration that the artist suffered trying to complete his commission. In his original designs, the tomb was to be an enormous rectangular structure decorated with over forty statues (among them the unfinished *Captives* in the Accademia in Florence). Pope Julius II quibbled over cost, his successor popes stalled out of jealousy, and Michelangelo never found the time or the money to finish what he had hoped would be his greatest work. Nevertheless, his central figure, the imposing **statue of Moses,** is a masterpiece. The anomalous goat horns protruding from his head come from a medieval misinterpretation of the Hebrew Bible. When Moses descended from Sinai with the Ten Commandments, according to Exodus, "rays" (similar to "horns" in Hebrew) shone from his brow.

Flanking the Moses statue are Leah and Rachel who represent the contemplative and active lives, respectively. Julius had wanted this to be the greatest funeral monument ever built; it remains either just or tragic that his body doesn't lie in the sarcophagus (his remains were scattered in the 1527 sack of Rome). Under the altar of the church dangle chains by which St. Peter was supposedly bound after having been imprisoned in the Tullianum prison on the Capitoline Hill. The two chains were separated for nearly a century in Rome and Constantinople, but when brought back together in the fifth century, the links united once again. This miracle is commemorated in the church's name: *vincoli* means "chains."

IL CENTRO STORICO

The Via del Corso, running north to south through the center of the city, forms the eastern boundary of the *Centro Storico,* the historic center of Rome, nestled into the elbow-shaped bend in the Tiber. This sprawling labyrinth of ancient streets and alleys is stuffed with monuments both great and small—proud Baroque churches, the ruins of ancient marble temples, vast open *piazze,* and shadowy picture galleries. Though there are plenty of attractions to keep an eye out for (among them the ancient Pantheon, Baroque Piazza Navona, and medieval Campo dei Fiori), you may have the best time simply wandering, letting the antique stores, chic *caffè,* romantic alleyways, and splashing fountains lure you in with their beauty.

▓ Piazza Venezia to Piazza Colonna

The straight **Via del Corso** runs for nearly a mile between Piazza del Popolo and Piazza Venezia. Many buses run from Termini to Piazza Venezia, including #57, 64, 75, and 170, among others. Following the line of the ancient Via Lata, the Corso takes its name from its days as Rome's premier racecourse, the site of the annual Carnival. Today you'll find a seemingly endless array of boutiques and shoe stores—good window-shopping, especially on Sundays when the street is closed to traffic; otherwise you'll have to brave the apocalyptic onslaught of buses and scooters roaring by inches from the sidewalk. **Piazza Venezia,** anchoring the southern end of the street, is a deadly expanse of asphalt where all the aspiring Mario Andreottis of Rome try to hit fourth gear before re-entering the medieval labyrinth of the historic center. This glorified traffic circle is dominated by the bombastic white **Vittorio Emanuele II Monument** (see p. 148). The crumbling **Palazzo Venezia,** on the right of the *piazza* as you face the monument, was one of the first Renaissance *palazzi* built in the city—not hard to imagine, as its plain, battlemented façade shows a healthy attachment to the Middle Ages. Mussolini occupied the building and delivered some of his most famous speeches from its balcony. Mussolini also had the Via dei Fori Imperiali across the *piazza* (see Fori Imperiali, p. 156) cleared to provide a good view of the Colosseum from his office.

The **Museo Nazionale del Palazzo Venezia,** Via del Plebiscito, 118 (tel. 69 99 42 16; open Tues.-Sat. 9am-2pm, Sun. and holidays 9am-1pm; admission L8000, under 18 and over 60 free), can be accessed by the entrance on Via del Plebiscito around the right of the *palazzo* as you face the façade on the *piazza.* The museum maintains a permanent collection of papal art objects, furniture, ceramics, sculpture, and various other collections from different historical periods, but is supplemented by more exciting exhibits held in three large rooms. One of these rooms, the **Sala del Mappamondo,** was the office where Mussolini deviously left his light on all night long, to earn the title of "Sleepless One." The *loggie* of the interior courtyard and of the **Church of San Marco** (church interior open daily 8:30am-noon and 4-7pm; enter from P. di San Marco, to the right of the Vittorio Emanuele monument as you face it) date from the Renaissance. Inside the dark and gloomy church, which was founded in 336 and remodeled in the 15th century along with the *loggie,* Melazzo da Forlì's pensive *Portrait of St. Mark* hangs in the chapel to the right of the altar. The mosaic in the apse (set up in 829 AD) depicts Christ and Pope Gregory IV holding a model of the recently restored church.

Facing Via del Corso, turn right on Via C. Battisti, which soon becomes Via Quattro Novembre; at the end, turn left on Via del Pilotta. Four thick arches connect the back of the **Palazzo Colonna** with the gardens of the **Villa Colonna** (closed to the public). To the left, at the end of the street at #17, the **Galleria Colonna** (tel. 679 43 62) opens its doors every Saturday morning from 9am-1pm (admission L10,000, L8000 with student ID). The decor of the *palazzo* is as opulent as the paintings themselves, having been designed in the 17th century for the express purpose of showing off the family goods. The central gallery, lined with ancient statues, is dazzling. The chaos of the ceiling fresco celebrates the victory of Marcantonio Colonna over the Turks at the Battle of Lepanto in 1571. The ebony desk in the next room is adorned with ivory reliefs of Michelangelo's famous *Last Judgement.* The throne room, built for Martin V, preserves a modest portrait of the portly pontiff. The chair is kept turned to the wall so none but the papal tush might sit in it.

Passing under the arches, take your first left to Via del Vaccaro, which leads to the Piazza dei S.S. Apostoli. Here, Palazzo Colonna sits to your left, with the **Church of the Santi Apostoli** (open daily 7am-noon and 4-7pm) tucked in the corner. Byzantine lions guard the entrance to the church which is filled with glass chandeliers and coated in Baroque and Rococo goo. The *palazzo* was built in the 15th century for Pope Martin V, first in a long line of overachievers from an ancient Roman family. The present decoration dates from the 18th century.

Leaving the *piazza,* Via S.S. Apostoli leads back to the main drag of the Corso, where the façades of two churches, one black with soot and the other pristine, flank the street. On the right stoops the recently restored **Church of San Marcello** (open Sept.-June Mon.-Sat. 7:15am-noon and 4:30-7pm, July and Aug. 7:15am-noon and 4:30-7pm, Sun. 8:30am-noon and 4-7pm). The tomb of Cardinal Michiel, dating from 1503, rests by the door. The third chapel on the right contains a 16th-century fresco, while the fourth chapel on the same side contains a 15th-century wooden crucifix that survived a fire in the church in 1519. Legend has it that the artist killed an unlucky passerby and watched his death throes for inspiration. Across the street and down to the left, restorative scaffolding hides the facade of the **Church of Santa Maria in Via Lata,** a spooky little shrine open daily 5-9:45pm.

Via Lata, off the Corso between the two churches, leads into Piazza del Collegio Romano, where the stalwart **Palazzo Doria Pamphili** hides the Rococo frivolity of the **Galleria Doria Pamphili** (tel. 679 73 23; open Fri.-Tues. 10am-1pm; admission L12,000, L9000 with student ID). Gallery 1 unfolds counter-clockwise around a charming enclosed courtyard. Hunt along the jam-packed walls for Titian's *Spain Succouring Religion* (#10) and *Salome with the Head of St. John the Baptist* (#29); Caravaggio's *Mary Magdalene* (#40), *Rest on the Flight to Egypt* (#42), and *Young John the Baptist* (#44); and a Raphael, too (#23). The next long gallery is highlighted by Carracci's *St. Jerome* (#120) and *Pietà* (#137). At the end of the gallery a series of small rooms juts off the right. The first—officially "Room II"—holds the hilarious *Nativity* (#180) by Ortdano, in which a blasé baby Jesus looks all too bored with the hubbub, while Room III boasts a Parmigianino *Madonna and Child* (#207) as well as a breathtakingly beautiful ceiling. An assortment of Breughels bespeckles Rooms IV and V: *Vision of St. John in Patmos* (#280) and *Snow Scene* (#316) by the Younger, and *Earthly Paradise* (#295) and *Battle in the Bay of Naples* (#317) by the Elder. The cabinet at the end harbors some engaging Dutch still lifes. Back in the Gallery, a third corridor holds wonderful sculptures and ceiling scenes depicting gods and humans in various acts of aggression. The corridor ends at Cabinet II, wherein reside the museum's stars, Bernini's *Bust of Innocent X* and Velazquez's painting of the same (#339). On the way out through the last gallery are Claude Lorraine's *Sacrifice at Delphi* (#348) and Carracci's *Assumption* (#357).

Some of the best paintings, tapestries, and sculptures are shown in the private apartments, open only by guided tour (an additional L5000 and worth it, usually at 11am and noon). The **Room of Andrea Doria** contains not pieces of the shipwreck,

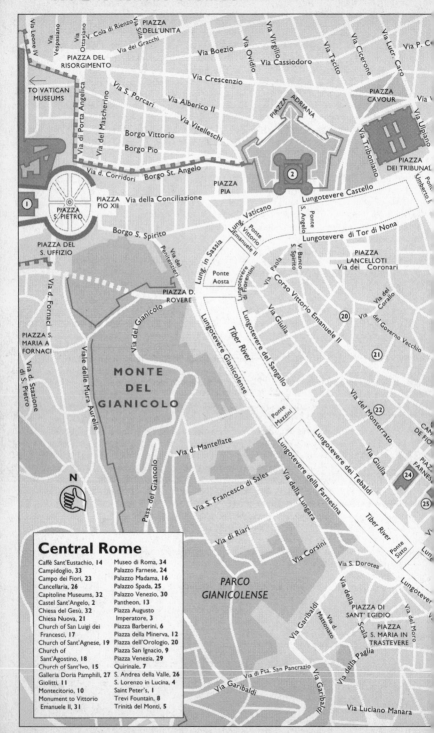

PIAZZA DELL'UNITA

Via Leone IV
Via Vespasiano
Via Octaviano
V. Cola di Rienzo
Via Silla
Via dei Gracchi
Via Boezio
Via Virgilio
Via Ovidio
Via Cassiodoro
Via Tacito
Via Cicerone
Via Luci. Caro
Via P. Ca

PIAZZA DEL RISORGIMENTO

Via Crescenzio

PIAZZA CAVOUR

TO VATICAN MUSEUMS

Via di Porta Angelica
Via del Mascherino
Via S. Porcari
Via Alberico II
Via Vitelleschi
Borgo Vittorio
Borgo Pio

PIAZZA ADRIANA

Via Ulpiano
Via Triboniano

PIAZZA DEI TRIBUNAL

Via d. Corridori
Borgo St. Angelo

PIAZZA PIA

Lungotevere Castello

Pon.
Umber.

①
PIAZZA S. PIETRO
PIAZZA PIO XII
Via della Conciliazione

Lung. Vaticano
S. Angelo
Ponte
S. Angelo

Lungotevere di Tor di Nona

PIAZZA DEL S. UFFIZIO

Borgo S. Spirito

Lung. in Sassia
Lung. Ponte Vittorio Emanuele II
V. Banco S. Spirito
Via Paola

PIAZZA LANCELLOTI
Via dei Coronari

Via d. Fornaci
Via del Penitenzieri

PIAZZA D. ROVERE

Ponte Aosta
Lungotevere in Fiorentini
Via Fiorentini
Corso Vittorio Emanuele II
Via Giulia

Via del Corallo
②⓪
Via del Governo Vecchio

PIAZZA S. MARIA A FORNACI

Via d. Stazione di S. Pietro

Via del Gianicolo

Tiber River
Lungotevere del Sangallo

②①

MONTE DEL GIANICOLO

Viale delle Mura Aurelie

Lungotevere Gianicolense

Via del Monserrato
②②

Ponte Mazzini

CAM
DE FIO

Via Giulia
Lungotevere dei Tebaldi
②④

Via d. Mantellate

N
🖐

Pass. del Gianicolo

Via S. Francesco di Sales

Via della Lungara

Lungotevere della Farnesina

Tiber River
②⑤

PIAZ
FARNES

Via di Riari

Via Corsini

Ponte Sisto
Lung

Via S. Dorotea

Lungotever

PARCO GIANICOLENSE

PIAZZA DI SANT' EGIDIO

Via della Scala
Via Garibaldi
Via d. Mattonato

PIAZZA S. MARIA IN TRASTEVERE

Via del Moro

Via della Paglia

Via di Pta. San Pancrazio
Via Garibaldi

Via della Paglia

Via Luciano Manara

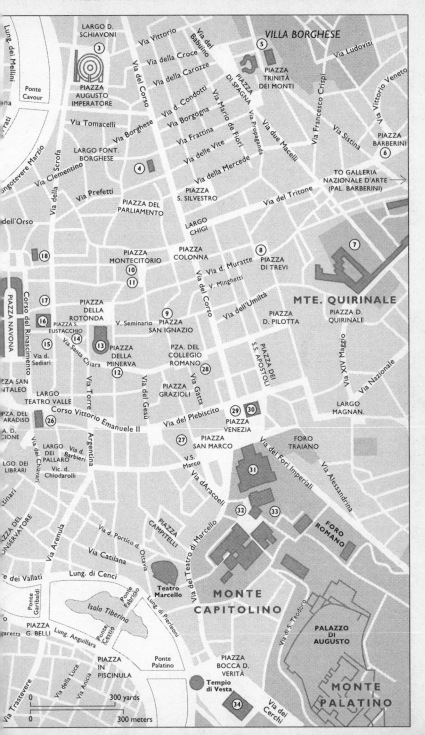

but two Brussels tapestries and some of Andrea's personal possessions. The **Green Salon** houses a gorgeous cradle from the 18th century, as well as Filippo Lippi's *Annunciation*.

From the gallery, walk up Via del Collegio Romano and turn left onto Via del Caravita which leads north into the lovely Piazza di Sant'Ignazio, a showcase of playful 18th-century Rococo design. The Jesuit **Church of Sant'Ignazio di Loyola** (open daily 7:30am-12:30pm and 4-7:15pm) that lends the *piazza* its name demonstrates, by contrast, the Baroque bombast of the Counter-Reformation. Inside, Padre Andrea Pozzo painted his famous *trompe l'oeil Triumph of St. Ignatius* along the vault of the great, aisle-less nave. Taking his inspiration from Michelangelo's Sistine ceiling and its intricate, logic-defying architecture, Pozzo went one step further. Instead of the Sistine's flat central scenes, the figures on Pozzo's ceiling exist in the same space as the architecture, and the painter's mastery of perspective makes their foreshortened forms seem to float in the air above the nave. The church was originally meant to have a grandiose dome, as magnificent as the one at the Gesù, Sant'Ignazio's sister church, but the Jesuits ran out of money during construction. Pozzo saved the altar from domelessness by painting a deceptively realistic *trompe l'oeil* cupola on the flat ceiling of the unfinished drum.

North of Piazza di Sant'Ignazio is Via del Burro, which leads directly to **Piazza di Pietra** and the remaining pieces of the **Temple of Hadrian,** part of the façade of the *Borsa* (the now-defunct stock exchange). The temple was built to honor the newly deified emperor in 145 AD. Exit the north side of the *piazza* to reach **Piazza Colonna,** named for the colossal **Column of Marcus Aurelius** that occupies its center. Though designed in imitation of the emperor Trajan's earlier triumphant column (see Fori Imperiali, p. 156), Marcus Aurelius' monument actually represents one of the more tragic moments in the history of the Empire. Trajan's victories across the Danube in the first years of the second century AD (which his column celebrates) had pushed the boundaries of Roman power as far as they would ever go. Only 40 years later, Marcus Aurelius found himself governing an empire so large and far-flung that it couldn't be defended. With barbarians encroaching on every frontier, the philosopher-emperor could barely keep his vast armies fed and paid. His campaigns against the Germans and Sarmatians, fought between 169-76 AD, saw the first defeat of a Roman army in over three centuries. Although the spiral reliefs on the column lionize the legions for their efforts, the praise rings hollow and the triumphal monument seems more like a tombstone marking the start of Rome's decline. Sixtus V had the statue of St. Paul added to the top of the column in the 16th century.

On the opposite (western) side of the Piazza Colonna, **Palazzo Wedekind** grins sheepishly through the restorative scaffolding which partially blocks its façade. Now home to the newspaper *Il Tempo,* it was built in 1838 with Roman columns from the Etruscan city of Veio. Check out the clock supported by four strange human figures. **Palazzo Chigi,** built in the 16th and 17th centuries, forms the north side of the *piazza.* Guards hovering around the door prevent public entrance (it is now the official residence of the Prime Minister), but you can look through into the lovely courtyard. The northwest corner of Piazza Colonna flows into **Piazza di Montecitorio,** dominated by Bernini's **Palazzo Montecitorio,** now the seat of the Chamber of Deputies. The obelisk in front of the *palazzo* was once the centerpiece of a giant sundial that was part of Augustus' Ara Pacis complex (see p. 189). Exiting southwards, Via in Aquiro leads into Piazza Capranica, from which you can see the **Piazza della Rotonda,** more commonly known as **Piazza del Pantheon,** down the Vicolo degli Orfani.

■ The Pantheon

The majestic **Pantheon** (tel. 36 98 31; open June Mon.-Sat. 9am-6pm, Sun. 9am-1pm; July-Aug. Mon.-Sat. 9am-6:30pm, Sun. 9am-1pm; Oct.-May Mon.-Sat. 9am-4pm, Sun. 9am-1pm, Sun. Mass 9:45-11:15am; free) has stood here for nearly 2000 years, with its marble columns and pediment, bronze doors, and soaring domed interior (save superficial decorative alterations) all unchanged from the day it was erected. While centuries of political chaos and urban neglect corroded most of ancient Rome's great monuments into ruins, the Pantheon has remained whole, a proud but bittersweet reminder of the eternal city's former glories. The temple has drawn visitors for centuries, in part because it's one of the few Roman ruins that won't strain the imagination; the vast, serene interior not only preserves its perfect architectural proportions, but also retains the power to mystify and inspire.

The building as it stands today is the product of Emperor Hadrian's fertile architectural imagination. Though it's unclear whether the emperor actually drew up the plans himself, it's certain that the second-century AD philosopher-king, who also takes credit for the revolutionary design of the Temple of Venus and Rome in the Forum, for the sprawling fantasies of his Villa Adriana at Tivoli, and for his own mausoleum, now Castel Sant'Angelo, had a hand in its design. The temple, dedicated to "all the gods," was conceived as a celebration of the abstract spatial harmonies and celestial order that the divine powers had bestowed on the universe. It's a study in very carefully planned contrasts and very cleverly concealed surprises. The classically proportioned façade, with its traditional triangular pediment, inscribed dedication, and Corinthian columns, was designed to deceive the first-time visitor into expecting an equally traditional interior. Note the large, functionally useless rectangular brick element that rises behind the pediment: its only purpose is to hide the dome from the view of those approaching. If you imagine that the level of the pavement outside in the *piazza* was some 7m lower during the Empire so that the temple was approached by steps, you can see how completely the dome was concealed. Deceptive, too, is the inscription across the architrave on the façade: "Marcus Agrippa made it in his third consulship" Indeed he did build a temple here in 27 BC, dedicated to all the gods. Hadrian later tore it down and started from scratch in 119 AD, but had the old inscription copied here, apparently to avoid accusations of overweening pride.

Once inside, however, all notions of modesty disappear. Even if you have spotted the dome from outside, the dusky, soaring interior and luminous central oculus (the big hole in the ceiling) come as a shock. The effects of light and shadow on the recessed coffers endow the vast space with a dizzying power. On hot summer days, particularly, the cool stillness of the air indoors offers a sense of the perpetual sacredness of this ancient temple. The dome itself has both a radius and a height of 21.3m, representing a perfect half-sphere. It was constructed entirely out of poured concrete, without the support of vaults, arches, or ribs. Archaeologists and architects have puzzled for centuries over how the thing was actually erected. The central oculus (9m in diameter), which once provided the only source of light for the entire building, also supports the weight of the dome, as all the inward forces of the sloping concrete are trapped in an eternal ring of tension around it. The sunlight, which pours through the hole like a divine ladder, was used as a sundial to indicate the passing of the hours and the dates of equinoxes and solstices.

It's not surprising that such an extraordinary building was preserved over the centuries, even as its lesser marble and brick cousins fell into disrepair. It seems that from the beginning the usually lackadaisical Romans knew they had something special. Though the Senate voted to close all pagan temples during the fifth century AD, the emperor Phocas (whose column stands in the Forum) gave the Pantheon to Pope Boniface IV for safekeeping in 609 AD. Converted to the **Church of Santa Maria ad Martyres** (the title it retains to this day), the temple weathered the Middle Ages with few losses, though it sometimes moonlighted as a fortress and even a fishmarket. Later artists and architects adored and imitated the building, which served as the inspiration for countless Renaissance and Neoclassical edifices, including Bramante's Tempietto, Palladio's Villa Rotonda, and America's own Jefferson Memorial. Michelangelo, using the dome as a model for his designs in St. Peter's Basilica, is said to have designed his own dome about two meters shorter in diameter than the Pantheon's, out of respect for his ancient model. The 17th century wasn't quite so deferential. When the vainglorious Pope Urban VIII Barberini melted down the bronze revetments from the roof of the portico to make cannons for Castel Sant'Angelo (and the *baldacchino* over the altar of St. Peter's), horrified Romans remonstrated: "What the barbarians didn't do, the Barberini did." Adding injury to insult, Urban had Bernini add two clumsy turrets to either side of the pediment (visible in the famous Piranesi prints of the temple), which were almost immediately tagged the "ass-ears of Bernini." Saner minds removed the turrets in the 19th century. Later additions to the interior of the temple include several modest Renaissance frescoes, the tombs of Italy's first two kings, and the simple tomb of the Renaissance master Raphael Sanzio.

In the *piazza* before the temple, Giacomo della Porta's playful, recently renovated, late-Renaissance fountain supports an **Egyptian obelisk,** which was added in the 18th century, when obelisks, popular among ancient Romans, were once again in fashion. Around the left side of the Pantheon, another obelisk marks the center of tiny **Piazza Minerva,** supported by Bernini's curious, winsome elephant statue. Behind the obelisk, the unassuming façade of the **Church of Santa Maria Sopra Minerva** (open daily 7am-noon and 4-7pm) hides some of Renaissance Rome's artistic masterpieces. To the right of the entrance, six plaques mark the high-water level of floodings of the Tiber over the centuries. Inside the church, stained-glass windows cast a soft radiance on the Gothic interior and its celestial ceiling. The chapels in the right hand aisle (the south side) house a number of treasures, including, in the fifth chapel, a panel of the *Annunciation* by Antoniazzo Romano, a pupil of Pinturicchio, and, in the sixth chapel, a statue of *St. Sebastian* recently attributed to Michelangelo. The south transept houses the famous **Carafa Chapel,** with a brilliant fresco cycle by Filippino Lippi. The altar of every Catholic church houses a holy relic and Santa Maria Sopra Minerva has a great one—the body of St. Catherine of Siena, the famous 14th-century ascetic and church reformer who died in a house nearby. To the left of the altar another medieval great, the painter Fra Angelico, lies under a tomb surrounded by a bronze-leaved fence. Just to the left of the altar, Michelangelo's *Christ Bearing the Cross* stands guard.

Standing in Piazza della Rotonda, with your back towards the Pantheon, head northwest to Via Giustiniani in the upper left corner of the *piazza.* Take it to its intersection with Via della Scrofa and Via della Dogana Vecchia, halfway to the Corso del Rinascimento. Here stands the simple, sooty façade of the **Church of San Luigi dei Francesi** (open Sun.-Wed. and Fri. 8am-12:30pm and 3:30-7pm; Thurs. 7:30am-12:30pm; Sat. 8am-12:30pm and 3:30-6:30pm), the French National Church in Rome and home to three of Caravaggio's most famous ecclesiastical paintings. The controversial Baroque artist decorated the last chapel on the left, dedicated to the Evangelist Matthew, between 1597 and 1602. *The Calling of St. Matthew,* to the left of this chapel's altar, is the most famous of the three. You have to pay L200 for a light to shine on it, since it's impossible to see otherwise. Here you can see Caravaggio's revolutionary attention to everyday detail (see Caravaggio, p. 14). While his Baroque compatriots were busy painting up sweet madonnas on pastel clouds, Caravaggio didn't hesitate to imbue even Biblical scenes with the dark and dirty atmosphere of his own day. Unlike the idealized models of both Renaissance and Baroque painting, the figures in Caravaggio's works seem like plain street people, from their carefully detailed period clothing down to the dirt under their fingernails. But Caravaggio's real brilliance lies in his virtuosic ability to express in oils the play of light on surfaces, from the mellow gleam of a glass goblet to the rough texture of a wooden table, giving every scene a clarity of more than photographic realism. Notice how Caravaggio painted the shaft of light that falls on the bewildered figure of St. Matthew at the moment of his calling to the Christian faith so that it continues the line of the real light pouring in from above the altar. Not surprisingly, Caravaggio's insistence on warts-and-all portraiture wasn't always pleasing to his patrons. His first rendition of the central *St. Matthew and the Angel,* in which an angel helps the aged saint compose his Gospel, was an example of his relentless effort to make the most legendary scenes seem real to his viewers. Caravaggio had imagined the apostle as an elderly man for whom the task of writing so holy a book was nearly overwhelming. He painted the angel as a symbol of divine grace and inspiration, as Matthew's opposite, a charming, youthful figure who seemed almost to mock the old man's difficulty. The chapel's patrons, on seeing the work, cried foul and demanded a more respectful treatment of the subject, which you can see hanging over the altar. The third painting in the series, to the right of the altar, depicts St. Matthew's agonizing *Crucifixion.*

Continuing past the intersection onto Via Salvatore, turn left at Corso del Rinascimento. On the left, the celestial **Church of Sant'Ivo** (open daily 9am-noon; closed in summer) parades its famous corkscrew cupola over the Palazzo della Sapienza, the original home of the University of Rome, founded by Pope Sixtus IV in the 15th century. The entrance to the **cloister** on Corso del Rinascimento (#40) provides the best view of Borromini's intricate façade and cupola, designed in 1660 and recently restored. Inside, Borromini's obsession with geometry and its perfect, abstract forms climaxes in the hexagonal symmetry of his gleaming white dome. Unlike his rival Bernini, Borromini rarely incorporated sculpture into his works, preferring to manipulate and decorate a space with his mastery of architecture alone. When he did choose to use figures, he opted for stark, six-pointed stars and odd little cherubs, the closest things to terrestrial beings that you'll find in the otherworldly Sant'Ivo. Across the street from the *palazzo,* Via dei Canestrari leads into Piazza Navona.

▨ Piazza Navona

Contrary to popular belief, Emperor Domitian (81-96 AD) never used this 30,000-person stadium to shred naughty Christians; later emperors can take credit for that. Instead, Domitian used the site of modern-day **Piazza Navona** as a racetrack. From its opening day in 86 AD, the stadium witnessed daily contests of strength and agility: wrestling matches, javelin and discus tosses, foot and chariot races, and even mock naval battles. For these seafaring fracases the stadium was flooded and floated with fleets of convicts. Nowadays, the only water in the *piazza* is confined to the three graceful fountains, each with an aquatic theme.

As the empire fell, real-life battles with marauding Goths replaced staged contests, and the stadium fell into disuse. Resourceful Romans used its crumbling outer walls as foundations for new houses, thus preserving the original outline of the stadium. Large crowds returned to the *piazza* during the Renaissance, when from 1477 to 1869 the space hosted the city's general market. Festivals and jousts were commonplace, as was the contest of the *cuccagna,* in which contestants shimmied up a greased pole to win fabulous prizes. These days, the market, selling plastic manger scenes, marzipan fruit, and *Befane* of every size, comes to the *piazza* only at Christmas time until the Epiphany (January 6); caricaturists, though, roost here year-round, joined at night by musicians and roving crowds. Throw money to the wind in the many *caffè* and throw fate to the readers of *tarocchi.* Female travelers have no problem getting lights for cigarettes or company for strolls, as prowling Romeos vie to test their virility and their English.

One of the great examples of Baroque city planning, Piazza Navona owes its beauty and fame to a case of pure one-upsmanship. Innocent X, the Pamphili Pope who came to the papal throne in 1644, was only too eager to distract the Roman people from the achievements of his predecessor, the ubiquitous Urban VIII Barberini. Innocent cleared out the old stadium, where his family had had a palace for centuries, and set about constructing a new *piazza* and palace to rival those of the Barberini across town (see Piazza Barberini, p. 192). Innocent's desire to please the people of Rome (and not just his own ego) determined the appearance of the present *piazza;* it was, and is, a place for people to congregate, circulate, and celebrate, all under the watchful eye of the Pamphili dove.

The towering, rippling bodies in Bernini's **Fountain of the Four Rivers** *(Fontana dei Quattro Fiumi)* command the center of the *piazza* with the grandeur that Innocent intended. In an effort to sabotage his nemesis, the Pope managed to divert the flow of a previously repaired channel, which had been supplying the Fontana del Tritone in Piazza Barberini. Having stolen old Urban's watery thunder, Innocent commissioned Bernini to make something impressive out of it and the artist responded with this exuberant work. Each of the four male river gods represents one of the four

SIGHTS

continents of the globe (as they were thought of then): the Ganges for Asia, the Danube for Europe, the Nile for Africa (veiled, since the source of the river was unknown), and the Rio de la Plata for the Americas.

According to an old story, Bernini designed the Nile and Plata statues to shield their eyes from the sight of his arch-rival Borromini's **Church of Sant'Agnese.** The legend continues that Borromini then made his statue of St. Agnes on the façade look haughtily out beyond the *piazza,* not deigning to drop her gaze to Bernini's work. Unfortunately, at least half of the story seems to be a load of pole grease, since the fountain was finished in 1651, before Borromini had even started work on the church.

At the southern end of the *piazza,* the **Fontana del Moro** attracts pigeons and small children alike. Originally designed by Giacomo della Porta in the 16th century, Bernini renovated it in 1653 and added *Il Moro,* the central figure perched precariously on a mollusk while struggling with a fish (carved by Antonio Mari, one of Bernini's pupils). The tritons spitting water from shells around the edge of the fountain were moved to the Giardino del Lago in the Villa Borghese in 1874 and replaced by copies. Adding balance to the whole scene is the **Fountain of Neptune,** flowing in the north end of the *piazza.* It too was designed by della Porta in the 16th century and spruced up by Bernini, but was without a central figure until 1878. Antonio della Bitta then added the Neptune from which the fountain takes its name. The ruler of the sea stands ready to spear his prey, while sea nymphs frolic around him with seahorses and a cockeyed octopus.

The *piazza* has more than fountains; it was also the site of a genuine *miracolo,* marked by the **Church of Sant'Agnese in Agone.** According to Christian legend, Saint Agnes said no to the lascivious son of a low-ranking magistrate; consequently, she was stripped naked in Domitian's stadium. When her hair miraculously grew and covered her sinful nudity, the powers that were tried to burn her at the stake. When the flames didn't even singe her, the efficient Diocletian decided to cut her head clean off. This time it worked. The church marks the spot where she was exposed and houses her severed skull (referred to as the *Sacra Testa,* or Holy Head) in its sacristy. Girolomo and Carlo Rainaldi reconstructed the now run-down church in 1652, but it was Francesco Borromini who orchestrated the complex façade, with its soaring dome embraced by twin bell towers, between 1653 and 1657. The inside of this Baroque marvel is dominated by the airiness of its tall, frescoed cupola. Statues take the place of paintings on most walls; Maini's monument to Innocent X, who is buried here, is above the entrance.

The region to the north of Piazza Navona, traversed by winding cobbled streets, vaulted alleyways, and crumbling ancient arches, harbors some of the most magnificent churches in Rome, well hidden behind ivy-covered walls. Exiting the *piazza* at its northern end on Via Agonale, cross through Piazza delle Cinque Lune to the right to Via di Sant'Agostino, which opens up to the simple Renaissance façade of the **Church of Sant'Agostino** (open daily 7:45am-noon and 4:30-7:30pm). The plain exterior is juxtaposed with an ornate interior, as its 15th-century design has been encrusted with the usual layers of Baroque and Rococo stucco and frippery. Keep an eye out for Raphael's magnificent *Prophet Isaiah,* painted on the third pillar of the left aisle, and Caravaggio's compellingly shadowed *Madonna of the Pilgrims,* another striking example of the Baroque artist's insistence on realistic representation.

Via della Scrofa, to the right of the church, leads north to Via dei Portoghesi, where the Rococo **Church of Sant'Antonio dei Portoghesi** (the Portuguese national church) is all shine inside. Electric bulbs glimmer off the clusters of gilt throughout the church. Antoniazzo Romano conveniently gave his 15th-century painting of *Mary, St. Francis, and St. Anthony* a gilded background. To top it off, Canova's somber funeral painting is framed in gold. Although there are some fanciful serpentine sculptures above the altar, this elegance is countered by a number of cheesy statues with haloes.

At the fork in the road, bear right on Via dell'Orso and meander past reliefs of lions, boars, and other wild beasts. Up the stairs at the end of the street, on the corner of Via Zanardelli and Via di Monte Brianza, the **Museo Napoleonico** (open Tues.-Sat.

9am-7pm, Sun. 9am-1:30pm; L3750, students L2500; free last Sun. of every month) caters to anyone with a short-man complex or fetish. Rooms are dedicated to the vertically challenged emperor and many of his little relatives (most of whom lived in Rome). There's even the couch on which Pauline, his nutty sister, posed naked for the sculptor Canova. Across the *lungotevere,* on the **Ponte Umberto I,** you can catch a breathtaking view of St. Peter's and Bernini's oval *piazza,* with the stern battlements of Castel Sant'Angelo standing guard over the foreground.

From the Piazza di Ponte Umberto I, take the steps near the museum back down Via dei Soldati, which makes its way back to Piazza di Tor Sanguigna in front of Piazza Navona. Here along the outer curve of Piazza Navona you'll see the last remains of Domitian's ancient stadium, including an arch and a decaying stairwell, preserved beneath a 20th-century building. Follow the curve right along Via di Tor Sanguigna, which shortly becomes Via dell'Anima. Under the arch to the right, Vicolo della Pace approaches the charming semi-circular porch of the **Church of Santa Maria della Pace,** the product of Baroque architect Pietro da Cortona's playful imagination. His 17th-century facelift made the church so popular among Rome's upper crust that the *piazza* soon became jammed with carriages of the *crème de la crème* on their way to pray. A nightmare for city planners, commuters, and pedestrians alike, the *piazzetta* was finally expanded to let carriages turn around—an improvement so popular that a Latin inscription was put up declaring that no stone in the *piazza* could be changed thenceforth. At night, the *piazza* brims with less pious crowds of Italian stallions and tourists sipping *espresso.*

To enter the church, pass through **Bramante's cloisters,** a masterpiece of Renaissance harmony designed in 1504, at Vicolo della Pace, 5. The open courtyard and surrounding buildings are still frequented by crimson-clad nuns. Portions of the church are undergoing restoration—and have been since time immemorial—because of humidity in the subsoil, and the dome is blocked off. Still, you can marvel at Raphael's gentle *Sibyls* in the Chigi chapel (the first on the right). The painting of the Virgin over the altar supposedly bled when hit by a stone, and the church was built in commemoration. Check out the 15th-century wooden cross.

To the right of the porch of Santa Maria della Pace and across the street hides the unassuming entrance (#20) to the **Church of Santa Maria dell'Anima** (open Mon.-Fri. 8am-7pm, Sat. 8am-6pm, Sun. 8am-1pm and 3-7pm; you may have to ring the bell to get in), the German National Church in Rome. Don't be deceived by the simple façade of the building—after passing through a fragrant courtyard, you'll find the dark, echoing interior of the church deserted and spooky. Keep an eye out for the bizarre skull-cherub reliefs everywhere, the imitation of Michelangelo's *Pietà,* and the statue reclining as if watching TV (actually resting on a tomb). On the opposite side of the ivy-covered *piazza,* Via del Teatro Pace leads into Piazza Pasquino.

■ Via del Governo Vecchio

In **Piazza Pasquino,** a scarred torso is all that remains of poor **Pasquino,** a communal bitchboard ever since Cardinal Caraffa put him here in 1501. The "talking statue" was plastered by early activists with satirical comments against city authorities, the Pope, and other perennial targets—mass media in the days before CNN. You may still find some graffiti on Pasquino, though present-day authorities try to keep him clean. From Piazza Pasquino, Via del Governo Vecchio, an ancient street now lined with off-beat art and antique galleries, vintage clothing stores, and cheap *trattorie,* heads west toward the Vatican. It used to be a papal thoroughfare, lined with the townhouses of prosperous bankers and merchants. Though you probably won't be bumping into His Holiness anytime soon, you can still gawk at the medieval mansions overhanging the street, now filled with trendy boutiques. The once grand, now abandoned **Palazzo del Governo Vecchio,** built by Cardinal Stefano Nardini in 1473, sits at #39; pass an eye over the ornately carved, but ill-kept, Renaissance doorway.

A left on Via della Chiesa Nuova leads into the *piazza* of the same name. The **Chiesa Nuova** (open daily 8am-noon and 4:30-7pm), originally founded in the 12th century as Santa Maria in Vallicella, was the home base for Counter-Reformation leader Saint Philip Neri's congregation of Oratorians. He remodeled the church, and in 1605 the refurbished building was called the "new church;" it was further restored in the 19th century. During the building process, St. Philip had a vision of the Virgin rescuing churchgoers at a mass-in-progress by supporting a section of the old church that was about to collapse. This mini-miracle is represented in a stucco ceiling painted in 1644 by Pietro da Corona, the man responsible for much of the other art in this Baroque interior. Don't miss the early Rubens (1608) paintings in the chancel. The chapel on the left holds the remains of St. Philip Neri and is consequently decorated with bronze, marble, mother-of-pearl, and gold. Next door the **Oratory** (closed for restoration), where St. Philip's followers met to make music, is graced by Borromini's intriguing brick façade, a symphony of convex and concave surfaces for which the geometrically-minded architect is famous. The courtyard and walkways are also worth seeing.

Back around the church to the left as you face it, Via dei Filippini leads back to the end of Via del Governo Vecchio in **Piazza dell'Orologio,** where Borromini's Baroque clock tower stands guard—when it's not shrouded in scaffolding. Don't miss the beautiful virgin supported by cherubs, carved into the rear corner of the **Oratorio dei Filippini** below the clock tower on the *piazza*.

Continuing along Via Banchi Nuovi (the extension of Governo Vecchio after P. dell'Orologio), you'll end up in **Piazza Banco di Santo Spirito.** In the 15th century the *via* and *piazza* made up a banking district that attracted moguls from all over Italy. Not only did they change and hoard money, they also acted as bookies, taking bets on anything from Papal behavior to sporting events. The **Palazzo di Banco di Santo Spirito** was a working mint until 1541 and now functions as a regular bank (Banca di Roma), despite the fact that its ornate façade is crumbling and sprouting weeds. The **Palazzo Niccolini-Amici** (at Via dell'Arco della Fontanella, 40), now also a Banca di Roma, boasts a columned balcony and was built for the Strozzi by Jacopo Sansovino in the 16th century. The **Arco dei Banchi** (on the left down Via di Santo Spirito, toward the Tiber), a grotty little tunnel, leads to the Chigi bank and houses a Virgin and lamp to which Roman passers-by say a quick *Hail Mary*. Just inside the entrance and to the left, the arch shows the height of the Tiber when it flooded in 1277. Via di Santo Spirito opens out onto an amazing view of the Ponte and Castel Sant'Angelo. From Piazza Ponte S. Angelo in front of the bridge, Via Paola crosses Corso Vittorio Emanuele II into Piazza d'Oro and the beginning of Via Giulia.

■ Via Giulia

As part of his campaign in the early 1500s to clean up Rome after the "Babylonian Captivity" (when the popes moved to Avignon and the city fell into serious disrepair), Pope Julius II commissioned Bramante to construct a straight road leading directly to the Vatican, giving birth to **Via Giulia,** an elegant, even revolutionary contrast to the narrow and winding medieval streets. Throughout the 16th century, this luxurious expanse remained a refined neighborhood, as later architects built the expensive residences in accordance with Bramante's restrained, classical vision. In the 17th century, however, Innocent X built a prison here in order to down-market this area, and to make the neighborhood that he commissioned himself around Piazza Navona stand out. Nevertheless, the tiny neighborhood attracted popes, Roman nobility, and artists, including Raphael, who lived at #85. Today, this street parallel to the Tiber remains one of the most peaceful and exclusive in Rome, with well-maintained *palazzi*, antique stores, and art galleries.

Near the beginning of Via Giulia in the Piazza d'Oro, the **Church of San Giovanni dei Fiorentini** (open Mon.-Sat. 7-11am and 5-7pm; Sun. and holidays 7:30am-1pm and 5-7:30pm) has a particularly prestigious history. Pope Leo X, a Medici from Florence, decided to illustrate the glories of his hometown and build a Florentine church in Rome. All the most famous Renaissance artists competed for the privilege of building it, and Jacopo Sansovino beat out the likes of Peruzzi, Michelangelo, and Raphael.

Started in the 16th century, the work was continued by Antonio da Sangallo and Giacomo della Porta and finally wrapped up by Carlo Moderno in 1614. Two busts were done, one by *the* Bernini (Gianlorenzo), on the right, and one by his lesser known father (Pietro), on the left. A pupil of Bernini's, Antonio Raggi, contributed a set of marble statues. The tombs were designed by Borromini.

Down Via Giulia at #66 is **Palazzo Sacchetti,** designed in 1543 by Sangallo the Younger, the Farnese Palace architect. The courtyard features several stone busts and a relief of a Madonna and Child illuminated by an enormous candle. In the two blocks between Via del Gonfalone and Vicolo del Cefalo, giant stone blocks known as the "Via Giulia sofas" protrude from the bases of the buildings on the left. They were to provide the foundation for the never-completed law courts of Julius II. A quick jaunt one block north to Via dei Banchi Vecchi reveals Alexander VI's **Palazzo Sforza Cesarini** with its own little *piazza.* Back down Via Giulia, note Pope Innocent X's dread **prison** (1655) at #52. The prison was converted into a museum of criminology, reputedly filled with old papal torture instruments, which never opened. Fittingly, the prison is now the U.N. Interregional Crime and Justice Research Institute.

Continuing along Via Giulia, watch carefully for the turn toward the river on Via di Sant'Eligio; it's worth the detour to visit the miniature **Church of Sant'Eligio degli Orifici** (open Sept.-July 10am-noon; Oct.-June Sun. mass at 11:30am; ring around the corner at Via S. Eligio, 9). Raphael designed this 16th-century Greek-cross church which was continued by Peruzzi, who added the cupola. Further along Via Giulia on the right is the **Palazzo Falconieri,** expanded by Borromini; it has been the Hungarian Academy since 1928. The Falconieri is easily recognizable by the giant falcons with breasts that roost on each corner. Next door to the *palazzo* lies the **Church of Santa Maria dell'Orazione e Morte** (open Sun. and holidays for 6pm mass), which was revamped by Ferdinando Fuga from 1733-37 and carries the *vanitas* skull motif and some Corinthian columns.

Perhaps the most striking of all sights in this area is the ivy-draped **bridge** that spans Via Giulia from the back of the Palazzo Farnese and extends to the embankment of the river. Michelangelo designed the bridge, which was originally intended to be the first leg in a longer bridge that would cross the Tiber to connect the *palazzo* with the **Villa Farnesina** on the other side (see Villa Farnesina, p. 207), but the funds dried up and Pope Paul passed away. After passing under it, steal a glance through the iron and glass gate (to the east of the *palazzo*) at the lush gardens and Giacomo della Porta's beautiful façade of the Palazzo Farnese. Off the southeast corner of the *palazzo,* just before the end of Via Giulia (at #253), lurks the **Fontana del Mascherone.** Though erected by the Farnesi, the immense marble mask of the bloated face and the granite basin are ancient Roman. Across from the fountain, Via del Mascherone leads away from the river and into Piazza Farnese.

▨ Piazza Farnese

Piazza Farnese is dominated by the huge, stately **Palazzo Farnese** (look for the French flag hanging in front; not open to the public), begun in 1514 and considered the greatest of Rome's Renaissance *palazzi.* The Farnese, an obscure noble family from the backwoods of Lazio, parlayed Pope Alexander VI's affair with Giulia Farnese into bishophood for her son Alessandro, a fling at the papal throne, and eventually duchies in Parma and Piacenza. Alessandro Farnese refounded the Inquisition as Paul III, the first Counter-Reformation pope (1534-1549), and (more humanely) commissioned the best architects of his day—Antonio da Sangallo, Michelangelo, and Giacomo della Porta—to design his dream abode.

Although Sangallo's façade and entrance passage are remarkable, the most impressive part of the building is Michelangelo's elaborate cornice, modeled on ancient Roman architectural fragments and running the length of the *palazzo*'s flat roof. Note the band of *fleur de lis* that runs around the building. Since 1635, the French Embassy has rented the *palazzo* for one *lira* per 99 years in exchange for the Grand Opera House in Paris, home of the Italian Embassy. In the 16th and early 17th centuries, the Farnese family hosted great spectacles in the square and had the two huge tubs (later converted into the present-day fountains) dug up from the Baths of Caracalla to serve as "royal boxes" from which members of the self-made patrician family could look on. In the west side of the *piazza* stands the **Church of Santa Brigida,** whose ornate portal curiously upstages its *palazzo* façade. Saint Bridget lived here for 19 years before her death in 1373. Go around the back of the Palazzo Farnese for a glance at the gardens and Michelangelo's beautiful vine-covered bridge over Via Giulia (p. 178).

Galleria Spada

Behind the elaborate Baroque façade of the **Palazzo Spada,** in Piazza Capo di Ferro to the left (east) of the Palazzo Farnese as you face it, you'll find the jewel-like picture collection of the **Galleria Spada** (tel. 686 11 58; open Tues.-Sat. 9am-6:30pm, Sun. 9am-12:30pm; admission L4000, under 18 and over 60 free). Seventeenth-century Cardinal Bernardino Spada bought up a grandiose assortment of paintings and sculpture, then commissioned an even more opulent set of great rooms to house them. Time and good luck have left the palatial apartments nearly intact, and a visit to the gallery offers a glimpse of the luxury that surrounded Baroque courtly life.

 The *palazzo* is a treasure in itself. The outer façade and inner court are masterpieces of Baroque stucco work, recently restored to their original creamy-white frothiness. Outside, eight ancient Roman kings, generals, and emperors stand proudly under Latin legends describing their achievements. Inside, eighteen even less modest Roman gods surround the court—every last one of them, down to the usually prudish Vesta, buck-naked. Bernardino commissioned the elaborate decoration to make up for the relatively puny size of his palace, but even swaggering stucco couldn't keep the poor cardinal from feeling boxed in on all sides by distressingly banal neighbors. To ease his discomfort, Borromini, the master architectural illusionist, designed an ingenious colonnade beyond the library on the left side of the courtyard. From the court, the colonnade seems to stretch far back through a spacious garden, framing a life-size classical statue. In reality, Borromini manipulated perspective by shrinking the columns and pavement dramatically—the colonnade is only a few yards long, the statue stands three feet tall, and the spacious garden is no more than a narrow alley, full of fighting cats, between the *palazzo* and its next-door neighbor. You can see the colonnade from the courtyard.

 Bernardino proved no less self-serving in assembling his **picture collection;** in the first of the gallery's four rooms he hung three portraits of himself, by Guercino, Guido Reni, and Cerini. The following rooms (each stacked with complete lists of the numbered paintings and furniture) hold more interesting 16th- and 17th-century subjects. Before leaving the first room, witness a frog's dream-come-true in #28, Chiari's *Latona Changes Frogs into Lycian Shepherds.*

 In the portrait-studded **Room 2,** look for paintings by the Venetians Tintoretto and Titian. Number 60 is Titian's pensive *Portrait of a Musician,* and #86 a copy of his portrait of the aged Pope Paul III. Number 75 marks Tintoretto's *Portrait of the Archbishop Zara Luca Stella.* Lavinia Fontana, one of the few women painters whose work has survived from the 16th century, painted the stark *Cleopatra* at #90. Despite the work's flatness, Fontana managed to paint a covertly interesting background with a snake rising from a jar clasped by a disembodied hand. Above the windows of Room 2 is a frieze painted by del Vaga and originally intended to be placed beneath Michelangelo's far less cherubic *Last Judgment* in the Sistine Chapel. It was rediscovered by Cardinal Bernardino in 1636.

 Grandiose **Room 3** houses 17th-century portraits and mythological scenes along its capacious walls—most of the overblown stuff doesn't merit a second look, but stop to take in Guercino's sumptuous *Death of Dido* (#132), in which the Carthaginian queen scorned by Aeneas throws herself simultaneously onto her sword and her funeral pyre. In the distance, Aeneas' ships set sail for Italy. Facing Dido on the opposite wall, Tornioli's *Cain Kills Abel* (#113) portrays the slaughter of the prostrate older brother with a vulture strapped about Cain's hulking torso, while the animals in the neighboring Flemish *Still Life of Badgers and Guinea Pigs* (#116) capture the sweeter essence of wild life. In **Room 4,** the father-daughter team of Orazio and Artemisia Gentileschi is represented by three canvases: Orazio's *David* (#155), and Artemisia's *Santa Cecilia* (#149, the patron saint of musicians) and *Madonna with Infant Jesus* (#166).

When you leave the gallery, follow the narrow street further away from P. Farnese along Via di Capo di Ferro, past a medieval house built out of an ancient temple; you can still see some weathered Ionic columns plastered into the wall. Via dei Pettinari leads right to the **Ponte Sisto,** one of Pope Sixtus IV's more useful constructions, which offers pedestrians a handy route to the medieval quarter of Trastevere. Right across the way stands another relic of the Baroque, the tiny **Church of Santissima Trinità dei Pellegrini** (*in restauro;* open for mass Mon.-Sat. 7:30-8:30am, Sun. and holidays 10am-1pm). It was built by Paolo Maggi from 1603 to 1616 and the façade was added in 1723 by Francesco De Sanctis. A left-hand turn on Via dei Arco del Monte takes you round the **Monte di Pietà,** an architectural collaboration by the Baroque masters Carlo Maderno and Francesco Borromini. Famous for centuries as a pawn shop, the building is now home to a bank and the *carabinieri.*

■ Campo dei Fiori

From the Monte di Pietà, you can pass onto the busy, window-shopping haven of Via dei Giubbinari, where a short jaunt to your left will bring you to the **Campo dei Fiori.** During papal rule, the area was the site of countless executions. In the middle of the Campo, a statue marking the death spot of one victim, Giordano Bruno (1548-1600), rises above the bustle, arms folded over his book. Scientifically and philosophically ahead of his age, Bruno sizzled at the stake in 1600 for taking Copernicus one step further: he argued that the universe had no center at all. Now the only carcasses that litter the *piazza* are those of the fish in the colorful **market** that springs up with plenty of fresh fruit, vegetables, fish, and flowers every day except Sunday (open approximately 6am to 2pm).

At the northern corner of Campo dei Fiori, Piazza della Cancelleria stretches to Corso Vittorio Emanuele II. On the left as you enter the *piazza,* an imposing stone coat of arms identifies the early Renaissance **Palazzo della Cancelleria.** Designed in 1485, it impressed an array of popes and cardinals who affixed their insignia to it. Today, the Cancelleria is the seat of the three Tribunals of the Vatican and is legally considered a part of the Vatican City. The building's designer remains unknown, but its unprecedented size and style have led the architecturally optimistic to suspect Bramante. The courtyard, ringed by three stories of *loggie* supported by Doric columns, resembles his masterful restoration of the adjoining **Church of San Lorenzo in Damaso** (no admittance beyond the Cancelleria's courtyard; open summer daily 7am-noon and 5-8:30pm, winter 7am-noon and 4:30-8pm).

Just next door, to the right as you reach Corso Vittorio Emanuele II from the *palazzo* and its *piazza,* the tiny **Palazzo della Farnesia ai Baullari** (also known as the **Piccola Farnesina**) manages to hold its own. Built in 1523 by Antonio da Sangallo the Younger for Thomas Le Roy, a French diplomat, it gets its name from a case of mistaken identity of the floral kind. Le Roy's brilliant career in Rome was rewarded when he was made a nobleman and given special permission to add the lily of France to his coat of arms. The lilies were mistaken for similar flowers representing the Farnese and so the *palazzo* got its name, *Farnesina,* or "little Farnese." Le Roy's castle is also called Farnesina ai Baullari; *baullari* refers to the trunkmakers' street nearby.

The interior, which was restored in the 19th century, houses the **Museo Barracco** (tel. 68 80 68 48; open Tues.-Sat. 9am-7pm, Sun. 9am-1pm; admission L3750, *ridotto* for students with ISIC L2500; enter from Via dei Baullari), a collection of Egyptian, Greek, and Roman statues donated to the city in 1902 by Senator Giovanni Barracco (1829-1914). Recently reopened after six years of restoration, the museum houses one of the finest collections of antique statuary in Rome. The museum differs from most in the city in that its small, manageable collection is meticulously labeled and exquisitely displayed over three floors of gleaming Renaissance palace. It's also almost entirely deserted and is a peaceful opportunity to scrutinize the miraculous details and brazen nudity of the collection. Once you enter, the din of traffic and tourists on the *corso* outside dies down to a dull roar and the sun streams through the tiled and frescoed *loggie.*

In the entry court, the massive, broken Hellenistic *Torso of Apollo of Omphalos* (#100) presides over the ticket office. On the first floor are Egyptian, Cretan, Cypriot, and archaic Greek sculpture. Look for the serene, 3000-year-old polished basalt *Head of Rameses II* (#19), who maintains his composure even though the right side of his head is cleaved off. The *Head of a Bearded Man* (#31) was once thought to be a portrait of Julius Caesar. Carved in Roman Egypt, it shows elements of both cultures' tastes in portraiture. Here you'll also find little Bes, the whip- and club-wielding Phoenician god represented both in sculpture (#60) and relief (#304) as an endearing sort of proto-Sumo-wrestler with pasta strands for a beard and a lion's face on his forehead. In the small room to the left, a mesmerizing painted *Cypriot Head* of a priest (#64; 6th-5th century BC) is a rare example of the coloring that once decorated statues in the ancient world. The middle chamber houses silky smooth Egyptian organ jars (#35, 309) for those with a morbid streak.

On the second floor, Roman and Greek statuary cohabitate. The so-called *Head of Alexander the Great* (#157) is the prototype for most Hellenistic portraiture: you can see the swirling locks of hair, upturned face, and distantly focused eyes repeated on statues around the room. To the left of Alexander, a gallery of well-known Greeks stares ahead, among them Sophocles, Epicurus, Euripides, and Demosthenes. An incredible collection of meticulously carved miniature heads stare back from a glass case in a neighboring room. On the wall between rooms, you can satisfy your long-held desire to see what a dancing hermaphrodite really looks like (#170). Passing through the two adjoining rooms, you will come to a rogues-gallery of head statues with the Thing of the ancient world, a *Forearm and Right Hand with a Discus* (#98), which was found in the Baths of Caracalla. In the small room on the second floor, beyond the stairwell, are Roman treasures, including a tiny *Head of a Julio-Claudian Prince* (#194), a funerary urn carved in the shape of a temple (#173), a fresco of a hermaphrodite playing a lyre (#214), and a 12th-century mosaic (#209) taken from the original Constantinian basilica of S. Pietro.

Across Corso Vittorio Emanuele II, in tiny Piazza San Pantaleo, the **Church of San Pantaleo** (open for mass Mon.-Sat. 7:30am and 7:15pm, Sun. 7:30am, 11:30am, and 7:15pm) dates from 1216. Giuseppe Valadier added the strange façade in 1806. Exit Piazza S. Pantaleo on Via della Cucagna, opposite Corso Vittorio Emanuele II, and take your first right into Piazza dei Massimi (if, instead, you continue straight, you'll enter Piazza Navona) to reach the soot-blackened façade of the **Palazzo Massimo,** designed by the Renaissance painter Baldassare Peruzzi in 1532. Note how the building, nestled in a narrow, oddly-shaped spot, cleverly follows the curve of the *corso*. The street itself, like the Via di Grotta Pinta in Campo dei Fiori (see p. 181), follows the line of an ancient theater, the Odeon of Emperor Domitian. Behind the *palazzo*, a solitary column remains from the ancient edifice, which once hosted concerts and theatrical performances. The back wall of the *palazzo* preserves a rare cycle of monochrome painting from the 16th century; most houses in Rome once boasted such intricate decoration, but few have resisted the assaults of wind and rain as well as this one. The palace saw its finest hour when it hosted the first printing press in Rome, set up by migrant German craftsmen in 1467 to serve the newly fashionable humanist tastes of the papal court.

Just past the *palazzo*, Via San Giuseppe Calasanzo leads to the south end of the Corso del Rinascimento and, to the right, the **Church of Sant'Andrea della Valle** (open Mon.-Sat. 7:30am-noon and 4:30-7:30pm, Sun. 7:30am-12:45pm and 4:30-7:45pm), begun in 1591 by Grimaldi and completed by Baroque bigwig Carlo Maderno. Rainaldi's recently restored 1665 façade is a sober Baroque production, with orderly rows of columns and pediments in place of the usual swirls and curls. Inside, pass by the twin wall tombs of the Piccolomini Popes Pius II and III (on either side of the nave right before the dome) to view Domenichino's colossal 17th-century frescoes of St. Andrew, crucified on his characteristic X-shaped cross. Puccini's opera *Tosca* opens in this church, continues in P. Farnese, and concludes in the prison of Castel Sant'Angelo, across the river at the end of the Corso Vittorio Emanuele II. Unfortunately, the restoration of this church is purely cosmetic; the funding allowed restorers to clean off the façade—which is now blindingly white—but they couldn't clean the interior or reinforce the structure.

Back across Corso Vittorio Emanuele II and through Largo dei Chiavari, Via dei Chiavari leads to Largo del Pallaro and the beginning of Via di Grotta Pinta, a dizzying canyon of curved *palazzi* built over the remains of the semi-circular **Theater of Pompey.** Pompey the Great, one of the power-hungry generals of the first century BC whose autocratic machinations helped destroy the Roman Republic, competed with his rival Julius Caesar both in war and peace. When Caesar's wildly popular victories in Gaul became too galling for the pompous Pompey, he distracted the populace by building a grandiose theater, the first of its kind in the city. The prudish Senate had outlawed permanent theaters because they feared they would corrupt public morals; Pompey outwitted the censors by building a small shrine at the top of the stands and calling the whole complex a temple. Though Caesar bested the hapless Pompey politically, the old general still got the last laugh: it was in Pompey's portico, built to surround his sumptuous theater, that Caesar was finally assassinated on the Ides of March, 44 BC. A note to serious archaeology nuts: on the back side of the theater on Via del Biscione, two restaurants, S. Pancrazio and da Costanza, have basement dining rooms built out of the 2000-year-old understructure of the theater and will gladly let you in during off-hours for a dusty look around.

Continue on Via di Grotta Pinta, which curves back into Via dei Chiavari. A short distance to the right is Largo dei Librari and the shop-lined Via dei Giubbonari, which opens onto P. Cairoli to the east (left) and its **Church of San Carlo ai Catinari** (open daily 6:30am-noon and 4:30-7pm), built from 1612 to 1620 by Rosato Rosati. The façade is in the style of the counter-reformation and the interior, with its Greek-cross plan, had the same decorating committee as neighboring Sant'Andrea della Valle, namely Domenichino, Lanfranco, and Corona. Just across Via Arenula from P. Cairoli, Via dei Falegnami leads to Piazza Mattei and the heart of the Jewish Ghetto.

▧ **Piazza Mattei and the Jewish Ghetto**

It was dirty, but it was Rome, and to anyone who has long lived in Rome even its dirt has a charm which the neatness of no other place ever had.
—William Wetmore Story (1862)

In **Piazza Mattei,** the graceful 16th-century **Fontana delle Tartarughe** (Tortoise Fountain) by Taddeo Landini marks the center of the **Ghetto,** the lowland quarter where Jews were confined from the 16th to the 19th centuries. While Dickens declared the area "a miserable place, densely populated, and reeking with bad odours," today's Jewish Ghetto is one of the most picturesque and eclectic, even chic, neighborhoods, with family businesses dating back centuries and restaurants serving up some of the tastiest food in Rome. The **Foro Olitorio** market for oil and vegetables and the **Foro Boario** for meats made the neighborhood a busy commercial center from the ancient days up until the 18th century, surviving even during Rome's severe Dark Ages. Today, of the 40,000 Jews who live in Italy, 16,000 call the eternal city home. In recent years, the community has been the target of international terrorism, suffering a bombing of its Synagogue in 1982. Since the Gulf War, well-armed *carabinieri* have been patrolling the area night and day.

The Ghetto is truly its own neighborhood, acting as a bridge between the *centro storico* to the west and north and the ancient ruins of the Tiber's flood plain and the Capitoline Hill to the south and east. The Renaissance *palazzi* and winding cobble-stoned alleyways, together with the crumbling remains of Imperial Rome and the occasional Kosher bakery give the Ghetto a unique, distinctive character and make the neighborhood a perfect stop on a tour of either of its neighbors, as well as a tour in itself. The SIDIC (Service International de Documentation Judeo-Chrétienne, an international library information center for Jewish-Christian relations) offers a half-day, English-language, **free walking tour** of the Ghetto environs organized on an irregular basis according to interest. The tours originate at the center, Via Plebiscito, 112 (tel. 679 53 07). Tours not given in July and August—call if you are interested.

The graceful, spritely boys on the **Tortoise Fountain** in the **Piazza Mattei** mark a good point of departure for your tour of the Ghetto. Designed by della Porta, the fountain wasn't graced with turtles until Bernini restored it in 1658. According to local legend, Duke Mattei, a notorious and incorrigible gambler, lost everything in one night. His father-in-law-to-be was so disgusted by the Duke's flagrantly idiotic behavior that he rescinded his approval of Mattei's marriage to his daughter. The Duke, in a bid to pull his name from the mud of scandal, had the fountain built in a single night to show that a Mattei could pull off anything, even when completely destitute. He got the girl, though she ended up blocking up her window so she would never have to see the fountain that got her married to such a *schlemiel*. The *piazza* itself is now home to the state-owned Italian Center for American Studies. There are no less than five Mattei *palazzi* in the area surrounding the Ghetto, traditionally controlled by that (ig)noble family.

Leaving the *piazza* on the east along Via dei Funari brings you past **Palazzo Mattei** (on the left). They made much of their money collecting tolls over the bridges to Trastevere, and later, from serving as gate-watchers for the Ghetto. The Mattei constructed their huge expanse of *palazzi*, often called the Island of Mattei, over a period of two centuries (15th-17th). A papal housing decree in 1574 required all new buildings to be attached in some way, by courtyard or wall, to another; thus the 16th- and 17th-century Mattei *palazzi* are not free-standing structures. The façades of Via dei Funari and Via Michelangelo are by Maderno. The Red Brigade kidnappers and murderers of Aldo Moro, the former Prime Minister of Italy, dumped his body here in 1978, and there are occasionally flowers and candles in commemoration. You can see Moro's likeness down Via Caetani (at #9), the street to the left of the Palazzo Mattei.

On the next block of Via dei Funari, the **Church of Santa Caterina dei Funari** (closed for renovation in 1996; they say it's been closed for ages) towers austerely above the street of the same name, titled for the rope-makers who worked here. St. Ignatius founded the church to provide homes for poor and orphaned girls, who were then married off to local artisans. The girls were blessed with a hefty dowry from an endowment by the richest courtesans in Rome. The church is a rare late-Renaissance specimen in Rome, built on the site of a 10th-century monastery, designed in 1554 by Guido Guidetti, one-time apprentice to Michelangelo, while he was reconstructing the Campidoglio. The bell tower is a sorry addition to the church, and adding insult to injury, the recent restoration attempts have made the top look like a wedding-cake decoration, now called "the sacrilege of St. Catherine."

Down to the right is **Piazza di Campitelli,** a lovely and harmonious example of the counter-reformation Church's efforts to beautify Rome above all other cities. To create the perfect space for the *piazza*, which is guarded by what were once some of the swankiest *palazzi* in town, the **Church of Santa Maria in Campitelli** (open Mon.-Sat. 7am-noon and 4-7:15pm, Sun. and holidays open for mass 7:30, 10, 11am, noon, and 6:30pm) had to be moved and rebuilt. Carlo Rainaldi designed the church, which is arguably his best work ever. Even more so than his Church of Sant'Andrea della Valle, this church exemplifies the theatrics of Baroque architecture by creating a grand sense of space. Hovering ominously over the rest of the church, the front altar seems to give the small interior more depth. The church was built in 1662 to give thanks to the Virgin for delivering the city from a plague in 1656. The church, a variation on the Greek-cross plan and full of Baroque art, still houses the statuette that dispelled the plague. Above the first window on the left is a tabernacle to Santa Maria in Portico and to Pius VI, which refers to this protectress of Rome. Pay L1000 for a recorded history and explanation of the church's works in English. From Via dei

Funari, take Via Sant'Angelo in Pescheria off Piazza Lovatelli toward the river to Via del Portico d'Ottavia.

Via Sant'Angelo emerges at the **Church of Sant'Angelo in Pescheria,** installed inside the Portico d'Ottavia (see p. 141) in 755 AD. It was here that the Jews of the Ghetto were forced to attend mass every Sunday from 1584 until the 18th century—an act of aggressive evangelism which they quietly resisted by stuffing their ears with wax. The church is rarely open. At #28 Via del Portico d'Ottavia, to the right of the old fish market, there is a plaque in memory of the 2,091 Roman Jews who died in the Holocaust. Several houses on this street, notably #13, #17, and #19, date from medieval times. Note the inscription on the building at Via del Portico d'Ottavia, 1; after the patriotic invocation *Ave Roma,* it praises the owner for beautifying Rome. At the end of Via del Portico d'Ottavia near the Tiber, the façade of the **Church of San Gregorio a Ponte Quattro Capi** (open Mon.-Sat. 8-11:30am and 4-7pm; mass Mon.-Sat. 8am, Sun. 11am) displays a Hebrew and Latin inscription admonishing Jews to convert to Catholicism.

Across the street from San Gregorio, the **Sinagoga Ashkenazita** (tel. 68 75 051; open only for services) stands at Via Catalana and Lungotevere Cenci, defiantly proclaiming its divergent heritage in a city of Catholic iconography and classical designs. This synagogue reflects the unity of the Jewish people in Rome. Built between 1874 and 1904, the synagogue incorporates Persian and Babylonian architectural devices, purposefully avoiding any resemblance to a Christian church. The building is topped by a large metal dome, which is one of the many domes visible from the top of the Gianicolo.

The inside of the temple has a strictly Orthodox seating plan, with the women sitting above the men in three ornamented balconies. Though the symmetrical interior avoids Christian elements, the massive marble columns are quintessentially Roman. The front of the temple is graced with seven massive gold menorahs below the exuberant rainbow-colored dome—the source of most of the synagogue's light. Notice the locked wooden boxes lining the prayer benches; worshippers can leave their sacred belongings inside so that they abide by the orthodox law which forbids carrying on the Sabbath. Services, to which anyone is welcome, are given entirely in Hebrew. Since the 1982 attack on the synagogue, *carabinieri* armed with machine guns and video devices keep terrorists at bay; all visitors must be searched and questioned before entering. On the left side of the entrance gates (opened only for services), a crater in the sidewalk filled with cigarette butts marks the spot of attack. To protect worshippers, the three heavy entrance doors are all locked and bolted from the inside when the synagogue is in use.

The synagogue also houses the **Jewish Museum** (tel. 68 40 061; open July-Sept. daily 9am-4:30pm; Oct.-June Mon.-Thurs. 9:30am-1pm and 2-4:30pm, Fri. 9:30am-1:30pm, Sat. 9:30am-noon; hours fluctuate widely and the administrators advise checking for changes—ask for a guide of the museum and synagogue in English; admission L8000; no cameras). Ceremonial objects from the 17th-century Jewish community as well the original plan of the ghetto are displayed here. Several objects, like the green morocco leather prayer book from 1325 AD, attest to the tenaciousness of the Jewish Sephardic community over the centuries. The original manuscripts, weathered prayer books, and other precious materials are still used by the synagogue. The collection, all that is left from the five schools (see below), was hidden in a *mikvah* (a Jewish ritual bath) during the nine-month Nazi occupation of Rome. The director of the museum, herself a Holocaust survivor, will be glad to share her knowledge of ghetto history in enthusiastic English.

Also note the **Palazzo Cenci,** on a slight rise (Monte Cenci) at the end of Via Catalana, named for the Spanish Jews who settled here. The *palazzo* was the scene of a September 9, 1598 scandal when Beatrice Cenci, aided by her brother and her stepmother, succeeded in having her father Francesco Cenci murdered. The whole clan was beheaded a year and two days later at the command of Pope Clement VIII, but the public sympathized with the group's plea of self-defense against the incestuous drug addict, Francesco. Every year on September 11, a mass is held in St. Thomas's at

Piazza Cenci for the wronged Beatrice. The *palazzo* now houses an art gallery an the Rhode Island School of Design European Honors Program, which sponsors a free bi-annual art exhibition of its American students' work (early May and early Decem ber). At the other end of Via Catalana is what remains of the Teatro di Marcello; fo low the street that curves around the theater to continue onto the sights of th ancient city (see The Velabrum, p. 141). To finish your tour of the historic cente head to the north end of **Piazza delle Cinque Scole.** Here, a clunky modern buildin has replaced what was originally five amalgamated Jewish synagogues, called *scuol* (from the Latin word for "synagogue"). There were five synagogues representing th separate populations of Roman Jews: Aragonese, Castillian, Catalan, Sicilian, an Roman. Although each *scuola* spoke a separate language, the *lingua franca* wa Ladino, a hybrid of Spanish and Hebrew spoken by Sephardic Jews. The buildin housing the five *scuole* was destroyed in 1910. From here, turn left on Via di S. Mari del Pianto and go right on Via Arenula to arrive at Largo di Torre Argentina.

■ Largo di Torre Argentina

Toward the beginning of Corso Vittorio Emanuele II lies **Largo di Torre Argentin** (affectionately known as Largo Argentina), a busy cross-street which sees a unhealthy portion of Rome's bus and taxi traffic scream through in polluted proces sion. The *largo,* named for the square *Torre Argentina* ("silver tower") that dom nates its southeastern corner, was a center of the medieval quarter of town, fille with similar towers and rustic houses. Mussolini demolished many of the surroundin streets in the 1930s to make way for a grandiose Fascist square, but constructio revealed a new obstacle—the **Four Republican Temples** known as the *Area Sacra d Largo Argentina*, which now repose in the gaping square below the street. Thei excavation is as much a testament to *il Duce*'s disregard for the city's medieval her tage as it is a tribute to his monumental love for Rome's antiquities. Archaeologist still don't know for sure to whom the temples were dedicated, but it is known tha the four were connected with the larger complex built around the theater of Pompe (near present-day Campo dei Fiori). Most of the time, the complex is closed to th general public, but recently extra funds have allowed the **Associazione Cultura** **dell'Italia** (tel. 39 72 81 86; fax 39 72 81 87) to initiate guided night tours of the ruin (45-min. tours in English, Italian, or Japanese; July-Sept. two nights per week L10,000; call for times).

Going east (right as you face the *largo* with the temples behind you) on Corso Vit torio Emanuele II, a short walk leads to the Piazza del Gesù and **Il Gesù** (open 6am 12:30pm and 4-7pm), the sumptuous Church of the Jesuit Order and clearly one o the richest churches in the city (on your left as Via del Plebiscito meets Corso Vittori Emanuele II). The Jesuits, the famous shock troops of the counter-reformation, wer given orders by Pope Paul III at the Council of Trent to combat the growing influenc of Protestantism. Their church, begun in 1568 according to designs by Il Vignola (a Michelangelo devotee), encapsulates their new concept of the church's role in th lives of its worshippers. The façade, by Giacomo della Porta, presents a stern and so emn front to the outside world, also drawing from some of Michelangelo's designs fo St. Peter's, including the paired pilasters (i.e., the pair of two-dimensional columns) Inside, della Porta's long, great nave was a deliberate departure from classically inspired circular and Greek-cross churches of the Renaissance, which, said the Coun cil of Trent, had subordinated the priest and his altar from their places at the head o the church. To combat this architectural corruption, the Council recommended a new set of standards. The aisle-less nave firmly directs the congregation's attentio ahead to the altar and the towering dome that illuminates it. The monogram "IHS" i the apse represents the first three letters of Jesus' name in Greek. The lighting here i almost theatrical; the nave remains relatively dark and, by contrast, the large win dows on the Eastern side of the church in the drum of the dome spotlight the alta with sunbeams. The Gesù became the prototype for countless churches built o rebuilt during the counter-reformation. The decoration of the interior, on the othe hand, done a hundred years later, expresses the success of the counter-reformation. An aggressive array of 17th-century colors highlights Il Bacaccia's fresco *The Triumph of the Name of Jesus* in the vault of the nave, no mean testament to the order's ambition. As you make your way to the front of the church, look to the left of the dome for the **Chapel of Sant'Ignazio di Loyola,** dedicated to the founder of the order, who lies buried under the gilded altar.

Il Gesù also anchors the eastern end of the bustling Corso Vittorio Emanuele II. Though named in 1876 for the first king of unified Italy, the roaring **Corso Vittorio Emanuele II** has a history that goes back well before the 19th century. Pope Sixtus IV, the 15th-century pontiff responsible for so much of Rome's Renaissance construction, first widened and straightened the street in the 1470s in preparation for the designated Holy Year of 1475. From Sixtus' time on, the street has been the favored address of sumptuous *palazzi* and churches and is still used for papal processions today. After Il Gesù and the end of the Corso Vittorio Emanuele II, Via del Plebiscito continues to the east and back into the din of Piazza Venezia.

EAST OF VIA DEL CORSO: PIAZZA DEL POPOLO TO THE NOMENTANA

▓ Piazza del Popolo

Piazza del Popolo was the first sight that greeted 19th-century visitors entering the city from the north through the Porta del Popolo. The "people's square" has always been a popular gathering place. Masked revelers once filled the square for the torch-lit festivities of the Roman carnival, and today the *piazza* remains a favorite arena for communal antics. After a soccer victory or the latest government collapse, the *piazza* resounds with music and celebration. The southern end of the square also marks the start of three streets: the central Via del Corso, which runs straight for over a mile to Piazza Venezia (you can see the gleaming white Vittorio Emanuele II Monument at the end), the Via di Ripetta, built by Leo X for service to the Vatican, and the Via del Babuino, cleared in 1525 by Clement VII, which leads to the Spanish Steps.

The great **Obelisk of Pharaoh Ramses II,** restored in 1984, commands the center of the *piazza*. The obelisk, some 3200 years old, was already an antique when Augustus brought it back as a souvenir from Egypt in the first century BC. Flanked on four sides by floppy-eared lions spouting water, its foundation provides a fantastic perspective of the three streets reaching into the city. Outside the Porta del Popolo (whose southern façade was designed by Bernini) is an entrance to the **Villa Borghese.** You can also cut across the switchback road that begins at the eastern end of the *piazza* and up the slope to the wooden steps that lead to the Pincio and the Villa Borghese.

At Napoleon's request, architect Giuseppe Valadier spruced up the once-scruffy *piazza* in 1814, adding the two travertine fountains on the western and eastern sides. Each fountain is accentuated by a triad of marble figures. To the west, a beefy Neptune splashes in his element with two of his Tritons; the opposite figures represent Rome flanked by the Aniene and the Tiber. Walls extend from either side of the fountains, forming two large semi-circles which encase the *piazza*. Each end of the walls holds a figure of one of the Four Seasons. The *piazza's* symmetry is reflected in Carlo Rainaldi's **Churches of Santa Maria di Montesanto** (open April-June Mon.-Fri. 5-8pm; Nov.-March 4-7pm) and **Santa Maria dei Miracoli** (open Mon.-Sat. 6am-1pm and 5-7:30pm, Sun. and holidays 8am-1pm and 5-7:30pm; Sunday mass at 7pm and daily mass at 7:30am, noon, and 7pm). If you look closely, you'll see that the Baroque twins aren't exactly identical. Santa Maria di Montesano (1662), on the left, is the older sibling, with a façade by Bernini. Santa Maria dei Miracoli was completed by Carlo Fontana in 1677.

Behind its simple early Renaissance façade, the **Church of Santa Maria del Popolo** (tel. 36 10 487; open daily 7am-noon and 4-7pm), situated on the opposite (north) side of the *piazza* and to the right of the Porta del Popolo, contains a number of masterpieces of the Italian Renaissance and Baroque. Immediately to the right after the main entrance, just near the Porta del Popolo, the **della Rovere Chapel** harbors an *Adoration* by the Umbrian Bernardino Betti, better known as Pinturicchio (1454-1513). The fresco, with its careful coloring of the figures and fine execution of the landscape and distant architecture, is complemented by lunettes (turn on the light on the right side of the chapel for a better view) depicting the life of St. Jerome. You can find more frescoes painted by Pinturicchio's pupils in the third chapel on the right. The gilded relief above the **main altar** depicts the heroic exorcism that led to the church's foundation. Pope Paschal II chopped down a walnut tree that marked the legendary spot of despotic Nero's grave, thereby allowing the terrified neighbors to live free of his ghost and clearing ground for the church. The **apse** behind the altar (sporadically accessible) was designed by Bramante—look for his signature shell pattern on the walls. Pinturicchio was at work again in the vault of the apse (architecture by Bramante), painting a cycle of the *Coronation of the Virgin,* accompanied by various saints, sibyls, and church MVPs. They're illuminated by 16th-century stained glass windows by the Frenchman Guillaume de Marcillat.

The **Cerasi Chapel,** immediately to the left of the main altar, houses two exquisite works of Caravaggio's. *The Conversion of St. Paul* depicts St. Paul seconds after being thrown from his horse, an experience that triggered his conversion to Christianity. In the *Crucifixion of St. Peter,* three faceless men drag the martyred first pope, still nailed to his upside-down cross. Caravaggio shunned traditional iconography, choosing not to include angels or other divine images in either work. Notice also the focus of the painting of St. Paul; the canvas is taken up almost entirely by the backside of a horse, while Paul lies in the lower corner. In both pieces, the light comes from an unknown source, shining directly on some faces and objects while leaving others completely obscured. This dramatic use of lighting, along with Caravaggio's earthy realism and psychological intensity, heralded the early Baroque style. Caravaggio's style strikes a great contrast to the comparatively bland, classical restraint of *Assumption of the Virgin* by his contemporary rival, Antonio Carracci, which hangs over the altar of the chapel.

The **Chigi Chapel,** second on the left, was designed by Raphael for the wealthy Sienese banker Agostino Chigi, reputedly the world's richest man. The sumptuous chapel is a riotous symphony of paintings, mosaic, sculpture, and precious marbles that foreshadows the theatrical compositions of the Baroque by at least a century. Raphael proved especially ingenious in his designs for the mosaic of the dome. Instead of representing the angels as flat figures on the surface of the vault, he used clever tricks of perspective and foreshortening to make them seem to stand on top of the chapel, peering down from their gilded empyrean. This technical breakthrough would be copied again and again by the illusionistic painters of the Baroque. Raphael designed the statue of *Jonah* (who stands with one foot in the mouth of the whale that swallowed him) and the tombs, inspired by the ancient Pyramid of Gaius Cestius outside the Porta San Paolo in Testaccio. Work on the richly ornate chapel ceased in 1520, when Raphael and Agostino Chigi died within days of each other. It was completed a century later by Bernini for Cardinal Fabio Chigi, the future Pope Alexander VII. Bernini added two medallions with protruding faces to the pyramids and the marble intarsia **figure of Death** in the floor. Outside the chapel, look for more gruesome portraits of Death in the wall tombs and the marble skeleton who sits behind bars beside the doors.

Tucked under the stairs to the right of the church is a covert little museum, the **Sala del Bramante** (tel. 32 30 426; open Tues.-Sun. 10am-7pm; admission L10,000, with student ID L7000), which unveils fascinating temporary exhibitions of works for view and, from time to time, for sale. In the past, they have exhibited paintings, drawings, and sculptures by Mark Chagall, Picasso, Goya, and Dalí. Browse through funky T-shirts and prints (L20,000-30,000) in the well-stocked gift shop.

■ Ara Pacis and Mausoleum of Augustus

From Piazza del Popolo, Via di Ripetta leads south toward the Tiber, ending in the **Piazza Augusto Imperatore.** The circular brick mound of the **Mausoleum of Augustus** once housed the funerary urns of the Imperial Roman family. The oversized tomb may originally have been crowned by a hill of dirt and planted with cypress trees in imitation of archaic Etruscan mound-tombs. The Middle Ages saw the mausoleum converted to a fortress, an amphitheater, and even a concert hall. After years of being closed to the public, the mausoleum has opened for tours, though hours are random.

To the west (the right, coming from the Piazza del Popolo) of the mausoleum, the glass-encased **Ara Pacis** (open Tues.-Sat. 9am-4pm, Sun. 9am-1pm; admission L4000) stands as a monument to both the grandiosity of Augustan-age propaganda and the ingenuity of modern-day archaeology. The altar, completed in 9 BC, was designed to celebrate Augustus' success in achieving peace after years of civil unrest and war in Gaul and Spain. The reliefs surrounding the marble altar include depictions of allegorical figures from Rome's most sacred national myths, as well as portraits of Augustus, his family, and various important statesmen and priests. One of the reliefs on the outer enclosure shows Aeneas, Augustus' legendary ancestor, sacrificing a white sow as part of his quest to found the Roman people. On the side walls, Augustus himself appears with members of his family and political entourage, on their way to perform a sacrifice of their own. Their act became, by association with Aeneas' sacrifice, a symbolic refounding of the city, thus transforming the establishment of monarchy into an act of service to the state. Linking the newly minted Julio-Claudian dynasty with the figure of Aeneas, its legendary patriarch, the altar redefined the upstart Augustus as a near-divine figure, endowed with ancestral authority and, quite literally, born to rule.

The altar, which originally stood alongside the ancient Via Lata (now the Via del Corso), was discovered in fragments over the course of several centuries and only pieced together within the last hundred years by Mussolini's archaeologists. The final stages of excavation were almost never completed, as it was discovered that the altar, buried some 30 feet underground, was actually supporting a substantial section of one of Rome's larger *palazzi*. To make matters worse, the water table of the city, having risen with the ground level over the past two millennia, had submerged the monument in over eight feet of water. Teams of archaeologists and engineers devised a complicated system of underground supports for the palace and, after permanently freezing the water with the help of carbon dioxide charges, painstakingly removed the precious marble fragments. Mussolini provided the colossal aquarium-like display case.

The mausoleum, the Ara Pacis, and the obelisk that now stands in Piazza Montecitorio once fit together into a strategically designed complex whose dimensions and orientation were dictated by celestial and solar phenomena. According to the organization of the structures, the shadow of the obelisk pointed directly at the center of the Ara Pacis on the day and hour of the anniversary of Augustus' birth. In the 2000 years that have passed since the construction of the complex, however, the mausoleum alone has remained in its original position. Head past the mausoleum and east down Via dei Pontefici to Via del Corso. Turn right on the Corso, then take your third left on Via Condotti which leads directly to Piazza di Spagna.

■ The Spanish Steps

Designed by an Italian, paid for by the French, named for the Spaniards, occupied by the British, and currently under the sway of American ambassador-at-large Ronald McDonald, the **Spanish Steps** (*Scalinata di Spagna*; located in the aptly named **Piazza di Spagna**) exude a truly international air as a tourist attraction and hangout for foreigners and Italians alike. When the steps were first built in 1725, Romans hoping to earn extra *scudi* as artist's models flocked to the steps dressed as the Madonna or Julius Caesar. Posers of a different sort abound today, few dressed like virgins or ancient conquerors. Each night, hordes of testosterone-injected adolescent males, along with drunken foreigners imitating their Italian counterparts, descend on the *piazza* in search of female tourists. These amateur Romeos are mostly harmless, but prone to making annoying catcalls and gestures. Equal in number, though less irritating, are the scruffy *artistes* who will give you a hair wrap or "write your name on grain of rice."

The Spanish Steps and the **Piazza di Spagna** were once quite literally Spanish. The area around the Spanish ambassador's residence, located in the western end of the hourglass-shaped *piazza* since 1622, was once granted the privilege of extra-territoriality. Wandering foreigners who fell asleep there were liable to wake up the next morning as grunts in the Spanish army. The 137 steps were constructed in 1723-1725 to link the *piazza* with important locales above it, including the Pincio, the Villa Medici, and the Church of Santa Trinità dei Monti. The beginning of May heralds the world-famous flower show, when the steps are covered with pots of azaleas and postcard photographers. The **Fontana della Barcaccia,** at the foot of the steps, was designed by Gianlorenzo Bernini's less famous father Pietro. The sculptor was inspired to carve the central basin in the shape of a sinking boat after he saw a barge washed up in the *piazza* after a Tiber flood. The fountain was built below ground level to compensate for meager water pressure.

Though today you're likely to see more con artists than true artists, the *piazza* has attracted many a creative spirit. Stendhal, Balzac, Wagner, and Liszt all lived near here; at **Caffè Greco,** the well-known establishment on swanky Via Condotti, Goethe, Gogol, Berlioz, and Baudelaire used to linger over cups of *espresso.* Henry James and the Brownings lived at different times on Via Bocca di Leone, a small side street in the area, while Rubens and Poussin took flats on Via del Babuino. Above Via Frattina, 50, amid the glitter and glamour of chic boutiques, you'll see a plaque commemorating James Joyce's former residence. Another small plaque on the side of the pink house to the right of the Spanish Steps (P. di Spagna, 26) marks the home where Keats died in 1821. The second floor now houses the **Keats-Shelley Memorial Museum** (tel. 67 84 235; open May-Sept. Mon.-Fri. 9am-1pm and 3-6pm; Oct.-Apr. Mon.-Fri. 9am-1pm and 2:30-5:30pm; closed 2nd and 3rd weeks of August; admission L5000). Some morbid curiosities include plaster casts of Keats's face, before and after he died of tuberculosis, a lock of his hair, his deathbed correspondence with his sister, and an urn containing the ashes of Shelley's bones. More scholarly (if less titillating) exhibits include facsimiles of original manuscripts and an extensive collection of books dealing with the work and lives of Keats, Shelley, and Byron. Touted as "the most famous relic of English literature" is a silver scallop reliquary once owned by Pope Pius V (who excommunicated Queen Elizabeth), which holds locks of Milton's and Elizabeth Barrett Browning's hair. Near the door hangs a list of many famous (and infamous) British and American expatriates and where they lived in Rome.

Despite its simple design by Carlo Maderno, the rosy Neoclassical façade of **Church of Santa Trinità dei Monti** (mass in Italian at 8:30am; French mass 11:30am; vespers Sunday at 5:30pm; confession in Italian or French Sun. at 11am) provides a worthy climax to a climb of the grand curves of the Spanish Steps, not to mention a sweeping view of the city. The interior is open 9:30am-12:30pm and 4-7pm, but the upper half is usually blocked by a gate. The whole church opens up only on Tuesdays and Thursdays from 4 to 6pm. The third chapel on the right and the second chapel on the left contain works by Michelangelo's star pupil, Daniele da Volterra. The last figure on the right of his *Assumption* is a portrait of his cantankerous grandmaster. His other painting here, *Descent from the Cross* was rated by Poussin as one of the three greatest paintings ever created. The fourth chapel on the left was frescoed in the 16th century by the Zuccari brothers. These same siblings built their *palazzetto* at the corner of the *piazza* on Via Sistina. The obelisk in the center of the *piazza* was brought to Rome in the second century when its hieroglyphics were plagiarized from the obelisk in P. del Popolo.

Along Viale Trinità dei Monti, to the left of Santa Trinità as you face it, the **Villa Medici** houses the **Accademia di Francia** (tel. 67 61 311; call for reservations and

nformation; times will vary). Founded in 1666 to give young French artists an opportunity to live in Rome (Berlioz and Debussy were among the scheme's beneficiaries),
the organization now keeps the building in mint condition and arranges excellent
exhibits, primarily of French art. Behind the villa's severe façade lie a beautiful garden
and an elaborate rear façade. The **Pincio,** a public park planted with formal gardens,
extends up the hill beyond the villa (see p. 208).

Back down the steps and to the left, at the southern end of the Piazza di Spagna
rises the **Column of the Immaculata.** The column is an 1857 celebration of Pope
Pius IX's acceptance of the notion of the Immaculate Conception. On December 8,
the Pope kneels at the base of the shaft, while Roman firemen climb their ladders to
place a wreath on the head of the Madonna, who stands atop the column. Just south
of the column stands the **Collegio di Propaganda Fide,** or, as the Latin inscription
high above the entrance reads, the Collegium Vrbanvm de Propaganda Fide. Though
it sounds like something left over from the fascist era, the college was actually
founded to train missionaries in the 16th century. The façade along Via di Propaganda, the street which intersects Piazza di Spagna leading to the column, is by Borromini.

Outside P. di Spagna to the south you'll find the **Church of Sant'Andrea delle
Fratte** (open daily 6:30am-12:30pm and 4-7pm; at Via di Sant'Andrea, 1, at the foot of
Via di Propaganda), with a Borromini bell tower on which eight delicate angels fold
their wings while tiny faces poke out of the Corinthian columns on the lower ring.
Inside, near the altar, stand two angels carved by Bernini that originally decorated the
Ponte Sant'Angelo (see Castel Sant'Angelo, p. 229). Across the mini-*piazza,* at Via
della Mercede, 12, a plaque commemorates the building, now full of offices, where
Bernini died. From here, follow Via di Sant'Andrea to Largo del Nazareno. Veer right
onto Via del Bufalo and follow it until via Poli appears on the left. Take this street
across Via del Tritone straight to the Trevi Fountain.

■ Trevi Fountain

Nicola Salvi's (1697-1751) famed and now sparkling clean **Fontana di Trevi** emerges
from the back wall of **Palazzo Poli,** dwarfing the already narrow *piazza* and soothing
the crowds with the sounds of its cascading waters. The water for the fountain flows
from the **Acqua Vergine** aqueduct, which also supplies water for the spouts in Piazza
Navona and Piazza di Spagna. The aqueduct's name derives from the maiden who
allegedly pointed out the spring to thirsty Roman soldiers. She is immortalized in one
of the bas-reliefs above the fountain. The opposite relief shows Augustus' right-hand
man, Agrippa, as he gives the go-ahead for the aqueduct in 19 BC. Completed in
1762, the present fountain, supposedly based on designs by Bernini, is a grandiose
elaboration of an earlier, simpler basin by Leon Battista Alberti. In the foreground of
the fountain, two enormous Tritons struggling out of the rough-hewn stone of the
fountain's base guide the winged chariot of Neptune. The unfinished stone spans the
length of the palazzo, cleverly incorporating the building into the fountain's dynamic
depiction of the fathoms below. Flanking the burly mermen are inset statues of Abun-
dance and Health. Meanwhile, the Four Seasons, each displaying her bounty, look
upon the scene from the top of the fountain, just under the Corsini family arms. In
Fellini's *La Dolce Vita,* the bodacious Anita Ekberg takes a midnight dip in the fountain with Marcello Mastroianni and a kitten. A jeep full of sleepy *carabinieri* now
keeps watch over the fountain through the night, preventing others from re-enacting
the famous scene.

Legend has it that the traveler who tosses a coin into the fountain will return to
Rome soon afterwards. Proper form is for the traveler to face away from the fountain,
tossing the coin with the right hand over the left shoulder. As the funds increase, so
do the rewards: the traveler who tosses two coins will fall in love in Rome. The more
ambitious visitor can throw three coins to be married in the city. Years of this practice have taken their toll on the fountain, however. The metal of the coins eats away
at the marble and stains the pool. Since the ten-year restoration, travelers are advised

not to partake of the custom. Instead, save your pennies for another plane ticket to Rome, and as for falling in love … well, there's always the Spanish Steps. Opposite the fountain is the Baroque **Church of Santi Vincenzo e Anastasio** (open daily 6:45-noon and 3:30-7:30pm), rebuilt in 1630. The crypt preserves the hearts and lungs of popes from 1590-1903.

Backtrack up Via Poli and turn right on Via del Tritone. Just across Largo del Tritone begins Via Francesco Crispi, home to the **Galleria Comunale d'Arte Moderna,** Via F. Crispi, 24 (tel. 47 42 848; open Tues.-Sat. 9am-7pm, Sun. 9am-1pm; admission L10,000; under 18 and over 60 free; wheelchair access from the entrance at Via Zucchelli, 7). The museum offers free guided tours with purchase of a ticket. Few visitors are to be found mid-week; in fact, there's a good chance you will find yourself alone with a few pacing guards in the seven-room gallery. Don't expect to find neon Marilyn Monroes or funky Dadaist abstractions here; Rome's concept of modern art includes works mostly from the late 18th and early 19th centuries.

■ Piazza Barberini

Rising from the modern hum of a busy traffic circle at the end of Via del Tritone, Bernini's **Triton Fountain** spouts a stream of water high into the air over Piazza Barberini. This cascade marks the fulcrum of Baroque Rome, as well as five major thoroughfares. Stretching north is the Via Vittorio Veneto (also known simply as Via Veneto), which has seen its *dolce vita* replaced by a flood of embassies and airline offices. This area was once the edge of the city, joining the papal Rome of the west with the gardens and villas to the east. Pushy real-estate developers and speculators at the turn of the 19th century managed to demolish many of the villas and gardens, including the gorgeous wooded preserve of the **Villa Ludovisi.** The speculator who bought the Ludovisi built himself a colossal palace in its place, but soon even he couldn't afford the upkeep and the enormous taxes, so the government repossessed the palace. The U.S. embassy now resides in this immense *palazzo,* traded for tons of war surplus material in 1945. The rise of the movie industry and postwar tourism in the 1950s heralded the height of Via Veneto's glamour and fame. The grand *caffè* and hotels attracted movie bigwigs like Roberto Rossellini and Ingrid Bergman, eager *paparazzi,* and wide-eyed Americans. Via Veneto's prominence has long since faded, though the overpriced *caffè* and restaurants still prey upon tourists in search of Sophia Loren.

Piazza Barberini is also home to Bernini's **Fontana delle Api** (Bee Fountain), which was intended for the "use of the public and their animals" and buzzes with the same motif that graces the aristocratic Barberini family's coat of arms. Walking up Via Veneto from Piazza Barberini, immediately after the Barberini metro stop on the right hand side of the street emerges the 1626 Counter-Reformation **Church of L'Immacolata Concezione** (open Fri.-Wed. 9am-noon and 3-6pm), a mausoleum housing the

---

Dem bones, dem bones

The bones of 4000 Capuchin friars (for whom *cappuccino* is named) decorate the four chapels of the Capuchin Crypt, making this one of the most bizarre and elaborately macabre settings in Rome. A French Capuchin monk inaugurated the crypt in 1528 but never saw his brilliant concept brought to its spooky completion because the crypt was not finished until 1870. Angels deck the halls, with hip bones serving as wings. The bodies of certain more recently dead friars stand, robed and hooded, beneath bone arches. Even the hanging lights are made of bones. Dirt was shipped in specially from Jerusalem to line the floors. The last chapel displays two severed arms with mummy-like skin hanging on the back wall. Also featured in this chapel is a child's skeleton plastered to the ceiling, holding a scale and a reaper, and accompanied by the uplifting inscription: "What you are now we used to be, what we are now you will be."

Piazza
Barberini

American
Embassy

SIGHTS

Via Lucullo
Via Torino
Via Umbria
LARGO
S. SUSANNA
PIAZZA DI
S. BERNARDO
Via Leon. Carducci
Via G. Bissolati
Via Barberini
S. Susanna
Via Firenze
Via Sallustiana
Via Friuli
Nicola da Tolentino
Salita S.
Via XX settembre
Via Versilio
Vicolo S. Basilico da Tolentino
Via di S. Basilio
Via S. Nicola da Tolentino
Via Barberini
Palazzo
Barberini
Via Molise
Via della Quattro Fontane
S. Carlo alle
Quattro Fontane
Via S. Piacenza
Via Andrea
Via Liguria
Via Vittorio Veneto
Barberini
PIAZZA
BARBERINI
S. Andrea
al Quirinale
Via Ferrara
Via S. Isidoro
Via del Cappuccini
Via della Purificazione
Via dei Giardini
GIARDINO DEL QUIRINALE
Via del Quirinale
Via Rasella
Via Avignonesi
Via del Tritone
Sistina
Via Zucchelli
Via del Traforo
TRAFORO Umberto I
Via Franco Crispi
LARGO DEL TRITONE
Via in Arcione
Via delle Scuderie
Via Gregoriana
Via Maroniti
PIAZZA DEL QUIRINALE
Via dei due Macelli
Via Capo le Case
Via della Panetteria
Palazzo del
Quirinale
Vicolo Scanderbeg
V. d. Propaganda
Via Sant'Andrea
Via del Nazareno
Vicolo Scavolino
Via del Lavatore
dei Modelli
Vicolo del Babuccio
Via della Dataria
Via Mario dei Fiori
Via della Mercede
Via della Stamperia
Via San Vicenzo
Via dei Lucchesi
Via Moretto
PIAZZA DI TREVI
del Montecello
PIAZZA DI PILOTTA
Via Frattina
Via della Vite
Via del Pozzetto
Poli
PIAZZA DI POLI
Via
Fontana
di Trevi
Via delle Vergini
V. d. Archetto
Via S. Marcello
Via del Gambero
PIAZZA SAN SILVESTRO
Via S. Claudio
Via del Tritone
Via S. Maria
Via dei Sabini
Via dei Crociferi
Via delle Muratte
Via Minghetti
Vicolo Sciarra
Via dell'Umiltà
Via S.S. Apostoli
Via Vaccaro
LARGO CHIGI
PIAZZA COLONNA
Via del Corso
Via del Corso

N

tomb of Cardinal Antonio Barberomo, who founded the church; the tomb's inscription reads "Here lies dust, ashes, nothing." For a more utilitarian view of death, head downstairs for the real attraction, the **Capuchin Crypt** (same hours as church; L1000 minimum donation requested).

■ Museo Nazionale d'Arte Antica

On the side of Piazza Barberini opposite the church, up Via delle Quattro Fontane, the sumptuous **Palazzo Barberini,** Via delle Quattro Fontane, 13, houses the **Galleria Nazionale d'Arte Antica** (tel. 48 14 430; open Tues.-Sat. 9am-7pm, Sun. 9am-1pm; admission to both galleries and apartments L8000; under 18 and over 60 free; free guided tours Sat. at 5pm and Sun. at 11am), a collection of paintings dating from the 12th to 17th centuries. The *palazzo* was begun in 1624 by Carlo Maderno on a commission from the prosperous Pope Urban VIII. After Maderno's death, it took Borromini and Bernini a decade to finish the palace. Bernini added the theatrical central porch in front, topped by attached columns and shallow pilasters. Borromini worked on the marvelous spiral stairs to the right and toyed with the building's perspective so that the upper-level windows look the same size as those on the first floor. Unfortunately, the main façade is practically invisible beneath a web of scaffolding which has been up since 1984. The impressive central stairway is by Bernini and buzzes with Barberini bees in all sorts of unexpected places.

The main floor (*piano nobile*) of the museum is undergoing major restoration, expected to be completed in the summer of 1997. This means that important works by Lippi, Raphael, El Greco, Carracci, Caravaggio, Poussin and others will be scattered, often at random, throughout the usually well-ordered, well-labeled 17-room museum. In fact, some of these works may temporarily be removed from display. Even so, there still promises to be a healthy portion of Renaissance and Baroque masterpieces on display at any given time to tide over the art-starved tourist. From the museum, continue up Via delle Quattro Fontane and take a right onto Via del Quirinale at the four-fountained intersection.

■ Piazza del Quirinale and Via XX Settembre

Piazza del Quirinale, at the southeast end of Via del Quirinale, occupies the summit of the tallest of Rome's seven hills. From the belvedere, the view takes in a sea of Roman domes, with St. Peter's in the distance. In the middle of the *piazza,* the heroic **statues of Castor and Pollux** (mythical warrior twins whom ancient Romans embraced as their special protectors) flank yet another of Rome's many obelisks. The fountain over which they preside was once a cattle trough in the Roman Forum. The President of the Republic officially resides in the **Palazzo del Quirinale,** a Baroque architectural collaboration by Bernini, Carlo Maderno, and Domenico Fontana. Maderno did the front, while Bernini set himself to the *manica lunga,* or "long sleeve," on Via del Quirinale. If you look through the portals on the *piazza* or on Via XX Settembre, you may see the white-uniformed, silver-helmeted Republican Guards (each of whom must be at least 6 ft. tall to get his job) and the *palazzo*'s lush gardens. The *palazzo* was once the papal summer palace and then a royal residence; it has hosted the president since 1947. The neighboring white stone **Palazzo della Consulta** houses the constitutional court.

Back down Via del Quirinale, Via Ferrara on the right leads down the steps to Via Milano. At the corner of Via Milano and Via Nazionale, the **Palazzo delle Espozioni,** Via Nazionale, 194 (tel. 48 85 465; open Wed.-Mon. 10am-9pm; admission L12,000, L6000 with student ID, L20,000 for the year), is an architectural behemoth that hosts an ever-changing array of exhibits. Look for the posters plastered across the city for full details. 1996 featured a Marlene Dietrich film festival, a massive exposition on Ulysses called *Myth and Memory,* and an exposition of the art of Ferlinghetti.

Back up Via Milano to Via Ferrara, Via del Quirinale runs northeast past the **Church of Sant'Andrea al Quirinale** to its right (tel. 48 90 31 87; open Wed.-Mon. 8am-noon and 4-7pm). One of Bernini's simpler Baroque designs, the oval-shaped interior departs from traditional church plans; the altar is along the long wall, making the nave wider than it is long. Bernini's theatrical orchestration of the central altar deserves more than a passing glance. St. Andrew, crucified in the painted altarpiece, rises on stuccoed clouds through the vault of his apse, headed for the cherubim-filled space of the central dome.

Further along the street, the marvelous undulating façade of Borromini's **Church of San Carlo alle Quattro Fontane,** often called **San Carlino** (open Mon.-Fri. 9:30am-12:30pm, 4-6pm and Sat. 9am-12:30pm; if the interior is closed, ring at the convent next door) provides a sharp contrast to Bernini's neighboring work. Borromini avoided the kind of mixed-media extravaganzas that Bernini had perfected and focused on architecture alone. As a result, San Carlino presents a relatively simple interior. The head of the religious order that founded this church even bragged, "Nothing similar can be found anywhere in the world." San Carlino is a triumph of rhythmical curves and concavities, its narrow interior governed by periodic pairs of pilasters. The triangle motif throughout is meant to symbolize the Trinity. The church also has the distinction of being Borromini's first and last work: though he designed the relatively simple interior early on in his career, he finished the more ornate façade just before his suicide. He also designed the **cloister** next door, which holds the **crypt** in whose curves he had hoped (unsuccessfully) to be buried.

The nearby intersection of Via del Quirinale and **Via delle Quattro Fontane** showcases one of Pope Sixtus V's more gracious additions to the city. In an effort to ease traffic and offer greater definition to the city's regions, the 16th-century pontiff straightened many of Rome's major streets and erected obelisks at important junctions. From the crossroads here, you can catch sight of the obelisks at Piazza del Quirinale, at the top of the Spanish Steps, and at Santa Maria Maggiore, as well as (in the distance) Michelangelo's famous Porta Pia. The four reclining figures in the fountains represent two virtues, Strength and Fidelity, and Rome's two rivers, the Tiber and the Aniene.

Via del Quirinale becomes Via XX Settembre at this point, which, after a few more blocks, opens into the Baroque **Piazza San Bernardo,** site of Domenico Fontana's colossal **Fontana dell'Acqua Felice.** The fountain, recently cleaned but already showing signs of new pollution, was built in 1587 at the point where the Acqua Felice aqueduct enters the city. The beefy statue of Moses is said to have been carved by Prospero Antichi, who nearly died of disappointment after seeing the finished product. Across the way, the **Church of Santa Maria della Vittoria** (open daily 6:30am-noon and 4:30-7pm; dress code cited but sporadically enforced), named for an icon of Mary that "won" a battle near Prague for the Catholics in 1620, houses Bernini's turbulent *Ecstasy of St. Theresa of Avila* (1652) in the Cornaro Chapel, the last chapel on the left. The masterpiece of marble depicts the young Spanish saint's cataclysmic vision, in which she felt an angel pierce her heart with a flaming arrow. She later wrote, "The pain was so great that I cried aloud but at the same time I experienced such infinite sweetness that I wished the pain would last forever … It was the sweet caressing of the soul by God."

The **Church of Santa Susanna** (now the American National Church; mass in English Mon.-Sat. at 6pm, Sun. at 9am and 10:30am), across the street to the right as you exit Santa Maria della Vittoria, has a distinctive Counter-Reformation façade by Carlo Maderno (1603). Inside, Maderno's frescoes of the biblical life of Susanna cover the walls; so do his four large statues of the prophets who stand atop pillars dating back to the ninth century. It is customary for the Archbishop of Boston to hold the title of Cardinal Priest of Santa Susanna.

■ Baths of Diocletian

From the church of Santa Susanna, cross the *piazza* diagonally and follow Via V.E. Orlando towards **Piazza della Repubblica,** one of Rome's fume-spewing piazze and home to the ruins of the **Baths of Diocletian.** Forty thousand Christian slaves took almost ten years, 298-306 AD, to build the grandest community center of the age. The public baths, which could serve 3000 Romans at once, contained gymnasiums, art galleries, gardens, libraries, and concert halls as well as a heated, marble, 30-person public toilet and pools of various temperatures. The cold pool *(frigidarium)* was the size of a small lake and open to the sky (2500 square meters).

The baths were modeled on Trajan's thermal baths, the first to abandon a strict north-south axis for a southwest-northeast orientation, which makes optimum use of solar energy. The *calidarium* (hot-water bath) faced southwest (but still required huge boilers to heat) and the *frigidarium* faced northeast. The complex fell into ruin in 538 when the aqueducts supplying the water for the baths were destroyed by Witigis and the Ostrogoths. Centuries later, a Sicilian priest had a vision of a swarm of angels rising from the baths and pestered Pius IV to build a church on the dilapidated site. As a result, the baths came to life again in 1561 when Pope Pius IV ordered Michelangelo, then 86, to undertake his last architectural work and convert the ruins into a church. Imitating the architecture of the baths, his original design used the remains of the *calidarium* as the church facade. This is how it appears today, although much of his interior plan was changed after both he and the Pope died three years later. The result is the **Church of Santa Maria degli Angeli** (open daily 7:30am-12:30pm and 4-6:30pm). Despite the departure from Michelangelo's plan and years of design screw-ups, the vast interior gives a sense of the magnitude and elegance of the ancient baths. The church was constructed in the ancient *tepidarium* (lukewarm baths); Michelangelo had scavenged material from the baths to construct the red porphyry columns that line the church interior. In the floor leading from the east transept to the altar is a sundial, which provided the standard time for Roman clocks for hundreds of years. A door marked "Sacristy" leads to ruins of the *frigidarium* and an exhibit on the stages of the construction of the church. This includes an excellent, illustrated history of the reconstruction of the baths, as well as plans drawn up by other famous Renaissance artists.

Turn right as you exit the church and head down Via Giuseppe Romita. In the building on Via Romita between Via Parigi and Via Cernaia, the Museo Nazionale Romano delle Terme (see below) has organized a special exhibit on the decorative sculpture of baths (open 10am-7pm; free). If you don't intend to make it to the museum itself, this 4th-century rotunda is worth visiting. Statues from the baths of Diocletian and other imperial baths stand in a ring around the vaulted octagonal room, which once served as a planetarium. Glass panels in the center and on the edges of the floor afford a view down into the baths. In the center of the room are two well-preserved bronze statues, a rare treat since most bronzes were melted down in the chaos of the Middle Ages. The *Hellenistic Prince,* who basks in the rippling glory of his own physique, was unearthed in the baths of Constantine but dates from the third century BC. Next to him, the seated first-century-BC *Pugilist at Rest* looks tired and pensive. The rest of the sculptures, all in marble and more savaged by time, are less impressive individually, but offer a scintillating account of the ancients' knowledge of anatomy.

Backtracking past the church and Piazza della Repubblica, follow the wrought-iron fence around the corner to Viale Enrico de Nicola (across the street from the buses lined up in front of Termini Station), where you'll find the **Museo Nazionale Romano delle Terme** (tel. 488 05 30; open Tues.-Sat. 9am-2pm, Sun. 9am-1pm; admission L12,000, EU citizens under 18 or over 60 free). The museum combines several important patrician collections with sculptures and antiquities found in Rome since 1870. The museum is located in the charterhouse built along with Santa Maria degli Angeli and utilizes some of the rooms from the ancient baths. Don't miss the **Sala dei Capolavori** (Room of Masterpieces) and the so-called Ludovisi throne, a Greek statue dating from the 5th century BC. The exquisite reliefs on the throne depict the birth of Aphrodite from the waves of the sea. The prized *Esquiline Diskobolos* in the adjacent room captures a discus-thrower in the dynamic, swiveled state just before the throw. Most of the collection that is open to the public resides in the cloister and garden just beyond the mosaic-lined entry hall. Some of the sculptures once housed here have been moved to the special exhibit on Via Giuseppe Romita (see above).

Via Nomentana

Hop on the #36 bus in front of Termini or head back to Via XX Settembre and catch the #60 to go up **Via Nomentana.** Via Nomentana, which begins at Porta Pia, one of the gates to the city, is lined with villas, embassies, and parks. The **Church of Sant'Agnese fuori le Mura** (tel. 86 20 54 56; open Mon. 9am-noon, Tues.-Sun. 9am-noon and 4-6pm; guided tours free with admission, L8000; English guide pamphlets available) stands at Via Nomentana, 349, about 2km northeast of the Porta Pia. The **catacombs** here, perhaps the best preserved in Rome, contain skeletons of the saint's Christian followers. Before descending into the catacombs, look above the apse for the extraordinary Byzantine-style mosaic of St. Agnes with a pair of popes. St. Agnes was the 12-year-old who was martyred by Diocletian for refusing to marry—her heart was pledged to God (see Piazza Navona, p. 175 for the whole story on St. Agnes). More fourth-century mosaics await in the **Church of Santa Costanza** next door. Originally built by Constantinia (the saintly daughter of Constantine I who was cured of leprosy when sleeping on St. Agnes' tomb and promptly converted to Christianity) as a mausoleum for herself, it was transformed into a baptistry and later a church.

About halfway between the Porta Pia and the church of Sant'Agnese is the **Villa Torlonia.** Once Mussolini's private estate, the house itself is now abandoned and somewhat dilapidated, while the grounds have become a public park. Though not as large as Villa Ada or Villa Borghese, it is just as peaceful and is frequented by the usual children, dogs, and affectionate Italian couples. Join the students from the nearby Villa Mirafiori, the language faculty of the University of Rome, for a picnic, a soccer game, or a nap before heading back to the chaos of the city within the walls.

THE AVENTINE, TESTACCIO, AND EUR

The Aventine Hill

The easiest approach to the Aventine is from the western end of the Circus Maximus (the end farthest from the metro station) at Piazzale Ugo la Malfa. From here, Via di Valle Murcia climbs past two lush, well-maintained parks. The first, the **Roseto Comunale** (open daily 8am-7:30pm), entices you up the hill with the scent and the spectacular colors of various types of carefully labeled flowers from around Europe. The roses that bloom in May will leave any hard-core gardener in tears. Just a bit further up the hill, the **Parco Savello,** sheltered by medieval fortress walls, offers an unobstructed view of the Tiber, St.Peter's, Trastevere, and Piazza Venezia, as well as of countless affectionate young Italian couples frolicking under the orange trees. A gate at the southern (uphill) end of the park leads into the courtyard of the **Church of Santa Sabina** (open daily 6:30am-12:30pm and 3:30-7:00pm), a basilica built in the same style as San Gregorio and Santa Maria in Cosmedin, with a porch of ancient columns and a towering *campanile.* Inside, the wooden doors on the far left date from the fifth century and contain one of the earliest depictions of the Crucifixion. The 24 columns of the nave were pillaged from a pagan temple and are in perfect condition.

Via di Santa Sabina continues along the crest of the hill past the **Church of Sant'Alessio** (open daily 8:30am-noon and 3:30-6:30pm; winter 8:30am-noon and 3:30-5pm) to the **Piazza dei Cavalieri di Malta,** home of the crusading order of the Knights of Malta. Piranesi designed the military trophies atop the walls. The keyhole

SIGHTS

in the pale-yellow gate on the right offers a perfectly framed view of the dome of St. Peter's. Across the street, the **Church of Sant'Anselmo** (open daily 8am-1pm and 2-4pm) has a peaceful garden courtyard and a weekly Gregorian chant mass (Sun. 9:30am). Head down Via di Porta Lavernale (to the left of the church) and take a left onto Via di Sant'Anselmo. Another left on Via Icilio through Piazza Albina leads to the **Church of Santa Prisca** and its tiny *piazza.* The church dates from the fourth century and is built atop an ancient crypt and mithraeum, discovered in 1958 but now closed indefinitely. Via di S. Prisca leads left as you exit the church across the busy Viale Aventino to Via S. Saba. Just a bit up the hill is the 11th-century **Church of Santa Saba** (open daily 7am-noon and 4-7pm). If the entrance is closed, enter from Piazza Bernini, 20 on the opposite side of the church. Stop to note the mosaic-ridged door before continuing in to see the remains of the 13th-century frescoes depicting the life of Saint Nicholas. The frescoes show good old Saint Nick from Bari, before he started delivering presents to well-behaved children, giving three gold balls to three naked women reclining in bed in order to save them from the fate of prostitution. As you exit the church, Via Annia Faustina leads to Via Baccio Pontelli and stairs down to crowded Viale della Piramide Cestia. Just to the left lie the remains of the Porta S. Paolo and the neighborhood of Testaccio.

■ Testaccio

South of the Aventine Hill, the working-class district of **Testaccio** (easily reached by Metro Linea B at the Piramide stop or by bus #27 from Termini at the Porta S. Paolo stop) is known for its cheap and delicious *trattorie,* its raucous nightclubs, and its eclectic collection of monuments. Past the forbidding, castle-like **Porta San Paolo** (in ancient times the Porta Ostiense and still the start of the road to Ostia Antica), the colossal **Pyramid of Gaius Cestius** (*Caio Cestio* in Italian) borders the burial plot of the Protestants. Gaius Cestius, tribune of the plebs under Augustus, got caught up in the craze for things Egyptian that followed on the Emperor's defeat of Cleopatra in the late first century BC. Like the collection of Egyptian statuary in the Vatican and most of the obelisks in the city, there's nothing Egyptian about this hulking white pyramid except its inspiration. Though it was built in less than 330 days, the close fit of its marble blocks ensured that it was never pillaged. When the Goths were marauding in the third century, the emperor Aurelian had the pyramid built into his city walls as a bastion. Nowadays it's a favored hangout of Rome's impeccably mod transvestite population.

Around to the right as you face the pyramid, Via Persichetti leads to Via Caio Cestio, which runs along the length of the peaceful **Cimitero Acattolico per gli Stranieri** (the Protestant Cemetery, or, more literally, the Non-Catholic Cemetery for Foreigners; open April-Sept. 9am-6pm, Oct.-March 9am-5pm; closed Monday; free, but donation requested), the final resting place for many English visitors to the city, as well as anyone else who wasn't Catholic or Jewish. Ring the bell for admission at #6. Crowded tombstones cluster in the shade of fragrant blooms and foliage, while teams of affection-starved cats meow for attention. In the distant corner between planted avenues of tombs, John Keats lies beside his friend Joseph Severn. The tombstone itself doesn't mention the writer by name; it merely commemorates a "Young English Poet" and records, "Here lies one whose name is writ in water." On the other side of the small cemetery (the "New Cemetery"), Shelley rests in peace beside his piratical friend Trelawny, under a simple plaque hailing him as *Cor Cordium,* "heart of hearts." Also buried here are Goethe's son Julius and Richard Henry Dana, author of *Two Years Before the Mast.* Henry James buried his fictional heroine, Daisy Miller, here after she died of malaria.

At the end of Via Caio Cestio and across Via Nicola Zabaglia looms the **Monte Testaccio.** In ancient times the area served as the docklands of Rome, where grain, oil, wine, and marble were unloaded from river barges into giant warehouses. After the goods had been transferred to storage, Roman merchants tossed the leftover terra-cotta urns into a vacant lot. The pile grew and grew, and today the bulbous

Testaccio

Via Pandosia
Via Illiria
Via Licia
PIAZZALE LATINA
Via di Cilicia
PIAZZA DI S. GIOVANNI IN LATERANO
S. Giovanni in Laterano
Campo Sportivo
Rotondo
Via d'Ipponio
Via Gallia
Via Pannonia
Viale Metronio
Via di S. Stefano
Via dell'Amba Aradam
Via d. Ferratella
PIAZZALE DI PTA. METRONIO
Via Druso
PARCO EGERIA
Via di Porta Latina
Via Annia
Via della Navicella
PARCO DI PTA. CAPENA
S. Sisto
PIAZZALE NUMA POMPILIO
Via d. Terme di Caracalla
Via Claudia
PIAZZA CELIMONTANA
Villa Celimontana
Terme di Caracalla
Viale Guido Baccelli
PARCO DEL CELIO
PIAZZA S. GREGORIO
Via di S. Gregorio
Via d. Terme di Caracalla
Campo Sportivo
LUNGO E. FIORITTO
Largo Porta
LINE B
PALATINE HILL
PIAZZA DI PTA. CAPENA
Circo Massimo
V. Guerrieri
Via G. Dardini
Stadio di Domiziano
Via dei Cerchi
Via Aventina
PIAZZA BERNINI
Viale Guido
Viale Marco Polo
Museo di Roma
Via del Circo Massimo
Viale Aventino
V. Ligorio
S. Saba
PIAZZALE DEI PARTIGIANI
PARCO DI S. ALESSIO
PIAZZA S. PRISCA
PIAZZA ALBANIA
LINE B
AVENTINE HILL
S. Sabina
Via di S. Alessio
PIAZZALE OSTIENSE
Lungotevere Ripa
Lungotevere Aventino
PIAZZA D. EMPORIO
Piramide
Cimitero Protestante
PIAZZA V. BOTTEGO
S. Cecilia
Porto di Ripa Grande
Via Marmorata
PIAZZA TESTACCIO
Via Nicola Zabaglia
PARCO TESTACCIO
PIAZZA MASTAI
Ponte Sublicio
Tiber River
Via Ginori
LUNGO G.B. MARZI
Palazzo di Esami
Min. d. Pubblica Intruzionia
Viale di Trastevere
Lungotevere

Monte Testaccio (from *testae,* or pot shards) rises 150 lush, dark green feet over the drab surrounding streets. Though grown over with grass, the hill is punctured every where by fragments of orange clay amphorae. The park is no longer open to the public, and pilfering of pot shards is illegal.

■ San Paolo fuori le Mura

From the pyramid, take Metro Linea B or grab bus #673, 23, or 170 down Via Ostiense to the eery **Basilica di San Paolo fuori le Mura** (take Metro Linea B to Basilica S. Paolo; open 7am-6:30pm), one of the churches in Rome with extraterritorial status (with S. Giovanni in Laterano, Sta. Maria Maggiore, and, of course, St. Peter's and the largest church in the city after St. Peter's. St. Paul, who was martyred near the modern **EUR,** is believed to be buried under the altar (his body, that is; his head is in S. Giovanni), and the church was considered, until the construction of the new St Peter's, the largest and most beautiful in Rome. Destroyed by fire in 1823, the present church is a modern reconstruction. It's been called cold and gloomy, but the shiny newness of the marble interior is probably the best representation of how the paleochristian basilicas of Rome looked when they were first constructed. The mammoth interior is an Egyptian cross (in the shape of a T) with two aisles flanking the nave on each side. The triumphal arch before the altar and the apse is set with the original mosaics (salvaged and reassembled after the fire) depicting Christ, angels, saints, and the Virgin. All along the basilica's periphery, circular portraits of all of the popes solemnly admire the sporadic tour groups. There is space for only eight more portraits and legend says that once the wall fills up, the world will end. The **cloister** (open 9am-1pm and 3-6:30pm) is a peaceful remnant of the original construction, lined with twisted pairs of Cosmatesque columns and enveloping a rose garden.

■ EUR

Rome is famous for monuments that harken back to ancient empires, but south of the city stands a monument to a Roman empire that never was. The zone is called **EUR** (pronounced AY-oor), an Italian acronym for Universal Exposition of Rome, the 1942 World's Fair that Mussolini intended to be a showcase of fascist and imperial Roman achievements. The outbreak of World War II led to the cancellation of the fair, and wartime demands on manpower and material ensured that EUR would never complete Mussolini's mission of extending Rome to the sea. Visit the area only to see the cavernous museums or the mechanistic, eerily symmetrical region where all the strapping young fascists would have lived had Mussolini had his way. EUR lies three Metro stops from the Basilica S. Paolo at the EUR-Palasport stop on Metro Linea B; you can also take bus #714 from Termini or bus #717 from Trastevere to Viale G. Marconi. **Via Cristoforo Colombo,** EUR's main street, runs roughly north to south and is the first of many politically sycophantic names like "Via Lincoln" and "Piazza Kennedy." From the metro stop, walk north up Via Cristoforo Colombo to **Piazza Guglielmo Marconi,** sprouting a 1959 modernist **obelisk.**

Located to the right of the Piazza Marconi, the **Museo Preistorico ed Etnografico Luigi Pigorini,** at Viale Lincoln, 14 (tel. 54 95 22 38; open Tues.-Fri. 9am-1:30pm, Sat. 9am-7pm, Sun. 9am-12:30pm; L8000), houses an anthropological collection focusing on prehistoric Latium. The deserted museum features objects from various parts of the Italian peninsula from the Stone, Bronze, and Iron Ages. Artifacts from other parts of the world are exhibited in the ethnographic collection. The paleontological exhibits are in need of an update, but the special exhibitions on the second floor are thorough and interesting. Located in the same building, through the entrance at Viale Lincoln, 1 (walk to the end of the building and up the stairs to the right of the snack bar), is the collection of the **Museo dell'Alto Medioevo** (Museum of the High Middle Ages; tel. 592 58 06; open Mon.-Sat. 9am-1:30pm, Sun. 9am-12:30pm; L4000; wheelchair accessible).

EUR's folk museum, **Museo Nazionale delle Arti e Tradizioni Popolari** (tel. 591 07 09; open Mon.-Sat. 9am-2pm, Sun. 9am-1pm; L4000), is across the parking lot; most of the artistic graffiti in the area is showcased on its façade. Between the two buildings which house these museums, Viale della Civiltà Romana leads to the **Museo della Civiltà Romana** (tel. 592 61 41; open Tues.-Sat. 9am-7pm, Sun. 9am-1:30pm; L5000) which features a plaster cast of Trajan's column and a scale model of Rome in the time of Hadrian, among other reconstructions of major Roman monuments. You may be able to get in free to these museums if you're a student, particularly if your studies pertain to the museum's content.

Continuing north, you will reach the Viale della Civiltà del Lavoro. To the east (right) stands the **Palace of Congress,** but the awkward **Palace of the Civilization of Labor,** at the west (left) end of the street, serves as EUR's definitive symbol. Designed by Marcello Piacentini in 1938, it anticipates the postmodernist architecture of such designers as Michael Graves, by wrapping arch-like windows around the "Square Colosseum" building, in an effort to evoke Roman ruins. Nearby, **Piazzale delle Nazioni Unite** embodies the EUR that Mussolini had intended: imposing modern buildings decorated with spare columns attempt to meld the ancient empire with that of Mussolini's.

Heading east from EUR, take Viale dell'Industria (on the right of Via C. Colombo) down to Via delle Tre Fontane. The **LUNEUR park,** an old-fashioned amusement park on Via delle Tre Fontane (tel. 592 59 33; open Mon.-Fri. 1pm-midnight, Sat. 4pm-1am, Sun. 10am-1pm and 3pm-midnight), features cheap thrills like the "Himalaya Railroad" for L3000. There's no admission fee to enter the park, but you must pay for each ride. Farther down the road, at the intersection of Via delle Tre Fontane and Via Laurentina, stands the **Abbazia delle Tre Fontane** (Abbey of the Three Fountains), where St. Paul is said to have been beheaded. According to legend, St. Paul's head bounced on the ground three times, creating a fountain with each bounce—hence the name. A millennium later, Saint Bernard stayed here during his 12th-century visit to Rome. The monks who live here today sell the monastery's own eucalyptus liquor (¼ liter for L6000) and special chocolate (L1000 per small bar; store open Mon.-Sat. 11am-5pm, Sun. noon-5pm.) South of EUR, across the lake (known simply as "the lake" or *il lago*) looms the **Palazzo dello Sport** designed for the 1960 Olympic Games.

ACROSS THE TIBER

▓ Isola Tiberina

The **Tiber Island,** situated between Trastevere and the *centro storico,* splits the Tiber's unsavory yellow-green flow with banks swathed in marble and brick. It's not surprising that the island seems more like a floating city than a natural landmark—it's been continuously inhabited for nearly 3000 years. According to Roman legend, the island shares its birthday with the Roman Republic—after the Etruscan tyrant Tarquin the Proud raped the virtuous Lucretia, her outraged husband killed him and threw his corpse in the river, where muck and silt collected around it. Lucretia's family then went about founding a new government, and the Tiber Island grew into dry land.

Tarquin's muddy remains may have deterred Republican Romans from settling on the island; the place was first used as a dumping ground for slaves who had grown too weak or sick to work. Abandoned by their masters, the pitiful slaves prayed to Aesclepius, the Greek god of healing. Legend has it that when the Romans took his cult statue from the sanctuary at Kos and dragged it up the Tiber in 293 BC, the god appeared to them as a snake and slithered onto the island. The Romans took this as a sign that this was where he wanted his temple and, with typical architectural overkill, encased the island in marble, building its walls in the shape of a boat to commemorate the god's arrival. You can see traces of the original travertine decoration on the

southeast side (look for the serpent carved in relief near the "prow"). The site h
been associated with healing ever since; the order of Fatebenefratelli ("do goo
brothers") monks established a hospital here in 154 AD. Expectant Roman mothe
consider the island the most fashionable place in the city to give birth.

The bridge leading from the east bank of the river, the sturdy **Ponte Fabricio,** is tl
oldest in the city, built by Lucius Fabricius in 62 BC. From the *lungotevere,* you c
see the inscription Lucius carved into the bridge to record his public service; it
commonly known as the **Bridge of Four Heads** *(dei Quattro Capi).* As you str
across the cobbled span, pay your respects, as Romans have done for two millenn
to the two stone herms (four-sided pillars, narrower at the base and with a bust at tl
top) of Janus, two-headed god of beginnings and endings. From the bridge, you ca
also catch sight of the beleaguered **Ponte Rotto** to the south, one of Rome's less fe
tunate ancient constructions. Built in the second century BC, the poor bridge und
went repair after medieval repair, each time succumbing again to the Tibe
relentless floods. Since its last collapse in 1598, it's been slowly disintegrating. No
all that remains is a single arch planted squatly, but proudly, midstream.

In the island's one *piazza,* the 10th-century **Church of San Bartolomeo** (op
daily 8:30am-noon and 3:30-6pm; façade currently *in restauro*) has been flooded a
rebuilt many times, making it an eclectic mix of a Baroque façade, a Romanesque b
tower, and 14 antique columns. The well cover may actually be a relic from the or
inal temple to Aesclepius. The Fatebenefratelli's hospital takes up the northern half
the island. English King Henry I's courtier Rahere reputedly recovered here fro
malaria, often a fatal disease in those pre-quinine days. He was so thankful that **l**
promised to build a church and a hospital in gratitude when he got back to Englan
and true to his word, he built the structures that still stand in London's Smithfield d
trict.

The **Ponte Cestio** (originally built by Lucius Cestius in 46 BC and rebuilt in 189
links the island to Trastevere. While it may not garner a superlative, the little brid
offers a good view of the Gianicolo and the bell tower of Santa Maria in Cosmedi
Stairs lead down to the bank on either side, where lovers, vagabonds, and graffiti a
ists alike enjoy secluded anonymity.

▓ Trastevere

Trastevere (from *trans Tiberim*, "across the Tiber") boasts a proud, independe
vitality, giving the neighborhood a character and atmosphere unlike that of the rest
central Rome. The *Trasteverini* claim to be descendants of the purest Roman stock-
Romani de' Roma, "Romans from Rome," so they say; some residents claim never
have crossed the river. Augustus Hare once declared the inhabitants to be "mo
hasty, passionate, and revengeful, as they are a stronger and more vigorous race"-
wisdom undisputed by Romans on either side of the Tiber.

The legendary founder of Ostia, King Ancus Martius, first settled Trastevere not
a residential spot but as a commercial and military outpost to protect the valuable sa
beds at the base of the Tiber. The hills beyond Trastevere also became important ou
posts for defending the city from Etruscan incursions. During the empire, sailors fe
the imperial fleet inhabited the area, building mud and clay huts along the river
banks. The success of Hadrian's commercial port lured Syrian and Jewish merchan
to set up camp in the neighborhood, and for a time, the maritime business flourishe
alongside such cottage industries as tanning, carpentry, milling, and prostitution. I
the Middle Ages, however, Trastevere's commercial activity began to wane and ma
of the area's residents retreated to the other side of the river, leaving only the poor
and working-class Trasteverini behind. In his itinerary of 1617, guidebook edit
Fynes Moryson warned readers, "because the aire is unwholesome, as the winde th
blows here from the South, it is onely inhabited by Artisans and poore people." Tr
popes took little interest in this proletarian neighborhood and rarely extended the
wealth to build grandiose churches or monuments here. Instead, the communi
remained wholly self-sufficient, even producing two of the major poets of the Roma

Trastevere

1 Botanical Gardens
2 Villa Farnesina
3 Piazza Trilussa
4 Piazza Cenci
5 Teatro Marcello
6 Piazza d. Campidoglio
7 The Forum
8 Bocca della Verità
9 Museo di Roma
10 Piazza S. Cecilia
11 Piazza G. G. Belli
12 Piazza Sidney Sonnino
13 Piazza Mastai
14 Piazza Porta Portese
15 Piazza S. Calisto
16 Piazza and Church S. Maria in Trastevere
17 Piazza S. Egidio
18 Villa Aurelia

PARCO GIANICOLENSE

Via Corsini
Vicolo Morroni
Via S. Dorotea
Via Garibaldi
Via della Scala
Via d. Mattonato
Via Garibaldi
Via A. Masina
Via Giacomo Medici
Viale 30 Aprile
Via Nicola Fabrizi
Viale Tambucino Glorioso
Via F. Casini
Via Dandolo
Via d. Calandrelli
Via Garibaldi

PIAZZA DI SANT EGIDIO
PIAZZA SANTA MARIA IN TRASTEVERE
Via del Moro
Via della Lungaretta
Via d. Paglia
Via Luciano Manara
PIAZZA DI S. COSIMATO
Via G. Sacchi
Via di San Francesco a Ripa
Via Natale del Grande
Via E. Morosini
Viale di Trastevere
Ministero d. Pubblico Istruzione
Via Dandolo

Ponte Sisto
Ponte Garibaldi
Lungo. dei Vallati
P. del Conservatori
Via Arenula
Lungotevere Sanzio
Lungotevere di Anguillara
PIAZZA G. BELLI
Via d. San Gallicano
PIAZZA MASTAI
Palazzo d'Assisi
Via G. Induno
Via della Luce
Via Anicia
Via di S. Michele
V. Mad. dell'Orto
PIAZZA MERCANTI
V. d. Porta

Tiber River

Ponte Fabricio
Isola Tiberina
Ponte Cestio
Lungotevere Cenci
Lungotevere di Pierleoni
Via d. Portico
Via Catilana
PIAZZA CAMPITELLI
Via del Teatro di Marcello

PIAZZA PISCINULA
Via d. Salumi
Via Genovesi
V. S. Cecilia
Porto di Ripa Grande
Ponte Sublicio
Lungotevere Aventino
Lung. Ripa
Ponte Palatino

Via S. G. Decol.
Via di S. Teodoro
Via d. Velabro
Via d. Greca
Via dei Cerchi
Via del Circo Massimo
Circo Massimo

200 yards
200 meters

N

dialect, G.G. Belli and Trilussa. In keeping with its independent spirit, Trastevere backed two revolutions: Mazzini's quest for a Republic in 1849 and Garibaldi's resurgence in 1867.

Since World War II, Trastevere has been the target of (or victim of) aggressive foreign-funded gentrification. A significant portion of the neighborhood's residents are actually native speakers of English and the number of true, salt-of-the-earth, *Roman di Roma* is dwindling. Today, Trastevere continues to attract hordes of expatriates, bohemians, and artists, but thanks to rent control and centuries of fiery patriotism, the area retains its local *gusto*. To keep the spirit of independence alive, the festival of **Noantri** ("We others" in dialect) is still celebrated in the last two weeks of July. Though a bit cheesy, the festival features a number of grand religious processions, a couple of kiddie rides, and the oft-invoked *porchetta* (roast pig) on every corner.

To reach Trastevere, take bus #75 or 170 from Termini, or bus #56 or #60 from Via Claudio in front of Piazza San Silvestro, near the Spanish Steps, to **Piazza Sonnino.** It is a walkable distance from most places in the historic center and you might find it more enjoyable to navigate through the *vicoli* and *piazze* or walk along Via Arenula towards the Ponte Garibaldi. Tourists flock to the area for its restaurants, pizzerias, bars, and movie houses. Rome's one English-language movie theater, Cinema Pasquino, is here at Vicolo del Piede, 19. Crowds of young people and students gather in the *piazze* at night to make this one of the most lively nocturnal centers in Rome. With all of its night-time foreignness, however, Trastevere still maintains an authentically beautiful provincialism that can best be seen earlier in the day. Its dark maze of medieval quarters, with webs of laundry slung across buildings, may give you a better sense of traditional Rome than any other part of the city.

■ Piazza Sonnino

Right off the Ponte Garibaldi stands the statue of the famous dialect poet, G. G. Belli, in the middle of his own *piazza*, which spills onto the busy Viale di Trastevere. On the left, the **Torre degli Anguillara,** dating to the 13th century, stands over a *palazzo* of the same name. Members of the Anguillara family were at the head of Roman activity as priests, magistrates, warlords, criminals, and swindlers. The building now houses the **Casa di Dante,** with readings of the *Divine Comedy* every Sunday from November to March. Just up the street, on the other side, the **Church of San Crisogno** (open daily 7-11:30am and 4-7pm) perpetuates a well-known Roman name, Cardinal Borghese's, etched into the façade. Although it was founded in the fifth century, the church has been rebuilt many times through the years. Twenty feet beneath the most recent structure lie the remains of the fifth-century church. To visit the ruins, walk into the room adjacent to the church to the left of the altar, where the attendant will lead you to the narrow wrought-iron spiral staircase that descends into the excavations (*offerta* L2000). Traces of the original wall paintings and some well-preserved sarcophagi and inscriptions are still visible.

■ East of Viale di Trastevere

Across the street from San Crisogno, turn left at the McDonald's and continue down Via dei Genovesi until it ends at the intersection where Via dei Vascellari becomes Via di Santa Cecilia; turn right on Via di Santa Cecilia. The **Basilica of Santa Cecilia in Trastevere** (open 10am-noon and 4-6pm) is up ahead on the right, behind the cars; through the gate, and beyond the courtyard full of roses and shrubs. The church was built on the site of Santa Cecilia's house. She converted to Christianity and managed to convert her husband and brother-in-law. Unfortunately, her husband and brother-in-law were then beheaded for their refusal to worship Roman gods. Cecilia inherited a considerable fortune from both of them, becoming one of the richest women in Rome and inciting so much resentment that the prefect of Rome ordered her death in 230 AD. She was locked up in her own fiery steamroom to die, but miraculously survived. They then tried to chop her head off with the three legal lops, but the executioners did a poor job of it and she survived for three days more, slowly bleeding to death and converting over 400 people to Christianity in the meantime. She bequeathed her palace to build this church. She is the patron saint of music—she was found singing after her three-day stint in the steamroom. On November 22, Santa Cecilia's day of martyrdom, churches hold a special musical service. The National Academy of Music in Rome is also named after her.

Pope Urban I first consecrated the church in her palace, but Pope Pascal I rebuilt it in 821 when, according to one Vatican account, he dreamed of St. Cecilia showing him her burial grounds in the catacombs of St. Calixtus. He had her body exhumed and transferred to the new church. After passing through the spacious courtyard rose garden and into the church proper, you can see the site of the old steamroom, the first room on the right as you enter. The choice artwork, however, is Stefano Maderno's famous **statue of Santa Cecilia** that reclines under the high altar. The marble sculpture apparently shows what she looked like when exhumed from her tomb in 1599, in Maderno's presence. Rococo restorers wreaked untold damage on the medieval frescoes by Pietro Cavallini which once covered the church. However, there are fragments of his magnificent *Last Judgement*, painted in 1293, in the adjacent cloister (open Tues. and Thurs. 10-11:30am). This highly sophisticated work, with an extraordinary array of colors and an intense expression, has no contemporary parallel anywhere in Europe. Beneath the church are the ruins of Roman buildings and possibly an ancient church. The excavations are accessible whenever the church is open. The entrance to the ruins is on the left as you enter the church and is marked by the sign *"cripta e scavi"* (L2000 *offerta*). Cardinal Rampolla, the man responsible for the excavations, is memorialized in a tomb in the last chapel outside.

Via di S. Cecilia merges here with Via di S. Michele. **Porta Portese,** home to the largest flea market in Rome, lies at the end of Via S. Michele. On the left before you arrive at Porta Portese, the **Chiesa Grande,** at #22 Via di S. Michele, is the temporary home of the painting collection of the **Museo Borghese** (p. 210). Make your way through the parking area up the stairs to the courtyard and turn left to find the collection, which is currently called the Galleria Borghese al S. Michele (tel. 581 67 32; open Tues.-Sat. 9am-2pm, Sun. 9am-1pm; hours may be extended as more staff becomes available; last entrance 30min. before closing).

The various 16th- through 19th-century works are crammed along the apse walls of a former chapel. Just past the ticket counter is Lukas Cranach's *Venus and Cupid,* as well as two pieces by Andrea del Sarto, *Madonna col Bambino* and *San Giovannino* on the right. In the right apse, Bernini showcases his penetrating gaze in three self-portraits as child, adult, and old man, while Rubens treats *The Deposition of Christ* and *Susanna and the Elders.* On the far wall of the right apse hangs Maestro Romana's *La Carità Romana* (Roman Charity).

The museum's highlights are a slew of splendiferous Caravaggios, including *Boy with Basket of Fruit, Self-Portrait as Bacchus, St. Jerome,* and the horrifying *David with the Head of Goliath.* To the left of the apse is a collection of 16th-century art, including Titian's *Venus Blindfolding Cupid, The Flagellation of Christ* and *Sacred and Profane Love.*

Exiting the museum to the right, scurry back up Via di S. Michele and find on your left Via della Madonna dell'Orto. Vignola designed a quirky façade for the **Church of Santa Maria dell'Orto** (closed until further notice) at the street's end. The six obelisks atop the building do make a statement, though it may be at odds with the rest of the flowing Mannerist design. Via Anicia runs left from the church (as you face it) to Piazza di San Francesco d'Assisi to find the **Church of San Francesco a Ripa** (open Mon.-Sat. 7am-noon and 4-7pm, Sun. 7am-1pm and 4-7:30pm), one of the first Franciscan churches in Rome. Inside, you'll find Bernini's *Beata Lodovica Albertoni,* a sculpture rivaling his *St. Theresa in Ecstasy.* Lodovica, carved at the moment of her death, lies in a state of divine euphoria.

SIGHTS

■ West of Viale Di Trastevere

From the church, take Via di San Francesco a Ripa across Viale Trastevere to Piazza San Calisto. This *piazza* spills into Piazza di Santa Maria in Trastevere, home to numerous dogs and expatriates, not to mention the **Church of Santa Maria in Trastevere** (open daily 7am-1pm and 3:30-7pm; Sun. mass at noon and 5:30pm). The church has the distinction of being the first of Rome's churches to be dedicated to the Virgin Mary. Though this structure dates from the 12th century, a basilica was first constructed on the site under San Calixtus (217-222). The mosaics of the Virgin and the 10 saintly women lining the exterior are only a warm-up for the ones inside. The 12th-century mosaics in the apse and the chancel arch depict Jesus, the Virgin Mary, and a bevy of saints and popes in rich detail.

To the north of the church, off Via della Paglia in Piazza Sant'Egidio, is the **Museum of Folklore and Roman Poets** (tel. 581 65 63; Tues.-Sat. open 9am-7pm, Sun. 9am-1pm; L3750), celebrating the dialect poets G.G. Belli and "Trilussa" (Carlo Alberto Salustri). This is not the most sophisticated museum, but kids often like it. There are hokey waxworks and tableaux of traditional Roman life, 19th-century paintings of the Roman carnival and its fireworks, and a ramshackle replica of Salustri's studio, as well as an exhibit introducing G.G. Belli to the uninformed. The building also serves as a cultural center and frequently hosts special exhibits. The employees are fairly helpful and can give you a good sense of the city life, past and present. Call ahead for a tour.

From Piazza Sant'Egidio, Via della Scala leads past a church of the same name, to the **Porta Settimiana.** The gateway is part of the Aurelian Wall, which incorporated Trastevere in its grasp and fended off invasions in the third century. Pass through the gate, where Via della Lungara leads north to the **Galleria Corsini,** Via della Lungara, 10, on the first floor of the Rococo Palazzo Corsini. The Galleria Corsini houses one half of the **Museo Nazionale dell'Arte Antica** (tel. 68 80 23 23; open Tues.-Fri. 9am-7pm, Sat.-Sun. 9am-1pm; L8000; tickets sold up one flight—take the stairs directly in front of you as you enter); the other half hangs in the Palazzo Barberini, (see p. 194). The gallery's seven rooms (numbered clockwise) boast no fewer than 41 portrayals of the Virgin Mary, but despite the consistency of theme the collection's haphazard arrangement is uninspiring. Concentrate on **Room 2,** with an eclectic assortment of 14th- to 17th-century masters. Here Fra Angelico's triptych of the *Last Judgement,* surrounded by other early Renaissance panels, shares wall space with portraits of the *Madonna and Child* by Andrea del Sarto, Murillo, and van Dyck. Titian's *Portrait of Philip II* and Pierino del Vaga's *Portrait of Alessandro Farnese* (Pope Paul III) recreate the 16th century, but the agonies of Rubens's *St. Sebastian Cared for by Angels* fail to distract Hans Hoffman's memorable (and clearly unperturbed) *Rabbit.* In **Room 3** (forward) is a little-known *St. John the Baptist* by Caravaggio and yet another *Madonna and Child,* this one by the Roman early-Baroque master Orazio Gentilleschi. There's not much else to see along the palace's packed walls except in **Room 5,** which houses a bronze model of Bernini's *Davide,* and in **Room 7,** which hosts Guido Reni's *Salome with the Head of John the Baptist* and sorrowful *Lucrezia* (the Roman matron whose suicide after rape by Etruscan king Tarquinius Superbus inspired the establishment of the Roman Republic). On your way out, don't miss Bernini's bust of Alexander VII in **Room I.**

Via Corsini, off Via della Lungara, skirts the side of the palace to meet Rome's beautifully maintained **Botanical Gardens,** at the Largo Cristina di Svezia, 24 (grounds open summer Mon.-Sat. 9am-6:30pm; winter Mon.-Sat. 9am-5:30pm. Greenhouse open Mon.-Sat. 9am-12:30pm; Closed Aug.; L4000). This impressive and well-maintained assemblage of worldly flora stretches from valleys of ferns, through groves of bamboo, to a hilltop Japanese garden. Of special interest are the *Garden of Rose Evolution,* preserving the two founding species from which a rose by any other name has sprung, and the *Garden for the Blind,* which holds some aromatic plants and others with especially tactually interesting leaves.

■ Villa Farnesina

Across the street from the Galleria Corsini stands the Renaissance **Villa Farnesina,** (open Mon.-Sat. 9am-1pm; free) the jewel of Trastevere. Baldassare Peruzzi built the magnificent suburban villa for the Sienese banker and philanthropist Agostino Chigi ("il Magnifico") between 1508-1511. Thought to be the wealthiest man in Europe, Chigi entertained the stars of the Renaissance papal court in his sumptuously decorated *salone* and extensive gardens. Artists, ambassadors, courtesans, cardinals, and even Pope Leo X partook of Chigi's extravagance, and the stories of his largesse are legendary. He once invited the Pope and the entire College of Cardinals to dinner in a gold-brocaded dining hall so imposing that the Pope reproached him for not treating him with greater familiarity. Agostino smiled, ordered the hangings removed, and revealed to his astonished guests that they'd only been eating in his stables. At one infamous banquet in his *loggia* overlooking the Tiber, Chigi led his guests in tossing the gold and silver dishes into the river after every course; needless to say, the shrewd businessman had hidden nets under the water to recover his sunken treasure. The interior decoration of the villa, with frescoes by Raphael, Peruzzi, il Sodoma, and Giulio Romano, smacks of the same decadence. But with the banker's death in 1520, the villa fell into disrepair and was later bought by the Farnese family, after whom it is now named. Today, the villa houses the *Accademia dei Lincei,* a scientific circle that once claimed Galileo as a member.

To the right as you enter the villa, past the security guard's room, you'll find the charming **Sala of Galatea,** painted by the villa's architect, Baldassare Peruzzi, in 1511. The vault displays allegorical and mythological symbols of astrological signs which, taken with the two central panels of *Perseus Decapitating Medusa* and *Callisto* (in a chariot drawn by oxen), add up to a symbolic plan of the stars in the night sky at 9:30pm, November 29, 1466, the moment of Agostino's birth. But the masterpiece of the room, on the long wall opposite the windows, is Raphael's perpetually vibrant fresco of the sea-nymph **Galatea,** plying the seas on a conch-shell chariot drawn by two nasty-looking dolphins. In the panel to the left, Sebastiano del Piombo's one-eyed giant Polyphemus gapes at the nymph with gargantuan lust. Del Piombo also decorated all of the lunettes with scenes from classical mythology except for the one featuring the giant monochrome head which has recently been attributed to Peruzzi. Legend once said that Michelangelo had painted it as a dig to Raphael, to show him that his figures were too small.

The stucco-ceilinged stairway, with its gorgeous perspective details, is reason enough to visit the villa. The stairs ascend to the *piano nobile,* with its two splendid *saloni,* decorated with frescoes to celebrate Agostino's wedding to a young Venetian noblewoman whom he had abducted and kept cloistered in a convent for several years. The **Sala delle Prospettive** is a fantasy room decorated by Peruzzi with views of Renaissance Rome between *trompe l'oeil* columns that are almost real enough to bump into. Above the doorways are eleven Olympian gods sitting atop vine-covered arches guarded by cherubs. The adjacent bedroom, known as the **Stanza delle Nozze** (Room of the Marriage), was frescoed by il Sodoma, who had previously been busy painting the papal apartments in the Vatican until Raphael showed up and stole the commission. Il Sodoma rebounded with an exuberant scene of Alexander the Great's marriage to the beautiful Roxanne. The side walls have other scenes from Alexander's life, in which you might spot a famous Roman ruin or two. Don't forget to take a gander at the original ceiling, decorated with tiny paintings of mythological episodes.

▓ The Janiculan Hill (Gianicolo)

Though you can reach the Janiculan Hill (Gianicolo, in Italian) by bus #41 from the Vatican, the easiest way to ascend the ridge is by the medieval Via Garibaldi on its torturous route up from the Via della Scala in Trastevere (about a 10-min. walk). At the first sharp turn left, a graceful entrance gate stands just off the road. Inside, the liter-

SIGHTS

ary society of **Arcadia** was founded in the early 18th century. The academy was a center for political discussion, simultaneously attempting to maintain the sanctity of the Italian language and set standards of taste in literature. Continue up the steep, swerving roadway and to the unfenced staircase on your right that cuts across the switchbacks. At the top of the hill, the **Church of San Pietro in Montorio** (open daily 9am-noon and 4-6:30pm) was built on the spot once believed to be the site of Saint Peter's upside-down crucifixion.

The church itself houses a *Flagellation* by Sebastiano del Piombo, painted on slate from designs by Michelangelo. Next door, in the center of a small courtyard (open the same hours as the church), is Bramante's tiny **Tempietto** (1499-1502). A brilliant architectural marriage of Renaissance theory and ancient architectural elements, it was constructed to commemorate the site of Peter's martyrdom and provided the inspiration for the larger dome of St. Peter's, built later in the century at the Vatican. From the belvedere before the Tempietto you can see all of Rome; the dome of the Pantheon, Bramante's inspiration, rises straight ahead.

Continue up Via Garibaldi, crossing in front of the fountain, to the Viale Aldo Fabrizi entrance to the **Passeggiata del Gianicolo,** Rome's lover's lane (and then some). This shaded tree-lined road empties out into Piazza Garibaldi, where an equestrian statue of the leader of the Resistance commands yet another spectacular view of the city. The other street leading south out of the *piazza* soon meets Via San Pancrazio, which, in turn, leads to the gravel road leading to the Villa Doria Pamphili. An obelisk marks the center of a circular flower bed which tilts before the towering triple-arch entrance. You can catch the #44, #75, or the #710 that stop near the entrance to the park to get back to Trastevere.

PARKS

Rome's many parks provide a well-deserved refuge from the claustrophobic heat and headache-inducing noise of the city center. Though the Roman sun can turn the grass yellow and crispy in the summer, you can still take advantage of the shade and the lack of concrete. Picnic, nap, or join the Romans in a *passeggiata,* the traditional evening stroll. One of the larger parks, the Villa Borghese, houses three of Rome's major museums. All parks mentioned here are open daily 7am-dusk.

▓ Villa Borghese

The park of the **Villa Borghese** occupies six quiet square kilometers north of the Spanish Steps and Via Veneto. The cool, shady paths, overgrown gardens, scenic terraces, and countless fountains and statues are a refreshing break from the fumes and noise of daytime Rome. Romans have uncharacteristically begun to adopt the American mania for running and you may see them puff their way through the shade of umbrella pines that grow along the paths of the park.

Cardinal Scipione Borghese (originally Scipione Caffarelli, nephew of Pope Pius V), in celebration of becoming a cardinal, hired an architect, Flaminio Ponzio, and a landscaper, Domenico Savino da Montepulciano, to build him a little palace. Completed by Dutch architect Jan van Santen in 1613, the building, with its numerous works of art, was bought by the state in 1902. The park's sculptures, reliefs, and knick-knacks were mostly looted in the 19th century, but a taste of its former stylish self remains with the sprinkling of Borghese dragons, grotesque masks, dilapidated fountains, and floral reliefs around the park.

Abutting the gardens of the Villa Borghese to the southwest is the **Pincio,** first known as the "hill of gardens" *(Collis Hortulorum)* for the monumental gardens the Roman Republic aristocracy built on it. It's graced with the *Moses Fountain,* which depicts the future spiritual leader as just a babe in a basket. In the Middle Ages, it served as a necropolis for those bodies denied a Christian burial. Emperor Claudius'

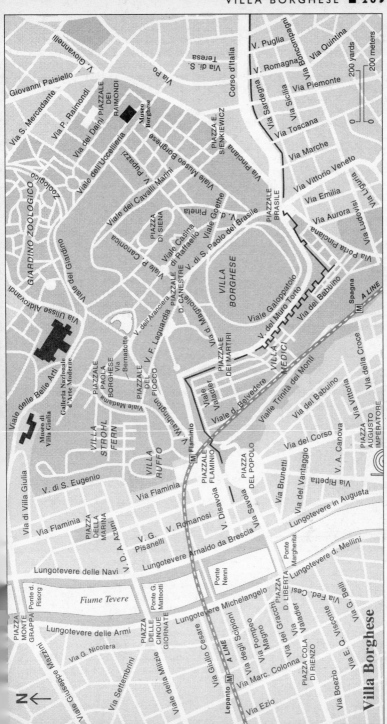

third wife, Messalina, created quite a stir in the nearby **Villa of L. Licinius Lucullus** by murdering the owner. When she later ran off with her lover, her infuriated husband sent his troops to kill her. The Pincio family took possession of the villa in the fourth century, giving the surrounding area its present-day name. Pincio, a favorite cruising and schmoozing spot of the 19th-century rich and famous, lured in fashionable people at sunset who preferred the view from the terrace of **Piazzale Napoleone.** Fleets of Vespas, skippered by gangs of crude teenagers, have replaced the Victorian carriages, but the view, which includes St. Peter's, is still one of the best in Rome. The elegant terrace of restaurant and *caffè* **Casa Valadier,** rising above Piazza del Popolo, offers an even better view, but nothing this good is free. This restaurant has fed an unusual clientele of politicians and celebrities, from Gandhi to Chaing Kai-Shek to Mussolini. The north and east boundaries of the Pincio are formed by the **Muro Torto,** or crooked wall, known for its irregular lines and centuries-old dilapidation. Parts of the wall have seemed ready to collapse since Aurelian built it in the third century. When the Goths failed to break through this precarious pile of rocks in the sixth century, the Romans decided Saint Peter was protecting it and refused to strengthen or fortify it.

The park contains three major museums: the Museo Borghese, the Museo di Villa Giulia, and the Galleria Nazionale d'Arte Moderna. To get to Villa Borghese, take Metro Linea A to **Flaminia,** four stops past Termini heading toward Ottaviano. To reach the **Museo Borghese** (tel. 854 85 77) without walking all the way from the Flaminia Metro stop, take bus #910 from Stazione Termini and get off at Via Pinciana. On the northwestern side of the park, along Viale delle Belle Arti, are the **Galleria Nazionale d'Arte Moderna** (tel. 322 41 54) and the **Museo di Villa Giulia** (tel. 320 19 51). Both are within easy walking distance of the main gate, but the footsore tourist can take tram #19 from Via Flaminia to Viale delle Belle Arti.

MUSEO BORGHESE

Unfortunately, the exquisite **Museo Borghese** (tel. 854 85 77; open Tues.-Sat. 9am-2pm, Sun. and holidays 9am-1pm; last entrance ½hr. before closing; L4000) has been undergoing extensive repairs since 1984, and there's no end in sight. It's all but covered up by a screen of ugly scaffolding. The ground floor and its remarkable sculpture collection remain open, but the gallery's first-floor (and first-rate) painting collection (a cache of Titians, Caravaggios, Raphaels, and Cranachs) has been shipped off for the interim to the Chiesa Grande di San Michele a Ripa in Trastevere (p. 205). Of the three museums in the Villa Borghese, this one caters most to English-speakers, with laminated multi-lingual cards explaining the contents of each room. The sculpture collection includes an extensive assemblage of Bernini's earliest works, mostly mythological in subject.

The temporary entrance to the museum deposits you in **Room 4,** which contains Bernini's exquisite *The Rape of Proserpina,* possibly a collaboration with his father. The sculpture depicts Pluto, god of the underworld, seizing the terrified Proserpina. The indentation where his hand presses her thigh and the single tear on her face are disconcertingly realistic. Pass through **Room 5,** the **Sala dell'Ermafrodito** (*in restauro* in 1996), for a titillating glance at something everyone can relate to, on your way to another Bernini father-son collaboration on a father-son subject, *Aeneas, Anchises, and Aschaniles,* in **Room 6.** Here also is Bernini's *Figure of Truth,* an atypically reclining figure that is not entirely finished; note the narrow marble webbing around the fingers. While **Room 7** remains closed for renovations, you must retrace your steps back through Room 4 to **Room 3.**

In this room, Bernini's *Apollo and Daphne* captures the nymph at the moment of her metamorphosis into a laurel tree. **Room 2** contains the other *David,* Bernini's famed Baroque-era representation of the biblical underdog. Sculpted when the artist was a tender 21 years old, the handsome, grimacing face is Bernini's own. The differences between Bernini's *David* in the Museo Borghese and Michelangelo's *David* in Florence serve as the standard academic comparison for differences between the Renaissance and the Baroque periods of art history. Bernini's *David* is about to release his slingshot; the energy and movement captured in this pose exemplify the intense energy and melodrama of Baroque sculpture. Compare this to the relaxed moment before action in Michelangelo's *David.*

Pauline Bonaparte, sister of the emperor and wife of a Borghese prince, was one of the villa's more eccentric inhabitants and lives on, naked, in **Room I** as *Venus Victrix* by Canova. Asked by a 19th-century tabloid writer if she felt uncomfortable posing disrobed, Pauline replied, "No, the room was quite warm." The *salone* at the villa's center contains some gruesome third-century mosaics of gladiator scenes by Turronuovo and an expansive ceiling fresco that places the visitor in the midst of hostile negotiations between Roman generals. Three Bernini models hide on the side of the room by the gift shop while back past Room 3, in the recently re-opened **Room 8,** a restored Raphael *Desposizione* resides in climate-controlled comfort.

GALLERIA NAZIONALE D'ARTE MODERNA

The **Galleria Nazionale d'Arte Moderna,** Via delle Belle Arti, 131 (open Tues.-Sat. 9am-7pm, Sun. and holidays 9am-1pm; L8000, over 60 or under 18 free) is housed in the forbidding **Palazzo delle Belle Arti,** designed by Cesare Bazzani in 1911 and enlarged in 1933. The white marble façade incorporates four sets of double pillars, and several large pieces of sculpture sit in the foreground, including Guerrini's primitivistic *Personaggi* (1974) and Colla's stark *Grande Spirale* (1952). Inside, the museum's rooms are filled with the best Italian art of the 19th and 20th centuries. The ongoing reorganization of the 19th-century collection makes navigating the museum a bit confusing, but the works on display definitely deserve a visit.

In addition to its splendid permanent display, the museum hosts intriguing special exhibits. Just past the ticket counter, the entrance hall is adorned with four towering impressions of *Spring* by Italian Art Nouveau painter Galileo Chini; try standing as far back as possible to see them as a unified series. The corridor to the right leads to a sequence of rooms housing art from the first half of the 20th century. Look for Gustav Klimt's *The Three Ages of Man* in **Room I.** In **Rooms 2** and **3** reality is completely shattered in Braque's Cubist *Still Life,* the Italian Futurist works of Giacomo Balla, and Mondrian's geometric color compositions, as well as in the fly-in-the-face constructions of Dadaist Duchamp. The **veranda** holds a mixed bag of 20th-century figure sculpture—a welcome interlude from Rome's ubiquitous ancient and Renaissance works. **Room 4** is home to Balla's clever *Noi Quattro nello Specchio (We Four in the Mirror),* in which the artist and his subjects stare out at you, while the painting on the canvas is from your perspective. Gregorio Sciltian's marvelous *Bacchus at the Hostelry* hangs with sleek lines and brilliant color in **Room 5,** along with works by Alberto Zivieri. Filippo de Pisis and his colleagues in **Room 6** show off Impressionist street scenes. The broad **salone** is broken up into numbered sections. In this wide range of works from the '20s, '30s, and '40s, Fortunato Depero's inlaid cloth *Festival of War* **(Enclave F)** mocks the hypocrisy of war. **Enclave D** pays tribute to women in paintings by Casorati, Conti, Campigli, and Tozzi.

On the other side of the entrance hall, the west wing of the gallery holds late 19th-century works. First, pass down a corridor and through a veranda of 1920s Impressionist country scenes. Several walls of the rooms are dominated by Gaetano Previati's expansive multi-frame works. In his sensational *Fall of the Angels,* a tempestuous trail of cherubs sweeps violently across a triptych of mustard-yellow canvases. Balla's more serene impression of the *Villa Borghese* adorns the back wall. Up the stairs from the veranda, there is a roll call of Impressionists—works by Cézanne, Van Gogh, Degas, Rodin, Courbet, and Monet—and a room full of busts by Vincenzo Gemito. The rest of the museum is under construction, but don't miss the beautiful garden tucked behind the entrance hall at the back of the building.

MUSEO NAZIONALE DI VILLA GIULIA

A short walk towards the river along Viale delle Belle Arti takes you back two and a half millenia to the **Museo Etrusco di Villa Giulia** (open Tues.-Sat. 9am-7pm, Sun.

9am-1pm; L8000), which houses the **Etruscan museum.** Etruscan art has undergone an interesting re-evaluation. In the 18th century, Etruscan sculpture was considered a crude derivative of Greek art, while today Etruscan art is extolled for its elegance, stylization, and expressiveness, which has a distinct affinity with modern forms. Villa Giulia was built under Pope Julius III, who reigned from 1550 to 1555. He was criticized by his contemporaries for leading a rather frivolous life in the middle of the Council of Trent. A poet of the day recorded for eternity the fiasco that erupted when Julius flightily appointed a 17-year-old monkey trainer to an official post. Julius's playhouse was designed by Vignola, with some input from Michelangelo, in 1551. More conservative popes have since stripped away some of the decorative sculpture; they did agree, however, to preserve Vignola's nymphaeum as a cool and attractive refuge from the heat. The villa now contains artifacts from pre-Roman civilizations. Every town from here to Florence seems to host an Etruscan museum, but Rome grabbed the best bits, all displayed here with care. Look carefully at the smaller bronzes: modern sculptors like Giacometti owe their inspiration in part to the tiny bronze warriors of Todi.

Immediately as you enter, just beyond the left portico, two rare, antiquated Etruscan sculptures of a centaur and of a youth riding a centaur welcome you to **Room 1.** Like most of the other Etruscan sculptures, the subject is animated, stylized, and upbeat, though these particular sculptures are actually funeral relics discovered in tombs. The Etruscans believed that the afterlife was as boring as the present life and were careful to supply the dead with objects that would keep them amused. A set of stairs in **Room 5** darts down to a reconstruction of a tomb dating from the sixth century BC, with two funeral chambers (they might be bigger than the double-rooms at your *pensione*), similar to the tombs in the necropolis at Cerveteri.

Room 7 contains strikingly realistic sixth-century BC statues of Apollo, one of the little tyke with his mother and the other of him grown up and fighting. They are set up in their original position, perched atop a temple roof silhouetted against the sky. The sculptures are supposedly the work of Vulca—the only Etruscan sculptor known today—whose reputation was so great that the king of Rome had him build the Temple of Jupiter on the Capitoline in 509 BC. **Room 9** contains a masterpiece of terracotta sculpture: a sarcophagus depicting a deceased man and his wife kicking back as though at a BBQ or cocktail party.

The Etruscans took great advantage of their wealth of copper and bronze, fashioning strikingly modern and kitschy pieces, such as chariot-shaped incense burners and urns shaped like huts. **Room 15** (after Room 10 they are numbered back to the entrance on the upper floor) holds the much-praised Chigi Vase (or wine pitcher), an exquisite example of proto-Corinthian handiwork from the seventh century BC, decorated with detailed hunting scenes and the judgement of Paris. **Room 31** hosts a long, hollow oak tree trunk once used as a coffin—the bones of the deceased are still inside as proof. For a more personal look at Etruscan life, **Room 33** exhibits 2,000-year-old cylindrical "beauty-cases" and their miraculous contents found in tombs in the region. Bronze mirrors and the small set of dentures on display were in these elaborately carved bronze cases. The largest ever found, the *Cistae Ficorini,* was probably a wedding gift given to a prominent couple. This is indicated not only by its overall size, but also by the size of the three bronze feet on which it stands.

Villa Giulia hosts **evening concerts** by the Santa Cecilia music society during the month of July; ticket prices vary greatly depending on the event. For concert information and schedules, visit the Villa Giulia or call 322 65 71. Tickets are available at the museum Tues.-Sat. 10am-2pm, Sun. 10am-1pm, and on the day of the performance from 6pm to intermission.

ELSEWHERE IN VILLA BORGHESE

If you come to Villa Borghese in the afternoon and find all the museums closed, do not abandon hope; art is rampant even along the paths. In the **Giardino del Lago** (Garden of the Lake), find Jacopo della Porta's Tritons looking suspiciously like the ones in Piazza Navona. These are the real thing, moved here in 1984—the ones in

Piazza Navona are copies. In the lake itself is a **Temple of Aesculapius.** Get a pictur-esque close-up from a rowboat (rentals daily 10am-8pm; L4000 per person per 20min., with a 2-person minimum.) Finally, there is an imitation medieval fortress, now known as the **Museo Canonica,** Viale P.Canonica, 2 (tel. 884 22 79; open Tues.-Sat. 9am-7pm, Sun. 9am-1:30pm; L3750, L2500 with student ID, over 60 and under 18 free), just off Via Canonica to the east of the lake. The home and studio of artist Pietro Canonica until his death in 1959, this museum houses a collection of his sculp-tures from the late 19th and early 20th centuries.

To see where the mildly wild things are, visit the **Giardino Zoologico** (tel. 321 65 64), the Villa's zoo, Viale del Giardino Zoologico, 3 (open summer daily 8:30am-7:30pm, winter 8:30am-5pm; L10,000, children under 1.3m and people over 60 free). The stroller-accessible zoo confines antelope, wolves, a giraffe, tigers, elephants, seals, and stray cats. There's even an aquarium with penguins. L10,000 may seem fairly steep for this little zoo, but admission also gets you into the **Museum of Zoology** (tel. 321 65 86; open daily 9am-1:30pm and 2:30-4pm), accessed from inside the zoo. Extensive mammal and bird specimens are on display, though reptiles, amphibians, and fish are poorly represented.

North of Villa Borghese are the **Priscilla catacombs,** Via Salaria, 430, before Via Antica crosses Via Ardeatina (tel. 86 20 62 72; open Tues.-Sun. 8:30am-noon and 2:30-5pm; admission L8000). The catacombs, along with the wilder **Villa Ada,** are most easily reached by the #57 bus from Termini or the #56 from Via del Tritone. Get off at Piazza Vescovio and walk down Via di Tor Fiorenza until you arrive at the Piazza di Priscilla, where you'll find the entrance to the park and the catacombs.

■ Other Parks

VILLA ADA

Once the gardens and residence of King Vittorio Emanuele III, the partially public park welcomes joggers and strollers alike with its wooded paths and ponds. Also in the park are the Egyptian Embassy and the **Priscilla Catacombs,** Via Salaria, 430 (p. 213). Villa Ada is located off Via Salaria in the north of the city. Take bus #57 from Ter-mini or #56 from Via del Tritone to Piazza Vescovio; walk down Via di Tor Fiorenza until you reach Piazza di Priscilla and the entrance to the park.

VILLA DORIA PAMPHILI

The Villa Pamphili sprawls behind the Gianicolo, among the hills west of Trastevere. The park, dotted with Roman umbrella pines, is a favorite among Romans for dog-walking and pick-up soccer. There are plenty of monuments, gardens, fountains, waterfalls, and statues, as well as surprising views of the cupola of St. Peter's. In sum-mer, concerts are held near the gate of Porta S. Pancrazio (see p. 235). From Largo Argentina or Trastevere, take bus #44, 75, or 710 to the city wall at the top of a big hill, then walk up Via Dezza to Via di Vascello to the park entrance.

BOTANICAL GARDENS

Though you may hesitate to pay for shelter from the summer heat, the Botanical Gar-dens in Trastevere are well worth the nominal price. Located at the end of Via Corsini in Largo C. di Svezia, just north of the Porta Settimania off the Via della Lungara, the gardens are filled with well-labeled specimens of trees and flowers, which remain green even when the rest of Rome is sick and yellow (open summer Mon.-Sat. 9am-5:30pm; winter Mon.-Sat. 9am-5pm; closed Aug.; greenhouse open daily 9am-12:30pm; L4000, children under 6 free).

GIANICOLO

The ridge of the Janiculan Hill is now the favored haunt of sex-starved Roman cou-ples, though this does not make the view of the city any less spectacular. On clear days you can see the Alban Hills and the mountains of Abruzzi. From the Vatican, take bus #41; from Trastevere, bus #44, 75, or 710 will take you to the residential district of Monteverde, a 10-minute walk south of the park. Or climb the tortuous Via Garibaldi from Via della Scala, off Via della Lungara in Trastevere.

CAMPIDOGLIO

Though the *piazza* itself may broil under the summer sun, the Campidoglio actually hides a very pleasant park, the **Belvedere di Monte Tarpeio**—the perfect spot for recovering from a tour of the Forum. With the Palazzo dei Senatori at your back, the Via delle Tre Pile climbs left from the front balustrade to the park at Piazzale Caffarelli. The southern side of the hill is planted with trees and traversed by paths open to the public.

AVENTINE HILL

The sacred precincts of the Aventine Hill shelter two formal gardens filled with orange trees and roses. The parks offer stunning views of the Capitol and of southern Rome. The Clivio Savello from Piazza di Bocca della Verità and the Clivio di Pubblico from the Circus Maximus converge on the gardens and their churches. Up Via di Santa Sabina, the **Piazza dei Cavalieri di Malta** hides Rome's famous keyhole with a perfectly framed view of the dome of St. Peter's.

PARCO DEL CELIO

A well-guarded secret, the Villa Celimontana and the surrounding Parco del Celio offer a verdant antidote to the dust of the Forum and the cantankerous tourists in the Colosseum. Once a private estate, the villa now welcomes Romans of all ages (particularly children, who come for the playground) to its fountain-filled avenues and flowering stretches of greenery. The park hosts concerts throughout the summer, including the summer program of the Alexanderplatz jazz club; call the club or check the *Trova Roma* section of Thursday's *La Repubblica* for dates and times. From the Colosseum or the eastern exit of the Forum, walk south on Via di Gregorio Magno toward the Baroque church of the same name. From there, the ancient Clivio di Scauro ascends to the park entrance.

CAMPO VERANO

For folks with a taste for the macabre, Rome's largest public cemetery makes an interesting stroll, with paths amidst funeral monuments both grandiose and humble. Stairs inside the Catholic cemetery's chapel lead to a maze of underground tombs lined with fresh cut flowers. Extraordinary landscape and architecture shifts as you move through the cemetery. The entrance is to the right of the Basilica San Lorenzo Fuori le Mura, in the San Lorenzo district (open daily 8am-6pm).

JEWISH CEMETERY

Located next door on the far side of the cemetery at Campo Verano (ask the entrance attendant for directions; open daily 7:30am-6pm, Oct.-March 7:30am-5pm). Take bus #492 from Termini to Piazzale Verano.

VILLA TORLONIA

This former estate of Mussolini is now a public park. The Neo-Classical house is on the verge of collapse, but palm trees and shady benches line the paths of the grounds. Take bus #36 from Termini or #60 from Trastevere and Via del Tritone to Via Nomentana. Get off four or five stops after Porta Pia.

Vatican City

Occupying 108.5 independent urban acres entirely within the boundaries of Italy's capital, the Vatican City is the last toehold of the Church that once wheeled and dealed as a mighty European power. Since the Lateran Treaty of 1929, the Pope has exercised all legislative, judicial, and executive powers over this tiny theocracy, but must remain neutral in Italian national politics and Roman municipal administration. As the spiritual leader for hundreds of millions of Catholics around the world, however, the Pope extends his influence far beyond the walls of his city. The nation manages to preserve its independence by minting coins (in Italian *lire* but with the Pope's face), running an independent postal system, and maintaining its own army in the form of the Swiss Guards, who continue to wear flamboyant uniforms designed by Michelangelo.

RECENT HISTORY

The Church came out of World War II with renewed strength and vigor and has since spread its message globally, particularly in Eastern Europe and Third World countries. However, in Rome (and in Italy—especially the North), the Church has lost much of its following: less than 10% of Roman citizens attend mass regularly. The Church's responses to modernity have been fraught with complications and contradictions. While Pope Pius XII insisted that the Church would not get involved with politics, a 1950s papal decree forbade all Catholics from associating with the Communist party and from publishing or distributing communist literature. The Church tried (unsuccessfully) to pressure the Christian Democrat party to join forces with the right-wing MSI party in order to block the election of Communist candidates, in spite of the fact that over one-third of Itlay was voting Communist and that in many other Western European countries the Catholic Church was directly affiliated with Socialist parties. Pope John XXIII ushered in moderation in the 1960s when he agreed to open dialogue with the Communist Party, showing a new commitment to amicable relations with non-believers.

In the wake of these liberalizing efforts, the Church called the **Second Vatican Council** in 1962. The aim of the ecumenical council was to reassess and improve relations with other religions and to make the church more accessible to the people. The most visible results of the Council, which disbanded in 1965, include the replacement of Latin in the mass with the vernacular, the increased role of local clergy and bishops in church administration, and the re-evaluation of scriptures.

Since 1981, Pope John Paul II's international approach to papacy, with his overt use of the media and his constant travels, has reflected the Church's intention to establish a more direct relationship with people without the interference of modern politics and parties. The fact that the current pope is Polish (note that Italian newspapers never call him Giovanni Paolo II, but always Wojtyla, his last name) also means that the church is even less tied to the vicissitudes of Italian politics and can commit to the pursuit of Catholic ideals at an international level. The Vatican operates a radio station (105FM, broadcasting daily news in English) and publishes a newspaper, *L'Osservatore Romano*.

Look out, Santa Claus

Ranking among the more bizarre achievements of Vatican II was the removal of certain saints from the official saint roster. St. Christopher, the patron saint of travelers, whose image hung on the rearview mirror of many a car, was deemed never to have existed. The sisters, Pudenziana and Prassede, whose churches stand on the Esquiline Hill (see p. 164), also turned out to be posers. Old legends die hard, though: the churches remain and the depiction of St. Christopher bearing Christ across the water continues to be a popular motif on keychains.

PRACTICAL INFORMATION

On the western bank of the Tiber, Vatican City can be reached from Rome's center by Metro Linea A to Ottaviano (after leaving the station, walk south on Via Ottaviano toward the distant colonnade) or by buses #64 or 492 from Termini and Largo Argentina, bus #62 from P. Barberini, #23 from Testaccio, or #19 from San Lorenzo. A bus connects St. Peter's to the Vatican museums (L2000; buy tickets on the bus), but the walk is only five minutes. The country also has a train station, San Pietro, for official use only.

Pilgrim Tourist Information Office, P. San Pietro (tel. 69 88 44 66 or 69 88 48 66; fax 69 88 51 00), to the left as you face the basilica. Ask for the sheet of useful information, aptly entitled "Useful Information," with just that about the Vatican City. Excellent English spoken by disgruntled people. Book tours of the otherwise inaccessible **Vatican Gardens** (2hrs.; Mon.-Sat. at 10am, except Wednesdays when the Pope's in town; L18,000; gardens open Mon.-Sat. 8:30am-7pm).

The Vatican Post Office, 2 locations in P. San Pietro: one on the left, near the tourist office and another on the right, near the middle of the colonnade. Service from the Vatican City is rumored to be more reliable than from its Italian counterpart. Open Mon.-Fri. 8:30am-7pm, Sat. 8:30am-6pm. Branch office on the second floor of the Vatican Museum (open during museum hours). No *Fermo Posta* available. Packages up to 2kg and 90cm, tied with string, can also be sent from the Vatican. Mail rates are the same as Italian rates.

Public toilets are found on either side of the basilica, near the post office and tourist office.

Papal Audiences are held Wednesday, usually at 10:30am. To attend a Papal Audience, apply in writing to the **Prefettura della Casa Pontificia,** 00120 Città del Vaticano specifying the number of people in attendance and the desired Wednesday date and alternate dates. Otherwise, stop by the office on the Monday or Tuesday before the audience you wish to attend and pick up tickets. The office is beyond the bronze doors to the right of the basilica at the beginning of the colonnade, past the Swiss guards (open Mon.-Wed. 9am-1pm; tickets are free). Audiences are held in the Audience Hall behind the colonnade to the left of the basilica. During an audience, delegates from various countries give readings in their respective languages, after which the Pope gives a message in several languages (Italian, English, French, Spanish, German, and Polish) to about 2000-3000 people, greets groups of pilgrims by name and country, and gives his blessing to all. Seating is limited, so arrive early. **Wear appropriate clothing:** dress formally and cover your knees, shoulders, and midriff! **Multilingual confession** is also available inside St. Peter's. Languages spoken are printed outside the confessionals towards the main altar.

SIGHTS

The pontiff's incomparable collection of architecture, painting, sculpture, decorative arts, tapestries, books, carriages, and cultural artifacts from around the globe merits enormous amounts of your time and energy. The official guidebook thoughtfully offers suggested itineraries for the faint-of-heart and the flagging; it's available at the Vatican Museums and at the tourist office (L12,000).

■ St. Peter's Basilica

St. Peter's is open daily from 7am-6pm from April to September and 7am-7pm from October to March. Admission is free. **Dress appropriately** when visiting—no shorts, miniskirts, sleeveless shirts, or even sundresses allowed, though jeans and a t-shirt are

N←

440 yards
400 meters

PIAZZA CAVOUR
PIAZZA COLA DI RIENZO
PIAZZA ADRIANA
PIAZZA PIA
PIAZZA DELL'UNITA
PIAZZA D. RISORGIMENTO
PIAZZA PIO XII
PIAZZA S. UFFIZIO
PIAZZA D. ROVERE
PIAZZALE DEGLI EROI
PIAZZALE S. M. D. GRAZIE
PIAZZALE GREGORIO VII
PIAZZA S. MARIA A FORNACI

Palazzo di Giustizia

Via Ulpiano
Via Lucr. Caro
Via Cicerone
Via Tacito
Via Virgilio
Via Ovidio
Via Boezio
Via Silla
Via Germanico
Via dei Gracchi
Via Cola di Rienzo
Via Valadier
Via Cassiodoro
Via Crescenzio
Via Alberico II
Via Vitelleschi
Via S. Porcari
Via Triboniano
Via Germanico
Via Leone IV
Via Ottaviano
Via Vespasiano
Via Sebastiano Veniero
Via Candia
Viale Vaticano
Viale Vaticano
Via della Meloria
Via Cipro
Via Angelo Emo
Viale degli Ammiragli
Via Luigi Rizzo
Via S. Simoni
Via di Bartolo

Via Ulpiano
Ponte Umberto I
Lung. Castello
Lungotevere di Tor di Nona
Via dei Coronari
Via del Governo Vecchio
Ponte S. Angelo
V. Banco S. Spirito
Corso Vittorio Emanuele II
Via Giulia
Lungotevere Sangallo
Tiber River
Ponte Vittorio Emanuele II
Lung. di Fiorentini
Ponte Amedeo Aosta
Lungotevere Gianicolo
Lung. in Sassia
Lung. Vaticano

Borgo St. Angelo
Borgo d. Corridori
Via della Conciliazione
Borgo S. Spirito
Borgo Vittorio
Borgo Pio
Via del Mascherino
Via di Porta Angelica

Via d. Stazione di S. Pietro
Via d. Fornaci
Piaz. d. Cavalleggeri
Viale Vaticano
Via II Paolo III
Via Nicolò III
V. d. Crocifisso
V. Leone IX
Via Nicolò V
Via Aurelia

GIANICOLO

CITTÀ DEL VATICANO

Campi Sportivi

Via Aurelia

Vatican City

1 Basilica San Pietro
2 Sacristia
3 Piazza San Pietro
4 Sistine Chapel
5 Vatican Museum entrance
6 Vatican Museum
7 Castel Sant'Angelo

VATICAN CITY

fine. Before braving the scrutiny of the clothing police, though, be sure to explore Bernini's sweeping, elliptical Piazza San Pietro. The obelisk in the center, originally erected by Augustus in Alexandria, is framed by two fountains. Via della Conciliazione, built in the 1930s by Mussolini to connect the Vatican with the rest of the city, opened up a view of St. Peter's that Bernini never intended. He had wanted the spacious marble piazza to greet pilgrims as a surprise after their wanderings through the medieval Borgo. One hundred and forty statues perch above the colonnade. Those on the basilica represent Christ (at center), John the Baptist, and the Apostles (excluding Peter).

The basilica itself rests on the reputed site of its eponym's tomb, and a Christian structure of some kind has stood here since the Emperor Constantine made Christianity the state religion in the fourth century AD. In 1506, with Constantine's original brick basilica showing its age, Pope Julius II called upon Donato Bramante, who designed a new one with a centralized Greek-cross plan—a decision which proved contentious for the next hundred years. When Bramante died before completing his project, Sangallo and Raphael usurped his design and changed St. Peter's to a Latin-cross (whereby one arm of the church is longer than the others). A stickler for symmetry, Michelangelo changed it back to Bramante's original plan in 1546, when, at the age of 72, he was handed the job. But Michelangelo, too, was finished before his project. Whether out of spatial necessity or a desire to best the brilliant architects who came before, the last architect, Carlo Maderno, lengthened St. Peter's nave, in effect turning the church into a Latin-cross plan once and for all. In 1626, 120 years after Bramante had torn down much of the ancient basilica, Pope Urban VIII consecrated the completed building.

As you ascend past the Swiss Guards to the portico of the basilica, gaze into the courtyard they protect. Here, in the first century AD, thousands of Christians were slaughtered—St. Peter was probably among them. The **Porta Sancta** (holy door), the last door on the right, can only be opened by the Pope, who knocks in its bricked-up center with a silver hammer every 25 years for the Jubilee; the next knocking will be in 2000.

St. Peter's interior measures 186m by 137m along the transepts. Metal lines in the floor mark the puny-by-comparison lengths of other major world churches. To the right, Michelangelo's sorrowful **Pietà** is protected by bullet-proof glass, after a hammer-wielding fiend attacked the famous sculpture in 1972, smashing the nose and breaking the hand off the Madonna. The sculpture was Michelangelo's first commission in Rome at the age of 25, and the only one he ever signed (on the sash falling across the Madonna's robe), reputedly after overhearing some onlookers who thought that it was done by a Milanese artist. Christ does not exhibit the physical signs of his violent martyrdom; his suffering is evident in the helpless, piteous way he lies in his mother's lap. This sculpture is significant in that it represents marks of pain, suffering, and death on a purely incorporeal, sublime level, anticipating the ethereal religious art of the Baroque.

Further down the nave on the right, towards the intersection of the two arms of the church, a medieval bronze **statue of St. Peter,** seated on a marble throne, presides over the crossing, his foot worn away by the attentions of the faithful. He is outfitted in full religious regalia on important holidays. The dizzying crossing of the vault is anchored by four niches with statues of saints; Bernini's **St. Longinus,** in the northeast niche, represents the centurion who skewered Christ on the cross and then came to have faith, as an allegory of the conversion of pagan Rome to Christianity. To the left of the altar is the **Treasury** (open Mon.-Sat. 9am-6:30pm; L3000, children L2000), which provides an intimate look at shiny sacred paraphernalia and the magnificent bronze tomb of Sixtus IV.

In the center of the crossing of the two arms, the *baldacchino,* another work by Bernini, rises on spiraling solomonic columns over the plain marble altar, which only the Pope may use. The canopy, cast out of bronze pillaged from the porch of the Pantheon, was unveiled on June 28, 1633, by Pope Urban VIII Barberini. Bees, the symbol of the Barberini family, buzz here and there, while vines climb up the twisting columns toward the cavernous vault of Michelangelo's cupola. The cupola was built with the same double shell as Brunelleschi's earlier dome in Florence, but made much rounder, on the model of the Pantheon. Out of reverence for that ancient architectural triumph, Michelangelo is said to have designed the cupola about a meter shorter in diameter than its predecessor.

In the four corner spandrels dwell exceptional mosaic renderings of Matthew, Mark, Luke, and John, the four reputed chroniclers of Christ. Before the *baldacchino* lies the sunken **confession,** a sumptuous altar marking the site of St. Peter's tomb. The sloping ramps were passionately decorated by Maderno and Martino Frescobaldi. In the apse, more Bernini treasures gleam in marble and bronze. The convoluted **Cathedral Petri** is a Baroque reliquary which houses the original throne of St. Peter. On either side, the **tombs** of Popes Paul III and Urban VIII slumber in mixed-media splendor. To the left of the altar, in the left aisle, and behind the statue of St. Veronica in the crossing, Bernini's last work in St. Peter's, the **monument to Alexander VII,** is enlivened by a bronze skeletal figure of Death raising an hourglass from a fluid marble drapery. Mass is said several times per day in the church, with a particularly beautiful vespers service Sunday at 5pm.

Steps at the crossing, below Bernini's spear-wielding statue of St. Longinus, lead down to the **Vatican Grottoes,** final resting place of innumerable popes and saints. The passages are lined with tombs both ancient and modern, and though the space is modernized and well-lit, it's still creepy. The grottoes lead you out to the entrance of the **cupola.** You can go up by stair or elevator to the walkway around the interior of the dome, or climb some more taxing stairs to the outdoor ledge around the very top of the cupola. From here, you will find perhaps the most expansive and breathtaking view of Rome, starting from the *piazza* in front of the basilica, over the Vatican gardens, all the way to the hazy Roman skyline. If you can't make it up the steps to the cupola, at least take the elevator and then walk along the interior rim of the dome; the view of the colorful floor below is amazing. The cupola closes one hour earlier than the church and may be closed when the Pope is in the basilica: often on Wednesday morning. Admission on foot L5000; by elevator—though there's still a hefty 330-step climb—L6000.

On the left side of the *piazza,* beyond a gate protected by Swiss Guards, is the entrance to the necropolis, one level below the grottoes. A double row of mausoleums dating from the first century AD lies here. Multi-lingual guides remind you that the center of the Catholic Church used to be a pagan burial ground, and tell the entrancing tale of the discovery of **St. Peter's tomb.** In 1939, workers came across ancient ruins beneath the Vatican, and the Church set about looking for St. Peter's tomb secretly because they weren't sure they'd find it. Twenty-one years later, they found the saint's bones in a small aedicule temple located directly underneath the altars of both the Constantinian and modern basilicas. Thus, a 1600-year-old mystery was solved. Archaeology buffs with L10,000 will want the whole tale. Only small, prearranged tours may enter. Apply to the *Ufficio Scavi* (excavation office), beneath the Arco della Campana to the left of the basilica a few days in advance (tel. 69 88 53 18; open Mon.-Sat. 9am-5pm). For those with foresight, an application may be requested before your arrival in Rome. Call the number above, or write to: The Delegate of the Fabbrica di San Pietro, Excavations Office, 00120 VATICAN CITY.

■ Vatican Museums

A 10-minute walk around the Vatican City walls (or the bus that drives from the *piazza* through the Vatican Gardens) brings you to the **Vatican Museums** (tel. 698 33 33 or 69 88 49 47). All the major galleries are open Mon.-Sat. 8:45am-1pm. Easter week, April, May, September, and October the museums are open Monday-Friday 8:45am-4pm, Saturday 8:45am-1pm. Last entrance 45 minuntes before closing. Museums are closed on major religious holidays. Last Sunday of every month open 8:45am-1pm; admission is **free.** Otherwise it's L15,000, L10,000 with an ISIC card, and children under 1m tall get in free.

The Vatican Museums constitute one of the world's great collections of art. Although the entrance price is steep, consider making more than one visit. If you have only one morning, invest some time planning your tour before you go—the galleries are so crowded and the distances between them so great that simply wandering will leave you more frustrated and exhausted than enlightened. The best known and most noteworthy attractions in the collection are the **Pio-Clementine Museum** with its celebrated masterpieces of ancient sculpture, the brilliantly frescoed **Borgia Apartments** and **Raphael Rooms,** Michelangelo's incomparable **Sistine Chapel,** and the eclectic **Pinacoteca,** or picture gallery. From the collections lying off the beaten track, you can choose to see the specialized galleries of **Egyptian, Etruscan, Greek,** or **Roman art,** each housing world-class collections of antiquities. There's also the more esoteric **Pio-Christian Museum** (with early Christian sarcophagi), the exhibition rooms of the **Vatican Library,** or the intermittently-open **Ethnological Museum** (with artifacts from cultures around the globe) and **Historical Museum** (with furnishings from papal households of the past). The remaining collections (tapestries, maps, rare books, and modern religious art) are housed in long corridors leading to and from the Sistine Chapel. You'll see them whether you want to or not.

In their most basic plan, the galleries function as a conduit for taking visitors from the entrance and the Belvedere Courtyard down to the papal apartments and the Sistine Chapel and back again. Two long, parallel corridors funnel the crowds through; at either end cluster the specialized galleries mentioned above. The museum management has laid out four color-coded tours, which you take by following the appropriate arrows. **Tour A** hits only the barest essentials, making a swift trip to the Sistine Chapel and back, while **tour D** hits absolutely everything. **Tour B** leads to a few more rooms than Tour A, but **Tour C** will take clock-conscious art buffs to the magnificent Roman sculptures and Raphael rooms that A and B ignore. Supplement this with your own jaunt to the Pinacoteca for a reasonably comprehensive tour. It's possible to pick and choose your way through. Remember that once you have passed a gallery, it's difficult to retrace your steps.

Just past the ticket-takers, there is a booth renting out portable cassette players with short audio tours: Tour A and the Sistine Chapel (L6000), the Raphael stanze and the Sistine Chapel (L6000), or just the Chapel (L4000). While these are not necessary (especially if you've purchased a guide book), it might help to focus matters amid the crowded bustle.

After the turnstiles, a courtyard sheltering the intricately carved base of Antoninus Pius' column confronts you with the choice of itineraries. Down the corridor and to the right are the **Pinacoteca,** the **Gregorian Profane Museum** (Greek and Roman sculpture), and the **Pio-Christian Museum** (early Christian sarcophagi); to the left, the Simonetti Stairway marks the start of the official routes. At the top and to the right of the first set of stairs is the entrance to the **Egyptian Museum,** with 10 rooms of Egyptian statuary, paintings, coffins, and mummies, and an assortment of ancient Roman statuary carved in Egyptian style.

A corridor skirts the **Cortile della Pigna** (Courtyard of the Pinecone), the uppermost end of Bramante's **Belvedere Courtyard,** once part of the papal summer palace. The structure atop the end of the building to the right is the **Tower of the Winds.** The sundial inside was used in the 16th century to cast doubt on the Julian calendar, leading to the adoption of the current Gregorian calendar. Wheeling about, steps lead down to the evocative **Chiaramonti Museum,** a 300m-long corridor which is really little more than a storeroom for the Vatican's collection of more than 1000 classical busts, statues, altars, and reliefs. Walking through the dusky gauntlet of vacant stares provides eloquent testimony to the grandeur and desolation of a ruined civilization. The **Braccio Nuovo** abuts the midpoint of the corridor. Here, a collection of life-size and larger statues includes the famous **Prima Porta Augustus,** a portrait of the emperor at the height of his political powers, a bust of Julius Caesar, and the piquant, reclining figure of the Nile surrounded by crocodiles, sphinxes, and sixteen *putti* representing the sixteen cubits of the river's annual flood. In the far end of the wing are busts of the more famous Roman emperors.

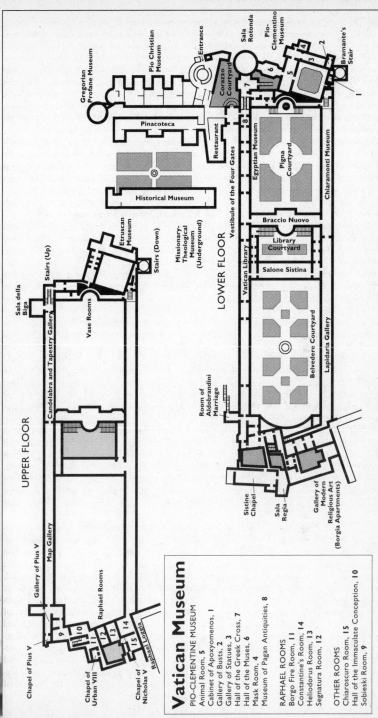

UPPER FLOOR

Gallery of Pius V

Map Gallery

Raphael Rooms

Chapel of Pius V

9

10

12 13 14

15

Raphael Loggia

Chapel of Urban VIII

Chapel of Nicholas V

Candelabra and Tapestry Gallery

Stairs (Up)

Sala della Biga

Etruscan Museum

Vase Rooms

Stairs (Down)

Missionary-Theological Museum (Underground)

Gregorian Profane Museum

Pio Christian Museum

Entrance

Pinacoteca

Restaurant

Historical Museum

Carrazzo Courtyard

Sala Rotonda

Pio-Clementino Museum

Bramante's Stair

4

2

3

5

6

7

1

LOWER FLOOR

Vestibule of the Four Gates

8

Egyptian Museum

Pigna Courtyard

Chiaramonti Museum

Braccio Nuovo

Library Courtyard

Salone Sistina

Vatican Library

Belvedere Courtyard

Lapidaria Gallery

Room of Aldobrandini Marriage

Sistine Chapel

Sala Regia

Gallery of Modern Religious Art (Borgia Apartments)

Vatican Museum

PIO-CLEMENTINE MUSEUM
Animal Room, **5**
Cabinet of Apoxyomenos, **1**
Gallery of Busts, **2**
Gallery of Statues, **3**
Hall of the Greek Cross, **7**
Hall of the Muses, **6**
Mask Room, **4**
Museum of Pagan Antiquities, **8**

RAPHAEL ROOMS
Borgo Fire Room, **11**
Constantine's Room, **14**
Heliodorus Room, **13**
Segnatura Room, **12**

OTHER ROOMS
Chiaroscuro Room, **15**
Hall of the Immaculate Conception, **10**
Sobieski Room, **9**

VATICAN CITY

■ Pio-Clementine Museum

Back-track through the corridor and up the stairs; straight ahead, a square vestibule marks the entrance to the stellar **Pio-Clementine Museum,** the world's greatest collection of antique sculpture. The placid, outdoor Octagonal Court opens off the first three small rooms. Here is where the Vatican Museums were born. Julius II filled the court, originally the centerpiece of the Belvedere Palace, with his first purchases of classical sculpture, thus beginning the long tradition of papal art collecting. In the corner niche to your left (since redecorated by Canova), stands the sublime **Apollo Belvedere,** probably the best-known work of ancient sculpture in existence and once called "the highest ideal of art." The god's placid features and posture (apparently he was holding a bow in one hand and drawing an arrow from his quiver with the other) inspired innumerable Renaissance copies both in stone and on canvas. Clockwise, in the next corner, stands the musculature of the tortured **Laocoön** family, a sculpture which was famous even in antiquity for its convincing grotesqueness. Virgil told the story of Laocoön in his *Aeneid:* the Trojan priest, advising his people against drawing the Trojan Horse into their city, was punished by Athena, the protectress of the Greeks, who sent two sea serpents to devour him and his sons. It is thought that the figures of Laocoön and the son to the left of him were carved from a single piece of marble. Laocoön's raised arm, flexed in a vain effort to escape the serpent, was only discovered and reattached in this century. Many art historians now debate the authenticity of the appendage; if you look closely, the proportions are somewhat off (the arm is smaller than it should be on the original body), and the marble seems to be a different color than the rest.

Two slobbering Molossian hounds guard the entrance to the **Room of the Animals,** a marble menagerie that reveals a lot about the Romans' predilection for verisimilitude in their art and brutality in their sport. Adjacent to the animals is the **Gallery of Statues,** home to Apollo, Hermes, Ariadne, and others, at the end of which are the stone faces in the **Room of the Busts** (with an engaging 1.25-m foot and calf muscle). The **Cabinet of the Masks,** also adjacent to the Room of the Animals, houses the **Venus of Cnidos.**

The **Room of the Muses** opens off of the animal room and is anchored by the inscrutable **Belvedere Torso,** a shattered work thought to represent Hercules sitting on his lion skin. It's said that while Michelangelo was painting his own colossal nudes in the Sistine Chapel, he was once found prostrate before the torso, abasing himself in solitary admiration. In the great **Round Room** beyond are colossal Roman statues, including two of Antinous, the ill-fated lover of Hadrian, one of the Emperor Claudius dressed in a general's uniform (his reputed obesity, lameness, and drool tactfully forgotten), and a breathtakingly atrocious gilded Hercules. The last room **(Greek Cross Room)** of the gallery contains the enormous red porphyry **sarcophagus of St. Helen,** mother of Constantine, in intricate fourth-century relief. Two statues of the lesser-known Egyptian demigods, Bartak and Blythu, hold up the ceiling and ogle a pair of sphinxes.

■ Etruscan Museum

The next flight of the Simonetti Stairway climbs to the recently reopened **Etruscan Museum,** filled with artifacts from the necropoleis of Tuscany and northern Lazio. Especially noteworthy is **Room II,** with the contents of the splendid **Regolini-Galassi Tomb,** a tumulus found intact and full of treasure outside the necropolis at Cerveteri. The case on the right holds the extraordinary bronze chariot and bed with which the deceased seventh-century BC couple were supplied for their journey to the other side. **Room III** contains the rare fifth-century BC bronze Mars of Todi, while in the rooms beyond lie smaller bronzes, terra-cotta, red- and black-figure vases (imported from Greece by wealthy Etruscan traders), and jewelry. At the end of the Etruscan Rooms you can visit the **Rooms of the Greek Originals,** the **Stairway of** the **Assyrian Reliefs,** and the **Vase Collection,** though you might do better to conserve your energies for the long walk ahead.

■ Other Assorted Galleries

Back on the landing of the Simonetti Staircase is the usually closed **Room of the Biga,** housing an ancient marble chariot outfitted with recent wheels and horses. There is also the entrance to the **Gallery of the Candelabra,** named for the ancient marble candle-holders housed there; it also contains more examples of Roman statuary and decorative arts. This is the starting point of the long trudge to the Sistine Chapel, through the **Gallery of the Tapestries,** the **Gallery of the Maps** (with diverting 16th-century views of Italy and the islands of the Mediterranean), the **Apartment of Pius V** (more tapestries—here there is a shortcut stair to the Sistine Chapel), the **Sobieski Room,** and the **Room of the Immaculate Conception** (with horrendous 19th-century murals).

■ Raphael Rooms

From the Room of the Immaculate Conception, a door leads into the first of the four **Raphael Rooms,** the sumptuous papal apartments built by Pope Julius II in the first decade of the 16th century. This is the old papal palace proper, just behind and to the right of the great basilica. Julius had abandoned the apartments of his predecessor Alexander VI Borgia one story below, saying he couldn't live under the portraits of the nefarious Spanish Pope painted there. Instead, he hired the best painters of his own day, including Perugino, Peruzzi, and il Sodoma to decorate a new suite of rooms for himself. Although they had already been working for several years, even these geniuses had to make way for the precocious talent of Raphael Sanzio, who painted the astonishing **School of Athens** as a trial piece for Pope Julius. The Pope was so impressed that he fired his other painters, had their frescoes destroyed, and handed the entire suite of rooms, with a total of 16 walls to be painted, over to Raphael. The commission marked the beginning of Raphael's brilliant Roman career, and on his untimely death in 1520, his students completed the decoration according to his designs.

A trip through the rooms can be confusing because you must view them in reverse chronological order; the flow of traffic is now diverted after the Stanza dell'Incendio, through an outdoor covered walkway, to the Sala di Constantino. To view the rooms in the intended sequence, take a detour from the Sala di Constantino to the **Room of the Chiaroscuri** and the **Chapel of Nicholas V.** The small chapel forms the oldest section of the apostolic palace and was delicately decorated by Fra Angelico between 1447-51, with frescoes depicting events from the lives of St. Stephen and St. Lawrence.

Retracing your steps to the Raphael Rooms, the **Sala di Constantino** (1517-24), mostly painted after Raphael's death, has as its main theme the church's victory over paganism. On the entrance wall, Constantine addresses his soldiers and sees the vision of the cross; on the wall opposite is the baptism of Constantine; on the window wall, Constantine donates the city of Rome to Pope Sylvester; on the wall facing the window, Constantine defeats Maxentius at the Battle of the Milvian Bridge. No slave to subtlety, Raphael's ceiling shows a striking meeting between two opposing icons in which a crumbled ancient pagan statue lies shattered and prostrate before a gleaming gold crucifix.

Next comes the **Stanza d'Eliodoro** (1512-14). The obscure subjects were chosen by Julius to illustrate the miraculous protection afforded by God to a threatened Church. The scenes depict, on the right wall, the Biblical story of the expulsion of Heliodorus from the temple; on the entrance wall is the miracle of Bolsena. Raphael painted Julius himself in the guise of Pope Urban IV who, after the miraculous appearance of blood on an altar linen at Bolsena, instituted the feast of Corpus Christi. Note the Swiss Guards, dressed just as they are today, kneeling on the right. On the long wall is Leo I expelling Attila from the city of Rome; on the fourth wall is

Raphael's depiction of the deliverance of St. Peter from the Tullianum Prison on the Capitoline Hill. Note the interaction of the three different types of light (from the moonlight, the angels, and the soldiers' torches) shining through the prison bars.

The **Stanza della Segnatura** (1508-1511), which popes once used as an office or possibly as a private library, was painted entirely by Raphael and is considered his masterpiece. The four walls represent four branches of learning—theology, law, philosophy, and poetry. On the wall opposite the entrance is the **Disputation of the Holy Sacrament,** in which celebrated doctors of the Church and theologians crowd around a monstrance holding the communion host. On the wall of the entrance itself is the splendid **School of Athens,** in which ancient philosophers and scientists (many of whom Raphael painted with the features of his friends and fellow artists) converse as they stroll through an airy architectural fantasy. In the center, Plato, with the features of Leonardo da Vinci, argues with Aristotle; Euclid, explaining geometry on the ground, has Bramante's face; to the far right of the composition stand Raphael, in three-quarter profile, and his friend and fellow artist, il Sodoma. In the center, the isolated, brooding figure of Heraclitus is thought to be a portrait of Michelangelo, added as an afterthought when Raphael had been given a sneak preview of the Sistine Chapel. Part of what is so remarkable about this fresco is the speed with which it was executed. Frescoes (literally meaning "fresh" in Italian) began with an outline, or cartoon. Then, the plaster was added (usually students did these kinds of menial tasks) and series of holes were poked through to illustrate the design. The plaster dried extremely quickly, so a fresco would have to be fully painted in a day; an artist would concentrate on one small section of a fresco for 15-20 hours. If you look closely at a fresco, you can often see these different sections (i.e. days) where an artist began and ended. In this case, Raphael supposedly drew up the elaborate cartoons in a matter of days. Furthermore, it appears that Raphael spent as much time working on the face of Heraclitus (Michelangelo) as he did on the entire left half of the fresco. The remaining scenes depict Mount Parnassus peopled by classical and contemporary Italian poets including Horace, Virgil, Propertius, Dante, Ariosto, Boccaccio, and Petrarch; opposite are the cardinal and theological virtues, represented by *Gregory IX Approving the Decretals* and *Justinian Publishing the Pandects.*

The final room is the **Stanza dell'Incendio** (the corner of which you passed through before) containing works by Raphael's pupils, including Giulio Romano. By the time of their painting in 1514-17, Pope Leo X Medici had taken up residence in the *stanze,* and portraits of his namesake predecessors dominate the room. The riotous *Fire in the Borgo* depicts a disaster which befell the Borgo in 847 AD and which was miraculously extinguished when Leo IV made the sign of the cross from the *loggia* of St. Peter's. The painting is notable for its depiction of the façade of the old Constantinian basilica, which was pulled down to make way for the new St. Peter's. Other scenes represent the coronation of Charlemagne by Leo I in 800 AD, the victory of Leo IV over the Saracens at Ostia, and, on the window wall, the oath of Leo III. From here you pass through the precious **Chapel of Urban VIII,** decorated by Pietro da Cortona in stucco and frescoes.

■ Borgia Apartments

Depending on the itinerary you are taking, a staircase leads down either to the Borgia Apartments and the Museum of Modern Religious Art or to the Sistine Chapel. The **Borgia Apartments,** named after the infamous Alexander VI Borgia, father of the even more infamous Lucrezia and Cesare, comprise six rooms decorated in 1492-95 by Pinturicchio. Today, all you can see of the decorations are the lunettes and ceiling vaults, as the walls have been covered by the Vatican's collection of modern religious art. The staircase descends into the **Room of the Sibyls,** named for the twelve lunettes, which depict pairs of classical sibyls and Old Testament prophets, foreshadowing Michelangelo's arrangement of the same subjects on the Sistine ceiling. Legend has it that it was in this room that Cesare Borgia had his brother-in-law Alfonso d'Aragone stabbed and then strangled, in order to free up his sister Lucrezia for marriage to Alfonso d'Este, the future Duke of Ferrara. One of Rodin's renowned and multitudinous *Thinker* statues squats nearby, trying to get the story straight. In the room to your left are two remarkable Rodin sculptures and a wall of Matisse drawings of the Madonna and Child.

The other rooms depict members of the Borgia court in the unlikely guise of saints and Biblical figures. Note, in the Room of the Mysteries (Room VI), in the Resurrection, the splendid portrait of the Pope himself, and the central soldier with a lance (possibly a portrait of Cesare). Above the door leading to the Room of the Mysteries, a *tondo* of the Madonna and Child by Pinturicchio may be a portrait of Giulia Farnese, Alexander VI's mistress and mother of the future Pope Paul III. A brisk walk through the collection of Modern Religious Art (mostly unwanted gifts to the Pope from fawning 20th-century artists) will carry you past church vestments designed by Matisse, some pots thrown by Picasso, and a Dalí.

■ The Sistine Chapel

Called "Sistine" after its founder, Pope Sixtus IV, this chapel has served as the chamber in which the College of Cardinals meet to elect a new pope ever since its completion in the 16th century. Its inclusion in the museum tour is somewhat deceiving, since the chapel is really part of St. Peter's Basilica. The door through which you enter is the west entrance, in the altar wall, while the opposite wall forms the proper entrance, opening onto the official state rooms of the Vatican Palace and the second-story *loggia* of the basilica.

The barrel vault of the ceiling, some 22m above the floor, gleams with the results of its recent, celebrated, and hotly debated restoration. Before craning your neck, first prepare yourself by taking in the frescoes on the side walls which predate Michelangelo's ceiling work. On the right wall, scenes from the life of Moses prefigure parallel scenes of the life of Christ, on the left wall. The cycle, frescoed in 1481-83, was completed by a team of artists under the direction of Perugino that included Botticelli, Ghirlandaio, Roselli, Pinturicchio, Signorelli, and della Gatta.

Down the right wall are the *Journey of Moses* (Perugino), *Flight from Egypt* (Botticelli), *Crossing the Red Sea*, *Tablets of the Law*, *Punishment of Korah, Dathan, and Abiram* (Botticelli), and the *Testament of Moses* (Signorelli); on the left wall are the *Baptism of Christ* (Perugino), *Temptation of Christ* (Botticelli), *Calling of the First Apostles* (Ghirlandaio), *Sermon on the Mount, Consignment of the Keys to Peter* (Perugino), and the *Last Supper* (Rosselli). Botticelli, Ghirlandaio, and Fra Damante painted the series of 26 early popes who stand in the niches between the high windows. On the right side of the far wall (the east entrance) is the *Disputation Over the Body of Moses,* by Matteo de Lecce, which replaces a lost work by Signorelli. On the left side of the wall is Arrigo Paludano's *Resurrection,* which fills the place once occupied by a Ghirlandaio piece.

THE SISTINE CEILING

Above stretches the undaunted genius, brave simplicity, and brilliant coloring of Michelangelo's unquestioned masterpiece; some have called these powerful frescoes the greatest works of Western art ever created. The fact that the Florentine sculptor and architect had the commission foisted upon him unwillingly (it's said that Bramante, worried that the genius might take over his project—the construction of the new basilica—hinted to Pope Julius that Michelangelo should paint the ceiling instead) only makes his brilliant success more impressive. The work is wholly Michelangelo's: he had never worked in fresco before and kept his assistants only long enough to learn the technique from them before settling down to a frenzied four years of solitary painting.

He painted not flat on his back, but standing up and bending backwards, and never recovered from the strain to his neck and eyes. The design of the frescoes is apparently Michelangelo's as well. The fledgling painter chose to depict the history of mankind before the coming of Christ, thus linking the ceiling decoration with the stories of Moses and Christ on the side walls. He divided the vault into a monumental architectural scheme, each enclosing a separate scene from Genesis. From west to east these are *Separation of Light from Darkness, Creation of the Sun, Moon and Planets, Separation of Land and Sea and the Creation of Fishes and Birds, Creation of Adam, Creation of Eve, Temptation and Expulsion from Paradise, Sacrifice of Noah, Flood,* and *the Drunkenness of Noah.* These are framed by the famous *ignudi,* contorted naked male youths who cavort among the decorative vaulting. In the four spandrels are depictions of *David and Goliath, Judith and Holofernes, the Brazen Serpent,* and *The Punishment of Hanan.* These are surrounded by monumental figures of Old Testament prophets and classical sybils, some pondering the events of Christian history to come and others holding aloft books of revealed wisdom.

LAST JUDGEMENT

The wall behind the altar, covered by Michelangelo's **The Last Judgment,** was at last revealed in 1994 after a lengthy restoration. He painted his turbulent vision of the apocalypse 23 years after the completion of the ceiling, and the events of the intervening years, including the sack of Rome and the Protestant Reformation, seem to have left the artist bitter and disillusioned. Many interpreted the turmoil in the Christian world at this time as divine punishment for the blatant corruption expanding throughout Europe. You'll notice that the location of *The Last Judgment,* above the altar, places the most sacred part of the church in the mouth of hell.

Amid the chaotic swarms of unclothed mortals, the figure of Christ as Judge hovers in the upper center, surrounded by Mary (who averts her eyes from the grotesque spectacle), and his saintly entourage. On the left, angels pull the lucky souls to heaven, while on the right, demons cast the damned souls into the abyss. The ferryman Charon carts the unfortunate crew of evil-doers across the river. In the lower right-hand corner, Minos, Master of the Underworld, sports a coiling snake and assears and bears a striking resemblance to Biagio da Cesena, who, speaking for Pope Paul III, pestered Michelangelo with objections to his use of "shameless nudity in a holy space."

After the renovation of the frescoes, art historians quibbled for years over whether the restoration had improved the works. Regardless of these speculations, however, the ceiling was on the verge of collapse from damage wrought by time and weather, and the frescoes were in danger of peeling completely away from the ceiling and walls. The restorers, whether they removed a crucial layer or not, reattached the frescoes and repaired the ceiling and walls. **Refrain from taking flash photos,** even if you see others around you doing it, since the light of the flash is detrimental to the frescoes. You can buy much better shots (cheaper than using your own film) on professional postcards. The best way to view the ceiling is by using a hand-held mirror, rather than craning your neck to look up, though the giddy feeling of staring straight up at superhuman beauty can be a treat in and of itself.

■ The Pinacoteca and Other Galleries

From the exit along the left-hand wall of the Chapel, a series of corridors returns you to the Galleries of the Library and the long walk back to the Belvedere. The corridors take you through rooms containing artifacts and reliquaries collected during the reigns of various popes. The second room, the **Chapel of St. Pius V,** might slow you on your way to the entrance for a glance into the reliquaries case to the left; the case contains fragments of saints retrieved from the treasury of Sancta Sanctorum. A short way up on the left, the **Room of the Aldobrandini Marriage** houses a series of rare ancient Roman frescoes, including the celebrated wedding scene, set in a flowering park filled with animals and architectural fantasies. The corridor continues past cases of awful modern religious art (try to miss the *Mute Swans of Peace*) and antique globes and maps. The Sistine Hall, leading off the main corridor to the right, is used for exhibits from the Vatican Library's superb collection of books and manuscripts. Although most visitors rush through this part of the museum, keep in mind that the

The Sistine Chapel Ceiling

East Wall: Exit

North Wall: Life of Christ

South Wall: Life of Moses

West Wall: Last Judgment (Entrance)

A B 10 C

17 21 E 20 E 11 15

F F F F F F

1 2 3 4 5 6 7 8 9

F F F F F F

16 18 E 19 E 6 E 12 D

13 14

BIBLE STORIES
A The Punishment of Hamen
B David Slaying Goliath
C Judith and Holofernes
D The Brazen Serpent
E Jesus' Forefathers
F The Ignudi

FROM THE CREATION TO THE FLOOD
1 God Separates Light from Darkness
2 Creation of Sun, Moon, and Plant Life
3 God Separates the Water and the
    Earth, and Creates Life in the Sea
4 Creation of Adam
5 Creation of Eve
6 Original Sin and Expulsion from the
    Garden of Eden
7 Noah's Sacrifice
8 The Flood
9 Noah's Intoxication

THE PROPHETS AND SYBILS
10 Zacharia
11 Delphic Sybil
12 Isaiah
13 Cumaean Sybil
14 Daniel
15 Libyan Sybil
16 Jonah
17 Jeremiah
18 Persian Sybil
19 Ezekiel
20 Eritrean Sybil
21 Joel

"one-way" system prevents you from returning to the corridors once you've gone to another part of the museum. When you reach the end of the corridor, you will find yourself again in the Vestibule of the Four Gates, from which the stairs on the opposite side lead up to the Sistine Chapel. On the left is the **Atrium of the Four Gates** and the **Court of the Pinacoteca,** which offers a sweeping view of St. Peter's Basilica.

The **Pinacoteca,** the Vatican's eclectic picture collection, is entered from the open courtyard to the right, immediately after the ticket booths. The Pinacoteca houses a collection of paintings and tapestries dating from the 11th to the 19th centuries. **Room 1** houses the oldest picture in the gallery, a curious keyhole-shaped wood panel of the *Last Judgement* dating from the 11th century (under restoration), which provides an interesting contrast to Michelangelo's monumental composition of the same subject in the Sistine Chapel. In **Rooms 2 and 3,** Gentile di Fabriano's *Scenes from the Life of St. Nicholas of Bari* is a treat. Look for the resurrection of three children who had been found cut up in pieces in a barrel. Stories of the same saint painted by Fra Angelico are here as well, along with his *Madonna and Child,* Filippo Lippi's *Coronation of the Virgin,* and Benozzo Gozzoli's *Madonna of the Girdle.*

Room 4 contains fragments of a huge fresco by Melazzo da Forlì which originally decorated the apse of the basilica of SS. Apostoli off the Via del Corso. Adjacent is another da Forlì fresco, which depicts Sixtus IV conferring the job of librarian on the humanist Bartolomeo Platina. The future Pope Julius II, dressed as a tonsured cardinal, stands at his uncle Sixtus' right hand. In **Room 6,** Vivarini's polyptych, *St. Anthony and Other Saints* is on the far wall. The startling **Pietà** of Carlo Crivelli is also here. **Room 7** contains Perugino's *Madonna and Child* and a *Coronation of the Virgin* by Pinturicchio. In **Room 8,** three important works by Raphael (from left to right: the *Madonna of Foligno,* the *Transfiguration,* and the *Coronation of the Virgin*) are surrounded by tapestries copied from the master's cartoons that were meant to hang along the lower walls of the Sistine Chapel.

Room 9 houses Giovanni Bellini's *Pietà* and a mutilated Leonardo da Vinci panel of St. Jerome. Prior to its discovery it had been cut in two pieces, one of which had served as a coffer lid, the other as a stool in a shoemaker's shop. This is a reproduction of the original, which is being restored. **Room 10** contains Titian's massive *Madonna of San Nicoletta dei Frari* (look for Titian's mark on the wall of the painting) and Veronese's elegant *St. Helena,* posing with noble reservevenear Paris Bordone's *St. George and the Dragon.*

In **Room 11** is Il Barocci's *Il riposo in Egitto.* **Room 12** brings you into the passionate but cruel world of Baroque devotional art. Here you can see Caravaggio's sensual and sensational *Deposition from the Cross* (note the unusual portrayal of the Virgin Mary as an old woman) and Nicholas Poussin's grisly *Martyrdom of St. Erasmus* (who had his intestines rolled out on a winch). **Room 14** contains a fanciful series of still lifes of fruit and flowers by Pietro Navarra. In **Room 15,** Pope Benedict XIV glowers down at the bewildered spectator, while Thomas Lawrence's full-length portrait of King George IV, in full coronation robes, seems wildly out of place. There is also a series of astronomical observations showing the various phases of the moon, executed for the observatory at Bologna by Donato Cretti. Animals, icons, and plaster maquettes by Bernini fill up the remaining three rooms.

The **Gregorian Profane Museum,** on the left as you make your way back to the museum entrance, is named for its collection of secular Greek and Roman art rather than for any naughtiness on display. Rarely visited, it makes a peaceful and low-key change from the bustle and bombast of the other museums. Look for the statues of Marsyas, the satyr who dared to play Athena's pipes (and was skinned alive for doing so), and the fragmentary *Chiaramonti Niobid.* Niobe, a mother of 14 children, had taunted Leto for only having given birth to only two. Unfortunately, the two were Apollo and Diana, and the outraged gods avenged their insulted mother by shooting down all fourteen of the Niobids. The statue shows one daughter turning to flee the heavenly assault; the crinkled folds of her flowing dress are a superb example of Hellenistic carving. The gallery also contains numerous, finely carved reliefs from imperial monuments (many of which represent actual buildings of ancient Rome) and, almost hidden in a sky-lit hemicycle toward the back, a breathtakingly noble and sorrowful *Dacian Captive* from Trajan's Forum.

The **Pio-Christian Museum,** with its entrance next door, displays artifacts of a fascinating historical synthesis—the marriage of the Greco-Roman sculptural tradition to the new iconography of the Christian Church. The sarcophagi and statuary here date from the earliest centuries AD, when the Roman Empire and its artistic vocabulary were still alive and well. Look for the small statue of the *Good Shepherd* among the many intricately carved sarcophagi. The **Ethnological-Missionary Museum** displays non-Christian religious articles alongside missionary-inspired works from Third-World cultures. The **Historical Museum** contains fairly recent papal artifacts, including armor, guard uniforms, and carriages.

■ Near Vatican City: Castel Sant'Angelo

A short walk down Via d. Conciliazione from St. Peter's stands the massive **Castel Sant'Angelo** (tel. 687 50 36; open winter daily 9am-2pm, summer 9am-7pm, but closed on 2nd and 4th Tues. of each month; L8000, EU citizens under 18 or over 60 free). Built by the Emperor Hadrian (117-138 AD) as a mausoleum for himself and his family, the edifice has served the popes of Rome, in the centuries since, as a convenient and forbidding fortress, prison, and palace. The towering complex consists of the mausoleum, a suite of palatial Renaissance apartments built on top, and concentric rings of fortifications, including the Leonine Wall extending to the Vatican Palace. Hadrian, an architect as well as emperor, designed the mausoleum in imitation of his predecessor Augustus' more modest tomb across the river. Later, as the city fell to barbarian depredations, panicked Romans quickly converted the imposing structure for defensive purposes.

When the city was wracked with plague in 590 AD, Pope Gregory the Great is said to have seen an angel sheathing his sword at the top of the citadel; the plague then abated, and the edifice was dedicated to the angel and has been called by his name ever since. During the sack of Rome in 1527, Pope Clement VII ran for his life along the covered wall between the Vatican and the fortress, while the imperial invaders took pot-shots at his streaming white papal robes. Pope Paul III used the fortress for more leisurely pursuits, building and decorating a sumptuous suite of apartments over the ancient foundations, which were used as a prison for heretics and other troublemakers, including the revolutionary astronomer Giordano Bruno and the thieving artist Benvenuto Cellini. The colossal fortress now contains a museum of arms and artillery, but the papal apartments and the incomparable panoramic view of Rome seen from them are the real reasons to pay a visit.

To enter the castle, walk past the front along the river from St. Peter's to the next side of its pentagonal bastions, and descend into the former moat. From the ticket booth, a ramp leads up to the fortress's ramparts and four circular bastions, each named for one of the four evangelists. From the ramparts you can see the massive cement remains of Hadrian's round base and bits of the travertine marble that once completely encased it. A bridge crosses into the base itself, where a ramp (built by Alexander VII) rises steeply over the tomb chamber of the emperor. The **Court of the Angel,** containing the original marble statue of the angel, leads into the **Sala di Apollo,** whose *grotteschi* frescoes were painted in imitation of ancient Roman designs. Two rooms adjoining the *Sala di Apollo* display 15th- and 16th-century paintings, while from the adjacent semicircular **Courtyard of Alexander VI** you can descend to a dank labyrinth of prison cells and storerooms (including endless rows of vats where oil was kept for boiling and pouring on besiegers) or stop to study the enormous crossbows and cannonballs that once served as the castle's defenses. Upstairs from the courtyard is the bathroom where Clement VII soaked in a tub fit for a Medici prince. Another stairway climbs to a **Gallery** that circles the citadel, decorated at intervals with *grotteschi*, stuccos, *loggie* built by Popes Julius II and Paul III, a bar, and a souvenir stand. Relax with a *caffè latte* (L2000) and write a postcard while you enjoy one of the best views in Rome.

Yet more stairs lead up to the extravagant **Papal Apartments,** including the over-decorated **Sala Paolina** (with wall paintings of Hadrian and the castle's patron angel), the **Camera del Perseo** and **Camera di Amore e Psyche** (frescoed and filled with period furniture), and the **Hall of the Library** (frescoed with scenes of cavorting sea gods and lined with an unusual set of stucco reliefs). Keep climbing through some dull exhibition rooms until you reach the broad **terrace.** Under the watchful eye of the bronze angel, the whole of Rome spreads out below. To the right is St. Peter's and the long wings of the Vatican Museums. You can also see the Pantheon, the Vittorio Emanuele II Monument, a dozen or more Baroque domes, the Tiber River, and the green parks of the Gianicolo. Outside, the walls of the fort now enclose a large park, while the marble **Ponte Sant'Angelo,** lined with Bernini's angels, leads back across the river.

Entertainment

Since the days of bread and circuses, Roman entertainment has been a public affair—concerts under the stars, street fairs with acrobats and fire-eaters, Fellini-esque crowds of slick Romeos, modern-day minstrels and maestros, and enchanted foreigners flooding *piazze* and *caffè*. Clubs are not necessarily an integral part of nightlife, especially during the summer, when the social scene spills out of doors. You're more likely to find Romans sipping beer or coffee in a bar, eating *gelato* near a fountain, munching on *cornetti* outside an all-night bakery, or contemplating a radical lifestyle in a *centro sociale*. By night, the monuments of Rome, including the Forum, the Colosseum, St. Peter's, and the Trevi Fountain, are flooded with light, making a walk, drive, or even a bus ride past these sights a spectacular finish to a day of touring. If you must have organized entertainment, however, look in Thursday's edition of **La Repubblica,** which includes *Trovaroma,* a comprehensive list of concerts, plays, clubs, movies, and special events in the city and the surrounding area.

■ Music Clubs

Rome's music clubs attract a hip Italian crowd; some even have dancing and are usually much cheaper than discos. If you're getting sick of the meat-market scene at the Pantheon, Spanish Steps, or at the foreigner-frequented pubs, music clubs usually have a more manageable Italian crowd. There are quite a few "Piano Bars" in the city, but unless you like to mingle with short, balding Italian men with lots of jewelry, many of these will not be particularly enticing; we've listed a few that are not garden variety cheese-'n-sleaze joints. Most are officially *associazioni culturali,* which means they are private; some require a "membership" requiring you to pay a one-time fee for a card. Memberships are usually not exclusive, but some of these clubs allow only members to enter on the weekends. Call before setting out; opening hours tend to change seasonally and/or at the manager's whim.

Alexanderplatz, Via Ostia, 9 (tel. 37 29 398), north of Vatican City. Take Metro Linea A to Ottaviano. From here, head west on Viale Giulio Cesare, take the second right onto Via Leone IV and then your first left onto Via Ostia. Night buses to Piazza Venezia and Termini leave from Piazzale Clodio; to get there from the club, just keep going north on Via Leone IV, which becomes Via della Giuliana. This is, without a doubt, *the* place to hear jazz in Rome and the only club that adheres to a strict jazz-only policy. A subterranean venue, which doubles as a restaurant, it captures the mythical setting of the underground European jazz club with its stuffy, smoky atmosphere, while maintaining its hep decor with sparkling walls and a funky bar. Read the messages left all over the walls by the greats who have played here, from old pros like Art Farmer and Cedar Walton to young stars like Steve Coleman, Christian McBride, and Josh Redman. You must buy a *tessera* the first time you go, but it is good for three months. Also watch for their free outdoor summer concerts at the Villa Celimontana. Open Sept.-June daily 10pm-1:15am. Shows start at 10:30pm.

Yes Brasil, Via San Francesco a Ripa, 103 (tel. 581 62 67), in Trastevere, off Viale di Trastevere on the left, as you come from the river. Foot-stomping live Brazilian music in crowded quarters. A favorite hang-out of young Romans. Drinks L8000-10,000. Open Mon.-Sat. 7:30pm-2am. Music 10pm-midnight.

Big Mama, Vicolo San Francesco a Ripa, 18 (tel. 581 25 51), around the corner from Yes Brasil in Trastevere. Excellent jazz and blues for the diehard fan. Weekend cover (L20,000) makes it more of a commitment; weeknights are just as fun, although less crowded. Open Oct.-June daily 9pm-1:30am (sporadically closed on Sundays and Mondays).

Down Town, Via dei Marsi, 17 (tel. 445 62 70). Take bus #11 or #71 to Piazzale Tiburtina or #492 from Termini to Via Tiburtina. From Piazzale Tiburtino, head down Via di Porta Labicana to Via dei Marsi. An Irish pub with a very non-Irish decor. Post-modern black, white, and yellow walls are covered with collages of pretty faces and pop culture icons. Live music by Irish bands; local and folk groups Fri.-Sun. Try their apple pie (apple/papaya juice, gin, and coffee; L8000). Lots of Irish beer. Open summer daily 9pm-2am, winter 8pm-3am. Closed part of July and Aug. Happy hour midnight-3am. No cover.

■ Discos and Dancing

Although Italian clubs seem to be filled with far more wall-flowers than actual dancers, Italians still pay over L20,000 to get into embarrassingly flashy discotheques that seem like they're from circa 1984. The really cool club scene changes as quickly as Roman phone numbers, so check under "Dolci Notti" in *Trovaroma,* which lists a day-by-day, play-by-play account of discos and happy hours. Many clubs are in the area near the notoriously unsafe Olympic Village, so think twice before going alone. The bigger clubs survive Rome's steaming summer by closing up shop and bounding beachward to **Fregene, Ostia,** or **San Felice Circeo.** Call before you head out.

The Groove, Vicolo Savelli, 10 (tel. 68 72 427), take your second left as you walk down Via del Governo Vecchio from Piazza Pasquino. Look for the black door and the small, probably unlit, neon sign. This cozy joint with pale yellow walls and vaulted ceilings serves up some of the grooviest dance music in Rome. Sip drinks (L10,000) at the bar, then boogie down to acid jazz, funk, soul, and disco downstairs. Best of all: no cover. Open Tues.-Sun. 10pm-2am and later. Closed most of August.

Gilda, Via Mario de Fiori, 97 (tel. 67 84 838 or 66 56 06 49), near the Spanish Steps. Gilda becomes **Gilda on the Beach,** Lungomare di Ponte, 11, in the summer. It remains an exhilarating, hip disco in Fregene, a beach which hosts its share of hedonistic Roman commuters. Open Tues.-Sun. 11pm-4am. Admission L40,000. Step aerobics and beach volleyball class also offered during the week.

RadioLondra, Via di Monte Testaccio, 67, just down the street from L'Alibi. Although this club (downstairs) is not explicitly gay, you will find a significant number of *family* here. The disco is small, in a cave-like bomb shelter where the music thumps, but a patio provides an escape from the close quarters. On weekends, the L15,000 cover includes a first drink. Mixed drinks L15,000. Beer from the tap L6000-8000. Upstairs is a pizzeria/pub where Italian cover bands play periodically. Pizza L7000-10,000, veggie burger L12,000, Bud and Miller in a bottle L6000. Club open Wed.-Mon. 11:30pm-4am. Pub/pizzeria open Wed.-Fri. and Sun.-Mon. 9pm-3am, Sat. 9pm-4am.

GAY AND LESBIAN ENTERTAINMENT

Rome has only a handful of gay and lesbian bars, and most keep late hours. Like straight nightlife in Rome, much happens outdoors, especially in the expatriate pockets of Rome. During the day, gay and lesbian Romans crowd the **gay beach** at "Il Buco" at Lido di Ostia, especially on weekends. The dunes along the beach are home to an amusing pick-up scene, with many middle-aged Italians standing gopher-like atop mounds of sand; the beach itself accommodates a more relaxed, younger crowd, mostly groups of friends. Take the train from Magliana (Metro Linea A) to Lido di Ostia (L700), then the #7/ bus to the *capolinea;* from there, walk 2km south along the beach. For a full list of the Roman gay bath scene, call ARCI-Gay (see Bisexual, Gay, and Lesbian Travelers, p. 54). The best resource for gay travelers is **Libreria Babele** (see p. 54) where you can pick up *Pianta Gay di Roma,* a detailed map with complete listings of cruising spots, bars, organizations, and baths in Rome. Check the gay magazines *Babilonia* and *Adam* for more info.

L'Alibi, Via Monte di Testaccio, 40-44 (tel. 574 34 48), in the Testaccio district (Piramide metro stop). Large, elegant, and diverse, the club's rooms spread over 3 levels, including an expansive, beautiful rooftop terrace. Especially during the summer, this is *the* gay club in Rome. Mostly men, but popular with women too. The #20N and 30N night buses pass nearby Piramide all night long, approximately every hr. and ½hr. respectively. Open Tues.-Sun. 11pm-4am. L15,000 cover includes first drink. Thurs. free.

Hangar, Via in Selci, 69 (tel. 488 13 97; fax 68 30 90 81). Centrally located (off Via Cavour where it bends near the Colosseum; take Metro Linea B to Cavour, or any bus down Via Cavour from Termini, or up from the Colosseum). Friendly John from Philadelphia runs this small bar, once the residence of Messalina, the wife of Nero. Though it is usually packed from wall to wall with men, the atmosphere is cool, neon blue, and laid back. Women are certainly welcome (except on Monday, which is dirty movie night) but might feel out-of-place. Music videos, modern lighting, and a cheery crowd. Located on a well-lit street. Membership is free, and the drinks are some of the cheapest in Rome. Open Wed.-Mon. 10:30pm-2am. Closed 3 weeks in Aug.

Joli Coeur, Via Sirte, 5 (tel. 839 35 23), off Viale Eritrea. Rome's primary lesbian bar is located a little out of the city center, east of Villa Ada. Kind of a seedy neighborhood; women often go together and split the cab fare. L15,000 mandatory first drink. Open Sat.-Sun. 10:30pm-2am.

Angelo Azzuro, Via Cardinal Merry del Val, 13 (tel. 580 04 72), off Viale di Trastevere, in Trastevere. Subterranean bar with a crowded dance floor and gelato. Black lights highlight a vast collection of trippy statuettes, nouveau art, mirrors, and plenty of dance space. Friday is women only. A little slow in getting started. Cover: Fri. and Sun. L10,000, Sat. L20,000. Open Fri.-Sun. 11pm- 4am.

RadioLondra, Via di Monte Testaccio, 67 (tel. 57 50 04). See p. 232.

Pantheon Club, Via Pozzo delle Cornacchie. A small club located one street north of the Pantheon. Women groove it up and disco on the last Saturday of every month. Open 11pm-2am.

▓ Pubs

If you're craving a Guinness, you should have no problem finding one. There are numerous pubs in Rome, many with some sort of Irish theme. The pubs cater to tourists and expatriates, but there's no shortage of Roman clientele. Drinks often go up in price after 9pm, so imbibe accordingly. If you want to meet Italians (that is, the kind that don't come to foreign bars to pick up Americans), you should probably avoid the pubs and head to a nightclub or jazz bar. The pubs and *birrerie* in Trastevere offer the best mix of foreigners and Romans.

Jonathan's Angels, Via della Fossa, 16 (tel. 689 34 26). West of P. Navona. Take Vicolo Savelli Parione Pace off Via Governo Vecchio. Jonathan is one wild and cuhray-zee guy, covered in tattoos and sporting a huge gold-like medallion around his neck. He has painted his likeness in all kinds of strange contexts on the walls, giving the place the atmosphere of a dark Disney ride. There's live music and a hip, young crowd, enjoying the campy, candlelit ambience. Medium beer on tap L10,000, cocktails/long drinks L15,000. Open 9pm-2am.

Julius Caesar, Via Castelfidardo, 49, just north of Termini near Piazza dell'Indipendenza. A cut above the trendy pubs popping up all over Rome. Conveniently located near the train station, backpackers and young tourists flock here (as do wide-eyed young Italian men) for live music, cheap drinks, and crazy fun. The upstairs features beer on tap (L5000-8000) amid Roman decor while the downstairs is filled with blaring live music every night except Sunday—usually vintage rock that you know all the words to. During happy hour (9-10pm), a beer and pizza are only L10,000. Pitchers L15,000, cocktails L10,000, wine L20,000 per bottle. Inquire about the *Let's Go* discount. Open 9pm-3am.

Druid's Den, Via San Martino ai Monti, 28 (tel. 488 02 58). Traveling south on Via Merulana from Via Santa Maria Maggiore, take your second right. An Irish hangout where Romans get to be tourists. Pints of Guinness and Strong Bow cider on draft L7000. Open summer 6pm-12:30am, winter 5pm-12:30am.

The Drunken Ship, Campo de' Fiori, 20/21 (tel. 68 30 05 35). Hipper than it was in its pre-renovation frat-house days, this slick establishment, complete with functional steel tables and chairs, warmly welcomes backpackers with special reduced prices on drinks and, a hold-out from the old days, jello shots (normally L2000).

The DJ spins mostly American favorites and all of the staff speaks English. Too much happiness for just one hour, so happy hour prices last from 6-9pm: pint of beer L5000, pitcher L15,000, sandwiches L8000, nachos L5000. Ask about student discount on Heineken. Open summer 6pm-2am, winter 5pm-2am.

Night and Day, Via dell'Oca, 50 (tel. 320 23 00), left off Piazza del Popolo. A fine Irish pub (curiously devoid of Irish employees), with great music that lives by the motto, "Guinness is good for you," posted outside the door. Happy hour 5-9pm. Pint of beer L5000, Guinness L6000; after 9pm, pint L7000, Guinness L8000. Open 5pm-5am. Closed for part of August.

Pigmalione, Via di Porta Labicana, 29 (tel. 445 77 40). Mellow rock and blues play under the watchful gaze of a massive one-eyed Buddha painted on the wall. An eclectic mix of Indian, Egyptian, and astrological decor; it's a bit cheaper than its Irish counterparts. Open 7pm-2am.

Victoria House, Via di Gesù e Maria, 18 (tel. 320 16 98), between Via del Corso and Via del Babuino, 3 blocks from Piazza Popolo. *The* English pub in Rome. "God Save the Queen," and all that. Shepherd and venison pies, jacket potatoes, salads, sandwiches, and snacks served. Community bulletin board inside listing apts. and services. Open daily 6pm-1am. Happy hour Mon.-Fri. 6-9pm, Sat. and Sun. 6-8pm; reduced-price pint of beer L5000, normally L7,500. Caffreys Stout served.

The Proud Lion Pub, Borgo Pio, 36 (tel. 683 28 41), 1 block up from Bernini's colonnaded square at St. Peter's. A decent Italian attempt at a Scottish pub—dim light, dark wood booths, plenty of plaid and pints to go around. Affiliated with the Italian Dart Club. Open Sun.-Thurs. 8:30pm-1am, Fri.-Sat. 8:30pm-2am.

▨ Centri Sociali

Centri Sociali, literally "social centers," are the latest entertainment craze in Rome among alternative young people. They started out as squatter settlements—socialist university students would take over an abandoned building in a poorer section of town, get their musician friends to play thrash, read and discuss socialist literature, and partake of controlled substances. In addition to featuring live music, *centri sociali* also organize film festivals and exhibits. Now they are slightly more established (and sometimes commercial), though the clientele remains on the cutting edge and the context remains political. You pay what you can; usually there's a minimal suggested donation. *Centri sociali* can be lots of fun and are very different from the usual tacky nightlife in Rome. As squatter settlements, they tend to move from abandoned building to abandoned building, but there always seem to be some in Testaccio, especially along the river near the old slaughterhouses. *Roma C'è* (available at most newsstands; L1500) usually contains a list of *centri sociali* locations and scheduled events. Advertisements for *centri sociali* are posted throughout the city.

Villagio Globale (ex Mattatoio), Lungotevere Testaccio. Take bus #27 from Termini, get off right before it crosses the river, and head left down the river. After midnight take night bus #20N/21N from Piramide back to Termini. One of the best known *centri sociali* in Rome. Live music some nights, but there's almost always something going on. Closed late July-mid-September.

Ex Snia Viscosa, Via Prenestina, 173. Take bus #15 or #81 from the Colosseum or bus #14 from Termini. Theater, live music, dance classes.

▨ Music, Theater, and Art

The best way to find out about upcoming cultural events is to keep your eyes peeled for posters advertising concerts, shows, and exhibits. Also valuable are the weekly cultural guides **Roma C'è** (L1500; available at newsstands) and **TrovaRoma** (included in each Thursday's edition of *La Repubblica*), which contain comprehensive lists of events and venues. *Roma C'è* also includes a section in English detailing the entertainment possibilities of special interest to English speakers. The touri office may have information or brochures on cultural activites, including *Un'Ospite a Roma.*

OPERA

The spectacular stage of the Terme di Caracalla used to host summertime opera performances, but this lively tradition was halted once it was discovered that performers' barreling voices brought the ancient house down—literally. During the regular season (Sept.-June), look for performances and tickets at the aptly-named **Teatro dell'Opera** in P. Beniamino Gigli (tel. 48 16 01). Tickets may be bought weeks in advance. Since 1995, summer performances have taken place in Piazza di Siena in the Villa Borghese. Also be on the lookout for the summer **Operafestival di Roma** (tel. 569 14 93), and occasional performances during the year at the Teatro Valle, the Teatro Manzoni, and the Loggia della Villa Medici.

CLASSICAL MUSIC

The **Accademia Nazionale di Santa Cecilia** (tel. 361 10 72) performs symphonies and chamber music in its auditorium at Via di Conciliazione, 4 (the street leading up to the Vatican). In summer, the company moves outdoors to the *nymphaeum* in the Villa Giulia. Tickets cost L15,000-L45,000.

The **Teatro Ghione,** at Via delle Fornaci, 37 (tel. 637 22 94), near San Pietro, hosts Euromusica, featuring classical concerts from Oct.-April with renowned international performers (tickets L15,000-25,000). Also during the winter season, the **Amici di Castel Sant'Angelo** (tel. 845 61 92) liven up Hadrian's Mausoleum with concerts Saturday nights at 9pm. Look for occasional concerts by the **Accademia Filarmonica Romana,** the **Coro Polifonico Romano,** and the **Associazone Musicale Claudio Monteverde.**

Summer

The classical music scene in Rome goes wild in the summer, with performances almost nightly in a variety of outdoor venues. It all starts with the Festa Europea della Musica, a weekend of non-stop music at the end of June, in various places throughout the city. In the month of July, the **Accademia Nazionale di Santa Cecilia** (tel. 361 28 73 or 679 36 17) holds concerts in the **Villa Giulia,** Piazzale della Villa Giulia, 9. All kinds of classical music are represented here, from Scarlatti to Gershwin, performed by soloists, chamber groups, and full orchestra. Buy tickets at Villa Giulia or from the Agenzia Tartaglia in P. di Spagna, 12 (678 45 83). The **Theater of Marcellus,** on Via del Teatro di Marcello, 44, near Piazza Venezia, is home to the **Concerti del Tempietto,** a series of nightly performances from mid-June to early October. Concerts start at 9pm; tickets are L26,000 and gain entrance to the otherwise inaccessible archaeological area. Check in *Roma C'é* to see what's on, or ask to see the hefty program at the door.

Bromante's cloister in the church of Santa Maria della Pace, Via Arco della Pace, 5, hosts a number of different concert series, including that of the **International Chamber Ensemble** (tel. 86 80 01 25) in July, and **Mille e Una Notti** in August, organized by **L'Ippocampo** (tel. 686 84 41). Be on the lookout also for concerts in Piazza Trinità dei Monti (at the top of the Spanish Steps) and in the gardens of the Pincio, overlooking Piazza del Popolo.

JAZZ

Rome is not a jazz-lover's paradise. If all you're looking for is a hip atmosphere where you can drink, smoke, and murmur softly to your sensitive companions, just head to one of the smaller clubs listed on p. 231, look in *Roma C'è* or *TrovaRoma,* or follow your ears to the nearest place in Trastevere or the historic center. True jazz cats, however, can take refuge at the **Alexanderplatz Jazz Club** (tel. 397 42 17, see p. 231). Occasionally, big names also come to some of the larger arenas, so be on the lookout for posters.

ENTERTAINMENT

In the summer Alexanderplatz organizes the **Jazz & Image** festival (tel. 77 20 13 11), in the **Villa Celimontana,** the lush, ruin-filled park that stretches from the Colosseum to the Baths of Caracalla. From mid-June to mid-August, jazz greats jam away every night at 10pm, while films about jazz and blues show on a huge outdoor screen at 9pm. Entrance is L7000, though the price may be hiked up a bit when big names perform. In 1996, the festival hosted McCoy Tyner, Branford Marsalis, Ray Brown, Cedar Walton, and Phil Woods, among others. Don't forget that Perugia, home to the world-renowned **Umbria Jazz Festival,** is only a few hours away by train or car. Last year's performers included Jao Gilberto, Joe Henderson, Jim Hall, Al Jarreau, and Sonny Rollins. Call (075) 573 33 63 for more information.

POPULAR MUSIC AND ROCK 'N ROLL

Once again, the best way to learn about upcoming concerts is to watch for posters and to scan *Roma C'è, TrovaRoma, Wanted in Rome,* and *Un'Ospite a Roma.* You can also visit the **ORBIS** agency at P. dell'Esquilino, 37 (tel. 474 47 76 or 482 74 03; open Mon.-Sat. 9:30am-1pm and 4-7:30pm) near S. Maria Maggiore, off Via Cavour. Otherwise head off to one of the music clubs on p. 231, a *centro sociale* (p. 234), or anywhere you pass by where the music's to your liking. Most big-time pop and rock performers play at the **Palazzo dello Sport** in EUR or at the **Foro Italico.**

In the summer, the city's pop and rock music scene grows out of control with outdoor concerts that last all night long. The **Live Link** festival (tel. 841 90 50 or 841 91 71) at the Foro Italico hosts your old favorites (emphasis on "old") every night from late June to late July. The 1996 roster included Tina Turner, Santana, David Bowie, Lou Reed, Bad Religion, and Iggy Pop. Head out to **Testaccio Village** on Via di Monte Testaccio, 16, for live music of all kinds from mid-June to mid-September every night starting at 9pm. In 1996 performers included the Wayne Shorter Quintet, Noel Redding, and Italian bands with such promising names as *Latte e i suoi derivati* and *Io vorrei la pelle nera.* In 1996, **Roma Incontra il Mondo,** a festival of world music and *"musica etnica,"* called the lake in Villa Ada home at Via di Ponte Salario (tel. 418 03 70). The festival runs from late June to early September with concerts starting at 6pm and lasting till the wee hours. Performers are from all over the world, from Cameroon to Macedonia to Egypt to the USA.

DANCE

The **Rome Opera Ballet** shares the stage and ticket office with **Teatro dell'Opera** (tel. 48 16 01 for the operator, 481 70 03 for tickets and info). The ballet company stages joint performances with the opera company in the summer, at Piazza di Siena in Villa Borghese (see Opera, p. 235). In the summer, there is also a festival of dance, art, and culture called **Romaeuropa** with venues throughout the city. Call 474 23 19 or 474 22 86 for information or pick up a program at the **Museo degli Strumenti Musicali** in Piazza S. Croce in Gerusalemme, one of the performance locations. 1996's program featured performances by William Forsythem, Hervé Robbe, the Martha Graham Dance Co., and others.

THEATER

For **theater** listings check with the tourist office or call the information number at **Teatro Ghione,** Via delle Fornaci, 37 (fax 637 22 94), which has both music and theater performances. For plays and musicals in English, check with the tourist office or check in *Wanted in Rome* or the English section in *Roma C'è.* Also be sure to speak with the native English speakers at the **Teatro Ghione,** Via delle Fornaci, 37 (tel./fax 637 22 94), near Saint Peter's. **Teatro Sistina,** Via Sistina, 129 (tel. 482 68 41) features musicals and plays from September to May.

CINEMA

First-run cinemas in Rome tend to charge about L12,000 and, though the movies are often American, they're generally dubbed into Italian. *Cineclubs* show the best and most recent foreign films, old goodies, and an assortment of favorites in the original language. For lists of what's playing where, check out any newspaper, *Roma C'è, TrovaRoma,* or the posters in most movie houses. A "v.o." or "l.o." next to any listing means *versione originale* or *lingua originale* (i.e., not dubbed).

The **San Lorenzo sotto le Stelle** film festival featured in 1996 an original language film series in July, **That's Cinema.** The films, which included mostly recent American flicks, were shown at 9pm and 11pm at the Villa Mercede, on Via Tiburtina 113, and cost L8000. If funding continues, so will the program. Look for posters, programs, and check out *Roma C'è.* During the rest of the year, head to any of the following cinemas:

Cinema Pasquino (tel. 580 36 22), Vicolo del Piede, 19A, off P. S. Maria in Trastevere. Rome's only exclusively English-language movie theater. Program changes daily, so call for the schedule or stop by and pick one up. L7000.

Alcazar (tel. 588 00 99), P. Merry Del Val, 14, in Trastevere. Films in *lingua originale* Mon.

Augustus (tel. 687 54 55), Corso Vittorio Emanuele II, 203. Films in "l.o." Tuesday.

Giulio Cesare (tel. 397 20 877), Viale Giulio Cesare, 229. "L.o." on Monday.

Lead-On (tel. 591 55 21), Via delle Montagne Rocciose, 62, in EUR. Original language movies Fri. at 5pm. Free but make reservations.

Majestic (tel. 679 49 08), Via SS. Apostoli, 20. "L.o." on Monday.

Nuovo Sacher (tel. 581 81 16), Largo Ascianghi, 1. "L.o." Mon. and Tues.

■ Shopping

FOOD AND GROCERIES

The cheapest eats in the city can be had at Rome's open-air **markets,** which carry a surprisingly fresh and varied array of produce, dairy, and meat products. For a list of these markets, see Markets, p. 134.

The produce at **supermarkets** is less fresh than at the markets, but you'll be sure to find the packaged foods and staples you need: **GS** in Piazza Bologna and on Via del Natale Grande in Trastevere; **SMA** in Piazza Bologna (Metro Linea B) and in Piazza Re di Roma, 15 (Metro Linea A); **CONAD** 24 hours per day, 7 days per week. In the Drugstore Termini complex underneath Termini station, accessible from Main Gallery of Termini (at night accessible from Metro entrance in P. dei Cinquecento). **STANDA,** at Viale di Trastevere, 60 and Via Cola di Rienzo, 173, is Italy's largest food chain with clothing and household goods; they take credit cards. If you can't face another plate of pasta or slab of pizza, take refuge at **Castroni,** Via Ottaviano, 55, near the Ottaviano Metro stop, about ½km from the Vatican. They sell a wide assortment of freshly made baked goods and sweets. More importantly, they have all your favorite American food, including taco shells, cake mixes, and Lucky Charms.

Italian delicacies of all kinds are available at specialty stores and make great souvenirs and presents, if you can manage to carry them (and not eat them) during the rest of your trip. **Tazza d'Oro,** Via degli Orfani, 84/86, near the Pantheon, not only serves up one of Rome's best cups of coffee, but also sells beans by the kilo and the *etto.* **Ai Monesteri,** P. Cinque Lune, 76, at the top of Corso del Rinascimento (across from the top of P. Navona) has a bewildering and arcane selection of liqueurs, wines, chocolates, and other spiritual aids produced by Italian monks. **Antica Enoteca,** Via della Croce, 76, sells fine wines, olive oils, expensive bottles of *grappa,* and brandies flavored with pickled fruit grown in the bottle.

CLOTHING AND SHOES

Compared to its more cosmopolitan cousins in the north, Rome is no shopper's paradise—if you'll be passing through Florence or Milan, save your *lire* for a spree up there. Rome's clothing, shoe, and leather boutiques offer a homogeneous (and often ho-hum) array of goods. Though prices are often lower than in the States, quality can be rock-bottom too, so shop critically. The best leather goods made in Italy are exported—you're more likely to find a gorgeous, high-quality Italian wallet in Miami than in Rome. Shopping for clothes in Rome can be a fun experience, however, and many of the same styles can be found over a broad range of prices. Italian shoes are deservedly world-famous, and you can find excellent values throughout the city, though women with larger feet will have a tougher time squeezing into the tiny sizes. Big-footed gals should head to **Louis** (tel. 679 16 77), Via Cavour 309, for a wide variety of shoes sizes 40 (US size 9) and up.

For the super-cheap and the die-hard bargain hunter, the **Porta Portese Flea Market** may be the best value (certainly the most chaotic) around. Open every Sunday from 7am to 2pm, the flea market stretches 4km from the Porta Portese bridge to the Trastevere train station. Used clothing, plastic shoes, t-shirts, bathing suits, CDs, pirated tapes, watches, as well as fake antiques, used books, bits of broken clocks, used (or stolen) mopeds, illegally cut videotapes, beauty supplies, and a bunch of other oddities are for sale here. **Guard your wallet carefully.** If you want the total bizarre bazaar experience, wait until about 11am; serious shoppers, though, should arrive early. If you can't get enough of the chaos, head to **Porta Portese 2,** a large offshoot of the original, on Viale Palmiro Togliatti in the Tor Sapienza district, near Via Prenestina. During the weekday mornings, you can buy clothes more cheaply (and more sanely) at the outdoor markets outside the **Porta S. Giovanni** (Metro Linea A to S. Giovanni in Laterano) or in **P. Vittorio Emanuele** (Metro Linea A to Vittorio).

The overpriced, but stylin' and profilin' chain stores **Balloon** (at Piazza di Spagna, 35, tel. 678 01 10) and **Benetton** (Via Nazionale, Piazza Colonno, everywhere) can have great deals if you catch them during a sale. If you need something cheap and in a hurry, head to one of Rome's chain **department stores,** where you'll find the kind of reasonably priced (though occasionally garish) clothing that Romans themselves wear every day. **STANDA** (see p. 237), **UPIM** (at Via Nazionale, 111, Piazza S. Maria Maggiore and Via del Tritone, 172), and **COIN** (at P. Porta San Giovanni; take Metro A to S. Giovanni in Laterano) all have extensive clothing sections. For a more upscale selection, try **La Rinascente** (open daily 9:30am-8pm; AmEx, MC, Visa), at P. Colonna on the Via del Corso. This is a bit closer to an American department store; in other words, it has fitting rooms and takes credit cards, though if you're going to pay their prices, you might as well go hunting for a boutique.

Boutiques abound in Rome, selling all kinds of moderately priced clothing, from the staid to the outrageous. Though you can't help but find stores on **Via Nazionale** and **Via del Corso,** the traffic and crowds may send you packing. You'll have a better time (and probably find better prices) casing the area around **Via Ottaviano** and **Via Cola di Rienzo,** near the Vatican (home to many of the same boutiques as in the center) or around P. Bologna, at the Bologna stop on Metro Linea B, and at the end of the #61 and 62 bus routes. In the streets around **Campo dei Fiori,** especially Via dei Giubbonari and Via dei Chiavari, you'll find numerous specialty boutiques, many of which sell hand-tailored or one-of-a-kind fashions at surprisingly good prices. The winding alleys of **Trastevere** hide similar stores, with plenty of funky accessories. Try Via di Lungaretta north of Viale Trastevere and Via di Paglia heading north toward Via della Scala. **Natraj,** Via della Mercede, 11 (tel. 679 59 05; fax 446 49 47; open Mon.-Sat. 9am-7:30pm, Sun. 3:30-8pm), is for those trying to save money for a store window outfit near Piazza di Spagna, but who simply can go no further in offensive clothes. Browse through this funky little import store and find flamboyant, cheap clothes. Silk tank-tops run for about L15,000, t-shirts are L13,000, and flowy pants cost L15,000. Look for wall tapestries (for those of you who brought your walls), jewelry, and incense.

MUSIC

If you simply cannot bear to listen to your music anymore and know the words to all of the songs on your *Eurotour Collection '97* tape, you might want to revive your brain cells and update your music collection with a tape or CD from one of Rome's music stores. Most of the smaller stores contain a limited stock of international music, but the ones listed below are all well-stocked and easily accessible. On the Italian scene, Luca Carboni, Pino Daniele, and Vasco Rossi are some of Italy's famous rock musicians, while the pop charts are topped by Jovanotti, Latte e i suoi derivati, Elio e le storie tese, 883, Eroz Ramazzoti, and Ligabue.

Ricordi Music Store, Via del Corso, 506 (tel. 361 23 70 or 361 23 31). Take Metro Linea A to Flaminio, go through Piazza del Popolo, and head down the Corso; or take any of the buses that go up the Corso, like #56 or 60. An enormous collection of national and international music on tapes and CDs, with all types of music sold—jazz, classical, easy listening, heavy metal etc. Look for *Prezzi Pazzi* signs for good deals on less mainstream music. Cassette tapes L14,000-23,000, CDs L20,000-30,000. There's also a listing of local concerts to be perused. Another location is on Via Cesare Battisti, 120 (tel. 679 80 22 or 679 80 23) just off Piazza Venezia where Via del Corso ends.

Messaggerie Musicali, Via del Corso, 123 (tel. 679 81 97). The 3-story music store specializes more in CDs and electronics than in affordable tapes for the wandering traveler. Still, their collection is well-chosen and often reasonably priced. Look for tapes in the *offerta speciale* (special offer) section (L8500). Foreign artists located in the *artisti stranieri* section. Tapes L8500-L22,000; CDs L20,000-L33,000. Classical and jazz music also available. Portable stereos, earphones, and electronics on the second floor. Open Mon.-Sat. 9:30am-1:30pm and 4-8pm.

SOUVENIRS AND RELIGIOUS PARAPHERNALIA

You can't turn around in Rome without seeing a souvenir stand. For **sacred objects,** the obvious place to look is the area around the Vatican, where countless booths and stores sell everything from miniscule saintly medallions to life-size plastic crucifixes. The stores on Via di Conciliazione and Via di Porta Angelica also sell calligraphic blessings; after you pay to have one filled out with someone's name, it's taken to a special audience and blessed by the Pope. There's plenty of papal equipment around too—John Paul II ashtrays, lollipops, thermometers, keychains, bottle openers, etc. **Fabbroni Colombo,** P. del Pantheon 69A (tel. 679 04 83), is a hole-in-the-wall stocked with the largest selection of postcards in Italy, including many from other Italian cities. On the north side of Corso Vittorio Emanuele II across from Il Gesù, **Via dei Cestari** brims with crucifixes. The area immediately surrounding Santa Maria Maggiore is full of both sinners and religious paraphernalia.

■ Sports

SPECTATOR

The best sources for sporting information are the tourist office and two magazines sold at newsstands, *Corriere dello Sport* and *Gazzetta dello Sport*. If you are in Rome between September and May, take in a **soccer (calcio;** CAHL-choh) game at the **Stadio Olimpico.** Of Rome's two teams, Roma and Lazio, Roma is the favorite, playing in the most competitive *serie A* league. If one of the two teams is playing *in casa* (at home), you'll witness a violent enthusiasm reminiscent of the Colosseum spectacles of yester-empire. The **Foro Italico,** at the Stadio, hosts the games. Each team sets its own price, which can be as much as L40,000. Lazio tickets can be purchased at Lazio Point, Via Farini, 24 (tel. 482 66 88). Roma tickets can be bought at Enjoy Rome, Via Varese, 39 (tel. 445 18 43). For soccer information in Italian call 84 911.

The **Concorso Ippico Internazionale** (International Horse Show) is held at P. di Siena in May. Go to the **Tor di Valle Racecourse** on Via Appia Nuova for the clay-court **International Tennis Championship of Italy,** held here at the beginning of May, which draws many of the world's top players. Tickets for many sporting events can be bought at the Orbis agency (tel. 482 74 03).

PARTICIPANT

Lace up your cross-trainers and head out to **Villa Borghese** for your daily run. **Villa Ada** also has places to run, along with an **exercise course** throughout the park. Villa Doria Pamphili has primitive exercise/obstacle course things, as well.

For chlorinated, wet relief from the Roman heat, ask at the tourist office for locations of public pools and check out the yellow pages under *piscine*. Otherwise, you can check in the newspaper or in TrovaRoma. Many major hotels in Rome open their pools to the public, but often for a large fee. Remember that bathing caps are usually required. At **Piscina della Rosa,** Viale America, 20 (tel. 592 67 17) in EUR, a full-day swim in the outdoor pool costs L15,000. A swim from 1-4pm, though, is only L6000. Open June-Sept. daily 9am-7pm. Take Metro Linea B to the EUR-Palasport stop.

If you prefer water in the solid state, the ice skating rink **Palaghiaccio di Marino,** on Via Appia Nuova, km 19 (tel. 930 94 80), has 1½-hr. rentals of skates and pads for L9000, on weekends L11,000. (1½-hr. rental sessions: Mon.-Fri. 5, 9 and 11pm; Sat.-Sun. 3, 5, 7, 9 and 11pm; Sun., also 11am.)

Or, if you just yearn for the feel of a bowling ball, try **Bowling Roma,** Viale Regina Margherita, 181 (tel. 855 11 84; open Mon.-Sat. 10am-11:30pm, Sun. 5pm-midnight), off Via Nomentana past the Porta Pia. This air-conditioned time warp to the 1960s comes replete with candlepins.

Even if you don't have a membership, you can still use the recreational facilities at Rome's YMCA (EEM-kah) in EUR at Viale dell'Oceano Pacifico, 13 (pool) and Viale Libomo, 68 (gym). For L30,000 you can use the Y's pool, gym, and tennis courts for an entire day, if you're under 45 years of age. Call 522 52 47 for more info. If all that *scamorza* is making you pudgy, you can head to an American-style athletic club:

Roman Sport Center, Via del Galoppatoio, 33 (tel. 36 14 358), in Villa Borghese. Take Metro Linea A to Spagna and follow the Via Veneto exit. This gym offers nonresidents a day of artificially induced sweating (aerobics, squash, pool, sauna, Turkish baths, weight room) for L25,000. Open Mon.-Sat. 9am-8pm.

Associazione Sportiva Augustea (A.S.A), Via Luciani, 57 (tel. 23 23 51 12), in Cinecittà. Take the Metro Linea A to Cinecittà or buses #558 or 54. Indoor pool (L10,000 for a day's swim), gym, tennis courts (L15,000).

■ Holidays and Festivals

Rome isn't world-renowned for its festivals; nonetheless, there are plenty of beautiful and sometimes bizarre Italian celebrations to participate in or gawk at. Most commemorate historical or religious events, and often include elaborate re-enactments. Rome also manages to attract its share of international arts and sports events. For more rural traditions, spend a lot of time in the Italian countryside and you will probably happen upon a few festivals without even trying. A food *festa* is rarely well publicized, but if your timing is good, you're in for a treat—local cuisine is celebrated by gorging to the accompaniment of music and dancing. The only official holiday specific to Rome is **June 29,** the feast day of Saints Peter and Paul. Rome and the rest of Italy officially close on the following dates: **January 1** (New Year's Day); **January 6** (Epiphany); **Easter Monday; April 25** (Liberation Day); **May 1** (Labor Day); **August 15** (Assumption of the Virgin); **November 1** (All Saints' Day); **December 8** (Day of the Immaculate Conception); **December 25** (Christmas Day); and **December 26** (Feast of St. Stephen).

JANUARY

1: The faithful light candles and make their way through the **catacombs of S. Priscilla;** the Pope gives a solemn High Mass at St. Peter's.

6: Epiphany: The *Befana*, the good witch of the Epiphany pays a visit and brings Italian children toys and candy. A fair, selling toys, candy, and miniature *befane* takes over Piazza Navona in mid-December and ends in mid-January.

17: Pet owners of Rome celebrate **St. Anthony's Feast Day** by gathering with their best friends for the traditional blessing at the **Church of Sant'Eusebio all'Esquilino** (patron saint of animals) in P. Vittorio Emanuele II.

21: You too can bless two lambs on **St. Agnes' Feast Day,** (at the church of Sant'Agnese fuori le Mura on Via Nomentana), whose wool will later be used to weave a sacred garment for the Pope.

FEBRUARY

Shrove Tuesday is the day to disguise yourself for the pre-Lenten **Carnevale** in the city's *piazze*. Onlookers watch precious *damine* ("little ladies"—8-yr.-old girls in poofy L300,000 gowns) parade around town, or get sprayed with shaving cream, confetti, and crazy string by tiny Mutant Ninja Turtle imposters.

MARCH

12: Anyone can buy insurance, but believers can have their cars blessed at the Piazzale del Colosseo on the Sun. after the **Festa di Santa Francesca Romana.**

19: Feast on *bignè* (cream puffs) at the **Festa di San Guiseppe** in the Trionfale district of the city northwest of the Vatican.

APRIL

Holy Week prompts the Good Friday **procession of the Cross** from the Colosseum to the Palatine, and the Pope's Easter Sunday *Urbi et Orbi* blessing in nearly 50 languages. **Civitavecchia** hosts a procession of the dead Christ; repenting sinners follow wearing white robes and dragging chains fastened to their ankles. April's spring festival features the **flower show** at P. di Spagna, with azaleas on the Spanish Steps. Spring blossoms with the **Fiera d'Arte,** an art fair in Via Margutta. An **International Horse Show** sprouts up in Villa Borghese's Piazza di Siena, the last week of April.

14-16: **Sagra del Carciofo Romanesco** (festival of Roman artichokes) in Ladispoli. Pyrotechnics and artifloats.

21: The anniversary of **Rome's founding** affords a rare opportunity to see the Palazzo Senatorio in Piazza del Campidoglio. Celebrations on the Capitoline Hill, Latin poetry, and more fireworks, set off from the Circus Maximus.

MAY

The **rose show** arrives in early May at Valle Murcia, on the Aventine Hill above the Circus Maximus, and lasts through June; the **Italian International Tennis Tournament** gets underway at the Foro Italico in late May.

JUNE

The hills of Rome are alive with the sound of music in June. There is a **Festival of Baroque Music** in Viterbo and the **Pontine Music Festival,** with concerts in the Caetani castle in Sermoneta. Nemi, in the Castelli Romani district, holds a **Strawberry Festival.** From mid-June to mid-July, French performers descend on the capitol for the **performing arts festival** at the French Academy at Villa Medici. From mid-June to early Aug., the **Rome Festival** features opera and classical concerts at the Piazza San Clemente (see Music, Theater, and Art, page 234).

23: Festa di San Giovanni at San Giovanni in Laterno sponsors a gluttonous banquet featuring stewed snails and roast pork.

29: The **Feast of Saints Peter and Paul,** an awe-inspiring religious ceremony for Rome's patron saint, takes place in the basilica of the church of the same name.

ENTERTAINMENT

JULY

During the first three weeks in July, the Tiber lights up with the sights and sounds of **Tevere Expo,** an annual national exhibition featuring industrial products, crafts, and foods of the various regions of Italy. Civic authorities organize a series of other cultural events under the rubric of **L'Estate Romana.** Pick up a program or check out what's happening in *Roma C'è* or *Wanted in Rome.* The **Festa di Noantri** comes to Trastevere for 10 days during the last two weeks in July. The **Romaeuropa** festival in July has dance, music, video, and art events at different locations all over the city. Pick up the schedule from the tourist office.

AUGUST

5: A blizzard of white flower petals represents a legendary out-of-season snow at the **Festa della Madonna della Neve** at S. Maria Maggiore.

SEPTEMBER

There's an **art exhibition** including the works of 100 painters in Via Margutta, piles of grapes and vats of wine at the **Sagra delle Uva,** in the Basilica of Maxentius in the Forum, and a torchlit **handicrafts fair** from late September to early October in the Via dell'Orso.

OCTOBER

The water in the fountains of Marino (in the Castelli Romani) turns into wine at a **wine festival,** the first Sunday in October. Rome plays host in October to both the **Film Fest Italia** and the **International Cinema and TV Festival—Eurovision 90.** An **antique fair** sets up on Via dei Coronari for the last two weeks of the month.

DECEMBER

The first week in December begins the sentimental, gaudy Piazza Navona **toy fair.** Overpriced Christmas knickknacks are for sale; a bejeweled Christ-child receives poems and speeches from children.

22: Fish cooked in cauldrons at the **Ciotto del Pesce** at the Mercati Generali in Via Ostiense; free samples.

31: New Year's Eve is also the **Feast of S. Silvestro:** If you get there by 5pm, you can watch the Pope participate in a ceremony at the church of the Gesù. New Year's merrymaking includes sparklers and tossing glass out the window. Expand your horizons by sampling the traditional pigs' foot dish, washed down with champagne, of course.

Daytrips

When the endless frenzy of Rome overwhelms you, head for the sanctuaries of rural Lazio. The cradle of Roman civilization, Lazio (originally *Latium,* home to Latin) stretches from the low Tyrrhenian coastline through volcanic hills to the foothills of the *abruzzese* Apennines. North and south of Rome, ancient cities, some predating the eternal city by centuries, maintain traces of the thriving cultures that were born there. Romans, Etruscans, Latins, and Sabines all settled here, and their contests for supremacy over the land make up some of the first pages of Italy's recorded history.

Latium has always been a rich land. Volcanic soil feeds farms and vineyards, and travertine marble quarried from the Latian hills built the Colosseum, St. Peter's, and most Roman buildings standing between them. With such resources, the territory attracted the notice of the Etruscan Empire in the ninth century BC, which set up colonies in Tarquinia, Cerveteri, and Veio. The less sophisticated Latin tribes dwelling in the hills (Colli Albani) around Lake Albano quickly rose to prominence in the south. While Rome was still a collection of mud huts on the Palatine, Etruscan and Latin towns enjoyed a sophisticated religious, political, and artistic society.

Trains for locations in Lazio leave from Termini, and one private line serves Viterbo from the Roma Nord Station in Piazzale Flaminio (outside P. del Popolo). **COTRAL** buses depart from Via Lepanto (outside the eponymous Metro stop on Linea A) for Tarquinia, Cerveteri, Bracciano, and Civitavecchia; from the Anagnina Linea A stop for the *Castelli Romani,* including Frascati and Albano; from the EUR-Fermi stop on Linea B for Anzio and Nettuno; and from the Rebibbia Linea B stop for Tivoli and Subiaco. **Hitchhiking** is not uncommon and rides are generally easy to come by; those who do hitch take a city bus onto the road that leads towards their destination. **Let's Go does not recommend hitchhiking. Women in particular should think twice about hitchhiking, and under no circumstances should they do it alone.** For an extended discussion of this issue, please see By Thumb, p. 86.

LAZIO

Daytrippers from the city are in good historical company. Roman bigwigs have been weekending in the surrounding towns since they quashed their neighbors in the third century BC. Though the ancient villas declined along with the Roman Empire, their remains inspired countless popes and nobles to build their own pleasure gardens, often on ancient foundations. The hill towns are known more for their relaxing pace of life, however, than for their sights. Medieval cobbled streets, belvederes overlooking sweeping views, and the crisp white wines of the region make each Latian hill town an ideal spot for a day of lazing and grazing. However, some of these towns are experiencing the rapid economic growth and construction that encroaches on most of Italy's old towns, and to top it off, many are now besieged by tourists as well. If you really want to escape the crush of modern Italian life, you may have to head further afield to Subiaco or Palestrina, where saints and composers kept quieter court, to the Etruscan ghost towns of Tarquinia or Cerveteri, or to Ostia Antica, the once bustling, now deserted port of ancient Rome.

▓ Tivoli

You can get to Tivoli by taking the Metro Linea B to the last stop, Rebibbia (L1500); exit the station to the COTRAL terminal above. Tickets to Tivoli (L3000) are on sale here, and the **buses** leave from Capolinea 1 about every 20-30 minutes. After passing through smoggy factory areas and travertine quarries, the bus climbs to the center of Tivoli, making a stop either at Largo Garibaldi or slightly beyond at Piazzale delle Nazioni Unite. At the *largo,* a grassy lookout with bursting fountains allows a view of expansive Roman suburbs. Here, visit the **tourist office** (tel. (0774) 31 12 99 or 33 45 22; fax 33 12 94; open Mon.-Sat. 9:25am-3pm), a round shack where the staff provides loads of historical information, maps with restaurant and hotel locations, and schedules of buses leaving Tivoli. Ask for a copy of the large yellow book entitled *Tivoli Down the Ages* to learn about countless Tiburtine sights.

Tivoli perches over the boundary between Lazio's hills and plains, providing dramatic views of Rome from its hilly streets and gardens. Here, where the Aniene River (the Anio in ancient days) pours over 120m of ravine and cliff on its way to meet the Tiber, water is the inspiration and the attraction. Ancient Roman *glitterati* came to enjoy the delicious cool of the cascades. Horace, Catullus, Propertius, Maecenas, and many others retreated to villas lining the ravine into which the Aniene river falls. Across town, the sparkling **Villa d'Este** siphons the river's overflow into a hundred spouting fountains lining a Renaissance-era formal garden, while in between lies a maze of medieval houses and churches, and a fortified castle, as well as two Republican-age temples presiding over some of the most impressive scenery in Lazio.

■ Villa d'Este

From Largo Garibaldi, follow the trail of souvenir stands through piazza Trento to the cool gardens and watery terraces of the **Villa d'Este** (tel. (0774) 31 20 70; open daily May -Aug. 9am-6:45pm; Sept.-April open 9am-approximately 1hr. before sunset; admission L8000, EU citizens under 18 and over 60 free). The entrance to the gardens passes through several frescoed rooms, notable primarily for their views of the gardens. The property was shaped by Cardinal Ippolito d'Este (son of Lucrezia Borgia) and his architect Piero Ligorio in 1550; the idea was to recreate the feel of the sumptuous ancient Roman *nymphaea* and pleasure palaces. Spiral stairs at the end of the hall lead to the bar and gift shop where maps are sold for those interested in actually finding the fountains listed below. Outside, a terrace sprawls above the gardens and offers a spectacular view of the countryside and Rome in the distance.

Immediately below the terrace is the **Fontana del Bicchierone,** a shell-shaped goblet of Bernini's design. To the left (with your back toward the villa), a path leads down to the **Grotto of Diana,** a fine example of a *nymphaeum*—a stuccoed nook lined with pebbles, statuary, and mosses. Take another path (on the right) to the **Rometta,** or Little Rome, a series of fountains including one representing the Tiber (the boat with the obelisk is Tiber Island) as well as stuccoed miniatures of some principal temples and a statue of Roma herself, accompanied by the suckling Romulus and Remus. The **Viale delle Cento Fontane** runs the width of the garden, pouring endless streams of water from moss-covered masks into its narrow basins. At the other end from the Rometta, the **Fontana dell'Ovato** spurts one great sheet of water 5 meters into the air. Down the semi-circular steps from the center of the Viale delle Cento Fontane is the Fontana dei Draghi, a round pool from which four dragons with moss-covered heads emerge. Two great, stagnant fishponds spread out from this point amidst cypress and orange trees. To the left of the pond lurk the **Fontana di Proserpina** and the **Fontana della Civetta e degli Uccelli,** which is said to emit the chirps of birdsong.

Across the ponds, the architectural behemoth **Fontana dell'Organo Idraulico** once powered a water organ; it now silently sprays cool moisture onto overheated onlookers. Don't miss the **Fontana della Natura** with its colossal statue of **Diana of Ephesus** at the very bottom of the garden. Hidden to the right of the Fountain of Ovato is a papyrus **museum** containing a paper-making laboratory and relics of the various stages of development of books. The bar in the villa is expensive, but the gardens themselves are a great place to park yourself with some bread and a bottle; buy your picnic fixings before you enter. Bathrooms are located across from the ticket booth and beside the Fountain of Proserpina.

From Largo Garibaldi, follow Via Pacifici as it becomes Via Trevio and leads to Piazza Plebiscito. Continue straight down Via Palatina and then Via Ponte Gregoriano as it winds its cobblestoned way to Piazza Rivarola. To the left of the piazza lies nar-

Lazio (Around Rome)

10 miles
15 km

Fiuggi
TO L'AQUILA
TO NAPLES
Sezze
Latina
Subiaco
Palestrina
S. Cesáreo
Autostrada del Sole
Velletri
Castel Madama
Mandela
Vicovaro
Tivoli
Frascati
Grottaferrata
Rocca di Papa
Aprilia
Autostrada Rome–L'Aquila
V. Prenestina
V. Casilina
V. Tuscolana
Ciampino
Marina
V. Appia Antica
Appia Nuova
Pomezia
V. Nomentana
V. Tiburtina
V. Laurentina
Via Salaria
Tiber River
Rome
V. C. Colombo
V. Ostiense
Via Aurelia
Lido di Castel Fusano
V. Flaminia
Ostia Antica
Lido di Ostia
V. Cassia
Leonardo da Vinci Airport
Fiumicino
Rignano Flaminio
Civita Castellana
Nepi
V. Aurelia
Fregene
Circeo National Park
Sutri
Lake Bracciano
Bracciano
Cerveteri
Ladispoli
Lake Vico
Viterbo
Vetralla
Tarquinia
Tyrrhenian Sea
Civitavecchia
Tuscánia

row Via Sibilla which leads to the two Republican temples, the **Temple of Vesta** and the **Temple of the Sibyl,** commanding a high point overlooking the cascades of the Aniene. Though the true identities of the gods worshipped here remain a mystery, it's pretty clear that the deities have long since taken their leave. Nevertheless, the temples themselves (preserved as churches until this century) are among the best examples of Republican sacred architecture in Lazio, and the view of the echoing gorge below is awe-inspiring in itself.

■ Villa Gregoriana

The best view of the temples themselves is from the paths in the Villa Gregoriana. Back down Via di Sibilla and through Piazza Rivarola, where at times you can find a food and clothing market, take Ponte Gregoriano over the Aniene to Largo Massimo and continue into Largo S. Angelo. To the left in the piazza is the entrance of the **Villa Gregoriana** (open May-Aug. 10am-7:30pm, Sept. 9:30am-6:30pm, Oct.-March 9:30am-4:30pm, April 9:30-6pm; admission L2500, children under 12 L1000), a natural park with paths descending through scattered ancient ruins to a series of lookouts over the cascades. Gregory XVI had his engineers bore a tunnel, the **Traforo Gregoriano,** through Monte Catillo to combat flooding problems in the 19th century. Now, from the opening of the Traforo Gregoriano, the Aniene plunges 120m in the startling **Great Cascade.** The terrain gets wilder and wetter as you descend into the gorge. Past the gate marked *Ruderi della Villa,* a series of grottoes carved out by the rushing water gurgle with eery light and echoes. Bearing to the right of the gate takes you to the underside of the spectacular cascade. You can climb up the other side of the gorge, but the gate at the top is only intermittently open, and you may have to retrace your steps.

■ Hadrian's Villa (Villa Adriana)

In the valley below Tivoli, the remains of another villa can be visited. Emperor Hadrian, a sophisticated cultivator of art and architecture, built, according to his own unique design, his enormous **Villa Adriana,** the largest and costliest villa ever constructed in Ancient Rome. Some of the best-preserved imperial architecture near Rome lies here, amidst gardens and pools of Anio water.

To get to the Villa, take the orange bus #4 (not to be confused with bus #4/) from Largo Garibaldi (tickets L1250, available at the news kiosk) or take an hourly COTRAL bus headed for Giudomia (10min.; L1500) from Largo Massimo near Villa Gregoriana, and in either case, ask the driver to let you off at the **Villa Adriana** (open May-Aug. 9am-7:30pm, Sept.-April 9am-dusk; last entrance 1hr. before closing; L8000). Hadrian came to power in 117 AD, when the empire was at its largest and most powerful, and spent his time judiciously traveling through and enjoying the delights of his possessions. The restless emperor built each section of his villa at Tivoli in the style of some monument he had seen before, recalling his varied travels. Romans resented Hadrian for keeping his distance (they called him a "Greek lover"), but it is not difficult to imagine why he chose this serenely flat, dry land for his undertaking. As you walk through the crumbling remains, the spirit of the cosmopolitan emperor, who treasured his privacy above all else, seems still to pervade his curious retreats.

Just after you enter the gate, there is a small museum followed by a bar on the right side. Both have public bathrooms and the latter sells maps (necessary unless you are just out for a stroll) and contains a sizeable model of the villa. From there, the path leads you to the **Pecile,** a great, once-colonnaded court built to recall the famous Painted Porch *(Poikile)* in Athens where Hadrian's heroes, the Greek philosophers, met to debate. Various building complexes open to the left. At the northeast corner of the Pecile, the Philosopher's Hall, with seven niches that once held the sages' tomes, leads to the **Maritime Theater.** This was the emperor's private circular study and bedroom, cloistered inside a courtyard and protected by a moat.

Underneath the broad **Court of the Libraries** (south of the Maritime Theater), a shadowy **Cryptoporticus,** one of several in the villa, kept the emperor's army of slaves hidden from view as they ran the enormous complex. The rest of the **Imperial Palace** sprawls nearby in well-labeled enclaves. South of the Pecile, beyond the main buildings, the **Canopus,** a murky expanse of water surrounded by plasters of the original architecture and sculpture found here, replicates a famous canal near Alexandria in Egypt.

The **Serapeum,** a Baroque-like semicircular dining hall, anchors the far end of the canal. Here the emperor and his guests dined on a platform completely surrounded by water cascading down from the fountains at the back. On the walk back to the entrance, note the **small Thermae** and **great Thermae** (baths), which reside under the remnants of a dome suspiciously like that of the Pantheon.

■ Subiaco

From Tivoli, you can trace the Aniene back to its source in the stunning, untouched valley of **Subiaco,** a rocky town that dominates one of Lazio's emptier up-country quarters. As the road climbs inland, the sheer, forested crags of the Monti Simbruni rise above pastures and vineyards. Subiaco stands alone in this verdant wilderness, but the few human hands that have touched its rocky valley have left impressive marks indeed. The town owes its origins to Nero, who built an enormous villa at the foot of the hill and diverted the Anio to make a giant reflecting pool in front of it. The slaves and workers involved in the construction of the villa needed a place to stay, and so ancient Sublaqueum was born. Nero soon went down the tubes—and so did the lake when the last bit of the dam finally broke in 1305.

The real fame of the town is due to a more humble inhabitant—the young Benedetto di Norcia, a rich wastrel of the sixth century who gave up everything to live a life of penitential contemplation in a cave above the town. After three years of seclusion he emerged and founded a monastery, giving birth to the **Benedictine Order.** Though there had been Christian monasteries before Benedict, it was his Foundation and Rule, written from atop the cliff, that set the pattern for the great monastic movements that spread throughout medieval Europe. In the following centuries, a building boom of monasteries and convents along the hillside filled the valley with monks and nuns and made Subiaco a center of Christian scholarship. The **Convent of Santa Scolastica,** named for Benedict's twin sister, assembled a famous library and in 1465 hosted the first printing press in Italy. The **Convent of San Benedetto,** built over the saint's original cave, is decorated to this day with one of the most extensive assemblages of 13th- and 14th-century painting in central Italy. Though a tour of Subiaco and its precipitous monasteries involves some footwork, the artistic and architectural treasures secreted inside the cliffs are well worth the effort.

COTRAL buses to Subiaco from Rome leave from Rebibbia at the end of Metro Linea B about every 20-50 minutes, but only every 1-3 hours on Sunday (buses depart Mon.-Fri. 5:50am-10:10pm, Sat. 6:20am-10:10pm, Sun. and holidays 7:10am-9:40pm). If the scheduled time is followed by an "A" or "GRA" the bus is direct by highway (1hr.); otherwise the bus takes a longer but more scenic route (1½ hrs.). **Buses returning to Rome** leave from Piazza del Campo about every 20-60min., but only every 1-3 hours on Sunday (buses depart Mon.-Sat. 4:30am-8:30pm; Sun. 5am-7:30pm). **COTRAL buses from Tivoli to Subiaco** leave from the *capolinea* at Largo Massimo about every hour with a break from 2:30-4pm. Purchase your ticket right at the *capolinea* (L4900; buses leave Mon.-Sat. 6:10am-10:50pm, Sun., 6 buses only, 9am-10:10pm).

Before the bus passes through the **Arco Trionfale,** get off and head up the street (Via Cadorna) to #59, home of the **tourist office** (tel. (0774) 82 20 13; open Mon.-Sat. 8am-2pm). If you are feeling adventurous, you can take the bus, without stopping at the tourist office, all the way to the Capolinea at **Piazza della Resistenza.** From there, catch the TRL bus labeled "Jenne/Vallepietra" which stops near the entrances to the monasteries (departures Mon.-Sat. 6am and 10am, 2pm, and 7pm, Sun. 10am and 3:30pm; L1000).

To the left of the tourist office winds a road climbing to the forbidding **Rocca Abbaziale,** a medieval fortress dating from 1073 and once home to Rodrigo Borgia (later Pope Alexander VI) during his tenure as abbot of San Benedetto. Only the most energetic should climb the winding streets to view its walls. To get to the monasteries on foot, take Via Cavour to Via Papa Braschi out of town. Veer left on the road that leads up the hill. At Nero's Villa begins the **Percorso dei Monasteri,** a lovely but unkempt 2.5km path of stairways that cuts through the mountainside past both monasteries.

The **Convento di Santa Scolastica** (tel. (0774) 855 25; open daily 9am-12:30pm and 4-7pm; monk-led tours every ½hr.; admission free), a massive, architectural hodge-podge rises on the right. The complex is made up of three different cloisters, each centered around a well and a garden. In the first, a dull reconstruction of a Renaissance design, look for the words "Ave Maria" planted in artichokes. Pictures of visits from recent popes line the wall mirroring paintings of earlier popes on the opposite columns. The second courtyard features an intricately carved Gothic arch and faded frescoes; the third and earliest court is the work of the 13th-century Cosmati family, whose twisted columns and bright mosaic work found their way into most of the churches in Rome. Off this court, a Neoclassical church by Quarenghi (the Italian architect who designed much of Russian St. Petersburg) reposes in white-washed serenity. The library shelters the first two books printed in Italy.

When Pope Pius II visited the **Convento di San Benedetto** (tel. (0774) 850 39; open daily 9am-12:30pm and 3-6pm; admission free), another ½km up the hill, he likened the Gothic complex, clinging to its perilous cliff, to a giant swallow's nest. Petrarch was more generous (and no less accurate) when he said it seemed like the threshold of paradise. The monastery occupies one of the most spectacular hilltop sites in central Italy: from its honey-colored terraces, the peaks and valleys of the Monti Simbruni stretch far into the distance. The monastery was founded on the site of the **Sacro Speco,** the rocky grotto where St. Benedict lived in penitential solitude for three years. As the fortunes of the monastery grew, so did the church. Each generation of monks carved new chapels out of the rock and plastered them with frescoes. A descent through the several levels of subterranean shrines is like a ride on an art-history time machine. The *loggia* at the entrance to the upper church is decorated with the newest art in the place, a series of late-15th-century frescoes of the Madonna and Child and the Evangelists by the school of Perugino.

Inside, the first section of the upper church boasts an elaborate cycle of 14th-century frescoes by a member of the Sienese school, depicting the Crucifixion and the Biblical events surrounding it. The scenes, including *The Way of the Cross* and *The Kiss of Judas* (on the left wall), *The Crucifixion* (on the central arch), *Entry into Jerusalem, The Visit to the Tomb, Christ with Mary Magdalene,* and *Christ with Doubting Thomas* (on the right wall), are filled with a fascinating cast of medieval men, women, children, and beasts. Beyond, a cycle of 13th-century frescoes decorates the nave and transepts around the exquisite Cosmatesque high altar.

Stepping down from the altar, the lower church glows with the colorful paintings of Conxolus, a late 13th-century painter. The walls and vaults depict various scenes from the life of Saint Benedict, including his many miracles. Monks are on hand to explain. To the right, the **Sacro Speco,** Benedict's original grotto, sits within the mountainside, rocks and all, decorated only by a 17th-century marble statue of the monk (by Reaggi, a student of Bernini) and the basket which was used to deliver his daily bread and water rations.

A small staircase (often locked, but it's worth asking for admission) leads up to the **Chapel of Saint Gregory,** where more frescoes by Conxolus depict Pope Gregory IX consecrating the church. Behind the Pope on the wall beside the arched entryway stands a pensive, bearded monk, who appears again on the opposite wall. The man is Saint Francis, but the inscription, *Frater Franciscus,* suggests that it was painted around 1210, before the famous monk received his stigmata; if that is true, then the painting is the first known portrait of Francis. On the left hand wall, Antoniazzo

Romano's delicate *Pietà* is an obscure gem—a breathtaking example of the 15th-century Roman artist's quiet technical brilliance.

Fourteenth-century Sienese frescoes of *The Triumph of Death* line the next staircase down. Here the **Chapel of the Madonna** gleams with winsome scenes from the life of the Virgin—look for her leaning tenderly on Christ's shoulder in the angel-studded *Assumption*. On the lowest level, the **Grotto dei Pastori** is revered as the place where Benedict taught catechism to local shepherds. Fragments remain of an eighth-century Byzantine fresco of *The Madonna and Child*, the oldest painting in this speluncular treasure-house. But the most spectacular sight of all is out on the terrace, where the lush green mountains dominate the horizon and slip down to the Aniene River. The rose garden below has its own story to tell. Legend has it that St. Benedict resisted the temptations of Satan by throwing himself on a thorn bush. When St. Francis saw the thorns on his visit (some seven centuries later), he miraculously transformed them into roses, which took root and bloom to this day.

Back in town, head past the tourist office and out through the Arco Trionfale to Corso Cesare Battisti. The small, stone **Ponte di San Francesco** leads to the **Chiesa di San Francesco,** at the summit of a small hill. Overlooking the town's expansive, mausoleum-filled cemetery, this somber church is filled with notable paintings, including a triptych over the altar by Antoniazzo Romano, *St. Francis Receiving the Stigmata* by Sebastiano del Piombo, frescoes in the third chapel on the left by il Sodoma, and an altarpiece of the Nativity by Pinturicchio.

■ Ostia Antica

The romantic remains of ancient Ostia (tel. 56 35 80 99) offer a cooler, closer, and cheaper alternative to the more famous ruins at Pompeii and Herculaneum. At Ostia, lush greenery and fragrant vines envelop well-preserved traces of a once-thriving Roman city. The ruins are sparsely visited, even at the height of tourist season, so you'll have no trouble finding a secluded spot for a picnic—and you'll need to bring one (and a bottle of water), since exploring the site requires the better part of a day.

To reach Ostia Antica, take the Metro Linea B to the Magliana stop, change to the Lido train, and get off at the Ostia Antica stop (you'll need another ticket for this leg; it might get checked on the train). Cross the overpass, take a left when the road ends, and follow the signs to the entrance. The site is open summer daily 9am-7pm, winter 9am-5pm; last entrance is 1 hour before closing and admission is L8000. The Bureau of Archaeological Digs (tel. 565 00 22) offers free guided tours at the excavations every Sunday morning from July to October. The tours are in Italian and follow a different route every time. Look for the schedule in the Sunday edition of *Il Messaggero.*

The city, named for the *ostium* (mouth) of the Tiber, was apparently founded around 335 BC, when Rome was just beginning its rise to power. The very first Roman colony, Ostia's growth parallels that of its mother city's expansion into the world of Mediterranean trade and politics. First a mere fortified camp established to guard the salt fields of the Tiber delta, the settlement was developed as a commercial port and naval base during the third and second centuries BC. After Rome won control of the seas in the Punic Wars, almost every bit of food and material imported to the city passed across the docks of Ostia. By 45 AD, the wharves lining the river had reached their capacity, prompting the Emperor Claudius to dredge an artificial harbor to the northwest. Following ancient tradition, Rome's international arrivals still enter through Ostia: Fiumicino Airport lies only a few miles to the north of the city.

Ostia was a city of commerce, and the ruins that remain all speak of the thriving activity the port once saw. Warehouses, shipping offices, hotels, bars, and shrines to the polyglot religious cults of slaves and sailors fill the site. Ostia's fortunes declined as Rome's did. The port fell into disuse during the onslaught of the Goths, and the silty Tiber eventually moved the coastline a mile or so to the west. After the city was sacked by the Goths in the ninth century, Pope Gregory IV built a new fortified town on the road from the present-day entrance gate, and the ancient city receded into malarial swampiness. Fortunately, the mud affected a remarkable archaeological pres-

ervation. Once with a population of 80,000, the site was nearly desolate until papa
excavations began in the 19th century (there were only about 150 inhabitants as o
the mid-18th century); archaeologists continue to dig, having only uncovered abou
half of the city. Practical Ostia's buildings were built of brick; the site was thus quar
ried and pillaged far less than the monumental marble precincts of Rome. Wha
remains today is in many ways more impressive. Walking its main streets and narrow
alleyways, you can easily imagine the din and flow of ancient city life.

From the entrance gate, the **Via Ostiensis** (the same highway that now leads out o
Rome), paved with basalt blocks, leads through a **necropolis** of brick and marble
tombs. As in Rome, city law forbade burial within the city walls. The tombs here
were for officials and people of high rank. The road passes through the low remain
of the **Porta Romana,** one of the city's three gates guarded by a winged **statue o
Minerva Victoria.** The road now becomes the city's main street, the **Decumanu
Maximus,** and leads into the center of town. A few hundred yards inside, the **Baths o
Neptune** rise on the right. Climb the stairs for a view of the large entrance hall, pave
with a mosaic scene appropriate for a harbor town: Neptune driving his chariot, su
rounded by marine creatures. To the left below is the large colonnaded **palestra
where bathers strolled and played games. The warren of smaller rooms enclosed th
hot and cold baths.

Via dei Vigili leads off to the right of the baths to the **Caserma dei Vigili,** or Hous
of the Firemen, which housed one of Ostia's many trade guilds. The firemen ev
dently kept a fairly earnest imperial cult, as their main meeting hall is lined with statu
bases inscribed to various emperors. The street is now partially closed. Off the Dec
manus on the left of the Baths of Neptune, the **Via della Fontana,** a well-preserve
street lined with stores and apartment houses, leads back to a **Fullonica,** or ancie
"dry" cleaning shop. The deep pits were filled with clothing and fresh, antisept
urine, then agitated by the unlucky slaves whose job it was to jump in and splas
around.

The well-preserved but much-restored **Theater** is found next on the right. Its ou
side face housed several small stores; now it holds a souvenir stand and bar. A vaulte
passage leads underneath the stands to the semicircular *cavea.* The stage itself w
backed by a wall several stories high, which would have been decorated with c
umns, arches, niches, and statuary; only the low wall of its foundation survive
Beyond the theater, the expansive **Piazzale delle Corporazioni** (Forum of the Corp
rations) extends to the old river bank. Here importers and shipping agents from :
over the Roman world maintained their offices (about 70 in all). The sidewalk is line
with mosaic inscriptions proclaiming their businesses, the ancient precursors
modern welcome mats. The inscriptions tell the trade and the origin of each me
chant, and they are accompanied by amazingly intact mosaic pictograms (look f
fish and ships on the doorfronts of sailors). In the center of the piazza is a small sta
case and a few disembodied columns—all that remains of a temple to Ceres, the g
dess of grain, the lifeblood of Ostia's trade.

Several dozen meters from the Piazzale delle Corporazioni, on the theater side
the Decumanus, Via dei Molini leads to the **Casa di Diana,** the best-preserved Rom
house at Ostia and among the most complete in the world. Buildings like this, know
as *insulae* (apartment blocks), once filled Rome and every city of the Roman Empi
Unlike the large, single-family villas at Pompeii, an *insula* was a collection of thre
story apartments and rooms where several dozen people lived together, sharing t
courtyard and kitchen facilities. The ground floor housed *tabernae* (shops), each w
its own opening onto the street. The grooves in the thresholds show where slidi
wooden screens served as doors. One of the ground-floor rooms houses a restore
multi-colored fresco which provides some insight into the elaborate home deco
tions. The entrance to the complex leads to a long, dark hallway heading into the c
tral courtyard. The building gets its name from the terra-cotta relief of Diana found
the courtyard. At the back of the ground floor, a dark, windowless room hold
Mithraeum, a shrine to the Persian sun god Mithras, whose cult was celebrated
worshippers sacrificing and feasting while reclining on the two low couches. T

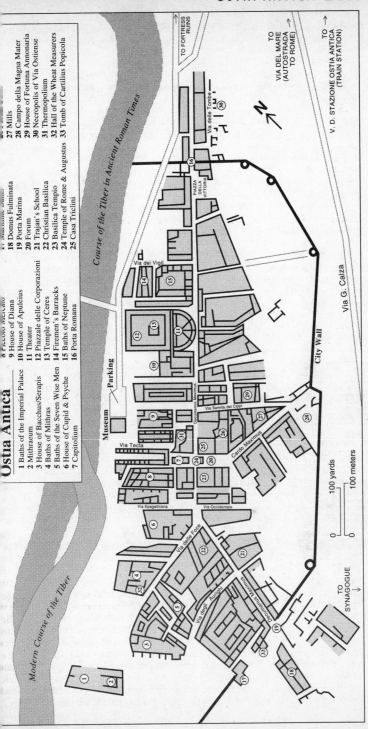

Ostia Antica

1 Baths of the Imperial Palace
2 Mithraeum
3 House of Bacchus/Serapis
4 Baths of Mithras
5 Baths of the Seven Wise Men
6 House of Cupid & Psyche
7 Capitolium
8 Piccolo Mercato
9 House of Diana
10 House of Apuleius
11 Theater
12 Piazzale delle Corporazioni
13 Temple of Ceres
14 Firemen's Barracks
15 Baths of Neptune
16 Porta Romana
17 Magazzini Grandi
18 Domus Fulminata
19 Porta Marina
20 Forum
21 Trajan's School
22 Christian Basilica
23 Basilica Tempio
24 Temple of Rome & Augustus
25 Casa Triclini
26
27 Mills
28 Campo della Magna Mater
29 House of Fortuna Annonaria
30 Necropolis of Via Ostiense
31 Thermopolium
32 Hall of the Wheat Measurers
33 Tomb of Cartilius Popicola

Course of the Tiber in Ancient Roman Times

Modern Course of the Tiber

Via delle Tombe

PIAZZA DELLA VITTORIA

Via dei Vigil

Via Tecta

Via Epagathiana

Via Occidentale

Decumanus Maximus

Via Semita dei Cippi

Cardo Maximus

Via degli Aurighi

Via della Foce

Decumanus Maximus

City Wall

Via G. Calza

Museum

Parking

TO FORTRESS RUINS

TO VIA DEL MARE (AUTOSTRADA TO ROME)

TO V. D. STAZIONE OSTIA ANTICA (TRAIN STATION)

TO SYNAGOGUE

N

0   100 yards
0   100 meters

DAYTRIPS

pumice stone adornments were supposed to imitate the cave in which Mithras was born. Upstairs there are more apartments and the foundations of stairs that led to as many as three more stories.

Down the Via della Casa, which cuts in front of the house and leads to the left, is the **Thermopolium,** the ancient ancestor of the cappuccino bar. Hot drinks were kept in the sunken clay jars and served across the marble bar. Ancient snackers consumed the fare in the small courtyard to the rear of the bar. A few yards down the Via dei Molini, on the right side of the House of Diana, the **molini** (bakeries), which produced bread for the markets of Rome, jut into the street. The volcanic-stone mills in which the bread was baked sit just behind the storefronts. Behind the House of Diana is the **museum** (open daily 9:30am-1:30pm; entrance included in the admission to the park), where a diverse collection of artifacts, both monumental and mundane, are on display. A colossal statue of Trajan (central room), several sarcophagi **(Room 9)**, bas-reliefs of various trades and businesses, a statue of Mithras slaying the Sacred Bull **(Room 3)**, and a spectacular set of fourth- and fifth-century AD polychrome marble panels with an early representation of a haloed Jesus **(Room 11)** are among the treasures. Those with an interest in male anatomy may gawk at the *Hero in Repose* in **Room 8**, with nothing more than a cloth draped over his knee.

Back on the Decumanus, past the House of Diana, the street then opens onto the **Forum of Ostia,** anchored by the imposing **Temple to Jupiter, Juno, and Minerva** (called the **Capitolium**). Climb to the top for an excellent panoramic view of the town. Across the Forum, a street leads to a **public latrine** (on the first left; no longer in service), and the vast **Terme del Foro** (Forum Baths), with their various hot and cold bathing rooms (second left). The Via del Tempio Rotondo runs parallel to the Decumanus and passes the third-century AD **Round Temple,** a miniature Pantheon, dedicated to the cult of all deified emperors, whose grand staircase is still intact. Via Epagathiana, across the Decumanus, leads back into the waterfront warehouse district. The **Horrea Epagathiana** on this street are marked by a delicate pediment and columns constructed entirely of brick.

At the fork in the Decumanus, the **Via della Foce** (which used to lead to the mouth of the Tiber) leads right to the sumptuous **House of Cupid and Psyche** (on the right) where the statue of the two lovers now in the museum was initially found. The house, amazingly intact, paneled in elaborate multi-colored marble, was home to one of Ostia's wealthier merchants. Further down the street and to the right on Via d Terme del Mitra, a staircase descends to another eerie subterranean **Mithraeum** again lined with banquet benches. Here you can also see the beginning of an endless maze of sewers and cisterns that spreads beneath the city.

Across the Via della Foce, the two-story **Casa di Serapide** has a central atrium with paintings and a relief of the god himself. Climb to the second story balcony for a par tially obscured view of the whole city—and the modern highway alongside the ruins The house opens into the **Baths of the Seven Wise Men,** named for a scatological fresco cycle found in one of the rooms. The circular mosaic hall was once heated b a system of hot air ducts and served as an exercise area for the bath. The next build ing as you pass through the baths past the circular room, the **Casa dei Aurigh** houses two frescoes of charioteers and an arcaded courtyard. This building comple may have served as a hotel. Take a left down Via degli Aurighi to reach the **Port Marina,** where debarking travelers entered the city a few meters down the Decu manus, at the western end of the city. Beyond the Porta Marina, on Via Serviana nea the ancient riverbank, the entrance to the **Synagogue** is marked by two steps whic lead into a vestibule. On the right, a section had been identified as the *mikvah*, or ri ual bath. Two architraves with well-known Jewish symbols led to the discovery tha these remains, which also include an oven and a podium for religious services, wer indeed once a Jewish synagogue.

There are cheap refreshments to be had at the **Caesar Bar**, just before the left tur that takes you to the ruins, next to the Sbarco di Enea (sandwiches L3000, ice crear L2000, Snapple© L3000). You can also try the bar just outside the station. Outside th archaeological park, there's little to see at Ostia. The modern village of **Ostia** (rel tively modern—it was founded in 830) has a few bars to slake your thirst. The **Castello San Giulio II** (tel. 56 60 002; open only on request—ring the bell at the entrance, Mon.-Sat. 9am-1pm), across the road from the car entrance to the park, was built by Pope Julius II in 1483-86, while he was still a cardinal. Opposite is the small Renaissance **Church of Saint Aurea.** Growling stomachs should find relief at **Al Monumento,** Piazza Umberto I, down the street from the castle and to the right (tel. 565 00 21), with pasta dishes for L8000-13,000 (wine L8000 per liter, *coperto* L2500; open Tues.-Sun. 12:30-3pm and 8-11pm). An **alimentari** next door sells bread, cheese, and gourmet chocolate. For curiosity's sake, peek in at the toga-wearing waiters and *Ben Hur* chariots at the **Sbarco di Enea** (on the way back to the train), named for the legendary site of Aeneas' landing in Italy.

■ Castelli Romani

Overlooking Rome from the volcanic Alban hills, the Castelli Romani are famous for their white wines, Renaissance villas, and annual festivals. The pace of life has slowed since the good old days when feuding medieval families built forbidding castles and slung insults across the hills; today there's not much to do in any of these towns except eat, drink, and watch the locals stroll by on their evening *passeggiata*.

All of the *castelli* can be reached by blue COTRAL **buses** from the Anagnina Station (tel. 722 21 53 or 722 22 34) at the end of Metro Linea A, and most of them are also connected to one another by bus; ask for bus schedules at the tourist offices in the towns. Buses for Frascati, Grottaferrata, Genzano, or Marino leave about every 30 minutes, 5:30am-10:30pm; a ticket costs L2000. Trains from Termini connect Rome to Frascati and Albano (departures throughout the day, L2700), but take longer than the bus.

■ Frascati

Frascati, famed for its fruity white wines, is the closest of the *castelli* to Rome, a mere 20 minutes away by bus. Its lofty position on an ancient volcanic ridge has attracted fugitives from the summer heat for centuries—Frascati's sumptuous patrician villas remain one of the town's finest attractions. The rich slopes outside the town also nurture acres of vineyards where Frascati wine was born; a visit to the town is incomplete without a taste or two of the local vintage.

The **tourist office** (*Azienda Autonoma di Soggiorno e Turismo;* tel. 442 03 31; open summer Mon.-Fri. 8am-2pm and 4-7:20pm, Sat. 8am-2pm; winter Mon.-Fri. 8am-2pm and 3:30-6:40pm) in Piazza Marconi, 1 (the **bus depot,** where bus schedules are posted, is a few doors down, also in P. Marconi) brims with maps and information on the area's villas. Ask here for a free pass to the gardens of the opulent **Villa Aldobrandini,** whose striking Renaissance façade, designed by Giacomo della Porta in 1598, dominates the hill over the center of town. Behind the majestic villa, fantastical marble creatures frolic in elaborate carved niches of a garden full of gnarled oak trees. Every corner of the estate and its garden sigh in reminiscence of past grandeur. The gardens are open summer Mon.-Fri. 9am-1pm and 3:30-6pm; winter, 9am-1pm only.

About 1km uphill on Guglielmo Massaia (beyond Villa Aldobrandini) is the **Chiesa dei Cappuccini** (Capuchin Church and Convent) which houses the unique **Ethiopian Museum** (tel. 942 04 00; open daily 9am-noon and 3-6pm; closed during church ceremonies; call for times), a collection of weapons, handmade crafts, and personal belongings of the bishop who founded it. He spent 35 years in Africa as a missionary, and now there's a brooding monument to him inside the church. The gardens of **Villa Torlonia,** adjacent to Piazza Marconi, are now a picnic-perfect community park.

Frascati's other villas lie on the outskirts and are often closed, but many of the gardens host evening concerts and plays. The tourist office can equip you with info. In town, the 17th-century *duomo,* its rough stone façade mostly reconstructed after extensive war damage, stands in P. San Pietro. The winding streets around the *piazza* bustle with restaurants, *caffè,* and the all-important **wine shops.** Pick up a bottle, then forage for picnic supplies at the **market** at Piazza del Mercato, off Piazza del Duomo. For the sedentary, reasonable sit-down meals are served with enormous vats of wine at **Trattoria Sora Irma,** Via SS. Filippo e Giacomo, 12. Open Wednesday through Monday, the restaurant is situated above the center of Frascati. From Piazza Marconi, take a left up the steps of Via Pietro Campana; Via S.S. Filippo e Giacomo is on your left. Another place to soak up the local culture—and wine—is at the **Cantina "Il Pergolato,"** Via del Castello, 20 (tel. 942 04 64; open daily 12:30-2:30pm and 3:30-6:30pm), off of Piazza del Mercato. They serve homemade wine and rustic food in the cave-like dining room.

If you're lucky enough to be in Frascati in October or November, you can't help but get caught up in the fevered dipsomania of the annual **vendemmia,** the celebration of the grape harvest. Vine-dressers line up their vats to receive the juicy fruits of the vineyards, to the slurred serenade of onlookers.

■ Tusculum and Grottaferrata

Beneath the Villa Aldobrandini, the road leading left out of town climbs 5km over winding country roads to the ruins of **Tusculum,** an ancient resort town that once hosted such Roman luminaries as Cato and Cicero along its rocky slopes. The town was destroyed in 1191 during a feud between its residents and the Romans, but the sparse remnants of its ancient foundations spread across the hill amidst romantic stands of wildflowers and olive trees. The climb to Tusculum is a tough one, and many succumb to hitching a ride up the hill. However you choose to go, it's worth climbing all the way to the top. Check at the tourist office to see if the sporadic guided tours are being given; if not, ask for a map. The citadel of Tusculum, now marked by an iron cross at the summit of the hill, affords a 360-degree view of southern Lazio, with Rome to the right, the flat countryside and beyond it the Tyrrhenian Sea in front, and to the left, the extinct volcano of Monte Cavo, whose steep slopes are home to the rest of the Castelli Romani. Seize the opportunity for a romantic picnic (and a chance to drink all the wine you've been buying), even if your only companion is a ball of mozzarella.

From the car park below Tusculum you can walk down the other side of the hill to **Grottaferrata;** buses run from Rome every 30-60 min.; they also run from Frascati to Grottoferrata about every 30-60 min. from 5:15-10:30am and at 1:30pm and 2:30pm (L1500). In the afternoon, buses run from Frascati to Albano, with a stop in Grottaferrata (L2000). Follow Corso del Popolo to its end to reach the town's Romanesque **abbey,** founded by the Greek Basilian monks St. Nilus and St. Bartholomew in 1002. History lingers tangibly within the walls of the Greek Orthodox community, from the wizened, white-bearded monks to the 1000-year-old wine kegs. The abbey stands surrounded by an impressive 15th-century moat and fortress, built by the cardinal who would later be Pope Julius II. Inside, the **Church of Santa Maria** has a well-preserved medieval portico and bell-tower. In the gloomy interior, the glimmering mosaics boast Greek inscriptions. The brighter **chapel of St. Nilus** off the right aisle is famed for its 17th-century frescoes of the life of the saint by Domenichino.

A second gate guards the entrance to the monastery itself. Ring the bell and a monk will take you on a tour of the ancient gardens and the monastery's **museum** (tel. 94 93 09; open Tues.-Sun. 9am-noon and 4:30-6pm), where Byzantine mosaics and medieval frescoes taken from the church share space with fragments of ancient statuary and pottery excavated nearby. The rare Greek *stele* from the fifth century BC is the pride of the abbey. The abbey also maintains a school for Byzantine music and restores rare manuscripts. Visit the **library** (open Tues.-Sat. 8:30am-12:30pm), if not to see the precious manuscripts, then at least to walk through the silent, white arches of the monastery's interior. For a few hours a week the monks will help exercise your liver with wine from their cavernous wine cellar (to the left as you enter the gate) for about L3000 per liter. Bring your own vessel. Head down Via XX Settembre or Via Cicerone to find cheap *trattorie.* Keep an eye open for *vino produzione propria* (wine made on the premises) signs.

■ Around Lake Albano and Lake Nemi

A few kilometers across the hills from Frascati and Grottaferrata, the rest of the Castelli Romani cling to the sides of an extinct volcanic crater, now filled with the shimmering blue waters of **Lago Albano,** one of Lazio's cleanest and coolest swimming spots. Lake Albano, as well as its cousin to the south, Lake Nemi, and their towns are easily accessible from Rome. Crisp wines, clear mountain views, and a taste of Italian country life are the main attractions among the *castelli,* except during the autumn harvest festivals when the towns liven up.

The road from Frascati to **Albano Laziale** (or "Albano") passes through Grottaferrata, Marino, and Castel Gandolfo. Albano takes its name from the ancient Latin city of Alba Longa, once the capital of the indigenous Latin League and the parent city of Rome; it's thought that the metropolis sat on this part of the crater's ridge. Albano is one of the bigger *castelli* (that is, it has more than one street) and offers plenty of winding alleys for wandering and exploring. The central **Piazza Mazzini** is bordered on the right (as you enter from Rome) by a spacious public garden, the **Villa Comunale,** built over the partially visible remains of a villa of Pompey the Great. At the ends of the park's broad avenues you can catch views of the Roman countryside.

Impressive artifacts and pictorial reconstructions of the Paleolithic through the Renaissance ages (from Albano and surrounding areas) are housed in the **Museo Civico,** Viale Risorgimento, 3 (tel. 932 34 90; open Fri.-Tues. 9am-12:30pm; Wed.-Thurs. 9am-12:30pm and 4-7pm; L4000, L3000 for visitors over 60). Interactive computer graphics and vibrant displays make this place a modernistic treat. To reach the museum and conveniently located **tourist office** (tel. 932 40 82 or 932 40 81; fax 932 00 40), Viale Risorgimento, 1 (right next door), follow Corso Matteotti from Piazza Mazzini for a good while, take the stairs on the left when you see a sign for the museum, and Viale Risorgimento will be on the right (tourist office open Mon.-Fri. 9am-12:30pm and 4-7pm, Sat. 9am-12:30pm).

COTRAL **buses** depart for Albano and other *castelli* from the Anagnina metro stop in Rome about every half-hour throughout the day (L2000). If coming from Frascati, take a bus marked "Albano" from Piazza Marconi. They run every hour from 6:35am-8:35pm but aren't always reliable (L2000).

North of Albano and just free of Rome's suburban sprawl, tiny **Castel Gandolfo** owes its fame to the **Papal Palace** which occupies its volcanic ridge. The current Pope comes here every summer to relax and enjoy his famed gardens, which spread down the outer rim of the crater toward the sea. The palace is topped by a modern metal dome, the locus of the **Vatican Observatory.** The papal domains are closed to the public, but the town's public street and one tiny piazza, dominated by Maderno's early Baroque papal palace and watched over by Swiss Guards when the Pope is in residence, offer passing glimpses of the lake views and mountain scenery which have drawn pontiffs here for centuries. The *piazza* also houses the **Church of San Tommaso di Villanova,** an early work by Bernini, along with a Bernini fountain. Outside the center of town, the lake road opens out to several belvederes, where you can catch better views of Lake Albano and its volcanic outcroppings. A winding road (about 2km) leads down to the lake shore and a **public beach,** where sailboats and windsurfers are for hire; be careful of the lake's infamous and unpredictable gusts. Buses to the beach from Castel Gandolfo or Albano run every 60-90 minutes throughout the day (L1000).

South of Albano, the same lake road passes a spacious park (open April-Sept. 8am-7pm, Oct.-May 8am-5pm) and the curious **Tomb of the Horatii and Curiatii,** a republican-age funeral monument believed to mark the graves of the famous triplets whose duel secured Rome's supremacy over ancient Alba Longa. **Ariccia,** 1km east of Albano on the same road, isn't noted for much beyond the soaring 19th-century viaduct that brings you into town. The *piazza* is graced by the remains of a Republican temple, the medieval **Palazzo Chigi** (spruced up by Bernini in the 17th century), and an original Bernini work, the round **Santa Maria dell'Assunzione.**

From Ariccia, the road continues south to the towns of **Lake Nemi,** another flooded volcanic crater. Ancient Romans, marveling at Nemi's placid blue waters, called the lake "the Mirror of Diana" and graced its sloping shores with a famous temple to the goddess. Surrounded by a sacred grove, the temple was presided over by a eunuch priest who got his job by killing his predecessor and plucking a golden bough off of one of the grove's sacred trees. Life's a bit less strenuous these days on the ridges surrounding the lake. At **Genzano** (a 3km walk or take the frequent COTRAL bus, L1500), the sloping streets that radiate from the central P. Tommaso Frasconi host the annual **Infiorata,** a festival of floral extravagance. Artisans spend weeks arranging yards of blossoms in artistic and geometric patterns; on the Sunday after Corpus Christi (the ninth week after Easter), the town deploys them in a frenzy of horticultural pride. Across the lake, tiny, secluded **Nemi** (avoid the torturous, poorly marked uphill path by taking the COTRAL bus from Genzano, L1500) clings to its rocky perch over the lake. The vertiginous village boasts more staircases than streets, but its miniature strawberries *(fragoline di Nemi),* grown along the shores of the lake, are the town's real glory. A bowl filled with the tiny fruits and topped with a dollop of fresh *panna* (cream) is a specialty at the several bars that line the belvedere overlooking the lake. In late June and early July, the town hosts a **Festival of Strawberries** that lasts several weeks.

Along the shores of the lake, the **Nemi Museum of Ships** (open Tues.-Sun. 9am-2pm; L8000) is 15 minutes down the road from Nemi. The barn-like museum was built to house two complete Roman barges which were dredged up from the lake in the early part of this century. The well-preserved barges, made of wooden planks and still outfitted with their metal hardware, rope riggings, and marble and mosaic floors, were an incredible archaeological find. Each one was over 75m long and 20m wide. It's thought that the emperor Caligula used the boats as scenes for his debauched orgies. Unfortunately, the ships were torched by the Nazis as they retreated from Italy at the end of World War II. Today, the museum houses two scale models of the barges and the few bits of lead and bronze that weren't melted in the blaze.

The lake road continues north to the summit of Monte Cavo, where **Rocca di Papa,** the highest of the Castelli Romani, glowers over Lake Albano and the spreading Roman countryside beyond it. The town doesn't offer much in the way of architectural sights, but the views of the lake, of Frascati and Tusculum to the north, and of Rome and the Tyrrhenian Sea to the west, are stunning in themselves. On the other side of Monte Cavo, **Marino** closes the circle of *castelli* to the north. If you're in town on the first Sunday in October, you'll see the town's fountains flowing with wine during the annual **Sagra dell'Uva;** otherwise, Marino's a good place to make COTRAL **bus** connections back to Rome (L2000).

■ Viterbo

The quiet city streets of Viterbo wind unexpectedly into quirky *piazze* and hidden stairwells, alluding to a romantic medieval past. Imposing, tinctured walls still surround Viterbo, sheltering the relics of its medieval grandeur, partially destroyed by Allied bombing. The city began as an Etruscan center but earned prominence as the papal refuge from Frederick Barbarossa's siege on Rome in the 12th century. The real architectural splurge commenced during the next century, as Viterbo became a Guelph stronghold in the aristocrats' civil war. It was here that the (literally) torturous process of papal elections first took shape. The *capitano* (city dictator) locked the cardinals in their palace until they chose a new one. Threats to cut off food deliveries and to remove the roof from the conference room (so that the cold could creep in more easily) were added incentives for a quick decision. Today Viterbo serves as an induction point for draftees of the Italian military; its streets brim with an eclectic mix of boys in uniform, window shoppers, and senior citizens (but notably few tourists). Yet it still draws some curious and perhaps ailing sightseers to its sulphurous hot **Bulicane spring** (3km from the center), famous for its curative powers. During the winter, the soothing waters are used to fill a large, public swimming pool.

The simplest way to get to **Viterbo** from Rome is to take the **Rome-Viterbo train line** from Termini. The first train to Viterbo from Termini is at 5:35am (L16,000 roundtrip), and the last train leaves Viterbo for Termini at 9:20pm. From Viterbo you can also reach **Bracciano** (L4200, 45min.) on the train line heading to Rome.

To get to Viterbo from Rome by **bus** take Metro Linea A to Flaminio. From the Flaminio station, follow the signs to the Roma Nord train station outside. There, buy a combination train/bus ticket to Viterbo. The train goes first to Saxa Rubra (15min.; deserted at night); then you board a COTRAL bus to Viterbo (1½hr.). The last bus to Rome leaves Viterbo at 7pm. You may want to call the Saxa Rubra station to confirm prices and times (tel. 332 83 33).

ORIENTATION AND PRACTICAL INFORMATION

Enter the city through the arched thresholds of the great stone wall. At first glance, the inner city might intimidate you with its incongruous passages, but yellow signs and a well-labeled map from the tourist office direct the way to the sights. The town is easily navigated: **San Francesco** and **Santa Rosa** are in the northeast region (right inside the **Porta Fiorentina**), **San Sisto** and **San Pellegrino** (the historical center) in the southeast, and **San Lorenzo** west of center. **Piazza dei Caduti** is just north of **Piazza del Plebiscito** (which is practically dead center). The **bus station** is located just outside the northeast corner.

The EPT office is a bit of a walk from the center, near the San Pellegrino neighborhood, but its free maps and information are invaluable. When you arrive at the bus or train terminal, turn right on Viale Trieste, a busy street which lies outside the city walls. Walk along the wall to the first opening, Porta Fiorentina (on the left), and descend along Via Matteotti, just across from the entrance. At the bottom of the hill is Piazza Verdi where you will find Corso Italia, the second street to the right. Follow this street as it passes the Fontana dei Leoni, turns into Via Roma, and finally ends up at Piazza del Plebiscito. Continue in the same direction across the *piazza* to Via San Lorenzo and follow this street as it winds down to Via Cardinale La Fontaine on the left. From here, take your first right and walk straight to Piazza San Carluccio and the tourist office.

Tourist Office: EPT, P. San Carluccio, 5 (tel. 30 47 95; fax 22 09 57). All sorts of printed materials, including a map (just ask for a *mapa*) and self-guided tour of Viterbo. Terse but informed non-English-speaking staff. Open Mon.-Sat. 9:30am-1pm and 3:30-5pm, Sat. 8:30am-2pm. **Azienda Autonoma Cura,** P. Verdi, 4/A (tel. 22 66 66; fax 34 60 29). No English, but a helpful wall map. Open Mon.-Sat. 8am-2pm.
Telephones: TELECOM, Via Calabresi, 7. Open Mon.-Fri. 8:10am-7:50pm, Sat. 9am-12:30pm. Also on Via Cavour, 31, just south of P. del Plebiscito.
Buses: Tickets can be purchased at the theater/snack bar at Viale Trento or at the COTRAL (tel. 22 65 92) on Via Sauro (1 block east). All buses board passengers across from the theater. Buses to: Orvieto (1½hr., L5000); Civitavecchia (1¾hr., L5600); Tarquinia (1hr., L4300); Caprarola (L1800); and Bolsena (L3500); as well as other cities in Etruria.
Emergencies: tel. 113 or 118. **Police: Polizia Stradale,** Via Palmanova, 4 (tel. 34 31 07). **Hospital: Belcolle,** Strada Sammartinese (tel. 30 58 73), 2km from the center. **Medical Emergencies:** tel. 30 40 33 or 112.
Post Office: Via Ascenzi, 5 (tel. 23 48 06), down from P. del Plebiscito. Hours vary depending on the service you want. Open Mon.-Sat. 8am-6:40pm. Another branch at P. della Rocca. **Postal code:** 01100.
Telephone code: 0761.

ACCOMMODATIONS AND CAMPING

There are not many *alberghi* within the old city walls which are accommodating to the modest traveler, but those which are are in beautiful rustic buildings where your weary bones will almost surely rest if you make a reservation. The plentiful (and prohibitively priced) three-star establishments in town charge about L90,000 for a single and L140,000 for a double in high season, but a bit of searching around Via della Cava may turn up a more reasonably priced option.

Albergo Roma, Via della Cava, 26 (tel. 22 72 74; fax 22 64 74). Comfy, old-fashioned quarters at 2-star prices. Some rooms have mini-fridges and TVs. Reasonable English spoken. Singles L45,000, with bath L65,000. Doubles L65,000, with bath L98,000. Triples with bath L130,000. Quads with bath L160,000. Rates may drop if they're not busy. AmEx, MC, Visa.

Camping: The nearest campgrounds are on the immaculate beach of **Lago di Bolsena,** 30km north. Most accessible by public transportation are those in Bolsena itself (COTRAL bus, L3000): **Il Lago,** Viale Cadorna (tel. 79 91 91), L7500 per person, L11,000 for tent and car; open March-mid-Oct. Prettier campgrounds near Bolsena off the Cassia in the towns of Capodimonte and Montefiascone. The tourist office has a list of campgrounds in the province of Viterbo (tel. 79 91 52).

FOOD

Local specialties include *lombriche* (earthworm-shaped) pasta and a chestnut soup known as *zuppa di mosciarelle.* Try Viterbo's native *sambuca,* a sweet anise-flavored liqueur. One of the most celebrated local wines exults in the effervescent name *Est! Est!! Est!!!,* with which a duke tippled himself to death (see Est! Est!! Rest (in Peace)!!!, p. 132). Pope Martin IV experienced doom of a different sort—the sufferings of purgatory, according to Dante—for his weakness for another local dish, roasted eel from Bolsena. Less exotic, if no less sinful, freshwater fish flourish in the towns surrounding Lake Bolsena. *Alimentari* can be found along Via dell'Orologio, or check out the huge **outdoor market** (Sat. 7am-2pm) in Piazza Martiri d'Ungheria, adjacent to the EPT. There is a **Supervivo supermarket** on Via Marconi, 40, just before P. dei Caduti on the left (open daily 8am-1pm and 4:30-8pm, closed Thurs. afternoon).

Trattoria all'Archetto, Via San Cristoforo, 1 (tel. 32 57 69), off of Via A. Saffi, at the open end of a dead end. Peppe cooks up traditional and local Italian delights which you can enjoy outside under a rustic, medieval arch. Outdoor tables rain or shine. *Primi* L6000. *Secondi* L9000-L14,000. L20,000 *menù* includes ¼-liter of wine. Open Mon.-Sat. 9am-9:30pm.

Porta Romana, Via della Bontà, 12 (tel. 30 71 18), in the southeast, near the Porta Romana gate. You tell Tina how much you're willing to pay, she tells you how much you're entitled to eat. Provincial specialties lauded by locals in a tavern atmosphere. *Primi* generally L10,000-15,000, *secondi* L15,000-20,000, full meals about L30,000. House wine L7500. Cover L2500. Open Mon.-Sat. 12:30-2:30pm and 7:30-11:30pm.

Taverna del Padrino, Via della Cava, 22. Tasty pizzas and a lively atmosphere. Popular with the locals. Pizzas average L8000. Cover L2000. Open daily 6:30pm-2am.

SIGHTS

Towards the southern end of town is the medieval quarter's administrative center, **Piazza del Plebiscito.** The medallion-decked building with the tall clock tower is the **Palazzo del Popolo,** across from the **Palazzo della Prefettura.** Large stone lions, the symbol of Viterbo, guard both. Between them lies the **Palazzo Comunale** (open 8am-2pm; free) in full Renaissance sprawl. The odd frescoes in the **Sala Regia,** painted in 1592, depict the history of Viterbo, mixing in Etruscan, Classical, Christian, and medieval legends. Go upstairs to the office straight ahead and ask to have the Royal Room opened. Peak into the **capella dei Priori** on the right at the top of the stairs for Sebastian del Piombo's compelling paintings of *The Flagellation of Christ* and the *Pietà.* Visit the *loggia* for a dazzling peek at the community garden and the tower of **Chiesa della Trinità** in the distance.

Outside, across from the large clock tower, the façade of the **Church of Sant'Angelo** incorporates a late Roman sarcophagus that contains the body of the beautiful and virtuous Galiana. When she refused to marry an amorous Roman baron, he besieged the city, promising to spare it if she came to the wall. As soon as Galiana appeared, the baron shot her with an arrow, thereby ensuring her fidelity.

Curious *palazzi* line **Via di San Lorenzo,** which winds its way from P. del Plebescito into Viterbo's medieval heart, P. San Lorenzo. As you walk down the street, enter **Piazza del Gesù** on the right, crowned by the medieval **Borgogne Tower.** A plaque on the seemingly peaceful thousand-year-old stone façade of the **Chiesa del Gesù** here recounts family murders that took place during a morning mass in 1271.

At the bend of Via San Lorenzo after Via Cardinale la Fontaine is the tree-lined, ever-so-charming yet unfortunately-named **Piazza della Morte** (Square of Death), whose center contains a vibrant fountain as well as the 13th-century **Palazzetto di San Tomaso.** Note the medieval balcony next to the **Church of Santa Giacinta,** also on the square. Just north of P. della Morte, to the right off of Via San Lorenzo, Via Cardinale La Fontaine leads, by way of Via San Pietro, to Via San Pellegrino, and stumbles its way through the medieval quarter of **San Pellegrino.** Churches and towers block the path completely, whittling the sky to a scant strip of blue between the dark *peperino* walls of the volcanic rock native to the area. Shadows dance in the yawning arches and narrow alleys of this perfectly preserved medieval scene.

In the Siena-influenced bell tower of the **cathedral** in Piazza San Lorenzo (at the end of Via San Lorenzo, coming from the Piazza della Morte), pairs of slender, arched windows climb to a sharp peak. The **Loggia dei Papi** (open Mon.-Sat. 10am-12:30pm), topped by a row of tooth-like merlons, fills the far end of the piazza. From the *loggia,* enjoy a bird's-eye view of a complex of early Christian churches. This has been the site of three papal conclaves, including the one in which the roof was almost removed to freeze the clergy into a decision. The **Museum of Sacred Arts** inside the curia of the church contains medieval sculpture and painting (opendaily 9:45am-1pm; free).

Towards the other side of town, Via Cavour and Via Giuseppe Garibaldi converge near the Porta Romana at the **Piazza Fontana Grande,** the appropriately named home to the city's largest, most luxurious fountain. Steps surround the Great Fountain which is crowned by a magnificent Gothic spire.

Back near the bus station at the northern end of town, the solemn **Basilica of San Francesco** contains the tombs of two popes who died in Viterbo: Adrian V (1276, whom Dante put in hell with the misers) and Clement IV (1265-68). Both mausoleums boast exemplary 13th-century sculpture (open daily 3:30-7pm). In the Crocetta district, at the nearby **Church of Santa Rosa,** the 700-year-old corpse of Viterbo's celebrated saint is preserved in a glass case. The people of Viterbo honor the saint every September 3 at 9pm, when 100 burly bearers carry the *Macchina di Santa Rosa,* a towering 30m-high construction of iron, wood, and *papier-mâché,* through the illuminated streets. The bearers of the tributary lug it around town and then sprint uphill to the church. In 1814 the *macchina* fell on the bearers, and in 1967 it had to be abandoned in the street because it was too heavy. Several days of frenzied celebration surround this event.

Directly inside the Porta Fiorentina, the **National Archaeological Museum,** P. della Roca, 21 (tel. 32 59 29), contains exhibits on Viterbo's Etruscan heritage. (Open Tues.-Sat. 9am-2pm, Sun. 9am-1pm. Admission L5000.)

The **Festival Barocco** brings excellent classical music to Viterbo's churches in June. Ask at the tourist office about tickets (L12,000) and schedules.

■ Near Viterbo

Villa Lante (tel. (0761) 28 80 08; open Tues.-Sun. 9am-7:30pm; March-April and Sept.-Feb. 9am-5:30pm. Tours of the inner gardens every ½hr., L4000), in the picturesque town of **Bagnaia** outside Viterbo, is a particularly enjoyable example of the grandiose villas that were *en vogue* among 16th-century church bigwigs. Designed by Vignola, the villa is framed by a park once used as a hunting reserve for popes and cardinals and is now open to the public. The local (orange) bus #6 leaves Viterbo from P. Martiri d'Ungheria every half hour for Bagnaia (15min.; L1300; last bus back leaves Bagnaia at 8:30pm). From the piazza where the bus drops you, walk uphill and enter the villa's right-hand gate. To enter the gardens next to the villa, however, you must ring at the gatehouse (on the left as you enter) and wait for a keeper to give you a tour of the verdant glories within. In a manner characteristic of Renaissance gardens, water rushes down the hill behind the villas through a sequence of elaborate fountains before disappearing underground.

Farther along the same road lurks a pleasure garden of a different sort: the **Parco dei Mostri** (Park of the Monsters; tel. (0761) 92 40 29; open daily 8:30am-7:30pm; L12,000). Blue COTRAL buses depart from Viale Trento in Viterbo (6 per day, L1400) and drop you off in **Bomarzo,** 1km from the park, 3km from the farmhouse *pensione* outside of town. From where the bus leaves you, walk downhill and follow the signs for **Palazzo Orsini** (*not* Parco dei Mostri). Turn left down the stairs marked Via del Lavatio, and continue downhill to the park. If the picturesque towns and landscape of this region have left you longing for a tourist trap, this off-beat 16th-century Disney World supplies the diversion. A surreal wilderness of grotesque forms mocks the overly refined aristocratic sculpture gardens of the time (e.g., Villa Lante's). A walk through the mossy paths is anything but pastoral, as you amble into the mouths of snarling beasts and past one giant ripping another apart limb by limb.

The Orsini who commissioned the gardens may also have owned what is now Bomarzo's only lodging, the **Pomigliozzo** (tel. (0761) 92 44 66), a converted 16th-century hunting lodge. Its new owners have two comfy rooms which rent for L39,000 per person, L75,000 for two people (each room accommodates up to 4 people). They also grow their own organic produce and offer camping (L7000 per person, L8000 per tent) and use of the kitchen. Horseback riding, tennis, and swimming facilities are nearby.

NORTH TO UMBRIA

■ Orvieto

Set atop a volcanic plateau, the town of Orvieto lies hidden from the rolling farmlands of southern Umbria. The dark closeness of its streets recalls its origin as one of the cities of the Etruscan *Dodecapolis,* but it is the medieval legacy that colors the city more strongly today. A papal refuge from the Middle Ages through the Renaissance, Orvieto reached its historical peak in the 13th century. While Thomas Aquinas lectured in the local academies, crusades real and imagined were planned within the city walls. A well-preserved medieval center provides the backdrop for the stunning 13th-century *duomo,* which has rewarded Orvieto's piety with touristic fame and wealth. Oenology has held special import for the region ever since it saved the city from a Barbarian sack in the early centuries AD. Local lore tells that marauders stealing off with precious chalices from the ancient temples were amazed when their booty transmogrified into "liquid gold"—actually the local wine. Nonplussed, the barbarians partook of the miracle until they were quite drunk and the locals drove them down the city cliffs. Make sure to sample the product that saved the city, the excellent white *Orvieto classico* wine.

Though Orvieto is a popular tourist stop, its residents are far from embittered by aimless wanderers. They are proud to share their rich history and have directed much of their energy into the creation of ceramic art, hand-crafted at nearby factories. The streets are lined with beautiful ceramic displays sold at fairly affordable prices.

ORIENTATION AND PRACTICAL INFORMATION

Orvieto lies midway on the Rome-Florence line. The first train to Orvieto from Termini is at 6:55am and several leave throughout the day. The last train back to Rome leaves at 8:06pm. From the Orvieto train station, cross the street to take the funicular tram up the volcano. When you reach the top you can walk up **Corso Cavour** to the city center (10min.) or take a **shuttle,** which waits at the top of the tram, to Piazza del Duomo (funicular departs every 15min.; L1100, with shuttle L1400). Corso Cavour is the town's backbone, site of most of the city's restaurants, hotels, and shops. **Via Duomo** branches to the left off C. Cavour and ends at **P. del Duomo.**

Tourist Office: P. del Duomo, 24 (tel. 34 17 72). The shuttle drops you at the door. Friendly and patient staff, but the office is often crowded. Get the incredibly complete pamphlet on hotels and restaurants, sights, and practical information. Complete information on trains and buses; city **bus tickets** for sale. Open Mon.-Fri. 8am-2pm and 4-7pm, Sat.-Sun. 10am-1pm and 3:30-6:30pm. The **Tourist Information Point** on Via Duomo will help you find a place to stay (L1000) and **exchange currency** (5% commission).

Guided Tours: Escursioni da Orvieto, Corso Cavour, 139 (tel. 34 46 78). 3 fascinating 2-3hr. itineraries leading through the underground caves, into the *duomo,* and around the city (L20,000-25,000).

Trains: To Florence (L15,000); Rome (L11,700); and Perugia (L8800). **Luggage Storage:** L5000 for 12hrs.

Buses: COTRAL, P. Cahen. 7 per day to Viterbo (L5400). **ATC,** P. Cahen, 10 (tel. 419 21), runs 1 daily bus from the train station to Perugia (5:55am, L10,700) and Todi (1:40pm, L7700). Buy tickets in the ticket office, at the *tabacchi* up Corso Cavour, or on the bus.

Emergencies: tel. 113. **Police:** P. della Repubblica (tel. 400 88). **Hospital:** P. del Duomo (tel. 30 91).

Post Office: Via Cesare Nebbia which begins after the Teatro Mancinelli, next to Corso Cavour, 114 (tel. 412 43). **Stamps** are available at tobacco shops and mail drops dot the town. Open Mon.-Sat. 8:15am-6:40pm. **Postal code:** 05018.

Telephone Code: 0763.

ACCOMMODATIONS

Da Fiora, Via Magalotti, 22 (tel. 410 83 or 411 19), just off P. della Repubblica through small P. dell'Erba (take minibus B from P. Duomo or P. Cahen to P. Erba). Best deal in town. Not technically a hotel; the friendly proprietress rents private rooms filled with spotless antique furniture. Prices go down in winter. L20,000 per person.

Hotel Duomo, Vicolo di Maurizio, 7 (tel. 418 87), off Via Duomo, the first right once you leave the Piazza. New owners rent out spacious, light, well-ventilated rooms just steps of the towering *duomo.* Singles L38,000. Doubles L51,000, with bath L79,000. Triples L66,000, with bath L103,000. Some have bathtubs. Breakfast L8000.

Camping Orvieto (tel. 95 02 40), on Lake Corbara 14km from the center of town. From the station, take the local bus Orvieto-Baschi and ask to be dropped off at the site (the stop is 200m from the entrance). Swimming pool and hot showers included. L9000 per person, L7500 per tent, L3500 per car. Open Easter-Sept.

FOOD

Most of the fixings will fix you for broke. At least the wine is cheap. An excellent *alimentari* sits below P. della Repubblica at Via Filippeschi, 39 (open Mon.-Tues. and Thurs.-Sat. 7:30am-1:30pm and 5-8pm, Wed. 7:30am-1:30pm).

Cooperativa al San Francesco (tel. 433 02), on Via Bonaventura Cerretti. Walk down Via Lorenzo Maitani from the front side of P. del Duomo. Follow the large signs, your nose, or the crowd. Extremely popular with locals. A huge restaurant, self-service cafeteria, and *pizzeria* all rolled into one. Cheap and wholesome. Dine at shady outdoor tables on a peaceful *piazza* or indulge in the cavernous interior. Pizza (at night only) and wine L11,000. Pasta L6500-11,000, *bruschetta con pomodoro* L4000. Open daily 12:30-3pm and 7-10:30pm. MC, Visa.

Da Fiora, Via Magalotti, 24 (tel. 411 19). Just below her rent-a-room residence, Signora Fiora has established a bustling restaurant with the best deals in town. The all-inclusive menù (L14,000) will fill you as you take in a spaghetti Western on TV or enjoy the company of what appears to be the local Boys Club.

SIGHTS AND ENTERTAINMENT

A first glance at the 1290 **duomo** (open 7am-1pm, but the afternoon hours vary each month—2:30-5:30pm is a safe bet; free), Orvieto's pride and joy; promises to be overwhelming: its fanciful façade, intricately designed by Lorenzo Maitani, dazzles and enraptures the admirer with intertwining spires, mosaics, and sculptures. The bottom level features exquisitely carved bas-reliefs of the Creation and Old Testament prophecies and a final panel of Maitani's realistic *Last Judgment;* the bronze and marble sculptures (1325-1964) stand in niches surrounding **Andrea Orcagna's** rose window. The small head in the middle looks out from amid a circular web of colonettes, and together, they form a magnificent maze of sculpture that took 26 years to complete.

The fabulous mosaics provide a day-long performance of light and shadow. Thirty-three architects, 90 mosaic artisans, 152 sculptors, and 68 painters worked for over six centuries to bring the *duomo* this far, and the work continues; the bronze doors were only installed in 1970. The cathedral's 700th anniversary two years ago provoked a flurry of restoration that has left its masterpieces better than ever. The **Capella della Madonna di San Brizio** (sometimes called the **Capella Nuova**) is off the right transept, but undergoing lengthy restoration. Inside are Luca Signorelli's dramatic **Apocalypse frescoes,** considered to be his *chef d'oeuvre.* Begun by Fra Angelico in 1447, they were supposed to be completed by Perugino, but the city grew tired of waiting and enlisted Signorelli to finish the project. His mastery of human anatomy, dramatic composition, and vigorous draftsmanship paved the way for the genius of Michelangelo. On the left wall hangs the *Preaching of the Antichrist.* On the opposite wall, muscular humans and skeletons pull themselves out of the earth in the uncanny *Resurrection of the Dead.* Beside it is the *Inferno,* with Signorelli (a blue devil) and his mistress embracing beneath the fiery display. Rumor has it that the Whore of Babylon, being carried on the back of a devil above the masses, was modelled after a woman from Orvieto who rejected Signorelli's advances.

In the **Cappella del Corporale** off the left transept, Lippo Memmi's *Madonna dei Raccomandati* hangs with abashed pride. This chapel also holds the gold-encrusted **Reliquary of the Corporale** (chalice-cloth), the raison d'être of the whole structure. The cloth inside the box caught the blood of Christ which dripped from a consecrated host in Bolsena in 1263, thereby substantiating the doctrine of transubstantiation, which was not fully accepted by the Christian community.

The austere 13th-century **Palazzo dei Papi** (Palace of the Popes) sits to the right of the *duomo.* Here, in 1527, Pope Clement VII rejected King Henry VIII's petition to annul his marriage with Catherine of Aragón, condemning both Catherine and English Catholicism to dim prospects. Set back in the *palazzo* is the **Museo Archaeologico Nazionale,** where you can examine Etruscan artifacts from the area, and even walk into a full-size tomb (open Mon.-Sat. 9am-1:30pm and 3-7pm, Sun. 9am-1pm; L4000, under 18 and over 60 free).

Return to Corso Cavour and continue to P. della Repubblica where the **Church of Sant'Andrea** initiates the **medieval quarter.** The church, founded over the ruins of an Etruscan Temple, served as a cultural meeting place or commune during the time of the medieval republic of Orvieto. Its Gothic portal, rosette window, and massive bell tower set it off as one of the most important churches in the town. Inside, the crypt at the beginning of the right aisle contains recently excavated remains from the Etruscan Temple.

From Piazza della Repubblica, take Viale dei Mercanti down into the medieval quarter and turn right onto Via Ripa di Serancia. The **Church of San Giovanni** at the end of the road sits just inside the ancient city walls and offers a truly (and we mean it) stunning view of the tame vs. untame countryside below. This simple church, built under the supervision of Pope John X in 916, was once home to the Hermits of St. Augustine. The beautiful cloister next door is now cultural exhibition center. The soils of the verdant slope below P. San Giovanni are enriched by the graves of thousands who perished in the Black Death of 1348.

On the eastern edge of town, down Via Sangallo off P. Cahen (to the left of the tram station; you can take the shuttle back) you can descend the **Pozzo di San Patrizio** (St. Patrick's Well; open daily 9:30am-7pm, winter 10am-6pm. L6000, L10,000 includes the Museo Greco). Having fled just-sacked Rome, Pope Clement VII wanted to ensure that the town did not run out of water during a siege and in 1527 commissioned Antonio da Sangallo the Younger to design the well. After cooling off in the clammy well shaft, enter the **Fortezza,** where a fragrant sculpture garden and lofty trees crown battlements overlooking the Umbrian landscape (open daily 7am-8pm, Oct.-March 9am-7pm).

For the most complete tour of Etruscan Orvieto, consider the **Underground City Excursions** departing from the tourist office. Spelunking guides lead groups on a labyrinthine path past tunnels, quarries, cellars, wells and cisterns that were dug from the tufa 3000 years ago (tour lasts 1hr., L10,000, students L6000).

On Pentecost (42 days after Easter), Orvieto celebrates the **Festa della Palombella.** Small wooden structures filled with fireworks and connected by a metal wire are set up in front of the *duomo* and the Church of San Francesco. At the stroke of noon, a white metal dove shoots across the wire to ignite the fireworks. In June, the historic **Procession of Corpus Domini** celebrates the Miracle of Bolsena. **Concerts** are held in the *duomo* on August evenings. From late-December through early-January, Orvieto's theaters, churches, and *palazzi* turn their attention to the hep sounds of the Umbria Jazz Festival's low-season counterpart, **Umbria Jazz Winter.**

THE PONTINE ISLANDS

A weekend playground for city-weary Romans, the Pontine Islands are Lazio's most splendid assets. After housing a series of exiles from ancient Rome, this stunning volcanic archipelago, with its mountain spines and its turquoise water, was given to Bourbon King Charles III of Naples by his mother Elisabetta Farnese in 1734. The Islands' subsequent inhabitation by wood-hungry Neapolitans led to the contemporary landscape of tiny, terraced, rocky vineyards. Though crowded on weekends in July and during all of August, the islands are geared mainly to Italians—a welcome change from the rampaging Germans on Elba and the international mayhem of Caprì. By making the trek to the islands, you'll see that the spectacular beaches and grottoes of Ponza and Ventutene put to shame the dirty stretches of sand on the coast near Rome.

GETTING THERE

From Rome, the best option is the train to Anzio (L5000) and then the CAREMAR ferry (L19,400-20,500). The islands can also be reached by **ferry** from Anzio, Terracina, and Formia. Companies run *aliscafi* (hydrofoils) and the slower, less expensive *traghetti* (larger ferries that also transport cars). **CAREMAR** has offices in Anzio (tel. (06) 983 08 04; fax (06) 984 62 91), Formia (tel. (0771) 227 10; fax (0771) 210 00), and Ponza (tel. (0771) 80 98 75; fax (0771) 851 82). **Linee Vetor** only uses *aliscafi* and has offices in Anzio (tel. (06) 984 50 85; fax (06) 984 50 97), Formia (tel. (0771) 70 07 10; fax (0771) 70 07 11), Ponza (tel. (0771) 805 49), and Ventotene (tel. (0771) 851 95). **Mazzella** runs cheaper but less frequent ferries from Terracina to Ponza (Ponza tel. (0771) 80160, Terracina (0773) 723 97 98).

Anzio-Ponza: CAREMAR 2 ferries daily each way, L19,400-20,500 (from Anzio at 8:30am and 2pm; from Ponza at 11:15am and 5pm). Schedule varies on Wed. Trip takes 2½hrs. **Linee Vetor** has 3-5 departures per day from 8:30am-5:30pm June-Sept., 70min., L35,000.

Formia-Ponza: CAREMAR *traghetti* departures at 9am and 4:30pm, 2¼hrs., L18,900. Returns at 5:30am and 1:30pm. **Linee Vetor:** one hydrofoil daily in each direction in the early afternoon, L35,000.

Formia-Ventotene: CAREMAR departures Fri.-Wed. at 8:45am, Thurs. 1pm, 2¼hrs. Return 5:30pm (L14,000 one way). If no one is at the information booth at the Ventotene port, inquire at the bar next door. **Linee Vetor:** 3 *aliscafi* per day from 8:30am-5:30pm, 55min., L26,000.

Ponza-Ventotene: Linee Vetor departure at 3pm. **CAREMAR** *aliscafi* departure at 6:10am, 35min., L20,000. Return 7pm.

■ Ponza

PRACTICAL INFORMATION

Tourist Office (Pro Loco): at Piazza Carlo Pisacane, 5, off Via Dante (tel. 800 31), at the far left of the port (looking from the ocean). Walk up the steps under the "Ponza Municipio" sign on the long yellow building with arched entrances. Useful brochure with hotel listings available. *Affita camere* listings as well. You do the calling. Open daily 9am-2pm, 4-8pm. 9am-2pm only in winter.

Banco di Napoli: also in P. Pisacane. Open Mon.-Fri. 9:05am-1:05pm. **ATM** accepting credit cards and Cirrus at Monte Paschi di Siena, Corso Piscane, 85.

Autolinee Ponzesi: Buses leave from Via Dante. Follow Corso Pisacane until it becomes Via Dante; you will see the bus station to your left. Buses depart to Le Forna every 15-20min. until 1am (L3000 roundtrip). There are no official stops, so be sure to flag down buses anywhere along Via Panoramica.

Pharmacy: in Piazza Piscane under the portico. Open Mon.-Sat. 8:30am-midnight.

Emergencies: dial 113. The **police** are at Molo Musco (tel. 801 30); **First Aid,** Via Campo Inglese (tel. 806 87).

Post Office: 3 doors to the left of the tourist office, at P. Pisacane. Open Mon.-Fri. 8:15am-1:30pm, Sat. 8:15am-noon. **Postal code:** 04027.

Telephone code: 0771.

ACCOMMODATIONS AND CAMPING

Ponza isn't the fishing village it used to be. Prices have skyrocketed over the past few years due to the evolution of tourism, and unauthorized **camping** was outlawed years ago due to fire hazards. There are two helpful agencies to save you the trouble of searching for a room: **Agenzia Immobiliare "Arcipelago Pontino,"** Corso Piscane, 49 (tel. 806 78), and **Agenzia Afari "Magi,"** Via Branchina Nuova, 22 (tel. 80 98 41). They can help you find a room in *affitta camere* (private homes) for L45,000 and up per person per night in July and August, much less during the off-season. Hotels are spread out across the island and many require almost super-human climbs up steep hills; consider taking a taxi.

Pensione-Ristorante "Arcobaleno," Via Scotti D. Basso, 6 (tel. 803 15). Go straight up the ramp, follow the street until it ends, then veer right until you pass the Bellavista Hotel. Turn left and follow the signs up, up, up. As you ascend the numerous stairs, you may be cursing the writer who sent you here. When you reach the summit, however, you'll understand why you came: wonderful people, the best views in Ponza, and excellent food. Immaculate rooms and a lovely garden terrace. Half-pension mandatory. L80,000 per person, L90,000 in July and Aug. Call ahead in summer.

Casa Vitiello, Via Madonna, 28 (tel. 801 17), in the historic part of town (to the left when facing away from the port). Walk up the ramp from Piazza Piscane, take a left at the top, then a right. Follow the signs to La Torre dei Borbini; it's across the street. The comfortable, tidy rooms are graced with splendid views. They also have 4-person apartments to rent for longer stays. Between L45,000 and L55,000 per person per night.

FOOD

The Pontine Islands are known and loved for their lentil soup, fish, and lobster. Several restaurants and bars line the port and spark the island's nightlife. They set up tables along the boardwalk, and the fun lasts well into the morning. For grocery and fruit stores, take a stroll along Corso Pisacane and Via Dante.

Pizzeria del Ponte, Via Dante, 2 (tel. 803 87), next door to the bus station. With pizza at L2000-3000 per piece, you can save up for your hotel and a boat tour. You'll think eggplant was invented especially for their vegetarian pizza. Round pizza too. Open summer daily 5am-1am.

Ristorante Lello, Via Dante, 10 (tel. 803 05), on the other side of the bus station. Many regional dishes. Their *zuppa di lenticchie* (lentil soup) is especially tasty (L9000). *Secondi* L12,000. Open summer daily 12:30-3pm and 7:30pm-midnight.

SIGHTS

Ponza abounds with grottoes and hidden beaches. Explore on foot or by renting a boat (L80,000 and up). Guided boat tours are L40,000 per person. At the port look for offices offering *una gita* (JEE-tah) *a Palmarola* to get a tour of Ponza's coastlines and a neighboring island, **Palmarola.** The clear, turquoise water and white cliffs (tinted red by iron deposits and yellow by sulphur) of the island make for an exotic experience. As you approach Palmarola, you will see Dala Brigantina, a natural amphitheater of limestone. Most trips go through the Pilatus Caves, an ancient breeding ground for fish.

The spectacular beach and surrounding white cliffs at **Chiai di Luna** are a 10-minute walk from the port. Follow the main road right along the water and turn left at the inlet full of motorboats before the tunnel. Take the road to a path through a series of ancient tunnels to the beach. The **Piscine Naturali** (natural swimming pools) provide excellent views of the white-washed houses of Le Forna to those bronzing in the sun and swimming past caves and grottoes. Take the bus to Le Forna and ask to be let off at the Piscine. There's a hefty walk down to the sea, but it's worth it.

You can also rent kayaks, paddle-boats, pontoon boats *(gommoni),* scuba equipment, and more. Check **Ponza Mare** (tel. 80 679; Via Banchina Nuova) for rentals, and **Scuola Sub "Nautilus"** (tel. 80 87 01) at Piscine Naturali for scuba lessons. There are also scooter rental companies near the port.

▓ Ventotene

If the crowds of the Eternal City are driving you mad, tranquil Ventotene provides a refuge to rejuvenate your travel-weary bones. The tiny, typically Mediterranean island seems to be populated primarily by the shrubs and cacti that thrive in the red, rocky, volcanic soil, while the coast hides more grottoes and natural arches.

The tiny **tourist office, Centro Servizio Ventotene,** Via Pozzo di S. Candida, 13 (tel. (0771) 852 73), is located right at the port (follow the signs with the *i*) and is managed by an affable English-speaking staff. They'll help you find a room in a hotel or an *affitta camera* (a private home) for L35-45,000 per person in high season. (Open March-Nov. daily 9am-1pm and 4:30-7:30pm; only 3 days a week in winter).

At **Albergo Isolabella,** Via Calarossano, 5 (tel. 850 27), Signora Santomauro and her family pamper the weary with large, clean rooms and terrific sunset views. (L85,000 per person in high season, with mandatory half-pension). To reach the hotel, walk up the ramps from the port to **Piazza Alcide de' Gasperi** and the yellow church. Go right, pass Caffè Freddo, take another right, then a left.

For an elegant meal, walk to Via Olivi, 45, from Piazza del Castello, where **Ristorante Il Giardino** (tel. 850 20) serves a wonderful *zuppa di lenticchie* (lentil soup) for L12,000, and *fusilli con zucchini* (pasta twists with zucchini, L8000), along with a variety of seafood selections. For basic staples, head to the grocery store in the *piazza.*

The **Archaeological Museum** is also in P. Castello. (Open daily 9:30am-1pm, 6-8pm, and 9:30pm-midnight. Admission L4000. During the winter call 850 29 and ask for Pino to open the museum.) Here you can inquire about Italian-language guided tours of archaeological sites, **Villa Giulia** (1½hr., L6000), **Cisterna Romana di Villa Stefania** (L5000), and the **Carcere of Santo Stefano** (2½hr.). **Coraggio** on the Porto Romano rents rowboats (L10,000 per day), motorboats (L50,000 per day), and scuba equipment (L35,000 per day). Three splendid **beaches** flank the port, including **Cala Nave** and **Parata Grande**.

For the week leading up to September 20, the day of their patron saint Santa Candida, the residents of Ventotene celebrate with hot air balloons, dancing, and rowboat races.

ETRURIA

The origin of the Etruscans, a tribe who dominated north-central Italy from the ninth to the fourth century BC, remains as mysterious as their written language. Though the wealthiest of their citizens enjoyed trade and communication with Greek colonies to the south, Etruscan culture (which may have had roots in Asia Minor) was quite its own—in fact, Rome itself owes much of its early artistic and architectural development to this mysterious nation. Apparently, however, the Romans weren't feeling too grateful when they demolished the Etruscan cities during their relentless drive to expand their empire. In the shadow of the new power to the south, most traces of Etruscan life disappeared.

Etruscans enjoyed life to the fullest. Their tomb paintings (at Tarquinia) celebrate life, love, eating and drinking, sport, and the rough, hilly countryside they called home. Vandalism and theft have forced the government to close many of the Etruscan *tumuli*. What artifacts have been excavated now reside in the Villa Giulia and Vatican Museums in Rome and in the national museums in Tarquinia and Cerveteri.

■ Cerveteri

Blue COTRAL **buses** run to Cerveteri at Via Lepanto in Rome (every 30-60min. L4900; take Metro Linea A or bus #70 from Santa Maria Maggiore or Largo Argentin to the Lepanto stop). The last bus returning to Rome leaves at 8:50pm. Fewer buses run on Sundays. There is a **tourist office** called Matuna at Via della Necropoli, 2 (tel. 995 23 04; open Tues.-Sun. 9:30am-12:30pm and 6-7:30pm). A smaller tourist office called Caere Viaggi, Piazza Moro, 17 (tel. 994 28 60; open 9am-1pm, 4:30-7:30pm) can be found across the street from the bus stop. There are no maps there but they answer your questions. From the village, it's another 2km to the necropolis along tree-lined country road; follow the signs downhill and then to the right. Whenever you see a fork in the road without a sign to guide you, choose the fork on the right but don't follow the Da Paolo Vino sign at the final fork. Bring a flashlight and a picnic lunch, with a bottle of Cerveteri's own wine—try the full-bodied red Cerveteri Rosso or the excellent white Cerveteri Nuova Caere. Bring courage, too—few sounds chill the heart like the flapping of the giant grasshoppers which lurk in the abandoned tombs.

The bulbous earthen tombs of the **Etruscan necropolis** (tel. 994 00 01) slumber in the tufa bedrock from which they were carved (open Tues.-Sun. 9am-7pm; Oct.-Apr. Tues.-Sat. 9am-4pm, Sun. 11am-4pm; L8000). The tombs are a curious mix—rough walls and grassy mounds outside speak of the Etruscans' monumental regard for their dead; inside, the simple chambers are carved to resemble the wooden huts in which living Etruscans resided. Archaeologists have removed the objects of daily life—chariots, weapons, even cooking implements—with which the dead were furnished, but the carved tufa columns and couches remain. As you enter a tomb, small rooms in the antechamber mark the resting place of slaves and lesser household members; the central room held the bodies of the rest of the family, and the small chambers off the back were reserved for the most prominent men and women. A triangular headboard on a couch marks a woman's grave, a circular one indicates a man's. Only some 50 of an estimated 5000 tombs have been excavated, mostly in a cluster of narrow streets at the heart of the ghost town. Don't miss the **Tomb of the Shields and the Chairs,** the smaller **Tomb of the Alcove** (with a carved-out matrimonial bed), and the row-houses where less well-to-do Etruscans rested in peace. Look for the colored stucco reliefs in the **Tomba dei Rilievi.**

Also worthwhile is the **Museo Nazionale di Caerite,** P. Santa Maria Maggiore, located in **Ruspoli Castle** (open Tues.-Sun. 9am-7pm; free), a fairy-tale edifice of ancient walls and crenellations, right next to the bus stop in town. The museum displays Etruscan artifacts dug from the Caere necropolis in the last 10 years. A quizzical boar fountain sits outside. The last bus for Rome leaves at 9:30pm. If you're stuck, the **Albergo El Paso,** Via Settevene Palo, 293 (tel. 994 30 33; fax 995 35 82; .5km away from the bottom left side of the main *piazza*) has singles for L65,000, doubles for L90,000, triples for L105,000 (shower included), and breakfast for L10,000. AmEx, MC, Visa.

NEAR CERVETERI

The COTRAL bus which runs to Rome makes stops in the small beach town of Ladis-poli (just 5min. from Cerveteri). Remember this if you feel the need to cool off after a day in the still heat of the necropolis (and chances are you will). Treat yourself to excellent seafood (much better than in Rome or Cerveteri) in any of the towns' cheap *trattorie* before catching the bus back to Rome. Also from Ladipoli, you can take the COTRAL bus to Civitavecchia which stops at the lovely beaches of **Santa Severa** and **Santa Marinella** for a dip in the blue waters off the rocky coast.

■ Tarquinia

When Rome was no more than a village of mud huts on the Palatine, Tarquin kings held the fledgling metropolis under their sway. The tables turned, of course. The Romans came back with a vengeance, and today little remains of the once-thriving Etruscan city or the dynasties that ruled it. The subterranean **necropolis** on the ridge opposite the city and the extraordinarily vibrant frescoes housed within are an enticing testimony to a fascinating culture.

Tarquinia is a local stop on the Rome-Grosseto **train** line; buses run from the station and beaches into town (5-min. ride, L1000; every 30min. until 9:10pm). Trains leave from Termini for Tarquinia starting at 6:13am; the last train back leaves Tarquinia at 9:43pm (1¼hr.; L9500 one way). **Buses** also go to Civitavecchia (30min., L3200).

Buses arrive in the Barriera San Giusto outside the medieval ramparts. The **tourist office** here (the Azienda Autonoma di Turismo, tel. (0766) 85 63 64; open Mon.-Sat. 8am-2pm and 6-8pm) provides a wealth of information, including bus schedules. English is spoken with a smile. In the adjoining P. Cavour stands one of the best collections of Etruscan art outside of Rome: the **Museo Nazionale** (tel. (0766) 85 60 36; open Tues.-Sun. 9am-7pm; closes earlier in winter; guided evening tours in summer, inquire at the tourist office; L8000). Inside the entrance loom the sepulchral monuments of many important Tarquinian families. The sarcophagi are crowned by full-length portraits of the dead that lie within. Look for the "magnate," whose dignified stone resting place still displays some of its colorful, decorative paints. On the second floor, the museum's dynamic mascot, a magnificent relief of *Winged Horses,* dates from the fourth century BC. The impressive array of Greek ceramics (imported by wealthy Etruscans and buried with them in their tombs) includes a cup shaped like a woman's head and a full case of vases depicting Etruscans in the timeless positions of physical intrigue. Also on the second floor are several reconstructed tombs with fine frescoes and a beautiful collection of delicate jewelry. Don't pass up the second-floor ramparts of the castle where you can sun yourself and catch great views of the sea.

The same ticket admits you to the **necropolis** (tel. 85 63 08; open summer Tues.-Sun. 9am-7pm ; 9am-2pm in winter), Tarquinia's main attraction. Take the bus from Barriera San Giusto (any that go to the "Cimitero" stop) or walk (15min. from the museum). Head up Corso Vittorio Emanuele from P. Cavour and turn right down Via Porta, passing the imposing, Gothic **Chiesa di San Francesco** on the left. Then take Via Ripagretta to Via delle Croci, which leads to the tombs. Small bungalows clutter a dry landscape; inside, each narrow staircase descends into an underground room. Because of their sensitivity to air and moisture, only four to six tombs may be seen on a given day (and even then, you can only peer at them from behind a metal railing in the doorway). All of the tombs are splendid works of art decorated with scenes of Etruscan life, including banquets, sacrifices, portraits of the dead, animals and geometric designs. Consider visiting here during the cooler hours of the day, since the open tombs can be somewhat distant from one another and English descriptions of the tombs are outside in the sun.

Tarquinia Lido, a beach 2km from where trains stop, is home to **Albergo Miramare,** Viale dei Tirreni, 36 (tel. 86 40 20). This hotel is right on the beach and rents beautiful doubles for L85,000.

BEACHES

During the summer, the beaches near Rome are crowded with city dwellers trying to escape the hustle and bustle of urban life. It used to be that all this traffic left the beaches dull and polluted, but recently, an effort to clean up the sand and waters has had a positive effect and made a day at the beach well worth the trip. The southern coast offers miles of clean and picturesque shoreline, along with some pretty towns and delicious fresh seafood. The further from the city you go, the better your prospects for sunning and swimming in relative peace, but be warned that in August you could go as far as Sicily and still find the beaches packed. **Sperlonga** (L9800 from Rome by train; take the Roma/Napoli line) and **Circeo,** though a bit of a jaunt from Rome, are the most aesthetically appealing beaches in the vicinity. **Santa Severa,** with its romantic castle looming above the coast, is more accessible, but not as clean. Many of Rome's discos close during the summer months and reappear at the beaches of **Ostia** and **Fregene;** head here for sun-baked nighttime revelry. Frequent bus and train connections make the beaches of **Anzio** and **Nettuno** easily accessible from Rome.

Another note: great stretches of the Lazio beaches lie under the thumb of nefarious *stabilimenti balneari*—private companies that fence off the choicest bits of beach and charge admission. The ticket comes with its perks, including the use of towels, beach chairs, showers, etc., but it's usually not worth the steep fee. Crashing a *stabilimento* is illegal and they have henchmen, but a little polite inquiring will point you to a *spiaggia libera*, the local public beach.

■ Anzio and Nettuno

The broad arc of beach stretching south of Rome is a natural extension of the Lido d Ostia, but the President of the Republic's vast seaside compound at Castel Fusano has effectively isolated the southern half of the shoreline. The train from Termini is the fastest way to get down to the beach (about 1hr.; 6:50am-9:30pm; returns 5am 9:50pm; L5000). When checking the train schedule at the station check for depar tures to Nettuno. The train stations in both Anzio and Nettuno lie one block inland from the beach and bus stops. You can also take the more scenic COTRAL buse (from the EUR-Fermi station near the end of Metro Linea B) that skirt inland of th presidential estate before heading seaward to Tor Vaianaca, the closest beach tow accessible to the public. (Buses depart 5:30am-10pm, every 30min.; L4700.) From here, the road stretches past 25km of *stabilimenti,* beaches, bars, restaurants, amusement parks, and the like—if sand is all you're looking for, hop off at the first appealing stop. Otherwise, continue to the end of the beach, where the twin towns of Anzio and Nettuno occupy a small promontory. The beaches here are prettier and cleaner than to the north, and the diversions are more abundant. The towns were the scene of an Allied invasion on January 22, 1944, and were mostly destroyed by the fighting; today the architecture is strictly postwar reconstruction.

Despite the present invasion of sun-worshippers, fishing is still **Anzio**'s main preoccupation, and the busy port is lined with trawlers and the scaly fruits of their labor. The bus stops at Piazza Cesare Battista; walk two blocks down and to the left to the tourist office in Riviera Zanardelli for maps and information on hotels and transport back to Rome. Anzio is a point of departure for Ponza, one of the grotto-filled Pontine islands. Unless you are a honky-tonk-beach-boardwalk or late-20th-century architecture fan, though, you'll want to move on quickly from Anzio to her more appealing sister, Nettuno.

Nettuno, 3km south of Anzio, sprawls along the coastline with modern bustle. Still, the little town managed to preserve more of its ancient foundations than Anzio did, including a walled medieval quarter and a Renaissance fortress. COTRAL buses and the local orange buses from Anzio stop along the beach road, which doubles as Nettuno's main street. Catch the bus from Piazza Cesare Battista to the side of the gas station (L1500). Ask the bus driver if the bus goes to Nettuno. Below the gaudy Palazzo Municipale, a busy marina teems with boats; the **public beach** lies to the left. The old medieval town, its walls now perforated by several vaulted passageways, preserves its limestone turrets and a minuscule *piazza,* where cheap *trattorie* serve up the morning's catch of seafood beneath an oasis of umbrellas. A few minutes' walk to the north brings you to the **Castello,** built in the 15th century by Antonio Sangallo the Elder for the infamous Borgia Pope Alexander VI. The castle's probably been under restoration since Alexander was alive, but the moat is open as a public garden.

Nettuno, like most Italian towns, has done its best to forget its war-torn past, but one somber reminder remains on Via Santa Maria: the **Sicily-Rome American Cemetery** stretches over 72 acres of parkland, donated to the U.S. by a grateful postwar Italian government. The spacious grounds, beautifully landscaped with umbrella pines, holm oaks, and a sober, cypress-planted island, hold the graves of over 7000 Americans who died during the 1943-44 Italian campaign, which began with the invasion of Sicily and ended with the liberation of Rome from Nazi occupation. The chapel at the top of the park contains a memorial to those whose bodies were lost in the fighting as well as extensive maps and descriptions of the Allied drive up the peninsula. An American custodian remains on duty to provide information and help locate graves. (Cemetary open Mon.-Fri. 8am-6pm, Sat.-Sun. 9am-6pm.)

Hotels in the area are prohibitively priced, but there are two **campgrounds** on Via Ardeatina in Anzio for the ardent nature-lover with a handy tent: **Internazionale Lido dei Pini** (tel. 989 01 01) charges L12,000 per person, L10,000 per car, L10,000 for a 2-person tent, and L13,000 for a 4-person tent; **Lido delle Ginestre** (tel. 989 01 04) charges L9000 per person, L13,000 for a small tent, L19,000 for a large tent.

■ From Nettuno to Terracina

The next great stretch of Latian shore, from Nettuno to Terracina, is also accessible from Rome by COTRAL buses (leaving from EUR-Fermi 6:20am-7pm, every 30min.; see prices below). **Latina** (L5700 by bus, or by train on the Roma-Napoli line), the inland provincial capital, sends local orange buses out to the shore towns of Borgo Sabotino, Foceverde, Capoportiere, and Borgo Grappa, all about 20km away. None of these modern beach magnets has much in the way of historic charm, but the sand is clean and the ocean's as wet as anywhere else.

Further down the coast, **Sabaudia** (L6700) is a modern agricultural center, founded by Mussolini in the 1930s as part of his very successful plan to drain the marshes south of Rome and render them habitable for Roman farmers. Sabaudia is part of the sprawling **Parco Nazionale del Circeo,** a national park named for the imposing promontory of Monte Circeo, which dominates this stretch of sandy shoreline. The town itself is separated from its beach by several modern reservoirs (crossed by bridges), and the mountain lies a few kilometers south across the bay. From Sabaudia's beaches you can walk, take one of the frequent local orange buses, or stay on the COTRAL bus from Rome (L6700) to the village of **San Felice Circeo,** which lies on the southern slopes of Monte Circeo. The few beaches here are pinched between the sheer, corroded cliffs of the mountain, but the scenery is fantastic. From the picturesque medieval village you can climb up to the mountain's summit, which has a bar and some of the more spectacular ocean views in Lazio. **Buses** from San Felice return to Rome every 30 minutes, 5:25am-8:05pm.

■ Terracina

South of San Felice, the town of Terracina was a Roman stronghold, sanctuary, and stopping-point on the old Appian Way. Medieval residents built a walled town over the old forum on the hill, and today a modern beach town occupies the low ground along the sea, in the shadow of the graceful Ausoni Mountains. To get here from Rome, take the bus from the *piazza* in front of the EUR-Fermi metro stop on Linea B (from Rome, 2hrs., L8300 with a bus change in Latina; San Felice Circeo, L1500; Formia L3000; Sperlonga L1500). The COTRAL **bus terminal** in Terracina is on Via Roma, with schedules posted outside. The bus from Rome deposits you in the Piazza XXV Aprile; a walk down Via Roma will bring you to the **Spiaggia di Levante** beach, where the sheer rock cliff, cut away by Trajan in the second century AD to make room for the Appian Way, dominates the shoreline. Across the canal, the larger **Spiaggia di Ponente** (just down Viale della Vittoria from the tourist office) stretches for four kilometers, with soft, golden sand and a view of the Pontine Islands. Both beaches are refreshingly clean, though quite crowded. The town has developed into a seaside resort lacking in small-town charm, but both the archaeological ruins and the beaches remain compelling. Two kilometers up the hill, the medieval town preserves its Roman origins in the pavement of the main *piazza* (once the forum); its **cathedral** houses a gorgeous set of inlaid mosaic decorations.

A half-hour walk up the hill above town (take Via Anxur out of Piazza Mazzini), the masonry foundation of the ancient **Temple of Jupiter Anxurus** occupies the highest ground around. The temple, thought to date from the first century BC, is long gone, but its vaulted foundations remain and make for a fascinating afternoon of exploration. The view from the temple at sunset is unforgettable.

The **tourist office** (tel. 72 77 59; fax 72 79 64; open Mon.-Sat. 9am-noon and 5-7pm) on Via Leopardi provides maps, brochures, and hotel lists (off Piazza Mazzini; from the bus stop, venture down Via Lungolinea Pio VI, and turn right on Viale della Vittoria, which leads to the Piazza). The **post office** is across the street (open Mon.-Fri. 8:30am-7:30pm; **postal code** 04019). **Public phones** are located at **SIP (TELECOM),** in P. Fontana Vecchia off of Via Roma (open 24hr.; **telephone code** 0773).

With a striking stretch of beach comes exorbitant hotel prices, but one hotel lusciously close to the coast is a viable option: **Hotel le Onde,** Via Abruzzo, 1 (tel. 73 15 75), is no-nonsense, spotless, and right off the boardwalk. Some rooms have sea views from balconies. All rooms have private baths. Singles L40,000; doubles L65,000; triples L110,000. If the hotels are full, try the local **campgrounds** accessible from the bus that goes to Sperlonga, including **Costazzurra,** Via Appia, km 104 (tel. 70 25 89; fax 70 08 39). Space for a tent, a car, and two people costs L49,000 in July, L51,000 in August, and L36,500 in June and September. In July and August, bungalows for four are L118,000-129,000.

Fix yourself a snack with supplies from local *alimentari.* If you have cooking equipment, buy the daily catch from the vendors on Lungo Linea Pio VI, and get veggies in the nearby market. To dine in style, try the pretty, pink-patioed **Pizzeria La Caverna,** Via Dino Savelli, 5 (tel. 72 42 81; open noon-3pm and 7pm-midnight; MC, Visa) at the corner with Via Gramsci, right near the bus stop. Full meals in this air-conditioned establishment cost L20,000-25,000. Pizzas from the wood-burning brick oven are a less expensive option (L6000-10,000). **Punto Giallo,** Via Due Pini, 18, offers a large assortment of *pizza al taglio* (L1200-2600 per *etto*) in a setting of teens and 20-year-olds just hanging out (open 10am-1am). Whatever the meal, walk it off with the rest of Terracina on **Viale della Vittoria,** and, while you're at it, stop at **Bar Trieste** in P. Mazzini for the best ice cream in town (cones L2000-3000).

■ Gaeta and Formia

Gaeta and Formia dominate their own craggy bay some 60km south of Rome. Here the steep cliffs and rocky promontories are closer in feel to the spectacular landscapes of the Bay of Naples than they are to the flat shores to the north; the scenery gets more precipitous as you travel south, and in the waters off the shoreline you'll find plenty of stony grottoes and caverns. Only 1½ hours by train from Rome, the area offers a dramatic change of scenery, but one that can get dramatically congested in the height of summer. The train from Termini deposits you in **Formia** (departures about every hour; L11,700), a modern town you'd do best to pass over—though there is a **tourist office** at Unità d'Italia, 32 (tel. (0771) 77 14 90; open Mon.-Fri. 8am-2pm, Sat. 8am-noon), offering a helpful guidebook to the area. From the port of Formia, there are **ferries** to the Pontine Islands, Caprì, and Ischia. For information about the Pontine Islands see p. 263.

From the station, walk north about .5km to Formia's **public beach,** which stretches beneath a great mounded hill crowned by the first century BC **Tomb of Munatius Plancus.** Fish is what to eat in Formia, and **Alla Vecchia Fontana** at Piazza Testa (tel. (0771) 212 63; open noon-2:30pm and 7:30-11:30pm), is where to eat it. Entrees, including the house specialty, *fritto misto*, are L12,000-19,000. Find a snack for the ferry ride elsewhere at a cheap fruit stand in this *piazza*.

For those with more than a few hours to spend in the area, head over to the other side of the mound (accessible by the bus, called the *pullman*, rather than *autobus;* every 30min. from Formia's train station to Gaeta's *Quartiere Medievale* stop; 10min.; L2000 round-trip), to the old section of **Gaeta.** The *pullman* drops you off in Piazza Tranielo where you can find the **tourist office** (tel. (0771) 46 27 67; fax 46 57 38; open Mon.-Fri. 9am-noon and 5-8pm) on the second floor of the building. The broader shores of Gaeta offer better swimming and sunning possibilities—though again, *stabilimenti* have swallowed up the choicest spots. If you want to spend the night in Gaeta, **Da Civitina,** Salita de Leone, 8 (tel. (0771) 46 17 48) is there for you. From Piazza di Leone, (look for the statues of the mournful lion), one block inland from Piazza Traniello, walk up to the top of the steep stairs in the far right corner. To the right, marked only with the number "8", you will find beds for L25,000 per person. Rooms have four beds each and there are only two showers for the whole *pensione* (L2000 per shower). **La Saliera** (tel. (0771) 46 56 51; open noon-3am), on the Piazza Traniello, 30, provides superb seafood while you sit on a porch enclosed with vines (L20,000-25,000 for a full meal). They also have mongo-sized fish that will empty your wallet.

NORTHERN LAZIO: LAKES

During the summer months, the beaches of Lazio teem with Romans trying to escape the grimy heat of the city. The lakes of Northern Lazio provide a cooler and cleaner alternative to the often dusty and polluted beaches closer to Rome. Three craters of extinct volcanoes contain fresh waters which see a lot of Roman traffic, but they are large enough to accomodate plenty of swimmers and sun-bathers in a sufficiently calm setting.

DAYTRIPS

■ Lake Bracciano

Lake Bracciano, a huge sheet of water which lies gently in a valley surrounded by lush hills, is one nearby option for swimming. The shore is meager and the volcanic sand gritty, but the air is fresh, the water cool, and the locals a bit more relaxed than their Roman counterparts. The town itself is dominated by an impressive medieval castle and the scent of fresh lake fish and eel (the local specialty) being cooked up in the town's many *trattorie*. A ferry ride across the lake to nearby **Anguillara** or **Trevignano** offers some spectacular scenery.

You can take a **train** to Bracciano on the Rome-La Storta-Viterbo line (first train leaves Termini 5:35am, last train back leaves Bracciano for Termini 10:14pm; L5000 one way; note that some trains may leave from/arrive in stations in Rome other than Termini). A **COTRAL** bus from outside the Lepanto Metro stop (first bus leaves Rome 6:50am, last leaves Bracciano 8:40pm; approx. 1hr.; L3500 one way). The bus follows much the same route as #201 for Veio (see p. 273); consider combining the trips in a day.

The town is small enough that you could easily miss it. The bus lets you off at Piazza Roma after passing a Tamoil gas station and a green *lavanderia* sign on the left. The **tourist office** is at Via Claudia, 58 (tel. 998 67 82)—a five-minute walk down the road which leads into town. If arriving by train, exit the station to the right and walk down Via Odescalchi to Via Principe di Napoli. Take a left and continue down until Via Traversini on the right. Follow the street to Piazza Roma, where Via Claudia juts off straight ahead. There you can get current bus/ferry information, maps and brochures on sights in and around town, and a handy booklet with listings of accomodations, restaurants, and more (open Mon.-Fri. 8am-1:30pm and 4-7pm, Sat. 8am-1:30pm).

In order to get to Bracciano's main attraction, the **Orsini-Odescalchi Castle** (tel. 902 40 03), take Via A. Fausti from Piazza Roma to Via Umberto and turn right (open summer Tues.-Wed. and Fri. 9am-noon and 3-6pm, Thurs. and Sat. 9am-12:30pm, Sun. and holidays 9am-12:40pm and 3-6:40pm; winter Tues.-Wed. and Fri. 10am-noon and 3-5pm, Thurs. and Sat. 10am-12:30pm and 3-5:30pm, Sun. and holidays 10am-12:40pm and 3-5:40pm; tours are every hour on Tues., Wed., and Fri., every 30min. on Thurs. and Sat., and every 20min. on Sun.; L11,000; children under 12 L9000).

The castle was built in the late 15th century for the Orsini barons, an ancient, independent-minded Roman family who managed to provoke (and withstand) the jealous rages of a succession of autocratic Renaissance popes. Even Cesare Borgia, Alexander VI's Machiavellian son and commander-in-chief, never breached the castle's forbidding tufa towers; the castle only succumbed in the 1670s, when the Odescalchi family tried a more powerful weapon—cash. Inside, a series of great salons and chambers stretches around two picturesque medieval courtyards, their walls and ceilings frescoed with the Orsini arms and with a few stellar cycles by Antoniazzo Romano, Taddeo, and Federico Zuccari. The rooms also house an impressive collection of arms and armor and a great number of stuffed wild boars. The ramparts atop the castle provide a panoramic view of the whole lake and its surrounding towns.

To get to the lake itself, come down Via Umberto and turn right following the signs pointing to the Lago (about 1km). After the first sharp turn to the right (a small church marks the spot), a footpath sits off to the right, taking you on a steep shortcut down to the road below. Cross Via Circumlacuale and continue down to the lake. Sand stretches in both directions, though not far, and stands renting windsurfing equipment, paddle boats, and other diversions (L10,000 per hr.) line the shore. This beautifully swimmable lake sits serenely amidst green pastures and rolling hills and is likely to be quite crowded on weekends. There are public restrooms in the bar at the entrance to the beach.

Consorzio Lago di Bracciano, at the end of the street parallel to the beach, runs a ferry service to the neighboring towns of **Anguillara Sabazia** and **Trevignano Romano** on Sundays at 2pm, 3:30pm, and 5:15pm. Neither of these towns has much in the way of sights, but in their winding medieval streets, innumerable *trattorie* serve up grilled *coregone* (a lake fish) and delicious *ciriole alla cacciatora* (eels cooked over a slow fire). COTRAL runs **buses** between both towns and Bracciano (every hr.) or back to Rome (every 1-2 hr. from Anguillara with last bus to Rome at 10:19pm; runs several times per day from Trevignano with last bus to Rome at 8pm; L4400). The bus for these two towns leaves from the top of Via del Lago, just before the descent down to the lake. To catch the bus back to Rome from Bracciano, cross Piazza Roma to Vicolo del Pratoterra on the opposite side of Via Claudia. Follow this alley to Via Garibaldi, then turn left and continue past the bridge on your right directly to the bus stop. Buses leave every half-hour or hour, running more frequently in the afternoon. Consider stopping off at Veio on the way back to Rome.

▨ Veio

To get to Veio from Lake Bracciano, take a COTRAL bus headed for Rome (see above for details) and watch carefully for the stop on the main road in La Storta. Get off here, cross the busy street, and walk uphill to the bus stop where you can catch the #032 bus to Isola Farnese. The tiny feudal hamlet of Veio surrounds the **Castello Ferraioli** (tel. 379 01 16). Before the bus goes up to the *castello,* there will be an orange sign on the right side of the road marking the beginning of the Isola Farnese. Get off at the next stop and cross the road to a street marked with another orange sign reading *"Rovine di Veio (Città etrusca)."* Follow this road all the way to a waterfall where a tiny bridge crosses a brook near the ruins. From Rome, take the metro line A to Ottaviano. From there, catch bus #32 to Ponte Milvio in the Largo Maresciallo Diaz (the last stop). Get off the bus and catch the #032 La Giustiniana bus headed for Isola Farnese, and follow the directions above to the bridge. On the other side, the path on the right leads up to a large stone gate, the entrance to the **Etruscan excavations** (open Tues.-Sat. 9am-6:30pm, Sun. 9am-1pm; L4000). To the left, the original Roman road, paved with basalt stones, winds to the summit where temples once stood, with a stunningly romantic view of the surrounding fields and hills. This area provides a perfect spot for picnicking and hiking away from the dusty clamor of the city.

▨ Lake Vico

Further away, little Lake Vico is prettier, cleaner, and better supplied with amusements than Lake Bracciano. Take a car down the serpentine road, or get off at the bus stop on top of the hill and walk down 2km from Caprarola. A COTRAL **bus** runs from Saxa Rubra to this stop for L7500 (take Metro Linea A to Flaminio, where you can take the Roma Nord train to Saxa Rubra; departures every half-hour or hour, first departure 7:20am; 15min.). Call the Saxa Rubra station for times (tel. 332 83 33).

A **nature reserve** radiates from the lake for 22km, and is staffed by a young, eager management that offers **guided tours** (mostly in Italian) for a minimum group of four: on horseback (L15,000 per hr., per person); in a jeep (4-8hr., L20,000 per person); on mountain bikes (you must have your own bike; L7000 per hour; 4-8hr., L20,000); in a canoe (L10,000 per hr.); or by foot (½-day, L3000; full day, L5000). You can also take instruction in canoeing (L15,000 per hr.) and archery (L7000 per hr.). You must make a reservation in order to stay at the **campsite** (tel. (0761) 61 23 47; L5000 per person, L4000 per small tent, L6000 per large tent, L2500 per car). Call the "Centro Visite" (tel. (0761) 64 69 56) for further information.

POMPEII, HERCULANEUM, AND PAESTUM

▨ Pompeii

Mount Vesuvius's fit of towering flames, suffocating black clouds, and seething lava brought sudden death to the prosperous Roman city of **Pompeii** in 79 AD. The eruption buried the city—tall temples, narrow streets, patrician villas, massive theater and all—under 10m of volcanic ash. Archaeologists have worked for centuries to uncover the hidden city, and today a walk through the narrow, ancient streets, lined with two- and sometimes three-story townhouses, presents a view of city life largely unchanged by the last 1900 years. Archaeologists commonly believe that Pompeii was inhabited as early as the 8th century BC and that during the 7th century BC it fell under the influence of Greek colonists from the south of Italy, who developed it as a commercial center. By the 3rd century BC, Pompeii was a mature city with a prosperous economy, a population of nearly 20,000, and a sophisticated cultural life closely linked to that of the Greek cities in the south. Falling under Roman influence around 180 BC, the city developed further both as a trading port and as an aristocratic enclave, where high-falutin' Romans, including Cicero, built lavish country villas.

Life went on as usual on the fateful day of August 24, 79 AD—merchants and shoppers crowded the Forum, farmers completed chores on farms just outside the city walls, and the priests of Isis paused in the middle of their daily rites to eat a quick lunch in their private house. These and countless other everyday moments were frozen forever by the sudden eruption, which rained successive layers of ash, dust, pebbles, lava, and rock down on the surprised metropolis. The catastrophe happened so quickly that few residents were able to escape; most took shelter in their homes or in public buildings, where they were quickly asphyxiated by the concentration of deadly volcanic gases. Dust and ash thrown up by the volcano drifted into the town and solidified, encasing not only the buildings but also the bodies of the dead. These decomposed, leaving hollow spaces in the new volcanic rock; when archaeologists found the cavities, they filled them with plaster, creating the haunting casts of agonized and panicked figures (including an abandoned dog) which now haunt some of the city's sites.

In both Pompeii and Herculaneum, you'll find numerous examples of the classic patrician Roman house, known in Latin as a *domus* (*casa* in Italian). Presenting a harsh and undecorated façade to the outside street, the *domus* turns inward on itself, its rooms gathered around one of the three types of open space: the *atrium*, the peristyle court, or the formal garden. The front door (often guarded by a porter's cubicle) leads into the dark and airy *atrium*, the main vestibule of the house, where images of the family and household gods were kept, and where the *paterfamilias* greeted his guests. A rectangular opening in the roof, the *expluvium*, allowed light into the room, as well as rain water, which was collected in the *impluvium*, a stone basin let into the floor. While various chambers and storerooms were arranged around the *atrium*, the main rooms of the house usually lay beyond, including the *tablinium*, or master's study, across the atrium from the door, and the *triclinium*, or dining room, usually arranged near the back peristyle court. These courts, especially in the more lavish houses at Pompeii, were decorated with colorful frescoes, statuary, formal plantings, and fountains. The most elegant houses also harbored a colonnaded garden at the back of the house, where more greenery and running water provided a sumptuous retreat from the heat of the city. Keep an eye out in both cities for the more modest *insulae*, or apartment blocks, where several families lived together in three-story complexes with shared kitchen and bathroom facilities.

PRACTICAL INFORMATION

A comprehensive walk-through will probably take four or five hours; pack a lunch and a water bottle, since the local cafeteria is hideously expensive. **Guided tours** are expensive as well but are probably the best way to savor the gory details of life and death in the first century AD. Call **GATA Tours** (tel. (081) 861 56 61; fax 536 85 77) for information; **Assotouring** (tel. (081) 862 25 60) also offers tours. Tour guides have gotten wise to freeloaders, and go beyond evil stares to actually yelling at offenders. If a tour is too rich for your blood, consider buying the informative *How to Visit Pompeii* (L8000-12,000) from one of the booths outside the park.

Pompeii has two train stations that are located near entrances to the park. The state train that runs from Rome to Salerno (2 per day; L19,000) sometimes stops at the

MODERN
POMPEII

N

PIAZZA
IMMACOLATA

Via
Roma

Via Colle S. Bartolomeo

Porta di Sarno

Porta di Nola

Porta di Nocera

Porta di Stabia

Porta di Capua

Via Nocerina

Via dell'Abbondanza

Via di Nola

Via Stabiana

Via del Teatri

Via Minutella

S.S. N°18

Via Vesuvio
Vicolo del Vettii
Vicolo del Labirinto
Vicolo del Fauno

Via Consolare
Vicolo di Mercurio
Via della Fortuna
Via degli Augustali
Via dell'Abbondanza

Via Marina

Via Regina

Viale ai Teatri

S.S. N°18

Porta di Vesuvio

Porta Ercolano

Porta Marina

Via dei Sepolcri

Viale alla Villa dei Misteri

TO NAPLES

0   200 yards
0   200 meters

Pompeii

Amphitheater, 14
Antiquarium, 34
Basilica, 32
Brothel, 25
Building of Eumachia, 29
Central Baths, 10
Doric Temple, 21
Forum, 30
Forum Baths, 6
Gladiators' Barracks, 20
Great Palestra, 15
Great Theater, 18
House of the
Cryptoporticus, 16
House of the Faun, 7
House of the Golden
Cupids, 9
House of Julia Felix, 13
House of the Large
Fountain, 5

House of Loreius
Tiburtinus, 12
House of Marcus
Fronto, 11
House of Menander, 17
House of Pansa, 3
House of the Small
Fountain, 4
House of the Vettii, 8
Macellum, 26
Small Theater, 19
Stabian Baths, 24
Temple of Apollo, 31
Temple of Isis, 23
Temple of Jupiter, 27
Temple of Venus, 33
Temple of Vespasian, 28
Train Station, 35
Triangular Forum, 22
Villa del Misteri, 1
Villa of Diomedes, 2

DAYTRIPS

Pompeii station. The more frequent state train that goes from Naples to Salerno also stops at Pompeii. To get to the **archaeological site** from this station, head straight on Via Sacra, where you'll find a tourist office at number 1 (tel. (081) 850 72 55; open summer Mon.-Fri. 8am-3pm and 5-7pm, Sat. 8am-noon; winter Mon.-Fri. 8am-3pm). Pick up a free map and the informative pamphlet *Notizario Turistico Regionale*. Continue past the tourist office and turn left on Via Roma. A few hundred meters ahead on the right is the amphitheater entrance to the park. If it's closed, continue on the street now called Via Plinio and take your second right after the park area. This street will take you past another tourist office and to the gate of the Villa dei Misteri. Follow the signs for *scavi*.

You can also take the more frequent **Circumvesuviana train** line from Napoli Stazione Centrale (toward Sorrento; 35min.; L2700, Eurail passes not valid), which lets you off at the Pompeii-Scavi/Villa dei Misteri stop just outside the west entry. To get to the **archaeological site** of Pompeii, head downhill from the Villa dei Misteri station and take your first left. The archaeological park is open 9am until one hour before sunset. Admission is L12,000. Pompeii's **telephone code** is 081.

ACCOMMODATIONS AND FOOD

Unless you wish to tour Pompeii extensively, there is no reason to stay overnight in the dull, modern city. If you decide to stay, however, the **Motel Villa dei Misteri,** Via Villa dei Misteri, 11 (tel. 861 35 93), uphill from the *Circumvesuviana* station, is a wonderful option. They've got comfortable, clean, modern rooms (all with baths) and a terrific pool. Doubles with bath L70,000, extra bed L15,000; full-pension L80,000. **Soggiorno Pace,** Via Sacra, 29 (tel. 863 60 25), has a peaceful garden and nice rooms with private baths; L20,000 per person. **Pensione Minerva,** Via Roma, 137 (tel. 863 25 87), near the amphitheater entrance to the site, rents doubles for L60,000-65,000 and triples for L75,000. Rooms with showers are L5000 more. The cheapest alternative is to stay at one of the local campgrounds, which are all near the ruins. Unfortunately, they tend to be somewhat ruined themselves. **Camping Zeus** (tel. 861 53 20), outside the Villa dei Misteri *circumvesuviana* stop, will someday soon boast a swimming pool and restaurant (L7000 per person, L5000 per large tent, L3000 per small tent). Not far away, on Via Plinio **Camping Pompeii** (tel. 862 28 82; fax 850 27 72), with the same ownership and prices as Zeus, has attractive bungalows for L50,000 for two people and L90,000 for four. If you're desperate you can sack out on the floor of its indoor lobby for L6000 per night. These places are eager for customers, so you can usually bargain them down at least 15%.

Stock up at the **GS Supermarket,** Via Statale, km 24, (open Mon.-Sat. 8am-8:30pm, Sun. 9am-1pm; closes Thurs. at 2pm) on the main road between the east and west entrances to the archaeological site. They've got good prices and great air-conditioning. **La Vinicola,** Via Roma, 29, tempts with a pleasant outdoor courtyard and abundant *gnocchi con mozzarella* (potato dumplings with tomato and cheese, L5500). Also try the *zuppa di cozze* for L5000. (Cover L1500. Service 15%. Open daily 10am-midnight.) More expensive meals are found at the **Trattoria Pizzeria dei Platani,** Via Colle San Bartolomeo, 8 (tel. 863 39 73), down the street from the Museo Vesuviano. L9000 buys you a plate of *cannelloni*. The *menù* is L20,000, one drink included. Cover L2000. (Open Thurs.-Tues. 9:30am-10pm.)

SIGHTS

A word of warning: you may find your trip to Pompeii a bit frustrating. A majority of the sculptures, wall paintings, and mosaics have been carted off to museums in Naples, Rome, and England, though a few of the more notable pieces remain. Many of the houses in the site are closed or have blocked off rooms and areas that only employees can open. Some people tag along behind a tour (in a language other than English, so they can't be shooed away), since the guide may have access to otherwise inaccessible areas. The Villa dei Misteri entrance to the archaeological site leads past the Antiquarium (permanently closed since the 1980 earthquake) to the **Forum,** sur rounded by a colonnade which retains a portion of what was once a second tier. Once dotted with numerous statues of statesmen and gods, this was the commercial, civic, and religious center of the city. Showcases along the western side display a few of the gruesome body casts of the volcano's victims. To the right rises the **Temple of Jupiter,** mostly destroyed by an earthquake that struck 17 years before the city's bad luck got worse; to the left is the **Temple of Apollo,** with statues of Apollo and Diana (these are copies; the originals are in Naples) and a column topped by a sundial. To the left of the temple is the **basilica,** or law-court, whose walls are decorated with stucco to imitate marble. On the opposite long side of the forum, to the left of the **Building of Eumachia** (with its carved door-frame of animals and insects hiding in scroll-like plants), the **Temple of Vespasian** houses a delicate frieze depicting the preparation for a sacrifice.

Exit the Forum to the north by the cafeteria and enter the **Forum Baths** to the left on Via di Terme. The body casts displayed here are so complete that you can even see teeth through their grimaces. Decorating the rooms to the right are remarkable terra-cotta figures. Exit to the right, and on the left opens the **House of the Faun,** where a small bronze of a dancing faun and the spectacular Alexander Mosaic (now in Naples) were found. Before the door, the word *Have* ("welcome," usually written *ave*) is inscribed in a mosaic. Continue to the left on Via della Fortuna and turn left on Vico di Vetti to see the **House of the Vettii,** home to some of the most vivid frescoes in Pompeii. In the vestibule is a depiction of Priapus (the god of fertility) displaying his colossal member; phalli were believed to scare off evil spirits in ancient times, but now they seem only to invite hordes of tittering tourists.

Walk back on Vico di Vetti and continue on Vico del Lupanare, where there is a small **brothel** with several bed-stalls. Above each of the stalls a pornographic painting depicts with unabashed precision the specialty of the woman (or man) who inhab-ited it. Continue down the street to the main avenue, Via dell'Abbondanza. The **Sta-bian Baths,** privately owned and therefore fancier than the Forum Baths (just think: ritzy spa vs. YMCA), are to the left. The separate men's and women's sides each included a dressing room, cold baths *(frigidaria),* warm baths *(tepidaria),* and hot or steam baths *(caldaria).* Via dei Teatri across the street leads to a huge complex con-sisting of the **Great Theater,** constructed in the first half of the second century BC, and the **Little Theater,** built later for music and dance concerts. North of the theaters stands the **Temple of Isis,** Pompeii's monument to the Egyptian fertility goddess. Exit the temple to the right and pass two houses, the **House of Secundus** and the **House of Menander** (so named for the painting of the comic poet on the wall, not because he lived there). At the end of the street, turn left to return to the main street. The Romans believed that crossroads were particularly subject to evil spirits, so they built altars, like the one here, designed to ward them off.

Turn right down Via dell'Abbondanza and note the red writing scribbled on the walls. You'll see everything from political campaign slogans to declarations of love— apparently graffiti hasn't changed much in 1900 years. At the end of the street, the **House of Tiburtinus** and the **House of Venus** are sprawling complexes with wonder-ful frescoes and gardens replanted according to modern knowledge of ancient horti-culture. The nearby **amphitheater,** the oldest one still standing (80 BC), held 12,000 spectators, and the **Great Palestra** was a gymnasium.

Complete your day with a visit to the **House of the Mysteries,** outside the main complex and 10 minutes up the hill from the *Circumvesuviana* station. A renowned cycle of paintings (in the room directly to the right of the entrance) depicts an initia-tion into the cult of Dionysus. You don't need a separate ticket, but you can't return to the central site after you exit.

Many of the astonishing mosaics and other goodies carted away from Pompeii and Herculaneum ended up in Naples, at the **Museo Archeologico Nazionale** (tel. 44 01 66), in Piazza Cavour. If you have some extra time and wish to see some of these trea-sures, consider stopping off in Naples on the way to or from Pompeii. The museum is accessible by Metro from Naples' Central Railway Station; get off at the stop for Piazza Cavour. Since few pieces are adequately labeled, you should pick up an English guidebook at the souvenir shop (L10,000) or leave your passport at the information desk and borrow a copy of the museum's own guide (available in English). The tremendous sculptures of the Farnese collection are stored in the rooms upstairs to the right. The **Farnese Hercules** presents the hero at a rare moment of repose in his otherwise busy life, while the **Farnese Bull,** the largest known ancient sculpture, depicts the bull as it tramples Dirce (her punishment for mistreating Antiope, who stands by looking somewhat bemused). Upstairs on the mezzanine level, you'll find paintings and mosaics from the Vesuvian cities of Pompeii, Herculaneum, and Stabiae. Don't miss the tender *Portrait of a Woman,* the frescoes and furnishings from the Iseum at Pompeii, and the famous wall-size **Alexander Mosaic.** This mosaic, thought to be a copy of a Greek painting, depicts a young and fearless Alexander routing a terrified army of Persians led by King Darius. The top floor houses more paintings, some extraordinary statues taken from the Villa dei Papiri, and an extensive collection of ancient ceramics—vase-painting fans should definitely pay a visit. Unfortunately, many of the museum's exhibits close at inconvenient times (though groups are often admitted then anyway). Check at the info desk about tours leaving at 10:30, 11:30am, and 12:30pm. (Open Wed.-Sat. 9am-2pm, Sun. 9am-1pm; hours subject to change. Admission L12,000.)

■ Herculaneum

Herculaneum (Ercolano), on the other side of Vesuvius, endured a harder fate. Laid out along the sea in the shadow of the volcano, the town was swamped by a wall of molten lava and swallowed up without a trace. The cataclysm did, however, leave the city nearly intact; when the city went under, it was enveloped in the mud and protected. The townhouses and apartment blocks of the ancient city are almost perfectly preserved, with staircases and ceilings, wall paintings, mosaics, and even furniture still decorating their labyrinthine rooms. The city was discovered by 18th-century farmers sinking shafts for wells. Once scholars grasped the full import of their discovery, digging began in earnest both here and at the site of Pompeii, which had been identified by the analysis of ancient texts. Neatly excavated and impressively intact, Herculaneum contradicts the term "ruins." Once a wealthy residential enclave on the Roman coast road, Herculaneum doesn't evoke the same sense of tragedy that Pompeii does—all but a handful of its inhabitants escaped the ravages of Vesuvius.

PRACTICAL INFORMATION

Closer to Naples (12km), Ercolano (Herculaneum) would have a sublime seaside view if it weren't 10m underground. To get to Ercolano, take any *circumvesuviana* train toward Pompeii from Naples's central train station to the Ercolano stop (15min., L2000). Walk 500m down the hill from the station to the **ticket office.** (Open daily 9am to 1hr. before sunset; L12,000.) Before entering, consider purchasing the little blue *Istituto Poligrafico dello Stato* guide to Herculaneum, with an excellent map, reliable text, and some beautifully clear black-and-white illustrations (L10,000). Solo travelers and women should be on guard in the occasionally less-than-savory neighborhood surrounding the site.

SIGHTS

In a much less disorienting (and less crowded) tour than those offered in Pompeii, you can wind your way through the 15 or so houses and baths that are now open to the public. Herculaneum's ruins have suffered less pillaging, and most of the original household art is still on the walls it decorated for two millennia. There are no colossal buildings, temples, or off-color frescoes to grab your imagination here, but the houses, with their fresh interior decoration, attest to the cultural development of this affluent community. Two-thousand-year-old frescoes, furniture, mosaics, small sculptures, and even wood paneling seem as vital as the day they were made, preserved by a mud avalanche that tumbled off the volcano on a cushion of gas. The **House of the**

Deer, so named for a statue of a deer being savagely attacked by greyhounds, is one of the more alluring villas. Probably big partiers, the owners had a statue of a Satyr with a wineskin and an all-too-recognizable statue of the town's eponym Hercules in a drunken stupor, trying to take a leak. The **baths,** with their intact warm and hot rooms and a giant vaulted swimming pool, are among the most evocative ancient sites in Italy. Archaeologists have left unexcavated parts of the *tepidarium:* you can see the imprint of the wooden doors which the waves of boiling mud snapped off their hinges and carried along.

■ Mt. Vesuvius

It is once again possible to explore Vesuvius, the sleeping source of the death and destruction that plagued these ancient Roman towns—just hop on the blue SITA bus from Herculaneum to the volcano (6 per day, last return 5:50pm, L2000 one-way). Once there, you must buy a ticket for a tour (L5000). Hikers can take the orange city bus #5 (L1800 one-way) to the base of the mountain and climb from there; bring plenty of water and a decent pair of shoes. Geologists say the trip is safe—there has been no eruption since March 31, 1944.

▓ Paestum

Not far from the Roman ruins of Pompeii and Herculaneum, the Greek temples of Paestum are among the best-preserved in the world, rivaling even those of Sicily and Athens. Greek colonists from Sybaris founded Paestum as Poseidonia in the seventh century BC, and the city quickly became a flourishing commercial and trading center. After a period of Lucanian (native Italian) control in the fifth and fourth centuries BC, Poseidonia fell to the Romans in 273 BC and was renamed. Paestum remained a Roman town until the Appian Way was extended from Rome to Brindisi and trade began to bypass the city. Plagued by malaria and pirates, Paestum's last inhabitants abandoned the city in the 9th century AD, leaving the ruins relatively untouched.

ORIENTATION AND PRACTICAL INFORMATION

Getting to Paestum from Rome is a bit complicated, but definitely worth the effort. Head south on the train to **Salerno** (trains leave frequently from Termini, Ostiense, and Tiburtina stations; 3-4hrs.; L20,800). From Salerno, **buses** (every 30min. 6am-8pm; L4200) let you off on **Via Magna Graecia,** the main modern road; ask to stop at the ruins *(gli scavi)* or at your hotel to save yourself a walk. Be sure to check return bus times in advance. If you catch one of the infrequent **trains** (5 per day from Salerno, L4200), head straight out of the station and through Porta Sirena, the most intact of the ancient city gates. A short walk brings you to V. Magna Graecia. The last bus back to Salerno passes by at 7:30pm and the last train at 10:10pm. Another option is to take the bus to nearby Agropoli (L1800) where there are many other train connections. The **tourist office** is at P. Basilica 151/153 (tel. 81 10 16; open Mon.-Sat. 8am-2pm). You can also call **Cointur,** which is not in Paestum but can help with reservations over the phone (tel. 72 47 47; some English spoken). Paestum's **telephone code** is 0828.

ACCOMMODATIONS AND FOOD

Paestum makes a great daytrip from Rome, but if you want to spend the night, **Albergo delle Rose,** Via Magna Graecia, 193 (tel. 81 10 70), is a relatively inexpensive option with luxurious rooms. Singles L45,000. Doubles L80,000. Prices are L5000-10,000 lower from October to April. A 10-min. walk on Via Principe di Piemonte to the right past the ruins and toward the coast will bring you to numerous **campsites. Apollo** (tel. 81 11 78) provides a soccer field, bar, and *discoteca.* L6000 per person, L11,000 per tent. Four-person bungalows L60,000. Open May to September, **Dei Pini** (tel. 81 10 30) also keeps you well fed, with a *pizzeria,* bar, and food store on-site.

English spoken. Groups of four or more preferred. L40,000 for 4 people in low season; L60,000 in high season. Open year-round. Restaurants in Paestum are scarce, so you may want to pack a picnic lunch before you go. With outdoor seating under a large tent that looks like something from *Lawrence of Arabia,* **Oasi** (tel. 81 19 35) on V. Magna Graecia, 100m to the left of the museum, serves full meals (about L20,000) during the day and pizzas in the evening (from L5000). Cover L1500. Service 15%. (Open Jan.-Sept. daily and Oct.-Nov. Tues.-Sun. noon-3pm and 7pm-midnight.)

SIGHTS

The ancient Greeks built Paestum on a north-south axis, marked by the still-paved Via Sacra. (Looking at the ruins from the modern V. Magna Graecia, which runs parallel to Via Sacra, north is to your right.) Most guided tours start from the Porta Giustizia at the southern end of Via Sacra.

Paestum's three **Doric temples** rank among the best-preserved in the world. Built without any mortar or other cement, the buildings were originally covered by roofs of terra-cotta tiles supported by wooden beams. All the stone you see now was once painted. For a more detailed discussion of the history, architecture, and archaeology of the temples and site, look for *Paestum: Guide to the Excavations and Archaeological Museum* (ed. Matonti; available in any of the roadside shops, L6000).

When excavators first uncovered the three temples, they misnamed them. Although recent scholarship has led to new guesses for the temples' dedications, the old names have stuck anyway. The southernmost temple, the so-called **basilica,** is the oldest, dating to the second half of the sixth century BC. Its unusual plan, including a main interior section *(naos)* split in two by a single row of columns down the middle, has inspired the theory that the temple was dedicated to two gods, Zeus and Hera, instead of just one. The next temple to the north, the **Temple of Poseidon** (actually dedicated to Hera), was built 100 years after the "basilica," in the middle of the fifth century BC. The Temple of Poseidon incorporates many of the same optical refinements that charcterize the Parthenon in Athens. On the temple's roof are some small lions' heads; when it rained, water from the gutters came pouring out of their mouths. The third major Doric temple, the **Temple of Ceres** (whose dedication is now disputed), lies off to the north of the Forum. This temple was built around 500 BC (placing its construction date between those of the other two temples). It became a church in the early Middle Ages then was abandoned in the ninth century.

Continuing north on Via Sacra, you come to the Roman **Forum,** even larger than the one at Pompeii. The Romans leveled most of the older structures at the center of the city to make room for this proto-*piazza*, the commercial and political arena of Paestum. To the right, a large, shallow pit marks the site of the pool in an ancient **gymnasium.** East of the gymnasium lies half of the Roman **amphitheater** (the modern road buries the rest).

The **museum** on the other side of V. Magna Graecia houses an extraordinary collection of ancient pottery and paintings taken primarily from the tombs discovered in the area. Those well-versed in mythology can play guessing-games with sculptural panels from a sanctuary dedicated to Hera discovered 9km to the north of Paestum. According to legend, Jason and the Argonauts founded the temple. Also of note are the paintings from the famous **Tomb of the Diver,** rare examples of Greek wall painting. (Archaeological site open daily 9am-1hr. before sunset; ticket offices close 1hr. earlier. Museum open daily 9am-7pm. L8000 admits you to both ruins and museum.)

After visiting the ruins, you may want to worship the sun at the **beach** 2km to the east. The golden sand stretches for miles—unfortunately, much (but not all) of it is owned by resorts that require you to rent a chair for the day. Ask around for directions to a *spiaggia pubblica*, where you can take a free dip in the Mediterranean.

■ Caserta

There is little reason to visit Caserta, or rather, one very large reason: the magnificent **Palazzo Reale** (Royal Palace; tel. 32 14 00), locally called the "Reggia." To get to Caserta from Rome, take one of the frequent trains from Termini to Napoli Centrale, the main train station in Naples. From there, local and express trains run to Caserta (45min., L3400). Upon leaving the train station, you will see the palace smack dab in front of your face. Commissioned by the Bourbon King Charles III to imitate Versailles, the enormous building has 1200 rooms, 1790 windows, and 34 staircases. Frescoes and intricate marble floors adorn the Royal Apartments. Pass through the three libraries that hold original manuscripts, and you will come to the *presepe,* an immense Nativity scene set in an Italian market. (Open July-Oct. Mon.-Sat. 9am-1:30pm, Sun. 9am-1pm. Admission L8000.) Behind the Reggia are the vast **palace gardens.** Those who like to frolic barefoot in the grass, often do so (no, the caretakers do not condone such behavior): 3km of lush green lawns, fountains, sculptures, and carefully pruned trees culminate in a 75-m man-made waterfall. If you don't feel like attempting the long walk, take the bus (L1500) or a romantic horse-and-buggy ride (price varies). Pack a lunch and a bottle of water, especially if you plan to walk. Gardens open daily 9am-1hr. before sunset. Admission L4000. If you're around on July 26, catch the **Festival of Sant'Anna,** when music and fireworks light up the town. Early September brings concerts to Caserta Vecchia in a festival known as **Settembre al Borgo:** 20 nights of theater, comedy, music, and dancing.

One train stop from Casterta lies **Capua** and the remains of one of the most impressive Roman amphitheaters. Larger and more complete than Pozzuoli's amphitheater, this massive structure has a rival only in the contemporaneous Colosseum in Rome. From Caserta, take the train to the Santa Maria Capua Vetere stop (L2000). Walk straight one block, then make the first left onto Via G. Avezzana. Take your first left, then walk 150m and turn right onto Via E. Ricciardi, which becomes Via Amphiteatro. At the end, you can't miss the enormous ruins. Open daily 9am-1hr. before sunset. Admission L4000.

If you're too tired to trek elsewhere after touring the palace, gardens, or amphitheater, stay at **Hotel Baby,** Via G. Verdi, 41 (tel. 32 83 11), to the right as you exit the station. With friendly management and clean rooms, this hotel is a good choice in the somewhat run-down train station neighborhood. Singles L70,000. Doubles L80,000. Triples L110,000. Quads L140,000. Hungry after a long stroll in the park? Try **O Masto,** Via S. Agostino, 10 (tel. 32 00 42), which has such homestyle meals as tasty *spaghetti alla carbonara* (L7000). *Primi* L6000-L8000, *secondi* L8000. Open Tues.-Sun. 10am-midnight. **Tavola Calda Il Corso,** Corso Trieste, 221 (tel. 35 58 59), serves full meals with drink for about L18,000. Open Mon.-Sat. 10am-midnight. Caserta's **EPT** offices are located at Corso Trieste, 37 (tel. 32 11 37), at the corner of P. Dante; and in the Palazzo Reale (tel. 32 22 33). Pick up a brochure on the Reggia. Open Mon.-Fri. 9am-1pm. **Telephones** are at Via Roma, 53. **Avis Rent-a-Car** (tel. 44 37 56) is in the train station. Open Mon.-Fri. 9am-1pm and 2-6pm, Sat. 9am-2pm. The **post office** is on Viale Ellittico, to the left of P. Carlo III in front of the train station. Caserta's **postal code** is 81100; its **telephone code** is 0823.

Glossary/Appendix

■ Weights and Measures

1 millimeter (mm) = 0.04 inch	1 inch = 25mm
1 meter (m) = 1.09 yards	1 yard = 0.92m
1 kilometer (km) = 0.62 mile	1 mile = 1.61km
1 gram (g) = 0.04 ounce	1 ounce = 25g
1 liter = 1.06 quarts	1 quart = 0.94 liter

To convert from °C to °F, multiply by 9/5 and add 32.
To convert from °F to °C, subtract 32 and multiply by 5/9.

°C	-10	-5	0	5	10	15	20	25	30	35
°F	14	23	32	41	50	59	68	75	86	95

■ Climate

Month	Average Low	Average High	Rainfall in inches	Percentage of rainy days
January	39	55	3.3	34
February	41	57	2.9	35
March	42	59	2.0	33
April	48	62	2.0	34
May	55	70	1.9	22
June	60	77	0.7	11
July	66	82	0.4	3
August	66	82	0.7	5
September	61	79	2.8	10
October	54	70	4.3	19
November	46	61	4.4	27
December	41	58	4.1	31

■ Language

If you don't speak Italian, you'll probably be able to manage with English in Rome. More Italians are likely to know a smattering of French than English, and cognates often help Spanish speakers. Take a phrase book and practice with it before you leave or teach yourself with a tape and book set. Pronunciation is pretty much phonetic. **H** is the only letter that is ever silent.

VOWELS

There are seven vowel sounds in standard Italian. **A, I,** and **U** are always pronounced the same way; **E** and **O** have two possible pronunciations, either tense or lax, depending on where the vowel appears in the word, whether it's stressed or not, and regional accent (some accents don't even have this distinction). It's difficult for non-native speakers to predict the quality of vowels, but you may be able to hear the difference, especially with **E.** We illustrate below the *approximate* pronunciation of the vowels, but don't worry too much about **E** and **O.**

a:	*a* as in f**a**ther (*casa*)
e: tense	*ay* as in b**ay** (*sete*)
e: lax	*eh* as in s**e**t (*bella*)
i:	*ee* as in ch**ee**se (*vino*)
o: tense	*o* as in b**o**ne (*sono*)
o: lax	between *o* of b**o**ne and *au* of c**au**ght (*zona*)
u:	*oo* as in dr**oo**p (*gusto*)

CONSONANTS

Italian consonants won't give you many problems, except for the few quirks noted here. **H** is always silent and **R** is trilled.

C and G: before **a, o,** or **u, c** and **g** are hard, as in *cat* and *goose* or as in the Italian word *colore* (koh-LOHR-eh), "color," or *gatto* (GAHT-toh), "cat." They soften into "**ch**" and "**j**" sounds, respectively, when followed by **i** or **e**, as in the English *cheese* and *jeep* or the Italian *ciao* (CHOW), "good-bye," and *gelato* (jeh-LAH-toh), "ice cream."

CH and GH: h returns **c** and **g** to their "hard" sounds in front of **i** or **e** (see above); making words like, *chiave* (key-AH-vay), "keys," and *tartarughe* (tahr-tah-RU-geh), "tortoises."

GN and GLI: pronounce **gn** like the **ni** in *onion*, thus *bagno* ("bath") is "BAHN-yo." **Gli** is like the **lli** in *million*, so *sbagliato* ("wrong") is said "zbal-YAH-toh."

S and Z: An **s** found between two vowels or followed by the letters **b, d, g, l, m, n r,** and **v** is pronounced as the English **z**; thus *casa* ("house") sounds like "KAH-zah" and *smarrito* ("lost") like "zmahr-REE-toh." A double **s**, an initial **s**, or an **s** followed by any other consonant has the same sound as English initial **s**, so *sacco* ("bag") is SAHK-koh. **Z** has a **ts** or **dz** sound; thus *stazione* ("station") is pronounced "staht-see-YOH-nay," while *zoo* ("zoo") is pronounced "dzoh" and *mezzo* ("half") is "MEH-dzoh."

SC and SCH: when followed by **a, o,** or **u, sc** is pronounced as **sk**, so *scusi* ("excuse me") yields "SKOO-zee." When followed by an **e** or **i**, the combination is pronounced "**sh**" as in *sciopero* (SHOH-pair-oh), "strike." **H** returns **c** to its hard sound (**sk**) in front of **i** or **e**, as in *pesche* (PEH-skeh), "peaches," not to be confused with *pesce* (PEH-sheh), "fish."

Double consonants: The difference between double and single consonants in Italian is likely to cause problems for English speakers. When you see a double consonant, think about actually pronouncing it twice or holding it for a long time. English phrases like "dumb man" or "bad dog" approximate the sound of a double consonant. Failing to make the distinction can lead to some confusion; for example, *penne all'arrabbiata* is "short pasta in a spicy red sauce," whereas *pene all'arrabbiata* means "penis in a spicy red sauce."

STRESS

In many Italian words, stress falls on the next-to-last syllable. When stress falls on the last syllable, an accent indicates where stress should fall: *città* (cheet-**TAH**) or *perché* (pair-**KAY**). Stress can fall on the third-to-last syllable as well. It's not easy to predict stress, so you'll have to pick this up by listening to Italian speech.

PLURALS

Italians words form their plurals by changing the last vowel. Words that end in an **a** in the singular (usually feminine), end with an **e** in the plural; thus *mela* (MAY-lah), "apple," becomes *mele* (MAY-lay). Words that end with **o** or **e** in the singular take an **i** in the plural: *conto* (COHN-toh), "bill," is *conti* (COHN-tee) and *cane* (KAH-neh), "dog," becomes *cani* (KAH-nee). There are several exceptions to these rules; for example *braccio* becomes *braccia* in the plural. Words with final accent, like *città* and *caffè*, and foreign words like *bar* and *sport* do not change in the plural.

NUMBERS

1	uno	21	ventuno
2	due	23	ventitrè
3	tre	28	ventotto
4	quattro	30	trenta
5	cinque	40	quaranta
6	sei	50	cinquanta
7	sette	60	sessanta
8	otto	70	settanta
9	nove	80	ottanta
10	dieci	90	novanta
11	undici	100	cento
12	dodici	105	cento cinque
13	tredici	200	duecento
14	quattordici	800	ottocento
15	quindici	1000	mille
16	sedici	2000	due mila
17	diciassette	8000	otto mila
18	diciotto	100,000	cento mila
19	diciannove	million	un millione
20	venti	billion	un milliardo

■ Phrases

RESERVATIONS BY PHONE

Even without any real knowledge of Italian, it is possible to reserve a room.

Hello? (used when answering the phone)	*Pronto!*	PROHN-toh
Do you speak English?	*Parla inglese?*	PAHR-lah een-GLAY-zay
Could I reserve a single/double room with/without bath for the second of August?	*Potrei prenotare una camera singola/doppia con/senza bagno per il due agosto?*	POH-tray pray-noh-TAH-ray OO-nah CAH-meh-rah SEEN-goh-lah/DOH-pee-yah cohn/SENT-sah BAHN-yoh pair eel DOO-ay ah-GOH-stoh?
My name is...	*Mi chiamo...*	mee key-YAH-moh...
I will arrive at 14:30. (Remember, Italians use the 24-hour clock, so add twelve to afternoon/evening arrival times.)	*Arriverò alle quattordici e mezzo.*	ah-ree-vair-OH ah-lay kwah-TOHR-dee-chee eh MED-zoh.
Certainly!	*Certo!*	CHAIR-toh!
I'm sorry but...	*Mi dispiace, ma...*	mee dis-pee-YAH-chay, mah...
We're closed during August.	*Chiudiamo ad agosto.*	kyu-dee-AH-moh ahd ah-GOH-stoh.
No, we're full.	*No, siamo al completo.*	no, see-YAH-moh ahl cohm-PLAY-toh.
We don't take telephone reservations.	*Non si fanno le prenotazioni per telefono.*	nohn see FAHN-noh lay pray-noh-tat-see-YOH-nee pair tay-LAY-foh-noh.

You'll have to send a deposit/check.	*Bisogna mandare un acconto/un anticipo/ un assegno.*	bee-ZOHN-yah mahn-DAH-reh oon ahk-KOHN-toh/oon ahn-TEE-chee-poh/oon ahs-SAY-nyoh.
You must arrive before 2pm.	*Deve arrivare primo delle quattordici.*	DAY-vay ah-ree-VAH-ray PREE-moh day-lay kwah-TOHR-dee-chee.

TIME (AND SOURCES OF DELAYS)

At what time...?	*A che ora...?*	ah kay OHR-ah
What time is it?	*Che ore sono?*	kay OHR-ay SOH-noh
It's 2:30.	*Sono le due e mezzo.*	SOH-noh lay DOO-ay ay MEHD-zoh
It's noon.	*E' mezzogiorno.*	eh MEHD-zoh-JOHR-noh
now	*adesso/ora*	ah-DEHS-so/OH-rah
tomorrow	*domani*	doh-MAH-nee
today	*oggi*	OHJ-jee
yesterday	*ieri*	YAIR-ee
right away	*subito*	SU-bee-toh
soon	*fra poco*	frah POH-koh
already	*già*	jah
after(wards)	*dopo*	DOH-poh
before	*prima*	PREE-mah
early/earlier	*presto/più presto*	PREHS-toh/pyoo PREHS-toh
late/later	*tardi/più tardi*	TAHR-dee/pyoo TAHRdee
early (before scheduled arrival time	*in anticipo*	een ahn-TEE-chee-poh
late (after sched-uled arrival time)	*in ritardo*	een ree-TAHR-doh
daily	*quotidiano*	kwoh-tee-dee-AH-no
weekly	*settimanale*	seht-tee-mah-NAH-leh
monthly	*mensile*	mehn-SEE-leh
vacation	*le ferie*	lay FEH-ree-eh
weekdays	*i giorni feriali*	ee JOHR-nee feh-ree-AH-lee
Sundays and holi-days	*i giorni festivi*	ee JOHR-nee fehs-TEE-vee
day off (at store, restaurant, etc.)	*riposo*	ree-POH-zo
a strike	*uno sciopero*	SHOH-peh-roh
a protest	*una manifestazione*	mah-nee-fehs-taht-see-OH-neh

MONTHS

January	*gennaio*	jehn-NAH-yoh
February	*febbraio*	fehb-BRAH-yoh
March	*marzo*	MAHRT-soh
April	*aprile*	ah-PREE-lay
May	*maggio*	MAHJ-joh
June	*giugno*	JOON-yoh
July	*luglio*	LOOL-yoh
August	*agosto*	ah-GOH-stoh
September	*settembre*	seht-TEHM-bray
October	*ottobre*	oht-TOH-bray
November	*novembre*	noh-VEHM-bray
December	*dicembre*	dee-CHEHM-bray

DAYS OF THE WEEK

Monday	*lunedì*	loo-nay-DEE
Tuesday	*martedì*	mahr-tay-DEE
Wednesday	*mercoledì*	mair-coh-leh-DEE
Thursday	*giovedì*	joh-veh-DEE
Friday	*venerdì*	veh-nair-DEE
Saturday	*sabato*	SAH-bah-toh
Sunday	*domenica*	doh-MEH-nee-kah

GENERAL PHRASES

Hi/So long (informal)	*Ciao*	chow
Good day/Hello	*Buongiorno*	bwohn JOR-noh
Good evening	*Buona sera*	BWOH-nah SAY-rah
Good night	*Buona notte*	BWOH-nah NOHT-tay
Goodbye	*Arrivederci/ArrivederLa*	ah-ree-veh-DAIR-chee/lah
Please	*Per favore*	pair fah-VOH-ray
Thank you	*Grazie*	GRAHT-see-ay
You're welcome/Go right ahead/May I help you?	*Prego*	PRAY-goh
May I help you?	*Mi dica/Dimmi*	mee DEE-kah/DEEM-mee
Excuse me (if you want to interrupt or get someone's attention; if you bump into someone)	*Scusi*	SKOO-zee
Excuse me (may I get by?)	*Permesso*	pair-MEHS-soh
Pardon? (I didn't understand)	*Come?*	KOH-meh
Yes/No/Maybe	*Sì/No/Forse*	see/noh/fohr-say
I don't know.	*Non lo so.*	nohn low soh
Beats me!	*Boh!*	BOH
Okay, that's fine.	*Va bene.*	vah BEH-neh
I don't speak Italian.	*Non parlo italiano.*	nohn PAHR-low ee-tahl-YAH-noh
I don't understand	*Non capisco*	nohn kah-PEE-skoh
Is there someone here who speaks English?	*C'è qualcuno qui che parla inglese?*	cheh kwahl-KOO-noh kwee kay PAHR-lah een GLAY-zay
Could you help me?	*Potrebbe aiutarmi?*	poh-TRAYB-bay ah-yoo-TAHR-mee
which	*quale*	KWAH-lay
where	*dove*	DOH-vay
when	*quando*	KWAN-doh
why/because	*perché*	pair-KAY
who	*chi*	KEE
what	*che/cosa/che cosa*	KAY/KOH-zah/KAY KOH-zah
how	*come*	KOH-meh
more/less	*più/meno*	pyoo/MAY-noh
How do you say...?	*Come si dice...?*	COH-may see DEE-chay
What do you call this in Italian?	*Come si chiama questo in italiano?*	COH-may see key-YAH-mah KWEH-stow een ee-tahl-YAH-noh

BASIC NECESSITIES

I would like...	*Vorrei...*	VOH-ray
How much does it cost?	*Quanto costa?*	KWAN-toh CO-stah
Where is...?	*Dov'è...?*	doh-VAY
How do you get to...?	*Come si arriva a...*	KOH-meh see ahr-REE-vah
a ticket	*un biglietto*	oon beel-YEHT-toh
reduced price	*ridotto*	ree-DOHT-toh
student discount	*sconto studentesco*	SKOHN-toh stoo-dehn-TEHS-koh
one way	*solo andata*	SO-lo ahn-DAH-tah
round trip	*andata e ritorno*	ahn-DAH-tah ey ree-TOHR-noh
a pass (bus, etc.)	*una tessera*	OO-nah TEHS-seh-rah
the train	*il treno*	eel TRAY-no
the plane	*l'aereo*	lah-EHR-reh–oh
the (city) bus	*l'autobus*	LAOW-toh-boos
the (intercity) bus	*il pullman*	eel POOL-mahn
the ferry	*il traghetto*	eel tra-GHEHT-toh
the arrival	*l'arrivo*	la-REE-voh
the departure	*la partenza*	la par-TENT-sah
the track	*il binario*	eel bee-NAH-ree-oh
the terminus (of a bus)	*il capolinea*	eel kah-poh-LEE-neh-ah
the flight	*il volo*	eel VOH-loh
the reservation	*la prenotazione*	la pray-no-taht-see-YOH-neh
with bath/shower	*con bagno/doccia*	kohn BAHN-yo/DOH-cha
the bathroom	*il gabinetto/il bagno/la toletta*	eel gah-bee-NEHT-toh/eel BAHN-yoh/ lah toh-LEHT-toh
the consulate	*il consolato*	eel kohn-so-LAH-toh
the street address	*l'indirizzo*	leen-dee-REET-soh
the station	*la stazione*	lah staht-see-YOH-nay
the office	*l'ufficio*	loo-FEE-choh
the building	*il palazzo/l'edificio*	eel pah-LAHT-so/leh-dee-FEE-choh
the grocery store	*il negozio di alimentari*	ah-lee-men-TAH-ree
the market	*il mercato*	eel mair-KAH-toh
the church	*la chiesa*	lah kee-AY-zah
the telephone	*il telefono*	eel teh-LAY-foh-noh
the beach	*la spiaggia*	lah spee-AH-jah
the hospital	*l'ospedale*	los-peh-DAH-lay
the post office	*l'ufficio postale*	loo-FEE-choh poh-STAH-lay
open/closed	*aperto/chiuso*	ah-PAIR-toh/KYOO-zoh
the entrance/the exit	*l'ingresso/l'uscita*	leen-GREH-so/loo-SHEE-tah
a towel	*un asciugamano*	oon ah-shoo-gah-MAH-noh
sheets	*le lenzuola*	lay lehn-SUO-lah
a blanket	*una coperta*	OO-nah koh-PAIR-tah
heating	*il riscaldamento*	eel ree-skahl-dah-MEHN-toh

DIRECTIONS

Where is...?	*Dov'è...?*	doh-VEH
Do you stop at...?	*Ferma a...?*	FAIR-mah ah
What time does the ...leave?	*A che ora parte...?*	ah kay OHR-ah PAHR-tay
near/far	*vicino/lontano*	vee-CHEE-noh/lohn-TAH-noh
Turn left/right	*Gira a sinistra/destra*	JEE-rah ah see-NEE-strah/DEH-strah
straight ahead	*sempre diritto*	SEHM-pray DREET-toh
Stop!	*Ferma!*	FAIR-mah
here	*qui/qua*	kwee/kwah
there	*lì/là*	lee/lah
street	*strada, via, viale, vico, vicolo, corso*	STRAH-dah, VEE-ah, vee-AH-lay, VEE-koh, VEE-koh-loh, KOHR-soh

RESTAURANT BASICS

the knife	*il coltello*	eel cohl-TEHL-loh
the fork	*la forchetta*	lah fohr-KEH-tah
the spoon	*il cucchiaio*	eel koo-kee-EYE-yoh
the plate	*il piatto*	eel pee-YAH-toh
the appetizer	*l'antipasto*	lahn-tee-PAH-stoh
the first course	*il primo (piatto)*	eel PREE-moh pee-YAH-toh
the second course	*il secondo (piatto)*	eel seh-COHN-doh pee-YAH-toh
the side dish	*il contorno*	eel cohn-TOHR-noh
the dessert	*il dolce*	eel DOHL-chay
the breakfast	*la (prima) colazione*	lah (PREE-mah) coh-laht-see-YO-nay
the lunch	*il pranzo*	eel PRAHND-zoh
the dinner	*la cena*	lah CHEH-nah
the napkin	*il tovagliolo*	eel toh-vahl-YOH-loh
the glass	*il bicchiere*	eel bee-kee-YAIR-eh
the bottle	*la bottiglia*	lah boh-TEEL-yah
the waiter/waitress	*il/la cameriere/a*	eel/lah kah-meh-ree-AIR-ray/rah
the cover charge	*il coperto*	eel koh-PAIR-toh
the service charge/tip	*il servizio*	eel sair-VEET-see-oh
included	*compreso/a*	KOHM-pray-zoh/ah
the bill	*il conto*	eel COHN-toh

MEDICAL VOCABULARY

I have...	*Ho*	OH
...a stomach ache	*un mal di stomaco*	oon mahl dee STOH-mah-koh
...a head ache	*un mal di testa*	oon mahl dee TEHS-tah
...a cough	*una tosse*	OO-nah TOHS-seh
...a cold	*un raffreddore*	oon rahf-freh-DOH-reh
...the flu	*l'influenza*	lenn-floo-ENT-sah
...a fever	*una febbre*	OO-nah FEHB-breh
blood	*il sangue*	eel SAHN-gweh

allergies	*le allergie*	lay ahl-lair-JEE-eh
My foot hurts.	*Mi fa male il piede.*	mee fah MAH-le eel PYEHD-deh
the lump (on the head)	*il bernoccolo*	eel bear-NOH-koh-loh
the rash	*l'esantema /il sfogo/ l'eruzione*	leh-zahn-TAY-mah/ eel SFOH-goh/ leh-root-see-OHN-eh
the itch	*il prurito*	eel pru-REE-toh
the swelling/growth	*il gonfiore*	eel gohn-fee-OR-ay
the blister	*la bolla*	lah BOH-lah
the bladder	*la vescica*	lah veh-SHEE-cah
the skin	*la pelle*	lah PEH-lay
the gynecologist	*il ginecologo*	jee-neh-KOH-loh-goh
the wart	*la verruca*	lah veh-ROOK-kah
the venereal disease	*la malattia venerea*	lah mah-lah-TEE-ah veh-NAIR-ee-ah
the vaginal infection	*l'infezione vaginale*	leen-feht-see-OH-nay vah-jee-NAH-lay
I have menstrual pains.	*Ho delle mestruazioni dolorose.*	oh DEH-lay meh-stroo-aht-see-OH-nee doh-lor-OH-zay
I'm on the pill.	*Prendo la pillola.*	PREHN-doh lah PEE-loh-lah
I haven't had my period for (2) months.	*Non ho le mestruazioni da (due) mesi.*	nohn oh lay meh-stroo-aht-see-OH-nee dah (DOO-ay) may-zee
I'm (3 months) pregnant.	*Sono incinta (da tre mesi).*	SOH-noh een-CHEEN-tah dah tray MAY-zee

EMERGENCY AND SELF DEFENSE PHRASES

I lost my passport.	*Ho perso il passaporto.*	oh PAIR-soh eel pahs-sah-POHR-toh
I've been robbed.	*Sono stato derubato.*	SOH-noh STAH-toh deh-roo-BAH-toh
Wait!	*Aspetta!*	ahs-PEHT-tah
Stop!	*Ferma!*	FAIR-mah
Help!	*Aiuto!*	ah-YOO-toh
Leave me alone!	*Lasciami in pace!*	LAH-shah-mee een PAH-cheh
Don't touch me!	*Non mi toccare!*	NOHN mee tohk-KAH-reh
I'm calling the police!	*Telefono alla polizia!*	tehl-LAY-foh-noh ah-lah poh-leet-SEE-ah
Go away, cretin!	*Vattene, cretino!*	VAH-teh-neh creh-TEE-noh

■ Glossary

ART, ARCHITECTURE, AND GEOGRAPHY

Abbazia	also *Badia,* an abbey.
Aisle	sides of a church flanking the nave, separated from it by a series of columns.
Apse	a semicircular, domed niche projecting from the altar end of a church.

Atrium	an open central court, usually to an ancient Roman house or a Byzantine church.
Baldacchino	baldachin. A stone or bronze canopy supported by columns over the altar of a church.
Basilica	a rectangular building with aisle and apse but no transepts. Used by ancient Romans for public administration. The Christians later adopted the style for their churches.
Battistero	a baptistry; (almost always) a separate building near the town's *duomo* where the city's baptisms were performed.
Campanile	a bell tower, usually free-standing.
Cartoon	full-sized drawing used to transfer a preparatory design to the final work, especially to a wall for a fresco.
Castrum	the ancient Roman military camp. Many Italian cities were originally built on this plan: a rectilinear city with straight streets, the chief of which was called the *decumanus maximus*.
Cenacolo	"Last Supper"; often found in the refectory of an abbey or convent.
Chancel	the space around the altar reserved for clergy and choir; the area was usually enclosed by a screen in medieval churches, but most are now open.
Cloister	a courtyard; generally a quadrangle with covered walkways along its edges, often with a central garden, forming part of a church or monastery.
Comune	the government of a free city of the Middle Ages.
Corso	a principal street.
Cupola	a dome.
Diptych	a painting in two parts or panels.
Duomo	cathedral; the official seat of a diocesan bishop, and usually the central church of an Italian town.
Façade	the front of a building, or any other wall given special architectural treatment.
Fiume	a river.
Forum	in an ancient Roman town, a square containing municipal buildings and/or market space. Smaller towns usually have only one central forum, while large cities, such as Rome, can have several.
Fresco	*affresco*, a painting made on wet plaster. When it dries, the painting becomes part of the wall.
Frieze	a band of decoration in any medium. Architecturally, can also refer to the middle part of an entablature (everything above the columns of a building) between the architrave and the cornice.
Funicolare	funicular, a cable railway ascending a mountain.
Giardino	garden.
Greek Cross	a cross whose arms are of equal length.
Grotesque	painted, carved, or stucco decorations of fantastic, distorted human or animal figures, named for the grotto work found in Nero's buried Golden House in Rome.
in restuaro	under restoration; a key concept in Rome.
Intarsia	inlay work, usually of marble, metal, or wood.
Latin Cross	a cross whose vertical arm is longer than its horizontal arm.
Loggia	a covered gallery or balcony.
Lungo, Lung	literally "along," so that a *lungomare* is a boardwalk or promenade alongside the *mare* (ocean).

Lunette	a semi-circular frame in the ceiling or vault of a building that holds a painting or sculpture.
Mausoleum	a large tomb or stone building with places to entomb the dead above ground.
Nave	the central body of a church.
Palazzo	an important building of any type, not just a palace. Many were built as townhouses for wealthy families.
Piazza	a city square.
Pietà	a scene of the Virgin mourning the dead Christ.
Putto	(*pl. putti*) the little nude babies that flit around Renaissance art occasionally, and Baroque art incessantly.
Sinopia drawing	a red pigment sketch made on a wall as a preliminary study for a fresco.
Stigmata	miraculous body pains or bleeding that resemble the wounds of the crucified Christ.
Thermae	Ancient Roman baths and, consequently, social centers.
Transept	in a cruciform church, the arm of the church that intersects the nave or central aisle (i.e. the cross-bar of the T).
Travertine	a light colored marble or limestone used in many of the buildings in Rome.
Triptych	a painting in three panels or parts.
Trompe l'oeil	literally, "to deceive the eye," a painting or other piece or art whose purpose is to trick the viewer, as in a flat ceiling painted so as to appear domed.
Tufa	a soft stone composed of volcanic ash (*tufo* in Italian).
Via	a street.
Villa	a country house, usually a large estate with a formal garden. In Rome, *villa* refers to the grounds surrounding the estates that have become public parks.

FOOD

Types of Pasta

al pomodoro	in tomato sauce
all'arrabbiata	in a spicy tomato sauce
all'amatriciana	in a tangy tomato sauce with onions and bacon
alla bolognese	in a meat sauce
alla carbonara	in a creamy sauce with egg, ham, and cheese
alla puttanesca	in a tomato sauce with olives and capers
alle cozze	in a tomato sauce with mussels
alle vongole	in a clam sauce; *bianco* for white, *rosso* for red

Types of Pizza

margherita	plain ol' tomato, mozzarella, and basil
ai funghi	with mushrooms
con rucola (rughetta)	with arugala (rocket for the Brits)
con prosciutto	with ham
con prosciutto crudo	with cured ham (also called simply *crudo*)
con bresaola	with cured beef
ai carciofi	with artichokes
ai fiori di zucca	with zucchini blossoms
con melanzana	with eggplant
con alici	with anchovies

alla capriciosa	with ham, egg, artichoke, and more
quattro formaggi	with four cheeses
quattro stagioni	four seasons; a different topping for each quarter of the pizza, usually mushrooms, *crudo,* artichoke, and tomato

Common Dishes in Rome

saltimbocca alla romana	slices of veal and ham cooked together and topped with cheese
involtini al sugo	rolled veal cutlets filled with ham, celery, and cheese, topped with tomato sauce
osso buco	braised veal shank
fiori di zucca	zucchini flowers; either as a pizza topping or filled with cheese, battered, and lightly fried
carciofi alla giudia	fried artichokes
trippa	tripe; chopped, sautéed cow intestines, usually in a tomato sauce
filetto di baccalà	fried cod
pasta e ceci	pasta with chick peas
supplì	fried rice ball filled with tomato, meat, and cheese
animelle alla griglia	grilled sweetbreads
coda alla vaccinara	stewed oxtail

Side Dishes

insalata mista	mixed green salad
insalata caprese	tomatoes with mozzarella cheese and basil, drizzled with olive oil
fagiolini	green beans
fagioli	beans (usually white)
melanzana	eggplant
broccoletti	broccoli florets

■ Area Codes

Italy's country code is 39. To place a call to another province within Italy, dial the complete area code and then the phone number. From outside the country, dial the country code and then the regional area code minus the first 0. To call internationally from Italy, dial 00 and then the country code.

Rome	06		**Paestum**	0828		**Terracina**	0773
Formia and Gaeta	0771		**Pompeii**	081		**Tivoli**	0774
Orvieto	0763		**Ponza**	0771		**Viterbo**	0761

Brindisi	0831		**Milan**	02		**Perugia**	075
Cagliari	070		**Naples**	081		**Turin**	011
Florence	055		**Palermo**	091		**Venice**	041

Australia	61		**France**	33		**Spain**	34
Austria	43		**Germany**	49		**UK**	44
Canada	1		**Greece**	30		**USA**	1

Index

LET'S GO MAP GUIDE SERIES

This unique combination of pocket guide and street finder will be an essential tool for tourists, new residents, and natives alike.

Available Now:
- **New York City**
- **Washington, D.C.**
- **Boston**
- **San Francisco**
- **London**
- **Paris**

Coming in 1997:
- **Los Angeles** (March)
- **New Orleans** (March)
- **Rome** (March)
- **Chicago** (June)
- **Madrid** (June)
- **Berlin** (June)

Featuring:
- Detailed maps of the downtown area, neighborhoods, city overview, and transportation routes.
- Complete descriptions, addresses, phone numbers, and prices for restaurants, entertainment, sights, museums, and hotels.

★ Let's Go 1997 Reader Questionnaire ★

Please fill this out and return it to **Let's Go, St. Martin's Press,**
175 5th Ave. NY, NY 10010

Name: _____ **What book did you use?**_____
Address: _____
City: _____ **State:** _____ **Zip Code:** _____
How old are you? under 19   19-24   25-34   35-44   45-54   55 or over
Are you (circle one)   in high school   in college   in grad school
     employed   retired   between jobs
Have you used Let's Go before?   yes   no
Would you use Let's Go again?   yes   no
How did you first hear about Let's Go?   friend   store clerk   CNN
     bookstore display   advertisement/promotion   review   other
Why did you choose Let's Go (circle up to two)?   annual updating
     reputation   budget focus   price   writing style
     other: _____
Which other guides have you used, if any?   Frommer's $-a-day   Fodor's
     Rough Guides   Lonely Planet   Berkeley   Rick Steves
     other: _____
Is Let's Go the best guidebook?   yes   no
If not, which do you prefer? _____
**Which part of Let's Go do you feel needs most to be improved, if any
     (circle up to two)?**   packaging/cover   practical information
     accommodations   food   cultural introduction   sights
     practical introduction ("Essentials")   directions   entertainment
     gay/lesbian information   maps   other: _____
How would you like to see these things improved?
_____
_____

How long was your trip?   one week   two weeks   three weeks
     one month   two months or more
Have you traveled extensively before?   yes   no
Do you buy a separate map when you visit a foreign city?   yes   no
Have you seen the Let's Go Map Guides?   yes   no
Have you used a Let's Go Map Guide?   yes   no
If you have, would you recommend them to others?   yes   no
Did you use the internet to plan your trip?   yes   no
Would you buy a Let's Go   phrasebook   adventure/trekking guide
     gay/lesbian guide
**Which of the following destinations do you hope to visit in the next three
     to five years (circle one)?**   Australia   China   South America   Russia
     other: _____
Where did you buy your guidebook?   internet   chain bookstore
     independent bookstore   college bookstore   travel store
     other: _____

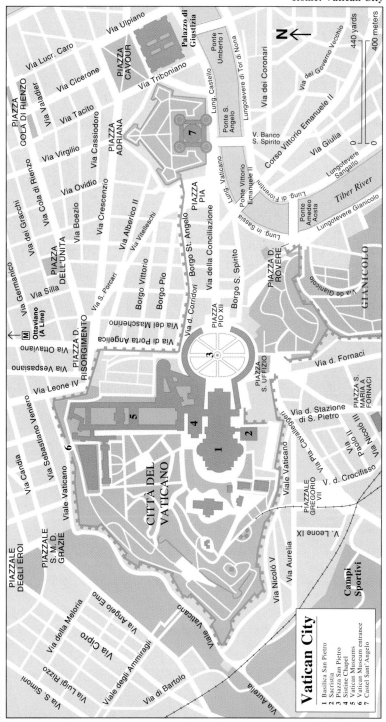

440 yards
400 meters

Vatican City

1 Basilica San Pietro
2 Sacristia
3 Piazza San Pietro
4 Sistine Chapel
5 Vatican Museums
6 Vatican Museum entrance
7 Castel Sant'Angelo

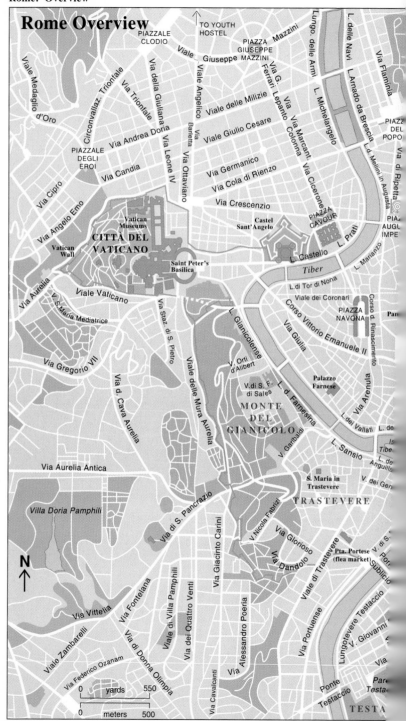

Rome Overview

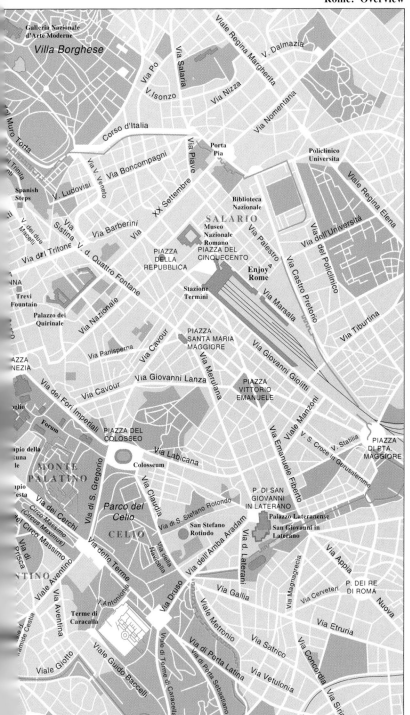

Rome: Transportation

Rome Transport

↑ TO YOUTH HOSTEL

VILLA BORGHESE

PIAZZA GIUSEPPE MAZZINI

Viale Giuseppe Mazzini

Viale delle Milizie

Viale Giulio Cesare

Viale Angelico

Via Leone IV

V. Ottaviano

Via G. Ferrari

Via Lepanto

Via Marcant. Colonna

Via Cicerone

Via Cola di Rienzo

Via Crescenzio

Via Giulia

PIAZZA DEL POPOLO

PIAZZA CAVOUR

Vatican

St. Peter's Basilica

Castel Sant'Angelo

Tiber

Via dei Coronari

PIAZZA NAVONA

Corso Vittorio Emanuele II

C. d. Rinascimento

Pantheon

PIAZZA ROTONDA

PIAZZA COLONNA

PIAZZA VENEZIA

Palazzo Farnese

Via Flaminia

Via di Ripetta

Via del Babuino

Via del Corso

Via del Corso

Corso

Viale del Muro Torta

Via V. Veneto

Via Piave

Via XX Settembre

Via Nomentana

Via Salaria

Viale Regina Margherita

Via Nizza

Via Po

Corso d'Italia

Via Sistina

Via V. d. Quattro Fontane

Via Nazionale

Via Barberini

Via del Tritone

Via del due Macelli

Via Condotti

Trevi Fountain

Palazzo del Quirinale

Stazione Termini

Via Marsala

Via Castro Pretorio

Via Merulana

V. Giov. Lanza

Via Cavour

A-LINE
- FLAMINIO
- SPAGNA
- BARBERINI
- REPUBBLICA
- TERMINI
- OTTAVIANO
- LEPANTO
- CINQUECENTO
- VITTORIO
- S. PIETRO
- CAVOUR

B-LINE
- SALARIO
- CASA PRETORIO
- TERMINI

SPAGNA

VITTORIO

Urban Train Service (F.S.)
S. PIETRO